HELLENISTIC ART

IN THE WALTERS ART GALLERY

HELLENISTIC ART

IN THE WALTERS ART GALLERY

ELLEN D. REEDER

with essays by Brunilde S. Ridgway, Andrew F. Stewart,

Roger S. Bagnall, and Beryl Barr-Sharrar

Published by the Trustees of the Walters Art Gallery

Baltimore, Maryland 1988

in association with

Princeton University Press, Princeton, New Jersey

This publication was made possible by grants from the National Endowment for the Humanities, the Martin Marietta Corporation, the Ensign C. Markland Kelly, Jr., Memorial Foundation, the Maryland Humanities Council, and the National Endowment for the Arts.

This catalogue accompanied the exhibition *From Alexander to Cleopatra: Greek Art of the Hellenistic Age* shown at The Walters Art Gallery, November 20, 1988–January 29, 1989.

Designed by Claude Skelton Design, Baltimore
Typeset by BG Composition, Inc., Baltimore
Printed by Collins Lithographing, Inc., Baltimore
Photography by Susan Tobin except pages 23, 25, 26, 52, 53, 55, 56, 57, 62, 63, which are by John Dean.
Maps by Richard Dowd
Edited by Troy Moss

Library of Congress Cataloging-in-Publication Data
Walters Art Gallery (Baltimore, Md.)
  Hellenistic art in the Walters Art Gallery.

  "In association with Princeton University Press, Princeton."
  1. Art, Hellenistic—Catalogs. 2. Art—Maryland—
Baltimore—Catalogs. 3. Walters Art Gallery (Baltimore,
Md.)—Catalogs. I. Reeder, Ellen D. II. Ridgway,
Brunilde Sismondo, 1929–   III. Title.
N5630.W334 1988   730'.0938'07401526   88-50742
ISBN 0-911886-35-4 (pbk.)
ISBN 0-691-04069-9 (Princeton University Press)

Cover: Detail of Catalogue No. 13.

Contents

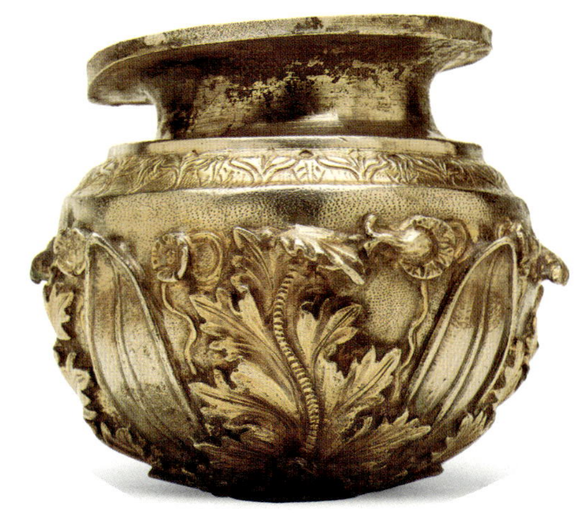

Catalogue number 67

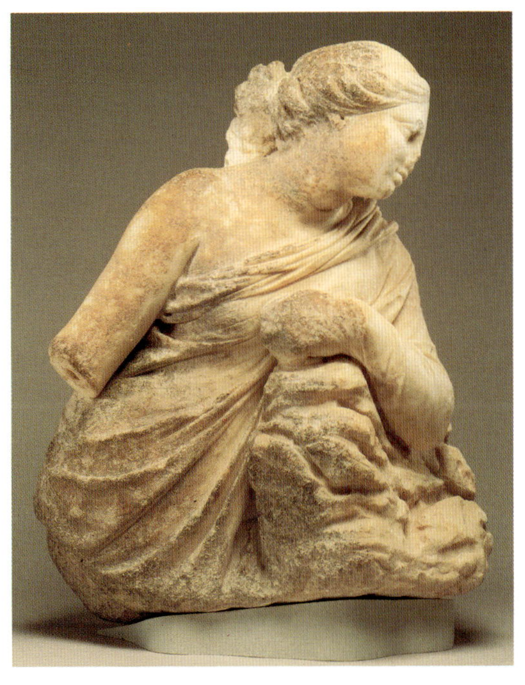

Catalogue number 25

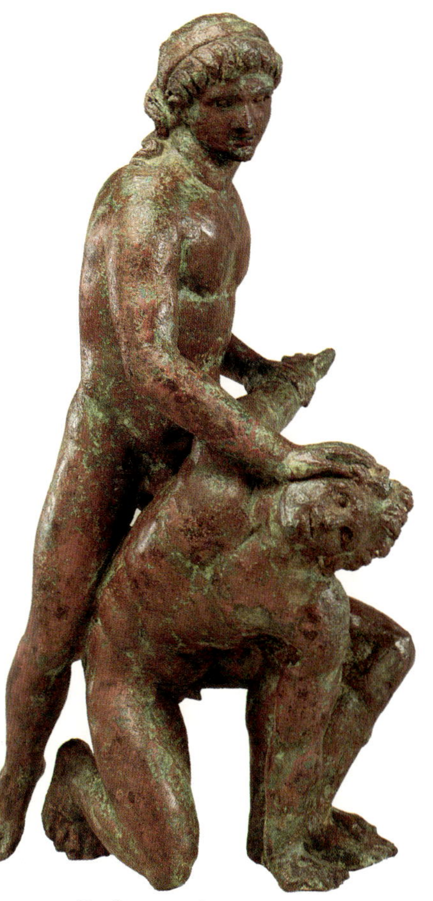

Catalogue number 63

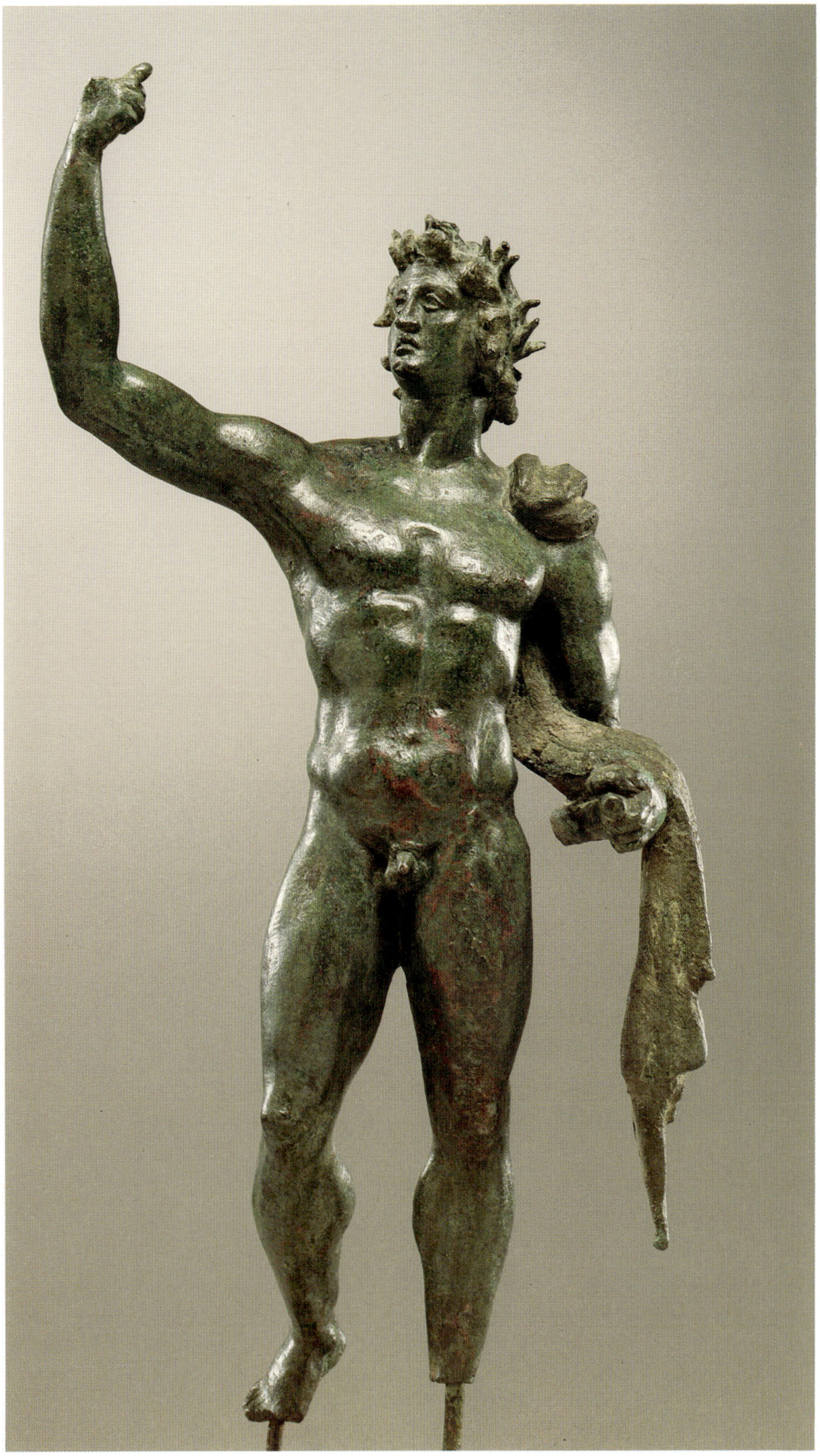

Catalogue number 61

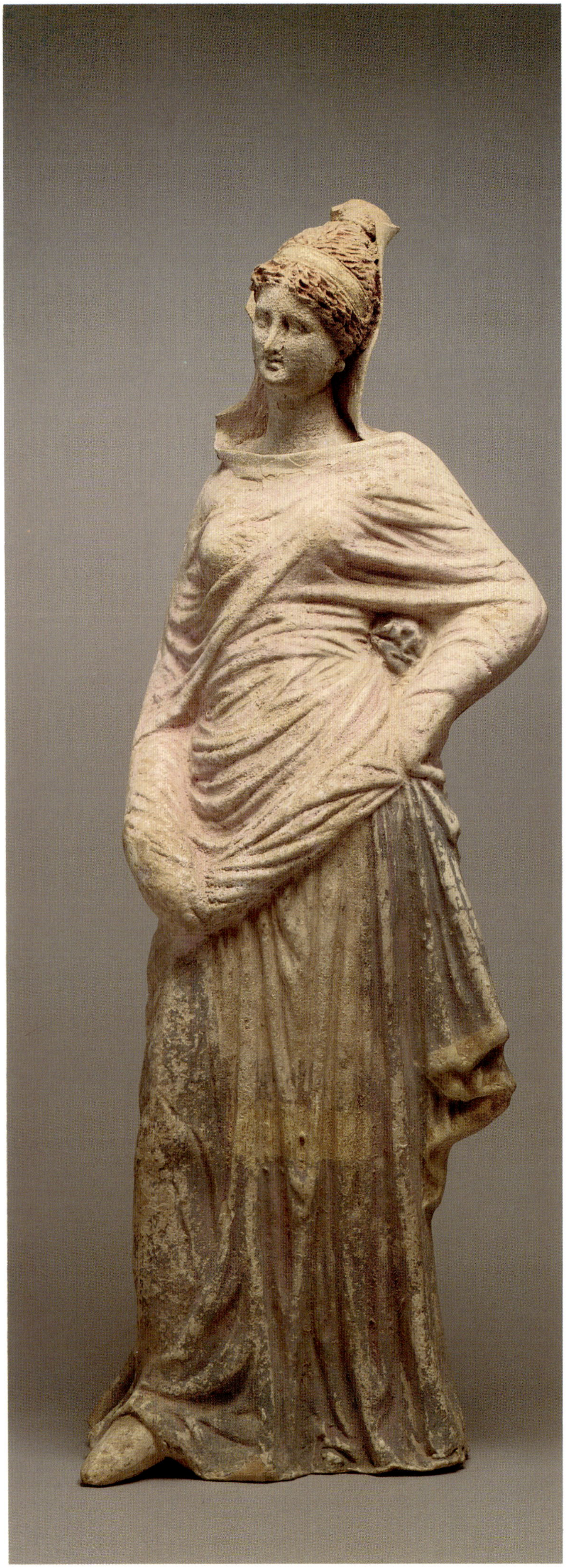

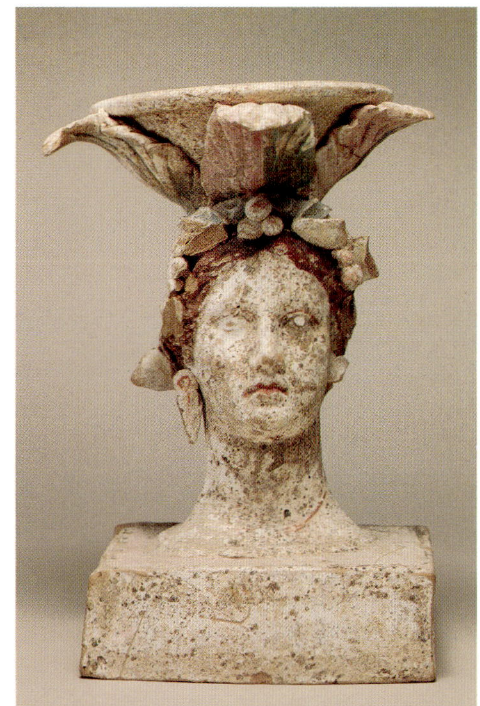

Catalogue number 87

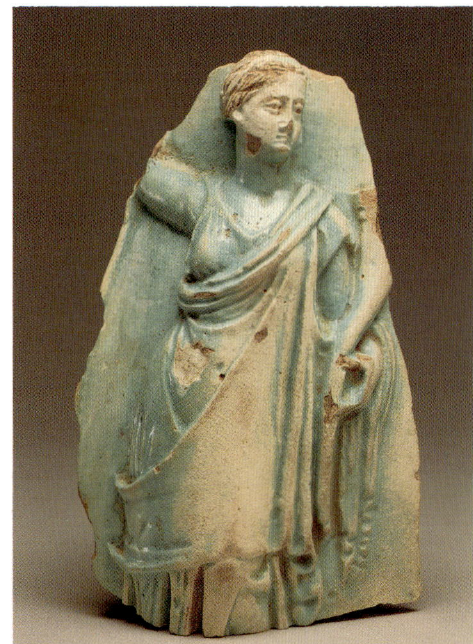

Catalogue number 104

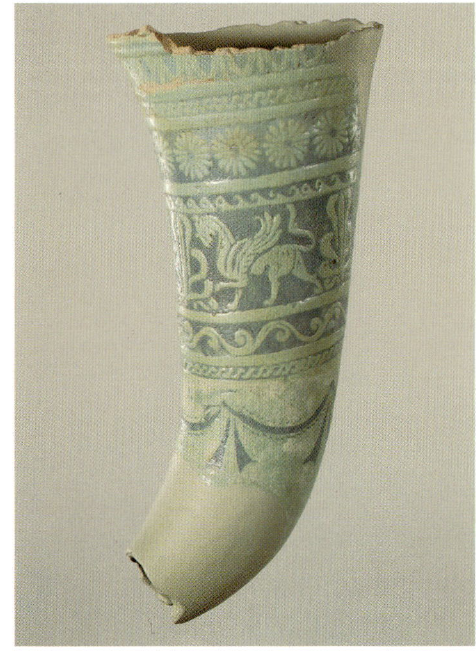

Catalogue number 105

Catalogue number 86

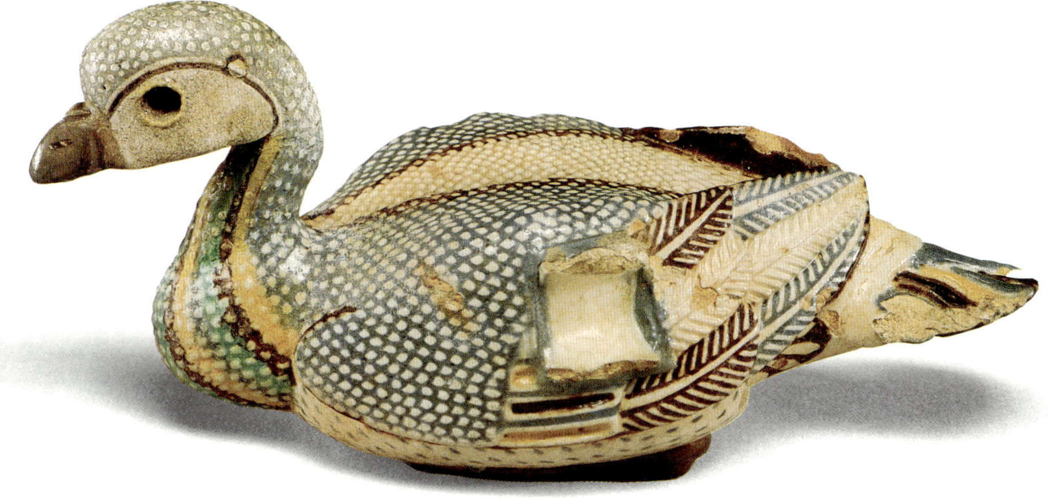

Catalogue number 109

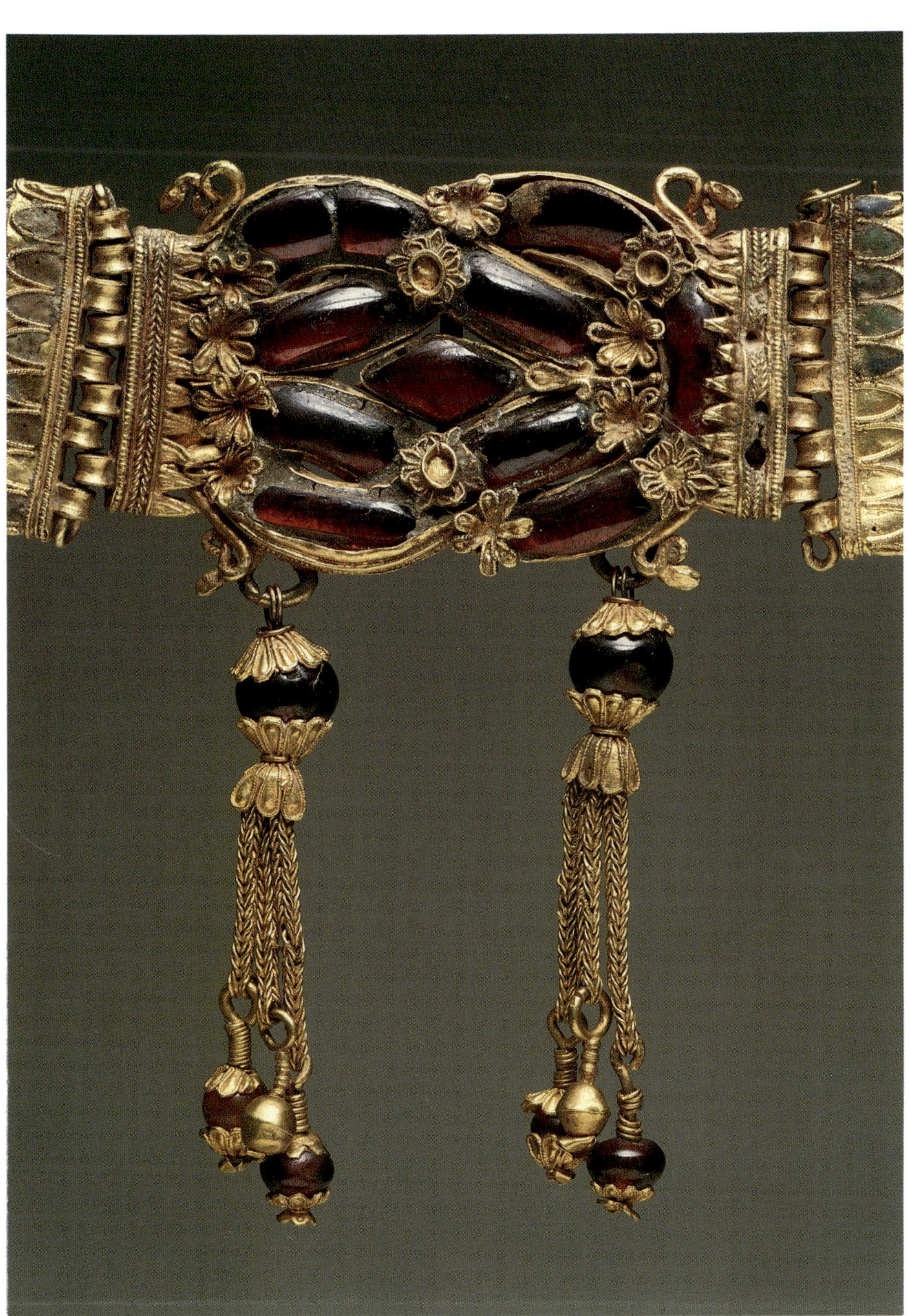

Catalogue number 127

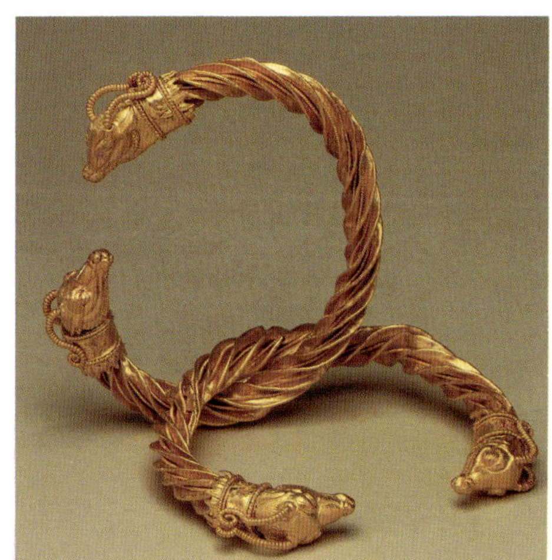

Catalogue number 116

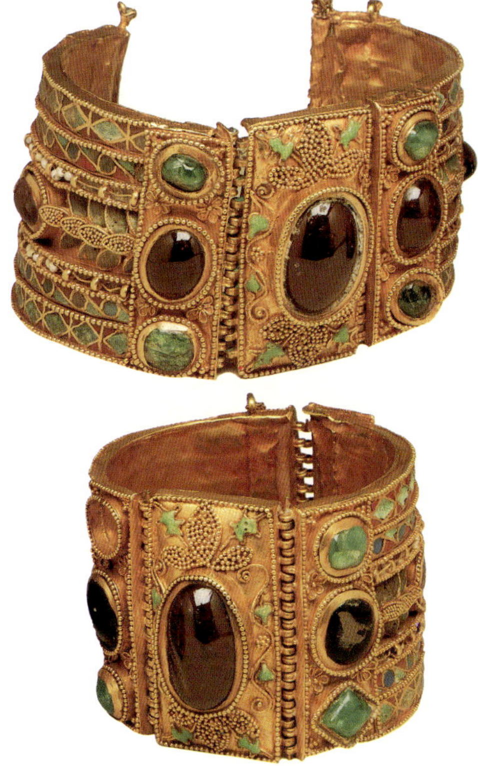

Catalogue number 131

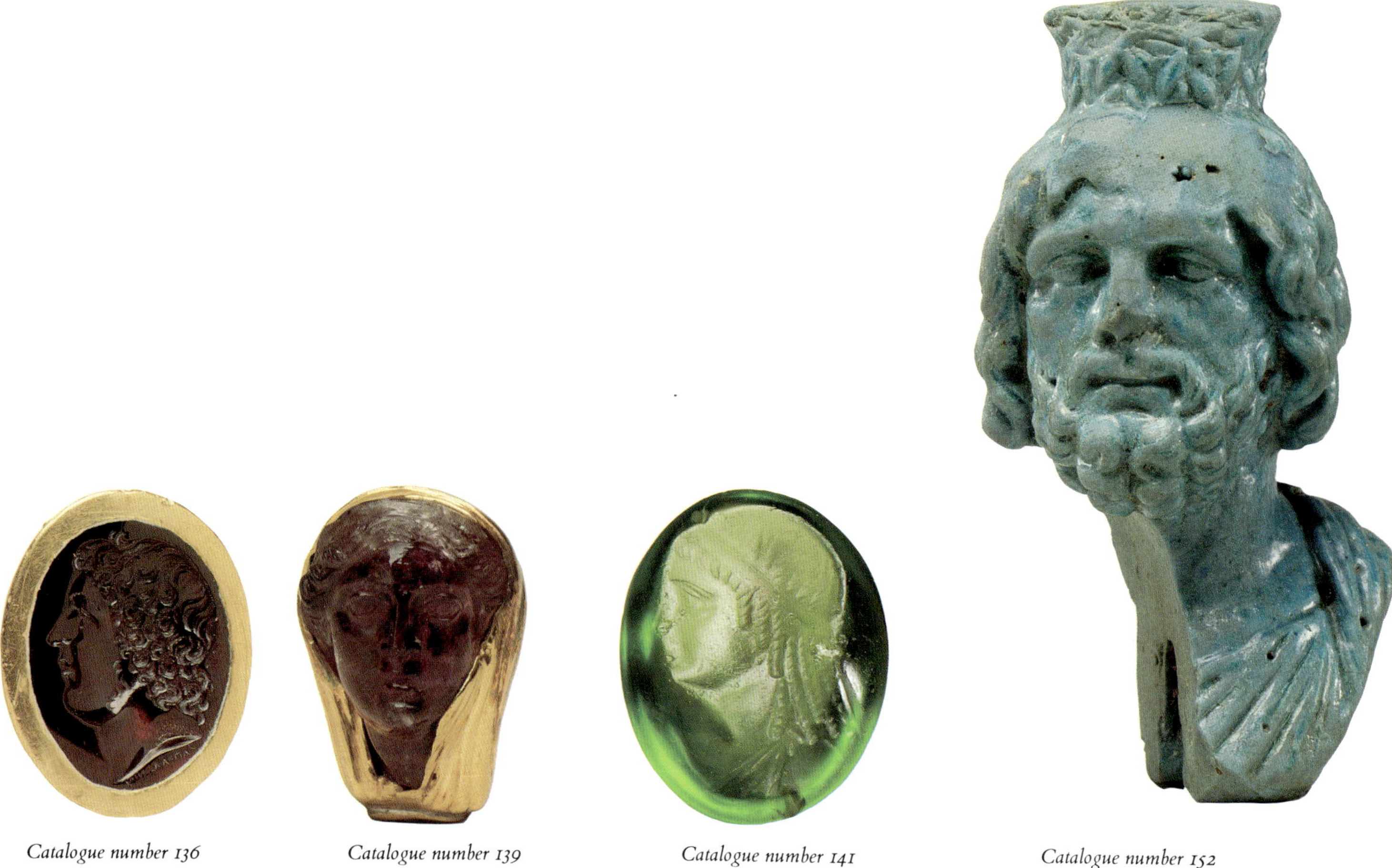

Catalogue number 136

Catalogue number 139

Catalogue number 141

Catalogue number 152

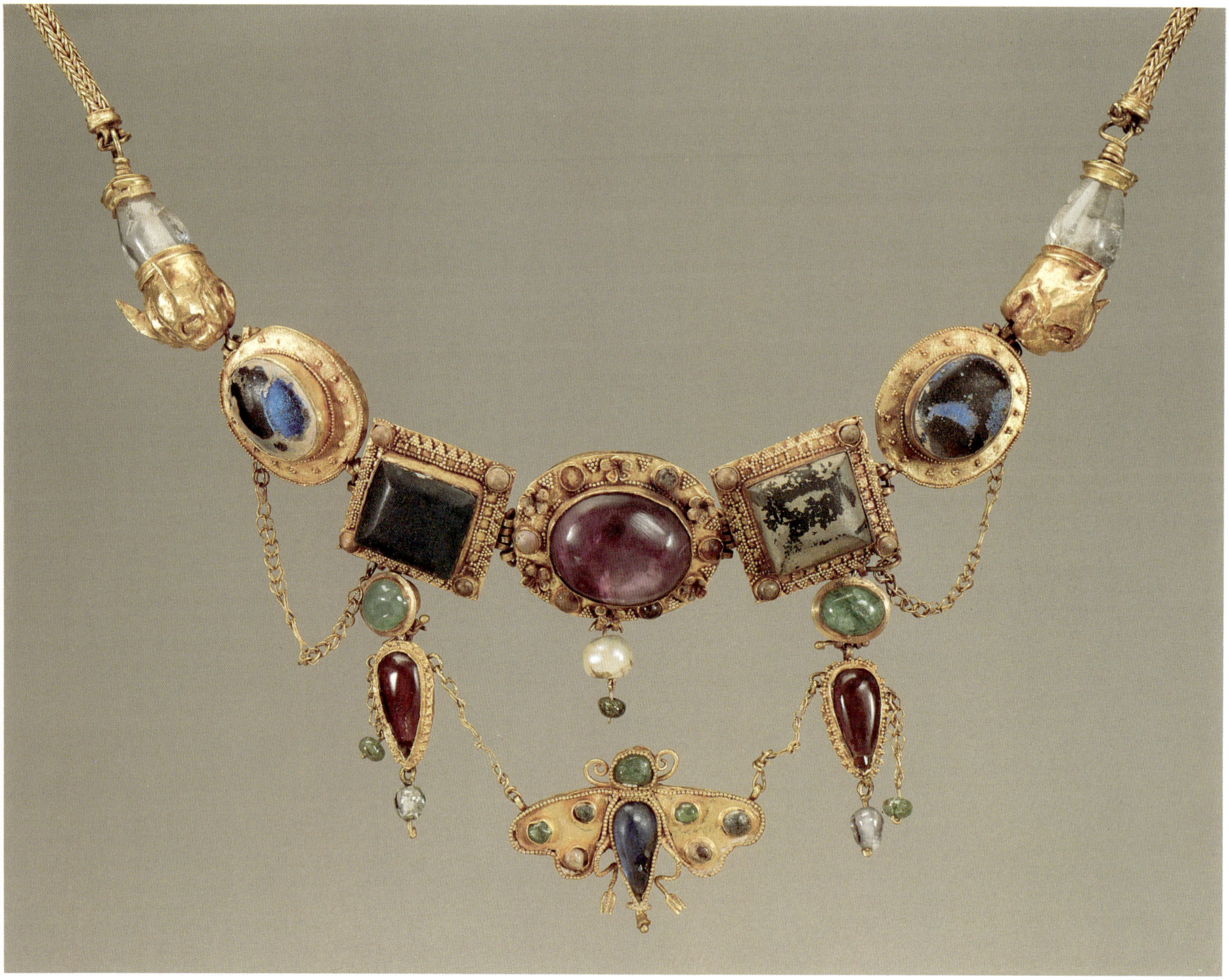

Catalogue number 132

FOREWORD

Robert P. Bergman

THE COLLECTION OF ANTIQUITIES formed by Henry Walters is one of the glories of the public museum that now bears his family's name. Among his earliest purchases in the 1890s was a group of ancient Near Eastern seals. His acquisition in 1902 of the great collection of Don Marcello Massarenti brought with it several hundred Greek, Roman, and Etruscan antiquities, including the seven magnificent Roman sarcophagi excavated from a tomb on the Via Salaria. Following World War I, his interest in ancient art continued unabated, and important purchases in the field were made right up until the time of his death in 1931. In the early years many works were purchased at auction, but acquisition through dealers gradually came to dominate: first Canessa, Picard, and Sambon, and later Hirsch, Brummer, and Kelekian. Of the approximately 22,000 works of art bequeathed to the public by Henry Walters serveral thousand were of Egyptian, ancient Near Eastern, Greek, Etruscan, and Roman origin. These were supplemented in the ensuing years by further significant gifts and purchases.

For the present volume—and for the exhibition organized concurrently with its publication—Ellen Reeder, curator of ancient art and the project's mastermind, has brought together the finest objects from the collection originating during the marvelously creative centuries between Alexander the Great and the Emperor Augustus. The Hellenistic period was an artistic epoch characterized by the spread of Greek forms—as well as ideas—throughout the Mediterranean world and beyond. The one adjective that to my mind captures the essence of Hellenistic art is exuberance, expressed in color, in boldness of design, in a penchant for highly expressive modes of representation, and in a clear love of virtuoso artistic expression. If the Hellenistic period is celebrated for broadening the iconographic repertoire of art it should also be recognized as fostering a wider range of expressive modes.

The Walters collection is rich in Hellenistic works of all types, but it is richest in smaller-scale arts such as bronzes, precious objects, and ivories. Many of these objects, because of their original context and function, resonate particularly powerfully with the spirit of personal or daily life in ancient times. Dr. Reeder and her collaborators have attempted to bring the collection into focus by viewing the objects in close relation to their original cultural and social contexts. This approach aims to benefit both scholars and the general public, and it is my hope that all will derive pleasure and edification from the enterprise.

In implementing the Hellenistic project, The Walters was fortunate to receive support from a number of quarters. The National Endowment for the Humanities provided a major grant, and additional funding was provided by the Martin Marietta Corporation, the Ensign C. Markland Kelly, Jr., Memorial Foundation of Baltimore, the Institute of Museum Services, the Maryland Humanities Council, the Getty Grant Program, and the National Endowment for the Arts. To each of these institutions, and to the individuals responsible, we extend our gratitude.

THIS VOLUME COULD NOT HAVE MATERIALIZED without the generous support of several granting organizations. Foremost among these are the National Endowment for the Humanities in partnership with the Martin Marietta Corporation, the Ensign C. Markland Kelly, Jr., Foundation, and the Maryland Humanities Council, which made possible: the exhibition itself, with its interpretative materials and programs; technical studies including thermoluminescence testing and marble isotopic analysis; the contributors' essays; and the publication of the catalogue. Funding from the Institute of Museum Services, the National Endowment for the Arts, and the Getty Grant Program enabled almost every work of art to undergo conservation treatment. Research was facilitated by a travel grant awarded by the National Endowment for the Arts.

Numerous individuals participated in the many aspects of the project and to all of them I express deep appreciation. Marsha Semmel of the National Endowment for the Humanities, Buzz Bartlett of the Martin Marietta Corporation, and Joanna Hitchcock of the Princeton University Press were particularly helpful and supportive. At the Walters, Beth Howell's efforts to secure funding for the project were tireless, and her optimism unfailing. Terry Weisser, Director of the Division of Conservation and Technical Research, supervised both the object conservation and the scientific testing, and worked together with Susan Schnepp, Rika Smith, Carol Snow, and Meg Craft in carrying out the conservation treatment. Susan Tobin photographed almost every object in the exhibition, often extensively, and always to her relentlessly high standard; Sara Glik was responsible for printing the photographs and Karen Matter organized their production. Richard Dowd supplied the maps, and Roger Wieck provided constant encouragement. Carol Benson deserves special thanks for sharing with me her knowledge of fourth-century and Hellenistic art, for functioning as an extremely competent curatorial and research assistant, and for coordinating the entire project with unflagging enthusiasm for every detail.

The catalogue involved contributions from a number of individuals. Essayists Brunilde Ridgway, Andrew Stewart, Roger Bagnall, and Beryl Barr-Sharrar shared with me their expertise with characteristic competence and generosity, and I thank them for interrupting their own projects to devote time to this volume. Numerous scholars outside the museum willingly supplied answers to questions I could not answer, and of these I particularly thank Susan Rotroff, John Oakley, Jeffrey Spier, David Mitten, Joan Mertens, Elizabeth Walters, Barbara Deppert-Lippitz, Andrew Stewart, F. W. Hamdorf, and George Switzer, who assisted in identifying the gems. Curators of museums I visited provided a model of curatorial hospitality, and I am especially grateful to Marion True, Marit Jentoft-Nilsen and Ken Hamma of the J. Paul Getty Museum, Arielle Kozloff of the Cleveland Museum of Art, and Kurt Luckner of the Toledo Museum of Art. The splendid observations of Andrew Oliver in the 1979 catalogue of the Walters jewelry formed the basis of my own descriptions of many of the pieces of jewelry. The tedious task of checking bibliographical data was cheerfully handled by several docents, interns, and volunteers, including Norma Blumberg, Ruth Pepper, Katia Sinis, Joy Riser, and Renée Kidd, who were led through the intricacies of the sales catalogues by Walters librarian Muriel Toppan. Meg Burns, Carla Brenner, and Carol Benson significantly improved the manuscript; the word-processing skills of Kathleen Sweeney and Nancy Koger produced a readable version of it. Muriel Toppan proved to be an exacting proofreader, Claude Skelton a particularly sensitive book designer. Above all, the volume is the product of editor Troy Moss, whose competence enabled me to enjoy a peace of mind for which I am most grateful.

An exhibition of this scope leaves almost no member of a museum staff untouched, and I thank everyone at the Walters who contributed to the project. Special mention is deserved by the installation staff of Eugene Gregorio and Paul Dion under John Klink, whose seasoned experience and imagination enriched the inspired design of ElRoy Quenroe and Allyson Smith of Quenroe Design Associates. Graphic designers Anne Jenifer and Theresa Segreti masterfully took in hand all the exhibition's graphics. The massive task of coordinating the traffic of objects from storage or display to conservation, photography, and installation was ably carried out by registrars Leopoldine Arz, Laura Johnson and Jennie Baumann. Art handlers Mark Ward and Bill Mead, accompanied the objects on their circuitous journey and then ably executed their final installation. The educational programs that accompanied the exhibition were largely conceived and completely organized by Diane Stillman. Efforts to publicize the exhibition were the work of Kate Sellers, Howard White, Richard Gorelick, and Laura Siegmeister.

The audiovisual presentation was a collaborative enterprise produced by Michael Gibbons, of BGW & Associates, Inc., with art direction by Gary Aten of Telesis. The photography of the Hellenistic sites was the work of John Dean whom I especially thank for his dogged perseverance and unfaltering equanimity. Assisting with the photographic permissions were William Coulson and Robert Bridges at the American School of Classical Studies, Athens, and T. Leslie Shear, Jr., John Camp, Homer Thompson, Jan Diamant, and Craig Mauzy at the Agora Excavations of The American School of Classical Studies. M. Olivier Picard generously extended the hospitality of the French Archaeological School's excavation house on Delos. Additional slides were generously provided by Lynn Abercrombie, and by Christy Swid and Barbara Shattuck of the *National Geographic Magazine.*

To several individuals I express special appreciation beginning with Robert P. Bergman and Gary Vikan, Director and Assistant Director, respectively, of The Walters Art Gallery, for their characteristic generosity in giving me complete freedom to envision the project and then to carry it out as I had conceived it. I also thank my predecessors at the Walters, whose work on the collection will always be the foundation of any publication of the material: Dorothy Kent Hill, and Diana Buitron-Oliver. Finally, and above all, I am grateful to Dorothy Burr Thompson, under whom I studied at Princeton and with whom I worked in the Athenian Agora. As much as I have valued the opportunity to benefit from her vast knowledge of Hellenistic decorative arts, I have appreciated her enthusiastic support of her students' efforts and her extraordinary generosity as a scholar and a person.

E.D.R.

AA	*Archäologischer Anzeiger*
AAA	*Athens Annals of Archaeology*
AJA	*American Journal of Archaeology*
Alessandria	*Alessandria e il mondo ellenistico romano: Studi in onore di Achille Adriani,* N. Bonacasa and A. Di Vita eds., 3 vols., Studi e materiale 4, 5, 6 (Rome, 1983–84)
Alexandre le Grand	*Alexandre le Grand. Image et Réalité.* Entretiens sur l'antiquité classique 22 (1976)
AM	*Mitteilungen des Deutschen Archäologischen Instituts, Athenische Abteilung*
AM-BH	*Mitteilungen des Deutschen Archäologischen Instituts, Athenische Abteilung. Beiheft*
ANRW	*Aufstieg und Niedergang der römischen Welt*
ANSMN	*American Numismatic Society Museum Notes*
AntK	*Antike Kunst*
AntP	*Antike Plastik*
AR	*Archaeological Reports*
ArchCl	*Archeologia classica*
ArchDelt	*Archaiologikon Deltion*
ArtB	*Art Bulletin*
ARV²	J. D. Beazley, *Attic Red-Figure Vase-Painters,* 2nd ed., (Oxford, 1963)
ASAtene	*Annuario della scuola archeologica di Atene et delle missioni italiane in Oriente*
Austin, *Hellenistic World*	M. M. Austin, *The Hellenistic World from Alexander to the Roman Conquest* (Cambridge, 1981)
BABesch	*Bulletin Antieke Beschaving. Annual Papers on Classical Archaeology*
BCH	*Bulletin de correspondance hellénique*
BEFAR	*Bibliothèque des écoles françaises d'Athènes et de Rome*
Bell, *Morgantina*	M. Bell, *Morgantina Studies I. The Terracottas* (Princeton, 1981)
Besques, *Grèce*	S. Besques, *Musée national du Louvre. Catalogue raisonné des figurines et reliefs en terre-cuite grecs, étrusques et romains. III: Epoques hellénistique et romaine: Grèce et Asie Mineure* (Paris, 1972)
Besques, *Italie*	S. Besques, *Musée national du Louvre. Catalogue raisonné des figurines et reliefs en terre-cuite grecs, étrusques et romains. IV. I: Epoques hellénistique et romaine: Italie méridionale - Sicile - Sardaigne* (Paris, 1986)
Bieber, *Sculpture*	M. Bieber, *The Sculpture of the Hellenistic Age* (New York, 1955)
Bol, *Liebieghaus*	P.C. Bol, *Liebieghaus Museum alter Plastik. Antike Bildwerke. Bildwerke aus Stein und aus Stuck von archaischer Zeit bis zur Spätantike* (Melsungen, 1983)
Breitenstein	N. Breitenstein, *Catalogue of Terracottas, Cypriote, Greek, Etrusco-Italian and Roman* (Copenhagen, 1941)
BSA	*The Annual of the British School at Athens*
BSR	*Papers of the British School of Archaeology at Rome*
BurlMag	*Burlington Magazine*
BWalt	*The Walters Art Gallery Bulletin*

BWPr	*Winckelmannsprogramm der Archäologischen Gesellschaft zu Berlin*
CJ	*Classical Journal*
CollLatomus	*Collection Latomus*
CP	*Classical Philology*
Davidson-Oliver	P. Davidson and A. Oliver, Jr., *Ancient Greek and Roman Gold Jewelry in the Brooklyn Museum* (Brooklyn, 1984)
De Juliis, *Taranto*	E. De Juliis, *Taranto. Il museo archeologico* (Taranto, 1985)
Deppert-Lippitz	B. Deppert-Lippitz, *Griechische Goldschmuck* (Mainz, 1985)
Furtwängler, *AG*	A. Furtwängler, *Die antike Gemmen. Geschichte der Steinschneidekunst im klassischen Altertum* (Leipzig-Berlin, 1900)
GazArch	*Gazette archéologique*
GBA	*Gazette des beaux-arts*
GettyMusJ	*The J. Paul Getty Museum Journal*
Goldman, *Tarsus*	H. Goldman, ed., *Excavations at Gözlü Kule, Tarsus, I: The Hellenistic and Roman Periods* (Princeton, 1950)
Greifenhagen, *Schmuckarbeiten I*	A. Greifenhagen, *Schmuckarbeiten in Edelmetall,* I (Berlin, 1970)
Greifenhagen, *Schmuckarbeiten II*	A. Greifenhagen, *Schmuckarbeiten in Edelmetall,* II (Berlin, 1975)
Hackens-Winkes, *Louvain*	T. Hackens and R. Winkes, eds., *Gold Jewelry: Craft, Style and Meaning from Mycenae to Constantinopolis* (Louvain, 1983)
Higgins, *Tanagra*	R. A. Higgins, *Tanagra and the Figurines* (Princeton, 1986)
Higgins, *Terracottas*	R. A. Higgins, *Greek Terracottas* (London, 1967)
Hill, *Bronzes*	D. K. Hill, *Catalogue of Classical Bronze Sculpture in the Walters Art Gallery* (Baltimore, 1949)
Hoffmann-Davidson	H. Hoffmann and P. Davidson, *Greek Gold. Jewelry from the Age of Alexander* (Mainz, 1965). The catalogue accompanied an exhibition under the same title seen at the Museum of Fine Arts, Boston, The Brooklyn Museum, and the Virginia Museum of Fine Arts, Richmond (November 1965–May 1966)
IEJ	*Israel Exploration Journal*
IG	*Inscriptiones Graecae* (Berlin, 1873–)
IstMitt	*Istanbuler Mitteilungen*
Ivory	R. H. Randall Jr., et al., *Masterpieces of Ivory from the Walters Art Gallery* (New York, 1985)
JAOS	*Journal of the American Oriental Society*
JARCE	*Journal of the American Research Center in Egypt*
JdI	*Jahrbuch des Deutschen Archäologischen Instituts*

JdI-EH   *Jahrbuch des Deutschen Archäologischen Instituts. Ergänz-ungsheft*

JEA   *Journal of Egyptian Archaeology*

Jewelry   *Jewelry: Ancient to Modern* (New York, 1979). The catalogue accompanied an exhibition under the same title seen at the Walters Art Gallery (October 13, 1979–January 20, 1980)

JHS   *Journal of Hellenic Studies*

JRS   *Journal of Roman Studies*

JWalt   *Journal of the Walters Art Gallery*

Leyenaar-Plaisier   P. G. Leyenaar-Plaisier, *Les terres cuites grecques et romaines: Catalogue de la collection du musée national des antiquités à Leiden* (Leiden, 1979)

LIMC   *Lexicon Iconographicum Mythologicae Classicae*

MAAR   *Memoirs of the American Academy in Rome*

MarbWPr   *Marburger Winckelmann-Programm*

Marshall, *BMCJ*   F. Marshall, *Catalogue of the Jewellery, Greek, Etruscan and Roman, in the Departments of Antiquities, British Museum* (London, 1911)

Esbroeck   E. van Esbroeck, *Catalogue du musée de peinture, sculpture et archéologie au Palais Accoramboni*, pt. 2 (Rome, 1897)

Macedonia and Greece   *Macedonia and Greece in Late Classical and Early Hellenistic Times*, B. Barr-Sharrar and E. N. Borza, eds., Studies in the History of Art 10 (Washington, D.C. 1982)

Mitten, *Bronzes*   *Master Bronzes from the Classical World*, Fogg Art Museum (Cambridge, December 4, 1967–January 23, 1968); City Art Museum of St. Louis (St. Louis, March 1–April 13, 1968); Los Angeles County Museum of Art (Los Angeles, May 8–June 30, 1968); catalogue D. G. Mitten and S. F. Doeringer.

MM   *Madrider Mitteilungen*

Mollard-Besques, *Myrina*   S. Mollard-Besques, *Musée national du Louvre. Catalogue raisonné des figurines et reliefs en terre-cuite grecs, étrusques et romains. II: Myrina* (Paris, 1963)

MonPiot   *Monuments et mémoires. Fondation E. Piot*

MüJb   *Münchner Jahrbuch der bildenden Kunst*

MusHelv   *Museum Helveticum*

Objects of Adornment   *Objects of Adornment: Five Thousand Years of Jewelry from the Walters Art Gallery, Baltimore* (New York, 1984). The catalogue accompanied an exhibition under the same title seen at the Cooper-Hewitt Museum; the Chrysler Museum; the Carnegie Institute Museum of Art; the San Antonio Museum of Art; the Philbrook Art Center; Honolulu Academy of Arts; New Orleans Museum of Art; Milwaukee Art Museum; Minneapolis Institute of Arts; the Toledo Museum of Art; The John and Mabel Ringling Museum; and The Walters Art Gallery (October, 1984–October, 1987)

OGIS   *Orientis Graeci Inscriptiones Selectae*

Oliver, *Silver*   *Silver for the Gods: 800 Years of Greek and Roman Silver*, The Toledo Museum of Art (Toledo, October 8–November 20, 1977); The William Rockhill Nelson Gallery of Art and Atkins Museum of Fine Arts (Kansas City, December 11, 1977–January 22, 1978); The Kimbell Art Museum (Fort Worth, February 18–April 2, 1978), catalogue Andrew Oliver, Jr.

Ori di Taranto   E. De Juliis et al., *Gli Ori di Taranto* (Milan, 1984)

Pollitt   J. J. Pollitt, *Art in the Hellenistic Age* (Cambridge, 1986)

Prakt.   Πρακτικὰ τῆς ἐν Ἀθήναις Ἀρχαιολογικης Ἐταιρείας

RA   *Revue archéologique*

Reinach, *Statuaire*   S. Reinach, *Répertoire de la statuaire grecque et romaine* (Paris, 1897–1930)

Reinsberg, *Toreutik*   C. Reinsberg, *Studien zur hellenistischen Toreutik; die antiken Gipsabgüsse aus Memphis*, Hildesheimer Ägyptologische Beitrage 9 (Hildesheim, 1980)

Ridgway   B. S. Ridgway, *Roman Copies of Greek Sculpture: The Problem of the Originals* (Ann Arbor, 1984)

RM   *Mitteilungen des Deutschen Archäologischen Instituts, Römische Abteilung*

Robertson   M. Robertson, *A History of Greek Art* (Cambridge, 1975)

Search for Alexander   *The Search for Alexander: An Exhibition,* The National Gallery of Art (Washington, D.C., November 16, 1980–April 5, 1981), exhibition catalogue (1980); Art Institute of Chicago (Chicago, May 14–September 7, 1981); Museum of Fine Arts (Boston, October 27, 1981–January 10, 1982), supplement by J. Herrmann, Jr. (1981); Fine Arts Museum of San Francisco: M. H. de Young Memorial Museum (San Francisco, February 20–May 16, 1982), supplement (1982); New Orleans Museum of Art (New Orleans, June 27–September 19, 1982), supplement (1982); Royal Ontario Museum (Toronto, March 5–July 10, 1983), supplement (1983)

Segall, ''Tradition''   B. Segall, ''Tradition und Neuschöpfung in der frühalexandrinische Kleinkunst,'' *BWPr* 119–120 (Berlin, 1966)

SIMA   *Studies in Mediterranean Archaeology*

Steindorff   George Steindorff, *Catalogue of the Egyptian Sculpture in the Walters Art Gallery* (Baltimore, 1946)

Stewart, *Attikà*   A. Stewart, *Attikà. Studies in Athenian Sculpture of the Hellenistic Age. Society for the Promotion of Hellenic Studies. Supplementary Paper 14* (London, 1979)

Tarn   W. W. Tarn, *Hellenistic Civilization*, 3rd rev. ed. (Cleveland, 1966)

Thompson, *Oinochoai*   D. B. Thompson, *Ptolemaic Oinochoai and Portraits in Faience* (Oxford, 1973)

Thompson, *Troy*   D. B. Thompson, *Troy. The Terracotta Figurines of the Hellenistic Period.* Supplementary Monograph 3 (Princeton, 1963)

Vermeule, *Sculpture*   C. C. Vermeule III, *Greek and Roman Sculpture in America* (Berkeley, 1981)

Vollenweider, *Geneva*   M. L. Vollenweider, *Catalogue raisonné des sceaux, cylindres, intailles et camées, Musée d'art et d'histoire de Genève 2* (Mainz, 1976)

Vollenweider-Boardman, *Oxford*   M. L. Vollenweider and J. Boardman, *Catalogue of the Engraved Gems and Finger Rings, Ashmolean Museum, Oxford* (Oxford, 1978)

Perhaps no area of greek and roman art history is currently experiencing greater ferment than Hellenistic art. Through scholarly reevaluation, archaeological excavation, and the application of such recently developed scientific procedures as isotopic analysis and thermoluminescence testing, our understanding of the Hellenistic world is rapidly advancing, a circumstance that both reflects and nurtures a renewed appreciation of Hellenistic art after many decades of neglect. As the focus of such intense and unprecedented scrutiny, Hellenistic art is the natural choice for an exhibition and catalogue to accompany the first-ever North American Congress of Archaeology, a convention in Baltimore from January 5 to 9, 1989, of members of the Archaeological Institute of America, American Philological Association, American School of Oriental Research, Conference on Underwater Archaeology, and Society for Historical Archaeology. The Walters collection is ideally suited to an endeavor of this kind, both because its extensive holdings in Hellenistic art claim an extraordinary breadth and quality, and because so many of the objects have been only cursorily published. The exhibition presented the opportunity not merely to bring these objects to the attention of the general public, but to produce a volume that, unlike many permanent collection catalogues, focuses on an era rather than a medium and incorporates interpretative essays by prominent scholars in the field.

The insight that the Walters collection affords into the Hellenistic era is somewhat different from that which results from the conventional concentration upon the major arts of architecture, wall-painting, mosaic, and monumental sculpture. By contrast, the Walters holdings mainly comprise works of art on a smaller scale: marble reliefs; statuettes in marble, bronze, and terracotta; and vases and other household objects in faience, ivory, bronze, gold, gems, and glass. These so-called minor, or decorative, arts were destined primarily for domestic use and thus illuminate both the private life of the Hellenistic age and the more public opulence of the Hellenistic royal courts. The wide variety of these objects invites us to reassess the age's artistic vitality, which, on the basis of its monumental sculpture alone, has often been dismissed as lacking in creative energy. In addition, the range and quality of this material enable us to evaluate the influence that Egyptian and Near Eastern traditions exerted on the minor arts, and to identify, if not regional schools, then the local flavor of the artistic expression of Alexandria, southern Italy, and Anatolia.

In conceiving this exhibition and catalogue, the traditional chronological parameters were observed, from 331 with Alexander's victory at Gaugamela, to 30 when Egypt's Ptolemies, the last Hellenistic dynasty, succumbed to Roman domination. A brief introductory section of the catalogue is devoted to the transitional era that preceded the Hellenistic period, on the grounds that aesthetic expression is shaped as much by deep-seated artistic traditions as by historical circumstances. Rome and its vicinity were the only geographical areas purposefully excluded, although no one would deny that Roman Republican art is closely related to Hellenistic art of the eastern Mediterranean. A great effort was made to include only those works of art that are Hellenistic in date or could be judged to be extremely reliable copies from the Roman period. The catalogue is not intended to be a complete reference to all the Walters holdings in Hellenistic art; some unquestionably Hellenistic objects were intentionally omitted in order not to diminish the impact of the exhibition. A few of these are lesser pieces that remain unpublished, and others have appeared in catalogues of the jewelry, ivories, and bronzes in the Walters collection.[1] Of those works of art included here, many have long been in storage; others have been subjected to scientific testing, and all have either been examined or cleaned by the Walters Conservation and Technical Research Division, and scrutinized with renewed interest and vigor.

This catalogue incorporates the contributions of two scientific techniques that have recently become important tools for scholars of the ancient world. Marble isotopic analysis was carried out on the relief with a procession of twelve gods (No. 38) by Norman Herz at the Center for Archaeological Science of the University of Georgia. The underlying principle of this technique is that every marble carries a specific isotopic signature comprised of the ratio of heavier oxygen and carbon isotopes to lighter ones. Because different marbles contain distinct isotopic mixtures, it is often possible to associate a marble sculpture with a specific quarry from which the stone was taken, and this information can be used to further our understanding of regional schools of sculpture. The information is also useful in determining the authenticity of a sculptural work, because many quarries worked today were unknown in antiquity.

A second technique, thermoluminescence testing, was carried out on a number of terracotta figurines (Nos. 10, 75, 88, 91) and two vases (including No. 96) by the Research Laboratory for Archaeology and the History of Art in Oxford, England. Quartz crystals in a clay matrix absorb nuclear radiation from the natural radioisotopes of uranium, thorium, and potassium embedded in the clay itself or present in the surrounding burial media. When a clay object is kiln-fired, the stored energy is driven off, but immediately begins to accumulate again. In thermoluminescence tests, a sample from a terracotta figurine or piece of pottery is heated to 500 degrees centigrade, at which point the stored energy is released in the form of light. Through measurements of this light, it is possible to determine, with accuracy of 6 to 20 percent, the date at which the piece was last fired, information that is a highly reliable indicator of an object's authenticity.

THE HELLENISTIC COLLECTION OF THE WALTERS ART GALLERY

The majority of objects in this catalogue were acquired between 1902 and 1931 by Henry Walters, a railroad financier and an active art collector at a time when many great European private collections were being dispersed. Some of the first works of art that Henry Walters acquired passed into his hands in 1902 with his purchase of the Massarenti Collection, which was housed in the Accoramboni Palace in the Piazza Rusticucci in Rome. This collection had been assembled by a priest, Don Marcello Massarenti, and included both paintings and antiquities, most of which were probably acquired from excavations conducted in Italy after 1870. Among the large number of objects included in this single purchase were the first Hellenistic works of art to enter the Walters collection: a relief amphora (No. 96) and a marble statue of a woman (No. 34).

In the years following the acquisition of the Massarenti Collection, Walters made extensive and regular purchases of Hellenistic material sold at auction in London and Paris. His profession did not permit him to travel more than two weeks of the year, and so he depended heavily on such dealers as Dikran Kelekian and Joseph Brummer. It is not always clear which auctions Walters attended himself; in many instances he must have made his choices known beforehand to dealers who bought these objects at auction and then sold them to Walters. In many cases dealers acquainted with Walters's taste must have independently purchased works of art at these auctions which they were confident Walters would subsequently acquire from them. A number of carefully marked auction catalogues survive from these transactions, but financial information is almost totally lacking because Walters preferred the object rather than its price to be its own legacy. From the years 1902 to 1931, purchases of Hellenistic art were made with great regularity and were shipped to the gallery in Baltimore that Walters had constructed in 1904. The Papposilenos (No. 51), and child boxer (No. 52), were obtained in 1905 from the Warneck Collection, which was sold at an auction in that same year, and in 1911 Walters purchased through Kelekian the statuette of Aphrodite (No. 35) from the Nelidow Collection, which was sold in that year at the Galerie Georges Petit in Paris. In 1912 Walters bought another statuette of Aphrodite (No. 33) and a gold necklace (No. 129) at the auction of the Dattari Collection at the Hôtel Drouot in Paris, and in the following year the Ptolemaic bust (No. 50) from the Dattari Collection was purchased from Kelekian together with two of the finest objects in the Hellenistic collection: the bronze warrior (No. 62) and the terracotta relief depicting boys at a cockfight (No. 90). Hellenistic material entered Walters's collection almost every year thereafter, with the most extensive purchases made in 1924 and 1925, when Walters acquired from Brummer a number of terracotta figurines (Nos. 80, 85, 93) including the Nike from Myrina (No. 94), the seated muse (No. 24), the bronze boxer (No. 66), and the krater by the Baltimore Painter (No. 95). The last Hellenistic material Walters purchased was in 1931, the year he died, and included the fine bronze group of wrestlers (No. 64).

Because so many crates remained unopened at the time of his death, the magnitude of Walters's bequest to the people of Baltimore was not fully comprehended until several years afterward. Organization of the ancient material in the Walters collection fell to the hands of Curator of Ancient Art Dorothy Kent Hill, who made significant additions to the Hellenistic holdings, both at auction sales, including that of Mrs. Henry Walters in 1943, and through individual purchases from dealers. The bronze bed (No. 68) was bought from Brummer in 1939, and a number of objects were acquired at the Brummer sale in 1949. Dorothy Hill's last major purchase of Hellenistic art was the pair of gold bracelets (No. 116), which arrived in 1973. Under her successor, Diana Buitron, the marble statue of a muse (No. 21) was acquired, as well as a grave relief (No. 23), and the lynx earring (No. 125), which was a gift from Cynthia and Lee Alderdice. In recent years the collection has been augmented by the acquisition of a marble head, (No. 13) and several terracottas (Nos. 87, 88, 89).

1. *Jewelry; Ivory;* Hill, *Bronzes.*

With Alexander's destruction of the Persian Empire in 331, the lands under his control stretched from Greece and Anatolia through Egypt and the Near East to India. So enormous was this expanse that its integrity could not survive Alexander's death, and his successors wrestled for years before several monarchies emerged from the fray: the Antigonids in Macedonia, upon which Greece was dependent; the Seleukids in the Near East; and the Ptolemies in Egypt. Smaller sovereignties, including Bithynia and Pontos, also existed, and during the second century the powerful kingdom of Pergamon acquired much of Anatolia. Complicating the unavoidable friction between these monarchies was the intrusion of Rome. By the end of the third century it had taken control of South Italy and Sicily and had already begun to interfere in the politics of the eastern Mediterranean. By the end of the second century Rome had annexed as provinces parts of Greece, Macedonia, and Anatolia, and in 30 the last Hellenistic monarchy, that of the Ptolemies, fell into Roman hands. This event is conventionally agreed to signal the end of the Hellenistic era.

The years between 331 and 30 are distinguished from the preceding centuries by the expansion of the Greek experience beyond the confines of Greece, the western coast of Anatolia, South Italy, and Sicily. Because the Hellenistic monarchs were oriented to Greek civilization or were themselves of Greek lineage, because they employed Greek mercenary soldiers, and because Greek settlement, intermarriage, and trade with the Near East and Egypt were more extensive than ever before, Greek culture came to penetrate the inner reaches of Egypt, Anatolia, and the Near East. Hellenism touched the lives of such disparate peoples as Syrians, Arabs, Jews, Iranians, Babylonians, and Egyptians, and a simplified form of classical Greek, the *koine,* became the common written and spoken language. The response of Greek culture to these changed circumstances and diverse peoples resulted in a civilization whose cross-cultural character is acknowledged by the modern term "Hellenistic."

From almost every point of view, the Hellenistic age is distinguished from the era of Classical Greece. One of the most basic differences is that most citizens of Hellenistic times lived under monarchs who controlled vast expanses of land, and who, through their authority to declare war and bestow royal favors, essentially held the well-being of their subjects in their personal control. The pivotal importance of the king is reflected in an unprecedented emphasis upon his individual personality, appearance, and divinized cult, and this phenomenon is vividly manifested in the prevalence of portraiture in Hellenistic art (Nos. 50, 135, 136, 139, 141, 148–50). In the absence of direct contact, these images established a link between the remote ruler and the ruled, allowing the sovereign to enter private homes and personal lives and, in so doing, forge a bond of loyalty with his subjects.

One important ramification of the new political structure was the tremendous wealth that the monarchs and the aristocracy of the royal courts enjoyed, and the opulent lifestyles these assets sustained. Royal wealth was derived from the enormous quantities of gold and silver that Alexander's conquests had introduced to circulation, from taxes on land and commerce, and from such state-owned enterprises as mines and quarries. The basis of aristocratic prosperity lay, as always, in land and occasional minor industry. Owners of large tracts, which were often enhanced through royal favor, were better insulated against agricultural distress than modest farmers, and this advantage enabled them to expand their landholdings and thereby widen the gap between rich and poor. The affluence of the ruling class, their Hellenic affiliation, and the vast scale of the kingdoms encouraged an extensive trade in both staple and luxury products which, in turn, offered even more opportunities for the acquisition of wealth.

The intensified trade that developed in Hellenistic times shifted the focus of Greek civilization away from mainland Greece to the eastern coast of the Aegean and Mediterranean and gave rise to enormous cities which profited from their role as centers of the transit trade. Among the sophisticated international metropoleis of the Hellenistic age were Antioch on the Orontes, Ephesos, Alexandria, and the islands of Rhodes and Delos. Through these centers passed a multitude of products: woven woolen cloth from Miletos, papyrus from Egypt, glass from Phoenicia (No. 151), and wine from Syria. Most valued and certainly most exotic was the trade from the Orient that was brought overland from China and then by boat from the mouth of the Indus River up the Tigris River to Seleukia before being transferred to camel caravan for the long trek to Damascus, Antioch, and Ephesos. Products hitherto unknown were now in tremendous demand: silk and furs from China; cotton and spices from India; and a wealth of colored

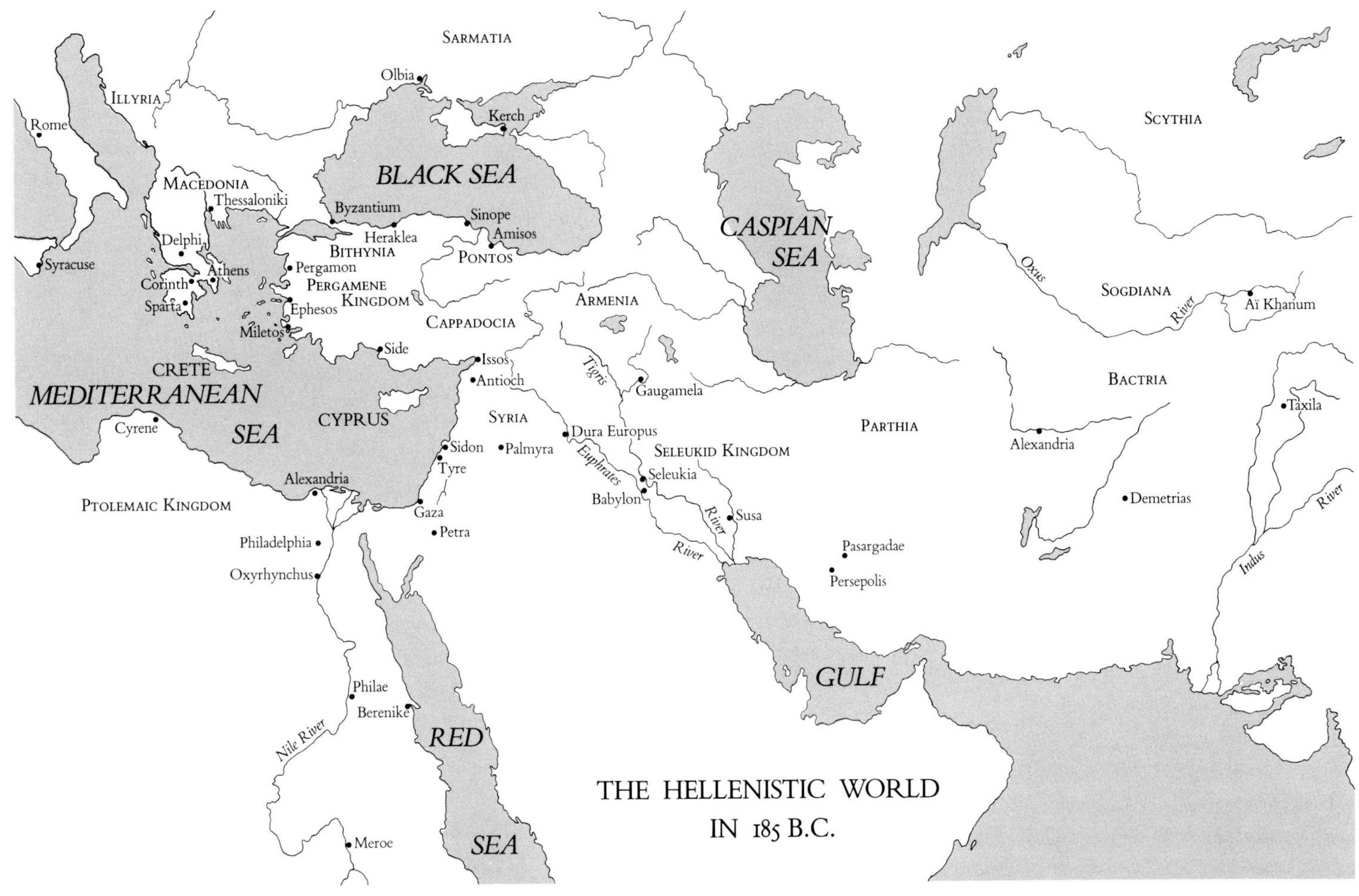

stones, which included emeralds from the Ural Mountains (No. 131) and garnets from India (Nos. 135, 136). Another trade route by land up the western coast of Arabia and overland to Damascus transported frankincense and myrrh from south Arabia and, from Africa, gold, ivory (No. 111), and slaves (Nos. 57, 58).

Fostered by international trade, cities such as Ephesos and Antioch grew prodigiously, their populations numbered in the hundreds of thousands, their grandeur and bustle a magnet for adventurers seeking wealth and excitement. Not only were foreign traders and exotic goods to be found in these metropoleis, but other transient groups as well: actors who circulated to various theatrical festivals, athletes competing in the numerous contests that flourished around the Mediterranean (No. 64), discharged professional soldiers of Macedonian, Greek, Syrian, and Iranian origin, travelers on their way to healing or religious sanctuaries on Kos and Samothrace, and scholars setting forth to study at Athens, Smyrna, Alexandria, or Pergamon. The stimulating cosmopolitan atmosphere nurtured a civic pride, which was manifested in the construction of theaters and gymnasia. These structures followed Greek architectural traditions and housed theatrical performances and educational programs that furthered the dissemination of Greek culture. The constraints placed upon a city's foreign policy by its relationship with the royal courts intensified a community's inward focus and resulted in a competition between cities that was expressed in beautification projects and the celebration of theatrical and athletic festivals. The individual generosity that sponsored many of these efforts was prominently acknowledged in monumental portrait statuary, which served as adornment to streets and public areas (No. 34).

The grandeur and Hellenic appearance of the metropolitan centers are too often allowed to obscure less visible aspects of Hellenistic life. Although urbanization was a primary objective of many Hellenistic monarchs, the vast hinterland of the Hellenistic world remained rural farmland punctuated by small villages. The lives of the inhabitants had altered very little under Assyrian and Persian rule, and under Hellenistic monarchs their traditional way of life remained intact and largely untouched by the process of Hellenization. Even within the large cities there is a somber side, for whereas opportunities for advancement were now shared by Greeks and those non-Greeks who embraced Hellenic customs, the lot of women and slaves had improved very little. Despite the preciosity of the world of the Tanagra figurine (No. 84), Tarn has argued that female infanticide was practiced throughout the Hellenistic era, and certainly the opportunities for female education did not improve noticeably. The institution of slavery flourished as never before, as seemingly unending strife and rampant piracy constantly replenished the supply of African, Syrian, and Anatolian slaves who were eagerly purchased by the affluent upper classes. Into these Greek and Macedonian households the slaves brought their native customs and, in turn, absorbed the Hellenic ways of their masters.

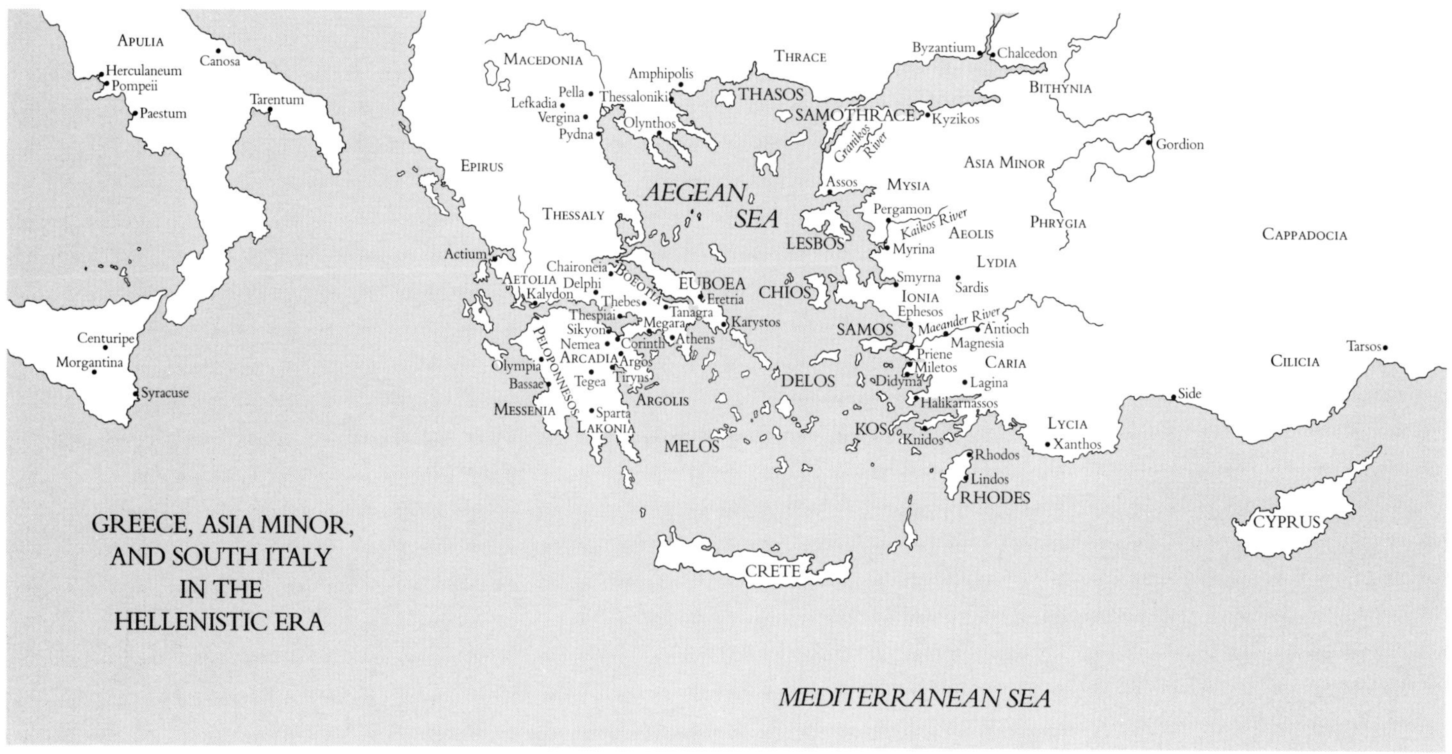

Fig. 2. Greece, Asia Minor, and Italy in Hellenistic times.

The monarchical system and the vast size of the Hellenistic kingdoms had a profound spiritual impact on the inhabitants of the post-Alexandrian world. In Classical Greece a citizen belonged to a city-state, or *polis;* as one of only several thousand citizens, he had a say in civic and foreign affairs, experienced a deep allegiance to the Olympian deities of his polis, and, in turn, acquired an identity through his position in this framework. In the new Hellenistic world, cities were often too large for a single individual's voice to be easily heard; at the same time, many cities experienced only a limited degree of autonomy from the kings, with the consequence that the city's prosperity was very much dependent upon royal approval. As a result of these changed circumstances, people believed themselves to have less control over their own lives than they had ever had before. The situation was complicated by the extensive intermingling of peoples that carried with it an exposure to other cultures, a phenomenon which intensified perceptions of individual insignificance.

Not unexpectedly, the mood that pervaded this new world was a complex one. The age's insecurity was voiced by Demetrios of Phaleron (Polybios 29.21) and such writers as Theophrastos, who adhered to the widely held sentiment that Fortune, not human will, guides man's destiny (No. 150). The eclipse of the insulating polis structure led to a reevaluation of the former conviction that the Greeks and their gods were superior to all others. Discouraged by the inability of the Olympian pantheon to respond to the needs of a new world, many people embraced non-Hellenic gods and goddesses, some of whom held connotations of salvation. Divinities of Egyptian origin, such as Sarapis (Nos. 70, 130, 152) and Isis (No. 73), became identified with Greek deities and acquired a many-faceted character that won them a broad following. The spread of their popularity both reflected and encouraged a growing predisposition toward monotheism that was the ideal breeding ground for Christianity. One of the greatest intellectual contributions of the Hellenistic age was made in the philosophical arena as codes of behavior were developed for dealing with the unsettling aspects of this new milieu. Stoics, following their leader Zeno (333–263), envisioned the universe as a single unit under a supreme presence known as Nature or Destiny, and advocated acceptance of this divine will in order to attain happiness. Adherents of the contemporary Epicurus (341–270) admitted the powerlessness of the gods and accepted death as a finite event not succeeded by an afterlife; happiness, the Epicureans asserted, could be attained by avoiding physical discomfort and mental distress.

Philosophy was only one sphere of an intellectual growth that was particularly nourished by royal patronage epitomized by the Mouseion (Museum) and Library in Alexandria, which Ptolemy I established about 300 as a center for scholarly contemplation and investigation. The Mouseion attracted some of the finest minds in the Hellenistic world, including the epic poets Apollodoros and Kallimachos, who wrote a variety of poetry including lyric and elegiac. An adjunct to the Mouseion was the Library, which accumulated a wealth of papyrus scrolls said to number in the hundreds of thousands. It was in the Mouseion and Library at Alexandria that the Old Testament was translated into Greek, the Seven Wonders of the Ancient World were codified, and Eratosthenes measured the circumference of the earth. It was here, too, that Euclid reviewed the progress of mathematics, Hero invented the steam engine, and Archimedes conducted experiments in engineering that resulted in the Archimedian screw for raising water, which is still in use today. A second, extremely prominent, intellectual center and library was established by the kings of Pergamon, which gave its name to the sheepskin, or parchment, used for the books that would eventually supersede papyrus rolls. The seclusion of these scholarly centers, which contrasts so markedly with the degree to which thinkers of the fifth century had been integrated into the affairs of the polis, gave rise to a scholarship whose pedantic nature and escapist leanings are still evoked by the term "Alexandrian." Even the dramatic scientific and technological advances were desultorily applied to the improvement of the quality of life, and the aloofness and irrelevancy of this intellectual exploration are intimated in Timon's description of the Mouseion as a "birdcage of the Muses" (Diog. Laert. 9.12.109–15).

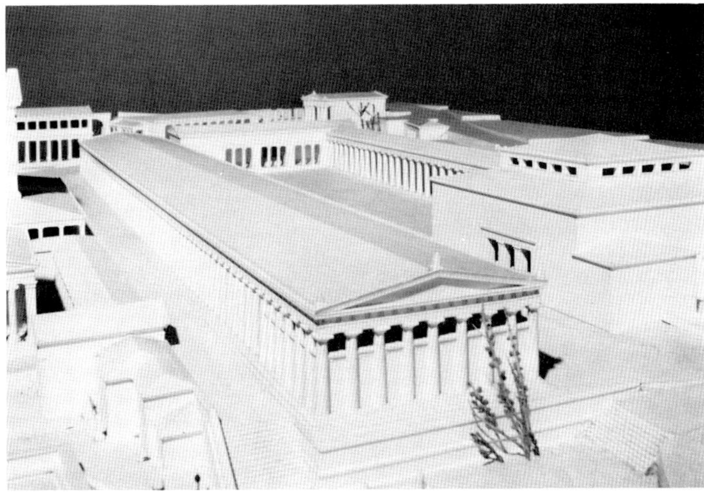

Fig. 3. Model of the Athenian Agora, ca. 100 B.C., Agora Excavations, American School of Classical Studies. Photograph, John Dean.

Hellenistic Art

Artistically, the Hellenistic age is easily recognized as a departure from the art of the Classical era, and this distinctiveness was so much at odds with late nineteenth- and early twentieth-century taste that only in the last few decades has Hellenistic art attracted its share of scholarly attention. The art of the Hellenistic era remains essentially Greek in its continued emphasis upon mankind, including the male and female form, and human character, activities, and preoccupations. Also typically Hellenic is its sense of humor, expressed both through sympathetic affection (Nos. 53, 55) and teasing jest (Nos. 45, 90). But at the same time as it is unmistakably Greek, Hellenistic art is easily contrasted with the inexpressiveness and languor of fifth- and early fourth-century art where figures are ageless and composed (No. 3), drapery subordinated to the human form (No. 1), and representations rendered either in low relief (No. 4) or, in the case of freestanding sculpture, composed in an almost two-dimensional manner (No. 6). The opposite point of view that permeates so much of Hellenistic art is probably partly a reaction to this Classical reserve, but an equally forceful catalyst was the diversified and invigorating atmosphere that resulted from the confrontation of Greek with non-Hellenic artistic traditions.

One of the most immediate results of the new international milieu was the widened range of subject matter which has no precedent in art before Hellenistic times. Frequently encountered are both the unorthodox elements of daily life such as hunchbacks (No. 54) and grotesques (Nos. 59, 101, 102), and more conventional denizens including children (Nos. 90, 91), animals (No. 109), and athletes (No. 64). Elements of a landscape setting are not only more prevalent in two-dimensional works (No. 48), but also appear in sculptural reliefs (No. 45). Another noteworthy feature is the degree to which the preoccupations of the age find their expression in contemporary art. The same yearning for escape sensed in Hellenistic literature is perceptible in such rural subjects as Pan (No. 53) and the Nymphs (No. 48), and in the withdrawn musings of the terracotta Tanagra figurines (Nos. 83, 84), the romantic pairings of amorous couples (No. 46), and the festive and spirited gestures of the wine-god Dionysos (No. 65) and the Silenoi, his semi-bestial followers (No. 51). The increased secularization of the traditional Olympian religious structure is apparent in the transferal of the banquet relief from the heroic world to the human one (No. 14) and in the many depictions of the nude Aphrodite (Nos. 20, 35, 71, 72). The erotic and romantic connotations that underlie many of her representations are elsewhere apparent in depictions of Eros (No. 89), and in the intermingling of male and female iconography in a female version of the Diadoumenos (No. 35). Contemporary philosophical explorations are mirrored in the representation of such abstract concepts as the Muses (Nos. 21, 22, 24, 25), and the pedantry characteristic of Alexandrian literature has its echo in such artistic monuments as a wrestling group that alludes to an age-old Egyptian motif of victor triumphing over victim (No. 63). The perennial Greek sense of humor expresses itself in parody; a cockfight is attended by little boys, one of whom assumes a languorous pose based on the stance of a Lysippan work that depicted Herakles exhausted by the magnitude of his many labors (No. 90).

A particularly prominent feature of Hellenistic art is the influence of the royal courts, which prompted a thirst for such previously scarce materials as ivory, glass (Nos. 128, 132), emeralds from the Ural Mountains (Nos. 125, 131–133), amethysts from India (No. 139), pearls from Bahrain (Nos. 131–132), and garnets from India and the Balkan area (Nos. 135, 136, 140). Court influence is also evident in the way that products made for royal use came to function as prototypes for imitations made in less expensive fabrics; precious metal vessels, for example, surely inspired both the ceramic moldmade bowls (Nos. 97–99) and the faience oinochoai with Ptolemaic portraits (Nos. 103, 104). Another area of court influence can be recognized in the extensive use of royal portraiture (Nos. 50, 135, 139, 140, 148–50), and in the resilient legacy of Alexander, whose image survives in a wide range of works of art including statuettes (Nos. 49, 61) and appliqués (No. 110). The portrait ring Alexander wore inaugurated a fashion for such royal accoutrements (Nos. 136, 140, 141), and the double-knot and diadem, so closely associated with him, enjoyed widespread popularity (Nos. 117, 127). Distinctive elements of Alexandrian portraiture, particularly the upward gaze, were assimilated into the portraits of Ptolemaic monarchs (No. 50) who claimed a Heraklean ancestry that not coincidentally affiliated this dynasty more closely with Alexander (No. 52). Another by-product of royal patronage was outstanding craftsmanship, particularly in metalwork and gold jewelry, surely a partial legacy of the goldsmiths who had been employed in the Persian courts. The inevitable emphasis in the royal courts on such appurtenances as drinking vessels and furniture encouraged production of objects which had a long artistic tradition in other cultures, and so it is not surprising that Hellenistic beds, bowls, and bracelets claim ancestry from the Persian world (Nos. 68, 97–99, 116), and faience vessels bear motifs and shapes of Egyptian origin (Nos. 105–106, 108).

Perhaps the thorniest problem intrinsic to the study of Hellenistic art lies in the area of style. The versatility and competency of the artists, coupled with the broad geographical area over which they were working, resulted in the absence of a sequential, easily recognized stylistic development. This phenomenon, compounded by a lack of unequivocably dated monuments, has resulted in a weak chronological footing that is still the subject of lively debate. Most scholars would agree, however, that works of the late fourth and early third centuries continue to adhere fairly closely to the style of the Classical era; the bearded head from a grave monument (No. 13), for example, recalls a mid fourth-century version (No. 5), but exhibits greater plasticity and an introduction of emotion that look forward to the art of succeeding centuries. Many early third-century terracotta figurines (Nos. 76, 80) are inspired by the late-Classical treatment of the body exemplified by the work of Praxiteles (No. 6). The Classical heritage is further apparent in the controlled rhythm and low relief of the tongue pattern on a silver bowl of the late fourth or early third century (No. 41).

The third century witnesses a greater interest in three-dimensionality, often in self-contained or centripetal silhouettes, exemplified by a dancer (No. 56) and a number of terracotta figurines (No. 83). Group sculpture becomes more prevalent, both figures interlocked as a single unit and adhering to a centripetal formula (No. 64), and figures not immediately juxtaposed but presumably grouped in a tableau or montage (Nos. 58, 62).

By the closing decades of the third century and through the second century, so-called baroque elements are introduced in the form of exaggerated movement, often in an open silhouette, exemplified by the standing Alexander (No. 61), the running soldier (No. 62), and the Myrina Nike (No. 94). The character of the age is also visible in the restless, plastic leaves of the floral ornament on a silver bowl (No. 67), the deep shadows and complicated drapery folds that envelop the standing Muse (No. 21), and the extensive decorative detail in the gold jewelry (No. 126).

By the mid-first century a classicizing trend had been introduced, manifested here in the classical pose of a bronze athlete (No. 74) and the allusion to the Polykleitan Diadoumenos in the marble statuette of a woman binding her hair (No. 35). The late Hellenistic period also saw the fabrication of works of art in an archaizing style that incorporated allusions to the style of the late sixth and early fifth centuries (No. 38). Contemporary with the archaizing style were neo-Attic works of art, usually decorative reliefs, which combined styles of the late Archaic period, mid-fifth, and later fourth centuries (No. 39).

Although attempts to recognize regional schools of Hellenistic sculpture have been marked by checkered success, most scholars would agree that certain identifiable features characterize the general artistic current of specific areas such as Alexandria, and the broader geographical expanses of South Italy with Sicily, and the western coast of Anatolia. Because of their predisposition to linearity and their appreciation of humor, Greek and Egyptian art shared a natural affinity that was strengthened in Hellenistic times with that era's wider interest in nature (No. 48) and the variant forms of humanity from slaves (Nos. 57, 58) to hunchbacks (No. 54) and dwarfs (No. 55). It is not surprising, therefore, to find that the art of Alexandria was inspired by traditional Egyptian motifs and styles: figures of grotesques betray influence from the age-old depictions of Bes (Nos. 101, 102), and a limestone representation of a Ptolemaic queen continues a long tradition of Egyptian portraiture, displaying such specifically Egyptian features as stylized frontality and corkscrew locks (No. 29). Contrasting with Alexandrian art was the Hellenistic art of South Italy and Sicily which developed an indigenous predisposition to flamboyance manifested in such varied creations as the elongated and elaborately coiffed terracotta figurines (No. 86), the baroque shape and ornament of the pottery (Nos. 95, 96), and the exaggerated details of a gold earring (No. 123). Still a different artistic flavor is perceptible along the western coast of Asia Minor where the sculptural tradition retained such vitality that even the bronze, marble, and terracotta statuettes adhere strongly to the style and iconography of monumental sculpture (Nos. 35, 90).

A final, novel characteristic of Hellenistic art, and one that looks forward to the Roman era, is the changing role in which works of art now functioned. In the Classical era sculpture was specifically commissioned as a public monument or private dedication, and terracotta and bronze figurines served as votive or burial offerings. In the Hellenistic age, by contrast, the emphasis shifted to the enhancement of the home with small-scale marble, bronze, and terracotta sculpture sold predominantly for a secular context as domestic decoration, the religious connotation in the iconography largely suppressed (Nos. 71, 72). The existence of many affluent consumers eager to enhance their private surroundings resulted in a wide range of such luxury products as ornamental furniture (No. 68) and mirrors (Nos. 46, 47, 48). As this clientele burgeoned, objects were mass-manufactured as never before, and major sculptural monuments were replicated through a mechanical method known as the pointing system. One outgrowth of

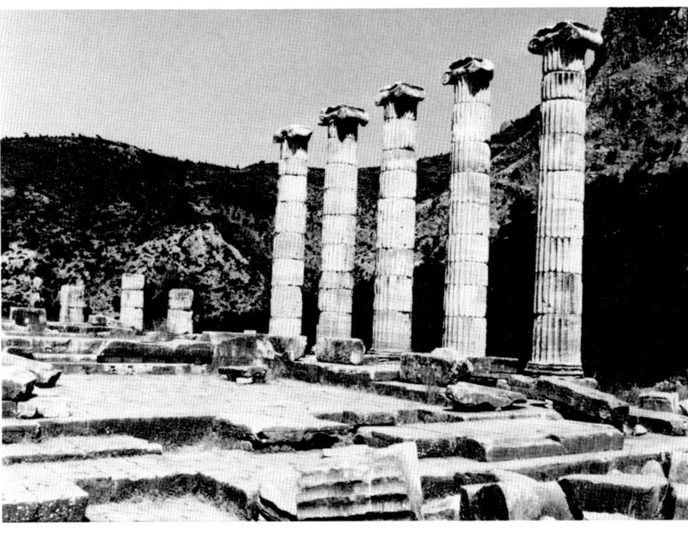

Fig. 4. The Temple of Athena Polias at Priene, fourth century B.C. Photograph, John Dean.

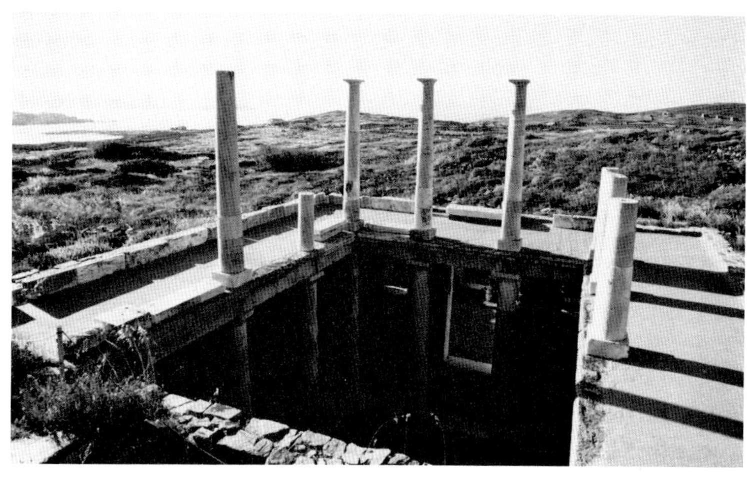

Fig. 5. The House of Hermes, Delos, second century B.C. Photograph, John Dean.

this expanded production was the appearance of the dispassionate professional craftsman; a second result was the generation of an international traffic in works of art. The art market intensifed in late Hellenistic times with the emergence of the Roman consumer, as wealthy businessmen in the eastern Mediterranean and prominent landowners in Italy made extensive purchases of objects for domestic adornment. Particularly popular were archaizing and neo-Attic works of art, some of which were probably sold to unsuspecting customers as genuinely Archaic or Classical pieces.

Because the Roman intrusion into the eastern Mediterranean can be documented as early as the late third century, Roman interaction with Hellenistic civilization is a matter of great interest. Politically and economically, the Roman presence left a marked imprint on the late Hellenistic world, but in artistic terms the Roman impact is far less easily substantiated. In the other direction, the influence of Hellenistic culture on Roman civilization was immense. From their encounter with Hellenistic monarchies, the Romans carried home with them notions of kingship that would dramatically shape the Roman imperial administration in aspects ranging from the divinization of the ruler and the accoutrements of court life to the reliance of the king upon his army, the effectiveness of ceremony and pomp, and the employment of royal portraiture as a political instrument of the state. The Romans absorbed and emulated the Hellenistic emphasis upon city life with its concern for beautification and the focus of its social life upon the gymnasium and the theater. In the sphere of religion, the increasingly ecumenical mood of the Hellenistic world culminated in Roman times in a more intensified assimilation of Hellenic and foreign deities that made possible the ultimate triumph of monotheism.

Within the larger dimension of the ancient world, the Hellenistic period has often been viewed as a bridge between the fifth century and the Roman period, a transmitter of Classical culture to the Roman world. A more accurate assessment is to describe Hellenistic civilization as an adaptation of Classical Greek culture by which the ordered, even austere, rhythm of an earlier age was adjusted to a more comfortable, less rigidly defined, way of life. That this was a colorful and more experimental world is immediately evident in the greater number of opportunities that enabled a Hellenistic citizen to make a living as a trader, soldier, scholar, athlete, actor, or craftsman. Moreover, the success of the Hellenistic formula is attested by its longevity; through the Roman period and well into the Byzantine era, the culture of the eastern Mediterranean, in its language, physical appurtenances, and cultural traditions, remained essentially Hellenistic.

BIBLIOGRAPHY

Austin, M. M., *The Hellenistic World from Alexander to the Roman Conquest* (Cambridge, 1981).

Bagnall, R. S. and P. Derow, *Greek Historical Documents: The Hellenistic Period* (Ann Arbor, 1981).

Bieber, M., *The Sculpture of the Hellenistic Age,* rev. ed. (New York, 1961).

Burstein, S., ed., *The Hellenistic Age from the Battle of Ipsos to the Death of Kleopatra VII* (Cambridge, 1985).

Charbonneaux, J., R. Martin, F. Villard, *Hellenistic Art* (New York, 1973).

Ferguson, J., *The Heritage of Hellenism* (New York, 1973).

Grant, F. C., ed., *Hellenistic Religions: The Age of Syncretism* (New York, 1953).

Gruen, E., *The Hellenistic World and the Coming of Rome* (Berkeley, 1984).

Hadas, M., *Hellenistic Culture* (New York, 1959).

Havelock, C., *Hellenistic Art,* 2nd ed., (New York, 1981).

Kidson, P., "The Figural Arts," in M. I. Finley, ed., *The Legacy of Greece* (Oxford, 1984).

Lewis, N., *Greeks in Ptolemaic Egypt* (Oxford, 1986).

Onians, J., *Art and Thought in the Hellenistic Age* (London, 1979).

Peters, F. E., *The Harvest of Hellenism* (New York, 1970).

Pollitt, J. J., *Art in the Hellenistic Age* (Cambridge, 1986).

Rostovtzeff, M., *The Social and Economic History of the Hellenistic World,* I–III, (Oxford, 1941).

Walbank, F. W., et al., eds., *The Cambridge Ancient History, VII, Pt. I,* The Hellenistic World, 2nd ed. (Cambridge, 1984).

Walbank, F. W., *The Hellenistic World* (Atlantic Highlands, N.J., 1981).

Welles, C. B., *Alexander and the Hellenistic World* (Toronto, 1970).

Welles, C. B., *Royal Correspondence in the Hellenistic Period* (New Haven, 1934).

IF WE WERE ASKED TO GIVE AN EXAMPLE of Hellenistic art, most of us would probably cite the Pergamon Altar (figs. 1, 2). This magnificent structure, discovered by C. Humann in 1873 and excavated by the Germans in the following years (1878–1886), is one of the main features of the East Berlin Museum, where it has been partly reconstructed and displayed in the most appropriate form to convey an idea of its architectural appearance and the extent of its two friezes—the pictorial "film-strip" development of the legend of Telephos in its interior, and the flamboyant, baroque Gigantomachy from the exterior of the high podium. The monumental staircase between projecting wings that leads to the Ionic colonnade surrounding the inner space is indeed a good example of the theatrical and volumetric effects attempted by Hellenistic architects, and the writhing coils, craggy faces, and bulging bodies of the fantastic creatures battling the Olympian gods and their allies epitomize what we consider the excesses of Hellenistic sculpture. The correspondence between art and literature provided by the Hesiodic cast of characters for the Gigantomachy frieze is considered symptomatic of the literary bent of the general period. Moreover the building, universally attributed to the reign of Eumenes II (197–159 B.C.), is generally dated between ca. 180 and 160 B.C. (a very precise chronological determination, for Hellenistic sculpture), and is identified as an altar to Zeus and Athena erected to commemorate the victories of the Attalids over the Galatians. Given the uncertainty that surrounds most of our attributions to the Hellenistic period, this amount of information for a single monument is remarkable indeed.[1]

Yet the Pergamon Altar exemplifies our notions of Hellenistic art in other ways as well, quite different from those cited and certainly not generally appreciated by the superficial student of the period—in the assumptions and controversy that underlie much of the established knowledge. The architectural layout may lend itself to variant reconstructions, and some elements of it, such as the score of diminutive akroterial (?) horses, have never been properly explained. Nothing was found of the presumed sacrificial platform in the interior, so that the structure, even in the traditionally accepted form, would represent only the outer casing for the altar proper. The continuous narrative and pictorialism of the Telephos frieze are so different from the baroque rendering of the Gigantomachy that some scholars have wondered whether the two should be considered contemporary. The fragmentary inscription has been integrated to read as Eumenes' dedication, but nowhere in the preserved portions does the name of the king appear, or the reason for the offering. The attribution to Zeus and Athena has been based on the presumed alignment of

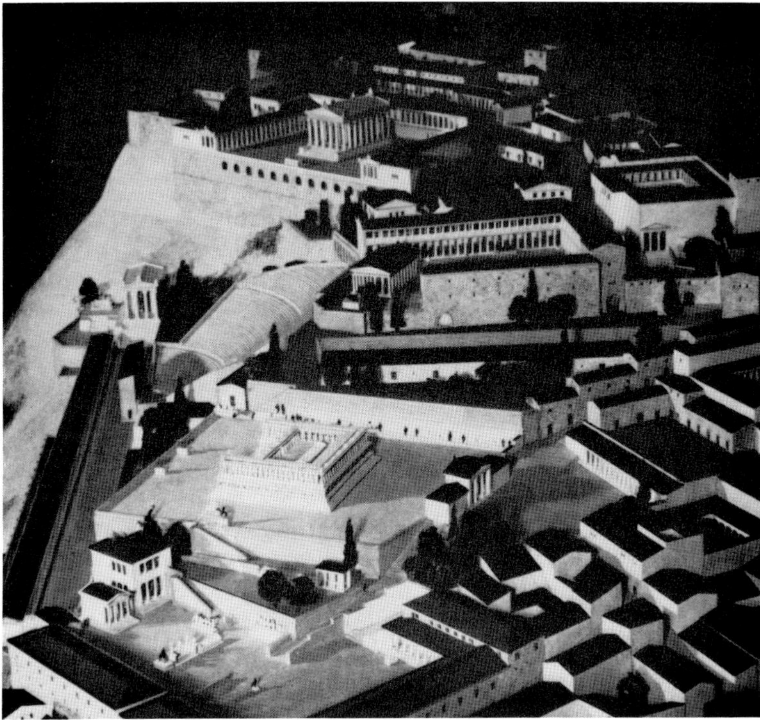

Fig. 1. Model of the Akropolis of Pergamon, by Hans Schleif (now lost), from E. Schmidt, *The Great Altar of Pergamon* (Boston, 1965), PL. 3.

the altar with the Temple of Athena at a higher level, but both structures could also be visualized as sited, not in relation to each other, but to the edges of their respective terraces with an aim to achieve the greatest possible visibility from the plain below. In addition, although Athena and Zeus are dramatically rendered on the east section of the Gigantomachy frieze, they do not lie on the direct line of vision of a viewer entering the precinct, who would instead have seen first Herakles fighting alongside the Olympians. Correlations with Christian sources mentioning a Throne of Satan and with representations on coins have not proved a perfect fit. Finally, recent studies have interpreted the presence of an apsidal structure within the foundations as evidence that the main building was not an altar but rather the Heroon of Telephos, and examination of pottery fragments found underneath the monument has suggested that construction did not begin until 166 B.C., a date later than usually postulated which would carry with it somewhat different historical connotations.[2]

These controversial issues are all the more disquieting because the Pergamon Altar has traditionally been considered a firm point in our studies of Hellenistic culture, a sort of artistic watershed for the establishment of relative chronologies, with monuments ranged on either side according to the degree of their presumed affinity (or lack of it) to this major example. Architecturally, its reconstruction has arbitrarily been taken as the basis for many other Hellenistic altars, to the point that Gigantomachy panels now known to have formed the coffers of the Temple of Athena at Priene were once attributed—on analogy with Pergamon—to the podium of its altar despite excavators' sketches that showed it as a low structure.[3] Sculpturally, another important monument, the famous Laokoon, has been alternatively considered melodramatic and one-sided or poignant and three-dimensional, according to whether it was dated as late as the first century B.C., in a revival of Pergamene style, or earlier, in the second century, approximately contemporary with the Altar. After the discovery of the mythological groups from the Sperlonga grotto, one of them carrying the names of the same sculptors who are said by Pliny to have made the Laokoon, even the latter has undergone revisionist analysis, and is now considered by many scholars a Roman re-elaboration of Hellenistic prototypes, being variously attributed from the Augustan to the Flavian period.[4]

Perhaps no other single event has had as much impact on our approach to Hellenistic art as the finding of the Sperlonga sculptures. In their obvious adaptation to the natural environment of the cave, they bespeak ad-hoc composition and manufacture, as a typical imperial program; yet in their dramatic style and epic content they seem closest to Hellenistic conceptions, at least as we understand them at present. It is this last point that needs review and perhaps modification, if we are to perceive the reasons for our current positions on the Hellenistic period as a whole, and Hellenistic art—primarily sculpture—in particular.

We may usefully begin with the term Hellenistic itself. As first used by Johann Gustav Droysen in his *Geschichte des Hellenismus* (1833), the word meant not simply "late Greek" but also "diluted" or "impure" Greek, to reflect the assimilation of non-Greek speaking peoples in the cultural koine created by the conquests of Alexander the Great. Droysen had the great merit of being the first to conceive of Greek history as a continuum stretching to the beginning of the Christian era. Before his day, as pointed out by Margarete Bieber, the last three centuries B.C. had been neglected by historians, philologists, and archaeologists alike, in the misconception that the manifestations of that period were debased and adulterated versions of the peak of culture that had been reached during the Classical phase.[5] To be sure, individual monuments—like the Melos Aphrodite (better known as the Venus de Milo), the Victory of Samothrace, the Laokoon itself—were greatly admired and perhaps even overly praised. But at first there had been a tendency to attribute to the fourth century those works that appeared "too good to be late," and the sculptural production of the period as a whole was considered inferior. This general belief that all Hellenistic art was decadent and degenerate has persisted until recent times, and a faintly apologetic tone has permeated studies of Hellenistic sculpture, which was either left out entirely from general surveys of Greek art, or was treated in much more abbreviated fashion and unfavorably compared, whether tacitly or openly, to the glorious renderings of the preceding centuries.

This critical approach can partly be explained on philosophical grounds. As natural science observed in all living things a definite cycle going from weak beginnings, through growth and strengthening, to full

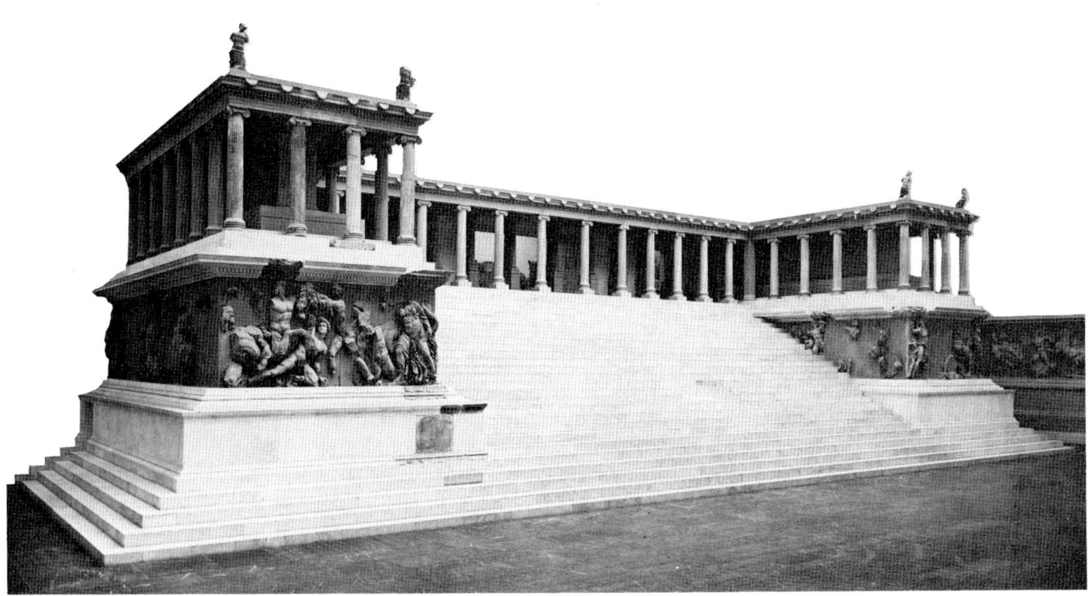

Fig. 2. The Pergamon Altar, ca. 180–160 B.C., as reconstructed in East Berlin, Staatliche Museen zu Berlin. Photograph, Staatliche Museen zu Berlin.

flowering and maturity, to be followed inevitably by decline and death, so historical and art-historical studies conceived of culture as following the same pattern, perennially repeated through the centuries, after each cycle was completed. Thus not only was Hellenistic regarded as the decadent period of Greek art, but Archaic suffered from the same strictures, being perceived as primitive and imperfect, a mere striving toward the aims and accomplishments of the Classical phase. Yet, whereas naturalism and pattern within the same Archaic sculpture, and hybrid Ionic and Doric forms in a single early building were ascribed to beginners' experimentation, the different renderings and the mixture of the orders in Hellenistic art were considered tired and misguided deviations from the golden norm.[6]

This conception was definitely promoted by influential scholars like Johann Joachim Winckelmann (author of the *Geschichte der Kunst des Altertums,* 1764) and Adolf Furtwängler (*Meisterwerke der griechischen Plastik,* 1893), who respectively set the course of archaeological and sculptural studies for all subsequent generations, the first being considered the father of archaeology, and the second providing the *ipse dixit* in matters of sculptural attributions and styles. Yet a similar approach can be detected in the ancient sources, both Greek and Roman, with their emphasis on the "first discoverer"—the *protoeuretes*—and their sequential development even within the lives of individual artists, for each of whom a *floruit* or *akme* was established on the basis of the most important work dated by a specific Olympic year. That some of this information was erroneous or based on the wrong premises is irrelevant with regard to the impact that such ancient sources have had on modern scholarship, by the very authority lent to them by their being in Greek or Latin.[7] Pliny, Plutarch, and Pausanias are as removed in time from the subject of their writings as the modern art historian writing on Giotto or the sculpture of the Middle Ages; yet their pronouncements are taken at face value, and little attention is paid to the fact that their conception of the past is inevitably colored by the modes and habits of their own present.

This veneration for the classical writers has led to several problems, especially in connection to Hellenistic art. Because so little documentation remains for ancient monuments, we have clung to the extant Greek and Roman sources despite the fact that their intent is often polemic or propagandistic, apologetic or laudatory, and in general literary or historical, but rarely art-historical. Even Pliny, the most extensively used among our sources, wrote a *Natural History,* not a treatise on sculpture and painting per se. Pausanias, our most invaluable guide through the Greek sites, is just that—an ancient Baedeker or *Guide Bleu* meant to explicate some monuments and structures of antiquarian interest as the viewer stood in front of them, not to describe them for an armchair reader far removed in time and space. He was especially discriminating with regard to Hellenistic art, which he seldom mentioned in his accounts, perhaps because of the same evolutionary prejudices from which more recent scholars have suffered.[8] Yet we have persistently tried to "illustrate" these texts in the conviction that if something was important enough to be mentioned by the ancient writers, it should also have survived as at least an echo in the Roman copies. Conversely, we have consistently attempted to match the holdings of our museums to the "descriptions" of the sources.

To be sure, such descriptions are minimal, and seldom go beyond the mere listing; but modern scholars, undaunted, supply adjectives and emend texts so convincingly that their hypotheses become standard pronouncements of art-historical handbooks. Pliny's laconic mention of Epigonos's famous Trumpeter (*NH* 34.88), for instance, has been connected with another of his passages (*NH* 34.84), in which he speaks of an Isogonos who made "representations of the battles of Attalos and Eumenes against the Gauls." The names have been emended to match, and the statue has been identified as the Dying Galatian now in the Capitoline Museum, so that the "*Dying* Trumpeter by Epigonos" has now become a traditional caption for the piece, on Pliny's authority, despite the fact that no such description is ever given in his text. Yet the trumpet is a minor attribute inconspicuously placed on the base of the Capitoline marble replica, and the original bronze Trumpeter could be visualized in a variety of other poses emphasizing the instrument.[9]

A similar case in point is the so-called Doidalsas's Aphrodite (fig. 3), identified in a popular crouching type on a chain of assumptions that go from the emendation of a corrupt transcription to an unlikely transliteration of Bithynian names, a reference to historical figures and a numismatic connection, all ingeniously correlated to present a plausible reconstruction of events and places, but excluding whatever other evidence may cloud or alter the coherent picture.[10] Another example of modern ingenuity with regard to ancient sources involves the so-called Pasquino Group (fig. 4). This dramatic composition of a mature bearded warrior supporting the lifeless body of a young beardless companion was identified as Menelaos with the body of Patroklos on the tenuous grounds that the peculiar animals decorating the older man's helmet—a leopard and a snaky-tailed bird—were symbols of Libya and Aithiopia respectively, two countries where Menelaos was said to have wandered after he left Troy. The original monument was then attributed to Antigonos of Karystos because this Hellenistic sculptor, known to have written treatises on a variety of subjects, would have been learned enough for this allusion and for the general Homeric tone of the group. Both conjectures seem rather improbable, yet the identification of the figures, if not the attribution to a master, is today generally accepted or questioned only for individual replicas of the work in specific contexts.[11]

Many such cases could be cited. Suffice it here to state that whenever the intermediate steps and the bases for attributions and identifications are omitted, theories on major monuments are usually presented as established facts, to be unquestioningly accepted by subsequent writers. Generations of students have been brainwashed by handbook statements made familiar by constant repetition and long gone unverified and unchallenged, even in the light of more recent discoveries and new knowledge.

Such ingenuity in the making of these theories was made possible by several facts. Earlier scholars were much better acquainted with the literary sources than today's students, who usually have "little Latin and less Greek," to echo Ben Jonson's comment on Shakespeare. In addition, archaeology started as a step-sister of epigraphy and history, two powerful disciplines versed in extensive restorations of fragmentary inscriptions and major reconstructions of events based on dominant figures. European historians and art-historians of the nineteenth and earlier twentieth century were preconditioned by a general belief that powerful personalities could dominate vast political and cultural spheres—such as Napoleon, Bismarck, Hitler, or Cézanne, Renoir, Picasso. It was therefore possible, culturally and ideologically, to accept the conception of an Alexander who spread Greek civilization and art throughout the ancient world, and of masters like Skopas, Praxiteles, and Lysippos, who set the standards of sculptural renderings for the next three centuries.[12]

Hellenistic artists who did not belong to the Schools of the Great Masters were more nebulous creatures, at least in the classical texts—a situation abetted by Pliny's cryptic statement, *cessavit deinde ars* (*NH* 34.52)—that effectively eliminated from consideration most of the artistic production from the years between the 121st and the 156th Olympiad (ca. 296–293 and 156–153 B.C.).[13] Identification and dating of Early Hellenistic works thus had to be based primarily on indirect evidence. Scholars studied the few Hellenistic monuments decorated with architectural sculpture for which history and architecture occasionally provided outside information. Correlations were attempted between historical events and geographical areas likely to have produced major works. Finally, but perhaps most significantly in terms of consequences, traits and interests of Hellenistic culture were derived from Hellenistic poetry and literature and

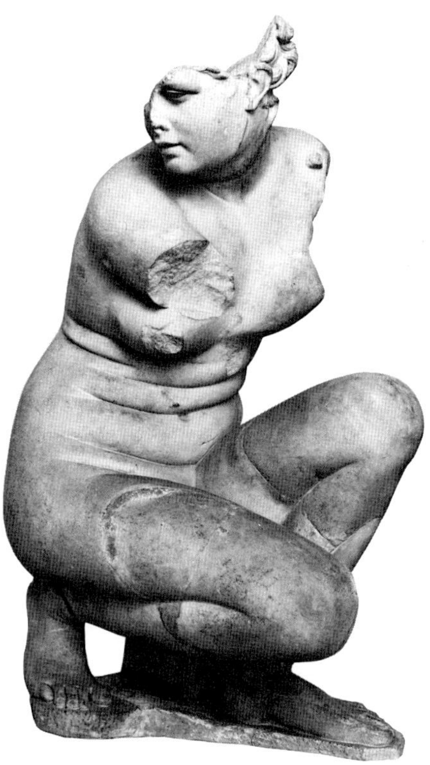

Fig. 3. Statue of Aphrodite, marble. Rome, Museo Nazionale Romano, Inv. no. 108597. Photograph, Deutsches Archäologisches Institut Rom, Neg. Nr. 66–1682

applied to extant sculptures, although such monuments were usually acknowledged as Roman copies of Hellenistic originals, found within Roman contexts and meant for Roman patrons. These identifications were all the more readily accepted in that little or no originality was attributed to masters working during the Roman Imperial period, except in matters of Imperial portraiture, historical reliefs, and funerary sculpture. We thus visualized a Hellenistic period filled with paradoxes and excesses, an art focusing on extremes and juxtaposing opposites: the very young to the very old, the beautiful to the ugly and deformed, the destitute to the ruler, the ridiculous to the pathetic, the epic to the mundane. And we acknowledged the many satyrs and nymphs from Roman gardens and villas as typical products of a Hellenistic culture that emphasized nature and pastoral life, despite the fact that no excavated Rhodian, Delian, or Prienian household had yielded quite the equivalent of these Roman decorative programs.[14]

To be sure, two factors had some bearing on this state of affairs. Quite a few early excavations had paid little attention to context and stratigraphy, focusing instead on major finds, and even then often listing them in excavation notebooks at the end of the day, by area, rather than on the spot and at the pertinent level. Moreover, many such finds had already been made outside legitimate investigations, either by chance (through the building of modern structures or tilling the fields) or by intent, in a sort of uninformed treasure hunt, as is common in lands that have seen continuous occupation from ancient to present times. No true distinction could then be made between sculptures from an earlier and those from a later context.[15]

A second factor was—and to some extent still is—the importance attributed to works of the minor arts, so-called not in terms of intrinsic value but of scale. It was taken for granted that if bronze and terracotta statuettes, metal vessels, jewelry, gems, and cameos depicted genre, rococo and baroque subjects, the same repertoire could be postulated for the major arts, regardless of the very different purposes for which such objects would have been made or the settings in which they would have been displayed. As is the case for literary works, luxury goods should rather be considered finite products typical only of themselves and their own environment. They certainly played a major role in the monarchical circles of the Hellenistic centers but were meant for a very restricted clientele and for private use. The same strictures apply to relatively less expensive pieces, like moldmade terracottas. They may have had wider circulation, and can contribute to our knowledge of stylistic effects and drapery treatment; but again it should be stressed that many elements of costume and coiffure did not cross over. Overall, the two productions—of the major and of the minor arts—remained distinct in content and function, so that only toward the end of the Hellenistic period can one be confident that some themes were shared by both.[16]

Another problem, not unique to Hellenistic studies but perhaps more acutely felt there for the relative lack of information, has been the often haphazard nature of sculptural restoration and display. Statues found during the Renaissance (or even later) were routinely integrated with alien appendages and attributes with the same concerned piety of doctors supplying patients with artificial limbs, and nonpertinent heads were often joined to headless bodies for the sake of completion, or to provide a patron with a more costly whole. Unless strong stylistic discrepancies resulted, such additions and restorations could barely be detected after one century or more had passed from their execution. In more recent times, shipment of crates to the British Museum or other European collections often met with natural disaster or accidental mixing, so that works collected in Ephesos could mingle with finds from Priene or Halikarnas-

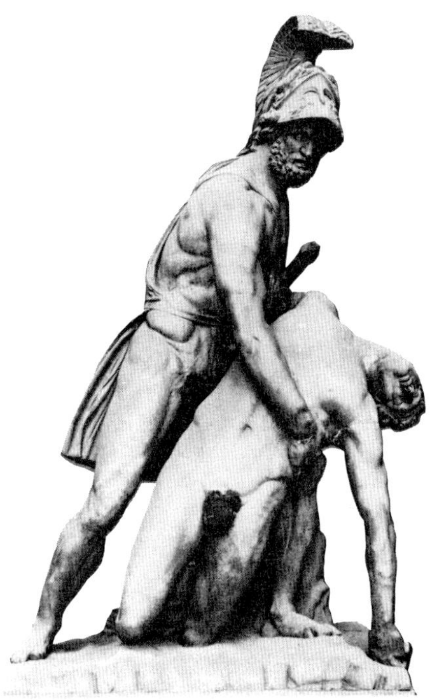

Fig. 4. The Pasquino Group, marble. Florence, Loggia dei Lanzi, from *AntP* XIV (1974) pl. 64b.

sos. Finally, unrelated pieces, albeit from the same monument or general context, could be joined in hybrid reconstructions that altered the appearance and thus often influenced the stylistic evaluation of the new whole: statues were put on the wrong bases, so that inscriptions provided misleading evidence for chronology, or fragments from different panels could be cemented together to produce a figure in countermotion because of improper juxtaposition of discrete elements.[17]

Several theories on the development of Hellenistic sculptural styles have been based on these erroneous restorations, most influential among them being the 1924 study by Gerhard Krahmer, *Stilphasen der hellenistischen Plastik.* Other flaws of this major essay were the indiscriminate examination of originals and copies commingled, and the arbitrary selection of a single replica among many, or of one among possible variants, in determining the appearance of a presumed Hellenistic prototype.[18] Another problem, the organization of the extant material according to formal criteria considered sequential and chronologically meaningful, can hardly be blamed on the German scholar alone. A major feature of previous studies of Classical sculpture had been the logical arrangement of the monuments according to a progressive development by which each period was seen to build on the stylistic and technical advances of the preceding phase—a method that sought, and found, justification in contemporary philosophical and theoretical positions of Greek writers and their Roman commentators. The same approach was then applied to Hellenistic sculpture, despite evidence that different styles could seemingly coexist on the same monument. Greater discrimination is applied today, yet Krahmer's "open" or "closed forms" are still identified as valid chronological criteria in attempting to place a specific sculpture.

Other scholars have resorted to a geographical system that equates historical importance with productivity in the arts, and sees distinct styles as the result of regional patronage or local preferences. Thus Alexandrian sculpture would have been characterized by illusionism and a sort of Praxitelean sfumato resulting from both taste and available media, Pergamon would have been responsible for the development of baroque, Rhodes was seen as a major center of "rococo"—terms borrowed from later periods of European art and of dubious application to Hellenistic forms and monuments. In addition, such styles were generally considered sequential, despite the fact that the presumed geographic distinction would allow coexistence, and the theory of regional preference was undermined by the recognition that artists traveled widely and often worked outside their place of origin. A more realistic assessment today shows that evidence is lacunose for many sites, especially the potentially all-important Alexandria, and major sanctuaries like Delos, despite careful excavation and abundant local documentation, seem almost to lack sculptural production for entire decades or half-centuries. The arts of the eastern regions, except for Asia Minor, are little known, or at least poorly integrated into the overview of what constitutes "mainstream" in our opinion. Even Magna Graecia and Sicily have yielded few major monuments that can be considered Hellenistic. When they exist and can be dated on external evidence, such as the pottery that accompanied Tarentine funerary structures, they surprise us in their baroque style *ante litteram,* unexpected in the early third century, almost one hundred years before the Pergamon Altar.[19]

None of the methods used in the past, and perhaps not even a combination of them, will resolve all our problems in the study of Hellenistic art, but the situation is today considerably better than even thirty years ago, the time when Margarete Bieber's *Sculpture of the Hellenistic Age* appeared in its first edition (1955). That monumental book already represented a major step forward in the gathering of sculptures, illustrations, and bibliography, and was a valiant attempt to put some order in the chaos of attributions and chronology, but its positions rested on traditional conceptions and assumptions. Subsequent works, perhaps reflecting the progress made by Hellenistic history and social history, have been somewhat more critical and innovative in their theories, more comprehensive in their coverage: T. B. L. Webster's *The Art of Greece: The Age of Hellenism* (1966), Christine Havelock's *Hellenistic Art* (first ed. 1971, second ed. 1981); J. Charbonneaux, R. Martin, and F. Villard's *Hellenistic Art* (1973); J. Onians's *Art and Thought in the Hellenistic Age* (1979)—the first and the last characterized by a strong dependence on the ancient sources and correlation of sculpture with Hellenistic literature. This approach has now attained excellent balance and presentation in J. J. Pollitt's *Art in the Hellenistic Age* (1986), with its awareness of chronological difficulties and sensible scrutiny of the evidence. The herculean enterprise of the *Lexicon Iconographicum Mythologiae Classicae,* currently in progress, is beginning to separate Greek from Roman monuments through an understanding of the underlying meaning of the images and their changes from period to period.

Also on the positive side is the fact that many new discoveries, besides Sperlonga, have increased our knowledge of the period. Primary among these are the results of excavations in Macedonia, which offer a new understanding of the luxurious court at the time of Philip II and Alexander the Great, with all the consequences that this revised assessment of Macedonian culture may have for evaluating its diffusion by the Diadochoi. Historians are here making the greatest strides, and art-historians may soon follow. In considering the impact of Alexander the Great and his portraiture, we have become aware of our own historical and philosophical biases, and in general the imperialistic and Nietzschean—i.e., heroic— conception of the events has been gradually replaced by a more democratic and even Marxist approach to the past, in which the lower classes and economic factors play as important a role as the rulers. In excavations and publications of sites, greater attention is being paid to pottery and other evidence, and architecture is seen as only one manifestation of style to be studied in all its possible phases of construction and reconstruction, in a new acceptance of mixed orders as expression of creativity and originality. Even buildings researched generations ago are being reinvestigated and reinterpreted, with occasionally dramatic redatings and conclusions. *Disiecta membra* carefully reassembled may lead to startling discoveries, such as the gradual recovery of the late fourth-century pedimental compositions from the Temple of Apollo at Delphi, once thought to be entirely lost to us, and which are likely to have had great stylistic and iconographic impact on much contemporary production.[20]

In the area of Hellenistic sculpture in particular, it seems now accepted that several different styles could coexist, and that innovative trends like ''baroque'' and realism flourished alongside classicizing and archaistic currents. More significantly, we are becoming aware of the Roman input on Hellenistic production—from the veristic portraits on Delos (true forerunners of the Republican statues on Italic soil) to the decorative neo-Attic works for the Campanian villas. Statues are no longer considered in isolation but as part of decorative programs, be these Roman or Greek in inspiration. Perhaps the most important questions to be asked of the material have in fact become: Why was it made? Where was it set up? If a work traditionally assigned to the Hellenistic period but known only through Roman copies could be conclusively shown to be out of place—both in function and meaning—in a proper Greek context, the time is perhaps right for revising our notions and asking whether the piece in question could rather be a Roman creation in Hellenistic style. It can confidently be said that today a Roman label no longer carries an implication of lesser quality, much as Hellenistic art is no longer considered less noble or appealing than Classical.

That we may have reached a crucial point in our approach to Hellenistic culture is perhaps shown by the fact that, even as I write, several symposia and congresses are being devoted to Hellenistic topics: ''Images and Ideologies: Self-Definition in the Hellenistic World,'' University of California at Berkeley, April 7–9, 1988; ''Hellenistic History and Culture,'' University of Texas at Austin, 19–22 October 1988; and the XIII International Congress for Classical Archaeology in Berlin, 24–30 July 1988, has the Hellenistic period as its theme and focus. New publications will result from such meetings, and we can already announce Peter Greene's forthcoming book on Hellenistic society, and my own review of late fourth/ early third-century B.C. sculpture, currently in press.

To be sure, not all new positions will be accepted or even acceptable, and much new evidence may be needed before some thorny problems may be solved. But every step forward is an achievement, and contributes to insure that the long-maligned Hellenistic production may at last find its own legitimate place within the history of ancient art.

1. The official publication of the architecture of the Pergamon Altar is J. Schrammen, *Der grosse Altar. Der obere Markt* Altertümer von Pergamon III.¹, (Berlin, 1906). For the frieze, see H. Kähler, *Der grosse Fries von Pergamon* (Berlin, 1948). The Hesiodic reading is given by E. Simon, *Pergamon und Hesiod* (Mainz, 1975).

2. The observation on the sighting of Herakles from the entrance to the Altar Terrace is due to my colleague, G. Ferrari Pinney, who will develop the point in a future publication. The theory on the Heroon of Telephos is by K. Stähler, "Überlegungen zur architektonischen Gestalt des Pergamonaltares," *Studien zur Religion und Kultur Kleinasiens* Festschrift F. K. Dörner, (Leiden, 1978) 838–867. For the dating of related sherds, see P. Callaghan, "On the Date of the Great Altar of Pergamon," *University of London. Bulletin of the Institute of Classical Studies* 28 (1981) 115–121.

3. On the Altar of Athena at Priene, see J. C. Carter, "The Date of the Altar of Athena at Priene and Its Reliefs," *Alessandria* 748–764, pls. 114–115; some of the positions are slightly revised in J. C. Carter, *The Sculpture of the Sanctuary of Athens Polias at Priene* (London, 1983), 181–209, despite the apparent discrepancy in relative date of publication (the Festschrift article was obviously written earlier than the latest version of the book).

4. For a recent discussion on the history of the Laokoon, see E. Simon, "Laokoon und die Geschichte der antiken Kunst," *AA* 1984, 643–672, and cf. 670–671 for comments on the Sperlonga sculptures. The official publication on them remains B. Conticello and B. Andreae, "Die Skulpturen von Sperlonga," *AntP* 14 (1975), but for more recent statements by the same two authors, see, e.g. B. Conticello, "Sul gruppo di Scilla e della nave nel Museo di Sperlonga," in *Allesandria* 611–623; B. Andreae, *Odysseus: Archäologie des europäischen Menschenbildes* (Frankfurt, 1982). For a dating of the Laokoon to the Augustan period, see E. E. Rice, "The Date of the Rhodian Sculptors of the Laocoon and Sperlonga Sculptures," *AJA* 90 (1986) 209, see also "Prosopographia Rhodiaka," *BSA* 81 (1986) 209–50.

5. Bieber, *Sculpture*, 3.

6. This attitude is still reflected, for instance, in the chapter headings given by W. B. Dinsmoor in his influential *The Architecture of Ancient Greece* (London and New York, 1950).

7. For similar comments, see e.g. M. I. Finley, *Ancient History: Evidence and Models* (New York, 1985), 10 and passim.

8. For a critical analysis of the ancient sources, see e.g. the introductory comments in J. J. Pollitt, *The Art of Greece 1400–31 B.C.* Sources and Documents in the History of Art Series, (Englewood Cliffs, N.J., 1965), ix-xviii.

9. For the complex issue of the Capitoline Trumpeter and related statues as copies of the Attalid dedication, see the summary in Pollitt 79–97.

10. The main challenge to the theory is by A. Linfert, "Der Meister der kauernden Aphrodite," *AM* 84 (1969) 158–164; criticism of the ancient sources and their emendation had originally been voiced by H. L. Urlichs, in K. Jex-Blake and E. Sellers, *The Elder Pliny's Chapters on the History of Art* (London, 1896), 239. For a brief account, see Pollitt 56–57 and fig. 50.

11. The main publication of the so-called Pasquino Group is B. Schweitzer, *Das Original der sogennanten Pasquino-Gruppe*, Abhandlungen der Sächsischen Akademie der Wissenschaften zu Leipzig, Philologisch-historische Klasse 43.4 (Leipzig, 1936). A recent discussion is by U. Hausmann, "Aias mit dem Leichnam Achills. Zur Deutung des Originals der Pasquino-Gruppe," *AM* 99 (1984) 291–300; for a brief summary of the standard theories, see Pollitt 118, fig. 119, and 124.

12. See, for instance, the important review of historiography, with regard to Alexander the Great, by E. Badian, "Some Recent Interpretations of Alexander," in *Alexandre le Grand:* 279–303 and discussion on 304–311. On the influence of the three great fourth-century masters, see e.g. Bieber, *Sculpture*, Chapters 2–3.

13. For a recent discussion of this debated passage, see e.g. F. Preisshofen, "Kunsttheorie und Kunstbetrachtung," *Le classicism à Rome aux Iers siècles avant et après J.C.* Entretiens sur l'antiquité classique 25 (Geneva, 1978), 263–277 and discussion on 278–282.

14. That contemporary poetry and literature may have had little or no influence on Hellenistic art is suggested, for instance, by the fact that the highly popular *Argonautika* by the third-century Apollonios Rhodios, although full of suggestive episodes of saga, found no echo in Hellenistic monuments, especially of sculpture: cf. *LIMC* II (1984), pt. 1, 599. For a discussion of modern attitudes toward Roman sculpture, see e.g. Ridgway chapters 1–2, 7–8. For the decorative programs of Greek and Roman gardens, see e.g. B.S. Ridgway, "Greek Antecedents of Garden Sculpture," 7–28, and D. K. Hill, "Some Sculpture from Roman Domestic Gardens," 81–94, in Ancient Roman Gardens (Washington, D.C., 1981).

15. To be sure, not all excavations were neglectful of stratigraphy. Dr. Donohue reminds me that H. Schliemann secured W. Doerpfeld's help at Troy precisely to investigate problems of stratigraphy, and that the identification of the Laokoon with the work mentioned by Pliny was partly based on its findspot. On the other hand, even attention to context often could result in misinterpretation of the evidence, and many cases exist, even in the more recent past, of excavation at classical sites being carried out more cavalierly than at prehistoric settlements, or with ruthless elimination of layers not of primary interest to the excavators.

16. On this point, see e.g. D. Willers, "Typus und Motiv. Aus der hellenistischen Entwicklungsgeschichte einer Zweifigurengruppe," *AntK* 29 (1986) 137–150. Cf. also J. Dörig, "Tonformen aus Tarent. Bemerkungen zum Verhältnis der Kleinkunst zur Grossplastik," in *Alessandria*, 680–685; A. Oliver, "New Hellenistic Silver: Mirror, Emblem Dish and Spoons," *Jahrbuch der Berliner Museen* 19 (1977) 13–22.

17. A typical example of this "healing" attitude is provided by the pedimental sculptures from the Temple of Aphaia at Aigina, which were extensively restored in 1816–1817 by B. Thorvaldsen; see C. Grunwald, "Zur den Aegineten-Ergänzungen," in *Bertel Thorvaldsen: Untersuchungen zu seinem Werk und zur Kunst seiner Zeit* (Cologne, 1977), 305–341. For the joining of unrelated fragments, see e.g. J. C. Carter, "The Date of the Sculptured Coffer Lids of the Temple of Athena Polias at Priene," *Studies in Classical Art and Archaeology in Honor of P. H. von Blanckenhagen*, G. Kopcke and M. B. Moore, eds. (Locust Valley, N.Y., 1979), 139–151.

18. The article by Krahmer was published in *RM* 38–39 (1923/24) 138–184; one of the erroneously reconstructed monuments on which he based some of his theories was indeed a coffer from Priene (note 17).

19. For a typical example of a geographical account, partly unfounded because based largely on Roman "copies" of presumed Hellenistic originals of unknown provenience, see G. Dickins, *Hellenistic Sculpture* (Oxford, 1920, published posthumously). For a helpful, modern overview of the art of the peripheral regions, by various authors, see *The Cambridge Ancient History, plates to Vol. VII, pt. 1. The Hellenistic World to the Coming of the Romans* R. Ling. ed. (Cambridge, 1984); each geographical section is preceded by a map and introductory comments; note also the lengthy captions of the plates. Tarentine monuments, with pertinent context, are discussed by J. C. Carter, *The Sculpture of Taras* Transactions of the American Philosophical Society 65.7, Philadelphia, 1975).

20. For recent Macedonian developments, see *Macedonia and Greece* and M. Andronicos, *Vergina: The Royal Tombs and the Ancient City* (Athens, 1984). Excavations continue to produce startling results, and historians are providing most helpful discussions. On the recovery of the pedimental sculptures from the Temple of Apollo at Delphi, see, most recently. F. Croissant, "Les frontons du temple du IVe siècles à Delphes: Esqisse d'une restitutions," *Archaische und klassische griechische Plastik*, H. Kyrieleis, ed. (Mainz, 1986). II, 187–196, and discussion on 197.

Hellenistic Art and the Coming of Rome

Andrew F. Stewart

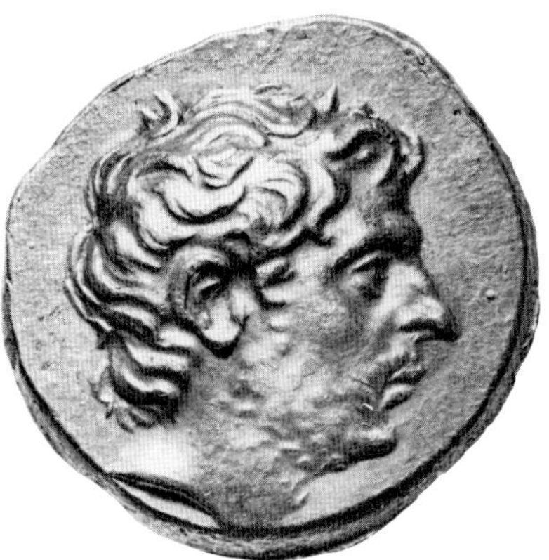

Fig. 1. Gold stater of T. Quinctius Flamininus, ca. 196–194 B.C.

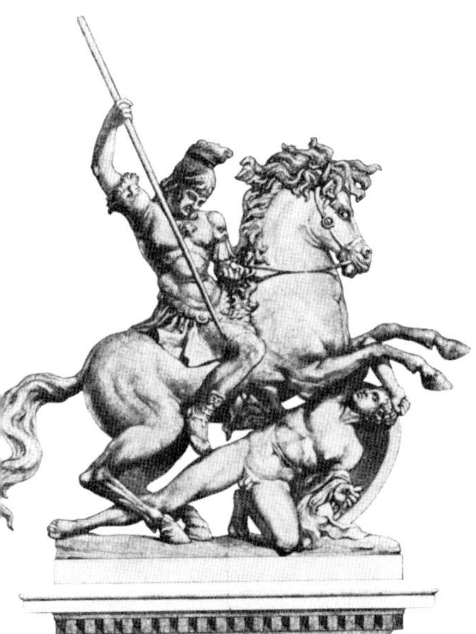

Fig. 2a. Monument of L. Aemilius Paullus, Delphi, 168 B.C. (restored by A. Tournaire, 1902).

IN THIS ESSAY I HAVE BEEN ASKED to consider the impact of the Roman domination of the Eastern Mediterranean upon late Hellenistic sculpture, painting, and architecture. For while the effects of the massive importation of Greek art into Rome are both well known and well studied, the eastern response to Roman penetration, despite one or two excellent studies of particular problems, remains essentially unsurveyed. Taking the Augustan period as our lower limit, it will be convenient to examine Greece and Asia Minor first, then to turn to three special cases: the activities of the supposedly fanatical Romanizer Antiochos IV Epiphanes (175–164), of the Italian community on Delos (ca. 146–69), and finally, of Herod the Great of Judea (37–4).

GREECE

The first Roman army to cross the Adriatic did so in 229, and thereafter the Romans were to intervene repeatedly in Greek affairs, to secure their interests and limit the power of Macedonians, Seleukids, Mithradates, and their allies, then finally to fight their own civil war over what was left. Formal Roman occupation, in the sense of the reduction of Greece to provincial status, came comparatively late: Macedonian and Illyrian independence ceased only after 146, Achaea was not made a province until 46, and many cities like Athens continued to remain at least nominally free until Augustan times.[1]

Viewed from this perspective, the Romans' main impact upon the late Hellenistic world and its art looks decidedly negative. Vast quantities of statues, paintings, embossed metalwork, and other treasures, not to mention enormous amounts of hard cash, were transferred to Italy as loot. And after the art, artists themselves soon followed, draining the East of talent to supply the ever-hungry markets of the West.[2] Finally, as the confiscations dwindled and the supply of originals began to run dry, both Greek and Italian entrepreneurs roamed the mainland in search of bargains to buy for their Roman clients,[3] and an entire copying industry sprang up, slavishly devoted to supplying decorative replicas and versions of "old master" paintings and sculptures to embellish the public buildings, piazzas, villas, and eventually the tombs of the new world conquerors.[4]

Yet the picture must not be painted too black. For not only did the Roman appetite for Greek art lead to the enormous enrichment of their own, but provided hitherto undreamed-of opportunities for artists of talent and initiative, opportunities that were fast decreasing in the East. In Greece itself, though the mass success of the copying industry can hardly have fostered a great sense of originality and self-worth among its practitioners, it is by no means clear that these qualities had been conspicuously prized among most Hellenistic artists and patrons before the Roman intervention. And in some genres, such as portraiture, the Roman presence offered unlooked-for opportunities to shine.

The earliest identifiable portrait of a Roman from either East or West is that of T. Quinctius Flamininus, on his rare issue of gold staters issued, perhaps by himself, shortly after his great victory over Philip V of Macedon at Kynoskephalai in 197 (fig. 1).[5] On its reverse the coin bears a Victory and an inscription in Latin, T. QVINCTI; this shows that the initiative behind the issue was certainly his, for it was to be many years until the Greeks understood that the Romans could not be identified simply by their *praenomina* alone. The portrait clearly follows his defeated opponent's coin portraits in type, but exaggerates the Roman's intense, aquiline physiognomy (Plutarch, *Flamininus* 1) almost to the point of caricature: the first glimmerings of the ultra-realist or "verist" style in Roman portraiture. To the cities, whose freedom he proclaimed in 196, the Roman was indeed fit to be ranked with kings: cults were inaugurated in his honor, and a bronze equestrian statue (hitherto a royal preserve) erected by the demos of Delphi in 191/90.[6] Its inscription praises his *arete,* goodwill, and benefactions to the Delphians, in conventional terms.

The statue started a trend: many more followed in the next two centuries, though being of bronze, all have now perished. Only their bases remain, among the most revealing of which is that of Aemilius Paullus, victor over Perseus of Macedon at Pydna in 168 (fig. 2). It was embellished with a frieze depicting the main stages of the battle, carved in high relief in an updated classical style that recalls the frieze of the temple of Athena Nike at Athens (ca. 420), and clearly caters to Aemilius's distinctly pro-Athenian, clas-

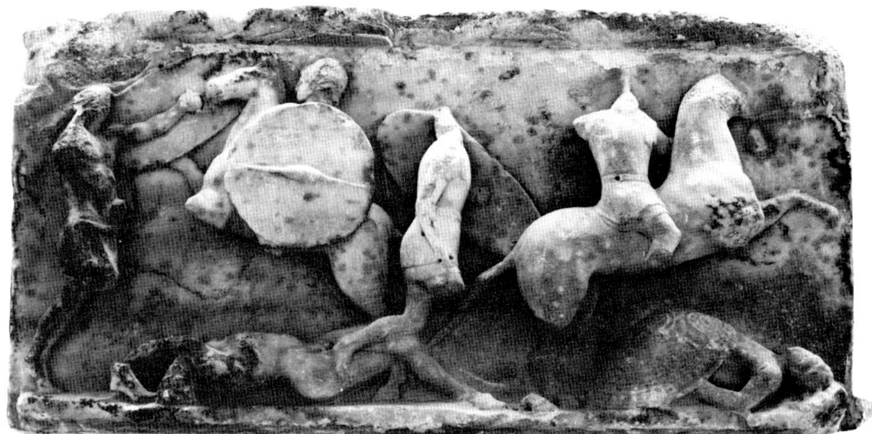

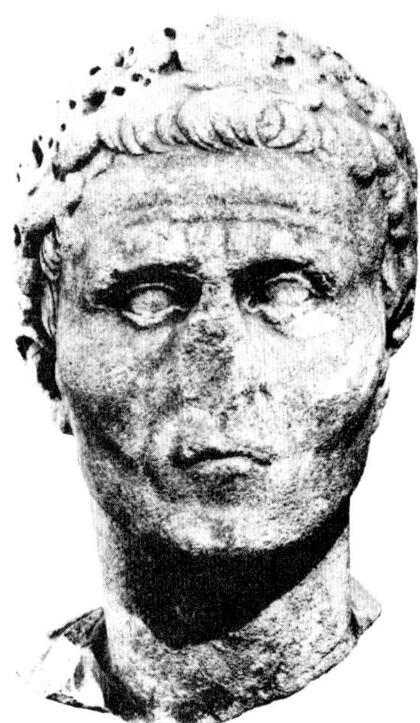

sicizing tastes.[7] As to the portraits themselves, it seems that *Graeca adulatio* led their Greek dedicators to favor the idealizing style of Hellenistic royal portraiture over Roman realism: for when Sulla and others were likewise honored at Oropos in the first century, a parsimonious demos was able simply to change the inscriptions on some third-century equestrian statues by the Lysippic school, and the deed was done.[8] Nor was this unique: the practice was sufficiently widespread by the mid-century for an apprehensive Cicero, angling for a memorial at Athens, to warn Atticus of his distaste for it (*ad Atticum* 6.1.23).

Clearly verism, being basically unflattering to Greek eyes, was not considered at all appropriate for their honorary portraiture, regardless of the subject.[9] Indeed, of the large number of late Hellenistic portraits discovered in Greece, only one known to me can truly be called verist: a battered head from Corinth, re-founded as a Roman *colonia* by Caesar in 44. Another often so described, a priest of Isis in Athens, has much more of the late Egyptian style than the Roman.[10] A rather larger number of pieces make some concession to verism, but seldom if ever at the cost of disrupting their overall regularity and pseudo-classical reserve: Caesar's own portrait, on a marble head with *corona civica* from Thasos (fig. 3), does just this, though as befits a cult image of a God Manifest (Θεὸς ἐπιφανής) the sculptor has cleverly infused the whole with the intensified charisma of a Hellenistic ruler.[11] Wholesale imitation of a Roman portrait style begins in Greece only with Augustus, whose neo-classical image was evidently designed to bestride both worlds, and succeeded brilliantly.[12]

Along with Roman generals, the Greeks also honored Rome itself. The cult of Roma, like the personification, is a Greek adaptation of the familiar city Tychai of Antioch, Alexandria, and so on, and as such both are thoroughly Greek in form from the beginning.[13] The earliest cult was founded at Smyrna in 195, to solicit Roman help against Antiochos III, and others soon followed. Though evidence is thin, it seems that at first the iconography is extremely variable and ad hoc. Thus, in a hasty and unsubtle attempt to conciliate their new masters after Perseus's defeat at Pydna in 168, the Macedonian cities replaced both his image and Alexander's on their coins with a female head, presumably Roma, wearing the hero Perseus's winged cap and accompanied by the name of the Roman quaestor.[14] On Delos, on the other hand, the Poseidoniasts of Berytos, an association of traders and shippers, chose a tranquil standing matron to represent their benefactor (εὐεργετίς), the guarantor of the peace and freedom of the seas.[15] The seated, armed type later to become canonical is not found until the early first century, in the context of the Mithradatic Wars, and once again the inspiration is purely Greek, from a Pheidian or neo-Pheidian Athena Nikephoros. Here one detects a pattern that was to be repeated time and again during these two centuries: confronted by the awesome power of Rome, and the massive disruption of Greek life that it all too often caused, the Greeks first tried to cope with it as best they could, but in the end all too often retreated into the comforting embrace of classicism. With its connotations of rationality, stability, dignity, nobility, and repose, and its aura of a glorious past reborn, this provided welcome solace in a disintegrating world.[16]

Finally, architecture. One of the Cossutii designed the temple of Olympian Zeus in Athens, given by Antiochos IV of Syria in 174 (fig. 4), and in 63–52 Ariobarzanes II of Cappadocia likewise hired two Italian architects to renovate Perikles' Odeion, destroyed in the siege of 86; fifty talents given by Pompey also helped toward the reconstruction of other buildings.[17] Yet these buildings were thoroughly Greek in style, as was the first major structure actually donated by a Roman, the Propylaion of Appius Claudius Pulcher at Eleusis, begun in 50.[18] Assessment of the Roman Agora at Athens, given by Caesar and Augustus, will have to await its forthcoming publication.[19] All in all, one senses that Athens, mesmerized as usual by classicism, was once again virtually closed to new ideas, from the West or anywhere else.

The opposite was true of the Roman *colonia* of Corinth. Though building hardly began before Augustan times, it is revealing that distinctive Roman building types and construction methods are found there both earlier and in greater abundance than at any other site in Greece. A basilica (always rare in the East) by the Lechaion Road, the Roman-style semicircular theater, the podium-temple dedicated to Tyche, and several bath-buildings all bespeak strong ties with Italy, as does the choice of the Tuscan order for the poros temple of Hermes, and the discreet use of concrete and reticulate brickwork in these and other structures.[20]

Such thoroughgoing yet still judiciously managed Romanization only serves to emphasize how unreceptive, by and large, was the rest of late Hellenistic Greece to what the West had to offer. Convinced of the superiority of their own culture, and reinforced in that belief by the Romans' insatiable thirst for any and all of its products, the mainland Greeks either simply ignored their new masters where they could, or sought to inscribe them within their own frame of reference when this proved impossible. Yet familiar though such attitudes are, they seem positively genial by comparison with the Romans' reception in Asia Minor.

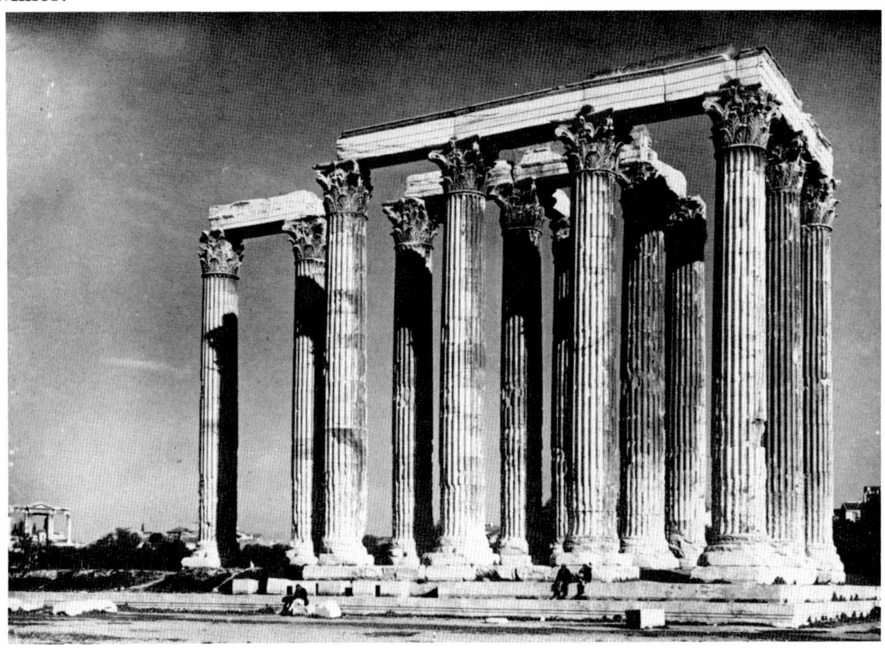

Fig. 4. The Temple of Olympian Zeus, Athens, designed by (Decimus?) Cossutius, 175–164 B.C., and completed by Hadrian.

ASIA MINOR AND SYRIA

Extensive Roman penetration of Asia Minor was both somewhat later, and rather different in character. The armies that defeated Antiochos III in 189 left almost at once, and until Pergamon passed to Rome after 133, only senatorial ambassadors and merchants were to be seen there. Yet once the kingdom was organized into a province (which took some time), Roman tax-collectors descended in force, as they also did in Syria when Pompey annexed it in 64. The bitter resentment they caused may be gauged from the enthusiastic response of much of the Greek populace of Asia to Mithradates VI's invasion of 88 (fig. 6), and their willing participation in his order to massacre all Italians (some 80,000) in the province. Sulla's counteroffensive and exaction of massive reparations, followed by yet more wars, and even a disastrous Parthian invasion, reduced some cities to their last extremities. Pompey's settlement of 63, renewed by Caesar after 47, provided only temporary relief, and it was left to Augustus to repair the damage in earnest.[21]

In this situation, it is not surprising to find that honors to individual Romans, usually including portraits, are rare before the early first century, but increase rapidly thereafter as the cities scrambled for favors from their new overlords. Bases form the main bulk of the evidence, but coin portraits of Roman notables begin by 60: represented are Pompey, Caesar, Mark Antony, and one or two lesser figures. As in Greece, the portraits seem to have been purely Hellenistic in both type and style, eschewing the excesses of verism for a rendering similar to that of the Caesar from Thasos (fig. 3).[22] ''Conversions'' of earlier statues are common, and a distinct dearth of equestrian monuments is perhaps to be explained by the fact that much is lost, and most Roman generals were by no means benefactors: thus, not one statue of Sulla is known, though both Pompey and (after Pompey's defeat at Pharsalos in 49) Caesar received

Fig. 5. Kings of Pontos and Cappadocia. a) Silver tetradrachm of Mithradates III of Pontos, ca. 246–190 B.C. b) Silver tetradrachm of Pharnakes I of Pontos, ca. 190–169 B.C. c) Silver drachm of Ariobarzanes I Philoromaios of Cappadocia, 96–63 B.C.

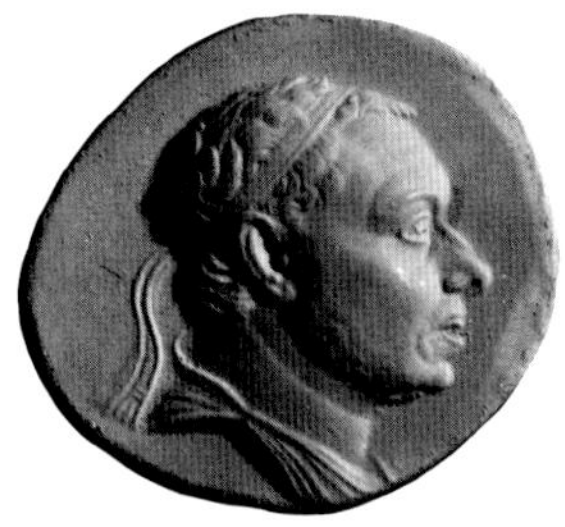

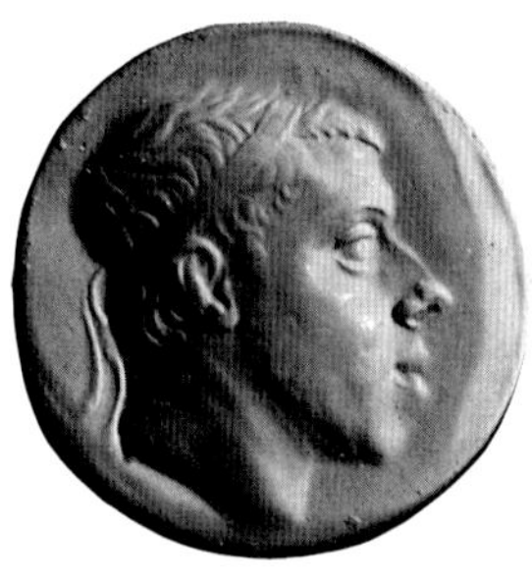

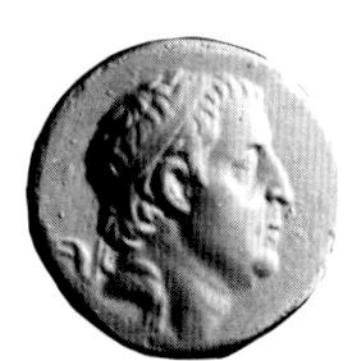

Fig. 6. Silver tetradrachm of Mithradates VI Eupator Dionysos of Pontos, 75 B.C.

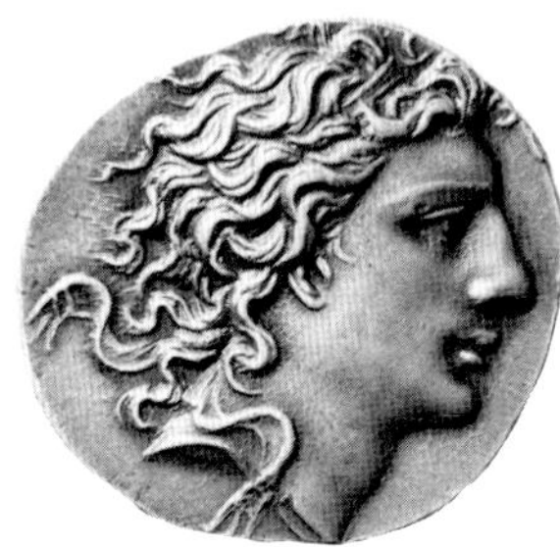

extravagant honors, equal for the first time to those formerly accorded to Hellenistic kings.[23] Cults of Roma are common, with over twenty recorded in the sources, though as remarked earlier, only after the defeat of Mithradates VI does the seated, armed type become canonical.[24]

Finally, a Hellenistic epigram tells us that Romulus and Remus appeared in person, together with their mother Servilia, in one of the nineteen panels (reliefs or paintings) that embellished the colonnade of a temple dedicated at Kyzikos by Attalos II and Eumenes II of Pergamon to their mother Apollonis, probably around 160.[25] Since the panel was grouped with another featuring Kleobis, Biton, and their mother Kydippe, the main point seems to have been to exalt the filial piety of the two men, but contemporaries would surely have recognized the compliment to Rome. Given that their kingdom owed its preeminence in western Asia after 188 largely to its alliance with Rome, the reference would have been clear.

With the exception of the honors paid to Pompey for his settlement of 63, all this seems lukewarm at best. Indeed, recent studies have shown that this very period saw the heyday of a populist, often virulently anti-Roman rhetoric in the cities, a final flowering of the florid, Asian rhetorical tradition.[26] As one might expect, the archaeological evidence splits right down the middle: on the one side (presumably the Greek), a variety of styles ranging from a tempered realism to various inflections of the baroque, but always with a touch of perplexity and pathos, and on the other, occasional examples of Roman verism, gruff, uncompromising, and hard.[27] Among non-Romans, the salient exceptions are the coin portraits of those remaining kings who, like Ariobarzanes I of Cappadocia (96–63), declared themselves "Philoromaioi" and threw in their lot with Rome (fig. 5c).[28] Yet even here the rendering is far less brutal, and continues a tradition popular with these Hellenized but racially non-Greek monarchs before any Roman army even set foot in Asia (fig. 5a-b).[29] Given the likelihood that the usual mode for Romans in the East was probably not verism anyway (see above), the motive could have been more negative—to distance themselves first from the Seleukids and Attalids, then later from Mithradates VI—than positive. For Mithradates VI represented himself as the apostle of this Asiatic Greek revival par excellence, appearing as a second, even more charismatic Alexander (fig. 6); his son Pharnakes tried the same tactic, until defeated by Caesar in 47.

Anathema to classicists and supporters of Roman rule, this resurgent Asianism seems to have quieted only under Augustus, when universal peace and relief from the excesses of republican rule brought widespread acceptance of imperial classicism as the appropriate style for a world reborn.[30] Yet even so, in sculpture at least it still refused to die: the "baroque" of the Rhodian masters of the Laokoon found favor among some circles in Rome even under Augustus and Tiberius, and from the mid-first century A.D. Aphrodisian sculptors were sending a constant stream of such work to the West.[31] By then, of course, any political connotations it may once have had were long forgotten.

As to architecture, though a few leading Romans of the last generation of the republic are reported to have endowed some cities on a scale approaching the munificence of Hellenistic kings, almost nothing is known of the details. Ephesos, Assos, and other cities were certainly beneficiaries, and Pompey's reorganization of Asia even led him to found new centers in Pontos.[32] Yet in Ephesos, as elsewhere, Italic styles and construction techniques do not appear until the Imperial period, neither do favorite Italian building types like baths, podium temples, semicircular theaters, and basilicas. Indeed, though the first three of these eventually came to enjoy wide popularity, only a handful of basilicas (in Greek, $\beta\alpha\sigma\iota\lambda\iota\kappa\alpha\grave{\iota}\ \sigma\tau o\alpha\acute{\iota}$ or $\alpha\upsilon\lambda\alpha\acute{\iota}$) are known from the whole of Asia.[33] No shrines of Roma have been recognized with certainty, though some small rectangular exedrae inserted into already existing porticoes and other buildings may have performed this function, by analogy with Roma's chapel in the Establishment of the Poseidoniasts on Delos.[34] Finally, Pompey's foundations were ad hoc administrative affairs, involving either completion of projects already begun by Mithradates VI, or synoecism of pre-existing villages.[35]

Signs of Romanization in those parts of the East under Roman domination prior to Augustus being somewhat elusive, it is perhaps time to turn to those three ostensibly more promising cases introduced at the beginning of this essay.

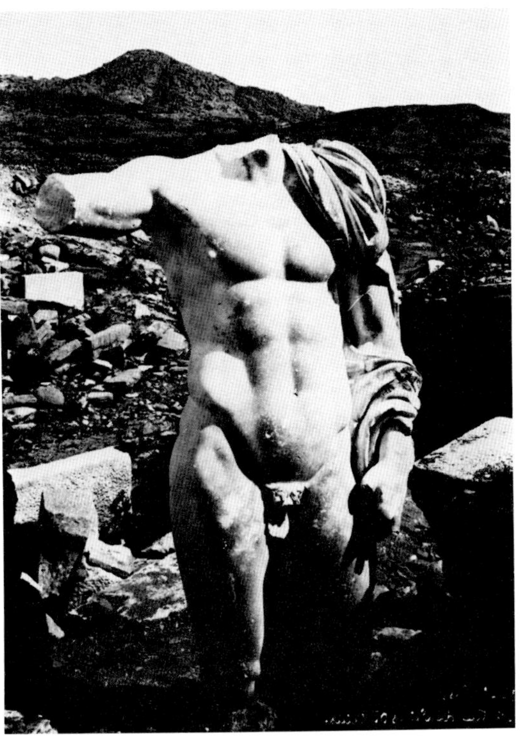

ANTIOCHOS IV EPIPHANES OF SYRIA (REIGNED 175–164)

Antiochos's long sojourn in Rome as a hostage after his father's defeat in 188 certainly left a permanent impression upon him, but his commitment to Romanization as a policy is much more problematical. His reputation as a fanatical Romanizer is derived mainly from Polybios's accounts of his unusual behavior—importing gladiators, dressing in a toga, soliciting election in Antioch as quaestor, and judging cases there like a praetor—and of his great festival procession at Daphne in 166, modeled, so we are told, on the triumph of Aemilius Paullus after Pydna.[36] Yet the first simply fits in with his other eccentricities and as such hardly constitutes a program (who would have taken it seriously?), and the procession was conceived in the immediate aftermath of his humiliating withdrawal from Egypt, forced upon him by a single Roman envoy at the very gates of Alexandria. Only his decision to equip 5,000 of his troops like Romans smacks of long-term policy: an army of such men had defeated his father, and modernization of this kind was simply common sense.

In fact, an unprejudiced reading of the sources suggests that Antiochos's aims were exactly identical to those of every Seleukid monarch before him—to increase Seleukid power and influence to the utmost—but with one crucial modification: nothing, he saw, must now antagonize Rome. Hence his immediate withdrawal from Egypt, hence his preoccupation with extending his power over Jews and Parthians, nations still of little or no interest to Rome at all.[37] A look at his religious and artistic programs only reinforces and amplifies this conclusion.

Antiochos's own portraits, both on coins and in the round, are conceived in the highly idealized, Apolline mode that had been canonical for Seleukid rulers from the mid-third century: no trace of the supposed *philoromaios* here. Yet whereas his predecessors had favored Apollo himself, the tutelary divinity of the kingdom, for the reverses of their coins, he chose a Pheidian-style Zeus as the symbol of his program of reconstruction.[38] Having built a new temple to the god in Antioch, and dedicated neo-Pheidian cult-statues of him there and at Daphne, he then proceeded to promote the cult elsewhere, foisting it upon Jews and Samaritans, and donating temples to cities far and wide. Those at Olba (modern Uzuncaburç) in Cilicia, Athens (fig. 4), and Lebadeia survive, and manifest not a trace of Western style—even though a Roman architect, Cossutius, was hired for the Athenian temple.[39] Their most striking feature is their novel use of an exterior Corinthian order, repeated on another of his benefactions, the bouleuterion at Miletos. Though the motive for this is still uncertain, where regional ties can be documented in this architecture they are clearly with Syria, not Rome.[40] Finally, the theater which he donated to Tegea, though badly preserved, was of Greek, not Roman form.[41]

Antiochos's cultural program, then, was overtly nationalistic and expansionist, looking for inspiration both to his native Syria and to Athens (now generally acknowledged as the ''education to Greece'' of Perikles' dreams). Far from prostrating himself at the Romans' feet, Antiochos exemplifies the resilience of Hellenistic culture in the face of Roman domination. Yet if no Italianate bias can be detected here, the opposite is true a half-century later, in the very different setting of late Hellenistic Delos.

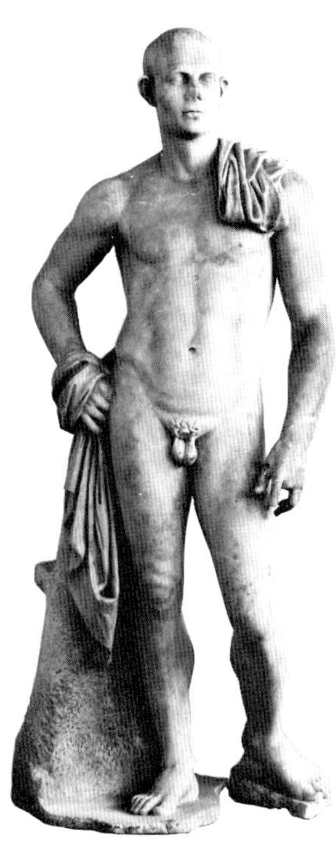

Fig. 8. Unfinished portrait of an unknown Italian merchant, from the House of the Diadoumenos at Delos, marble, ca. 100–88 B.C. Athens, National Museum, Inv. no. 1828. Photograph, Ecole française d'archéologie, Athènes.

Delos

As a part of their settlement of the Greek world in 166, after Pydna, the Romans declared Delos a free port. From then, and especially after the sack of Corinth in 146, it became the greatest slave-market in the Mediterranean, the mecca of Roman businessmen, and an almost obligatory port of call for Roman statesmen and generals on their way to the East. By ca. 100, large numbers of Italians had made the island their home, and had built their own Agora in which to conduct their affairs. Though the architecture of the Agora, a quadrangular space surrounded by two-storyed porticoes (donated by both Greeks and Italians) is wholly Greek in style, the numerous dedications of portraits constitute the first extensive evidence for the intrusion of Roman/Italian taste into the late Hellenistic Aegean world.[42]

In contrast to the standard "civic" portraits of Greeks on the island, where the subject was shown standing draped in a cloak, these men preferred a more assertive image: on horseback, standing in armor, or heroically nude. Inscriptions are often in both Latin and Greek, indicating that they were designed to speak to both elements of the population, though the image of a Roman slave-trader in the guise of a colossal Hermes, his naked body topped by a bald, jowly head in the hard-boiled verist style (figs. 7–8) would certainly have offended traditionalists among the Greeks, however much it appealed to Romans and their fellow-travelers. This eclectic but forceful union of a classical body and verist head may be an authentically Italian contribution to the art, but if so it must be attributed to Italian patrons, not to Italian sculptors. No Italians are documented among the numerous sculptors' signatures, the bulk of which are Athenian and Ephesian. It is suggestive that the Athenians seem to have undertaken almost no commissions on the mainland, supporting one's impression that these men formed something of a "dissident" group, out of sympathy with the stultifying neo-classicism prevailing in Athens. Furthermore, though Italy has yielded many parallels, especially after Mithradates VI sacked the island in 88 and the sculptors migrated elsewhere, only a handful have appeared in the Hellenistic East, all of them in centers where Roman *negotiatores* were especially active: Ephesos, Rhodes, and Antioch.[43]

As to the other arts, Delian frescoes of religious scenes often show sacrifices *ritu Romano* (fig. 9), though careful study of those depicting the Compitalia indicate a degree of syncretism with Hellenistic themes and practices even here.[44] In other respects, however, the foreigners seem to have blended quickly into the cosmopolitan atmosphere of late Hellenistic Delos. Their houses are no different from the rest, nor is the decor within, whether sculpture, mosaics, furniture, jewelry, or tableware.[45] This should caution one against ascribing certain developments in the minor arts of the late Hellenistic East, from preferences for red gemstones in jewelry to "Boethian beds," as products of a specifically Roman taste.[46] On Delos itself, the only exceptions to this general rule are the Italian amphorae found from the later second century, and in large quantities after the ruin of Knidian commerce by Mithradates VI's sack of 88: clearly the Italian community liked their own wine and oil, and took advantage of the situation to import it themselves.[47]

Like Knidos, Delos was severely damaged by Mithradates VI's forces in 88; though recovery was quite swift, a second sack by the pirates in 69 proved all but fatal. Merchants established themselves elsewhere, commerce melted away, and soon the town was but a shadow of its former self. The only art market in the east catering specifically to Italian taste had vanished as quickly as it had arisen.

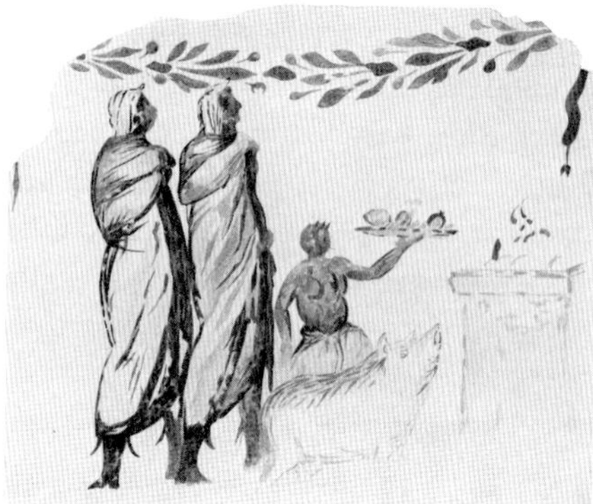

Fig. 9. Sacrificial scene *ritu Romano,* from an altar at Delos, ca. 100–88 B.C., from M. Bulard, *Exploration archéologique de Délos IX: Description des revêtements peints à sujets religieux* (Paris, 1926), pl. 19.

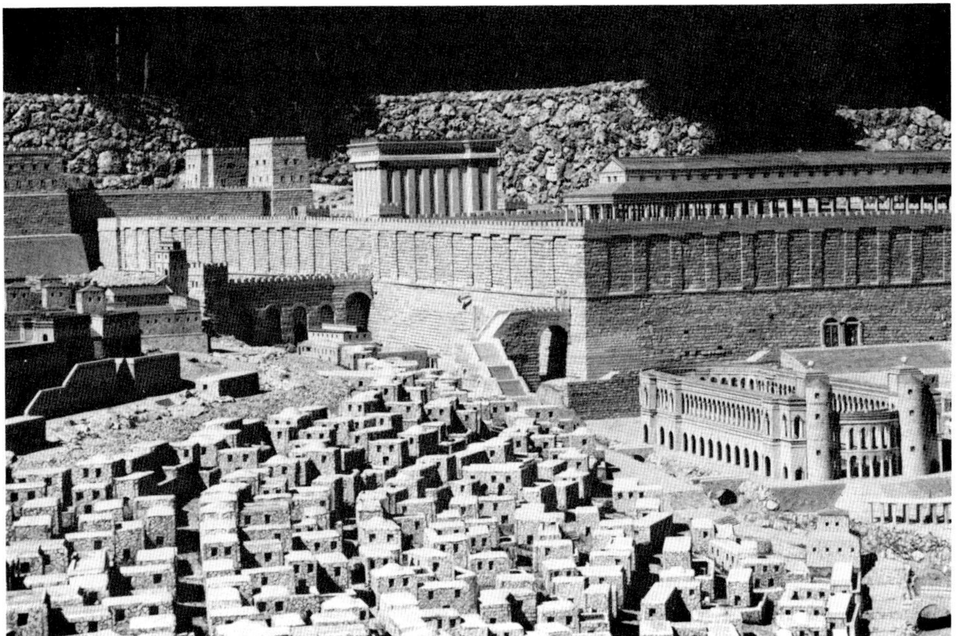

Fig. 10a. The Temple Mount, Jerusalem, seen from the Tyropoieon valley, 40–4 B.C. From the model in the Holyland Hotel, Jerusalem. Herod's temple is in the center, his basilica is to the right of it, and the Antonia fortress at the left rear.

Herod the Great of Judea

If the Italian community on Delos is a typical child of the republic in its strident assertion of Roman superiority and simultaneous capitulation on most fronts to Hellenistic taste, then the Judea of Herod the Great (reigned 37–4) announces the future. Disliked by the Jews, and perpetually insecure on his throne, Herod owed his position entirely to the support of Antony (from 40) and Augustus (from 31).[48] His massive building program, including extensive benefactions to the Greek cities of Syria, Asia, and Greece itself, represents the first thoroughgoing acceptance of Roman ideas and practices in the history of the Greek and Hellenized East.[49] Here, the lack of a strong indigenous tradition of monumental architecture evidently helped: Hellenistic and Hasmonean monumental building in Israel is largely confined to fortifications, and the Torah mandated that the Temple in Jerusalem must remain unique.

Accordingly, when Herod rebuilt the Temple, he did so in the prescribed (actually neo-Phoenician) manner, but surrounded it with Greek-style porticoes, and added a huge three-aisled, Italianate basilica on the south, over 600 feet long and in the Corinthian order (fig. 10). The temple mount was supported by vaults and approached by viaducts (on the west) and tunnels (on the south): all Roman, not Greek, innovations. A Roman-style quadrangular fortress dominated the complex from the North; as its name, the "Antonia," suggests, it was (not surprisingly) the first element in the scheme to be built.[50] Rapidly shifting gears in 31, he named his two palaces on the other side of the city the "Caesareion" and "Agrippeion." Though little remains of them except Josephus's description,[51] a sumptuous winter palace recently excavated near Jericho to some extent makes up for the loss. Employing much concrete and reticulate brickwork, incorporating a Roman bath and triclinium, and landscaped wholly in the Italian manner, it would have been quite at home in Campania.[52] The palaces at Herodium and Masada are more idiosyncratic, largely because of their precipitous sites, but still largely Italianate in construction and facilities, with hypocaust bath complexes much in evidence.[53]

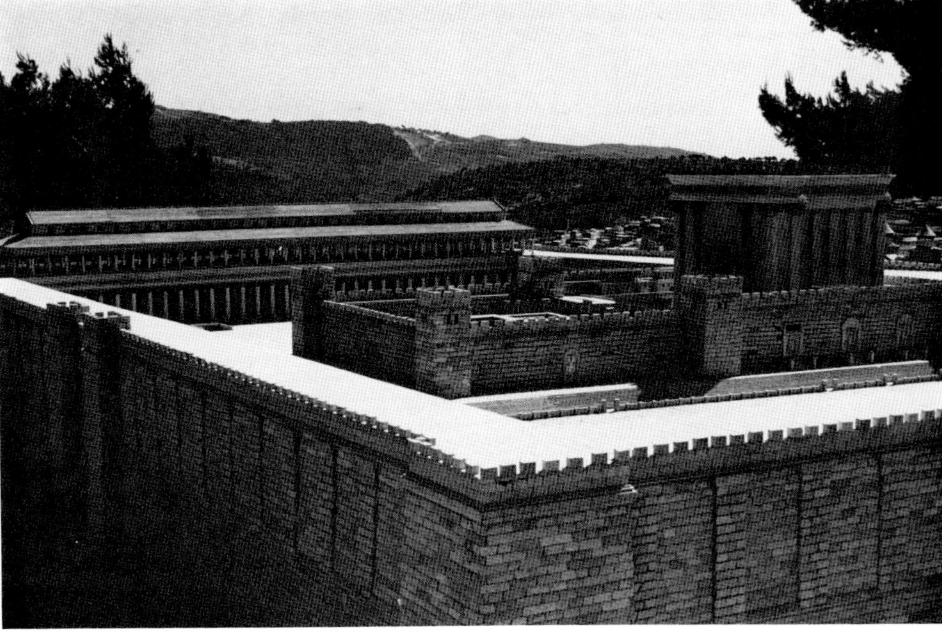

Fig. 10b. The Temple Mount, Jerusalem. View of Herod's basilica and temple from the northeast.

Herod's foundations of cities tell essentially the same story. Resettling Samaria (destroyed in 108) with mostly non-Jewish colonists, he renamed it Sebaste (= Augusta), re-fortified it, and built a temple of Rome and Augustus on the summit. It was thoroughly Italian in design, consisting of a large rectangular temenos terraced out on vaults, and enclosed on the front and sides by Corinthian porticoes; inside, a long flight of steps led up to the temple itself, which dominated the center axis. The temple was also Corinthian, but neither its colonnade nor that of the temenos continued around the back: as in Rome, where the whole arrangement had already been perfected in monuments like Caesar's forum, the entire stress was on the facade.[54] Later temple-complexes in both Israel and Syria follow essentially the same pattern.

At Caesarea, founded to give himself a secure harbor in a non-Jewish area, he laid out the town Roman-style, with cardo and decumanus meeting in a cross, and built another podium-temple to Rome and Augustus above the docks, again using vaults. The cult-statues imitated Pheidias's Zeus at Olympia and Polykleitos's Hera at Argos, making the project a synthesis of the best that both Greece and Rome had to offer. The theater was equally eclectic, blending a Roman-style vaulted auditorium of semicircular plan with a stage-building that, although somewhat obscured by later reconstruction, was less strongly articulated than normal in Italy, and terminated in colonnaded wings, recalling the theater of Dionysos in Athens.[55] The city was also provided with an amphitheater, a Roman building type hitherto unknown in the East. Chariot racing and the stage seem to have attracted Herod, who not only donated theaters and amphitheaters to several towns outside his kingdom, but even built one of each in Jerusalem, much to the annoyance of the orthodox.[56]

Herod's buildings are certainly in the vanguard of the Romanization of the East, and his enthusiasm for Roman tastes, including neo-classicism in sculpture, was certainly as politically correct and as calculated to please as the names he put on his palaces and towns. Yet among his own subjects, the impact of his sycophantically pro-Roman stance was uneven at best. While the Jewish elite had Hellenized since the mid-second century, and now to some extent began to Romanize, the orthodox stuck rigidly to traditional practice; even Herod himself strictly observed the prohibition upon representation of living things within the Jewish parts of his kingdom. As in the interior of Asia Minor, Romanization is barely noticeable in most parts of the Levant until well after the reign of Augustus.[57] The Jews may have offered the most extreme resistance to Roman ways, but they were certainly not alone. As the Greeks themselves had discovered, throughout the East, tradition died hard.

The pattern that emerges from all this is very much congruent with the conclusions advanced in the first half of this survey. Antiochos IV, far from being the fanatical Romanizer of modern tradition, turns out to have exploited Roman efficiency only as a means of strengthening his own hand, bolstering Greek pride and thereby stiffening Greek resistance to Rome. On Delos, the Italian community inaugurated a period of intense but extremely restricted Romanizing, essentially confined to one genre, portraiture, and to a limited period of two generations. This situation was virtually a microcosm of that to be found in Italy itself, where the local culture capitulated to the blandishments of Hellenism in the course of the second century. Finally Herod, an Edomite ruling Jews and others with few sentimental ties to Hellenism (rather the reverse), is the exception that proves the rule: sensing the winds of change, he simply altered course where it was expedient to accommodate them.

Hellenistic culture of the later second and first centuries B.C. is often described as being in a state of decline, even of complete collapse.[58] If this study has shown nothing else, it is that this is a gross oversimplification at best. In the Hellenistic world's steadfast resistance to Roman ways, and its consistent and largely successful efforts to inscribe the newcomers within its own frame of reference, one senses its continuing resilience and vitality, even as its political system was being assaulted, its treasure appropriated, and its morale eroded by the conquerors and their lackeys. Alternately awed and indifferent, intrigued and hostile, grateful and exasperated, and last but not least, sanguine and bitterly disappointed, the Greeks turned to their own culture for support, and were well rewarded. For if nothing else, there was the great solace that, in this sphere at least, it was they who were the victors:

Graecia capta ferum victorem cepit et artes intulit agresti Latino.[59]

This much was plain, and no one, least of all the conquerors, could deny it.

1. See, in general, E. S. Gruen, *The Hellenistic World and the Coming of Rome* (Berkeley, 1984); on Roman monetary policy as a reflection of official political policy, see M. H. Crawford, *Coinage and Money under the Roman Republic* (Berkeley, 1985), especially 116–132, 195–198. I am most grateful to Erich Gruen, John Pollini, and Christopher Hallett for reading and commenting upon the drafts of this paper, and for suggesting improvements and further references. If I have not followed their advice in every case, mea culpa.

2. The bibliography is vast. See especially O. Vessberg, *Studien zur Kunstgeschichte der römischen Republik* (Stockholm, 1941); J. J. Pollitt, *The Art of Rome,* Sources and Documents in the History of Art (Englewood Cliffs, N.J., 1966), 29–95; G. Alsop, *The Rare Art Traditions* (New York, 1982), 194–208; Gruen (note 1) 250–266, 288–315; Pollitt 150–163.

3. Pollitt 72–73, 76–79; E. Rawson, "Architecture and Sculpture: the Activities of the Cossutii," *BSR* 43 (1975) 36–47. As Crawford (note 1) 172 remarks, this shows that the flow of wealth was not all one-way: indeed, much of the tribute must have been repatriated to Greece and the East in one form or another, in return for goods and services.

4. G. Lippold, *Kopien und Umbildungen griechischer Statuen* (Munich, 1923); idem, "Antike Gemäldekopien," *Bayerische Akademie der Wissenschaften, München, Philosophisch-Historische Klasse. Abhandlungen* N.F. 33 (1951); L. Curtius, *Die Wandmalerei Pompejis* (Leipzig, 1929); K. Schefold, *Pompeianische Wandmalerei* (Basel, 1952); M. Borda, *La Pittura romana* (Milan, 1958); W. Fuchs, *Die Vorbilder der neuattischen Reliefs, JdI-EH* 20 (1959); idem, *Der Schiffsfund von Mahdia* (Tübingen, 1963); M. Bieber, *Ancient Copies* (New York, 1977); C. C. Vermeule, *Greek Sculpture and Roman Taste* (Ann Arbor, 1977); Pollitt 169–184.

5. C. M. Kraay-M. Hirmer, *Greek Coins* (London, 1966), pl. 175, no. 577—cf. no. 579 (Philip); J. M. C. Toynbee, *Roman Historical Portraits* (London, 1978), 19–20, fig. 5. On the circumstances of its issue, see Crawford (note 1) 124, who points out that Macedonian regal silver coins disappear from Greece at the same time, being either melted down or overstruck—at Flamininus's initiative? On the other hand, Roman coins do not appear in Greece until almost the end of the century (ibid., 128), and the denarius does not become the standard monetary unit there until the Athenian "New Style" coins decline to a trickle after the pirate sack of Delos in 67 (ibid., 197).

6. F. Chamoux, "Un portrait de Flamininus à Delphes," *BCH* 89 (1965) 214–219; H. R. Siedentopf, *Das hellenistische Reiterdenkmal* (Waldsassen, 1968), 23; Gruen (note 1) 167.

7. H. Kaehler, *Der Fries vom Reiterdenkmal des Aemilius Paullus* (Berlin, 1965); Stewart, *Attikà,* 46; Pollitt 155–158, figs. 162–164.

8. *IG* VII, nos. 264, 267, etc.; Siedentopf (note 6) 29; on this practice in general, see H. Blanck, *Wiederverwendung alter Statuen als Ehrendenkmäler bei Griechen und Römern* (Cologne, 1962).

9. A problem overlooked in the otherwise stimulating study of Roman verism by R. R. R. Smith, "Greeks, Foreigners, and Roman Republican Portraits," *JRS* 71 (1981) 24–38, where Greek hatred for the Romans after 190 is both oversimplified and overestimated; it all depended whose side they, and you, were on. See, in general, Gruen (note 1) 316–356.

10. For both, see E. Harrison, *Portrait Sculpture,* The Athenian Agora 11 (Princeton, 1953), no. 3, pls. 3 and 43c; A. Adriani, "Ritratti dell'Egitto greco-romano," *RM* 77 (1970) 78–79, pl. 37.

11. F. Chamoux, "Un portrait de Thasos: Jules César," *MonPiot* 47 (1953) 131–147, pl. 12; K. Tuchelt, *Frühe Denkmäler Roms in Kleinasien, Ist-Mitt* Beiheft 23 (Tubingen, 1979), 81 and 141 (Caesar Θεὸς ἐπιφανὴς at Ephesos); Toynbee (note 5) 37–38, figs. 36–37. On the others, see most recently my *Attikà* 80–88, pls. 24–28.

12. See, e.g., Harrison (note 10) nos. 7–9, etc.

13. R. Mellor, ΘΕΑ ΡΩΜΗ (Göttingen, 1975); C. Fayer, *Il Culto della Dea Roma* (Pescara, 1976); Mellor, "The Goddess Roma," *ANRW* II, 17, 2, 950–1030.

14. P. A. MacKay, "Bronze coinage in Macedonia, 168–166 B.C.," *ANSMN* 14 (1968) 5–14, pl. 3; on Alexander's apparent *damnatio memoriae* after Pydna see especially A. Giovannini, in *Alexandre le Grand,* 211–213 and idem, *Rome et la circulation monétaire en Grèce dans la IIe siècle avant J.-C.* (Basel, 1978). The Alexanders issued by the pro-quaestor Aesillas, evidently to mobilize Macedonian sentiment against either Thracian invaders or Mithradates in the 90s and 80s, are the exceptions that prove the rule: B. V. Head, *Historia Numorum* (Oxford, 1911), 240–241; R. Göbl, *Antike Numismatik* (Munich, 1978), pl. 47, nos. 689–691; cf. R. S. Fisher, *ANSMN* 30 (1985) 69–88; Crawford (note 1) 197, fig. 77; T. Frank, *An Economic Survey of Ancient Rome* 4 (Baltimore, 1938), 422–423; Livy, *Epitome* 70, 74, 76; Cicero, *In Pisonem* 84.

15. J. Marcadé, *Au musée de Délos* (Paris, 1969), 128–134, pl. 65; Stewart, *Attikà,* 65, pl. 12c.

16. See Stewart, *Attikà,* 34–64, 139–142. The "New Style" coinage of Athens, apparently produced to service the booming economy of Delos after Rome made it a free port and gave it to the Athenians in 167, should be added to the list of examples: see most recently Crawford (note 1) 125, fig. 43.

17. Vitruvius 5.9.1,7 Praef. 15; *IG* II², nos. 3426–7, 4099; Plutarch, *Pompey* 42; J. Travlos, *A Pictorial Dictionary of Ancient Athens* (London, 1971), 387–391, 402–411.

18. Cicero, *ad Att.* 6.1.27 and 6.2; G. Mylonas, *Eleusis and the Eleusinian Mysteries* (Princeton, 1961); J. B. Ward-Perkins, *Roman Imperial Architecture* (Harmondsworth, 1981), 263–264. Like the restoration activities of P. Servilius Isauricus on Kalymnos, Tenos, and perhaps also at Aegae (*OGIS* 449, n. 2; *IG* XII 5, no. 917; L. Robert, *Hellenica* VI [Paris, 1948], 38–39; and A. Degrassi, *Inscriptiones Latinae Liberae Rei Publicae* [Florence, 1957–63], 403–404) these are squarely in the Hellenistic tradition of royal liberality, and anticipate imperial gifts.

19. By Michael Hoff, of the American School of Classical Studies; provisionally, see Travlos (note 17) 28–36, and Ward-Perkins (note 18) 265.

20. See, in general, Ward-Perkins (note 18) 255–263. Corinth also boasts the only known amphitheater in Greece, but this was not built until the third or fourth century: Dio Chrysostom 31.121 describes the area as a sewer, and Pausanias does not mention it. See H.N. Fowler, R. Stillwell, *Corinth I, Pt. 1: Introduction, Topography, Architecture* (Cambridge, 1932), 88–91.

21. See, in general, D. Magie, *Roman Rule in Asia Minor* (Princeton, 1950); on monetary policy and politics, see Crawford (note 1) 152–160, 198–209, 250–255.

22. See, in general, Tuchelt (note 11); for the coins, cf. Toynbee (note 5) 31, fig. 24, 43, figs. 44–50, etc.; Crawford (note 1) 250–255, figs. 107–109. Contrast the much harsher, truly veristic style of the Western coin portraits of these men illustrated alongside them.

23. See Tuchelt (note 11) 124–125 for another explanation of the equestrian problem.

24. Mellor and Fayer (note 13), with S. Price, *Rituals and Power. The Roman Imperial Cult in Asia Minor* (Cambridge, 1984), 40–47.

25. *Greek Anthology* iii.19; R. Brilliant, *Visual Narratives* (Ithaca, 1984), 35–36, with earlier bibliography. John Pollini, to whom I owe this reference, also draws my attention to another, more conjectural Romulus and Remus on Chios: Price (note 24) 44.

26. E. Gabba, "Political and Cultural Aspects of the Classicistic Revival in the Augustan Age," *Classical Antiquity* 1 (1982) 43–65, especially 51–52.

27. G. Hafner, *Späthellenistische Bildnisplastik* (Berlin, 1954); the verist and semiverist portraits are collected by J. Inan and E. Rosenbaum, *Roman and Early Byzantine Portrait Sculpture in Asia Minor* (Oxford, 1966), nos. 135–138, 203, 284, and supplementary edition (Mainz, 1979), nos. 97, 122, 173, 248, and 312.

28. Suggested by Smith (note 9) 33 n. 88; cf. e.g. Kraay-Hirmer (note 5) nos. 769–772; Toynbee (note 5) 128, fig. 246.

29. Toynbee (note 5) 114, fig. 201; Pollitt 36, fig. 28a (Mithradates II/III of Pontos, ca. 220–185).

30. See Inan-Rosenbaum (note 27), passim; also the very early Augustan Zoilos frieze at Aphrodisias, K. T. Erim, *Aphrodisias* (London, 1986), 4–5, 80–82, 136–139.

31. Laokoon, etc.; Stewart, "To Entertain an Emperor: Sperlonga, Laokoon and Tiberius at the Dinner Table," *JRS* 67 (1977) 76–90; E. E. Rice, "Prosopographika Rhodiaka," *BSA* 81 (1986) 209–250; Pollitt 120–126, figs. 124–130. Aphrodisias: J. M. C. Toynbee, *The Hadrianic School* (Cambridge, 1934); M. Squarciapino, *La Scuola di Afrodisia* (Rome, 1943); Erim (note 30) passim.

32. Strabo 12.556, 560, 562; Appian, *Mithradatic Wars* 115; A. H. M. Jones, *The Cities of the Eastern Roman Provinces* (Oxford, 1937), 158–160.

33. In general, see Tuchelt (note 11) 127–128; Ward-Perkins (note 18) 273–306; Price (note 24) 133–169 (with important remarks on the reorganization of civic space around the imperial cult) and catalogue, 249–275.

34. Tuchelt (note 11) 29–33.

35. Jones (note 32) 158–160. As to coinage, Crawford (note 1) 201–209 and 243–255 discusses the successive Roman reorganizations of the monetary affairs of the East: they are complex, but the main point is that types and legends were invariably Greek until the Civil Wars, and often Greek thereafter; the mainstream coinage of Rome did not circulate freely in Asia until after 44, and in Syria and Egypt not until after 30.

36. Polybios 30.25–6; Livy 41.20, etc.; arguments on both sides are conveniently summarized and discussed in Gruen (note 1) 660–663.

37. See Gruen (note 1) 647–671, 745–751.

38. See O. Mørkholm, *Studies in the Coinage of Antiochus IV of Syria* (Copenhagen, 1963); A. Houghton, *Coins of the Seleukid Empire from the Collection of Arthur Houghton* (New York, 1983); on neoclassicism and his cultural program see Stewart, *Attikà*, 47, etc., though like others, I was too trusting of his supposed program of Romanization.

39. Vitruvius 7 praef. 15, 17; on [Decimus?] Cossutius [P.f.?] see Rawson (note 3) 36–38, with the suggestion that he was "one of Antiochos's low-born cronies" from his days of exile, perhaps trained in Campania. As John Pollini reminds me, M. Torelli, "Industria estrattiva, lavoro artiginale, interessi economici: qualche appunto," *MAAR* 36 (1980) 313–323 suggests that Antiochos may have been more interested in Cossutius's engineering skills (particularly necessary on a vast project like the Olympieion) than in his abilities as an architect; not only is a Cossutius found among the graffiti on a second-century aqueduct at Antioch, but the Cossutii were later heavily involved in marble-quarrying and transportation.

40. For a list of his benefactions, see Livy 41.20.5–9, with Ammianus Marcellinus 22.13.1; further references in Rawson (note 3) 43, and Stewart, *Attikà*, 47. Cf. G. Roux, "Le devis de Livadie et le temple de Zeus Basileus," *MusHelv* 17 (1960) 175–184; C. Williams, "The Corinthian Temple of Zeus Olbius at Uzuncaburç: a Reconsideration of the Date," *AJA* 78 (1974) 405–414; A. W. Lawrence and R. A. Tomlinson, *Greek Architecture* (Harmondsworth, 1983), 275–277, 355–357; for speculation on the symbolism of the orders, see J. Onians, *Art and Thought in the Hellenistic Age* (London, 1979), 72–79.

41. R. Vallois, "Le Théâtre de Tégée," *BCH* 50 (1926) 135–173, pl. 5–7.

42. Delos in general: P. Bruneau, *Guide de Délos,* 3rd ed. (Paris, 1983); see also Crawford (note 1) 125 and 197 on Delos and the "New Style" coinage: cf. note 16, above. Agora: E. Lapalus, *Exploration archéologique de Delos XIX: L'Agora des Italiens* (Paris, 1939); Lawrence-Tomlinson (note 40) 360. Portraits: C. Michalowski, *Exploration archéologique de Délos XIII: Les portraits hellénistiques et romains* (Paris, 1932); Marcadé (note 15); Stewart, *Attikà*, 65–78; reflections on local gravestones from Rheneia: M.-Th. Couilloud, *Exploration archéologique de Délos XXX: Les monuments funéraires du Rhénée* (Paris, 1973), 250, though as to tomb *types,* I see nothing particularly Italian about, e.g., the tomb of Tertia Horaria, ibid. no. 58 and figs. 3, 9.

43. References, Stewart, *Attikà*, 92 n. 28, and for the Ephesos head, Inan-Rosenbaum 1979 (note 27) no. 122, pl. 101; though some of the other heads listed in note 27, above, seem indebted to the Delian style in various ways, none is as close as this.

44. Against the extreme pan-Romanism of M. Bulard, *Exploration archéologique de Délos IX: Descriptions des revêtements peints à sujets religieux* (Paris, 1926), see P. Bruneau, *Recherches sur les cultes de Délos à l'époque hellénistique et à l'époque impériale* (Paris, 1970), 589–620; U. Bezerra de Meneses and H. Sarain, *Etudes déliennes, BCH* Suppl. 1 (Athens, 1973), 76–109; and Bruneau (note 42) 86, 87.

45. In general, Bruneau (note 42) 52, 92, etc., with his remarks in *Exploration archéologique de Délos XXIX: Les mosaïques* (Paris, 1972), 115–116.

46. On the luxury arts see R. A. Higgins, *Greek and Roman Jewellery* (London, 1961), 154–156; D. E. Strong, *Greek and Roman Gold and Silver Plate* (London, 1966), 107–125, 137–139. Beds: S. Boucher, in *Bronzes hellénistiques et romains: Tradition et renouveau* (Lausanne, 1979), 95–102.

47. J.-P. L'Empéreur, "Les anses d'amphores timbrées et les amphores: aspects quantitatifs," *BCH* 106 (1982) 225; idem, in Bruneau (note 42) 97–98.

48. See A. H. M. Jones, *The Herods of Judaea* (Oxford, 1938); E. Schürer, *The History of the Jewish People in the Age of Jesus Christ (175 B.C.– A.D. 135)*, rev. ed. (Edinburgh, 1973); E. M. Smallwood, *The Jews under Roman Rule* (Leiden, 1981), and, of course, Josephus.

49. With so much recently excavated and essentially unpublished, no synthesis of this material is currently in sight: see, in general, Ward-Perkins (note 18) 309–314; commentary and useful compendia of pictures in M. Avi-Yonah and E. Stern, eds., *Encyclopedia of Archaeological Excavations in the Holy Land* (Jerusalem, 1976), also in G. Cornfeld, ed., *Josephus, The Jewish War* (Grand Rapids, 1982).

50. Josephus, *AJ* 15.396–417; *BJ* 5.238–246; B. Mazar and others in Y. Yadin, ed., *Jerusalem Revealed* (Jerusalem, 1975), 25–35, 87–89 (Antonia); Mazar, "Herodian Jerusalem," *IEJ* 28 (1978) 230–237; idem, in A. Biran, ed., *Biblical Archaeology Today* (Jerusalem, 1985), 463–469.

51. *BJ* 1.402; 5.176–183.

52. E. Netzer, "The Hasmonean and Herodian Winter Palaces at Jericho," *IEJ* 25 (1975) 89–100.

53. Josephus, *BJ* 1.419–21, 7.290; E. Netzer, *Herodium: an Archaeological Guide* (Jerusalem, 1987); Y. Yadin, *Masada* (London, 1966).

54. Josephus, *BJ* 1.176, 414; *AJ* 15.217.292, 296–298; J. W. Crowfoot et al., *Samaria-Sebaste 1. The Buildings of Samaria* (London, 1942). Begun between 27 and 23.

55. Josephus, *BJ* 1.408–416; L. I. Levine, *Roman Caesarea, Qedem* 5.2 (Jerusalem, 1975); built 22–10.

56. Josephus, *AJ* 16.142–149, *BJ* 15.268.

57. So, e.g., Ward-Perkins (note 18) 328–329; the architecture of the present author's own site at Dor, just north of Caesarea, remains tenaciously Phoenician well into the first century A.D. A paved cardo, decumanus, and forum were not constructed until shortly before 100, and the Ionic podium-temple was not built until the second century.

58. Thus Bieber, *Sculpture,* 165 believed that the art was revitalized by Rome just when it was becoming "stale, dry, and degenerate"; J. Charbonneaux, R. Martin, F. Villard, *Hellenistic Art* (London, 1973), 333 speaks openly of "decline" and "collapse"; Robertson 564–565 detects a "falling off of artistic quality throughout the Hellenistic world in this period of incomplete subordination to Rome," rather strangely using Nemrud Dagh as his example; and most extreme of all, Onians (note 40) 180 opines that "As the Greeks lost the strength and the conviction which were necessary if they were to impose Hellenism, the Hellenistic period drew to a close. Yet even as they faltered they had the presence of mind to recognize their true successors. They thus ensured the continuance of much of what they had achieved."

59. Horace, *Epistles* ii.1.156–7.

The Hellenistic Minor Arts

Ellen D. Reeder

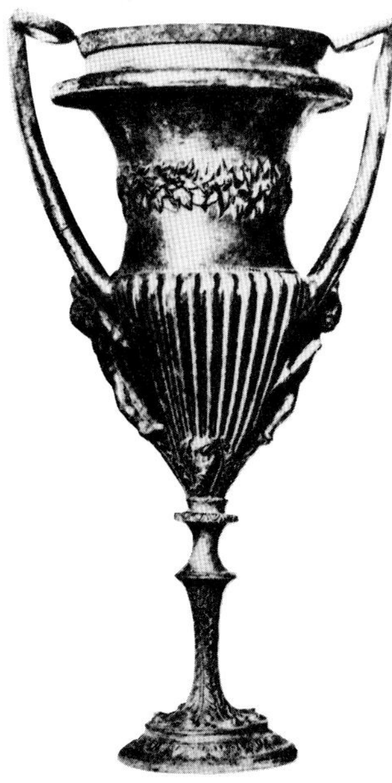

Fig. 1. Silver krateriskos from Taranto, ca. 300–275 B.C., private collection, from *Macedonia and Greece,* 126, fig. 7.

IN THE FIELD OF GREEK ART, most scholars would agree that there is a clear-cut distinction between the "major" and "minor" arts. The major arts comprise architecture, monumental sculpture, wall-painting, and mosaics. The minor arts include what is left: small-scale sculpture in bronze, marble, and terracotta; metal vessels and utensils; unpainted pottery; objects of faience, glass, ivory, coins, gems, and other jewelry. The only body of material not easily categorized is red- and black-figured pottery, which is generally grouped with monumental sculpture and architecture. With this one exception, the distinction between the major and minor arts is based on scale. The division is far more than an organizational aid, however, for intrinsic to the classification is the implication that the minor arts, from antiquity to the present day, have been of lesser importance.

It is, however, by no means clear that the ancient viewer used a yardstick to evaluate the importance of the arts; indeed, Michael Vickers has eloquently argued that the current inferior stature of the minor arts does not coincide with the ancient point of view, but is rather a modern notion ultimately attributable to the Arts and Crafts Movement.[1] In fact, if we ask which were the most highly valued arts in the Hellenistic age, based on the monetary worth of the works of art, the fields in which the most acclaimed artists of the day were active, and the kinds of objects most treasured by the patrons of artists, we find it impossible to relegate the minor arts to a lesser status. The value of gold and silver relative to clay and marble was so substantial that a gold or silver vessel had several hundred times the value of a finely painted clay vase or marble statue.[2] Vessels of precious metal were, in fact, a utilitarian form of the assets of Hellenistic kings, and were proudly paraded in lavish royal processions, as were ivory, precious stones, and fabric embroidered with gold threads. The legendary parade of Ptolemy II Philadelphos at Alexandria, for example, included many gold and silver vessels set with precious stones, and an impressive array of fabric including hangings, coverlets, and cloths.[3] The procession of Antiochos IV at Daphni featured gold and silver vessels, elephant tusks, and more gold threaded garments.[4] Obviously, these goods constituted some of the most monetarily valuable articles that these monarchs possessed.

An important indicator of the high regard in which the minor arts were held in Hellenistic times is the considerable personal value that ancient owners and patrons attached to their possessions. Upon his deathbed Alexander gave his ring to Perdikkas as a sign that the latter had been chosen as Alexander's successor, and Pyrrhos treasured an agate carved with a representation of Apollo and the Muses.[5] Minor arts also functioned as the currency for gifts exchanged between major powers. Ptolemy IX gave the Roman general Lucullus an emerald engraved with the Ptolemaic king's portrait, and the gift that the Syrian prince Antiochos designated for the Roman administration was a lampstand fashioned of precious stones.[6] It is also illuminating to consider the prominence of the artists who were commissioned to work in the minor arts. Alexander permitted no one other than Pyrgoteles to carve his image in emerald, and such engravers as Nikias and Apollonios were not only employed as gem-carvers and die-engravers, but also traveled between the royal courts and signed their names prominently on their work (Nos. 136, 140).[7] Quite clearly, the materials that claimed the highest value in their unworked state, gold, silver, and precious stones, were placed only in the hands of artists of the finest caliber, and were transformed into

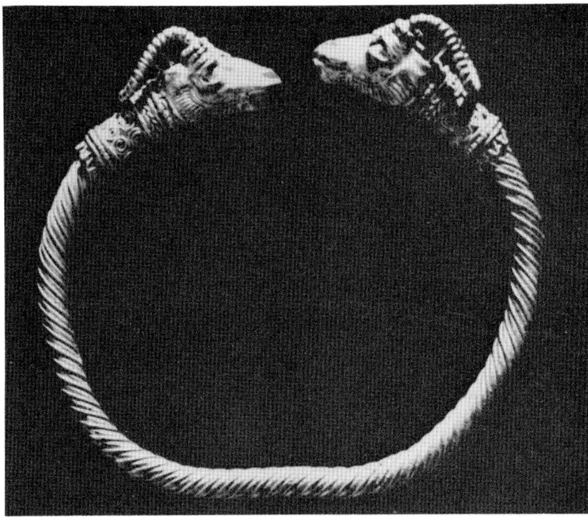

Fig. 2. Gold bracelet from Pasargadae, ca. 400–350 B.C., from D. Stronach, *Pasargadae* (Oxford, 1978), pl. 147a.

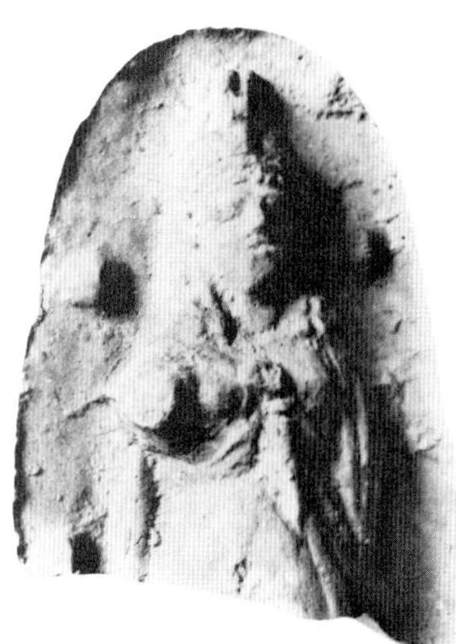

Fig. 3. Plaster piece-mold from Memphis, second or first century B.C. Cairo, Egyptian National Museum, Inv. no. 32.050, from C. Edgar, *Greek Moulds* (Cairo, 1903), pl. 22.

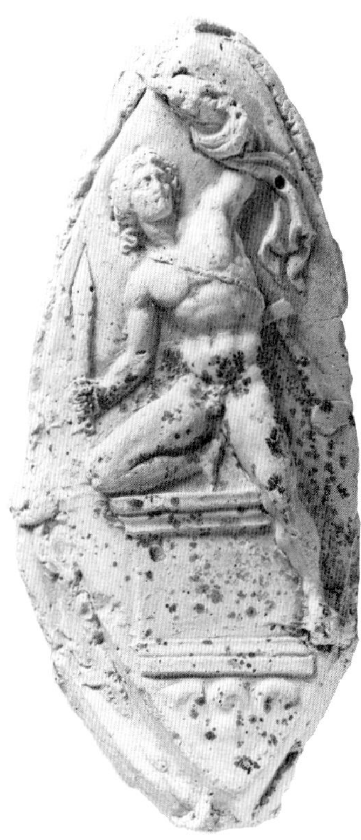

Fig. 4. Plaster cast of a Prometopidion, from Mit Rahine, ca. 150 B.C. Hildesheim, Pelizaeus Museum, Inv. no. 1145. Photograph, Pelizaeus Museum, Hildesheim.

works of art held in the utmost esteem. That this phenomenon was so before the Hellenistic period is certainly true, but in Hellenistic times the minor arts flourished as never before, due to royal patronage and an increased emphasis upon the individual and the home. To allow the minor arts to be eclipsed in a study of the Hellenistic age is to condone an unbalanced assessment of the era's artistic achievement.

Perhaps the major reason for the efflorescence of the minor arts in Hellenistic times was the existence of the royal courts with their traditional emphases upon such appurtenances as furniture, eating and drinking vessels, clothing, gems, and jewelry. The monarchical system had deep roots in Egypt and the Near East, and from the very threshold of the Hellenistic age the Greeks and Macedonians were exposed to royal treasuries of immense resources. At Persepolis Alexander encountered gold and silver vessels, together with richly embroidered drapery, and at first sight of these riches is said to have uttered the prophetic words: "So this is what it is like to live like a king!".[8] Undoubtedly included in this bounty were jeweled cups, because the treasury of Mithradates VI contained several that were said to have belonged to Darius, and, in a passage by Theophrastos, a soldier obviously discharged by Alexander claims to have such a jeweled vessel in his baggage.[9] Other Persian luxury objects included couches, such as that owned by Darius, which ultimately came into the possession of Mithradates VI.[10] Even greater opulence may have been encountered in India, where Alexander's army beheld multitudes of gold vessels adorned with emeralds and garnets.[11] That the lesson of ornamental finery was absorbed by the Macedonians is demonstrated by Alexander's funerary procession in which both the roof of his carriage and the animals' trappings were studded with precious stones.[12]

Ample literary and archaeological evidence attests to the alacrity with which Hellenistic monarchs embraced the eastern royal lifestyle. Mithradates VI had a three-by-four-foot game board made of precious stone that, Pausanias tells us, supported a thirty-pound gold moon.[13] He also possessed a ring cabinet, gold vessels inlaid with gems, two thousand drinking cups of gold and onyx (perhaps the *myrrhine* discussed by Pliny), and furniture, some of which had come from the Persian court and was made of precious stones and gold.[14] When the Syrian prince Antiochos traveled as an emissary to Rome, he packed in his personal belongings a jewel-studded cup together with a ladle carved from a single piece of stone and adorned with a gold handle.[15] One senses that such finery was commonly accepted as an attribute of leadership. When Demetrios Poliorketes died, his daughter Stratonike dedicated on Delos his necklace, arm bracelets, and leg bracelets; of uncertain disposition was his gold-and-purple mantle, which was so elaborate that none of his successors dared to claim it.[16] Even the Spartan leader Kleomenes III (260–219) acceded to convention and provided his company with silver bowls and drinking cups.[17] The literary record is amply supported by material evidence, for not all of the riches of these royal courts have disappeared. Silverware (Nos. 41–43), ivory appliqués (No. 110), and royal portrait rings (Nos. 113, 114) have survived, and excavation continues to enrich this legacy. The royal tombs at Vergina have yielded ivory furniture appliqués and silver cups, which speak eloquently for the elegance of the Macedonian court, and from Aï Khanum were recovered fragments of luxury vases of extraordinary richness, made of alabaster, amethyst, agate, and a host of other precious stones.[18] Also in this royal treasury were found jewelry and plaques of agate and rock crystal, apparently for furniture inlay.[19] Even the distant Parthian palace at Nisa yielded marble statuettes and ivory rhyta.[20]

Several circumstances proved particularly beneficial to the blossoming of the minor arts under the aegis of the Hellenistic royal courts. No insignificant catalyst was the rivalry between the courts, which were linked by intermarriage and by the mobility of artists (No. 136). The importance of the grand gesture, epitomized by the official gift, resulted in such opulent creations as the lampstand of precious stones that the Syrian prince Antiochos brought with him to Rome, and the magnificent decorations of the boat that Hieron II of Syracuse sent to Ptolemy Philadelphos.[21] The minor arts were also significantly affected by the intensification of international trade, which made available previously inaccessible goods and resulted in a fashion for works of art made from such exotica as amethysts (No. 139), garnets (Nos. 135, 136, 140), emeralds (Nos. 125, 130–132) and pearls (Nos. 130–131). These materials were often put to use in fashioning those tours de force that are almost an inevitable aspect of a royal milieu where a piece unique in fabric, workmanship, design, or use is especially prized; one thinks of the gold mountain replete with animals that belonged to Mithradates VI.[22]

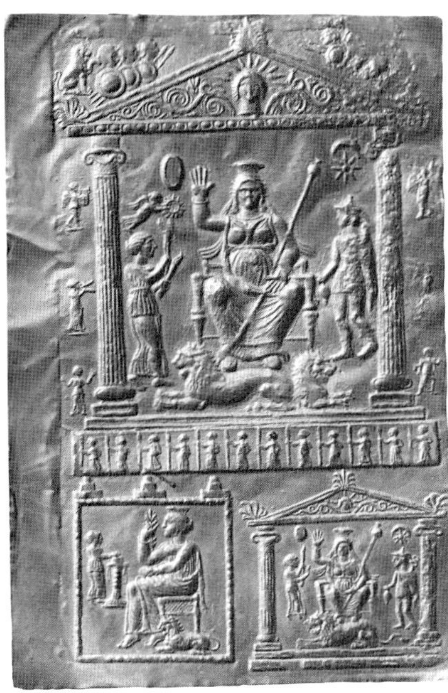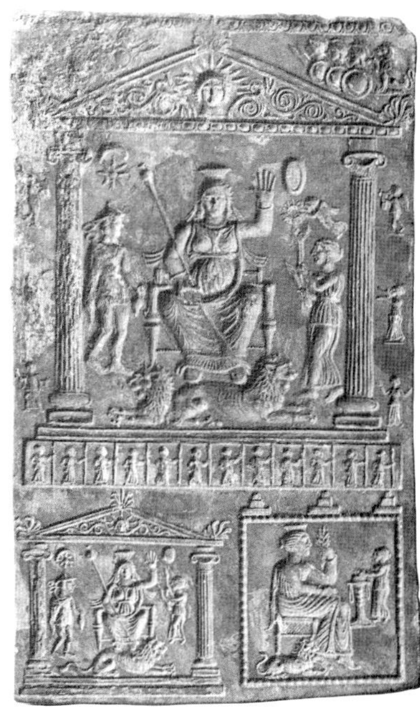

Fig. 6. Bronze matrix, second or first century B.C. New York, The Metropolitan Museum of Art, Inv. no. 20.2.24. Photograph, The Metropolitan Museum of Art, New York.

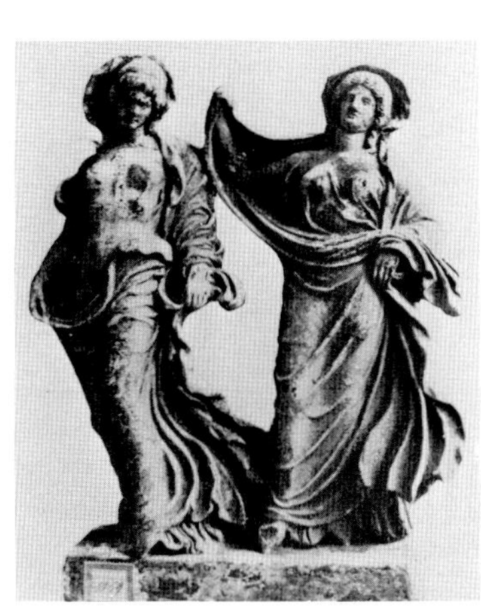

Fig. 5. Terracotta group of dancers, made in an Attic mold, found at In-Tepe, near Troy, ca. 370 B.C. Istanbul, Archaeological Museum, Inv. no. 1868, from *Proceedings of the Xth International Congress of Classical Archaeology* (Ankara-Izmir, 1973), III, pl.183.2.

The magnificence of Hellenistic royal patronage had far-reaching effects. Foremost among these was the unprecedented caliber of the workmanship. Gem-carving and metalwork, including vessels and gold jewelry, flourished as never before under such kings as Antiochos IV, who was said to spend his leisure hours frequenting the goldsmith shops of Antioch.[23] A second result was the impact that products and fashions conceived within the royal milieu exerted upon people of more modest lifestyles. As never before in ancient art, royal finery was adapted in design and fabric for customers with a wide range of financial resources. The ceramic moldmade bowls (Nos. 97–99) and faience oinochoai with Ptolemaic portraits (Nos. 103–104) are surely inexpensive versions of costly vessels made in precious metal. Certainly the clay amphora from Tarentum (No. 96) was inspired by examples of gold and silver (fig. 1), and terracotta and marble figurines (Nos. 15, 17, 18, 81–84) imitated more expensive counterparts in bronze. One long-lived legacy of the royal courts was the portrait ring, for which the prototype was an emerald belonging to Alexander that was carved with his own image.[24] Rings with portraits of Hellenistic rulers (Nos. 135, 140, 141) were bestowed as gifts, and affluent subjects emulated the practice to the extent that they were able (No. 136). Indeed, royal portraiture was an immensely influential phenomenon in the minor arts. Portraits of Hellenistic monarchs appear not only on vessels (Nos. 103, 104), rings (Nos. 135, 140, 141), and coins (Nos. 148–150), but also on bronze and ivory appliqués for furniture (Nos. 50, 110), and as free-standing statuettes (Nos. 61, 63). Divine affiliations are frequently extolled; Ptolemaic kings are identified with Dionysos (Nos. 50, 135) and Alexander (No. 50), and Ptolemaic queens wear the garments and insignia of Isis (Nos. 103, 104, 113, 114). One can imagine the willingness with which the concept of royal portraiture was embraced by ingratiating individuals favored by the court, and one can understand the popularity of the convention as monarchs realized its effectiveness as a political tool.

Given the location of the Hellenistic monarchies in lands ruled for millennia as kingdoms, one would expect substantial influence upon the Hellenistic minor arts from Near Eastern and Egyptian art. The dearth of freestanding sculpture in Assyrian and Achaemenid civilizations explains the minimal role of Near Eastern traditions in Hellenistic freestanding sculpture, but in the minor arts, where both Achaemenid and Egyptian art were strong, the legacy was, not surprisingly, extensive. After Alexander's destruction of the Persian Empire, the pure style of Achaemenid art evaporated, and many of the Greek artists who had worked at Persepolis were settled permanently in the vicinity of the palace.[25] Achaemenid artistic traditions lived on, however, in the Hellenistic world. Although Near Eastern influence was certainly detectable in Greek art by the early years of the fourth century, the orientalizing tendency grew much stronger in the following centuries. Hellenistic beds (No. 68) were undoubtedly inspired by Persian counterparts, and the ultimate prototype for the Hellenistic ceramic moldmade bowl (No. 97–99) was probably a Persian drinking vessel. The influence of Near Eastern art is particularly perceptible in jewelry. Bracelets with antelope head finials (No. 116) can be traced back to specific Persian prototypes (fig. 2), and the pair of bracelets from Olbia (No. 131) surely also owe their inspiration to the cuff bracelets seen in Assyrian or Persian reliefs. The hoop earring with animal head finial (Nos. 122–124) is also certainly of Achaemenid inspiration, and the popularity among women of the diadem (No. 127) is surely related to Alexander's adoption of this form of Persian regalia.

Egyptian influence in the Hellenistic minor arts is also quite prominent, especially in the widespread use of royal portraiture (Nos. 103, 104, 139, 140, 141) following an age-old Egyptian tradition, and in the inclusion on Hellenistic earrings of such Egyptian motifs as the Isis crown (No. 126). Noteworthy, too,

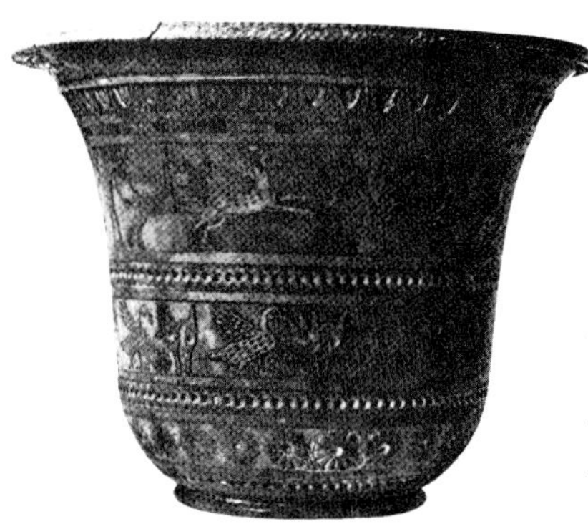

Fig. 7. Faience vessel from Thessaloniki, second century B.C. Thessaloniki, Archaeological Museum, Inv. no. 2829, from *JdI* 91 (1976) 143, fig. 9.

are Hellenistic faience vessels (Nos. 105, 106, 107, 108) which in shape and ornament were derived from the traditional Egyptian faience ware. In sculpture, Hellenistic figurines of grotesques (Nos. 101, 102) were inspired by images of Bes, and the age-old Egyptian motif of a victor triumphing over his collapsed victim was translated with renewed vigor into a Hellenized version (No. 63). The blending of Egyptian and Greek artistic traditions sometimes resulted in a curious style, as manifested by a diorite head of a man (No. 30), which reflects its Greek heritage in the modeling of some facial planes, but exhibits a characteristically Egyptian hairstyle.

One of the most striking features of the Hellenistic minor arts is an unprecedented trend to mass production. Contemporary with the exquisite, singular objects for court and aristocracy were those manufactured on a massive scale. Although the quality of these objects was often very high, the system by which they were made demonstrates remarkable labor-saving techniques. To a greater extent than ever before, terracotta figurines were made by interchanging heads, torsos, and limbs made in separate molds (Nos. 75, 76, 94). A similar phenomenon exists in metalworking where the wax models for bronze figurines were assembled from separate wax elements that had been made individually (fig. 3) in plaster piece-molds (No. 73).[26] Often limbs were cast separately and soldered or welded onto a cast bronze torso (No. 65). Multiple copies of a single bronze figure or group were not uncommon (No. 63), emulating a practice long established for terracotta figurines.

Within a workshop every effort was made to facilitate production. Workshop aids included plaster molds, bronze matrices, plaster impressions and casts from finished metalwork (fig. 4), and castings from incomplete images.[27] Virtually unprecedented is the traffic that developed in these workshop aids. Excavation at Pella uncovered a workshop that exported molds for terracotta figurines, and evidence exists for the export from Athens of figurine molds which in their final destination were used to manufacture reliefs (fig. 5).[28] From Egypt have come imported bronze matrices (fig. 6), and imported plaster casts from finished metalwork have been found in Begram.[29] One can also hypothesize the interchange of artists' handbooks containing working sketches. By late Hellenistic times, artisans such as Arkesilaos, working in Rome, could command enormously high prices for their clay and plaster working-models.[30]

The extensive trade in the minor arts that developed in Hellenistic times is documented not only by the attested traffic in these workshop aids, but also by the widely dispersed findspots of many finished products, which were, after all, highly transportable. Faience Naukratis ware (Nos. 105–107) has been recovered in Macedonia (fig. 7) and Tanagra, and metalwork made in Alexandria is known to have been sent to Italy (No. 50). Further proof of the intensity of the art trade lies in the uniformity of style. Late Hellenistic beds (No. 68) look very much alike whether found in Greece, Asia Minor, or Italy, and jewelry, particularly earrings (Nos. 118, 119) and diadems (No. 127), rarely exhibit a regional character. An especially difficult exercise is the identification of local schools in Hellenistic monumental sculpture.

At the same time, however, a certain flavor often informs the disparate works of art from a single locality. The art of South Italy exhibits an exuberance and inorganic decorativeness that is recognizable in the pottery (Nos. 95, 96), jewelry (No. 123) and terracotta figurines (Nos. 86–88). Along the western coast of Asia Minor the strength of the sculptural tradition is apparent in the faithfulness with which small-scale versions of marble, terracotta, and bronze adhere to their prototypes (Nos. 23, 35). Perhaps most distinctive are the works of art made in Ptolemaic Egypt, especially Alexandria. Enabling us to compile a profile of the Ptolemaic style are recorded Egyptian findspots (Nos. 44, 57), such technical evidence as the seams joining the disparate elements of a wax model, indisputably Egyptian fabrics such as the faience vessels with Ptolemaic portraits (Nos. 103–104), and subjects either inspired by daily Egyptian life (Nos. 54–56, 58) or related to traditional Egyptian iconography (Nos. 59–73). Frequently encountered in these pieces is a loose handling of the transitions between surfaces, which in some cases results in a bumpiness or roughness (Nos. 44, 58). Elsewhere we find abruptly angled planes that resulted from a careless finish of the wax surface; this hastiness in execution lends the figures a momentary, spontaneous quality (No. 59). Immediacy was also achieved by reworking by hand the drapery (No. 60) or facial features (No. 63) in the wax model before casting. Many of the statuettes are not organically convincing; the body forms are distorted (Nos. 61, 64), the limbs out of proportion, and the emphasis is on stylized, decorative detail at the expense of anatomical accuracy (Nos. 30, 50).

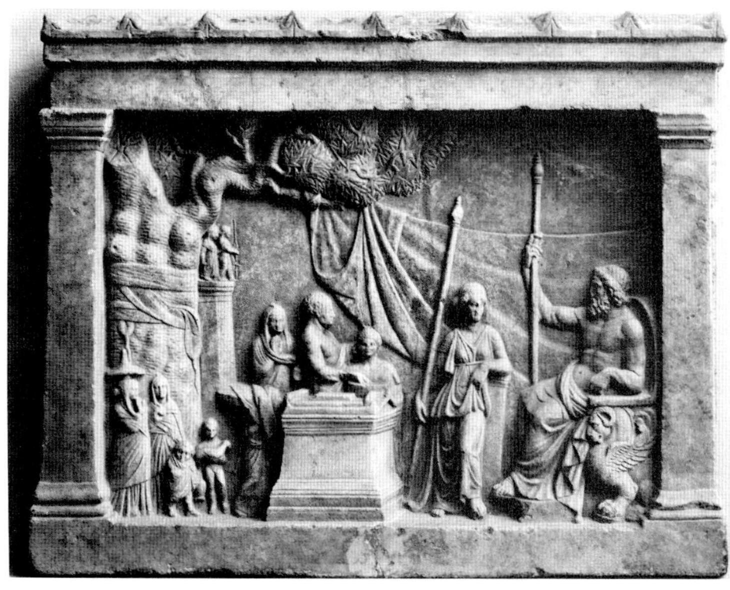

Fig. 8. Votive relief, marble, middle to late second century B.C. Munich, Glyptothek, Inv. no. 206. Photograph, Staatlichen Antikensammlungen und Glyptothek, Munich.

Most discussions of the extensive art trade during the Hellenistic era have focused upon the late Hellenistic period, when massive numbers of works of art, and artists, were imported to Italy.[31] No less significant in terms of the Hellenistic art market were the altered functions of the works of art and the broadened base of the clientele. Before Alexander, the adornment of the home was largely confined to painted pottery and metal vessels; small-scale sculpture in bronze and terracotta functioned as votive or burial offerings. In Hellenistic times, by contrast, the prominence of the royal courts and the increased focus on private life resulted in a new emphasis upon the purchase of objects for the home.[32] Little imagination is needed to understand the pleasure that these articles afforded. Ceramic drinking-bowls (Nos. 97–99) fit perfectly into the palm of the hand; faience bowls (Nos. 108) rest uneasily on their undersides and were obviously designed to be stored upside down so that their elaborately decorated undersides might be visible and their spherical contours invite the fingers' grasp. The smooth, undulating surfaces of bronze figurines offer enormous tactile appeal, as do the small glass vessels and ivory appliqués; these are objects intended to be handled with delight. For the first time in Greek art we encounter assemblages of terracotta figurines (Nos. 75–85) in modest households, and marble versions in more affluent homes (Nos. 15, 17, 18). Women were probably the collectors of the Tanagra figurines, which have also been found in female burials; one suspects that men were probably more attracted to the many bronze and terracotta statuettes of the nude Aphrodite, either in her Knidian pose (No. 19), or with her hands sensually uplifted to her hair in the Anadyomene type (Nos. 71, 72). The elimination from these images of any religious connotation marks a true departure from the art that predated the Hellenistic age; now demand and supply were fueled by popular taste, not religious impulse. The result were figures of dancing Silenoi (No. 5), crouching Pans (No. 53), or wistful Erotes (No. 89), and the manufacture of such disparate luxury products as repoussé mirrors (Nos. 45–48) and furniture adorned with elaborate appliqués (Nos. 50, 69, 110–111). The sensitivity of the artist to the vagaries of his patron's taste is reflected in the wide range of types—among Tanagra figurines, for example—and styles, particularly in earrings, that was now available.

The breadth and strength of the art market were partially responsible for the close relationship that developed between the major and the minor arts. Representations related to Tanagra figurines appear on such monuments as the Munich relief (fig. 8), and highly accurate, and by no means diminutive, replicas were made of such major works as the Knidian Aphrodite (No. 19), the Aphrodite Anadyomene (Nos. 71–72) and the Weary Herakles (No. 44).[33] Paired figurines (Nos. 78–79), multi-figured high-relief terracottas (No. 90), and individual figures that presuppose companion pieces (Nos. 58, 62, 115) were surely based on large-scale sculptural groups. So extensive was the multiple manufacture of some figures with political implications (No. 63) that it is not unlikely that monumental prototypes were also made in multiple, a hypothesis supported by the many images of Muses that were made not long after the statues that inspired them (Nos. 22, 25). The willingness of the koroplast and metalworker to interchange anatomical parts in order to facilitate the mass production of figurines probably had its counterpart in the major arts, and one can hypothesize without difficulty earlier Hellenistic antecedents to the neo-Attic sculptural workshops that produced such pastiches as the statue groups of Orestes and Pylades (fig. 9) and the Orestes and Electra (fig. 10).[34]

Because Rome played a prominent role in the eastern Mediterranean from the beginning of the second century B.C. it has been tempting to attribute to Roman influence certain stylistic changes in the late Hellenistic minor arts of this area.[35] Indeed, the evidence for Roman authority in the political and economic spheres is impressive; by the third quarter of the second century, Greece and Macedonia had been organized as Roman provinces, and Asia was added in 129 following the acquisition of the kingdom of Pergamon. In the eastern Mediterranean by the early first century B.C. the number of Roman administrators,

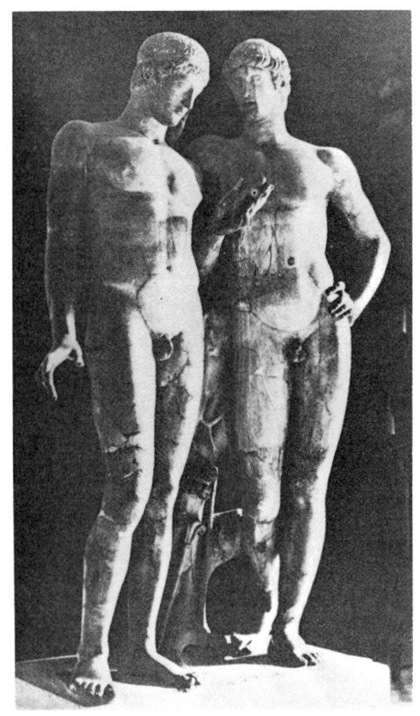

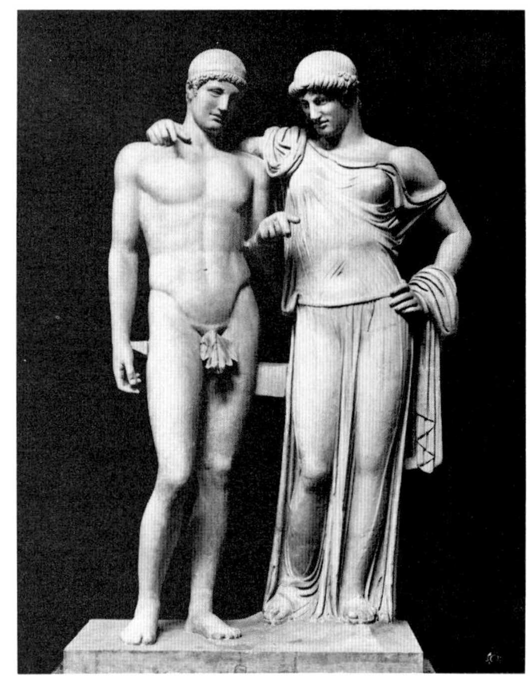

traders, and money-lenders was certainly substantial, and Appian tells us that the revolt of Mithradates VI in 88 precipitated the murder of eighty thousand Italian businessmen in Asia Minor alone.[36] In the artistic realm, however, the evidence for Roman impact on the minor arts is meager. Literary texts clearly state that most Italians, both in Italy and in the eastern Mediterranean, were not very familiar with Greek artistic traditions. According to Livy and Pliny, the Romans were first introduced to Greek sculpture with the triumphal procession that followed Marcellus's victory at Syracuse in 212, and fine silver first became known with Scipio's victory in 189.[37] The looting of Corinth in 146 brought painting and bronzes for the first time before the Roman people, who did not become familiar with pearls and gemstones until Pompey's triumph after his defeat of Mithradates VI in 87.[38] The Roman lack of a strong artistic background is epitomized by the rapacity with which Verres denuded sanctuaries in Asia Minor and Sicily and by the insensitivity with which Mummius supervised the plunder of Corinth. These actions were probably only extreme rather than anomalous examples of Roman behavior.[39] Given the weakness of the Romans' familiarity with traditions in the minor arts, and the particular heights that these arts had attained under the patronage of the royal courts, it is difficult to believe that the Romans could, or wished to, effect much change in objects they associated with a lifestyle to be emulated. This is especially true in the case of gemstones. Although the Roman appreciation of them is demonstrated by the importance Sulla attached to a carved signet, as well as by the collections of gems that Roman generals such as Scaurus, Caesar, and Marcellus eagerly accumulated, there is no reason to assume that this attraction was responsible for the increased use of gemstones in late Hellenistic jewelry.[40] Instead, the phenomenon is probably to be explained as a natural extension to jewelry of an enthusiasm for stones, which had been evident from early Hellenistic times in such royal objects as drinking vessels and horse trappings. The gem-studded bracelets and necklaces from Olbia (Nos. 131–33) were certainly locally made along the shores of the Black Sea well away from direct Roman influence, and they may not have been very dissimilar to the products of the nearby courts of Pontos and Bithynia.[41] Whereas Greek artists transported to Rome were undoubtedly affected by their exposure to art that had been made in the Roman capital over the previous two centuries, the eastern Mediterranean in late Hellenistic times surely saw few artists from Rome, and equally few Roman works of art were shipped out with the personal belongings of procurators or businessmen for whom there were less expensive ways of supplementing their belongings. Any source of Roman input within the artistic sphere could only rest with Italian patrons living in the East, and although those individuals may have been knowledgeable and opinionated about sculpture, they would hardly have had very sophisticated taste when it came to the refined designs and skilled execution of drinking vessels and jewelry. It is, in sum, very difficult to support a substantial Roman role in the evolution of the late Hellenistic minor arts outside the immediate vicinity of Rome.

No one today would question that the disdain which was accorded Hellenistic art only a few decades ago was largely a reflection of the background out of which scholars of the nineteenth and early-twentieth century emerged. Less recognized is the equally unfounded bias that still lingers against the minor arts, despite the tremendous vitality in design and craftsmanship which these arts demonstrated in Hellenistic times. Invigorated through contact with Near Eastern and Egyptian traditions, and fostered both by royal patronage and by an affluent, indulgent clientele, the minor arts attained a splendor that dazzled their Roman conquerors. A deeper familiarity with these works of art enables us to comprehend the stunning effect the Hellenistic monarchies made upon the Roman world, and, at the same time, to envision both the spiritual and the material character of private life in the Hellenistic age.

1. M. Vickers, ''The Influence of Exotic Materials on Attic White-Ground Pottery,'' *Ancient Greek and Related Pottery: Proceedings of the International Vase Symposium* (Amsterdam, 1984), 88. See also the same author in ''Artful Crafts: The Influence of Metalwork on Athenian Painted Pottery,'' *JHS* 105 (1985) 122–124; and in ''Value and Simplicity: Eighteenth-Century Taste and the Study of Greek Vases,'' *Past and Present* 116 (1987) 98–137.

2. Vickers, *JHS* 105 (1985) 116. Vickers, *Symposium,* 90.

3. Athenaeus, *Deipnosophistae* 5.196–202.

4. Ibid., 5.194–195.

5. For the ring given to Perdikkas, see Diodoros 18.2.4. For the agate of Pyrrhos, see Pliny, *NH* 37.3.5–6.

6. For the emerald given to Lucullus, see Plutarch, *Lucullus* 3.1. For the lampstand, see Cicero, *In Verrem Act.* II.4.28.64–65.

7. For Pyrgoteles, see Pliny, *NH* 37.4.8. For Nikias and Apollonios, see No. 136.

8. Plutarch, *Alexander* 20.8. For the finds at Persepolis, see Diodoros, 17.70.1–17.70.3.

9. For the cup belonging to Mithradates VI, see Pliny *NH* 37.6.14. For the passage by Theophrastos, see *Characters* 23.3.

10. Appian, *The Mithradatic Wars* 17.1 16.

11. Strabo, 15.1.69.

12. Diodoros, 18.27.4–5.

13. Pliny, *NH* 37.6.13–14.

14. For the ring cabinet, see Pliny, *NH* 37.5.1 1. For the drinking vessels and furniture, see Pliny, *NH* 37.6.14; Appian, *The Mithradatic Wars* 17, 115–116. For myrrhine ware, see Pliny, *NH* 37.17.18 and 37.8.21–22.

15. For the belongings of Antiochos, see Cicero, *In Verrem Act.* II. 4.27.62–3.

16. For the jewelry of Demetrios, see G. Macurdy, ''A Note on the Jewellery of Demetrius the Besieger,'' *AJA* 36 (1932) 27–28. For the mantle, see Plutarch, *Demetrius,* 41.4–5.

17. Plutarch, *Agis and Cleomenes,* 13.3.

18. M. Andronicos, *Vergina. The Royal Tombs and the Ancient City* (Athens, 1984), passim, especially 122–130; 132, figs. 88–90; 134, figs. 91–93; 207, fig. 169.

19. C. Rapin, ''La trésorie hellénistique d'Aï Khanoum,'' *RA* (1987) 60–63, 66.

20. Ibid., 67.

21. For the lampstand, see note 6. For the boat, see Athenaeus, *Deipnosophistae* 5.207c.

22. Pliny, *NH* 37.6.14.

23. Athenaeus, *Deipnosophistae* 5.193.

24. Pliny, *NH* 37.4.8.

25. Diodoros, 17.69.2–17.69.8.

26. E. Reeder Williams, ''A Bronze Statuette of Isis Aphrodite,'' *JARCE* 16 (1979) 100, n. 2. M. C. Edgar, *Greek Moulds,* Catalogue général des antiquités égyptiennes du musée du Caire 8 (Cairo, 1903).

27. For plaster molds, see Edgar (note 26). For bronze matrices, see E. D. Reeder, ''The Mother of the Gods and a Hellenistic Bronze Matrix,'' *AJA* 91 (1987) 423–440. For plaster impressions and casts, see Reinsberg, *Toreutik.* For castings, see A. Ippel, *Guss und Treiarbeit in Silber, BWPr* 97 (1937); A. Ippel, *Der Bronzefunde von Galjub.* Pelizaeus Museum zu Hildesheim wissenschaftliche Veröffentlichung 2 (Hildesheim, 1922).

28. For the workshop at Pella, see N. Winter, ''Newsletter from Greece,'' *AJA* 86 (1982) 548. For the export of molds, see S. Besques, ''Le commerce des figurines en terrecuite au IVe siècle av. J-C. entre les ateliers ioniens et l'attique,'' *Proceedings of the Xth International Congress of Classical Archaeology* (Ankara, 1973), II–III, 622–625.

29. For an imported bronze matrix, see Reeder, (note 27) 423–440. For plaster casts, see Reinsberg (note 27) 267; O. Kurz, *Nouvelles Recherches archéologiques à Begram,* Mémoires de la délégation archéologique française en Afghanistan, J. Hackin, ed. (Paris, 1954), II, 89–150.

30. Pliny, *NH* 35.45.155.

31. Ridgway 20.

32. Vickers, *JHS* 105 (1985) 114–115.

33. For the Munich relief, see Pollitt 197 and 196, fig. 210, dated mid- to late-second century.

34. Ibid., 175 and 177, figs. 185–186.

35. B. R. Brown, ''Questions about the Late Hellenistic Period,'' *Art Studies for an Editor: Twenty-five Essays in Memory of Milton S. Fox* (New York, 1975), 29–41. J. J. Pollitt, ''The Impact of Greek Art on Rome,'' *Transactions of the American Philological Association* 108 (1978) 155–174.

36. L. Jacoby, *Die Fragmente der griechischen Historiker* (Berlin and Leiden, 1923-), 434, F 22.9 by Memnon. R. Sherk, ed., *Rome and the Greek East to the Death of Augustus* (Cambridge, 1984), 66–68, no. 56.

37. For the procession of Marcellus, see Livy, 25.40.2 and 26.21.7–9; Plutarch, *Marcellus* 21.1–2. For Scipio's victory, see Pliny, *NH* 37.6.12.

38. For the destruction of Corinth and Pompey's triumph, see Pliny, *NH* 37.6.12.

39. For Verres, see Cicero, *In Verrem Act.* II. 1.20.53–54. For Mummius, see Velleius Paterculus, 1.13.4 and Ridgway 17.

40. For Sulla's signet, see Pliny, *NH* 37.4.9. For the collections of Scaurus, Caesar, and Marcellus, see Pliny, *NH* 37.5.11. For gemstones in late Hellenistic jewelry, see B. Pfeiler-Lippitz, ''Späthellenistische Goldschmiedearbeiten,'' *AntK* 15 (1972) 118.

41. For a late Hellenistic silver-gilt bowl from Olbia, see D. von Bothmer, *A Greek and Roman Treasury,* Bulletin of the Metropolitan Museum of Art 42 (New York, 1984), 51, no. 87; for a group of silver vessels from Prusias (Bithynia) dated 350–300, see 47, nos. 72–76.

The Hellenistic Environment

Roger S. Bagnall

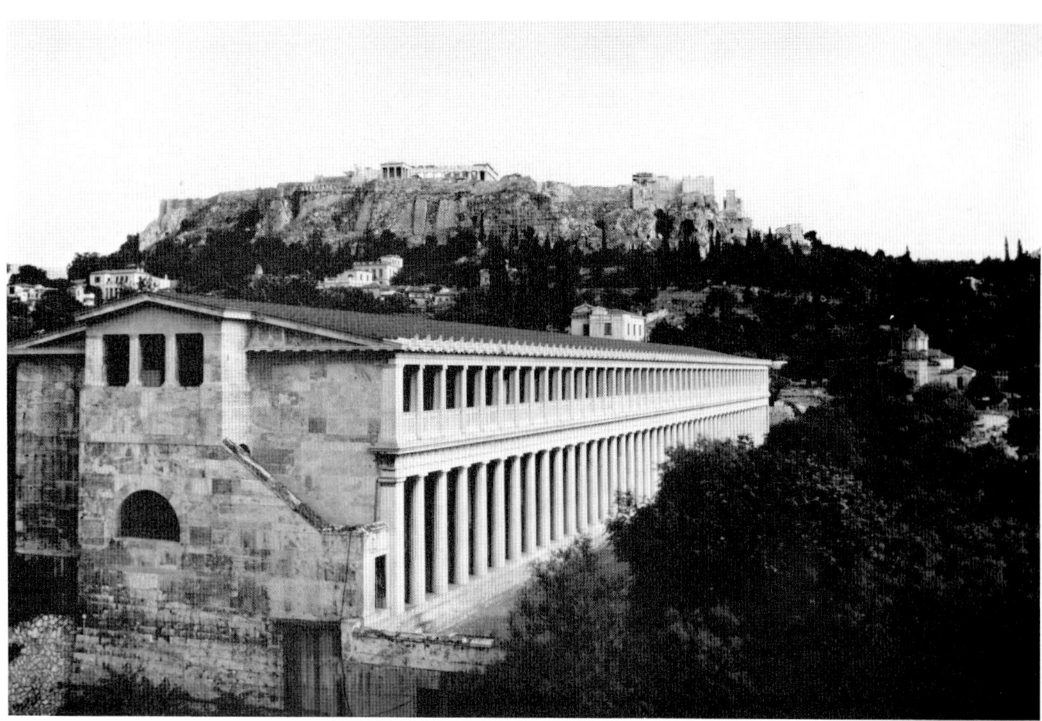

Fig. 1. The Stoa of Attalos, ca. 150 B.C., as reconstructed by the American School of Classical Studies, Agora Excavations, 1953–56. Photograph, John Dean.

THE VERY NOTION OF "HELLENISTIC," the term by which we describe the three centuries following the death of Alexander the Great in 323 B.C., is only a century and a half old. It was the German historian J. G. Droysen who introduced it to the language of scholarship, building on the notion of a "Hellenistic" language, Greek mixed with non-Greek elements, and the word first appears in English as a term for an age, according to the *Oxford English Dictionary,* in a book of J. P. Mahaffy published in 1874. The main point of the word when it came into the modern languages was one central to discussion of the period even today: the learning and use of the Greek language and Greek ways by the peoples of the eastern Mediterranean and the Near East.

Greeks were not a novelty in Egypt, on the Levantine coast, or even in Iran, by the time of Alexander. Their presence in the East had been continuous at least from the eighth century B.C., and there were certainly Greek-speaking natives of these regions more than a century before Alexander's arrival. But the conqueror's mighty work of destruction and slaughter had in a mere ten years toppled the Persian Empire, the last of the major regional states that had dominated the Near East for centuries, replacing it with rule by Macedonians and Greeks. And his death without an adult heir left little likelihood that any single world-state would survive him. His legacy, therefore, was a field of opportunities for smaller kingdoms inhabited mostly by non-Greek peoples but ruled by Greek-speakers—both Macedonians and Greeks, whose bitter differences at home soon became invisible when they were a tiny minority together abroad.

These basic facts are the framework for the civilization of these centuries. Substantial numbers of Greeks moved east to take advantage of opportunities for exploiting these new possessions, and where they went new Greek cities came into existence, usually founded by the kings. In institutions and physical shape, these cities were much like their predecessors in the Greek world of the Aegean, but they co-existed with a numerically dominant population of Egyptians, or Syrians, or Persians, or Bactrians. And their political horizon was dominated by the powerful figure of the king. In this environment, Greek culture lived in daily juxtaposition to indigenous people and civilization. Although the mixture of the two, of which Droysen and many after him wrote, was greatly exaggerated, the two worlds could not live side-by-side for centuries without both changing. The life of Greek cities of the Hellenistic period is in many ways very similar to that of cities of the Classical period, and the continuities of native life in the East—not only from earlier times to the Hellenistic period, but even down to the present—are striking. But the changes are more interesting.

Even with the Hellenistic period, it would be a mistake to suppose uniform conditions and development. There are enormous differences between an older Greek city of Ionia—Miletos, say—and a new settlement in Bactria. And the changes from the early third century to the later first century are at least as great. Egypt of the first two Ptolemies may almost suggest a state of apartheid between Greeks and Egyptians, but when the Romans came they largely lumped the two together as a single status, so difficult was it to untangle things. Civic democracy was widespread in the early Hellenistic period, but growing disparities of wealth and later the influence of Rome led to an increasingly oligarchic structure of city government through most of the Greek world.

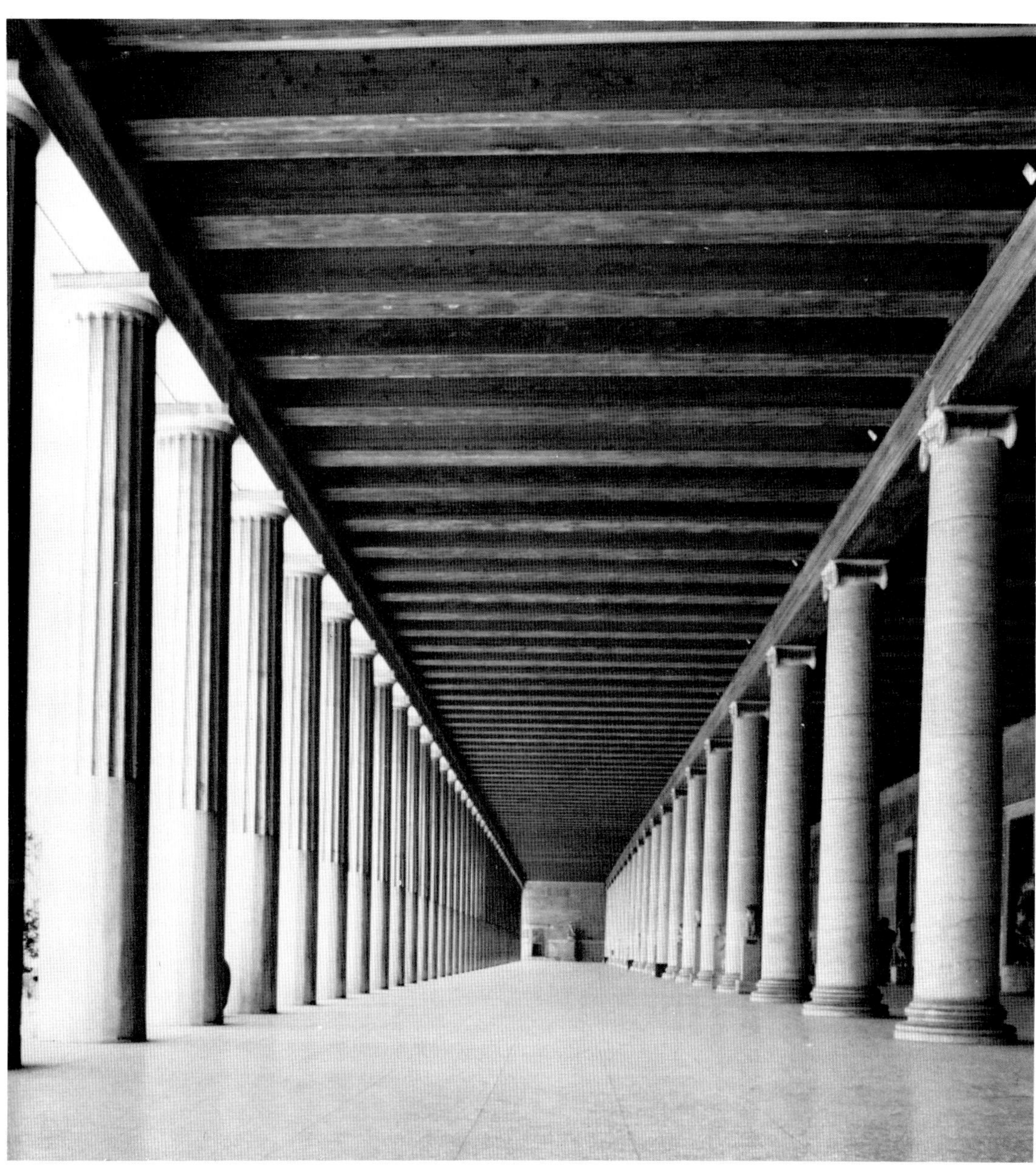

Fig. 2. The Stoa of Attalos, interior view. Photograph, John Dean.

The City Environment

Greek cities, old and new, big and small, were found over a tremendous geographical span—from Sicily to Afghanistan, from the Crimea to southern Egypt. In the older Greek world of the Aegean, distances from one city to its nearest neighbor might be very small, a day's walk or less. Further east, however, the density of cities was usually less. The Ptolemies, who were unenthusiastic about founding cities in Egypt, added only one (Ptolemais) to the old settlement of Naukratis and Alexander's famous foundation of Alexandria. Ptolemais, in Upper Egypt, was thus several hundred miles from any other Hellenic polity. Many of the Greek cities of the ''upper satrapies,'' the eastern parts of Alexander's empire such as Media and Bactria, were similarly distant from other cities and, given the sparsity of Greek population, very isolated. Ancient communications were slow, dependent on sailing ships, animals, and human feet. But Hellenism was powerfully dynamic: the excavations of Aï Khanoum in Afghanistan have shown that cities could flourish and maintain a staunchly Hellenic character even at such distances from the Greek homeland.

Most cities were small by modern standards. Even in a relatively large one, a resident could reach the center on foot from any point in no more than thirty minutes, and in the majority of towns, thirty minutes might suffice to walk around the outside of the walls. A total adult citizen population of ten to twenty thousand was perhaps typical, though we have reliable figures only very rarely. The land around a city and belonging to it was similarly manageable; in most cases a few hours' walk would bring one to the borders, and rare was the case of a radius greater than a day's walk. Though the physical environment varied with location, cities tended to pick hills of moderate height for building, thus providing for defense and avoiding the use of scarce arable land.

Inside the ubiquitous walls stood temples to the civic gods, the standard buildings of civic life, and domestic and commercial structures. Hellenistic cities do not quite convey the sameness of architectural character that we find in Roman towns, but they are well along in that development. Everywhere a visitor would feel at home, with theater, agora, porticoes, gymnasium, and government buildings like council-chambers. Life centered on these public areas, with an intensity hard for the inhabitant of a large, dispersed, and private modern city to imagine. Public architecture and public art were constantly visible to all men, a part of their daily world.

These public buildings were the setting for the corporate life of a city. Throughout the fourth century, as the city gained ground in Greece as a form of political organization, democracy became more prevalent as well: democracy of a limited and defined body of male citizens, to be sure, excluding from politics not only women and slaves but foreigners and those who did not meet whatever property qualifications were imposed in a given city. Many, perhaps most, cities suffered from periodic civil strife between the wealthier strata, who wanted a narrower franchise, and the poorer, who wanted it widened. The Hellenistic period saw the gap between rich and poor, which was mostly modest in classical times, become gradually greater, as the ever more dominant role of rich benefactors in the cities shows.

Yet we know little about the absolute level of prosperity of most citizens. The rise of mass-produced works of art, particularly terracottas, to prominence in the surviving art of the Hellenistic period suggests a wide diffusion of moderate means among the population. Equally, the large numbers of less modest surviving works of art point to the existence of a very wealthy aristocracy; thanks to the papyri from Egypt, we know something of the composition of this class in Alexandria, where royal officials and courtiers took the role that the local landed gentry would in smaller cities. Alexander's capture of the Persian treasuries was followed by the putting into circulation of gold and silver hoarded for centuries by the kings, as first Alexander himself and then still more his successors paid troops and made gifts for construction of temples and other public buildings. After long years of the deflationary effects of hoarding, this comparatively free spending produced economic expansion in the earlier part of the Hellenistic period. That this monetary growth was not then followed by any more sustained economic development is a natural result of other permanent factors in the ancient economy, notably the lack of basic technological progress (except in warfare) and the systematic use of slave labor rather than free hired labor.

The public spaces of Hellenistic cities came increasingly to be filled not only with buildings and art works but also with inscriptions on stone. A world lacking printing presses and electronic communication media had few choices for the popular dissemination of information and ideas. Public speech was by far the dominant means; in a small community it is, after all, perfectly possible to address all of one's fellow-citizens together as they sit in the theater. But for any lasting public record, stone inscriptions were the medium of choice; though hardly cheap to have cut, they endured. Many were handsome, and often they were parts of sculptural monuments, inscribed bases of statues, for example. This developing habit of inscription presupposes widespread, though not necessarily universal, literacy on the part of the citizens.

Communal life had many other aspects as well. The most important by far was religion, always central to the character of the Greek city. The calendar of a Greek city, though lacking the repetitive rhythm of our weeks, was sprinkled with festivals in honor of the various gods and heroes of the city. To the traditional ones were added cults of members of the royal house ruling the area at the moment. This public face of religion involved processions and public sacrifices, followed by eating the roasted meat of the victims. The community solidarity of the citizens was intimately bound up with these rituals, which furnished a staple social life for the population, including the women, who found themselves outside much of the other public activity of their city.

There was much entertainment linked to the religious festivals, too. Drama began at Athens as part of festivals of Dionysos, and he remained the patron of tragedy and comedy when their performance spread through the Greek world. The ''artisans of Dionysos,'' organized into regional synods, traveled from city to city providing professional performances. Greek drama embraced music and dance along with the spoken word and acting. Religious festivals commonly involved other musical performances as well. A few of the principal celebrations added substantial competitions in athletics—gymnastics, boxing, wrestling, and other contests—and often music (trumpeters, heralds, and the like). The most ambitious of these were modeled on the Olympic or Pythian games held every four years at Olympia and Delphi, but there were countless smaller and less ambitious sets of games. Cities competed vigorously for the prestige and international recognition of their festivals, and top athletes increasingly made a tour of contests. Athletics in Greek cities were as central to high culture as they were welcome to popular taste.

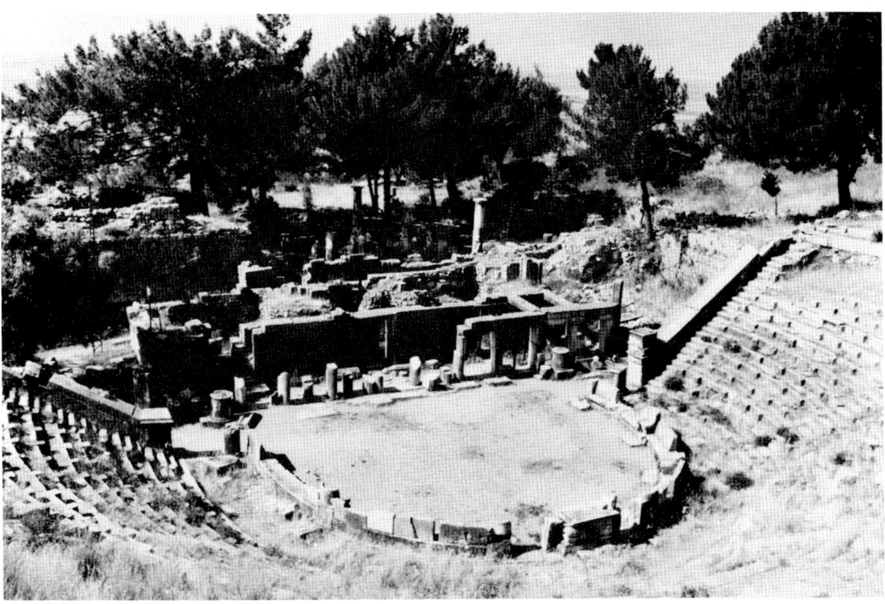

Private Life in the City

Behind all the flourishing public life visible in inscriptions, architecture, and literature, there lay the private life of the citizens. Our knowledge of this realm is less systematic than of the public, but it has often been observed that private activities seem more important in the Hellenistic period than in classical Greece. Certainly important changes are visible in Greek settlements in the East. The extremely tight-knit communities of the classical cities could not be replicated in new foundations with populations drawn from many quarters. The papyri suggest, for example, that women's lives in Ptolemaic Egypt became much less segregated; women made their own marriage choices much more than they once had, influenced perhaps by the freedom women had in Egyptian society as well as by their distance from their ancestral communities.

Households contained children, too. Middle-class families were likely to have slave pedagogues to take care of them in their earlier years. Hellenistic cities increasingly had provision for public support of elementary education for citizen boys, but higher education was always a private concern and expense; only the well-off were likely to go beyond grammar school. Whether the increased prominence of children in Hellenistic art indicates some change in their status in the family, or merely a shift in representational tastes, is hard to say; but there is much feeling in such depictions. The normal high mortality rate of infants and children did not anesthetize parents to emotional involvement in their offspring. It may even be that the partial deracination of emigrant society led people to find more of their emotional grounding in their families, less in the outer community. The pathos of death remains universal, as visible and poignant in funerary art of the Hellenistic period as it had been earlier.

Beyond the most basic needs, much varied with economic status. All households but the poorest would normally include slaves, whose relationship to their masters ran the full range from close affection to sullen hatred. Feeding the family might not be easy, even for the wealthy. Crop failures could and did leave whole cities vulnerable to famine; relief would come only from timely imports. Alexandria, with Egypt's resources behind it, must have faced this problem only rarely, but for island cities with poor land the shortages were perennial.

Even the poor households seem to have had more artwork than was found in the classical period; at least they had the mass-produced figurines so characteristic of the times. But it was in the richer homes that the change is more visible, in the works whose materials and workmanship were clearly very expensive and yet which cannot have been destined for a public place. Just as other aspects of life were more private than before, so was the experience of art. Accordingly, smaller objects become more common than they had been, things that would fit in a domestic environment rather than dominating a public place. Some of this, to be sure, was not just for display. In an economy that lacked most of the means by which the modern world holds, uses, and recycles wealth, such as stocks, bonds, and certificates of deposit, the rich—and even the middle class—would keep much of their wealth in gold and silver objects which could always serve as bullion. No matter how much the thought of melting down beautiful platters and bowls, not to speak of jewelry and figurines, may horrify a modern sensibility brought up to see art as almost sacred, these objects were the inert repositories of their owners' assets. They were relatively portable, always marketable, and comparatively easy to hide. Their bullion value, of course, is responsible for the small portion of them that have survived to the present.

Religion, too, had its place in the private sphere. Public festivals were often accompanied by smaller sacrifices on private home altars, sometimes on the roof. Many cults not part of traditional civic religion attracted worshipers. Greeks in a new land tended to pay attention to local divinities, on the prudent

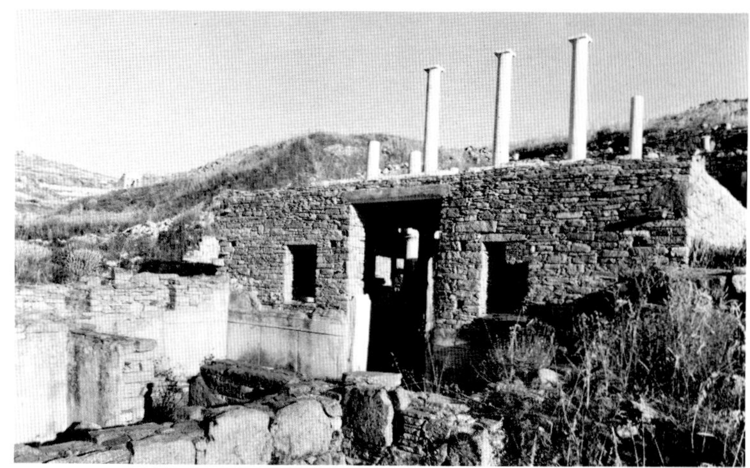

Fig. 4. The House of Hermes, Delos, second century B.C. Photograph, John Dean.

principle that any god the local residents had discovered to be powerful probably was and deserved propitiation. A number of Syrian and Egyptian gods gained a popularity, spread in the main by private initiative, far beyond their original homes; the process ultimately took them to virtually every corner of the Roman Empire. It is a modern superstition to believe that people of the Hellenistic period found religion less emotionally important than those of earlier or later times; the description of women at the festival of Adonis in Alexandria provided by Theokritos in his *Idyll* 15 shows how involved even spectators might be.

Getting close to private feelings, however, is usually difficult. Letters are businesslike rather than emotional, and court literature mostly obeyed canons of its own that cannot be assumed to reflect popular views. What are we to make, for instance, of the great increase in the popularity of erotic art, particularly female nudes? These ornamental statues were surely not meant for the agora; surely many, if not most, decorated homes. An increased importance for home and family life could well have led to a greater emphasis on eroticism in marriage, in contrast to attitudes prevalent in Classical Athens, where courtesans and boys occupy the center of attention when love is the subject. But it is hard to be confident of such interpretations; changes of taste could have other explanations.

There were other currents in taste. Not only eroticism but everyday experience in general becomes popular as a source of motifs; this is perhaps yet another reflection of the privatization of experience of which we find traces elsewhere. A wide variety of styles, often combined, turns up to reflect interests both broad in culture and deep in historical perspective. Greeks did not hesitate to borrow Egyptian artistic motifs in their houses and tombs, nor to imitate the art of several hundred years previously. This eclectic approach seems equally at home in literature, where the works of authors from Homer down to contemporaries circulated and the scholars of the Alexandrian Museum edited their predecessors at the same time as Egyptian and Jewish traditions were being translated into Greek.

The Larger World

The horizon of both individual and city was bounded, far more than in earlier periods, by permanent external forces. The most obvious and ubiquitous of these was the king. Whether in Greece or in Bactria, it was a rare city that spent many years free of control by one of the Hellenistic monarchies. There was a wide range of forms and degrees of royal control. At one extreme stood royal capitals like Alexandria, Antioch, or Pergamon, where the king was usually resident and utterly dominant. Political institutions coexisted to some degree with the royal court, but there could be no mistaking where the power lay. For most cities, however, the king was more distant. From that distance, and from the kings' need for the cities—as a source of manpower and taxes—came some balance in the equation. No city could stand up to the king, but neither could the king be everywhere at once if his burdensomeness caused pandemic revolt. Relations were generally conducted with considerable politeness on both sides, often by ambassadors behaving as if the two parties were on an equal footing.

The kings were eager to see their standing with their subjects rest on something more than coercion. Kings protected their domains in war, often from barbarians such as the Gauls who for many years threatened Asia Minor. Many public buildings in the cities were gifts of kings. A gymnasium here, a stoa there, and the king could acquire the reputation of generosity. In prominent cities like Athens, a significant part of its public face might be owed to such royal gifts. A competent and generous king could at least hope that his cities would consider his rule preferable to that of others, even if they would really have preferred no master at all.

Royal power was from the point of view of the city a remarkable phenomenon, difficult to comprehend within the framework of these small communities and even harder to domesticate. Where the cities' need to find a way of understanding the kings in their own terms met the kings' need to see the relationship develop beyond the purely businesslike we find the growth of royal cults. When Rhodes established a cult of Ptolemy I as Soter (Savior) after his extensive help to them in resisting a siege by Demetrios Poliorketes, it was choosing a form of relationship that recognized the more than human beneficent power displayed by Ptolemy. That does not mean that the Rhodians did not know the difference between the divinity of Zeus and the status they assigned to Ptolemy, but neither should we cynically suppose it was just so much empty show.

Royal propaganda tried as well to use other religious themes. Kings sought, for example, to adopt for themselves the image of Herakles, who was a paradigm of the human who through great deeds acquires immortality. In a society with the limited means of communication that antiquity possessed, putting across these connections was no simple matter. One key means of spreading widely the royal image and the links to it that the king wanted was coinage. What the average citizen thought of all this, we have little evidence; inscriptions tell us mostly what cities found it politic to say publicly.

Not all of the kings were as Hellenic as the major monarchies. A Greek city might be under the dominion of a king of Iranian background. This was, of course, no new experience for Greeks, for many of them in Asia had lived under Persian rule for significant portions of the preceding three centuries. The kings themselves, in places like Pontos and Bithynia, could hardly devote their energies solely to making their Greek subjects feel kinship with the rulers, since most of the kingdom was peopled with other than Greeks. The northern part of Asia Minor, heavily Iranized over centuries of Persian rule and virtually bypassed by Alexander, had Greek cities, mainly on the coast, but an Anatolian and Iranian population in the interior. The coins of the kings of these regions often display an only partially Hellenic character.

The centrality of military prowess in the royal image reflects Hellenistic reality. Reading Diodoros's account of the wars of succession after Alexander's death might well give one the impression that war was constant everywhere. The reality was far more bearable, but war was nonetheless always a threat in many places and sometimes a threat virtually everywhere. The historical record informs us mainly about the wars of kings against kings, but cities were often the proximate targets in these conflicts. Cities still campaigned against each other at times, mostly over disputed territory. And the external enemies, barbarians, menaced many areas from time to time. Upper Egypt rose against the Ptolemies several times and had to be subdued with considerable bloodshed.

Even in peace, however, most Greek cities of the East had to coexist with their non-Greek neighbors, that dominant fact of life that gives definition to Hellenism. Part of their relationship was exploitation: natives worked the fields around many cities in Asia Minor and Syria owned by Greek residents of the cities; and military "settlers" in Egypt, given the use of tracts of royal land for their support, mostly preferred to lease them to Egyptian peasants rather than working them personally. Slaves in Greek urban

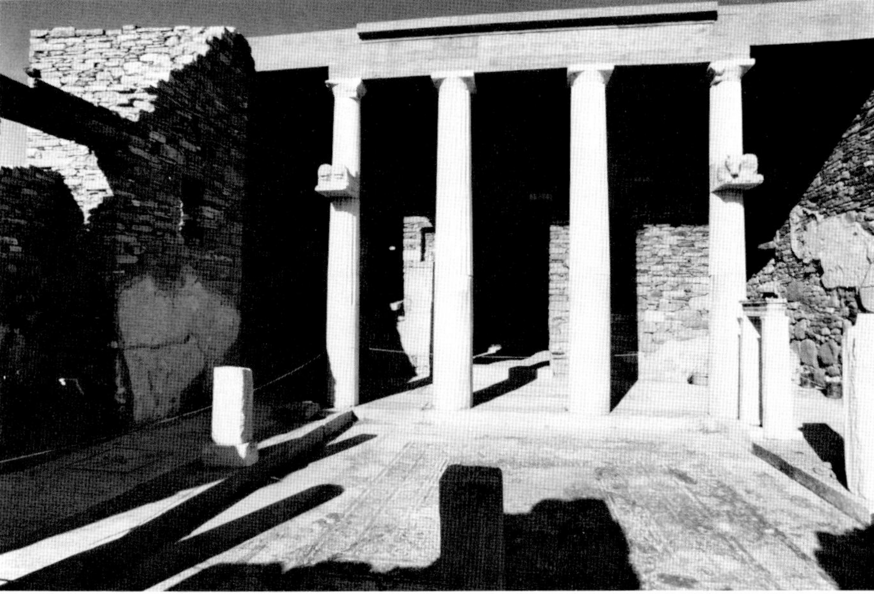

Fig. 5. The House of the Masks, Delos, second century B.C. Photograph, John Dean.

households were mostly, and preferably, barbarians of one sort or another. Greek underwriters made money by guaranteeing the amounts to be collected in taxes from the Egyptian peasantry.

On the other hand, it was Greek language and culture that counted, not "racial" identity. Natives discovered quickly that by learning Greek they could move up economically and eventually even socially. There was always a market for competent bilingual literate bureaucrats, for the kings needed administrators who could communicate both with the subjects and with the ruling cadres. And many existing privileged groups in native societies endured, such as the Egyptian priesthoods, the members of which collaborated with the king and helped give him legitimacy, in return for grants and privileges. Natives who became Hellenized did not necessarily, or even normally, lose their own cultural backgrounds; it is certainly in part to such bicultural people that we owe works of art and literature in which Greek and native elements are joined.

Movement in the other direction existed too, though no doubt to a lesser extent. Greeks mostly did not learn alien languages. Some did, however, marry native women. We can rarely see into the interior of such unions, but their offspring certainly could often operate in both spheres, blurring the lines to a substantial degree. This assimilation in both directions was certainly resisted by those whose positions it undermined. The most famous example of such resistance, of course, is the determined Jewish struggle to avoid Hellenization at the hands of Antiochos IV. Even there, however, the fight was as much internal—between those favoring Hellenization and those opposing it—as it was external. The more we learn about any particular Hellenistic society, the more complex the separateness and linkages of cultures appear. The coexistence of this complex diversity with broad common patterns of unity mark the Hellenistic world as one in which the *oikoumene,* the inhabited world, was united into one civilization without the suppression of any of its rich particularity.

Bibliography

Austin, M. M., *The Hellenistic World from Alexander to the Roman Conquest* (Cambridge, 1981).

Bagnall, R. S., and P. S. Derow, *Greek Historical Documents: The Hellenistic Period* (Chicago, 1981).

Bowman, A. K., *Egypt after the Pharaohs* (Berkeley and Los Angeles, 1986).

Fraser, P. M., *Ptolemaic Alexandria* (Oxford, 1972).

Préaux, C., *Le monde hellénistique. La Grèce et l'Orient de la mort d'Alexandre à la conquête romaine de la Grèce (323–146 av. J.-C.),* 2 vols. (Paris, 1978).

Rostovtzeff, M. I., *The Social and Economic History of the Hellenistic World,* 2nd ed., 3 vols. (Oxford, 1953).

Samuel, A. E., *From Athens to Alexandria: Hellenism and Social Goals in Ptolemaic Egypt,* Studia Hellenistica 26 (Louvain, 1983).

Tarn, W. W., *The Greeks in Bactria and India,* 2nd ed., (Cambridge, 1951).

Tarn, W. W., and G. T. Griffith, *Hellenistic Civilisation,* 3rd ed., (London, 1952).

Walbank, F. W., A. E. Astin, M. W. Frederiksen, and R. M. Ogilvie, eds., *The Cambridge Ancient History,* VII. Pt. 1, *The Hellenistic World,* 2nd ed. (Cambridge, 1984).

Walbank, F. W., *The Hellenistic World* (London, 1981).

Will, E., *Histoire politique du monde hellénistique,* 2nd ed. (Nancy, 1979–1982).

Wycherley, R. E., *How the Greeks Built Cities,* 2nd ed. (New York, 1962).

The Hellenistic
House

Beryl Barr-Sharrar

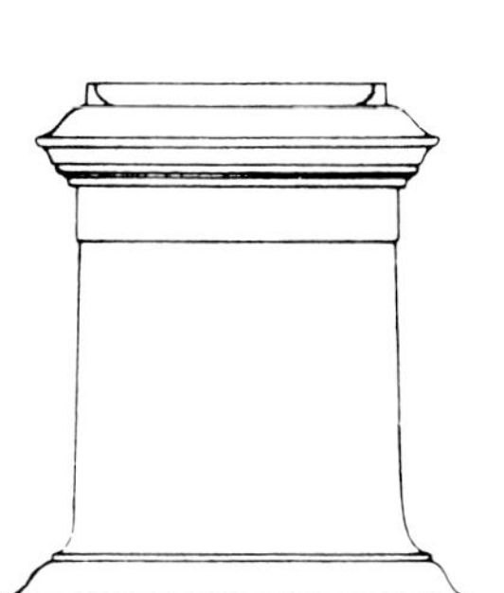

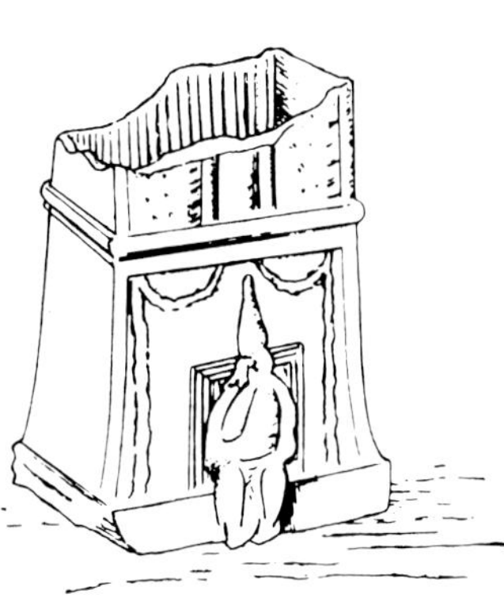

Fig. 1. Hellenistic stone altars for incense from Priene, from T. Wiegand and H. Schrader, *Priene* (Berlin, 1904), 377, figs. 477, 479.

LIKE THE CONSIDERATION OF so many manifestations of Hellenistic life, the search for the Hellenistic house[1] begins early in the late Classical period. The famous and elegant pebble mosaics and stucco-covered peristyle columns of late fourth-century Pella were not the earliest manifestations of innovation in domestic luxury in Greece, although it is possible that such manifestations may be found at Pella one day near palatial structures of earlier kings of Macedon. In the middle of the fourth century when Demosthenes admonished his fellow Athenian statesmen for being undemocratic enough to build private houses more stately than public monuments,[2] he may very well have been thinking of peristyle houses. For we know now that such houses existed as early as the first third of the fourth century B.C. in Eretria, and in the second quarter of that century in Olynthos, and very likely about the same time in Sikyon and other mainland cities, indeed perhaps including—although we have no proof of this yet—Athens and Corinth.

The striking contrast in Classical Greece between simple urban houses—huddled together in compact blocks with narrow, irregular streets—and the splendid public monuments of the city is, of course, entirely characteristic of that time. Tradition and civic pride dictated this discrepancy, subordinating private housing to the agora, the theater, gymnasia, temples, and other public buildings, just as domestic affairs were subordinated to the larger issues of political, social, and religious life.

Cities like Peiraeus and Olynthos were built, unlike Athens, according to the so-called Hippodamian scheme by which areas not occupied by civic monuments were divided into uniform rectangular blocks with parallel streets;[3] here the unimpressive aspect of the domestic area of the city was simply made uniform. Houses of approximately sixty meters square were built in rows out of mud brick on a foundation of stone rubble, sharing side walls, with roofs of tile, slate, stone slabs, or simply twigs and clay, with plain exterior walls with small, high windows onto streets which were untidy, but not filthy.[4]

Houses of more than one or two rooms were organized inward around a small open courtyard, a practice that continued for centuries. In general, Classical houses faced south, a prescription for sensible domestic architecture endorsed by both Xenophon and Aristotle,[5] which allowed the courtyard and the upper story built on the northern part of most houses to have maximum light in winter and relief from the sun in summer when the southern sun is high.

The only source of daylight into each room, however, was its double wooden door onto the courtyard. The top half of each panel, or leaf, of such a door could be opened separately inward, an architectural detail, like many others, provided by Attic vase-painting. Even so, life inside the house must have been dimly lighted at best, and it is likely that much of the housework—the daily grinding of the grain and perhaps even the weaving, a constant employment of the women of the household—took place outside in the small courtyard whenever possible. There were no gardens in the courtyards; their earth was covered with stones and some had marble altars (fig. 1), in Olynthos to Zeus Herkeios (of the courtyard).[6] Access to the partial upper story of the house was from the courtyard on uncovered wooden stairs.[7]

By 432 B.C.[8] the typical house in Olynthos had a canonical form with a long hall on the north, the *pastas,* partially open to the courtyard by means of a colonnade onto which opened the doors of the northern ground floor rooms. One of the rooms in this area was usually the *oikos,* considered the general living room for the entire family. In the middle of the hard clay floor was often an open hearth, as in the prehistoric megaron, around which the family may have eaten.[9] Cooking, and even the daily baking of the bread,[10] however, could also be done over portable braziers, mostly made of terracotta,[11] sometimes of bronze (fig. 2).[12]

The most important room in the Classical house, in that its canonical size (which varied from place to place) formed the basis for the proportions of all other parts of the house, was the *andron,* or banquet and symposium room.[13] This room, together with its anteroom, was traditionally reserved for the male owner of the house and his male guests, who were afforded complete privacy because the anteroom was entered from the courtyard (in Olynthos, from the pastas, and in Priene, from the prostas). A slightly raised area of the floor around the walls usually indicated the placement of the dining couches, or *klinai,* in Olynthos almost always seven in number as was common in the Classical period.[14] The presence of the andron in the houses of ordinary Greek citizens at this time may have been thought to have been of value politically in the democratization process,[15] rather than considered in terms of private comfort, luxury, or

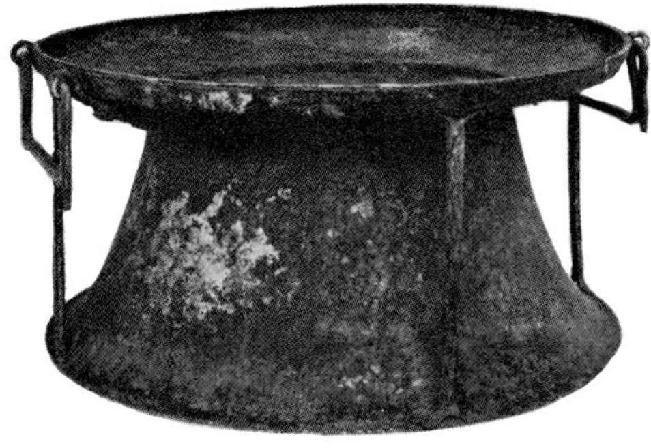

Fig. 2. Bronze brazier from Olynthos, ca. 400–350 B.C., from *AJA*
39 (1935) 235, fig. 3b.

pleasure (despite the vase-painting evidence), which would have been contradictory to conservative ideals. Nevertheless, it was in this area of the house where the first display of luxurious decoration as a manifestation of the prosperity of private individuals was to be seen.

Sometime after 379 B.C. there was an extension to the east of the so-called "new" city of Olynthos,[16] which had itself been built in 432 to the north of the old settlement, expanding Olynthos to five times its original size.[17] This was destroyed, with the entire city, by Philip II of Macedon in 348 B.C. In houses in this region of Olynthos, thus dated between 379 and 348 B.C., androns and their anterooms were ornamented with lively pebble mosaics with light gray and ochre patterns, often figural, on dark browns and grays.[18] Walls were painted with colored stucco of as many as four colors (red, yellow, black, and white) in patterns that duplicated the construction of the wall: socle (or plinth), orthostats, string course, and ceiling or upper main zone, with incised lines outlining the "masonry" panels and dividing the zones.[19]

Evidence also comes from the ancient city of Eretria, where a peristyle house discovered in 1972 revealed in an *andronitis* (andron and anteroom) mosaic floors of great elegance carefully executed with small black, white, and red pebbles, that could be dated by both earth fill and a destruction level to the first third of the fourth century B.C. (fig. 3).[20] An adjacent square room with a plain pebble mosaic floor, like the andronitis off the north portico of the courtyard, also had a reserved area around the walls for klinai. This reserved area as well as the room's location and shape—all three aspects those of the later, Delian major oikos—indicated that it had been used as a second banquet and symposium room. The surviving portions of the walls in this room were covered with red, yellow, and gray-white stucco.[21]

There are, quite naturally, many more surviving pebble mosaic andron and anteroom floors which appear to be from private houses of this period than there are wall fragments sufficiently preserved to reconstruct the contemporary stucco murals.[22] Pebble mosaic andron and antechamber mosaics in Sikyon,[23] Corinth,[24] and Peiraeus,[25] may be more or less contemporary to those in Olynthos and Eretria; others in Sikyon[26] and Corinth,[27] and one in Megara,[28] are probably somewhat earlier.[29] This suggests that by around 360 B.C., when, in fact, there is a strange coincidence in Greece of new luxurious decoration in public architecture[30] and a demonstrated taste for it in the minor arts,[31] such ornamentation of private symposium rooms was well established and fairly widespread.

Alterations or improvements made at this time in the architectural construction of existing houses may well have been borrowed from public buildings, just as floor and wall decorations may have been also. A window inserted into the wall of the andron in a Classical house in Peiraeus dates to the early fourth century B.C. according to the excavator. A ledge jutting out from the wall in high relief supported a Doric architrave with a pillar at each end and an Ionic half-column in the middle.[32] Window openings on each side of the half-column were forty centimeters; the height of the window is not known, nor is the height of the ceiling, which in androns may well have been considerably higher than in other rooms on the ground floor. To have natural light in the banquet room from a source other than the door, which could now be shut, must have been a welcome luxury.

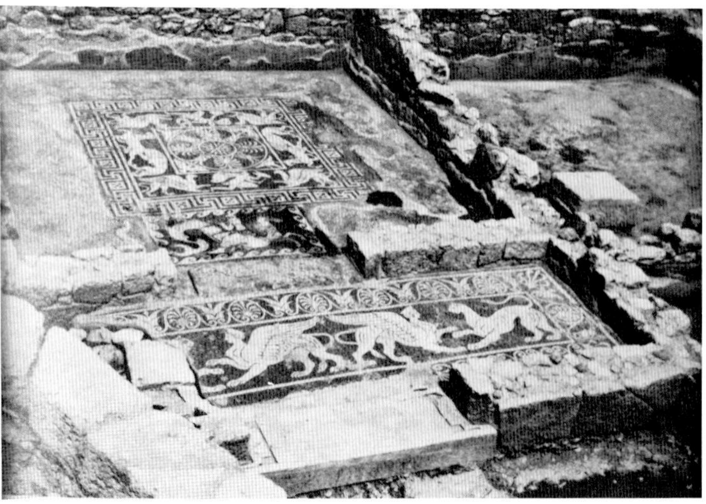

Fig. 3. Vestibule and andron from a
house in Eretria, 400–370 B.C.,
from *AntK* 22 (1979) pl. 1, 3.

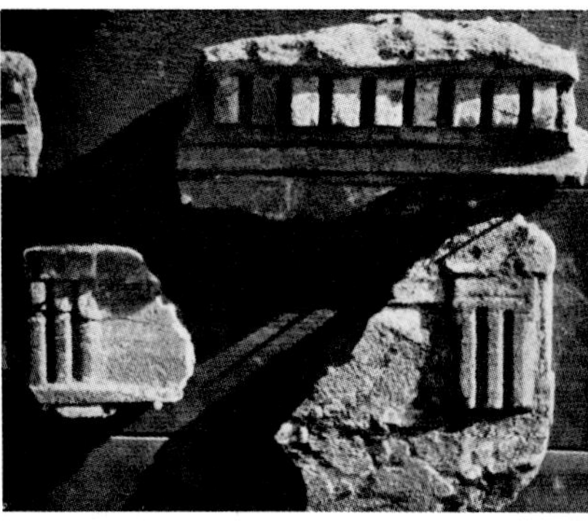

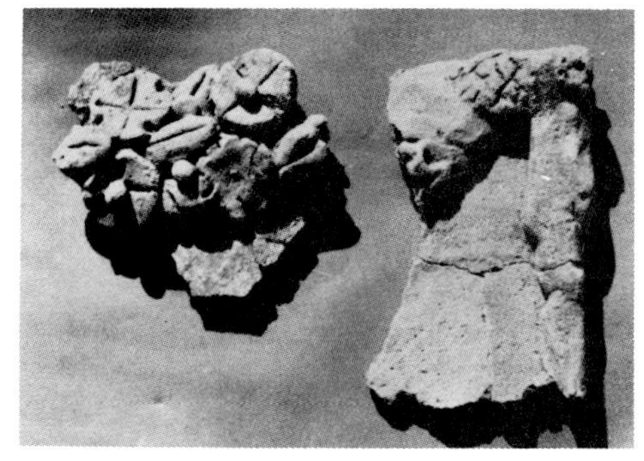

Fig. 4. Stucco reliefs from a Hellenistic house in Priene, from M. Schede, *Die Ruinen von Priene,* 2nd ed. (Berlin, 1964), 97, fig. 112.

Fig. 5. Stucco garland from a Hellenistic house in Amphipolis, from *Prakt.* 1983-A, pl 42a.

Perhaps the most dramatic architectural innovation in private housing, and one that perhaps for the first time decisively and visibly separated the prosperous homeowners from the less well-to-do because of its implication of space, was the peristyle. In a second phase of building in a house in Olynthos, sometime in the first half of the fourth century, a peristyle was created by moving the andron and its anteroom from their traditional Classical location near the house entrance in the south, to the northwest corner of the courtyard, and annexing half of the house to the east next door. The two wooden pillars (not columns in Olynthos) which opened the pastas to the court became the two northwest supports of the ten-pillared peristyle.[33] (Capitals were of wood or, sometimes, fieldstone.) In some houses built after 379 B.C. (and before 348), peristyles were part of the original construction.[34] The "House of the Mosaics" in Eretria discussed above was built before 360 B.C. with a four-sided peristyle and, although there is little evidence from this period, it is conceivable that peristyle houses were as ubiquitous by the middle of the fourth century as pebble mosaic andron floors. In any case, the fundamental characteristics of the Hellenistic house were certainly well established by this time, if not somewhat earlier.

In the hillside city of Priene on the coast of Asia Minor, the single-family row houses of the Classical period built, at least partially, of the abundant stone on terraces cut out of the sloping ground were almost all entirely or partially rebuilt, repaired, or altered in some way sometime after 188 B.C. when Priene and Samos became independent allies of Rome.[35] Although the character of the city changed to one of greater variety, and large houses developed in the center of the city with smaller, poorer ones remaining on the outskirts, the fundamental organization of the houses did not change radically. Most remained oriented towards the south, around a court paved with stone, a two-story living area on the north entered through a portico, called the *prostas,* with a small andron at one end of it[36] and an oikos and other rooms off it on the ground floor. The oikos in some houses may have been two stories high; the front of the existing second story perhaps had an open loggia off of which opened bedrooms (*thalami*) and dressing rooms, presumably the private area for the women of the house, the *gynaikonitis.* Across the court, and sometimes on one or both sides, were arranged other rooms, including rooms for storage and perhaps for slaves. Bathrooms, identified by their terracotta tubs, were infrequent.

The entrance to the house was usually on the south, through a small porch (*prothyra*) as sometimes in Olynthos, recessed into the wall of the house. Colonnades were erected on one, two, or three sides of the courtyard. One house had an extensive four-sided peristyle; another one next door had a Doric colonnade during the second century and, again rebuilt in the first half of the first century B.C. after a fire, was given a rectangular peristyle and expanded to more than double its earlier size.[37]

Although there were no figural mosaic floors in Priene (floors were hard-packed yellow clay), there were highly elaborate and colorful stucco walls with simulated masonry. Above the orthostat zone, these walls now had frieze zones with narrow panels painted to look like marble revetment interspersed with multiple stucco relief courses. Some stucco courses included continuous relief motifs: kymatia, meander, egg-and-dart; others were organized in panels, and still others had triglyphs and metopes (fig. 4).[38] Crowning the frieze zone was often a white stucco trompe l'oeil colonnade.[39] Walls with such architectural components in relief, known in Macedonian public buildings[40] and in Macedonian tombs[41] from the fourth century B.C., have been found in domestic houses elsewhere, most notably in Pella,[42] Amphipolis (fig. 5),[43] Delos,[44] and recently Pergamon.[45] There is some evidence that colored stucco walls with incised lines like those from Olynthos lie under the second-century architectural relief walls in Priene.[47]

It is on Delos where the growth of domestic architectural luxury in the Hellenistic west can best be documented. Here the remains of slender marble columns indicate rooms of considerable height behind peristyles as high as four meters; floor mosaics made from colorful marble chips and remaining fragments of wall paintings with stucco architectural relief elements and eye-level friezes of figurative painting suggest elegant and richly decorated interiors.

Private houses on Delos were essentially reconstructed in 166 B.C. when the city lost its independence to Athens, and Athenian citizens (and probably Roman merchants) went to live there. It is possible, perhaps likely, that the Athenians brought with them from Athens the concept of private housing represented on Delos after this date.[47] As Delos was almost completely destroyed in 69 B.C. in the second Mithradatic war, Hellenistic domestic architectural remains can be dated to between 166 and 69 B.C.

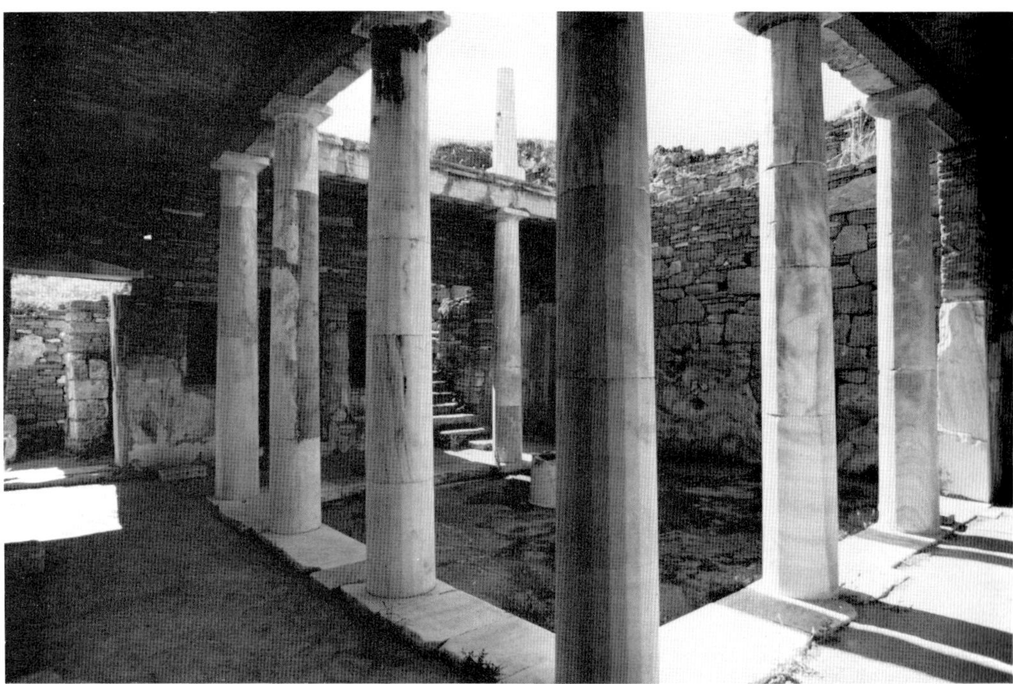

The courtyard was still the common feature, and the rectangular peristyle, forming covered galleries on all sides onto which opened the various ground-floor rooms, the most characteristic (figs. 6, 7). Most houses had a second story on several wings, not only on the north, and some had a partial third story, often a towerlike structure like those that appear in so-called "second style" wall painting.[48] As in Priene, stairs were within the house, allowing protected access to the rooms upstairs, and the best lighted rooms must have been those on the upper stories, their double doors opening to the covered loggia formed by the columns and piers carried upon the peristyle.

Many of the most elaborately decorated rooms were still on the ground floor, however, including at least the major oikos, which with some exceptions was located on the north side of the court, facing south, as in Priene. With its central doorway, often flanked by windows, the oikos was clearly the most important room: wide, elaborately decorated, and as the reserved, but not elevated, area around the wall for klinai sometimes indicated, serving as the symposium or main banquet room. Usually there was a second oikos in the same or an adjoining wing. Perhaps introduced from the East were the frequent *exedrae*: small rooms off the court and open to it on one side, frequently in the west.[49] Kitchens were a separate room on the ground floor with a high corner hearth. Families may have eaten around tables, perhaps the elaborately inlaid round tables found on Delos (fig. 8),[50] as well as in Pella.[51] However, crude stone buckets (which like the frequent latrines on Delos were also found in Dura Europas)[52] here replaced the elegant marble vessels with shallow tablelike containers (sometimes with drains) on fluted pedestals found throughout Priene[53] (fig. 9) and occasionally in Olynthos;[54] these containers of water were placed near the entrance to the reception area (here the major oikos) for guests to wash, or be washed by a servant, before entering to recline.[55]

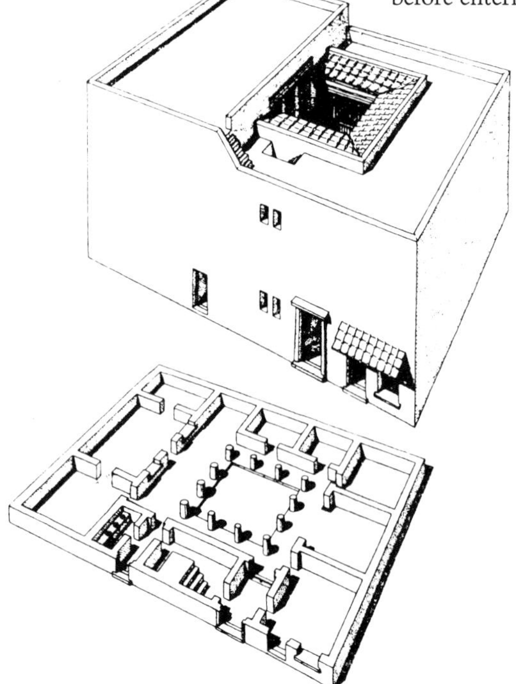

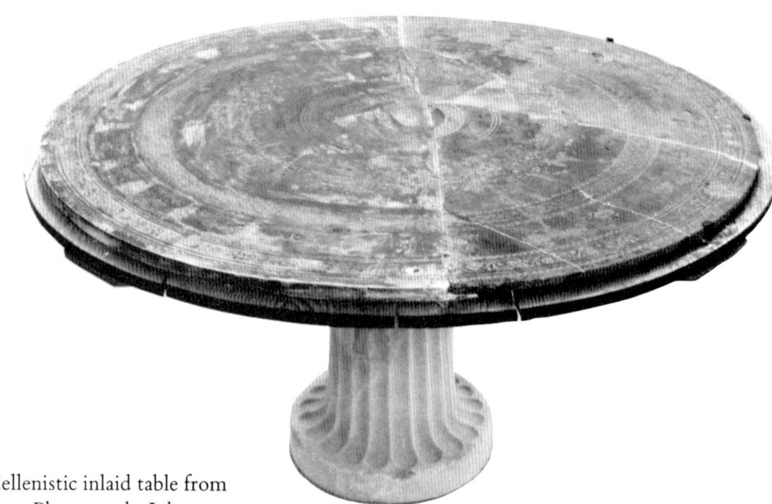

Fig. 8. Hellenistic inlaid table from Delos, slate. Photograph, John Dean.

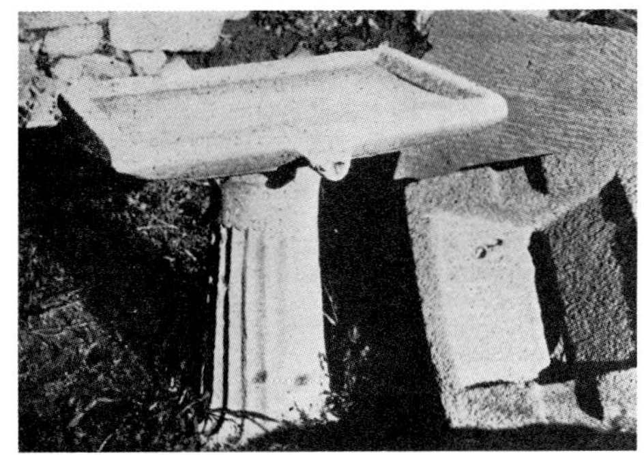

Fig. 9. Hellenistic marble water basin from Priene, from T. Wiegand and H. Schrader, *Priene* (Berlin, 1904), 376, fig. 474.

Most houses were irregular in ground plan, but often as big as 600 meters square, twice the size of the average fourth-century house (200–300 meters square).[57] Walls, most of fieldstone and some of granite from quarries on the island, were constructed on foundations of rock. Columns, stylobates, and capitals of the peristyles were usually marble, sometimes stone with stucco. There were usually eight or twelve columns, occasionally only four, one at each corner. In the courtyard enclosed by the peristyle was often a mosaic pavement, and beneath the courtyard floor was a cistern for rain water, conducted by lead pipes from the roof down one of the columns. The columns on the north side of the peristyle, forming the deeper portico facing south, were sometimes larger and higher than the others, as occasionally in Priene. Brackets received the entablature from the adjoining lower sides, thus allowing the major oikos and perhaps other rooms on the north to have a ceiling level that was higher than that found in the ground-floor rooms in other wings. Such an architectural design conforms to Vitruvius's description of the "Rhodian peristyle."[57]

These houses, with their marble-columned courtyards, large high-ceilinged banquet rooms, and numerous smaller rooms open to the courtyard both at ground level and above, were settings for considerable lavish ornament. Richly colored marble mosaics in the courtyard, the oikoi, the exedrae, and other rooms were frequently figural, sometimes emblematic (fig. 10). The murals on walls in rooms both on the ground floor and above were designed in colored stucco with the frequent inclusion of white stucco reliefs of architectural elements (like those discussed above from Priene, Pella, Amphipolis, and Pergamon),[58] and, by the end of the second century on Delos, included in the frieze zone narrative figural paintings. Averaging about fifteen centimeters in height, such continuous paintings were framed by several of the other courses in the frieze zone: kymatia, egg-and-dart, meander motifs, metopelike panels, etc., sometimes painted, sometimes modeled in relief. The subjects of these figural paintings were scenes of actors, battle scenes, and so-called peopled garlands, painted with loose brushwork on dark or light backgrounds.[59]

Little is known about the ceilings of Greek houses. In poorer late Classical and Hellenistic dwellings, the wooden beams were probably simply left exposed. In richer houses, however, it is almost certain that at least the ceiling of the andron, and later that of the major oikos, was decorated in some way. There were probably painted wooden coffers on the ceilings of some rooms.[60] Further, the painted ceiling designs, derived from woven textiles, of some late Classical and early Hellenistic tombs (the chamber and the antechamber of which, on some level, may have represented an andronitis) suggest that it may have

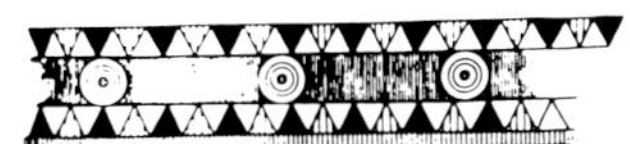

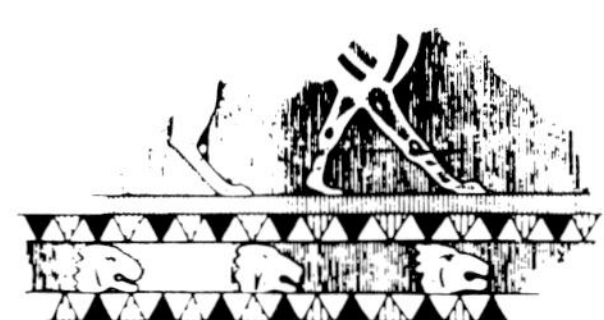

Fig. 11. Drawing after a wall painting in a Hellenistic chamber-tomb in Dion, Macedonia, 250–200 B.C., from *Antiquity* 44 (1970) 143, fig. 1.

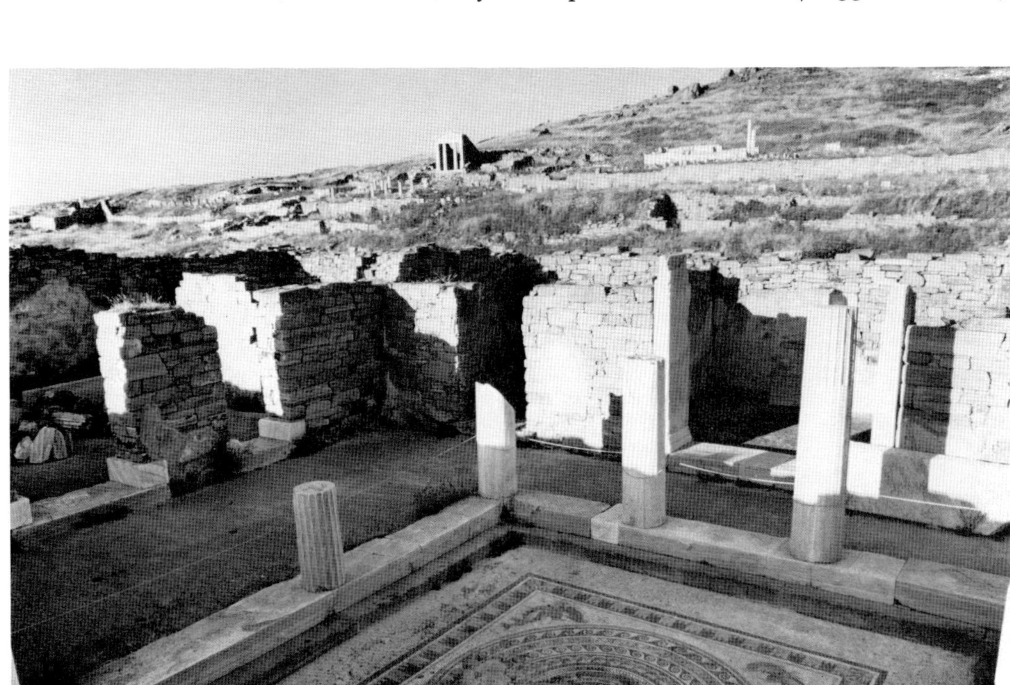

Fig. 10. Hellenistic mosaic pavement from the House of the Dolphins, Delos, second century B.C. Photograph, John Dean.

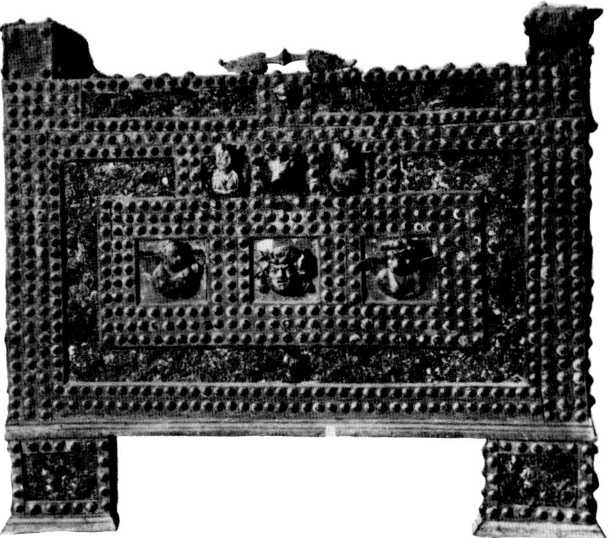

Fig. 12. Chest with bronze appliqués, from Pompeii, early first century A.D., from E. Pernice, *Die hellenistische Kunst in Pompeji 5: Hellenistische Tische Zisternenmündungen Beckenuntersätze Altäre und Truhen* (Berlin, 1932), pl. 52.1.

been a common practice in homes to hang woven fabrics not only on the walls, but above, covering the rafters of the ceiling, draped and tacked to hang like a canopy (fig. 11). This was probably most practicable in rooms with high ceilings.[61]

Household furniture of the Classical period was entirely made of wood with painted and ivory decoration, and has, of course, almost completely disappeared. Stone klinai and thrones from fourth-century tombs, often with textiles painted on their stone mattresses and pillows, corroborate what we know from earlier and contemporary vase painting about the appearance of this furniture.[62] By some time early in the third century B.C., parts of wooden klinai—the legs and all ornament—were cast in bronze, however, and among the most spectacular objects found in private houses in Hellenistic Priene, Pella, and Delos are such bronzes.

From Priene came fragments of a kline leg,[63] a cast bronze attachment with a horse's head protome for the decoration of the edge of the fulcrum, or leaning headrest, of a kline,[64] and a bronze bust of Artemis from the lower end of another such attachment.[65] Three bronze fulcrum attachments were found in Pella: two with busts of Dionysos and upper protomes of mule's heads, a third with a portraitlike bust of a garlanded hero and a horse's head.[67] Several bronzes with a secure *terminus ante quem* based on a burned level of the second quarter of the first century B.C., including a kline leg and two Silenos busts from klinai, were found in the Skardhana quarter of Delos.[67] These are probably local products, for there may well have been on Delos a workshop for the production of klinai.[68] The kline leg now in the Delos Museum may be compared to the legs of the famous and nearly complete kline in The Walters Art Gallery (No. 68), from Italy, which may have been produced about the same time.[69]

Other bronzes surviving from these cities contribute to our knowledge of the Hellenistic household. Two bronze decorative busts (Hermes and a youthful satyr), found together with a lock and key and fragmentary bronze feet on Delos,[70] allow the reconstruction of a late second-century chest for the storage of valuables or household linens similar to Roman examples found in Pompeii (fig. 12).[71] Bronze pulls to open the lids of such chests found in Priene are similar enough in form to later pulls from Pompeii to suggest that certain aspects of furniture changed very little during the first century B.C.[72]

Hellenistic bronze oil lamps, typically with bulbous body on a low foot and a long spout-like nose balanced by an elaborate and extensive handle, were found in quantity both in Priene (fig. 13) and on Delos.[73] These were placed on high bronze or marble stands as were their counterparts in terracotta, found in even greater abundance in both sites. Versions of the characteristic three-legged wooden table which stood before each kline during a meal, known from the second and first centuries on both painted and carved relief funerary stelai (fig. 14), may well have existed in metal, or with cast bronze legs, but no remains survive from the excavated cities discussed here.[74] Numerous marble legs, some in the form of Hermaphrodites, exist from Delos, but such tables had other functions.[75]

Whereas some families had bronze and even silver drinking vessels, the best reserved for festivals and sacrifices,[76] the common tableware was glazed ceramic of the period: red-figured and black-glazed ware, west slope style pottery, white-ground Lagynos ware (Priene and Pergamon), and the ubiquitous Megarian bowls. In most cities, pottery was both imported and locally made.

Although it is the Romans, not the Greeks, who are generally considered big spenders in the realm of domestic luxury,[77] it is clear that the reasonably prosperous city dweller in the Hellenistic period likewise demonstrated his wealth and taste in the decoration and furnishings of his house. It might be expected that it was in the andron and later the major oikos on which the greatest expense was lavished. Illuminated by one or two windows by day and the flickering light of oil lamps by evening, the center of the banquet room floor—the focus of the klinai lining the walls—presented the guest with a bold figural or

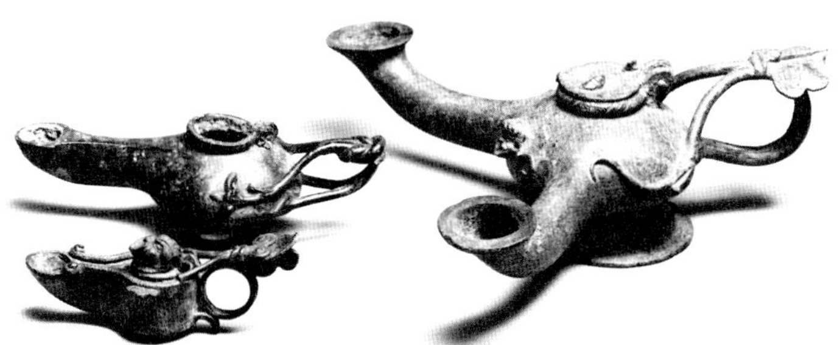

Fig. 13. Hellenistic bronze lamps from Priene, Berlin, Staatlichen Museen Preussischer Kulturbesitz, Inv. nos. 10049–51. Photograph, Antikenmuseum Berlin, Staatliche Museen Preussischer Kulturbesitz.

emblematic mosaic. The klinai themselves were piled with luxurious mattresses and pillows covered with vividly colored woven fabrics with woven or embroidered geometric designs, the busts and equine heads on their sloping headrests adding animation and the luster of polished bronze. Brightly painted terracotta masks—perhaps a Gorgon, Silenos, satyr, or leering theater caricatures[78]—were hung low on the richly stuccoed walls as added decoration. Other terracotta faces may have looked down from the metopes of a red and blue stucco relief frieze,[79] or, instead, a painted frieze may have presented to the reclining viewer a row of lively little figures of masked, gesticulating actors.[80] Above, very likely, was a stately colonnade made of stucco, but appearing like white marble against a clear blue sky, and then, above it all, may have appeared the looping folds of a colorful canopy or a ceiling of painted coffers. Painted terracotta figurines of lyre-playing centaurs, satyrs, or some other subjects suitable to the banquet and symposium, perhaps erotic, were undoubtedly placed on ledges built out from the walls, or in niches in them, and flying clay Erotes may have hung on ribbons from the ceiling.[81] Somewhere in the room, probably near the door, was the elegant polished bronze or glazed pottery krater, on its high stand, from which the wine was served.

No generalizations can yet be made about the presence of marble sculpture in the Hellenistic house, but enough small, late Hellenistic statuettes of Dionysos, Ariadne, Aphrodite with Eros, Aphrodite, Apollo, Hermes, and other deities were found in domestic areas in both Priene[82] and Delos[83] to suggest their considerable popularity. Like terracottas, small marble statuettes were placed in niches, on shelves, and possibly on marble stands, probably in many areas of the house. Some statuettes of deities were undoubtedly connected with household cults.[84] Herms may have appeared in hallways, the courtyard, and if Classical tradition continued, in the entrance porch.[85]

The original location of the larger marbles found in houses on Delos is more problematic.[86] Recent research suggests that by the late Hellenistic period on Delos, marble statuary could be found throughout the house, on all floors, and on the ground floor, at least, often placed with an eye to visibility from the entrance and other vantage points.[87] A fragment of a statue base, inscribed Praxi(teles), found in the major oikos of a house, raises intriguing questions about copies of Classical sculpture placed in symposium contexts.

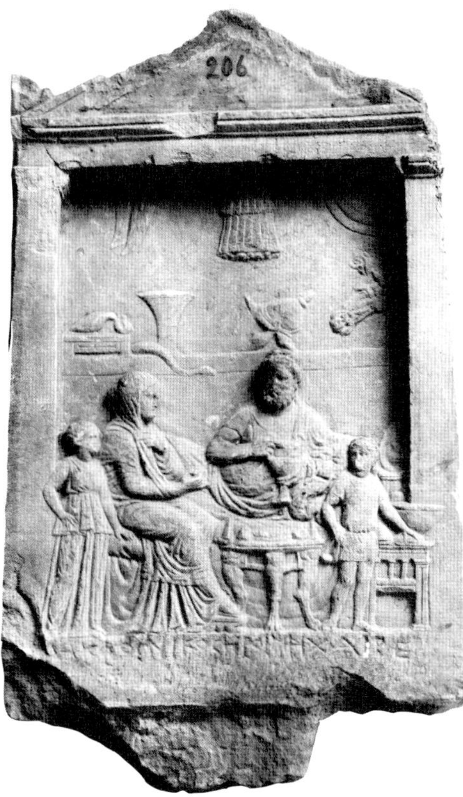

Fig. 14. Marble funerary relief from Samos, ca. second century B.C. Photograph, Deutsches Archäologisches Institut Athen, Neg. Nr. GR 813.

1. Given temporal and regional differences, there is no such thing, of course, as *the* Hellenistic house. I have tried to comply with Dr. Reeder's challenging and imaginative request by focusing on aspects of urban residences during the Hellenistic period in Eretria, Olynthos, Pella, Priene, and Delos with the hope of documenting my necessarily summary remarks with well-excavated material covering a discrete span of time. I am indebted to the new book by Wolfram Hoepfner and Ernst-Ludwig Schwandner, *Haus und Stadt in klassischer Griechenland* (Munich, 1986), for considerable background material.

2. Demosthenes, *Third Olynthiac*, 25–29.

3. Credited to Hippodamus, a Milesian. Aristotle, *Politics* 1267b.

4. Dirty water drained from freshly washed floors and infrequent bathtubs was channeled onto the streets, but refuse, including that from chamberpots, the only sanitation facility in Classical houses, was collected by a public garbage agency, at least in Athens, and deposited in a prescribed place outside the city walls. Hoepfner and Schwandner (note 1) 266. Cf. Juvenal, 3.279. For drainage and sanitation in Athens, see also H. A. Thompson and R. E. Wycherley, *The Agora of Athens: The History, Shape and Uses of an Ancient City Center,* The Athenian Agora 14 (Princeton, 1972), 194–197.

5. Xenophon, *Memorabilia* 3.8.9; Aristotle, *Politics* 1267b (on Hippodamus).

6. D. M. Robinson and J. W. Graham, *Excavations at Olynthus 8. The Hellenic House* (Baltimore, 1938), 160. In Priene there were no large altars in the courtyards, only small portable stone or terracotta altars for burning incense. Hoepfner and Schwandner (note 1) 180. T. Wiegand and H. Schrader, *Priene: Ergebnisse der Ausgrabungen und Untersuchungen in den Jahren 1895–1898* (Berlin, 1904), 367 and 377 sq.

7. Hoepfner and Schwandner (note 1) 261.

8. Hoepfner and Schwandner (note 1) 34 and 42–52.

9. Hoepfner and Schwandner (note 1) 273.

10. Athenaeus, *Deipnosophistae* 3.115.

11. Found in Olynthos, Priene, Delos, and elsewhere; for an extant, complete example, J. Raeder, *Priene. Funde aus einer griechischen Stadt* (Berlin, 1983), 16, fig. 6.

12. D. M. Robinson, "The Third Campaign at Olynthos," *AJA* 39 (1935) 235, fig. 3b.

13. The dinner proper was the *deipnon*, the *symposion* the drinking party and conversation after the meal was over.

14. There were seven participants in Plato's *Symposium*. There were also dining rooms for three, five, nine, ten, eleven, twelve, thirteen and even more couches. The smallest, the three-klinai room, which was standard in Priene, gave its name to the Roman *triclinium*, the size of which was not consistent. The Pinakotheke in the Propylaia on the Athenian akropolis, identified as a dining room by John Travlos, could hold seventeen klinai.

15. Hoepfner and Schwandner (note 1) 48 and 271.

16. Hoepfner and Schwandner (note 1) 52.

17. Hoepfner and Schwandner (note 1) 34.

18. Robinson and Graham (note 6) passim. Also D. M. Robinson, *Excavations at Olynthus 2: Architecture and Sculpture: Houses and Other Buildings* (Baltimore, 1930) and idem, *Excavations at Olynthus 12: Domestic and Public Architecture* (Baltimore, 1946), and "Mosaics from Olynthos," *AJA* 36 (1932) pl. 3 and "Archaeological Notes," *AJA* 38 (1934) pls. 29 and 30. Also M. Robertson, "Greek Mosaics," *JHS* 85 (1965) 72–89, pl. 18, 1 and 2. The identification of the famous "House of Good Fortune" as a private residence is disputed by Hoepfner and Schwandner (note 1) 53–54.

19. Robinson and Graham (note 6) 176. The walls of a chamber tomb from Olynthos are painted in a similar manner: D. M. Robinson, *Excavations at Olynthos 11: Necrolynthia* (Baltimore, 1942), 117–119, pls. 53–58.

20. P. Ducrey and I. R. Metzger, "La Maison aux mosaïques à Erétrie," *AntK* 22 (1979) 3–21, pls. 1–4; idem, "The House of the Mosaics at Eretrie," *Archaeology* 32 (1979) 34–42.

21. Ducrey and Metzger (note 20).

22. Fragments of a wall with a red stucco socle zone and gray-white orthostat level, with incised lines dividing panels and zones, were found recently in an early Hellenistic level ("Phase II") of a house in Pergamon. There may have been a frieze zone of red and greenish mottled lines (marble imitation?). W. Radt, "Pergamon 1985," *AA* (1986) 428–429.

23. D. Salzmann, *Untersuchungen zu den antiken Kieselmosaiken* (Berlin, 1982), 111–112, nos. 116–118, pls. 19–22; idem, "Ein wiedergewonnenes Kieselmosaik aus Sikyon," *AA* (1979) 290–302; M. Robertson, "Greek Mosaics: a Postscript," *JHS* 87 (1967) pl. 24.

24. Salzmann (note 23) 95–96, nos. 64–65, pls. 23–24, 1. Also C. K. Williams II and J. E. Fisher, "Corinth 1975," *Hesperia* 45 (1976) 114, n. 12, pl. 24; T. L. Shear, "Excavations in the Theatre District and Tombs of Corinth," *AJA* 33 (1929) 526–527, fig. 10.

25. Salzmann (note 23) 109, nos. 107–108, pl. 25. Also M. K. Donaldson, "A Pebble Mosaic in Peiraeus," *Hesperia* 34 (1965) 77–78, pls. 23–24, and 77, n. 2.

26. Salzmann (note 23) 95, no. 119, pls. 10–11.

27. Salzmann (note 23) 95, no. 63, pl. 9. Also C. K. Williams II, "Corinth Excavations, 1979," *Hesperia* 49 (1980) 115–116, pl. 19. Dated by Williams to the first quarter of the fourth century B.C.; by Salzmann to the end of the fifth to the beginning of the fourth century.

28. Salzmann (note 23) 97, no. 71, pl. 12,1. Also K. Votsis, "Nouvelle mosaïque de Sicyone," *BCH* 100 (1976) 586, figs. 15 and 16.

29. Dated to the late fifth to early fourth century B.C. by Salzmann. Salzmann (note 23) 23. Some mosaics in the older areas of Olynthos are probably also from this period.

30. The tholos at Epidauros was enlarged about 360 B.C. with elaborately carved floral and geometric decoration added throughout, and an abundant use of black and white marble flooring. Pausias, the flower painter from Sikyon, whom Pliny said also painted coffered ceilings (*NH* 35.123–127) is associated with the interior.

31. Black-glazed ware reached its apogee, and gold-decorated black-glazed ware originated about this time. B. A. Sparkes and L. Talcott, *Black and Plain Pottery of the Sixth, Fifth and Fourth Centuries B.C.,* The Athenian Agora 12 (Princeton, 1970); G. Kopcke, "Golddekorierte attische Schwarzfirniskeramik der vierten Jahrhunderts v. Chr.," *AM* 79 (1964) 22–84.

32. Hoepfner and Schwandner (note 1) 31. Such a window may be indicated in the wall of the temple in the Hellenistic relief in the British Museum of Dionysos visiting a mortal.

33. House AV 6. Hoepfner and Schwandner (note 1) 62 and 68; floor plans, 69.

34. Houses FIII 8 and AXI 10; perhaps the "Villa of Good Fortune," but see note 18. Hoepfner and Schwandner (note 1) 63, 68.

35. Hoepfner and Schwandner (note 1) 181 and 183–186.

36. Large enough for three klinai only. Hoepfner and Schwandner (note 1) 179.

37. Hoepfner and Schwandner (note 1) 186.

38. Raeder (note 11) 61; M. Schede, *Die Ruinen von Priene: kurze Beschreibung* (Berlin and Leipzig, 1934), 97, fig. 112. It is not clear whether triglyph and metope courses existed together with the marble imitation courses, or instead of them. Probably many variations existed.

39. Raeder (note 11) fig. 1. Reconstructed by Marina Heilmeyer. This is the "masonry style," a term first introduced by C. M. Dawson and later proposed to designate such walls outside Italy by Vincent Bruno ("Antecedents of the Pompeian First Style," *AJA* 73 [1969] 305–317) or the "architectural relief style," perhaps a more descriptive term suggested by S. Miller (*Hellenistic Macedonian Architecture* [Diss. Bryn Mawr College, 1970], 120). For similar walls in Italy the term "first style" is used for August Mau's original "incrustation style."

40. The interior wall decoration of the Hieron on Samothrace: P. W. Lehmann, *Samothrace 3. The Hieron* (Princeton, 1969), pl. 106.

41. The Great Tomb at Lefkadia. P. Petsas, *O taphos ton Lefkadion* (Athens, 1966).

42. For a reconstructed wall from Pella similar to the wall from Priene in its double-level plan with colonnade (here Doric with a sky-blue background) and its inclusion of marble imitation, see M. Siganidou, "Excavations at Ancient Pella," *Archaeologia* (1982) 34, fig. 5. I owe this reference to Stella Miller. There are many unpublished wall fragments from old excavations at Pella. Among these are remains of several painted walls with relief stucco segments of leafy garlands with flowers, or tainias. These must have been part of the frieze zone.

43. The Amphipolis wall is published by G. Touchais in "Les Chroniques des fouilles en 1982," *BCH* 107 (1983) 800–803, fig. 110. The stucco Ionic colonnade sits on the floor and reaches to a height of 1.40 meters; trompe l'oeil polychrome marble "masonry" revetment and a frieze of panels with linear design are revealed between the columns. Touchais dates it, without giving his reasons, to the second century B.C. Another room has a pseudo-isodomic stucco wall 3.65 meters high with incised and painted red and black lines between white "blocks." Touchais, "Fouilles en 1983," *BCH* 108 (1984), fig. 118. Associated with this house is the north side of a Doric peristyle, 7.05 meters long, with stucco-covered stone columns and poros capitals. A large part of the courtyard of this house was paved with plain pebble mosaic. See also G. E. Mylonas in *Ergon* (1982), 16–17, figs. 17–18; D. I. Lazaridis, *Prakt.* (1983) 35–37, pl. 39; and H. W. Catling, "Archaeology in Greece, 1984–1985," *JHS* 105 (1985) 49, fig. 87. Fragments of plaster reliefs of garlands and Erotes were found in this house: Lazaridis, *Prakt.* (1983) 37, pl. 42a.

44. M. Bulard, "Peinture murales et mosaïques de Délos," *MonPiot* 14 (1908) 91–188; J. Chamonard, "Fouilles de Délos," *BCH* 25 (1906) 456–606; idem, *Exploration archéologique de Délos VIII.2: Le Quartier du theâtre* (Paris, 1924), 357–391; idem, for the Maison des Masques, "Fouilles à Délos," *BCH* 57 (1933) 98–169. A. Plassart, "Le Quartier du Stade à Délos," *BCH* 40 (1916) 144–256; P. Bruneau, C. Vatin and U. Bezerra de Meneses, *Exploration archéologique de Délos XXVII: L'Ilot des comédiens* (1970) 151–193, pls. 21–26. Also U. Bezerra de Meneses, "La peinture," in P. Bruneau and J. Ducat, *Guide de Délos,* 3rd ed. (Paris, 1983), 55–61.

45. Fragments discovered in a house from the major Hellenistic period in Pergamon ("Hauptphase") have a stucco sima with dentils and lion's heads, and marble imitation over a black socle zone. W. Radt (note 22) figs. 11 and 12.

46. Hoepfner and Schwandner (note 1) 178.

47. Hoepfner and Schwandner (note 1) 241 and 245–246.

48. Hoepfner and Schwandner (note 1) 244. For a discussion of the towers, H. Lauter, *Die Architektur des Hellenismus* (Darmstadt, 1986), 225–226.

49. Hoepfner and Schwandner (note 1) 245. Lauter (note 48) 148–150, associates them with the peristyle, especially in public buildings.

50. For an inlaid marble table from Delos: W. Deonna, *Exploration archéologique de Délos XVIII: Le Mobilier délien* (Paris, 1938), pl. 26. These may have been used, rather, for sacrificial purposes.

51. A table from Pella is illustrated in Siganidou (note 42) 34, fig. 7.

52. Hoepfner and Schwandner (note 1) 228 and 245. For the stone buckets, 228, figs. 225 and 226; 245, fig. 249.

53. Weigand and Schrader (note 6) 375 and 376, fig. 474.

54. Where they were also made of terracotta. Robinson and Graham (note 6) 317–320.

55. In Plato's *Symposium* the guest Aristodemos is washed by a servant before reclining. (*Symposium* 175A).

56. Hoepfner and Schwandner (note 1) 243.

57. Vitruvius 6.7.3. In 1935, A. Rumpf, "Zur hellenistischen Haus," (*JdI* 50 [1935], 1 sq.) thought he had discovered a house in Delos which fit Vitruvius's description of a three-peristyle house, with andronitis, gynaikonitis, and guest residence (hospitalia). The German scholar Martin Kreeb has recently pointed out that all of this was actually for three separate households: "Das Delische Wohnhaus: Einzelprobleme," *AA* (1985) 93–111. The features that Vitruvius described did not belong to typical private houses, in any case, but—with spacious peristyles, gardens, reception areas and guest rooms—were, instead, characteristic of Hellenistic palaces. Vitruvius's description of the Greek house is a combination of many sources from different periods of time, and is not historical. See Hoepfner and Schwandner (note 1) 246, where they point out the many confusions in terms of Vitruvius's text.

58. Above, notes 39–45.

59. The recent book by V. Bruno, *Hellenistic Painting Techniques: the Evidence of the Delos Fragments* (Leiden, 1985), discusses the figurative friezes of Delos in careful detail. Bruno, 4, thinks that such friezes were part of the design of walls throughout Hellenistic Greece.

60. In Aristophanes' *Wasps* (1208–1215) it is clear that the ceiling in a home was decorated in such a way that it could be admired by a guest. For the ceilings of Hellenistic public buildings, see Lauter (note 48) 248–252. The ceiling of the tholos at Epidauros was decorated with carved marble coffers.

61. Horace (*Satires* 2.8.54) describes an episode in which a canopy spread above diners comes crashing down from the ceiling. A tomb at Lefkadia (K. Rhomiopoulou, "A New Monumental Chamber Tomb with Painting of the Hellenistic Period near Leukadia [West Macedonia]," *AAA* 6 [1973] 87–92) has in the antechamber a ceiling painted with a highly decorative multicolored floral motif which in design may be compared to the fourth-century B.C. gold and purple textile found in Tomb II at Vergina and in color to the dyed felt fabrics from the frozen barrows of the Altai, at Pazirik in Russia, dated to the fifth century B.C. (For the Vergina cloth, M. Andronicos, *Vergina. The Royal Tombs and the Ancient City* [Athens, 1984], figs. 156–157; recently published by S. Drougou in the Andronicos Festschrift, *ΑΜΗΤΟΣ* [Thessaloniki, 1987], 303–316, pl. 63–69. The Altai fabrics have been most recently published in the catalogue of an exhibition in Venice: *Tesori d'Eurasia. 2000 anni di storia in 70 anni di archeologia Sovietica* [Milan, 1987], figs. 131–133, 139–143.) In the burial chamber in the tomb at Lefkadia the ceiling is painted plain yellow, conceivably representing gold fabric. J. Boardman in "Travelling Rugs," *Antiquity* 44 (1970) 143–144, figs. 1–3, pointed out the similarity of a frieze painted above the marble klinai on the back wall of the late fourth-century Soteriades tomb in Dion (Macedon) to the leather appliqués and felt saddle blankets from the Altai barrows. The relationship of tomb architecture, with its complicated heroizing aspects, and domestic architecture is complex, and only the most general analogies can be made. However, it is clear from tomb finds in Macedon, including quantities of gold, silver, and bronze vessels, as well as both wooden and marble klinai, that some sort of belief in banquets in an afterlife prompted the indications of material security, both real and symbolic. The working marble double doors in the facades of such tombs—which in the fourth century at least usually swing inward on metal tracks—can afford us some notion of the actual wooden double doors at the main entrances to homes contemporary to them. In the late Classical period, their bronze fixtures—door nails, locks, and both vertical and lion-head ring door pulls—are identical to finds from excavations of dwellings. T. Macridy, "Un tumulus macedonien à Langaza," *JdI* 26 (1911) 193–215; see also the limestone door in the Archaeological Museum in Thessaloniki from a tomb in Petriotika-Potidaea. Cf. finds from Olynthos in Robinson and Graham (note 6) 258 and pl. 71.2. Similar parallels can be drawn in the Hellenistic period. Lauter (note 48) 221, n. 78, cites a Hellenistic grave facade that seems to imitate a normal domestic dwelling (*AAA* [1973] 116).

62. As does the occasional find. See the *diphros*, or stool, with four round legs made of wood and covered with silver from a cist grave in Stavroupolis, Thessaloniki: *Treasures of Ancient Macedonia*, Archaeological Museum of Thessaloniki (Thessaloniki, 1970), no. 292; 76 and pl. 39. 1970.

63. The only surviving one is from House XVII, now in the Antikenmuseum in Berlin. Raeder (note 11) 70, cat. no. 321, fig. 8a; Wiegand and Schrader (note 6) 382, fig. 483.

64. Once in the Antikenabteilung (Pergamonsammlung), Staatliche Museen zu Berlin. Wiegand and Schrader (note 6) 378–381, figs. 480, 481. Now lost.

65. Wiegand and Schrader (note 6) 381 and fig. 482. Probably from the late second century B.C.

66. Probably all to be dated to within the late third to early second century B.C. FA 4 (C 80), FA 5 (C 82), and FA 2 (C 171bis) in B. Barr-Sharrar, *The Hellenistic and Early Imperial Decorative Bust* (Mainz, 1987), 163–164 and pls. 78 and 81. Pertinent publication references, op. cit., 52–53 and 76. M. Lilimpaki-Akamati, who published the garlanded hero fulcrum attachment in "Xalkino fulcrum apo tin Pella," *ArchDelt* 34, 1980 (1986) 138–149, pls. 52–54, believes it to date to the middle of the second century B.C. based on the style of the bust.

67. G. Siebert, "Mobilier délien en bronze," *Etudes déliennes, BCH* Suppl. 1 (1973) 555–587. For the kline leg after cleaning, G. Siebert, "Delos. Le quartier de Skardhana," *BCH* 100 (1976) 814, fig. 25.

68. According to Pliny (*NH* 33.144; 34.9), Delos was famous in antiquity for its production of bronze beds. See Siebert (note 67) for a discussion of the local workshop.

69. Catalogue No. 68. Said to have been found in a chamber tomb in Canosa. D. K. Hill, "A Bronze Couch," *JWalt* 15–16 (1952–53) 49–61. Dated there to the first century B.C. I have recently suggested this date be narrowed to the first half of the first century B.C. Barr-Sharrar (note 66) 63 and 103.

70. Siebert (note 68) 555–587.

71. For vase painting depictions of Greek household chests, E. Brümmer, "Griechische Truhenbehalter," *JdI* 100 (1985) 37–168. They were sometimes used as children's cribs. The Hellenistic chests were less massive than the Roman: E. Pernice, *Die hellenistische Kunst in Pompeji* 5. *Hellenistische Tische, Zisternenmündungen, Beckenuntersätze, Altare und Truhen* (Berlin and Leipzig, 1932), pl. 52. Also T. Kraus, *Pompeii and Herculaneum* (New York, 1973), 158, no. 184.

72. A Hellenistic bronze pull from Priene: Raeder (note 11) 60, no. 310; 69, fig. 7a. An Augustan pull: Barr-Sharrar (note 66) 49, cat. no. C 67, pl. 22.

73. Priene: Raeder (note 11) 57, cat. nos. 279–280; 70, fig. 8b (two from the left). Delos: *Exploration archéologique de Délos XXVI: Les Lampes* (Paris, 1965), no. 4409.4417, pl. 26; cat. no. 4779.4780, pl. 35.

74. As these tables were removed after the *deipnon* (n. 13 above and Xenophon, *Symposium* 2.2), they had to be of light construction. For a painted example, see the marble stele from Demetrias in Thessaly from the third to the second century B.C. in the Archaeological Museum in Thessaloniki: *Macedonia and Greece*, 124, fig. 1. For examples in relief, see E. Pfuhl and H. Möbius, *Die ostgriechischen Grabreliefs* I (Mainz, 1977), and II (Mainz, 1979), passim.

75. Necessarily stationary, they were perhaps used for sacrificial purposes. J. Marcadé, "Reliefs déliens," *Etudes déliennes, BCH* Suppl. 1 (1973) 345; W. Deonna (note 50) 18, fig. 16; pl. 17, figs. 116, 119.

76. Xenophon, *Oeconomicus* 9.6.

77. Cicero's letters to Atticus, for example, constantly testify not only to his strong interest in decorating his several houses (*Letter* 20), but to the debt he incurs because of them. He is, nevertheless, conscious of their investment value and the social position they afford him (*Letter* 1, 13).

78. Along with fragments of Silenos and satyr masks from the square banquet room in the House of the Mosaics in Eretria was found a Gorgon mask, 31.5 cm high. Ducrey and Metzger (note 20) color photo page 37. Theater masks of slaves and a brothel host were found in houses in Priene. Raeder (note 11) 35, cat. nos. 19, 20, 21; color plate 4b and figs. 18a and 18b.

79. Raeder (note 11) 61–62, cat. no. 354, fig. 10.

80. The Frieze of the Actors in oikos N of the Maison des Comediens. Bruno (note 59) pl. 3–7. Many of the figurative friezes are believed to have been in upper story rooms.

81. Raeder (note 11) 34–39, cat. nos. 2–69; pls. 72–76 and 82–84.

82. Raeder (note 11) 33.

83. J. Marcadé, *Au musée de Délos* (Paris, 1969), passim; idem (note 75) 343.

84. Cybele was popular in Priene. In a niche in a corridor wall in a house in Delos, 1.30 meters high, was a rectangular base with a dedicatory inscription from Spurius Stertinius, probably a Roman, to Artemis Soteira. M. Kreeb, "Figurliche Ausstattung delischer Privathäuser," *BCH* 108 (1984) 328 and 327, fig. 11. Dionysiac herms were particularly popular on Delos. Marcadé (note 83) 377.

85. Thucydides 6.27.1.

86. Marcadé (note 83) 105, 367.

87. Kreeb (note 84) passim.

Almost every work of art is treated individually. Exceptions are the closely related Nos. 71, 72; 78, 79; and 113, 114 which, in each case, are discussed in a single entry. Each entry has the following format: item number, item title, date. The first paragraph gives the inventory number, the material, and reputed provenance which is presented within quotations and should occasionally be regarded with caution. Also included are the previous ownership, preserved dimensions, and present condition of the piece. The abbreviations employed for dimensions, which are metric measurements, are: D = diameter, L = length, W = width, Ht = height, Th = thickness, Depth = depth, max = greatest. The second paragraph describes the object. The third paragraph, under the heading, *Exhibitions and Catalogues,* lists the object's previous history of exhibition, and catalogue, where it exists. The fourth paragraph, entitled *Publications,* lists all other publications of the object, in chronological order. These paragraphs are followed by a general discussion of the item and finally, by numbered notes. This format is a master plan; minor variations occur in individual entries where information is not available or particularly extensive. In addition to the list of abbreviations on pages 16 and 17, subsequent references to a publication within a single entry may use a short form of the title. All dates are B.C. unless otherwise specified.

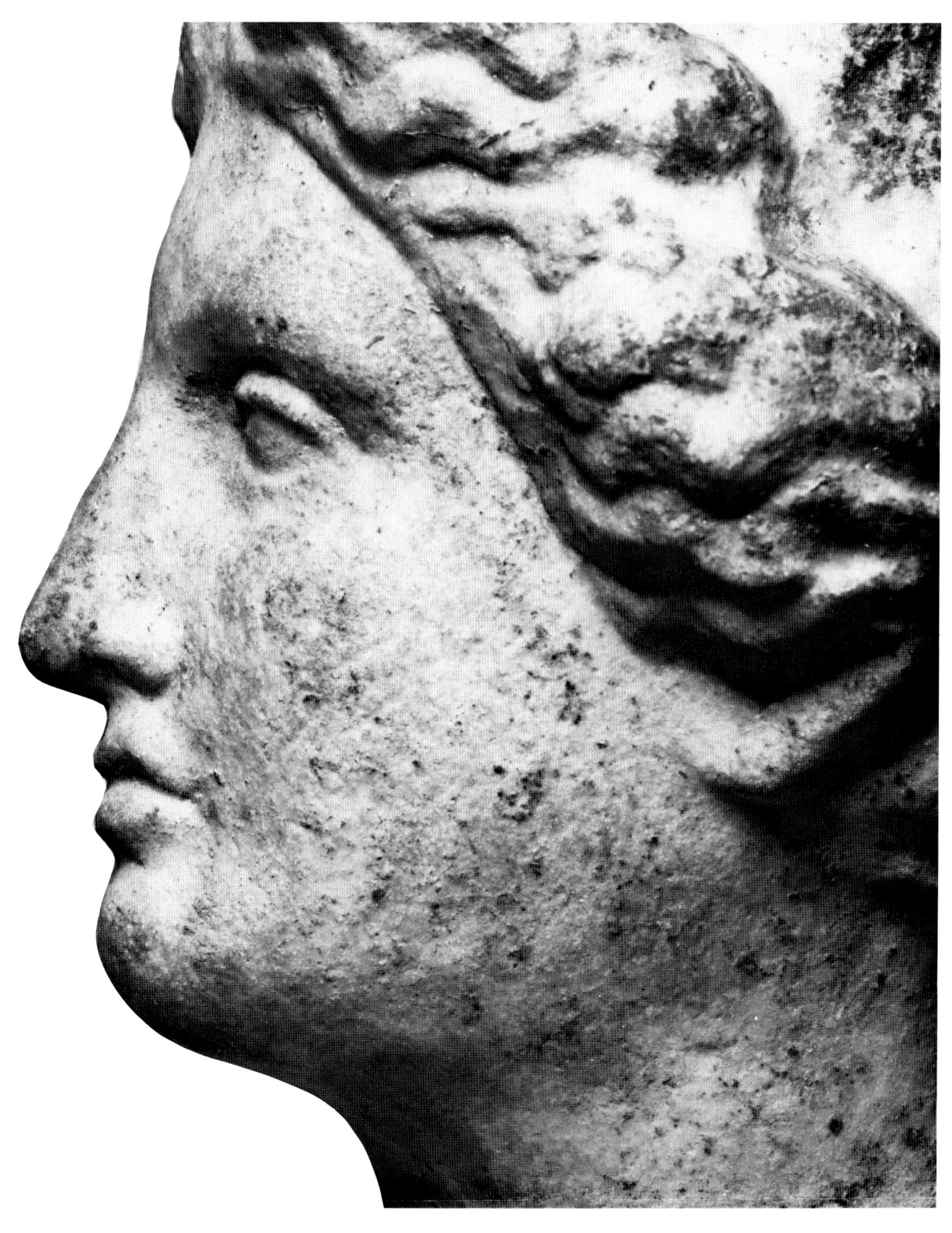

FRAGMENT OF A STELE WITH LEANING ATHENA
Ca. 400

23.177. Marble, probably Pentelic. Purchased from Brummer, 1925. Ht, 50.8 cm; max W, 20 cm; Th, 16.6 cm. Broken down each side and chipped across front.

Athena turns slightly to her right with her weight on her right leg and her left leg relaxed. Her right arm hangs at her side and her left forearm rests on a waist-high pillar, over which her aegis is draped. She wears a belted peplos with overfold and sandals. On the molding beneath her feet are inscribed the letters: NEPI; on the projecting molding above her head are the letters: NOΣ.

Illustrated on this relief is the so-called Leaning Athena type, which is first seen on a decree relief of Apollophanes of Kolophon, dated 427/6, where Athena rests her left arm upon a shield.[1] That fragment is so badly damaged that the goddess's dress is unclear, but on the decree relief of 410/9 for the Neapolitans of Thrace, the Leaning Athena wears a belted sleeveless chiton with overfold and without her aegis.[2] That this is the dress primarily associated with the type is confirmed by the reappearance of the Leaning Athena in this dress on statuettes and reliefs of the later fifth and early fourth century, as well as on a kotyle in the Kerch style of ca. 370.[3] The variant dress Athena wears on the Walters relief was undoubtedly influenced by that of the Erechtheion Caryatids, and the Leaning Athena appears again in the same garb on a pyxis in the Kerch style from the first half of the fourth century.[4]

On the Walters relief, the shield that conventionally belongs with the Leaning Athena type has been replaced by a pillar, which was probably inspired by the one against which Aphrodite leans in the type of the Aphrodite of Daphni, which is generally agreed to follow a lost original, the so-called Aphrodite of the Gardens, created ca. 435.[5] A later fifth-century conflation of the two types of leaning goddesses is suggested by a late fifth- or fourth-century decree relief of Dippos in the Epigraphic Museum in Athens, where Athena leans against her shield with her feet at such a distance from it that her body is no longer vertical but resembles the posture of the Aphrodite of Daphni.[6]

The pillars that accompany both the Daphni Aphrodite and the Athena on the Walters relief probably allude to the appurtenances of a typical sanctuary,

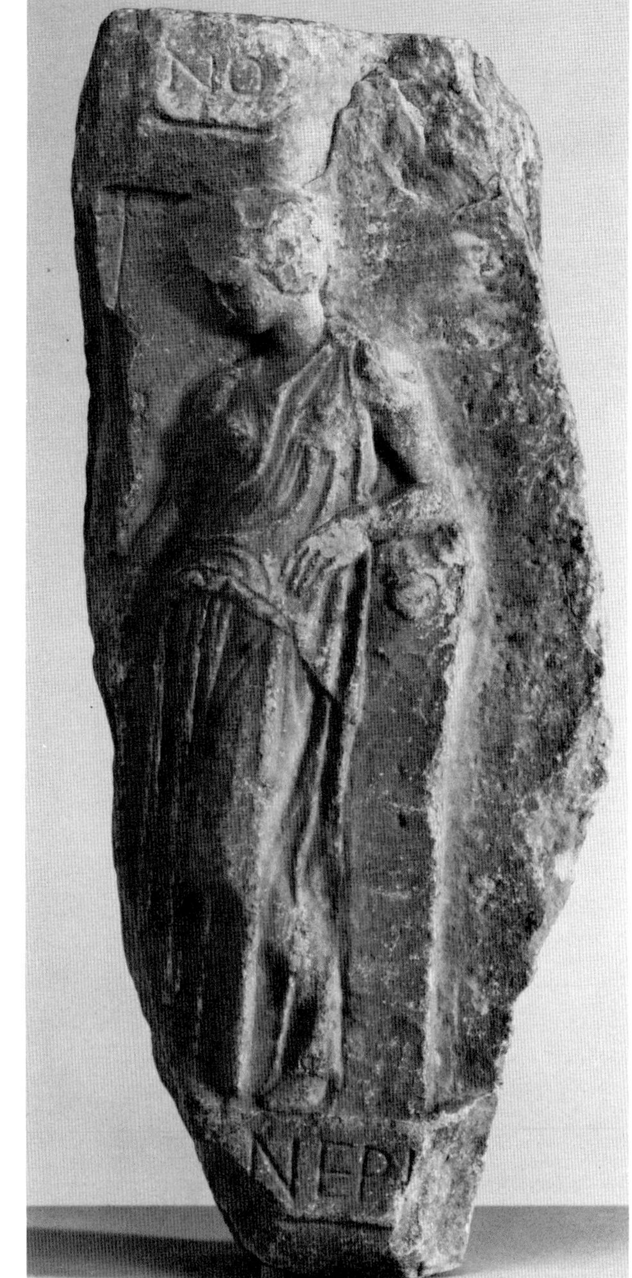

1.1

because on a late fifth-century votive relief in Athens, Persephone rests her elbow upon a similar pillar with a crowning element reminiscent of a pinax or votive relief.[7] Similarly, on the Lansdowne relief dated to the first century, a narrower pillar is crowned by a molding and surmounted by Athena's owl.[8] The inclined glance of the Walters Athena suggests that her gaze was directed at a worshiper who was conventionally depicted in reduced scale; if this is so, then the Walters relief was itself a votive offering, which was reused and reinscribed in Roman times. The Walters relief looks forward to the Hellenistic period in its use of a supporting element which, in the form of a pillar or shield, was introduced into freestanding sculpture between about 440 and 430. The innovation presages the non-figural elements that play an increasingly important role in fourth-century and Hellenistic sculpture.

1. Svoronos, J. N., *Das Athener Nationalmuseum* (Athens, 1903–37), 665, no. 431.4, pl. 207; S. Karouzou, "Two Statues on a Vase," *Essays in Memory of Karl Lehmann*, L. F. Sandler, ed. (New York, 1964), 155, ill. 2.
2. Svoronos (note 1) 663, no. 427, pl. 204; E. Berger, "Eine Athena aus dem späten 5. Jahrhunderts v. Chr.," *AntK* 10 (1967) 85, no. 12, pl. 24.4.
3. Karouzou (note 1) 153, fig. 4. See also Svoronos (note 1) 288–289, no. 66, pl. 37.5.
4. Karouzou (note 1) 153, fig. 6.
5. *LIMC* II (1984) pt. 1, 29–31, especially 29, no. 185 and 31, no. 200; A. Delivorrias, "Die Kultstatue der Aphrodite von Daphni," *AntP* 8 (1968) 19–31.
6. Svoronos (note 1) 670, no. 2787, pl. 224; Karouzou (note 1) fig. 9.
7. Svoronos (note 1) 437, no. 131, pl. 59.
8. *LIMC* II (1984) pt. 1, 976, no. 198.

STATUE OF NARKISSOS
*Roman copy after original
possibly of the late fifth century*

23.26. Coarse-grained marble. Purchased from Brummer in 1922. Ht, 63 cm; W, 26 cm. Part of a strut survives on the outside of the left thigh just above the break. Missing head, right arm, left arm above elbow and genitals. Both legs broken off above the knees. There are dowel holes on the outside of the left thigh and in each arm for attachment, and a modern dowel hole in the neck. Three additional holes are on the right buttock and one is on the right shoulder. The end of an iron pin remains for the attachment of genitals.

A nude youth stands on his right leg, with his relaxed left leg advanced. His left shoulder is upraised and the left upper arm lies against his side.

The type is familiar from as many as forty Roman copies, several of which are mirror reversals.[1] On better-preserved versions, the left arm hangs down vertically and the palm of the left hand is pressed against the top of a pillar; the right arm rests behind the right hip. Although most of the Roman copies present a boyish form, the muscular torso of a plaster cast recovered from Baiae argues that the original work depicted a more mature youth.[2] Robertson suggests that the prototype represented an exhausted athlete, to whom the nudity and pillar are appropriate, and was made in the late fifth or early fourth century, a contention supported by the appearance of a closely related type on the early fourth-century stele of Telesias.[3] It is unclear whether the prototype was a votive or grave monument.

The figure type is particularly interesting because it demonstrates the degree to which a supporting element had become incorporated into a sculptural composition by the early fourth century. The youth is also of special significance because his similarity to the Weary Herakles (Nos. 44, 45) identifies him as a precursor to the Lysippan work, which establishes a stronger antithesis between physical strength and exhaustion while introducing deeper philosophical connotations.

We know that the relationship between the two statues was recognized in antiquity because on several copies of the Narkissos type, the youth grasps an apple in his right hand.[4] Some of these replicas were intended for a garden setting or other decorative, domestic context; others apparently developed the intimations of melancholy inherent in the posture and functioned as grave monuments.

The name by which the type is known was assigned in the last century by Wieseler in reference to the mythical youth's obsession with his appearance. That identification was soon after rejected, and a recent suggestion of Hyakinthos has not met with widespread acceptance.[5]

1. P. Zanker, *Klassizistische Statuen* (Mainz, 1974), 26; D. Arnold, *Die Polykletnachfolge, JdI-EH* 25 (1969), 54–64, 91–93, 252–259; C. von Hees Landwehr, *Die antiken Gipsabgüssen aus Baiae,* Archäologische Forschungen 14 (Berlin, 1985), 100, nos. 59–62, pls. 58–59.
2. Landwehr (note 1) 102.
3. Robertson 334, 387. For the stele of Telesias, see B. Vierneisel-Schlörb, *Glyptothek München. Klassische Skulpturen* (Munich, 1979), 199; K. Schefold, "Die thronende Euthesion und Antigenes," *AntK* 13 (1970) 111; A. Conze, *Die attische Grabreliefs* (Berlin, 1900), II, no. 1036, pl. 208.
4. Robertson 467. Arnold (note 1) 256, no. 23 in Genoa and 258, no. 34 in Naples.
5. Arnold (note 1) 91–93, especially note 335.

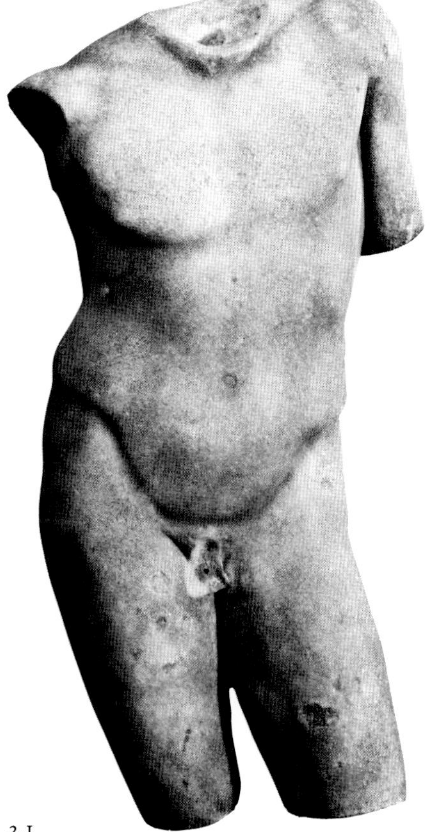

2.1

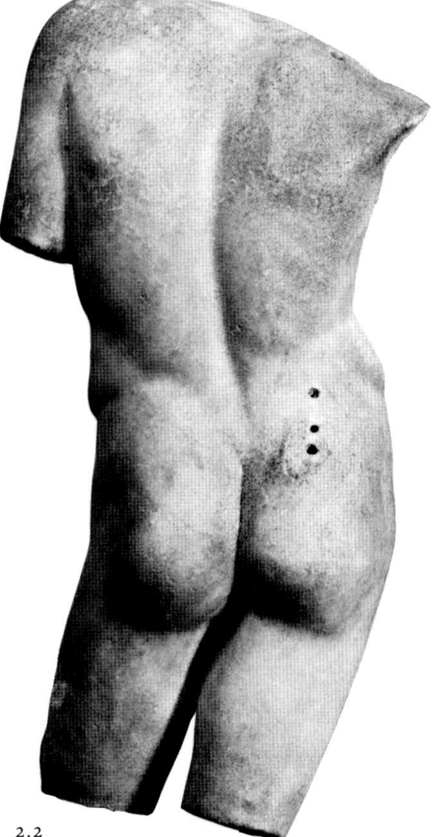

2.2

FEMALE HEAD FROM A
GRAVE RELIEF
400–375

23.220. Marble, probably Pentelic. Collections of
William Hepburn Buckler, Georgina Grenfell Buck-
ler (sale catalogue, Oxford, E. J. Brooks and Son,
October 8–9, 1953, 12, no. 234). Collection of
Ludwig and Renata Edelstein; bequeathed to the
Walters in 1965. Ht, 14.6 cm; W, 12.6 cm; Depth,
8.4 cm. Broken across neck; deposit over surface.

Female head in left profile, carved in high relief, is
broken away from the background. Her hair is
center-parted and rolled back from the face with the
ends gathered at the nape. The back of her hair is
roughly worked.

Exhibitions and Catalogues: *Ancient Art in American
Private Collections,* Fogg Art Museum (Cambridge,
December 28, 1954–February 15, 1955), catalogue
George M. A. Hanfmann, ed., 27, no. 154, pl. 40.

Publications: D. K. Hill, ''A Beautiful Greek
Head,'' *BWalt* 18 (1966) no. 5; D. K. Hill, ''Greek
Head in Baltimore,'' *Archaeology* 19 (1966) 288.

The head is certainly from an Attic grave
relief of the first quarter of the fourth century and illustrates the changes which
have taken place since the execution of the
Parthenon frieze (442–438). The trend of
development is toward a subtler delineation of the lower lid, recession of the
inner corner of the eye, narrowing of the
cheeks, and leveling off of the corners of
the lips, which are no longer downturned
as so often seen in the figures on the Panathenaic frieze. The result is a bland and
rather sweet expression. Color would
have enhanced and concealed the rough
surface of the hair.

The position of the neck and the forward gaze of her eyes indicates that the
woman was probably depicted as seated,
and facing a smaller servant figure at the
viewer's left. Slightly earlier in carving
details but very close in the treatment of
the face and hairstyle is the head of the
seated woman on a stele in the Louvre,
dated ca. 390.[1] Strikingly similar in facial
features and execution is the head of a
standing woman in profile view on the
recently excavated multi-figure relief
from Rhamnous, which has been dated
380–370.[2]

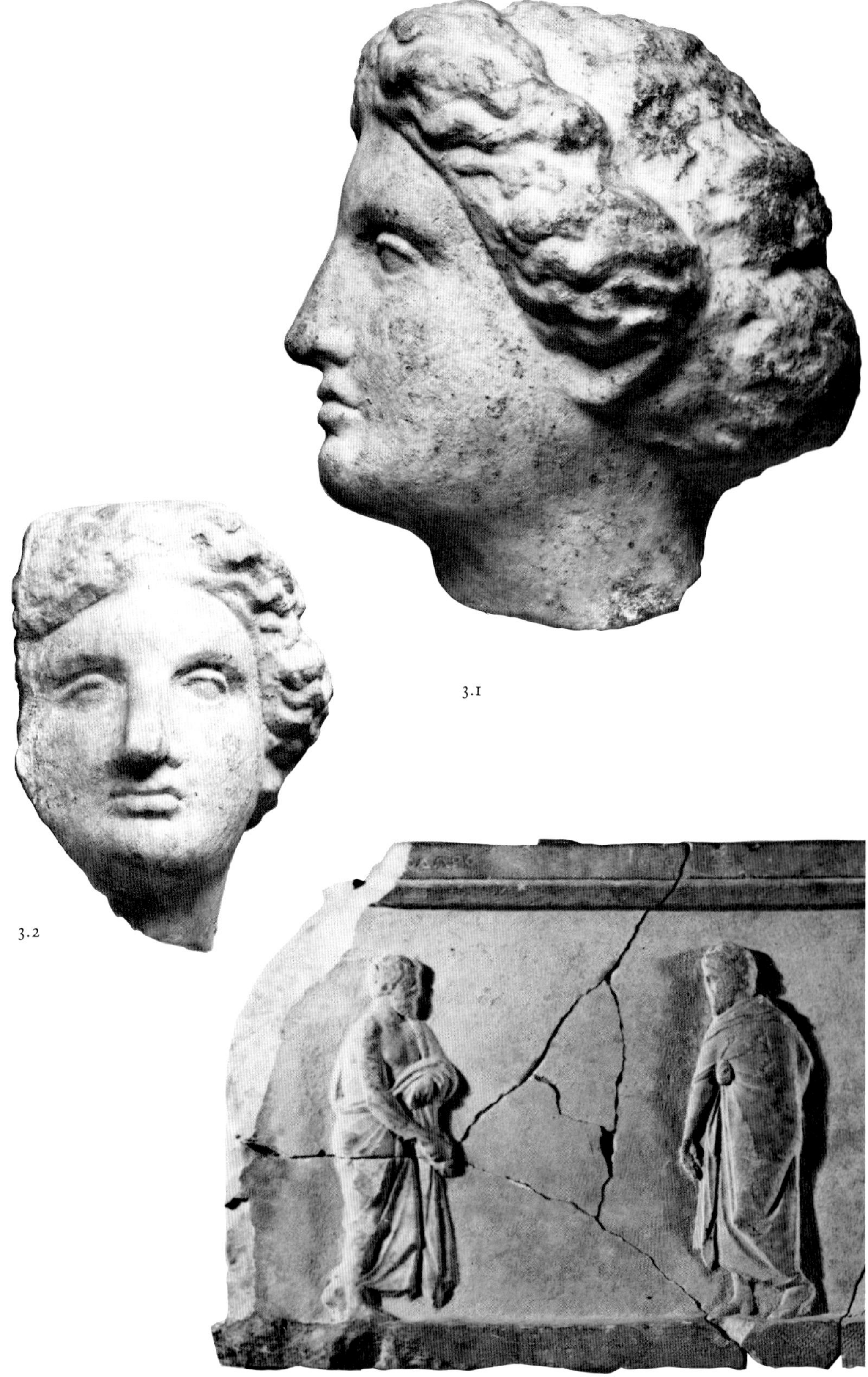

3.1

3.2

4.1

1. Paris, Louvre, Ma 830, Stele of Myrtia and ''Kephisia,''
   see most recently, J. Papaoikonomou, ''Η ΣΤΗΛΗ
   ΤΗΣ ΜΥΡΤΙΑΣ ΚΑΙ ΤΗΣ ''ΚΗΦΙΣΙΑΣ,'' *AAA* 14
   (1981) 95–104.
2. B. Petrakos, ''ΑΝΑΣΚΑΦΗ ΡΑΜΝΟΥΝΤΟΣ,''
   Prakt. (1976) pt. 1, 5–60.

Base from a Funerary Monument

360–340

23.185. Marble. Purchased from Brummer in 1926. L, 185.4 cm; Ht, 48.2 cm; Th, 10 cm. Mended from several pieces with sections missing from surface including left forearm of third figure from viewer's right. Broken at left edge; upper corner of opposite end chipped. Two clamp cuttings on upper surface, one in the middle, the other above the standing woman.

Eight figures appear in high relief above a projecting rectangular fascia which serves as a groundline. The molding above their heads has a projecting fillet above a cavetto. Letters are inscribed on the fillet above each figure's head. From the viewer's left: a bearded male stands in right profile with his weight on his right leg, his left foot resting only on the toes behind him. His right arm is extended and his left forearm is held in front of his waist and appears to rest on a staff which may have been indicated in paint. A mantle is drawn over his left shoulder, brought behind his back, and wrapped clockwise over his left forearm; the ends fall to his ankles. On the molding above his head are the letters:]ΟΔΩΡΟ. Facing him is a second bearded man who stands in left profile with his left leg relaxed, his left arm hanging at his side. His mantle is draped over his body revealing only his left forearm. The figure's posture and a bunch of drapery beneath the left elbow suggest that a staff (which was probably indicated in paint) rested under his left arm. Above his head: ΘΕΟΜΗΔΗΣ. In a group of three persons, a woman is seated on a klismos, in right profile, her feet on a stool. She wears a chiton beneath a mantle which frames her shoulder and is draped over her lower body; her hair is pulled back to the nape in a bun. Her left forearm is upraised to her chin; her right arm is extended to clasp the extended right hand of a facing bearded man. His left relaxed leg rests slightly behind him. His mantle covers his lower body; the ends are thrown over the left shoulder and expose his right breast, right arm, and his left arm beneath the shoulder. Other folds are bunched beside his left elbow. Behind the seated woman is another bearded man turned three-quarters to his left, who relaxes his advanced left leg. His left forearm is upraised to his beard; his right arm is bent at the elbow with the hand resting upon the drapery on the right side of his waist. His mantle is draped over his left shoulder and lower body, exposing the right arm and chest. Above the figures' heads are the inscriptions from left to right: ΙΠΠΟΜΑΧΟΣ ΘΕΟΜΝΗΣΤΗ ΚΗΦΙΣΟΔΩΡΟΣ.

The last group consists of a standing bearded man turned slightly to his left with the right leg relaxed. His mantle is draped over his left shoulder and is brought across his body beneath his chest; the folds extend to his ankles. The hand of his extended right arm clasps the right hand of a bearded male seated on a klismos, his feet resting on a footstool. His torso is turned three-quarters to his left; his legs are in left profile. His mantle hangs down his back and lies across his waist and lower legs; his left forearm rests along the back of the klismos. Behind him stands a woman turned three-quarters to her right, her relaxed right leg slightly advanced. Her left arm lies across her waist; her right hand is upraised to her chin. She wears a chiton or peplos beneath a mantle that is draped over her left shoulder and arm and covers the body to midcalf. She has short curly hair. Above the figures' heads are the letters: ΜΟΙΡΟ‖ ΓΕΝΗΣ ΜΟΙΡΙΑΣ ΚΛΕΑΓΟΡΑ.

Publications: A. Brueckner, "Archäologische Gesellschaft an Berlin. Sitzung vom 20 April 1926," *AA* (1926) 274–276, fig. 4; *IG* II–III[2], pt. 3, 11646; B. Schmaltz, "Zu einer attischer Grabmalbasis des 4. Jahrhunderts v. Chr.," *AM* 93 (1978) 90–91, pls. 30–31; E. Kaninia, "ΑΝΑΓΛΥΦΗ ΒΑΣΗ ΕΠΙΤΥΜΒΙΑΣ ΣΤΗΔΗΣ ΣΤΟ ΜΟΥΣΕΙΟ ΤΟΥ ΠΕΙΡΑΙΑ," *ArchDelt* 32 (1977) 257–258; Vermeule, *Sculpture*, 107, no. 77; C. Clairmont, *Patrios Nomos, Public Burial in Athens During the Fifth and Fourth Centuries, B.C.,* BAR International Series 16 (Oxford, 1983), pt. 1, 69, note 57 and pt. 2, 274–275, pl. 7.

Both the anathyrosis and the clamp cuttings on the back tell us that the relief formed part of a monument, which we know was fairly large because the total length of one side was nearly two meters. The proportions and moldings suggest that the relief belonged to the socle of a grave monument similar to one recently discovered in Kallithea and dated to the second half of the fourth century.[1] The base of this monument was surmounted by sculpture in the round flanked by columns, and the entire structure was almost eight meters high. The funereal character of the Walters relief supports a similar use, and finds parallels in a relief from Sigeion, now in the British Museum, a fragment from Athens, and a

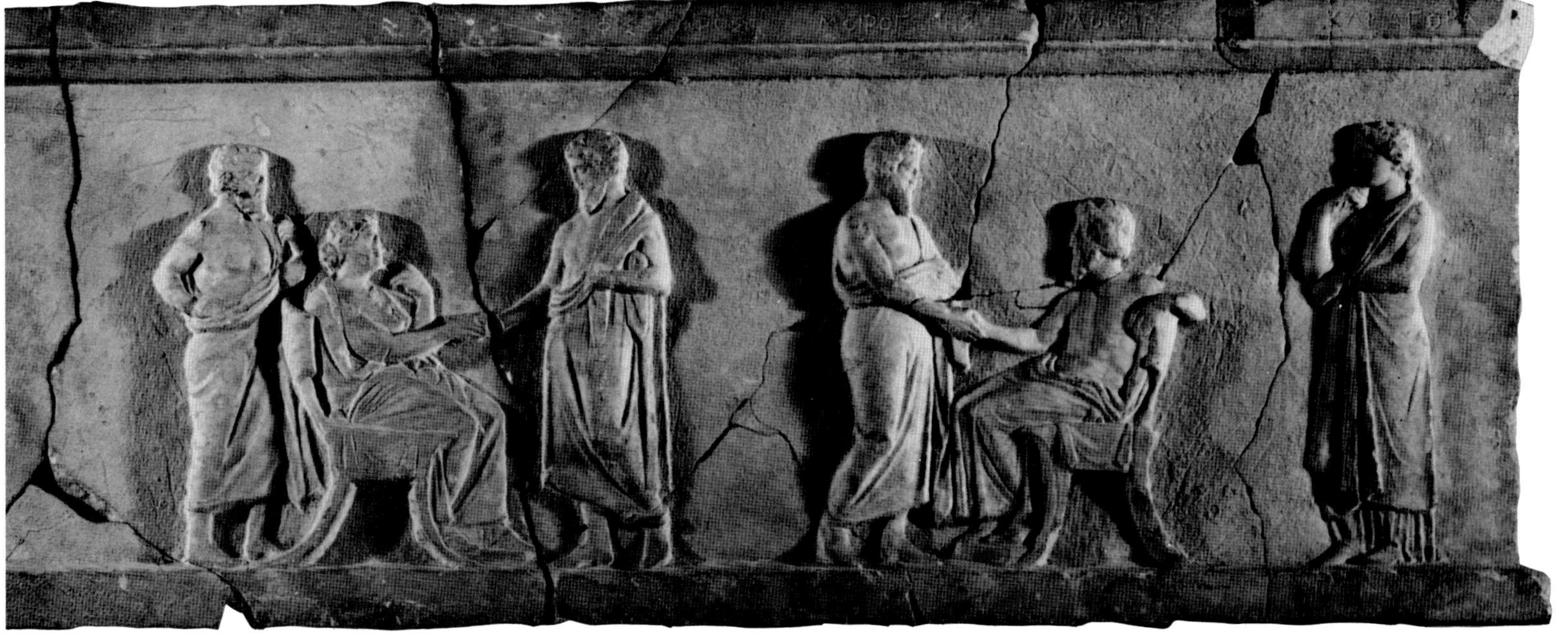

recently discovered relief from Nea Smyrni, now in the Piraeus Museum.[2] These four reliefs are strikingly similar in the wide spacing between the figures and in their poses, gestures, and garments. The seated woman on the Walters relief, for example, has parallels on the Nea Smyrni and Sigeion reliefs, and both the gentleman addressing her and the standing woman reappear on the relief from Nea Smyrni; similarly, the woman with the offering tray on the Nea Smyrni relief has a close counterpart on the Sigeion example and also compares well with the maiden on the fragmentary relief in Athens. Stylistic and iconographic analogies with Attic marble lekythoi and loutrophoroi place the Walters and Nea Smyrni reliefs among the Attic grave monuments of the middle of the fourth century, of which the Sigeion relief is certainly an Ionian adaptation.[3] The wide spacing of the figures looks forward to the monument of Lysikrates of 334 and suggests a date for the Walters relief between ca. 360 and 340.

In Attic grave iconography, the seated female is generally recognized as the deceased, and she is almost certainly to be identified as such on the Nea Smyrni and Sigeion reliefs where she is the central, focal figure.[4] On the Walters relief all the figures are commemorated by inscriptions executed by the same hand; the most logical explanation is that at the time the base was commissioned, stock figures were selected to correspond with deceased family members whose names were then inscribed on a monument which was intended as a family memorial.

Figural scenes on the bases of Attic grave monuments have forerunners in cult statue bases, but are probably more directly inspired by the East Greek tradition of funerary monuments, familiar from Xanthos, Gjölbaschi, and the Mausoleum of Halikarnassos. The Walters relief, then, contributes further evidence for the influence that the East Greek world exerted on late Classical mainland art, a phenomenon of which the Erechtheion is a prime exponent. At the same time, the easy repetition of stock figures on the Walters relief and its parallels reveals an exhaustion with the formulaic solutions of the Classical era, an attitude that would prove responsive to the revitalizing spirit of the Hellenistic age.

1. E. Tsirivakos, "Kallithea. Ergebnisse der Ausgrabung," *AAA* 4 (1971) 108–110; C. Clairmont, *Patrios Nomos,* 69–70.
2. For the Sigeion relief, see E. Pfuhl and H. Möbius, *Die ostgriechischen Grabreliefs* (Mainz, 1977), 34, no. 86, pl. 21; Clairmont (note 1) 69–70; H. Möbius, "Eigenartige attische Grabrelief," *AM* 81 (1966) 154, fig. 86. For the fragment, see K. Dabaras, "ΑΝΑΣΚΑΦΑΙ ΠΕΡΙΣΤΔΔΟΓΗΣ ΚΑΙ ΤΥΧΑΙΑ ΕΥΡΗΜΑΤΑ," *ArchDelt* 20B (1965) pt. 1, 118, no. 7, pl. 89. For the Nea Smyrni relief, see E. Kaninia, *ArchDelt* 32 (1977) pl. 83; H. W. Catling, *AR* (1982–83) 10, fig. 10.
3. B. Schmaltz, *AM* 93 (1978) 86–88.
4. Ibid., 85, 92.

FRAGMENT OF A GRAVE RELIEF

360–340

23.174. Marble, probably Pentelic. Purchased from Brummer in 1924. Ht, 52.7 cm; W, 52.7 cm; Th, 12 cm. Sides smooth with moldings continuing from front; top and back rough. Broken down left side and across bottom.

Within a naiskos with side antae are the head and upper torso of a bearded man turned to his right, his head in left profile and inclined. His mantle is draped over his left shoulder. Beside him in lower relief is the frontal face of a girl with short curly hair. The edge of her mantle is visible over her left shoulder. Above their heads is a low architrave bearing the letters:] ⋀⋀ ΤΗ ΚΛΕΟΜΑΧΟΤ ΘΤΓΑΤΗΡ ΦΕΙΔΙΠΠΟΤ ΓΤΝΕ The architrave is surmounted by a fascia resembling a sima, or roof edge, lined with antefixes. In the center of the triangular space above is a frontal winged siren, her left arm at her waist, her right hand uplifted to her brow. In the corner is a dove in left profile, its head turned back in right profile; only the chest of its counterpart survives in the opposite corner.

Publications: *IG* II–III[2], pt. 3, 11865a; Vermeule, *Sculpture,* 126, no. 97.

The composition conforms to a well-known type in which a standing male in three-quarters view gazes down at a seated female, who is attended by a frontal servant figure standing between them. Although inscriptions might identify almost any figure in a composition as the deceased, the seated female in this compositional type is usually thought to be the commemorated individual, an assumption here confirmed by the inscription which can be completed: "Kallistrate, daughter of Kleomaxos, wife of Pheidippos." The Classical rendering of the man's facial features, combined with the frontal face of the servant, supports a date for the relief in the middle of the fourth century. Typical of grave reliefs of this date is the grieving gesture of the siren, which was a being long associated with the world of the deceased. The mournful mood is here reinforced by the dove whose head, nestled in its wing, injects emotional content into the age-old device of symmetrically

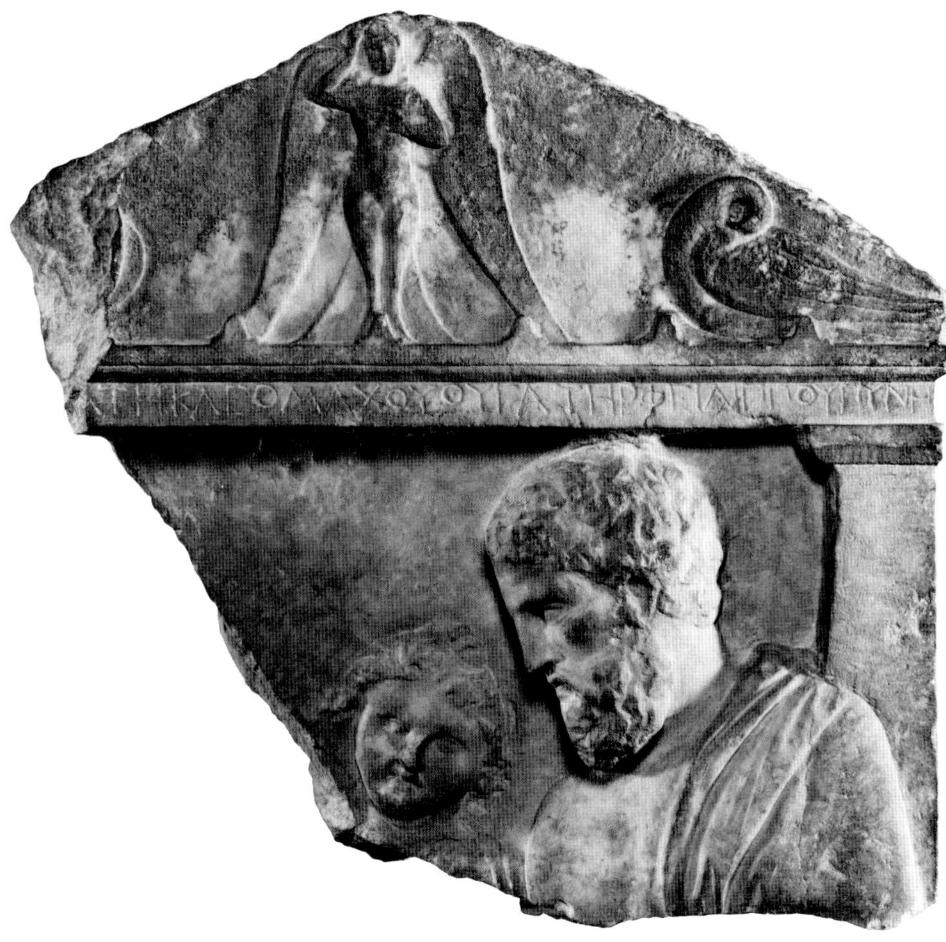

5.1

flanking animals with heads reversed.[1] Although their overt display of sorrow presages the emotion of Hellenistic art, these pedimental figures are still very much in the Classical tradition wherein grief was expressed primarily through posture and gesture.

The head of the man shows strong similarities with a head on another fragmentary stele in West Berlin, dated by Blümel to the third quarter of the fourth century; this stele is also crowned by a siren.[2]

1. For stelai crowned by a siren flanked by doves, see D. Woysch-Méautis, *La représentation des animaux et des êtres fabuleux sur les monuments funéraires grecs* (Lausanne, 1982), 123, nos. 238–249.
2. C. Blümel, *Die klassischen Skulpturen der Staatlichen Museen zu Berlin* (Berlin, 1966), 42, no. 41 (K 45), fig. 58.

STATUE OF A POURING SATYR

Roman copy, possibly after a bronze original of ca. 370–360

23.22. Marble, probably Pentelic. Found at Porto d'Anzio in the 1890s. Mengarini Collection. Purchased from Brummer in 1928. Ht, 106.7 cm; W, 37 cm. Hole in side of left buttock for attachment of left forearm; another, smaller hole below small of back. Back of left thigh smoothed away for statue support. Broken below knees. Right arm broken at shoulder. Part of left upper arm survives. Right ear broken away as well as two clusters of berries, one above forehead, other above left eye. Chipping across abdomen and front of left thigh. Several cracks over surface. Top of buttocks restored in plaster.

A nude youth stands on his left leg, his right knee bent and slightly advanced. His left upper arm hangs close to his side; his right arm was raised. His head is turned three-quarters to the left and inclined. His left ear has a pointed tip. He has short curly hair and wears a tainia just above the brow, and a narrower one above it to which three clumps of berries (korymboi) were attached. The hole in the small of his back probably served for the attachment of a tail.

Publications: W. Klein, *Praxiteles* (Leipzig, 1898), 192, no. 12, figs. 30, 31 on 198–199; A. Maviglia, "Del Satiro versante e della sua attribuzione a Prassitele," *Bollettino della commissione archeologica municipale* 38, fasc. II–III (1910) 5, fig. 1; F.Weege, *Der einschenkende Satyr aus der Sammlung Mengarini,* 89 *BWPr* 89 (1929), passim, figs. 2–5, pls. I–II; G.Rizzo, *Prassitele* (Milan, 1932), 17–20, pls. 24–25. *Handbook of the Collection: The Walters Art Gallery* (Baltimore, 1936), 30; R. L. Shoolman and C. E. Slatkin, *The Enjoyment of Art in America* (Philadelphia, 1942), pl. 44; C. Picard, *Manuel d'archéologie grecque* III.2 (Paris, 1948), 429, pl. 170 and 430–431, pl. 171; G. M. A. Richter, *The Metropolitan Museum of Art: Catalogue of Greek Sculptures* (Cambridge, 1954), 110, no. 108; D. K. Hill, "The Roman Collection of the Walters Art Gallery," *Archaeology* 10 (1957) 21; D. K. Hill, "The Spectacular in the Classical," *Apollo* 84 (1966) 453–454; P. Gercke, *Satyrn des Praxiteles* (Hamburg, 1968), 1, no. 1, and passim; G. Lippold, *Die griechische Plastik,* Handbuch der Archäologie III.1, 5th ed., W. Otto and R. Herbig, eds. (Munich, 1950), 237, note 4; R. Muthmann, *Statuenstützen und dekoratives Beiwerk an griechischen und römischen Bildwerken* (Heidelberg, 1951), 32–33.

About twenty-four statues or fragments of the Pouring Satyr type have been identified, of which the Walters example is considered to have the finest head. All but two examples were found in Italy, including the Walters satyr, which was discovered in the 1890s during construction of the Villa Mengarini in Antium. Nearby was a niche where the figure presumably stood, almost certainly serving the same decorative, domestic function to which most of the Italian examples can be assigned; three, for example, flanked the staircase of Domitian's villa at Castel Gandolfo.[1]

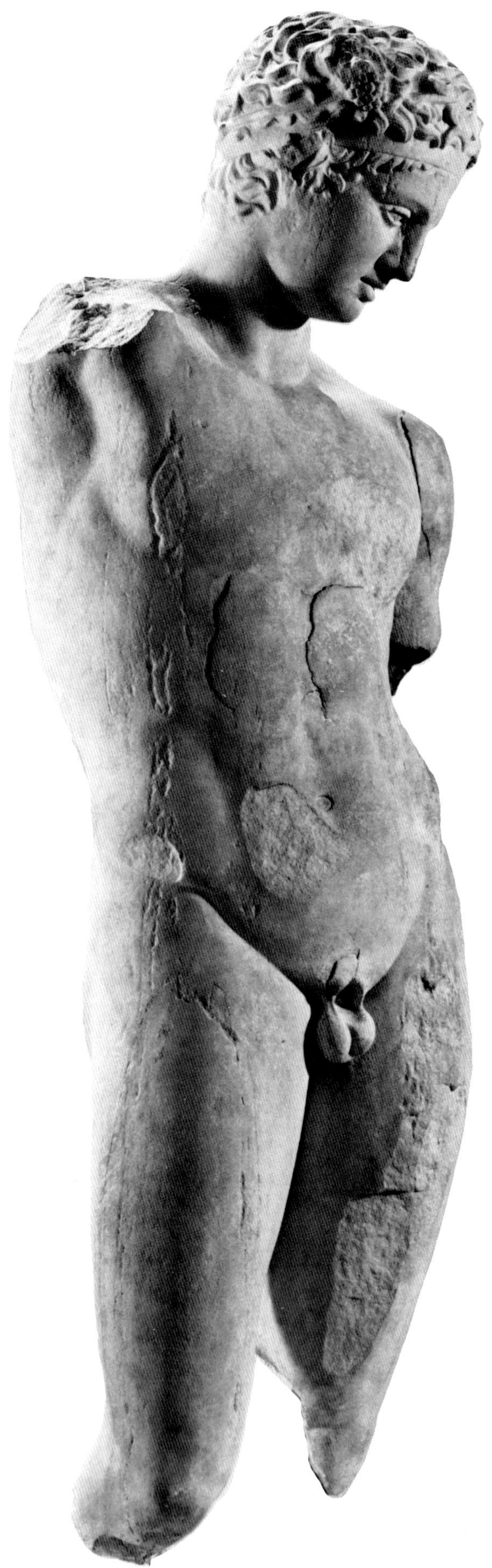

6.1

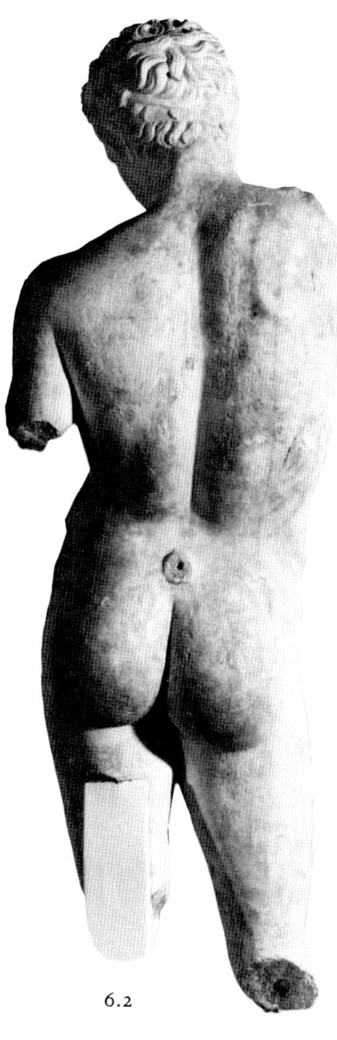

6.2

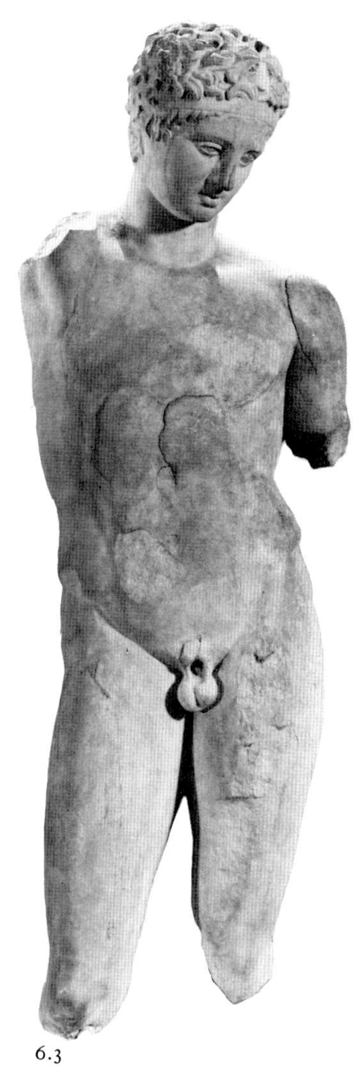

6.3

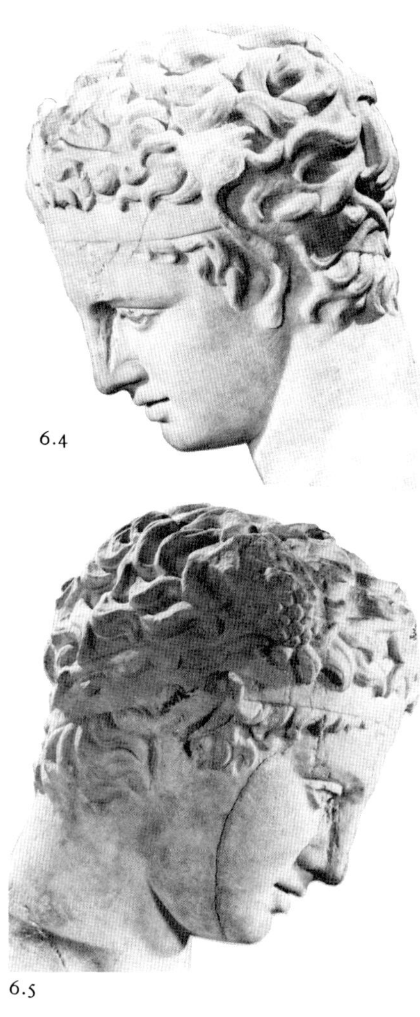

6.4

6.5

The prototype of the statues of the Pouring Satyr type was almost certainly bronze because the struts on the marble copies are in unsightly positions at the left thigh or extend from the head to the upraised left arm. Not all the copies had a tail, which may not have existed on the prototype, although the survival of more than ten heads confirms the existence of satyr ears. Fragments of a jug in the right hand of one example and, on another, the outstretched open left palm tell us that the satyr was in the act of pouring from a jug in his upraised right hand to a phiale in his extended left hand, a gesture easily traced back to the fourth century where youths in the act of pouring are seen on grave reliefs and a hydria handle.[2] Still unattested, however, is a fourth-century example of a pouring satyr.

On statues of the Pouring Satyr the adolescent form, the refined Classical features, and the sweet expression have long suggested Praxitelean influence. The attribution of the original Pouring Satyr to Praxiteles himself has been argued on the basis of literary references to satyrs exe-

cuted by Praxiteles, specifically a passage in Pausanias who, after speaking of a satyr by Praxiteles in the street of the Tripods, refers to a pouring "satyr pais" in the temple of Dionysos.[3] It has not always been recognized that Pausanias is actually speaking of two different works; furthermore, it is not at all certain that Pausanias attributes the "satyr pais" to Praxiteles.[4] Given both the textual ambiguity and that satyrs in the fourth century were still rendered with bestial features, one cannot discount the possibility that the prototype of the Pouring Satyr, whether the same or a different work from the pouring "satyr pais," was a later Hellenistic or Roman creation in the Praxitelean style.

Of uncertain relation to the Pouring Satyr are the statues of the Oil Pourer of the Munich-Dresden type, which have been attributed to a post-Polykleitan statue that is claimed as the prototype of the Pouring Satyr. The Oil Pourer type has also been identified as a work of the Lysippan school, in which case it could be derived from either a fourth-century type of pouring youth, or, should he have then existed, of the Pouring Satyr.[5]

1. For the most recent summary of the subject, see P. Gercke, *Satyrn*, 1–17.

2. For the grave reliefs, see J. N. Svoronos, *Das Athener Nationalmuseum* (Athens, 1903–37), I, 533–542, no. 195, pl. 84; C. C. Vermeule, *Sculpture in Stone: The Greek, Roman and Etruscan Collections of the Museum of Fine Arts, Boston* (Boston, 1976), 55, no. 82. For the hydria handle, see J. Charbonneaux, *Greek Bronzes* (London, 1962), 64, pl. 9.1.

3. The satyr by Praxiteles is mentioned in Pausanias 1.20.1. The satyr "pais," located in the temple to Dionysos, is mentioned in Pausanias 1.20.2.

4. See the discussion in Gercke (note 1) 71, 75, 81, 84; Robertson 390 and 688, notes 80–81.

5. Ridgway 85, pls. 112–113; A. F. Stewart, "Lysippan Studies 2. Agias and Oilpourer," *AJA* 82 (1978) 301–313; J. Inan, *Roman Sculpture in Side* (Ankara, 1975), 72–74, no. 20, pls. 32–33; D. Arnold, *Die Polykletnachfolge, JdI-EH* 25 (1969) 240–241, pls. 29–31; C. C. Vermeule, "Greek, Etruscan and Roman Sculptures in Boston," *AJA* 68 (1964) 327, pl. 100, fig. 10; D. Ohly, *The Munich Glyptothek: Greek and Roman Sculpture* (Munich, 1974), 36, pl. 13.

HEAD OF EROS
Roman copy of original by Lysippos of 340–336

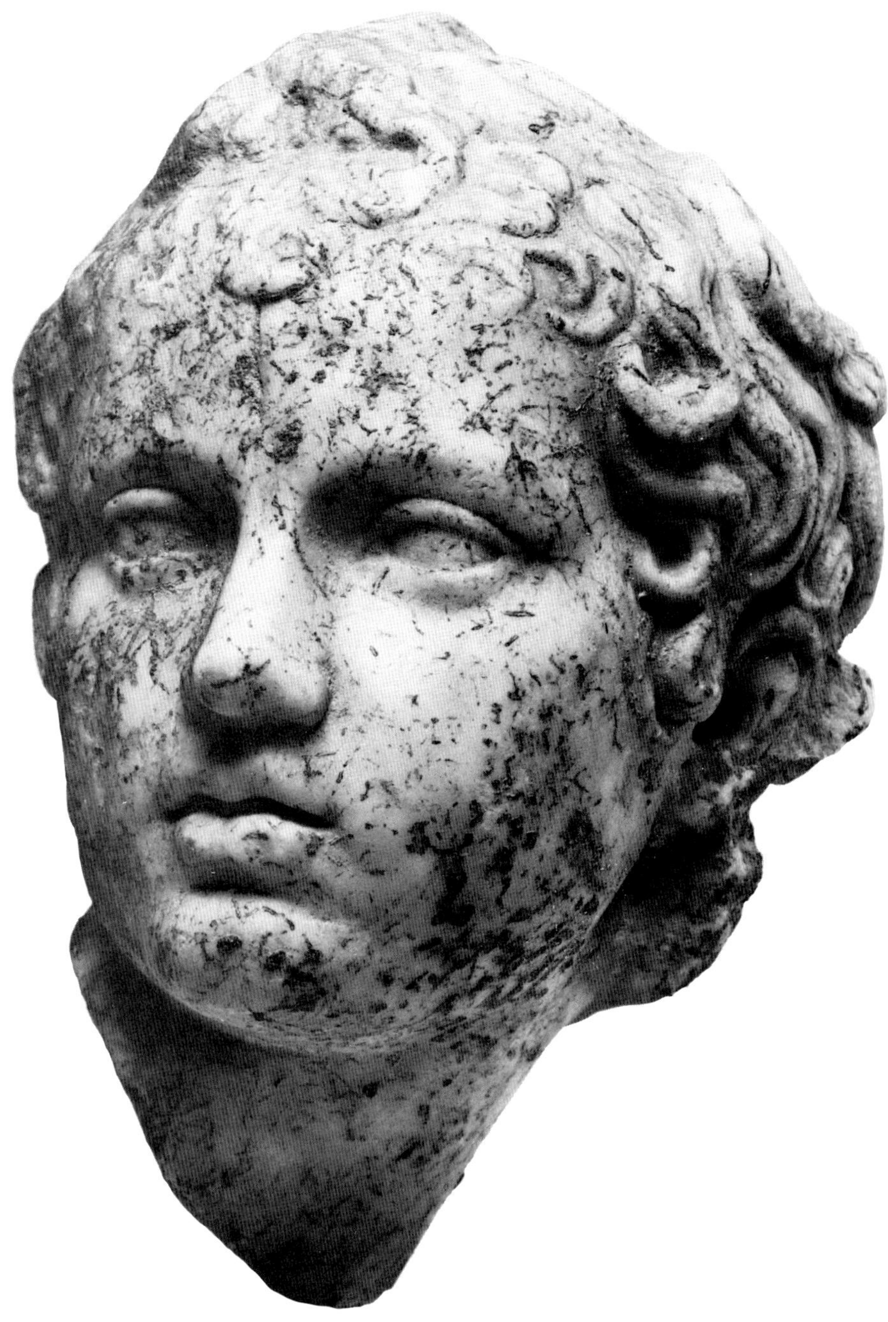

7.1

23.25. Marble. "From Capua." Purchased from Canessa in 1917. Ht, 26 cm; W, 17.8 cm; Depth, 19.9 cm. Broken across neck; encrustation over surface.

A boy's head is turned to his right on a sharply angled neck. He has a braid drawn back from his forehead over the top of his head; short curly hair is rolled up at the nape.

Publications: G. W. Elderkin, "A Marble Head of Eros," *Art in America* 5 (1917) 192–193; F. P. Johnson, *Lysippos* (Durham, 1927), 107, no. 9; Bieber, *Sculpture,* 38, n. 36, fig. 88; D. K. Hill, "More About Hellenistic Sculpture," *BWalt* 15 (1963) no. 7; Robertson 703, n. 49; H. Dohl, *Der Eros des Lysipp—Frühhellenistische Eroten* (Diss. Göttingen, 1968).

The statue to which this head belonged was a Roman copy of a work that represented Eros with his bow. The prototype is generally believed to be a bronze statue that, according to Pausanias, was created by Lysippos for the sanctuary of Eros at Thespiae.[1] Also seen by Pausanias at Thespiae was a Praxitelean statue of Eros which has curiously not been identified in copies, in contrast with the more than forty examples that have been recognized of the Lysippan work.

The Lysippan Eros may have been approximately contemporary with the sculptor's most famous work, the Apoxyomenos, which is dated to 340–330 and which displays the same pose and gesture, with the weight about to be transferred to the right foot and the arms brought forward and across the torso.[2] Also comparable in both works are the reliance on ancillary objects to complete the meaning of the composition, and an abrupt angularity, seen in the turn of Eros's head and in the thrust of the Apoxyomenos's right hand, which grasps the strigil. Also common to both is the momentary nature of the action, although a recent study of stringing and unstringing scenes suggests that Lysippos's Eros may only be testing the tautness of the bow.[3] Regardless of the specific activity in which Eros is engaged, there is a notable absence of any tension or effort in the countenance, which exhibits only a placid, musing expression that is not conventionally associated with Lysippos, although the full, short lips are also seen on the Apoxyomenos.

The Walters head is recognized as one of the finest copies of the Lysippan work, ranking with examples in Benghazi, London, Paris, Venice, and Rome. The sweetness of the countenance looks forward to the Hellenistic fascination with children's faces, but the boyish form favored by Lysippos contrasts with Hellenistic depictions of Eros as a baby (Nos. 89, 90).

1. Pollitt 48, fig. 40. Pausanias, 9.27.3; Bieber, *Sculpture,* 38; Robertson 466; Ridgway 74. See also B. F. Cook, *The Townley Marbles* (London, 1985), 30, fig. 29.
2. Pollitt 47.
3. T. Seki, "Eine neue Schale mit Bogenschützen," *AA* (1981) 52–53.

Attic Red-Figure Bell Krater by the Painter of Vienna 1089
Early fourth century

48.73. Clay. Massarenti Collection. Purchased in 1902. Ht, 37.2 cm; D, mouth 38.5 cm; D, base 18.8 cm. Relief lines for profiles of faces and some other contours on side A. Dilute glaze for some details of hair, drapery, wings, headgear, and for the anatomy of the winged figure. Flesh of Eros white. Glaze chipped. Body of Eros abraded. Ancient repair for part of rim.

The base has splaying sides with reserved bands around top and bottom. Between the handles is a figured scene above a band of three or four stopt meanders alternating with a checkerboard square. A laurel band runs above the picture. Around the base of the handle attachments is a band with dotted pattern. Side A depicts a nude winged Eros seated three-quarters to the right, his right leg crossed over the left, who gazes behind, his head in right profile, his arm resting on drapery which is spread beneath. He has short curly hair with long locks to the shoulder surmounted by a headband. Above and below are leafy stalks. Meeting the gaze of this figure is a woman standing three-quarters to her right, a striped scepter leaning against her left shoulder and resting against her left hand at her hip. Her right forearm is raised and her hand fingers the drapery. She wears a peplos which has a wave motif around the neckline and an overfold girded by a belt whose four corded ends terminate in knobs. Her hair is swept back from her brow beneath three narrow strings with leafy attachments and is gathered at the back of her head. She also wears a bracelet and ball earring. Behind her is a nude youth seated slightly to his left, his head turned back in left profile. A staff grasped in his right hand is also supported by his left hand which rests against his knee. His mantle, or chlamys, is draped beneath him. There is a petasos behind his left shoulder and upon his short hair he wears a headband with leafy attachments. Standing to Eros's right is a maiden turned slightly to her right, her head turned back in right profile, her weight on her right leg with the left leg relaxed and the knee advanced. Her right elbow is bent with the forearm upraised and the fingers at her shoulder; her left elbow rests upon a chest with scroll-like decoration. She is dressed similarly to her counterpart beside Eros. She wears a necklace, bracelets, and earring, and her long hair is gathered behind her neck beneath a headband with leafy attachments. To her right, standing in right profile, is Hermes, his left arm at his side with the fingers extended and his right hand, extended in front of his waist, holding a kerykeion. His chlamys is fastened at his throat and thrown over his left shoulder and behind his back; his winged petasos hangs behind his shoulder. He wears a headband to which leaves are attached.

On Side B, three standing youths wear their mantles fastened on the left shoulder, exposing the right shoulder and covering the rest of their bodies to the ankles. The figure to the viewer's left stands in right profile, a strigil in his outstretched right hand. In front of him, also in right profile, is a youth with right arm and hand outstretched. Facing him in left profile is a youth holding in his right hand a cord from which an aryballos (?) is suspended. Another one hangs on the wall behind.

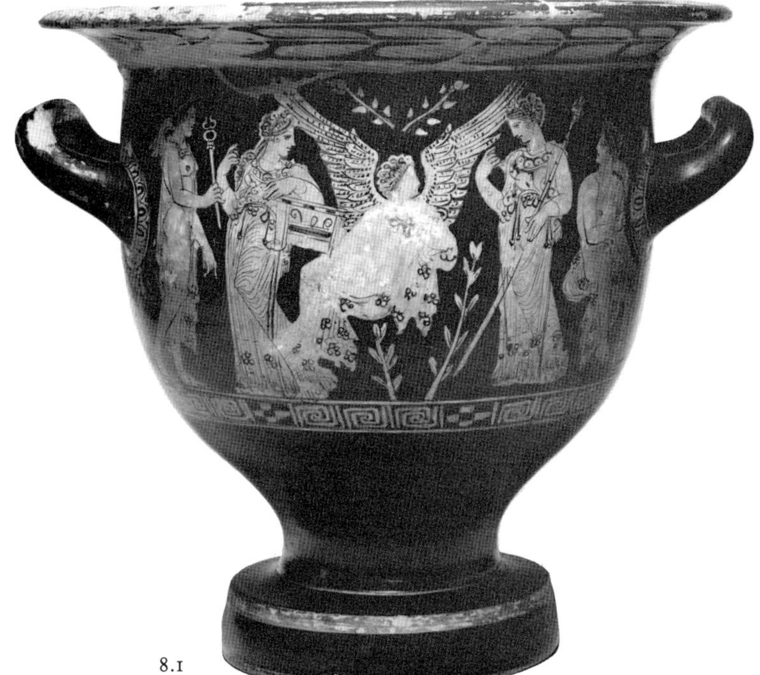

8.1

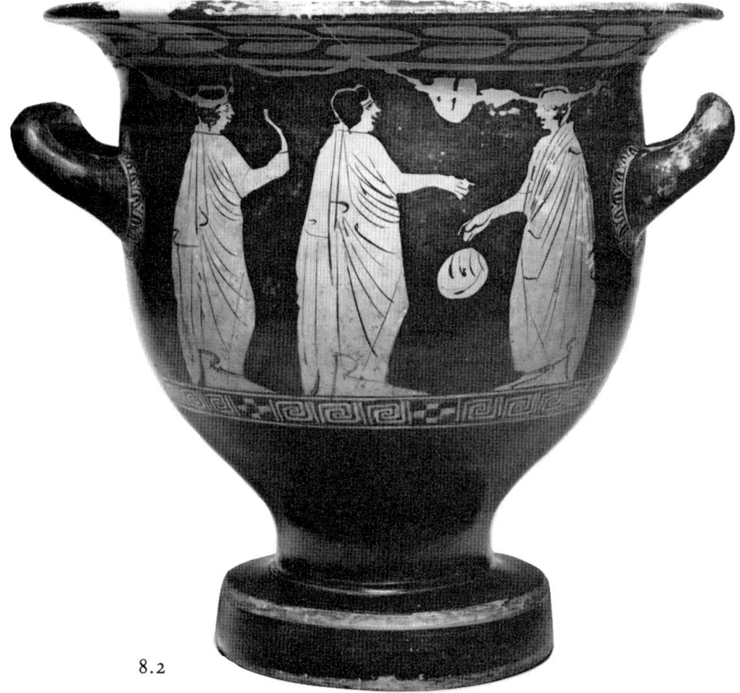

8.2

Beazley attributed this vase to the Plainer Group and specifically to the Painter of Vienna 1089, perhaps an early stage of the Painter of Louvre G508.[1] The subject is uncertain. To Eros's right stands Hermes and a goddess with a chest; to his left are a seated youth and a goddess whose staff suggests that she is Aphrodite. Typical of early fourth-century vase-painting are the languorous gathering of figures with stock, and often affected, poses and gestures, the absence of a consistent ground line, the proliferation of small lines in the rendering of garment folds, and the multi-plicity of decorative detail on the garment edges. The composition is clearly additive, and where two figures overlap, the juxta-position is awkward, particularly in the way Eros's left foot is bisected by the goddess's leg. The lack of seriousness in both subject matter and execution fore-shadows the demise of the red-figure tradition.

The conventional and sketchily executed scene on the reverse may depict a palaestra scene to which the aryballos and strigil are appropriate.

1. *ARV*[2], 1423.

Publications: Esbroeck, pt. 2, 32, no. 171; *ARV*[2], 1423, no. 2.

RED-FIGURE LEKYTHOS IN
THE KERCH STYLE BY THE
APOLLONIA PAINTER
360–350

48.84. Clay. Found in Apollonia, Thrace, in 1884–
85. Collections of Prince Boris Chatohoskoy; N. M.
Pacha; von Branteghem. Purchased about 1909. Ht,
35.6 cm; D, base 13.2 cm; D, rim 10.5 cm. Women's
garments in heavy paste, now green. Relief line and
dilute glaze for interior markings. White slip for
bodies. Traces of gilt. Pigment on bodies of women
abraded. Green on cloak of seated woman with
astragaloi and on cloak of standing woman behind
satyr. The woman with a bird in each hand has a
blue mantle and gold stephane. Gold on the wings of
the Erotes, blossoms of the plants, and the legs of
the klismos. Green and gold on the satyr's leafy
wreath. Neck and handle repaired.

The lekythos has a carinated shoulder; the base is
ribbed with the lower rib reserved, the upper one
glazed. Beneath the figural scene and between narrow reserved bands is a band of four stopt meander
squares alternating with a checkerboard pattern. A
woman seated three-quarters to her right in a high-
backed chair with turned legs leans forward, her
right arm extended and the fingers outstretched.
Above and below her hand are dots indicating
astragaloi. She wears a chiton beneath a mantle
which is brought over her left shoulder, frames her
back, and lies over her waist and legs. Her feet rest
on a footstool. She wears two bracelets on each arm
and a necklace. She gazes at her hand, her head
turned three-quarters to her right, her hair pulled
back from her face and gathered in a knot above her
brow. Holding a laurel wreath above her head with
the outstretched left hand is a nude, frontal winged
figure, the right arm extended out to the side, the
curly hair knotted at the crown with headband and
earring. Opposite the woman is a satyr seated on a
pile of rocks in right profile, his left leg drawn back.
His right arm is outstretched in front of him with an
astragalos resting on top of it; his left arm lies across
his waist with wrist bent, the palm and extended
fingers facing the viewer. He has a pointed ear, a
beard, curly hair to his shoulders, and a leafy wreath.
Standing behind him is a frontal woman who gazes
to her left, her right hand fingering her mantle
above her shoulders, her left elbow possibly resting
against a tree trunk. She wears a chiton which slips
off her right shoulder and a mantle which is brought
over her left shoulder and across her body. Part of
the mantle or a separate veil is draped over her head.
She wears a bracelet, earring, and beaded necklace.
At her right shoulder is a second flying nude figure
with arms outstretched, wavy hair gathered in a
knot at the crown. A thin stalk with clusters of blossoms grows beneath him. To the right side of this
figure a nude youth stands in right profile, his left
knee bent with the foot resting only on the toes
placed behind his right foot. He leans forward upon
a staff surmounted by his drapery, which is placed
beneath his left arm. His right elbow is bent with
the forearm resting beneath his armpit. His head,
seen in right profile, is inclined; he has short curly
hair beneath a laurel wreath.

On the viewer's right behind the seated woman is
a woman standing on rocky terrain, her left arm at

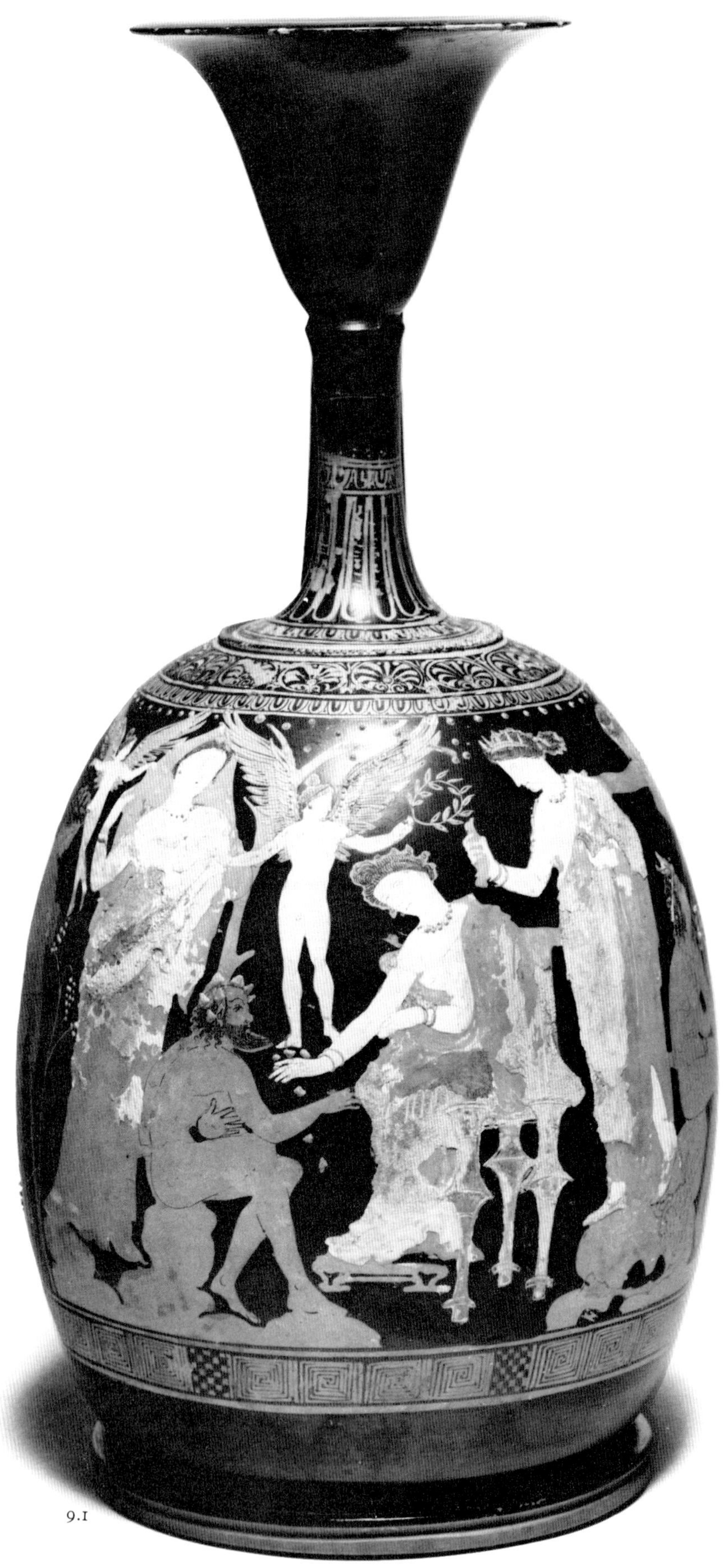

9.1

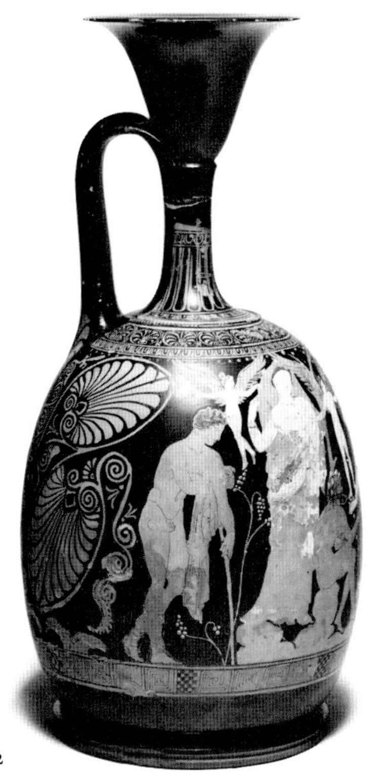

9.2

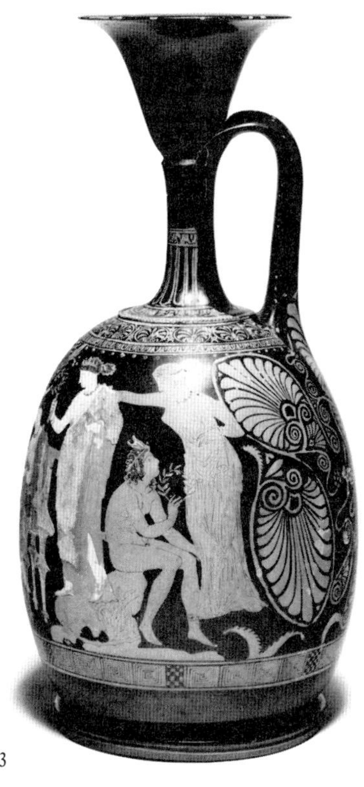

9.3

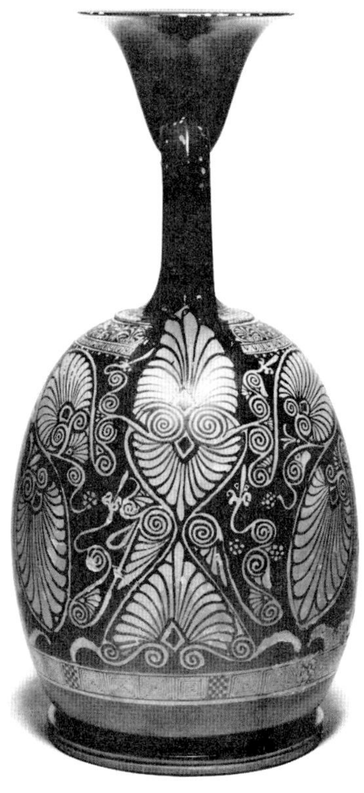

9.4

her waist, a bird in each hand. She wears two bracelets and a necklace. Above her chiton her mantle
passes over her left shoulder and covers her body to
her ankles. She gazes at the seated woman with her
head in left profile. Beneath a spiked diadem her hair
is pulled back to a knot above the nape. Behind her
and seated on a rocky terrain over which his
fawnskin is draped and on which his club is resting is
a nude Pan in right profile with goat horns, animal
tail, and pointed ears, wearing a narrow fillet to
which berries are attached. With his right hand he
offers a laurel crown; his left arm disappears behind
the draped leg of a standing woman turned to her
right and wearing a peplos. Her right arm is outstretched to the shoulder of the maiden in front of
her. She wears two bracelets, an earring, and a necklace. Beneath a fillet her hair is swept back from her
face to a knot at the back of her head. Above the figures is a row of dots in relief beneath bands of
tongue, palmette, and a raised beaded ridge. The
neck of the lekythos is encircled by a row of elongated tongues between rows of narrow ones.
Beneath the handle and enclosed by scrolls are three
palmettes, an inverted one beneath the uppermost.
On each side are two angled palmettes with elaborate scrolls between them.

Exhibitions and Catalogues: *The Taste of Maryland,*
The Walters Art Gallery (Baltimore, May 18–
August 19, 1984), 63, no. 128.

Publications: *Handbook of the Collection: The Walters
Art Gallery* (Baltimore, 1936), 34; G. M. A. Richter,
review of K. Schefold, *Untersuchungen zu den Kertscher Vasen* (Berlin-Leipzig, 1934), in *AJA* 39 (1935)
280–281; H. Metzger, *Les représentations dans la
céramique attique du IVe siècle, BEFAR* 172 (1951) 398,
n. 3; D. K. Hill, "A Late Athenian Vase," *BWalt* 7
(1954) no. 1; E. Simon, "Daphnis and Nymphe,"
JWalt 25–26 (1962–63) 29–37, figs. 1–4; K. Schefold,
Die Griechen und ihre Nachbarn (Berlin, 1967), 228,
pl. 22; K. Schefold, *Der Göttersage in der klassischen
und hellenistischen Kunst* (Munich, 1981), 286–287 and
287, fig. 408; *LIMC* II (1984) pt. 1, 30, no. 191, pt.
2, pl. 22.

This vase was discovered at Apollonia, a
city on the Thracian coast of the Black
Sea, which has yielded a number of examples of Kerch ware, a style of Attic pottery that was exported widely to the
Black Sea area between ca. 370 and 330.
Two vases found in Apollonia and now in
Berlin and Leningrad undoubtedly came
from the same workshop and have given
their name to a group which now numbers about eight examples and to which
the Walters lekythos has been attributed
by Simon.[1] The vase is a superb example
of Kerch ware, which is recognized by the
abundant use of short lines and the generous application of added color.

The subject of the scene is clearly amorous although the participants cannot all
be identified. In a rural setting a nymph,
seated on a throne usually associated with
brides, triumphs at knucklebones, which
is a game of love oracles that she plays
with a satyr wearing an ivy wreath.
Behind her stands a maiden holding the
traditional love-offering of a bird, and a
figure of Eros who extends a laurel
wreath. That wreath is identical to one
being proffered by a second Eros to a nude
youth leaning upon the staff traditionally
associated with the head of a household
and which, accordingly, suggests that he
is a bridegroom. To the youth's left and
flanked by the two Erotes stands Aphrodite, while on the viewer's far right a
seated Pan grasps the leg of another
maiden, certainly a nymph, while offering
her still another laurel wreath.

The proffering of laurel wreaths to all
but the unsuccessful satyr and the energetic participation of Erotes suggested to
Simon that the youth is Daphnis, whose
name means "Laurel," a mortal shepherd
whose love for a nymph was celebrated by
Theokritos.[2] Simon believed that the
rocky setting denotes the slopes of the
Akropolis where Pan was worshiped and
where was also located a sanctuary of the
Nymphs that was traditionally linked
with brides.[3] Another shrine in this area
was dedicated to Aphrodite and may have
housed the statue that served as the prototype for the figure of Aphrodite on the
vase.[4]

The positioning of the figures at different heights, the broken lines, and the
emphasis upon added color convey a restlessness that heralds the end of the red-
figure vase-painting style. Looking
forward to the Hellenistic age are the
bucolic and romantic themes as well as the
focus upon Aphrodite, nymphs, satyrs,
and Pan, all of whom became popular
subjects in Hellenistic art.

1. For the Apollonia Painter, see *ARV*[2], 1482. The example
   in Berlin is 1482,5; the vase in Leningrad is 1482,6. See K.
   Schefold, *Kertscher Vasen,* 102–4; K. Schefold, *Göttersage,*
   287; E. Simon, *JWalt* 25–26 (1962–63) 29.
2. Theokritos, *Idyll* 8. Simon (note 1) 30–37.
3. J. Travlos, *Dictionary of Ancient Athens* (New York, 1971),
   361.
4. *LIMC* II (1984) pt. 1, 30, no. 191.

Figurine Vase of a Nike
Ca. 390–350

48.2022. Terracotta. Ht, 18.4 cm; W, 11.7 cm; D, 5.6 cm. Collection of Joseph Brummer (sale catalogue, New York, Parke-Bernet Galleries, June 8–9, 1949, pt. III, 4, no. 18). Black glaze on mouth and back. Traces of white slip on body. Red in hair and on mouth. Left forearm missing and right arm broken above elbow. Broken across right thigh and left lower leg. Missing wings, vase mouth and handle. Hole in back. Authenticity established through thermoluminescence testing.

A maiden dances or flies with legs extended. She wears a sleeveless chiton which is fastened only on the right shoulder, exposing both breasts. An overfold flares out across the waist. Below the waist the garment blows open to expose the torso. A mantle is draped over her left elbow with the folds framing her back. Her head, worked in high relief on the vase neck, is slightly tilted to her right. She has center-parted hair with a lock on each shoulder, disc earrings, and a stephane adorned with rosettes alternating with leaves.

From the later fifth through much of the fourth century, figurine vases were made in the workshops of Attic koroplasts.[1] Using types and molds for terracotta figurines, artists crafted vases with glazed, unmodeled backs following the contemporary enthusiasm for high relief metal and terracotta vases. Most examples functioned as grave offerings and domestic decoration to which the Nike of the Walters example is appropriate. Better-preserved examples inform us that her wings were widespread and that she was almost surely intended to be hung. The distinctive style of the vases finds its closest sculptural parallels in the frieze of the

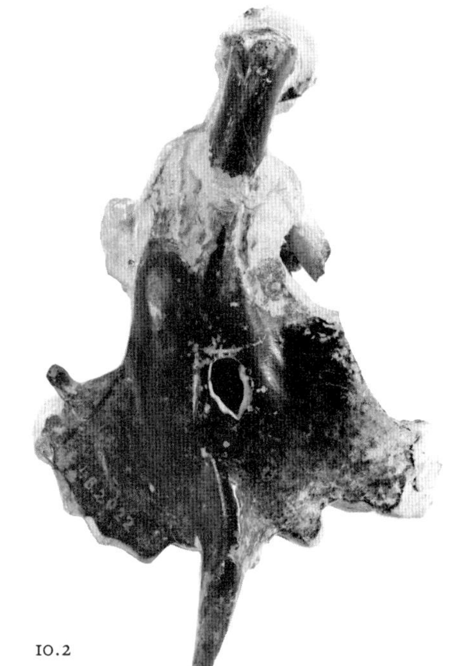

10.2

temple at Bassae (ca. 390) where we also find the same windblown, inflated drapery as well as the ruffled folds whose ends form the stylized outline of an omega.[2]

Following conventional practice, this figurine vase was made by using piece-molds, either in the construction of the figure or of the patrix from which the mold was impressed. This method of manufacture often resulted in an awkward juxtaposition of elements of independent lineage, here noticeable in the uncomfortable juncture of head and neck. Also typical of figurine vases is the considerable amount of handwork executed before firing, such as the retouching to the locks of hair and the addition of the ruffled band across the waistline.

In their quality and workmanship, figurine vases represent some of the finest koroplastic work of the first half of the fourth century; both for this reason and because of the subject matter and their destination for private rather than votive use, the vases look forward to the emergence of the Tanagra figurine in the last third of the century.

1. M. Trumpf-Lyritzaki, *Griechische Figurenvasen* (Bonn, 1969); E. Reeder Williams, "Figurine Vases from the Athenian Agora," *Hesperia* 47 (1978) 356–401; *Antiquities and Islamic Art,* Sotheby's (New York, February 8–9, 1985), no. 123.
2. C. Hofkes-Brukker, *Der Bassai-Fries* (Munich, 1975).

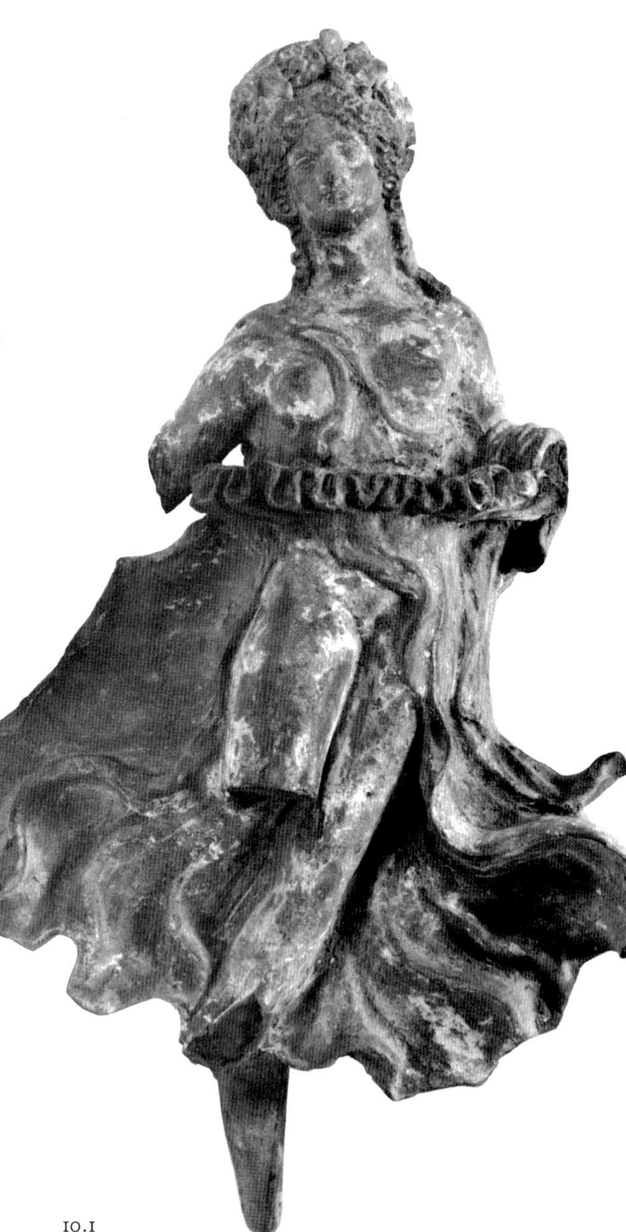

10.1

II

GROUP OF SILENOS WITH DIONYSOS
Ca. 350

48.302. Terracotta. Purchased in 1925. Ht, 12.7 cm; W, 7.6 cm. White slip; pink over Silenos's left ankle and face, and over Dionysos's upper torso and face. Vent hole at center back.

Nude squatting Silenos with animal ears supports on his left knee a child wearing a mantle over the lower torso, sandals, and a wreath, and holding an object in the extended right hand. The Silenos rests a cup on his right knee and gazes forward; he has short curly hair, a long mustache, and a beard in corkscrew locks. A round base, 1 cm high, is molded together with the figures.

This figurine represents a conflation of two well-known types. The crouching Silenos with hands on knees appears in Boeotian and Rhodian terracottas as early as the sixth century, and survives well into the Hellenistic period.[1] Popular in the fourth century was a type of standing Silenos who carries on his arm the youthful Dionysos, recognized by the cornucopia in his arm as well as by the cluster of grapes in the Silenos's right hand.[2] The Walters figurine substitutes for these attributes drinking cups suggestive of the young god's association with the vine, and softens the traditional bestial representation of the Silenos through influence from the stylized visages of votive masks. In this refined version the Silenos's lineage is betrayed only by his large head and features, thick lips, and the exaggerated curve of his brow.[3] Terracottas of the Hellenistic period develop several of the themes explored by this piece: the grouping of two or more figures (No. 90), and the depiction of a child together with his mentor (No. 91).

1. B. Schmaltz, *Terrakotten aus dem Kabirenheiligtum bei Theben* (Berlin, 1974), 17–19, pl. 2; see also G. Daux, ''Chronique des fouilles et découvertes archéologiques en Grèce en 1958,'' *BCH* 83 (1959) 712, fig. 6.
2. P. C. Bol and E. Kotera, *Liebieghaus, Vol. 3, Bildwerke aus Terrakotta* (Melsungen, 1986), 101–102, no. 53; Higgins, *Terracottas*, 197–198, no. 736, pl. 97; A. Peredolskaya, *Attische Tonfiguren aus einem südrussischen Grab. AntK* Beiheft 2 (1964) 29, pl. 14.1–2.
3. Schmaltz (note 1) 180, no. 347, pl. 27.

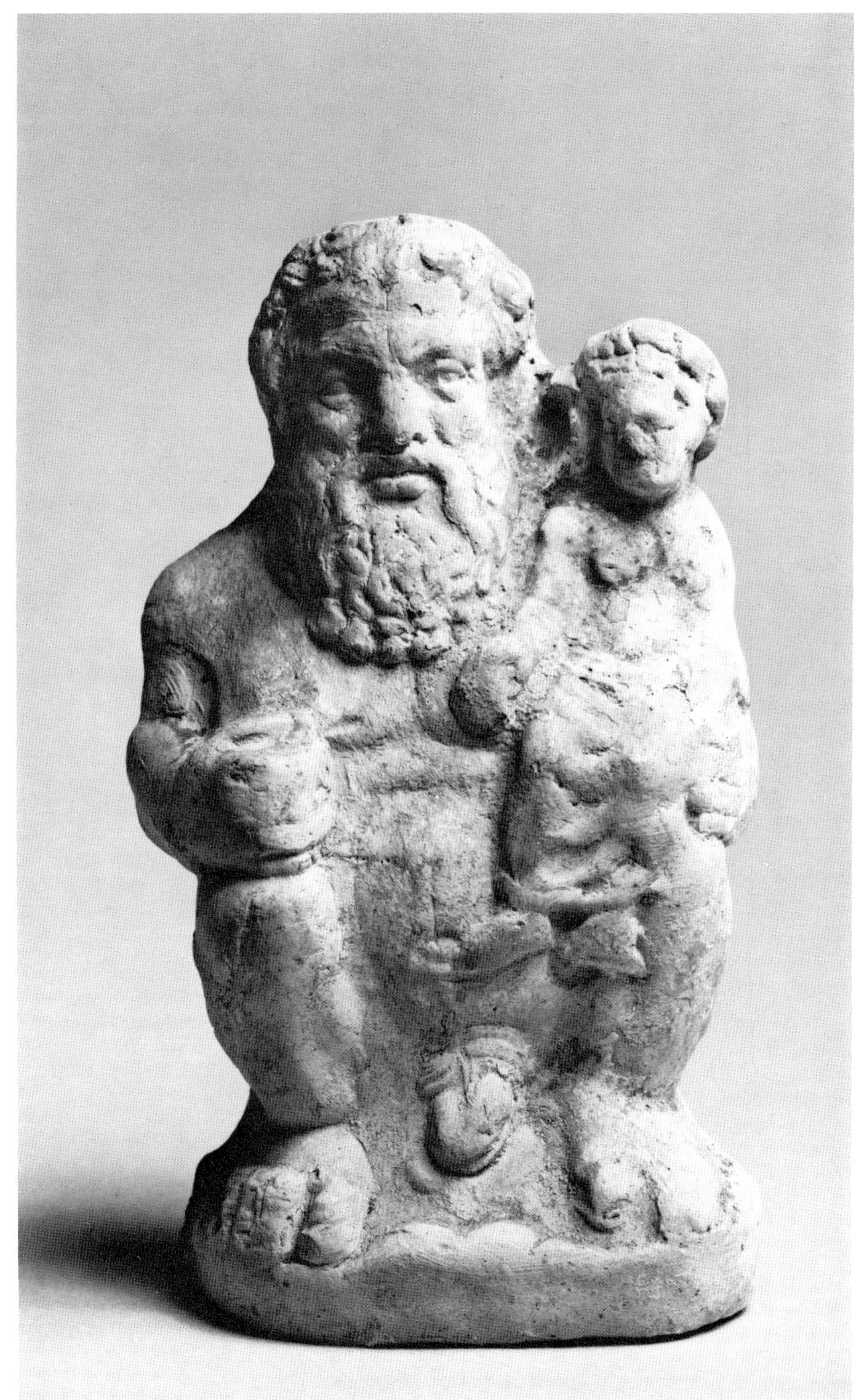

II.1

Appliqué Relief of a
Running Maiden
Ca. 350

48.2538. Terracotta. Purchased in 1986. Ht, 9.4 cm; W, 7.4 cm; Th, 1.5 cm. Back smooth and slightly concave.

The maiden runs to her left, her left leg advanced, her torso and legs in three-quarter view, her head turned back in three-quarter left profile. Her left elbow is bent with the forearm upraised and the palm at chest height with fingers extended. Her right arm is uplifted with the elbow bent and the fingers clasping folds of drapery above her right shoulder. She wears a girded peplos with overfold and a mantle which passes behind her back and billows out behind her. The ends are brought forward over her left elbow. She has short wavy hair.

Although it is not impossible that this piece was a type of furniture appliqué related to later ivory examples (Nos. 110, 115), this relief most likely belonged to a type of pottery distinguished by its separately molded relief appliqués. The closest parallels lie in unglazed Apulian oinochoai and pyxides of the fourth and third centuries, but pottery of this general type was widely manufactured in Hellenistic times.[1] An unglazed variety is known from Pergamon; black-glaze versions include the Calenian ware of South Italy and the plakette vases associated with Alexandria; also made in Egypt were counterparts in faience.[2] The direct prototypes for all this ware probably were metal vases with cast or repoussé relief decoration similar to the Derveni krater; a Hellenistic silver cup in Malibu, however, bears separately cast relief elements, and it is possible that metal vessels of this type existed at an earlier date.[3] Although the reliefs applied to the clay versions of the Walters type only occasionally display the crispness and detail that characterize a direct impression from a metal relief, the quality of the Walters fragment is so high that the relief was almost certainly made in a mold fabricated by impressing clay against a metal vessel worked in repoussé. Confirming the derivation of the Walters relief from a metal source is the prominence of the blowing drapery in the silhouette. Whereas this feature is effective on a metal vase where the drapery ends could be executed in low relief, the resulting thickness on a separately made clay relief is overly emphatic and obtrusive.

The origin of clay relief ware can be traced back to the fifth century when Attic workshops imitated contemporary metal vessels by fashioning pottery imitations with separately molded reliefs.[4] We can assume that the Walters fragment came from a vase that closely followed this Attic tradition because the iconography and style of the piece have close Attic affiliations, specifically with the frieze of the temple of Apollo at Bassae, the Attic associations of which are well known.[5] Here we also find three-quarter views of the faces, affected gestures, blowing drapery with upturned overfolds, and agitated and stylized drapery hems. Especially interesting both at Bassae and on the relief fragment are the drapery folds which neither articulate nor model, and therein look forward to the Hellenistic age; most noticeable on the clay relief is the ridge which forms a reverse "S" over the maiden's right knee.

The appearance of the motif of the running maiden in metalwork of the fourth century is elsewhere attested on a gold gorytos from Macedonia.[6] That piece was made by matrix hammering, a technique which facilitated mass production and so undoubtedly accelerated the dissemination of motifs such as this one into other media and over a broad geographical area.

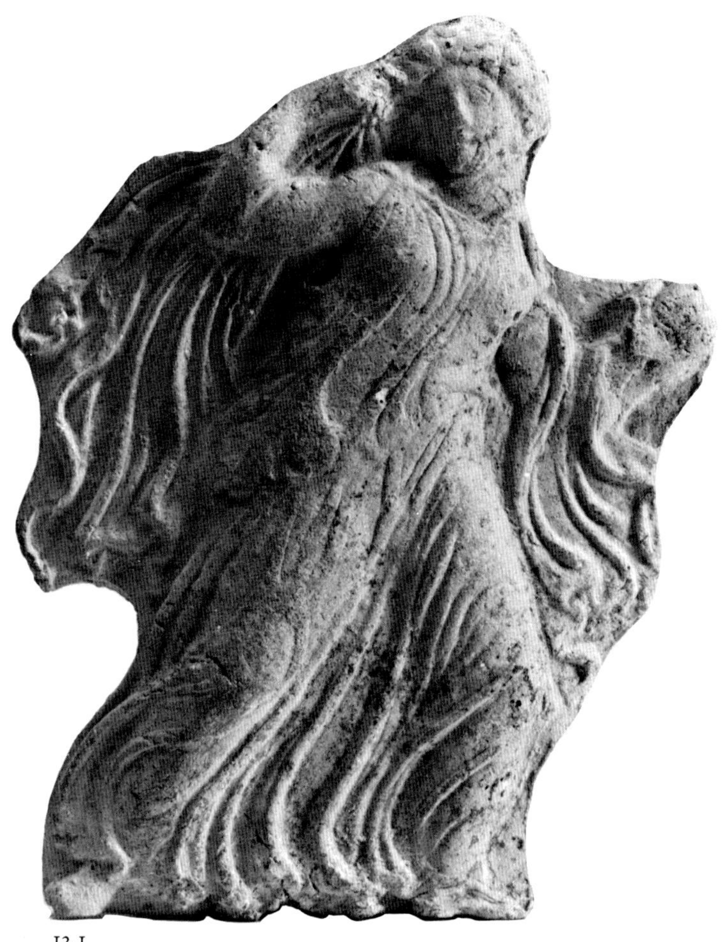

12.1

1. F. L. Bastet, "Zwei Neuerwerbungen des Rijksmuseum van Oudheden in Leiden," *BABesch* 57 (1982) 155–158; J. Eisenberg, *Art of the Ancient World IV* (New York, Royal-Athena Galleries, 1965), 51, no. 165, dated third century.

2. For the Pergamene ware, see *Antiken aus rheinischem Privatbesitz*, Bonn, Rheinisches Landesmuseum (Cologne, 1973), 74, no. 103; J. Schäfer, *Hellenistische Keramik aus Pergamon*, Pergamenische Forschungen 2 (Berlin, 1968), 87, fig. 5.3. For the Calenian ware, see R. Pagenstecher, *Die calenische Reliefkeramik* (Berlin, 1909). For the plakette vases, see K. Schefold, *Die Göttersage in der klassischen und hellenistischen Kunst* (Munich, 1981), 287–288 and 359, nos. 620–623. See also B. Barr-Sharrar, "Macedonian Metal Vases in Perspective: Some Observations on Context and Tradition," *Macedonia and Greece*, 134, fig. 20. For the faience vases, see Nos. 103, 104. See also A. Hochuli-Gysel, "Kleinasiatische glasierte Reliefkeramik," *Acta Bernensia* 7 (1977) 16.

3. For the Getty vase, see A. Oliver, "A Set of Ancient Silverware in the Getty Museum," *GettyMusJ* 8 (1980) 160–161, figs. 10–12.

4. E. A. Zervoudaki, "Attische Polychrome Reliefkeramik," *AM* 83 (1968) 1–88, especially pls. 11, 12, 16, 17. See also Schefold (note 2) 286, figs. 406–407.

5. C. Hofkes-Brukker, *Der Bassai-Fries* (Munich, 1975), 58–59, no. H6–530.

6. *Search for Alexander*, 182, no. 160. Compare M. Artamonov, *Treasures from Scythian Tombs* (London, 1969), 128, no. 186.

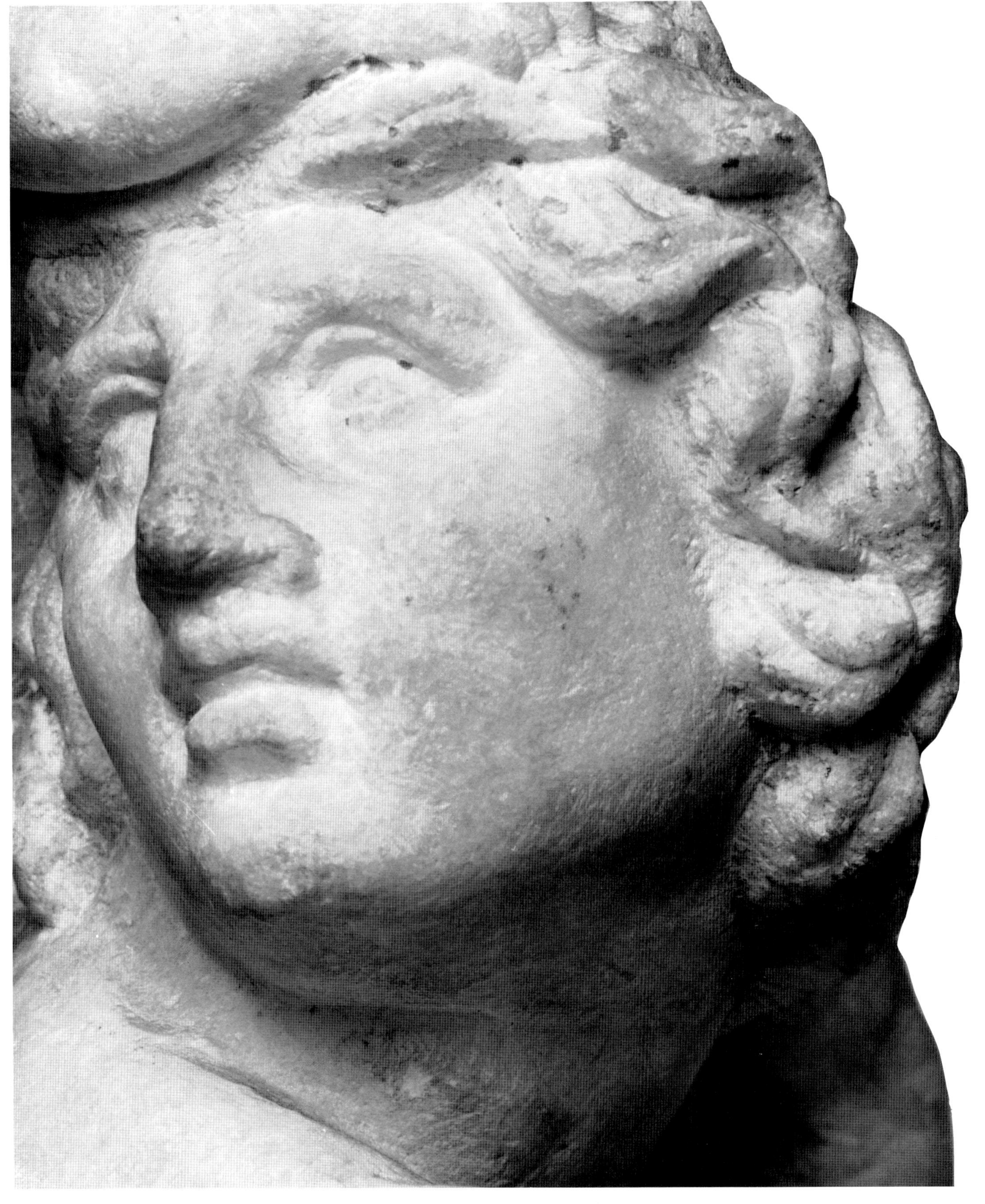

Bearded Head from a Funerary Monument

Ca. 325–317

23.239. Marble. Collection of E. Wolff. Purchased in 1986 through the W. Alton Jones Foundation Acquisition Fund. Ht, 32.3 cm; W, 18.7 cm; Depth, 20.3 cm. Broken across neck; nose missing; abrasions over surface.

A bearded head turns slightly to his right. The hair on the top of the head and above and behind the right ear is summarily carved. The back of the head is roughly blocked out.

Publications: E. Reeder Williams, ''From the Athens of Aristotle,'' *BWalt* 39 (1986) no. 4.

This head belongs to a type of Attic grave monument that presented images of family members in a tableau framed by a stagelike niche. The earliest examples of the late fifth century are small and in low relief (see No. 5), but gradually the figures became larger and more three-dimensional and the compositions more complex, with the result that the monuments came to cost as much as a private house.[1] The series disappears abruptly following the political upheaval precipitated by the death of Alexander the Great, when Athenian democracy gave way to a more repressive government under Demetrios of Phaleron. His anti-luxury decree of 317 effectively terminated the funerary monuments and therewith debilitated the Athenian sculptural industry.[2] Because the Walters head is one of the largest known heads from a grave monument and is worked completely in the round, the piece can be dated to the years immediately preceding 317 and can be viewed as the final product of a workshop tradition stretching back to the great Akropolis building program of the fifth century. The Walters head is remarkable among grave monuments of this late date in the degree of finish accorded all areas that were intended to be seen; by contrast, much of the grave sculpture from the series's end was executed in haste, either because of the intensity of customer demand or in anticipation of the forthcoming decree.[3]

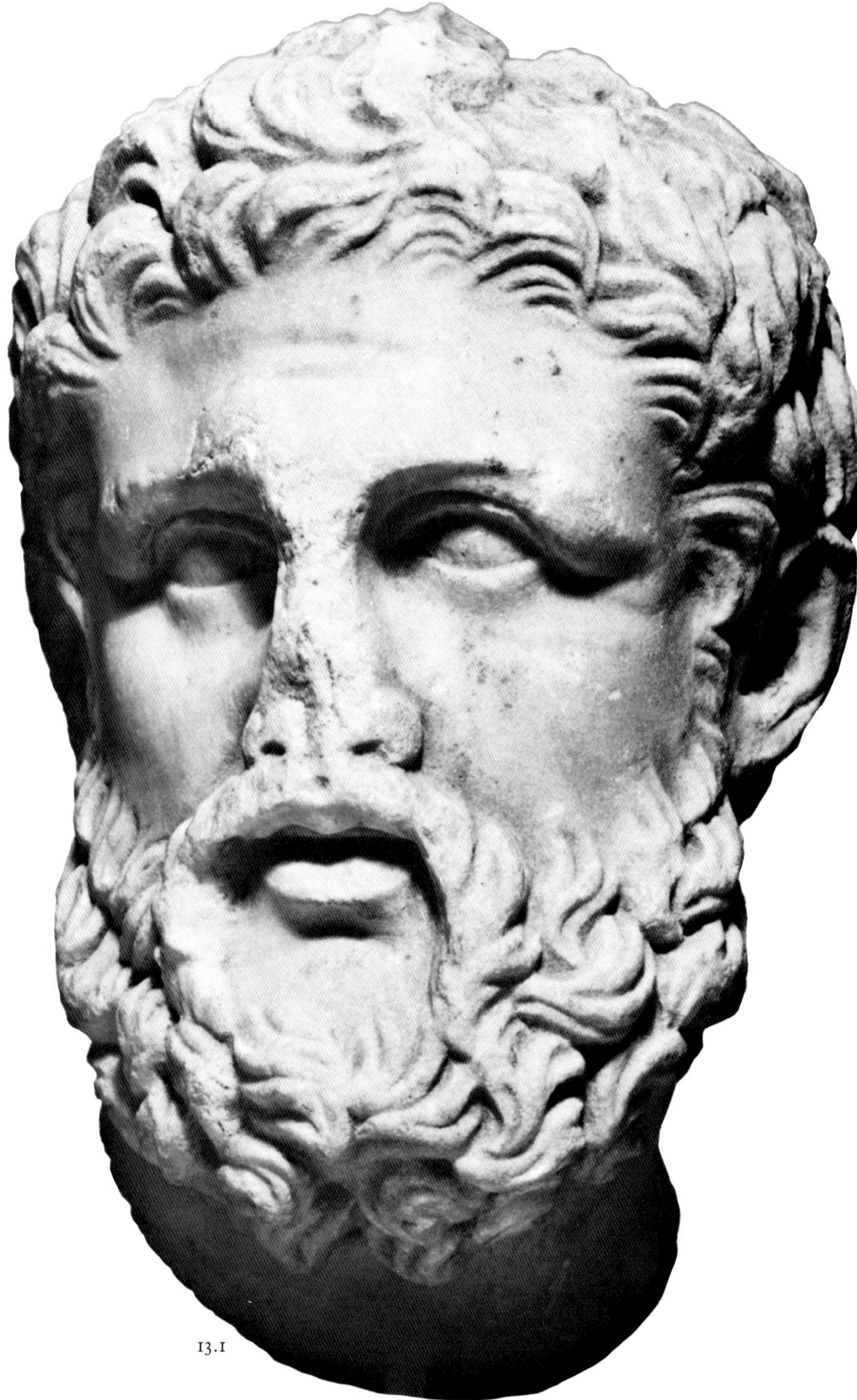

13.1

The head includes such so-called Skopasian elements as deep-set eyes, a fleshy overhang above the outer corner of the eye, a furrowed brow, and an open mouth.[4] Intensifying these suggestions of inner unrest are the energetic curls of hair and beard. The head exhibits no features of advanced age such as are seen in the contemporary Alexos or the old man on the Ilissos relief, but rather displays the countenance of a mature individual, an early Hellenistic version of a Classical type exemplified by the Poseidon of the Parthenon's east frieze.[5] The closest parallels are a grave relief from Eleusis, representing a standing cuirassed warrior attended by a small boy, and a monument in Budapest where a nude male with a boy at his side turns to clasp the hand of a standing woman at his right.[6] In each case the man is undoubtedly the deceased who is presented in ripe maturity accompanied by his family. The Walters head probably belongs to a composition similar to the Budapest example because, when turned to its right, the unfinished sides and back of the head are not visible and the plasticity and rhythm of the beard on the left side of the jaw are most effective. Because the head belonged to a tranquil domestic group, its emotional overtones are not motivated by the physical violence of Skopas's Tegean pediments, but rather by an interest in psychology which looks forward to later Hellenistic art and brings to mind the approximately contemporary Weary Herakles of Lysippos (No. 44).[7]

The formulaic iconography and the modifications to the identifying inscriptions tell us that the Attic grave monuments were not intended to be portraits of specific individuals.[8] The Walters head is thus only a generic representation of a mature bearded man, and as such, his similarity to a third-century statue from Kos casts doubt upon the identification of that work as a portrait of either Hippokrates or a prominent citizen.[9] Similarly, the Walters head encourages us to re-evaluate Roman sculptures which have traditionally been regarded as copies of portraits executed at about the same time as the funerary monuments. It is often assumed, for example, that the resemblance between a head in Copenhagen from a grave relief and a Roman copy of Plato is due to the influence of monumental sculpture on grave monuments, but the reverse direction is equally probable given the likeness which another head in Copenhagen, also from a grave relief and thus executed before 317, bears to Roman copies of Demosthenes attributed to an original of about 280.[10] Obviously, the experimentation with portraiture in the last third of the fourth century and beginning of the third century, so well attested in the literary sources, was heavily dependent upon the tradition of non-specific images produced for the funerary monuments.[11]

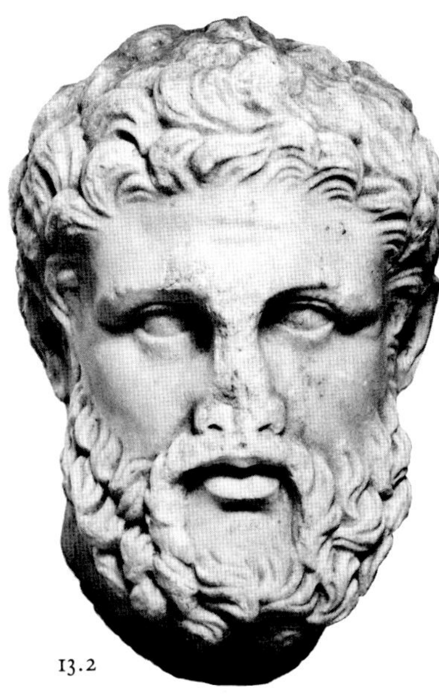

13.2

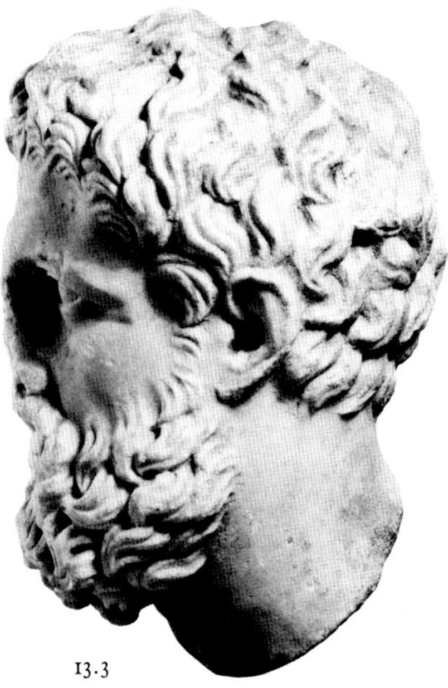

13.3

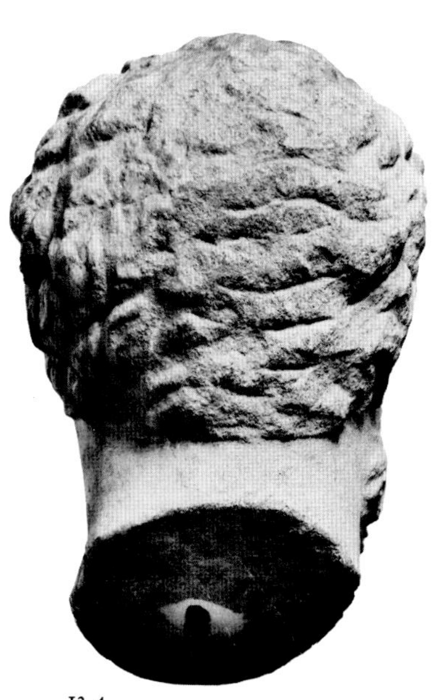

13.4

1. B. Schmaltz, *Griechische Grabreliefs* (Darmstadt, 1983), 138–141.
2. Schmaltz (note 1) 31; D. C. Kurtz and J. Boardman, *Greek Burial Customs* (London, 1971), 163, 166.
3. Compare an example in the Ashmolean discussed in O. Palagia, ''An Attic Head in Oxford,'' *Boreas* 3 (1980) 5–11. See also J. Frel, *Les sculpteurs attiques anonymes* (Prague, 1969), pl. 47.
4. A. Stewart, *Skopas in Malibu* (Malibu, 1982).
5. For Alexos (NM 2574), see R. Lullies, *Griechische Plastik* (Munich, 1956), pls. 240, 241, and K. A. I. Braun, *Untersuchungen zur Stilgeschichte bärtiger Köpfe auf attischen Grabreliefs und Folgerungen für einige Bildniskopfe* (Munich, 1966), 63; the Ilissos relief (NM 869) is discussed on 68. For the Poseidon, see F. Brommer, *Der Parthenonfries* (Mainz, 1977), pl. 80.
6. For the Eleusis relief, see A. Conze, *Die attische Grabreliefs* (Berlin, 1900), II, 217, no. 1023, pl. 201. For the Budapest relief, see A. Hekler, *Die Sammlung antiker Skulpturen* (Budapest, 1929), 36, no. 25; Braun (note 5) 75.
7. C. Havelock, *Hellenistic Art*, rev. ed. (New York, 1981), 119–120, no. 81.
8. Schmaltz (note 1) 117, 211; Kurtz (note 2) 136.
9. H. von Heintz, ''Die Statue des Epikur,'' *Alessandria*, 765–769. P. Bol, ''Die Hippokrates-Statue in Kos,'' *AntP* 15 (1975) 65–72, pls. 29–34.
10. For copies of Plato, see G. M. A. Richter, *The Portraits of the Greeks* (London, 1965), II, 164–170, and G. M. A. Richter, *The Portraits of the Greeks*, rev. ed. (Ithaca, 1984), 181–186. For the similar head in Copenhagen (inv. no. 1816), see ''Aus skandinavischen Museen,'' *AA* (1962) 91, fig. 12; Braun (note 5) 58; J. Frel, *Greek Portraits in the J. Paul Getty Museum* (Malibu, 1981), 20. For the second head in Copenhagen (inv. no. 214) see F. Poulsen, *From the Collections of the Ny Carlsberg Glyptotek* (Copenhagen, 1938), II, 11, fig. 8. For the statue of Demosthenes, see Richter (1965) 215–223.
11. Stewart, *Attikà*, 9.

BANQUET RELIEF
Ca. 350–300

23.222. Marble. Purchased in 1967 from Spink and Son (*Octagon,* Winter, 1966, 8; *Illustrated London News,* November 19, 1966, 29). L, 57.4 cm; Ht, 41 cm; Th, 8.2 cm. Sides smooth with moldings continued from front; top also smooth; back rough. One corner palmette missing. Deposit over front.

Within an enclosure of stoa form with side antae and an architrave crowned by six antefixes of palmette shape, is a banquet scene with seven figures. A couch with thick rectangular feet is overlaid by fabric; upon it reclines a bearded man with frontal torso and head, who rests his left elbow upon two pillows. In his left hand he clasps a wreath; his right hand, which is extended toward the viewer, holds a phiale. He is nude except for his mantle which is draped over his waist and lower legs, frames his left shoulder, and spills over his left arm. Seated at his feet in right profile is a maiden whose crossed feet rest on a footstool. An open incense box rests in her left hand; her right hand is extended toward an incense burner on the table before her. She wears a chiton or peplos beneath a mantle which is draped over her shoulder and upper arms, and brought across her waist and legs; the pleated folds of her undergarment emerge beneath the mantle at her feet. She has short curly hair. In front of the couch is a table upon which have been placed an incense burner, a flask, three pyramid-shaped cakes, and several round objects. Resting on the ground at the foot of the kline is a volute krater; behind it and gazing at it is a nude frontal youth whose head is turned slightly to his right. Beside him is a man seen in three-quarters right profile, his right arm bent, and his mantle framing his shoulders and wrapped around his body exposing only his bare chest. Behind him is a second mantle-wrapped figure. In front of them stand two smaller figures draped in their mantles with the right elbow bent. The exposed chest of the figure by the krater identifies him as a male.

Publications: D. K. Hill, "Accessions of American and Canadian Museums," *Art Quarterly* 31 (1968) 205 and ill. on 209; D. K. Hill, "A New Greek Relief," *BWalt* 20 (1968) no. 4; Vermeule, *Sculpture,* 109, no. 79.

The banquet scene, recognized by the reclining male on a kline, the seated woman, and the smaller attendants, has its origin in the ancient Near East, and is especially familiar in Assyrian and Achaemenid art whence it was introduced into the Greek world in the sixth century. There its greatest popularity begins in the late fifth century when a distinctive version was developed in Athens that was widely imitated in the islands, Asia Minor, and South Italy, and continued to

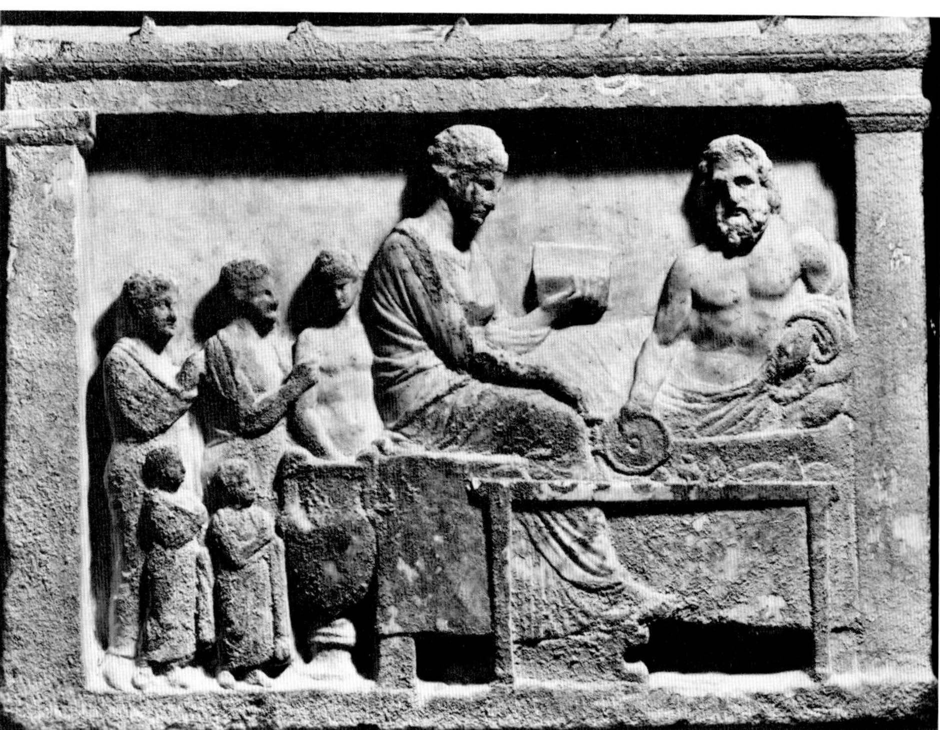

14.1

be made well into the second century. Such elements in the scene as an altar, modios, cornucopia, rhyton, and snake unequivocally denote the hero's realm and, for this reason, the pyramidal cakes and small round fruit are to be understood as votive offerings.[1] During the fifth and much of the fourth century the type functioned as a votive dedication to a local hero or helping god, and examples were dedicated in hero sanctuaries or in the cult centers of Pan and the Nymphs. During the fourth century the banquet relief came increasingly to serve as a grave relief with the reclining male presented as the heroized deceased, and the cakes and fruits now an allusion to the traditional grave offerings.[2] In Asia Minor at this date the reliefs were used primarily as grave monuments, and after the third century the reliefs are rarely found anywhere in a votive context.[3]

The Walters example represents a later fourth-century stage in the series when the reliefs still enjoyed both votive and funerary use. Distinctive of examples of this era are the frontal torso of the male who extends his phiale not to the female companion but to the viewer, and the profile position of the maiden who is now seated on the kline, not a klismos, and places balls of incense in a burner on the table. Also noteworthy are the diminished role of the serving boy and the diminutive sizes of the attendants or adorers.[4]

The banquet reliefs are a vivid illustration of the secularization of the Hellenistic age when cult practices, iconography, and attributes formerly reserved for mythical and divine beings were transposed to the human world. Although intimations of the process can be detected before the time of Alexander, it was the Hellenistic confrontation of Hellenic and Oriental cultures that facilitated the erosion of the boundary between divine and human. The heroization of the dead that takes place over the course of the banquet-relief series is part of the same phenomenon that would witness the deification of the deceased, and finally of the living, ruler.

1. R. N. Thönges-Stringaris, "Das griechische Totenmahl," *AM* 80 (1965) 1–14, 19, 52–54; H. Heres-von Littrow, "Vier Totenmahlreliefs der Berliner Antiken-Sammlung," *Berlin, Staatliche Museen, Forschungen und Berichte* 10 (1968) 103–112; L. Marangou, *Ancient Greek Art. The N. P. Goulandris Collection* (Athens, 1985), 181.
2. Thönges-Stringaris (note 1) 60–61.
3. Ibid., 62.
4. Ibid., 15–18

Head of a Maiden
Ca. 325

23.137. Marble. Purchased from Kelekian in 1929. Ht, 10.8 cm; W, 6.1 cm; Depth, 7.4 cm. Back summarily carved. Broken across neck. Brown encrustation over surface.

Head and neck of a maiden turned to her left. Her hair is arranged in a melon hairstyle with a long coil of hair circling the back of the crown.

Exhibitions and Catalogues: *Our Ancient Heritage,* Philbrook Art Center (Tulsa, October 7–November 27, 1963), no. 281. *From the Shipwreck of Time: One Hundred Greek and Roman Antiquities,* Staten Island Museum (New York, February 14–March 28, 1965), no. 2.

Publications: D. K. Hill, ''Greek Heads,'' *BWalt* 19 (1967) no. 5.

This maiden's hairstyle represents an early stage of the melon hairstyle, which would prove enormously popular throughout the Hellenistic period. On this example, the braids are not at the back of the head, but are wrapped around the head in a manner resembling a tiara. The style appears on an Attic grave relief in Boston, dated 330–320, and an approximately contemporary terracotta head from the Athenian Agora.[1] The Walters head is probably of the same date, and looks forward to later Hellenistic sculpture in the deep-set inner corners of the eyes, the Venus ring across the neck, and the angle at which the head is tilted.

The statuette to which this head belonged measured just under two feet, a height that became popular in the Hellenistic period, possibly because statuary of this size was suitable to a domestic setting. Decorative marble statuary of this size is not usually thought to have been made as early as the late fourth century, but it is likely that there existed marble counterparts to the contemporary terracotta Tanagra figurines.

1. For the relief in Boston, see C. C. Vermeule, *Greek and Roman Sculpture in America* (Berkeley, 1981), pl. 87. For the terracotta from Athens, see D. B. Thompson, ''Three Centuries of Hellenistic Terracottas,'' *Hesperia* 21 (1952) 138, pl. 36, and compare a figurine in New York, discussed on 139, pl. 36.

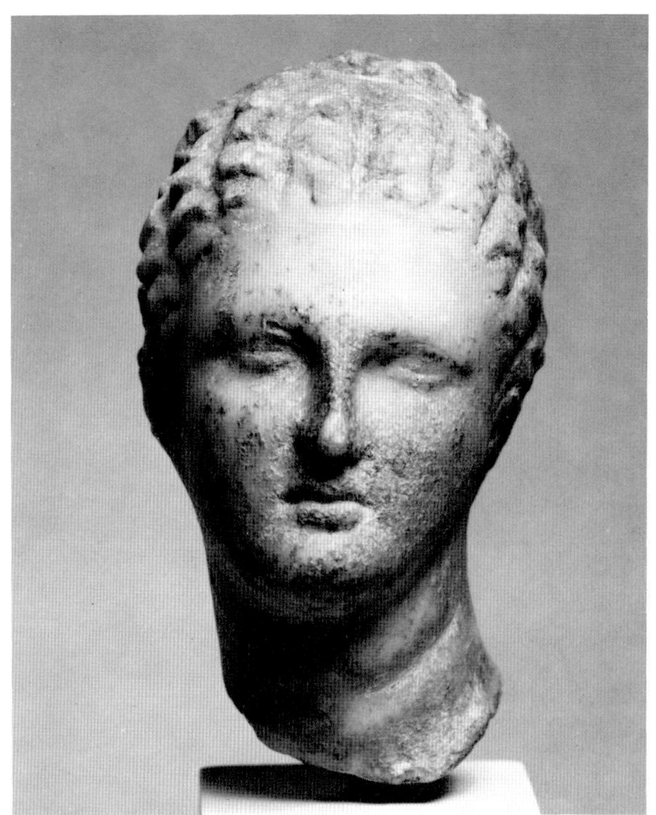

15.1

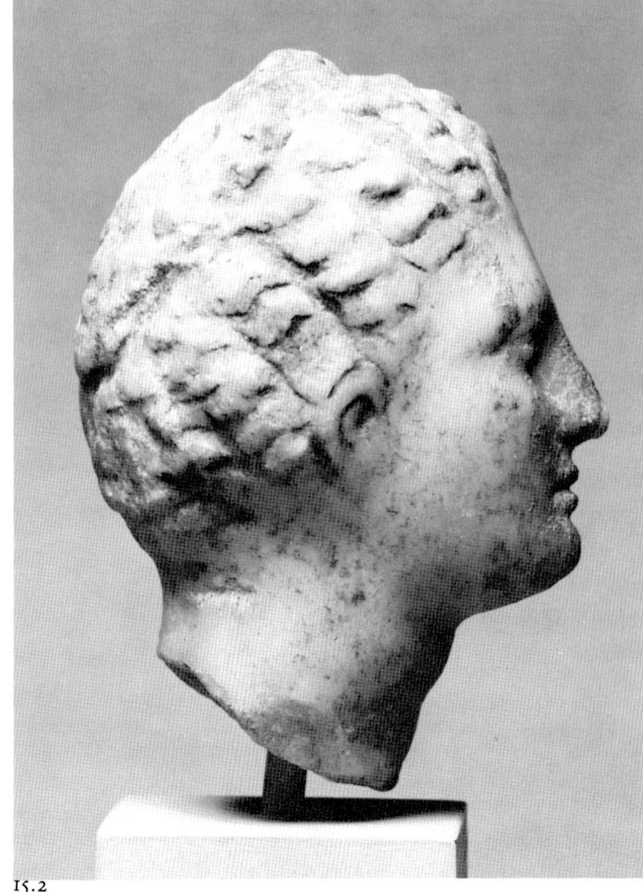

15.2

HEAD OF A MAIDEN
Third to second century

23.140. Marble. "From Rome." Purchased from Kelekian in 1931. Ht, 29.2 cm; W, 14.6 cm. Most of nose missing. Abrasions above left ear and on right cheek. Base of neck broadened and thickened for insertion into a statue.

The neck and head of a young girl turned slightly to her right. Her wavy hair is gathered in a knot at the crown of her head; short wisps edge the back of the neck.

The head, which was made separately for insertion into a statue, is a Hellenistic version of a late Classical type best represented by the statue of a maiden in New York, which belonged to a late fourth-century Attic grave monument.[1] Strongly contrasting with the New York head and indicative of a later date for the Walters piece are the deeply drilled topknot, the plastic and energetically waved locks of hair, and the minimal modeling of facial contours with a small, receding bow-shaped mouth. Particularly noteworthy is the groove at the base of the skull just above the nape, which may be the result of careless workmanship, but also brings to mind the similarly positioned groove believed to have been used for silver inlay on the bronze head of a Nike from the Athenian Agora.[2] The Classicizing features of that head coupled with the high relief and animation of the Nike's hair suggest that both the Agora bronze and the Walters head represent a Hellenistic nod to monuments of the Classical era. The Walters head is probably to be dated in the third or second century when the Attic grave monuments again began to exert influence upon the reviving Attic school of sculpture.[3]

The hair of both the Walters and the Agora maiden is gathered into a topknot at the crown of the head; the Metropolitan maiden wears a modification of the style wherein the topknot is accompanied by long locks of hair drawn back at the nape. The style was already known in the fifth century, but enjoyed special prominence in the fourth century and Hellenistic period when Dicaerchos, a pupil of Aristotle, commented that the beautiful women of Thebes gathered their blond hair onto the top of their head in a style that they termed the little torch or "lampadion."[4]

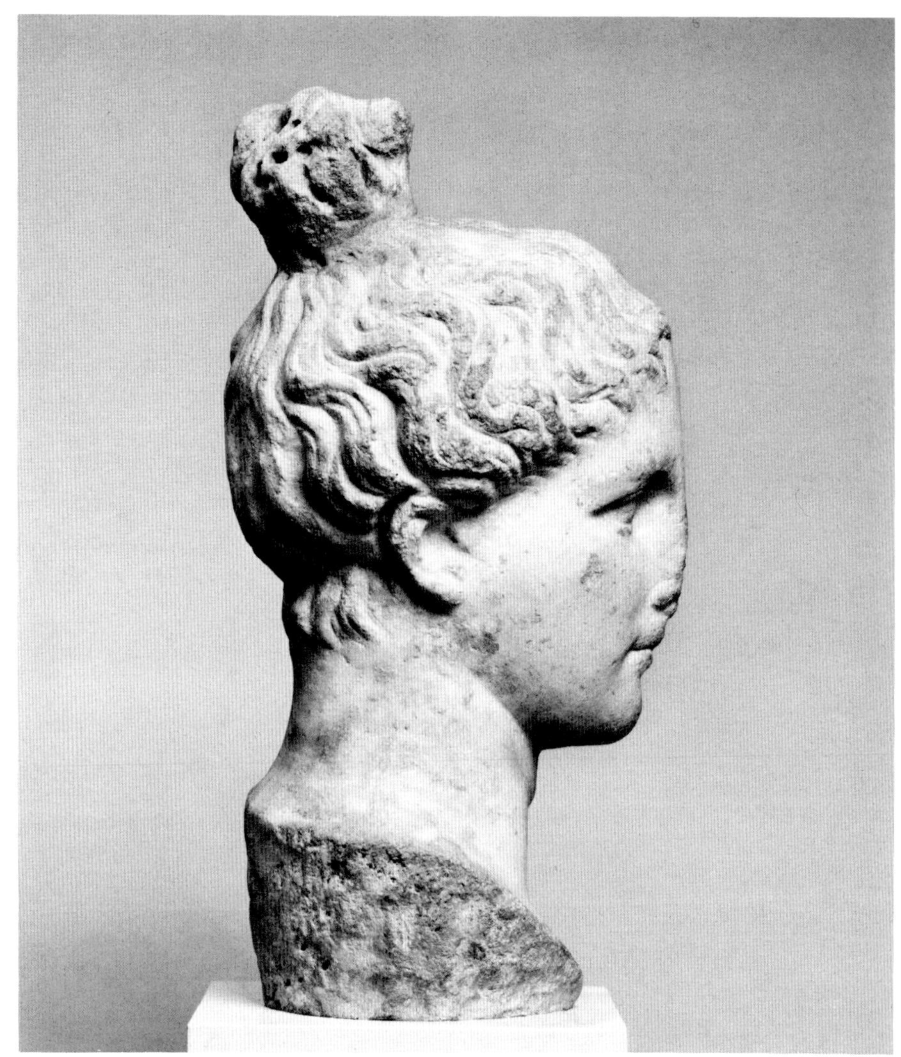

16.2

1. G. M. A. Richter, "Two Greek Statues," *Hesperia* 48 (1944) 234 and 236, fig. 11.
2. T. L. Shear, "The Sculpture," *Hesperia* 2 (1933) 519–520, 522–523, 525.
3. Stewart, *Attikà*, 11, 79, 140. See also Richter (note 1) 239.
4. Thompson, *Troy*, 41.

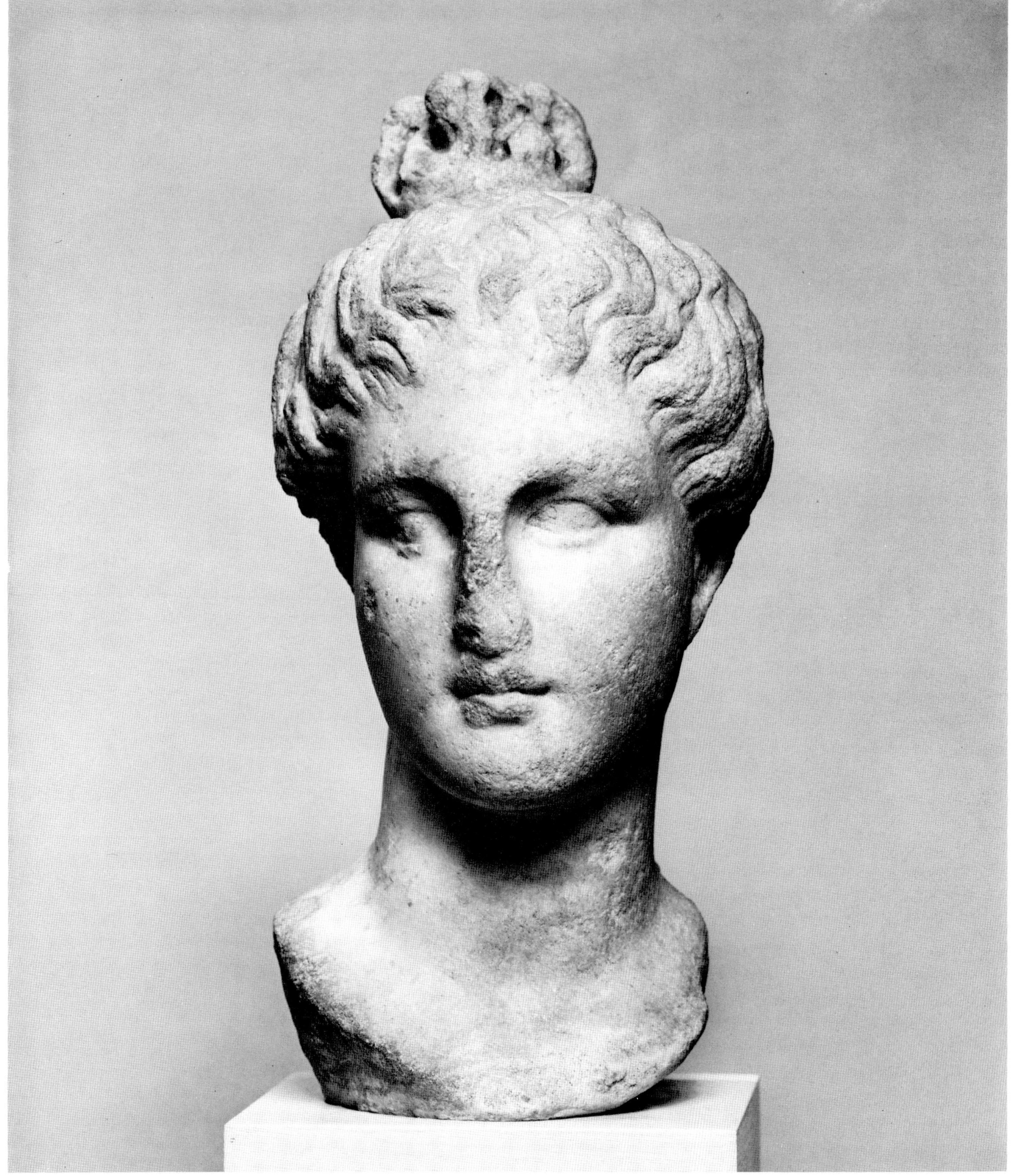

16.1

Head of a Maiden
Third century

23.155. Marble. Purchased from Kelekian in 1927. Ht, 5.9 cm; W, 4.3 cm. Broken across neck. Red pigment on mouth and left eye. Chip missing from hair above left ear.

A maiden whose hair is center-parted and drawn back over the ears to be bunched at the nape turns her head slightly to the right. She has Venus rings across her neck and wears a double fillet.

Exhibitions and Catalogues: *Our Ancient Heritage,* Philbrook Art Center (Tulsa, October 7–November 27, 1963), no. 282.

The elongated eye, bow-shaped mouth, slightly fleshy cheeks, and pronounced Venus rings identify the head as a Hellenistic refinement of the Praxitelean style. The twist of her head and the inclined glance communicate a pensive quality appropriate to a Nymph or Muse. It is possible that the head belonged to a marble version of terracottas of the Tanagra type, and, as such, the statuette may have served as domestic decoration, either placed on a ledge around the wall at shoulder height, or displayed within a niche.[1]

1. J. Raeder, *Priene. Funde aus einer griechischen Stadt* (Berlin, 1983), 22.

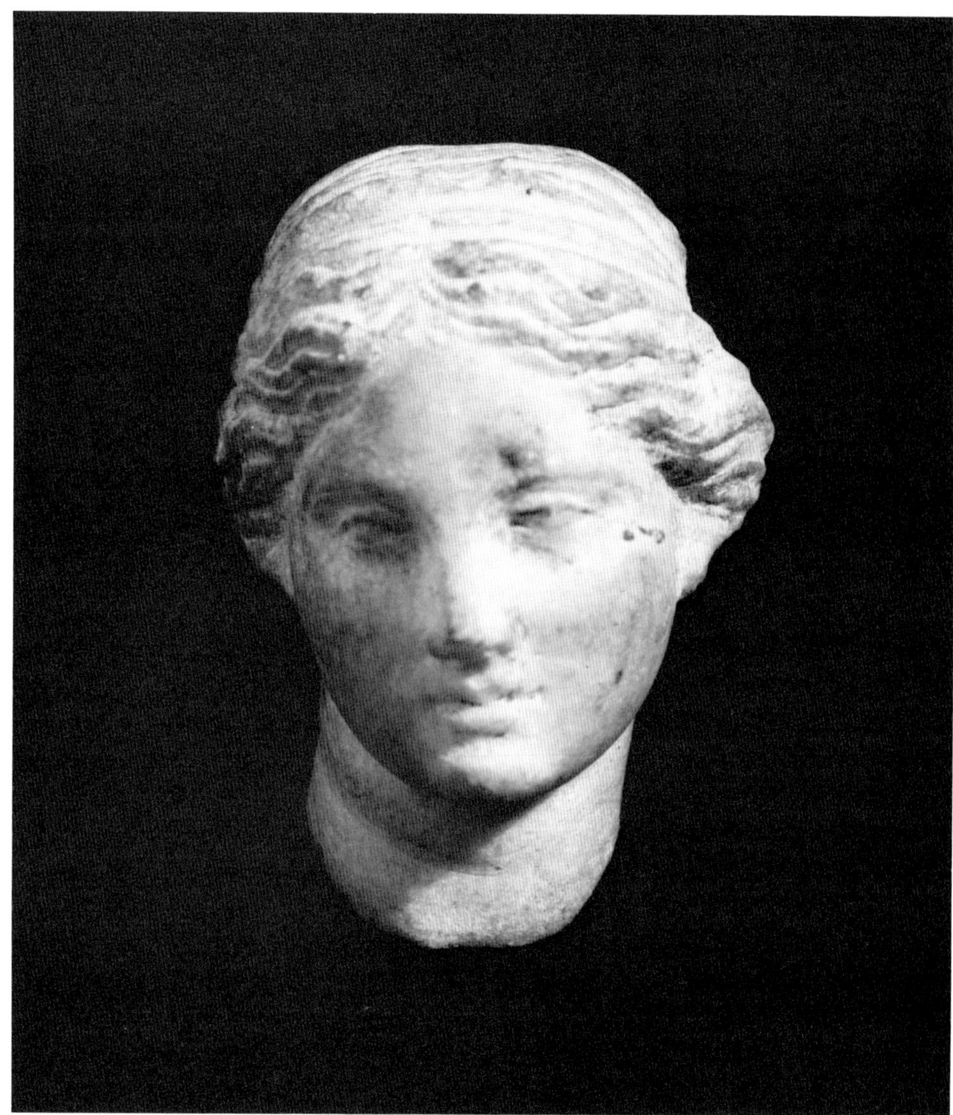

17.1

FRONTAL HEAD OF A
MAIDEN
Third to second century

23.141. Marble. Warneck Collection (sale catalogue, *La Collection Warneck,* Paris, Hôtel Drouot, June 13–16, 1905, 1, no. 3, fig. 3, pl. 1). Purchased before 1931. Ht, 13.7 cm; W, 8.8 cm; Depth, 10.3 cm. Broken across neck; brown patina over surface.

The frontal head and neck, with Venus rings, of a maiden has center-parted hair drawn back over the ears to the nape, with locks falling down behind.

Publications: A. Thomas, ''La collection Warneck,'' *Le Musée* 2 (1905) 129, fig. 3, pl. VIII.

Probably later than No. 17 is this head, whose classicizing character is expressed through the frontal gaze, full mouth, and the position of the eyebrow just above, and parallel to, the eyelid. The piece is significant as further evidence for the extensive production of Hellenistic small-scale sculpture that was surely destined for domestic use.

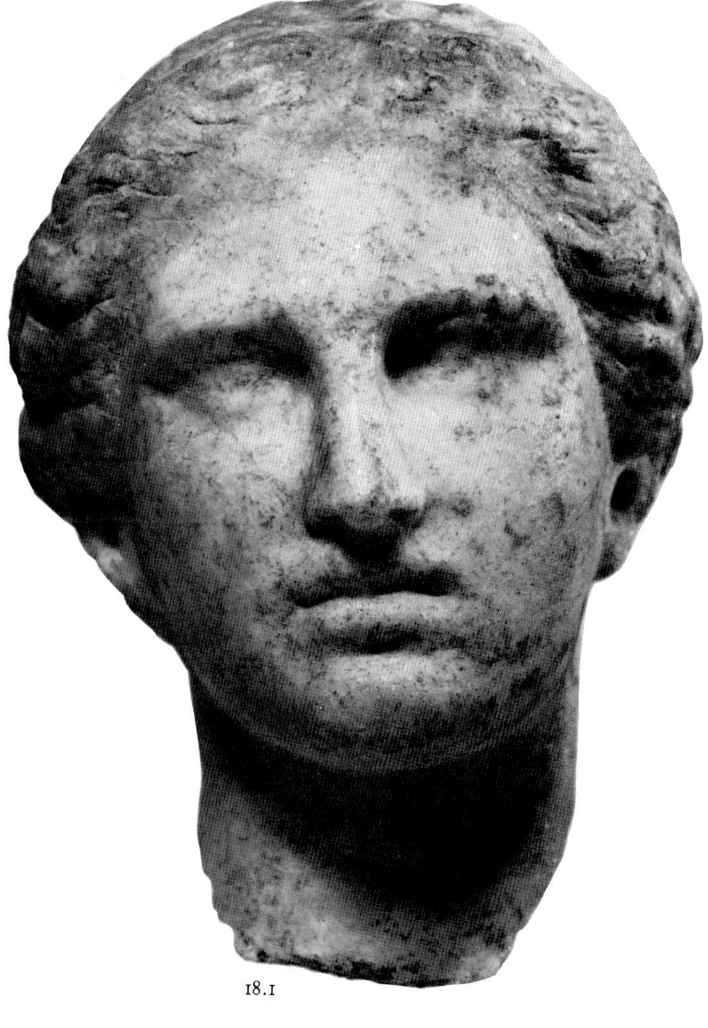

18.1

STATUETTE OF THE
APHRODITE OF KNIDOS
Third to second century after
marble original by Praxiteles
of the fourth century

23.98. Marble. "From Sidon." Collection of Mrs.
Wood of Brooklyn. Probably purchased shortly after
1905. Ht, 24.2 cm; W, 7.9 cm. Back of drapery
smooth. Intact. White with yellowed surface, dull
and pitted.

A nude maiden stands on her right leg, her left leg
relaxed with the foot slightly behind her right foot.
Her left hand holds folds of fringed (?) drapery
which fall down her left side and behind a vessel.
Her right arm is brought over her torso with the
thumb and fingers slightly touching the side of the
left thigh. Her head is turned to her left and is
slightly inclined; her wavy hair is center-parted and
drawn back from the face to a knot at the nape. The
round base is carved in one piece with the figure.

Publications: A. Sambon, "Une nouvelle réplique de
l'Aphrodite de Cnide," *Le Musée* 2 (1905) 79–80, pl.
III; Reinach, *Statuaire* 4 (1910) 216, no. 7; D. K.
Hill, "Venus in the Roman East," *JWalt* 31–32
(1968–69) 7–12, and 11, figs. 6 and 7.

This statuette reproduces a Praxitelean
work of ca. 355–330 that was one of the
most celebrated sculptures of antiquity
and the first example in the round of a
nude Aphrodite.[1] The deity is depicted at
the moment when she has just finished
disrobing for her bath and is surprised by
an intruder. Her instinctive gesture of
modesty underlines the invasiveness of the
visitor's entrance and contrasts strongly
with the demeanor of the Aphrodite of
the Parthenon's east pediment, whose
pose betrays the deliberation behind her
partial undraping. The Praxitelean work
exposes the goddess without her consent,
and by emphasizing her vulnerability,
introduces a hubristic note that reflects
the growing secularization of the Olympian pantheon. At the same time, the scenario provides what was apparently
perceived as a necessary motivation for the
unprecedented nudity.

Pfrommer has persuasively argued that
the most accurate rendering of the lost
Praxitelean original is represented by the
Belvedere Venus and a statuette in
Malibu; the Walters statuette also belongs

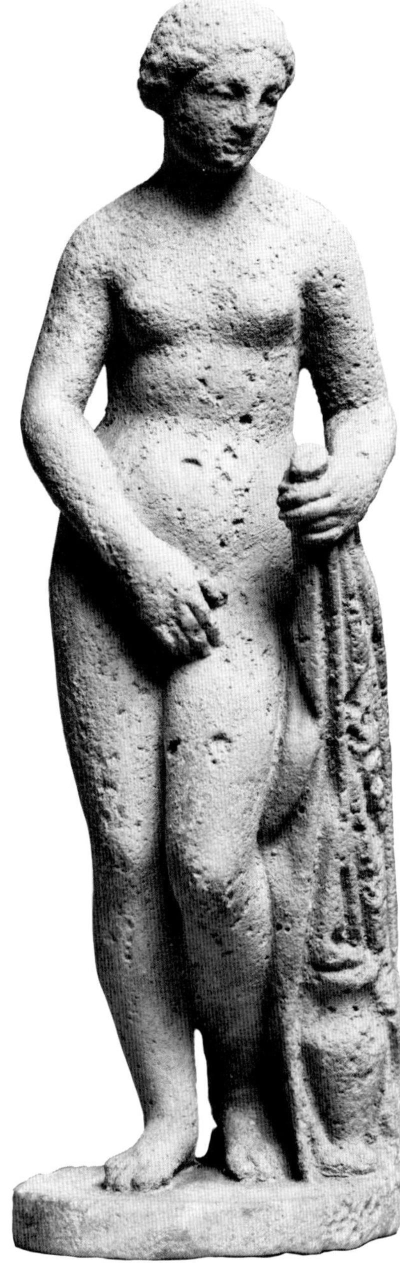

19.1

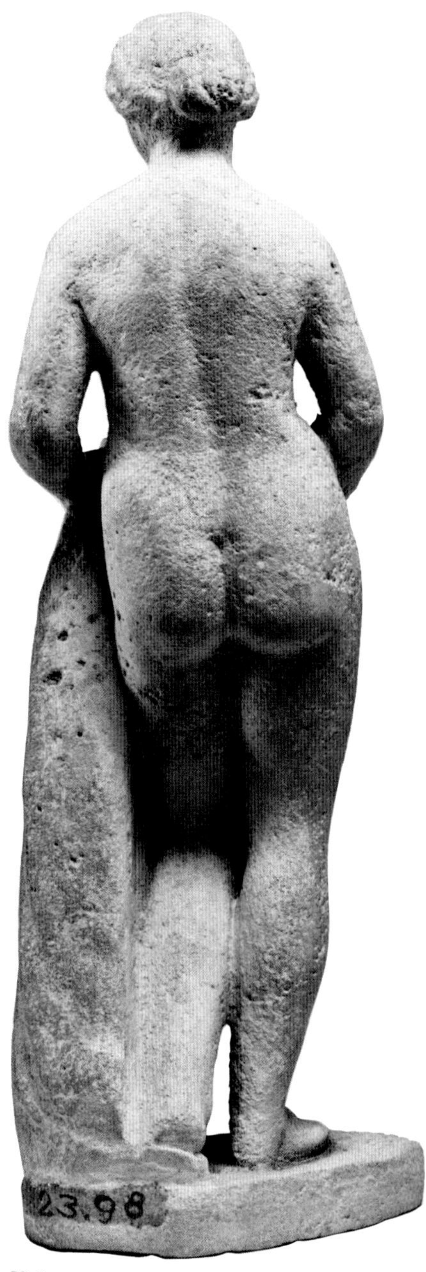

19.2

to this type.[2] Unlike the Venus Colonna
type, traditionally regarded as the most
reliable representation of the original, the
goddess here holds up the ends of her
mantle so that the folds fall vertically and
give the impression that she has only just
removed her garment. A further contrast
with the Venus Colonna type is the
diminutive size of the water vessel, an
indicator of its reduced importance or
even its absence in the original; this feature finds parallels in terracotta figurines
from Myrina of the first century.[3] The

reputed provenance of the Walters statuette together with its small scale and the
mediocre quality of the stone suggest that
the piece was made in the eastern Mediterranean, possibly under influence from
imported terracotta figurines.[4]

1. Robertson 392–93; *LIMC* II (1984) pt. I, 49–52.
2. M. Pfrommer, "Zur Venus Colonna," *IstMitt* 35 (1985)
173–180.
3. Mollard-Besques, *Myrina*, 15, no. LY1588, pl. 15c; 15, no.
B80, pl. 15e; 18, no. LY1553, pl. 17a.
4. On this subject, see J. C. Carter, *The Sculpture of the Sanctuary of Athena Polias at Priene* (London, 1983), 197.

STATUE OF THE
APHRODITE OF KNIDOS
*Copy of ca. first century after
marble original by Praxiteles
of the fourth century*

23.217. Large-grained marble. Purchased from Spink
and Son, in 1963. Ht, 50.5 cm; W, 22.8 cm; Depth,
17.2 cm. Broken across neck, left upper arm and
front of shoulder, right wrist, and above knees.
Abrasion on outside of left thigh where support element has broken away. Back is smooth, with heavy
encrustation.

A nude female of half-lifesize scale stands on her
right leg with her left thigh slightly relaxed and
advanced. Her torso leans forward. Her left arm was
held slightly away from her body; her right arm was
brought across her abdomen. The remains of a
thumb and three fingers protrude from her inner left
thigh. At the back of her neck her hair is gathered
into a short thick mass.

Publications: D. K. Hill, ''A Replica of the Knidian
Aphrodite,'' *BurlMag* 107 (1965) 49, figs. 58–59; D.
K. Hill, ''Statuette of Aphrodite,'' *BWalt* 16 (1964)
no. 6; D. K. Hill, ''More About the Aphrodite of
Cnidus,'' *BWalt* 16 (1964) no. 7.

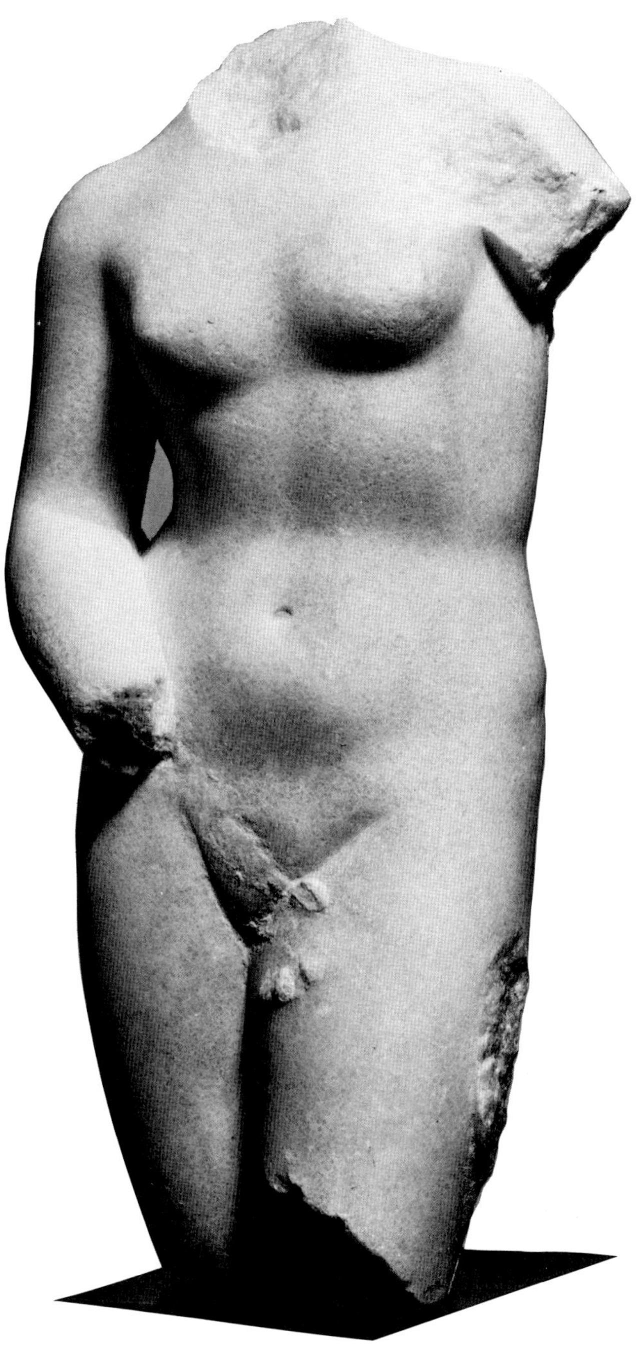

20.1

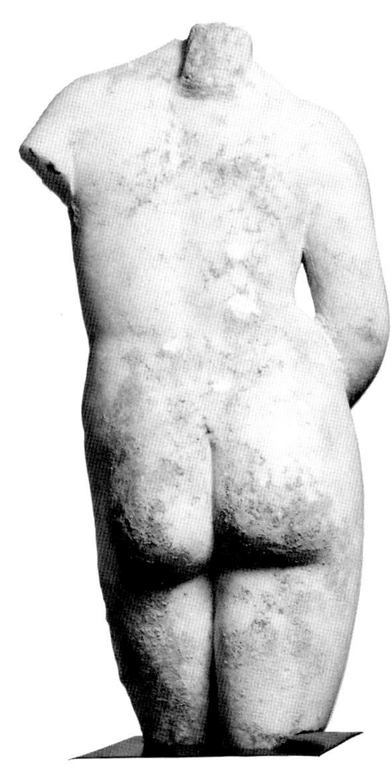

20.2

This statue differs from its prototype (see
No. 19) in the smaller size, the addition of
a strut at the left thigh, and the arrangement of her hair at the nape. Particularly
noteworthy is the greater accuracy with
which the female form is rendered, a manifestation of the broader experience that
later Hellenistic artists had acquired in
rendering the nude female; now the
breasts are more correctly positioned and
the forms slimmer with softer transitions.[1] The sensuality calls to mind such
other Hellenistic types of the nude Aphrodite as the Aphrodite Anadyomene (Nos.
71, 72) who is not only comfortable with,
but even exults in, her nudity. The size of
the Walters statue suggests that it served
as domestic or garden statuary.

1. See Ridgway 75. See also G. M. A. Richter, *The Metropolitan Museum of Art: Catalogue of Greek Sculpture* (Cambridge, 1954), 83, no. 146, pl. 107.

Statue of Standing Muse of Bookroll Type
Roman copy after a type of the second century

23.229. Marble. Collection of Grace Rainey Rogers. Bequeathed in 1943 to Cosmopolitan Club. Purchased in honor of Dorothy Kent Hill in 1977. Ht, 141 cm; W, 48.8 cm; Depth, 24.6 cm. Back is summarily worked. Missing head and neck, right arm, left forearm, left foot and the right leg with drapery below the knee where recutting is apparent. Dowel hole in neck for attachment of head. Two holes in right side for attachment of right arm; above them is an open drilled channel. Small hole behind right shoulder. Remains of dowel for attachment of left forearm. Crack in drapery over left elbow. Abrasions over surface.

A maiden stands on her right leg with her left leg relaxed. Her left arm was extended slightly behind her and to the side. She wears a U-necked undergarment, the folds of which cover most of her left foot. Her mantle is wrapped around her back, and is brought forward under her right arm with the lower hem passing from the right knee to the left hip and the upper edge forming a roll between the breasts and passing over the left shoulder. The mantle folds completely cover her left arm and the tasseled tips hang down behind her left shoulder.

Exhibitions and Catalogues: *From the Shipwreck of Time: 100 Greek and Roman Antiquities*, Staten Island Museum (New York, February 14–March 28, 1965), no. 3.

Publications: D. Buitron, "A New Statue of a Muse," *BWalt* 30 (1978) no. 4.

Since the days of Homer, the Muses as the source of inspiration to creative thinkers had been described in literature, and occasionally depicted, as beautiful maidens. It was a longstanding convention for poets to summon the Muses in the opening lines of their poems. Thus Theokritos, writing in the third century, opens his *Dirge of Daphnis* with the words, "Begin my country song, dear Muses," and Bion cries "Let Love call forth the Muses: . . . Let the Muses give me song."[1] In the Hellenistic period, a popular demand for images of the Muses was engendered by the celebrity of, and the many emulating versions after, the great Mouseion at Alexandria, which was literally the first temple or shrine to the Muses, a scholarly complex in a gardenlike setting. The popularity of the Muses in Hellenistic times was also due to the age's preoccupation with abstract forces, a phenomenon whose most familiar manifestation was the statue of the Tyche of Antioch (ca. 296), a personification of chance or luck. (See No. 148.)

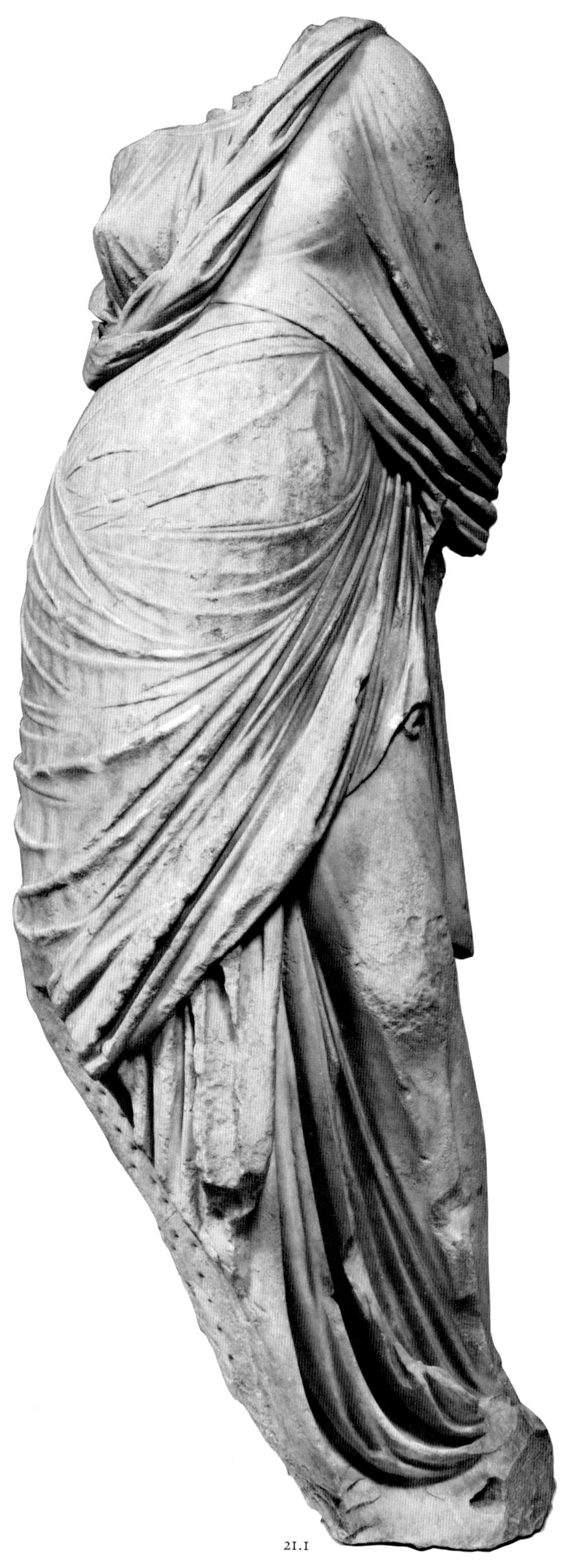

21.1

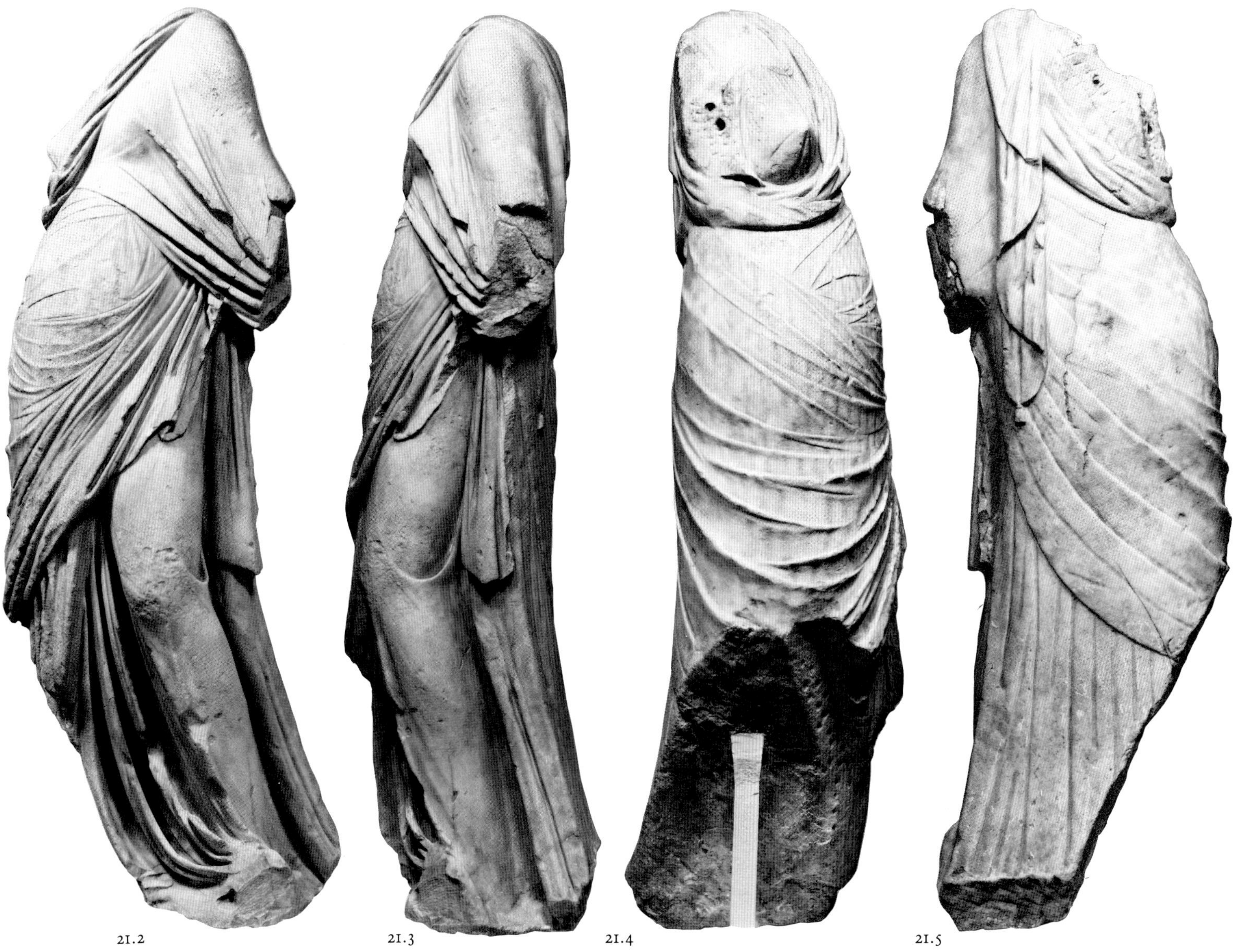

21.2   21.3   21.4   21.5

The Walters statue was probably inspired by a Hellenistic work based on a prototype that had not been made much earlier. The first known appearance of the type is in contexts that unequivocally identify her as one of the Muses: the Archelaos relief (ca. 220–150) and the Halikarnassos Base (ca. 120).[2] Enough copies of the type survive to allow us to restore a bookroll in the right hand, but the attribute is not specific enough to identify the prototype as Klio, the name by which the type is generally known. Indeed, because the Muses did not receive specific identities before the Augustan period, the prototype probably did not denote any one specific Muse.[3] The Book-roll type was particularly popular, with many copies coming from Rhodes or western Asia Minor (especially Kos and Ephesos), where it is likely that the proto-type originated, probably as part of a Muse cycle.[4] Hellenistic and Roman copies were acquired both individually and in groups for domestic and public set-tings.

The figure wears a thick woolen dress, thought to be the peronatris (Theokritos, *Adoniazusae* 5.21) beneath the diaphanous byssos which was made of linen or silk. The transparency of the overgarment con-stitutes a display of sculptural virtuosity not seen before the later third century.[5] Typically mid-to-late Hellenistic are the elongation of the torso, the high waist and broad hips, the backward inclination and sideways torsion of the upper body, and the manner in which the drapery seg-ments the figure into discrete areas of pat-tern, deliberately avoiding the articulation of the body which is familiar in sculpture of the Classical era. Identifying the statue as Roman work are the shallow, concen-tric grooves that define the drapery folds in back, and the grooves radiating from the right nipple.

1. Theokritos, *Dirge of Daphnis* I. 64; Bion 14.
2. D. Pinkwart, *Das Relief des Archelaos von Priene und die "Musen des Philiskos"* (Kallmünz, 1965), 99–101, pls. 2, 5. See also Bieber, *Sculpture,* 128–130 and figs. 499–501. For an example from Myrina, see Mollard-Besques, *Myrina,* 88, no. Myr 204, pl. 108a, dated second half of first century. See also G. Merker, *The Hellenistic Sculpture of Rhodes, SIMA* 40 (Göteborg, 1973), 28, no. 44, pl. 12, figs. 26–28. For the Archelaos Relief, see also Pollitt 15, fig. 4.
3. See Pinkwart (note 2) 78, 179.
4. See Ridgway 50, 101.
5. D. B. Thompson, "A Bronze Dancer from Alexandria," *AJA* 54 (1950) 371; J. C. Carter, *The Sculpture of the Sanc-tuary of Athena Polias at Priene* (London, 1983), 195, 197.

STATUETTE OF STANDING
MUSE OF BOOKROLL TYPE
Ca. second century

23.100. Large-grained marble. Purchased from
Brummer in 1928. Ht, 70.3 cm; W, 23.4 cm;
Depth, 17.6 cm. Most of back summarily worked;
area behind legs rough-picked. Missing head, right
arm above elbow, left forearm beneath elbow.
Dowel holes for attachment survive for all these
losses. Also missing are drapery folds down left side,
and the front of both feet. The drapery is chipped all
over.

A maiden stands on her right leg, her left leg relaxed
with the foot to one side. She wears a U-necked
peplos, the folds of which splay out upon the
ground. Her himation passes behind her back and is
draped across her torso with the lower hem passing
from the right calf to the middle of the left thigh,
and the upper border brought in a roll between the
breasts, passing over the left shoulder, and covering
the left arm.

Publications: D. K. Hill, "Some Sculpture from
Roman Domestic Gardens," *Ancient Roman Gardens*
(Washington, D.C., 1981), 88, pl. III.4.

As a Hellenistic replica of the Muse with a
Bookroll (see No. 21), this example
enables us to assess the variations that
could exist between copies, and, accordingly, their reliability as replicas of their
prototype. Whereas the pose, gesture,
proportions, and basic organization of
drapery are the same as seen on No. 21,
the smaller work exhibits a less complicated arrangement of the drapery folds,
and less torsion in the pose. Absent also
are the rendering of the folds of the
undergarment as seen through the diaphanous mantle, and the long folds which, on
the larger version, flank the outside of the
left leg to isolate that limb in deep vertical
troughs of darkness. The simplified form
of this replica as well as its smaller scale
may indicate a date closer to its prototype;
noteworthy is the consistency in style
between this piece and the following
entry (No. 23), of undoubted second century date.

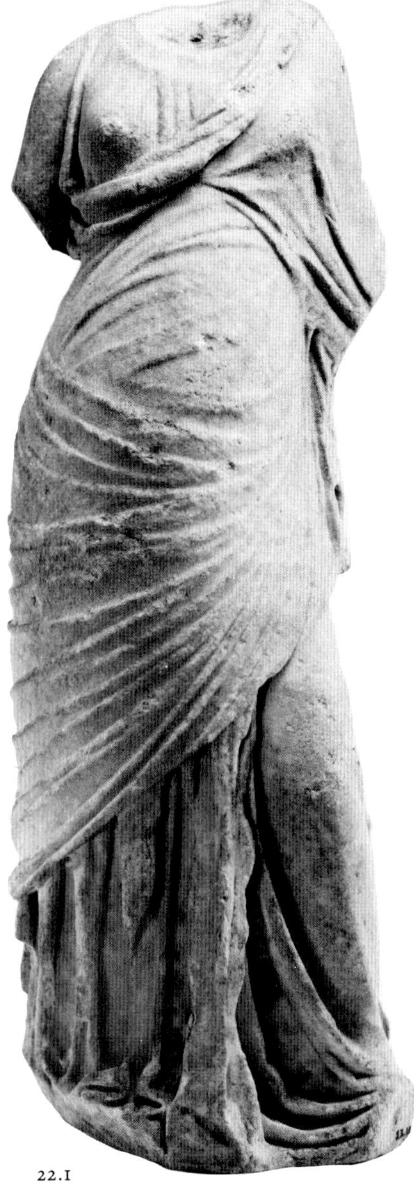

22.1

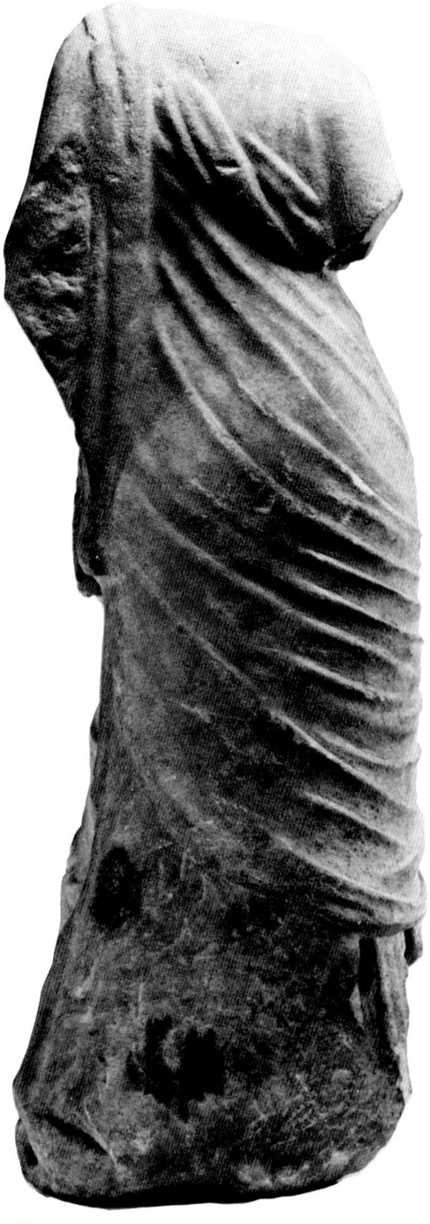

22.2

EAST GREEK GRAVE
RELIEF
Second century

23.230. Marble. Purchased in 1980. Ht, 75 cm; W, 43.2 cm; Th, 15.8 cm. Sides smooth with moldings continued from front. Missing top of stele with neck and head of largest figure. Both vertical sides of naiskos largely broken away. Most of head of servant and front of object she holds are missing. Chipped around base and abraded over surface with sections missing from left knee, right hip, and right hand of larger figure. Reddish discoloration on surface.

The stele is of naiskos form with plain vertical fasciae at the sides. The figures stand on a plain horizontal fascia surmounting a cavetto and flat base. Within is a standing frontal female, her weight on her right leg, her left leg relaxed with the foot to the side. Her right arm is bent at the elbow with the right hand resting upon her chest; her left arm hangs by her side. She wears a U-necked chiton beneath a mantle which is brought across her body completely covering her right arm and her left arm to the wrist. The lower edge passes from below the right knee across to her left hip. Beneath the mantle emerge the folds of the chiton which fall to the ground exposing only the toes of her right foot. Her left foot is concealed by the body of a standing female attendant seen almost from behind, her right knee bent with the toes of the right foot, seen in left profile, resting on the ground behind her. Her upraised left hand supports an open chest (?) which she is presenting to the other figure. She wears a belted long-sleeved garment with an overfold that extends to mid-thigh. The ends of her mantle hang down over the right shoulder to her calf. Her hair is drawn back to her nape in a bun.

The size and subject matter identify this relief as a product of East Greece, particularly the region around Smyrna where the closest parallels have been found, most of them dated to the second century.[1] Of special interest on the Walters example is the figure of the woman, who is a very accurate rendering of a type of draped maiden known as the Small Kithara Holder, which has been linked with a hypothetical group of Hellenistic statues depicting the nine Muses.[2] Although the inclusion of the type in unambiguous Hellenistic representations of Muses verifies the figure's origin as a Muse, it is not possible to link this type with any one specific Muse, and it is very likely that no such correlation was intended at the time when the type was created, probably in the second century.[3] As one of the most accurate Hellenistic reproductions of the Small Kithara Holder and one which could not have been made long after the creation of the prototype, the Walters relief strengthens the contention that this Muse type originated on the western coast

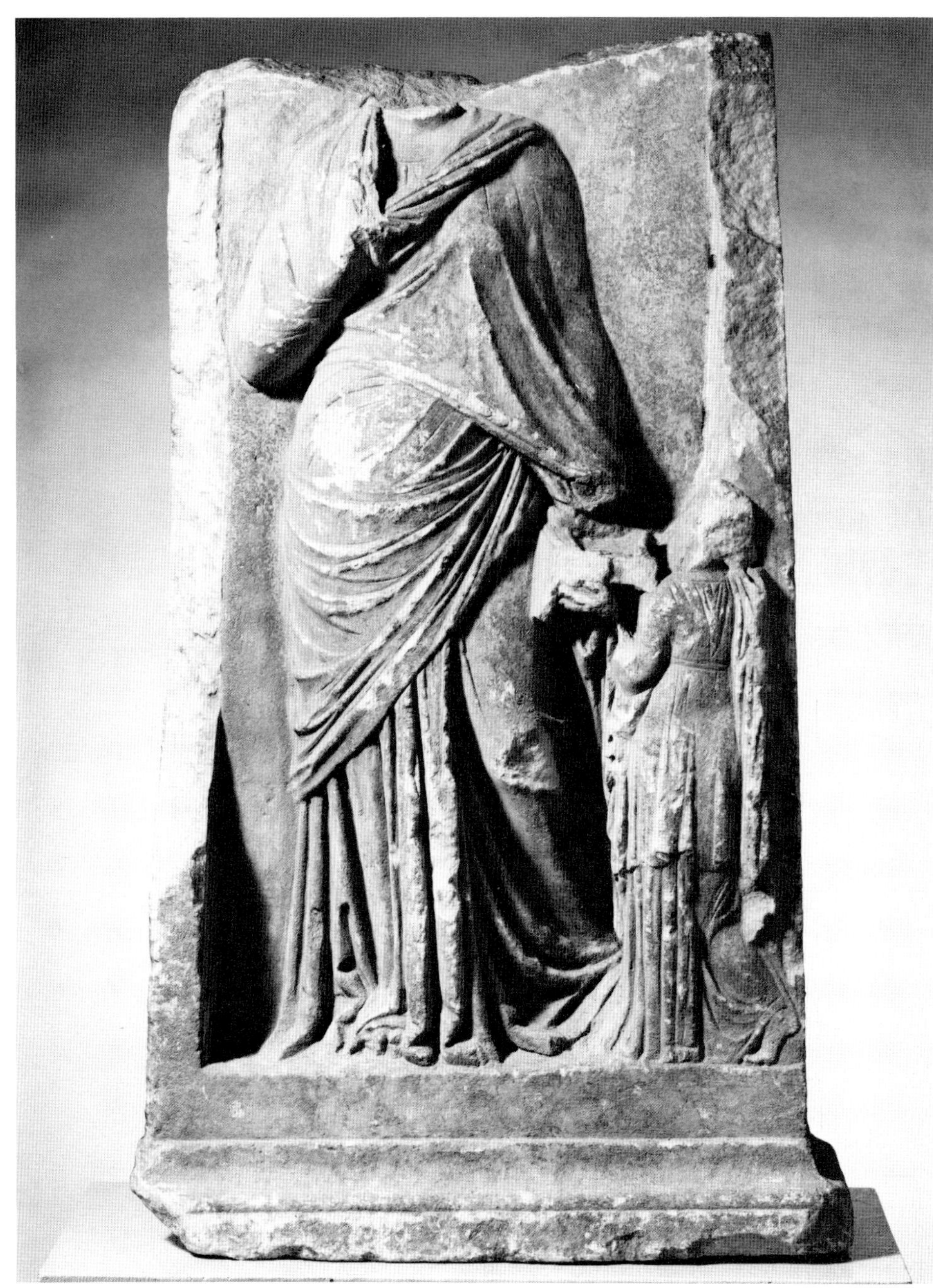

23.1

STATUETTE OF A SEATED MUSE OF URANIA TYPE
*Roman copy after an original
of the early third century*

of Asia Minor. Moreover, the accuracy of what is almost a contemporary replica testifies to the close relationship between large- and small-scale Hellenistic sculpture in this area, a phenomenon further attested by the appearance of the type among terracottas made in Myrina and Smyrna from the second century to the first century A.D.[4]

The scene on the relief is clearly a Hellenistic interpretation of a representation familiar from Classical Attic grave reliefs, in which the deceased woman is accompanied by a servant girl. In keeping with the Hellenistic period and distinctive of East Greek grave reliefs are the strict frontality, even isolation, of the woman, and the diminutive size of the servant girl who overlaps the anta and is presented in profile with particular attention to the left leg, which is not convincingly related to either the anatomy or the drapery.

The presence on a grave relief of a figural type denoting a mythical being follows a practice attested on grave reliefs from the Classical period, where the deceased might be represented in the guise of such divinities as Aphrodite.[5] The Walters relief honors that tradition by introducing a type that was also intended to be easily recognized, and the confidence in the allusion to a statue which could not have been created long before this relief offers thoughtful confirmation to the acclaim that the prototypical Muse statue must have been accorded almost immediately after its creation.

1. E. Pfuhl and H. Möbius, *Die ostgriechische Grabreliefs* (Mainz, 1977), fig. 989, pl. 149; fig. 944, pl. 141; fig. 882, pl. 130; fig. 414, pl. 68; fig. 382, pl. 62.
2. D. Pinkwart, *Das Relief des Archelaos von Priene und die "Musen des Philiskos"* (Kallmünz, 1965), 101–103, pl. 3.
3. Pinkwart (note 2) 78, 179.
4. Mollard-Besques, *Myrina*, 106, no. B66, pl. 126a; Leyenaar-Plaisier 420, no. 1165, pl. 152.
5. B. Schmaltz, *Griechische Grabreliefs* (Darmstadt, 1983), 221–222.

23.84. Marble. Purchased from Brummer in 1924. Ht, 65.7 cm; W, 29.2 cm; Depth 26.7 cm. Back almost completely finished. Missing left forearm, for which fragment of iron dowel survives in elbow, and right foot, for which dowel survives in lower leg. Hole behind left shoulder.

The maiden is seated on a rock, the contours of which are indicated as a series of semicircular overlapping outcroppings curved like flower petals. Her right knee is brought over her left knee and her right elbow is bent and rests upon her right thigh with her right hand cupping her chin such that the head is turned three-quarters to her right. Her left arm was extended slightly away from her body. Above a chiton or peplos her himation is draped around her torso from neck to mid-thigh; the folds are brought over her right upper arm, exposing only her forearm, and then pass over her left forearm. Her hair is center-parted and gathered in a knot at the back of her head.

Publications: D. K. Hill, ''Some Sculpture from Roman Domestic Gardens,'' *Ancient Roman Gardens* (Washington, D.C., 1981), 88, pl. III.5.

This figure reproduces a type that is generally agreed to represent one of the nine Muses and that is first documented with this identity on the Altar of Athena Polias at Priene, which Carter has convincingly redated to the late third century. The prototypical work, probably early Hellenistic in date, is thought to have been made somewhere on the western coast of Asia Minor where many replicas have been recovered.[1] The type takes its name from a Roman copy in Malaga on which the maiden holds a globe, an attribute that by the Roman period was identified with the Muse Urania, who was associated with astronomy, or heavenly knowledge.[2] It is by no means clear, however, that the prototypical work possessed the same attribute, because the seated Muse on the Halikarnassos Base (ca. 120) holds a diptychon, and copies in Liverpool and Broadlands are seen with bookrolls.[3] The appearance of a similar seated figure on a fourth-century Attic grave relief indicates that this Muse type had a late Classical prototype from which the Tyche of Antioch is surely also derived.[4]

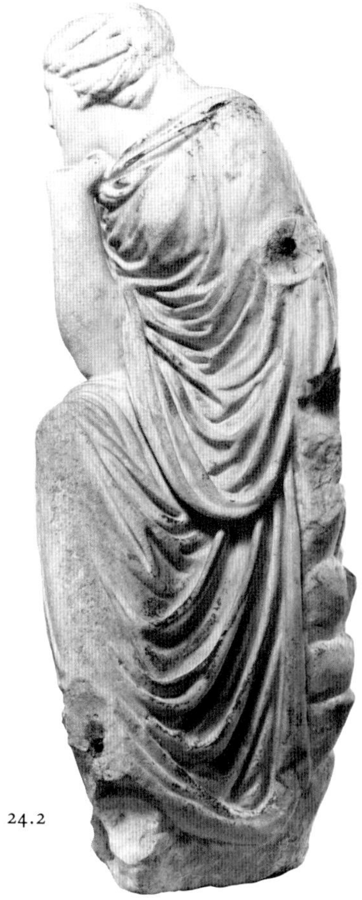

24.2

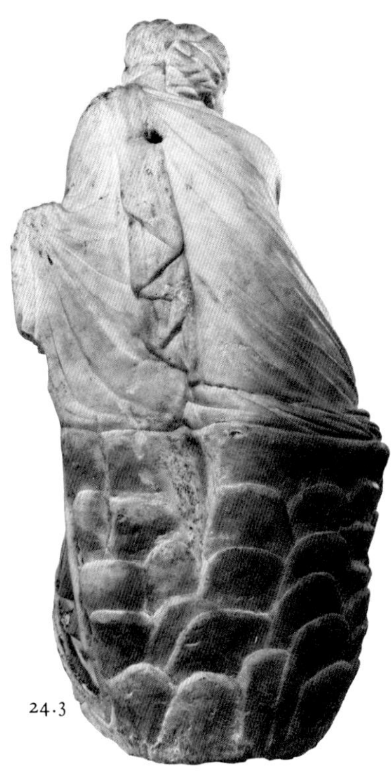

24.3

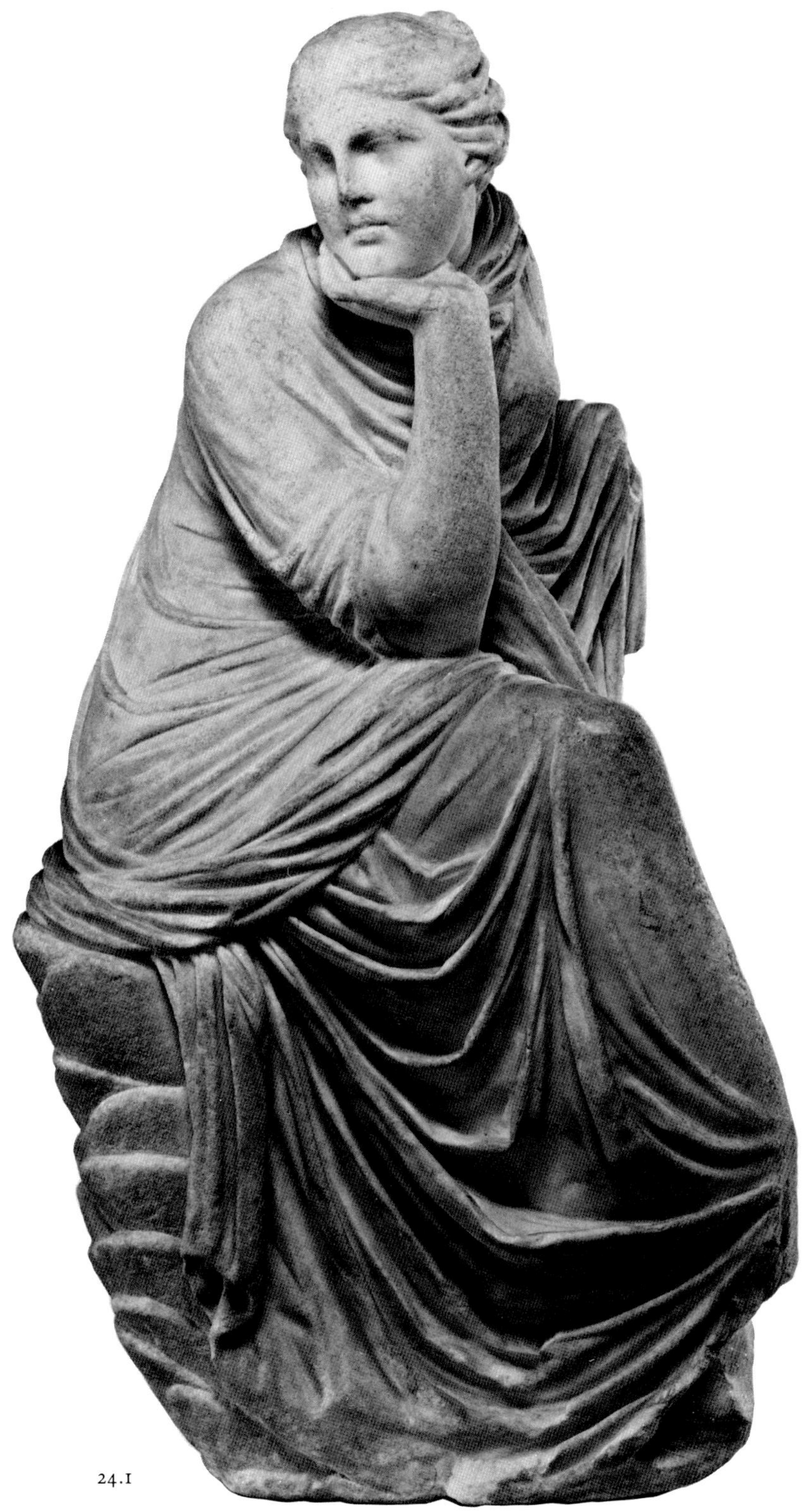

24.1

Although the Walters example does not exhibit all four tasseled ends of drapery, an omission that diminishes her accuracy as a copy, the piece is one of only two examples (the other is in Malaga) to retain her head, and is, therefore, important evidence that on the prototypical work the maiden gazed to her right and not to her left, as in the Tyche of Antioch. The scalloped treatment of the Walters figure's rocky seat recalls the handling both of tree trunks on Roman statuary and of the rocky promontory beneath the Tyche of Antioch as seen on Roman coins.[5] The Walters muse was probably displayed in a public area, such as a bath, mouseion (outdoor garden), or nymphaeum (fountain or pool area); alternatively, she was possibly intended for a private terraced or peristyle garden.

1. For the Altar of Priene, see J. C. Carter, *The Sculpture of the Sanctuary of Athena Polias at Priene* (London, 1983), 193. For other copies of the type, see D. Pinkwart, *Das Relief des Archelaos von Priene und die "Musen des Philiskos"* (Kallmünz, 1965), 163. See also a fine terracotta version from Delos, dated to the second century in A. Laumonier, *Exploration archéologique de Délos XXIII: Les figurines de terre cuite* (Paris, 1956), 195, no. 685, pl. 69 and T. Dohrn, *Die Tyche von Antiochia* (Berlin, 1960), 45, pl. 44.1. A terracotta mold for the head, hand, and bust of this type, showing the same hairstyle, is in the Louvre and is dated to the late fourth or early third century. Besques, *Grèce,* 73, no. D454, pl. 99. Also on Delos are a small-scale marble statuette of the type, missing its head, and a battered head with part of the hand at the chin, which in its fleshy cheeks and the arrangement of the hair is very close to the Walters version. See J. Marcadé, *Au musée de Délos* (Paris, 1969), 195–197, nos. A4131, pl. 33, and A999, pl. 34. See also Bol, *Liebieghaus,* 128, no. 36.

2. See Carter (note 1) 193; Pinkwart (note 1) 78–79, 139, 178.

3. For the Halikarnassos Base, see D. Pinkwart, "Die Musenbasis von Halikarnass," *AntP* 6 (1967) 89–93, pls. 53–57. For a discussion of the other copies, see Pinkwart (note 1) 139, 205, and Carter (note 1) 193.

4. For the grave relief, see H. Diepolder, *Die attischen Grabreliefs* (Berlin, 1931), 55, fig. 12 and Dohrn (note 1) 42, pl. 35.1. For the Tyche, see Pollitt 3, fig. 1.

5. For tree trunks, see P. Zanker, *Klassizistische Statuen* (Mainz, 1974), pl. 8; F. Muthmann, *Statuenstützen und decoratives Beiwerk an griechischen und römischen Bildwerken* (Heidelberg, 1951), pls. 20–21. For the Tyche, see Dohrn (note 2) 16, no. 7, pl. 22.1–2 and 31, pl. 30.5.

Statuette
of a Leaning Muse
Third to second century

23.90. Marble. Collection of Dr. B. and M. C. (sale catalogue, Paris, Hôtel Drouot, May 19–21, 1910, 6, no. 45, pl. 4); Durighello Collection (sale catalogue, Paris, Galerie Georges Petit, June 12, 1924, 11, no. 15, pl. II). Purchased from Kelekian in 1927. Ht, 30.6 cm; W, 26.3 cm; Depth, 20.2 cm. Roughly worked in back of waist; hole in right ear probably for earring. Missing right forearm with elbow; dowel hole remains in arm. Broken off below hips; rough tooling and a dowel hole in underside. Missing tip of nose; chipped above right eye.

Head to hips of a standing draped maiden who leans with her left side against a rocky surface, her left arm resting on top with the elbow bent. The right arm lies close to the body; the head is turned in right profile. Her himation is brought around the back and passes under the right arm and over the left shoulder with folds completely covering the left arm and hand. Her hair is center-parted and gathered in a knot at the nape, with locks extending to the shoulder.

Publications: D. K. Hill, ''Some Sculpture from Roman Domestic Gardens,'' *Ancient Roman Gardens* (Washington, D.C., 1981), 88, pl. II.3.

The leaning pose with the upper body weight pressed against a support can be traced back at least to the fourth century with an Attic patrix for a terracotta figurine.[1] The rocky support of the Walters piece coupled with the tilted head and downcast glance suggest that the maiden is a Muse. Certainly her hairstyle and facial features can be compared with the seated Muse, No. 24, and her pose recalls that of the Muse type known as the Poly-

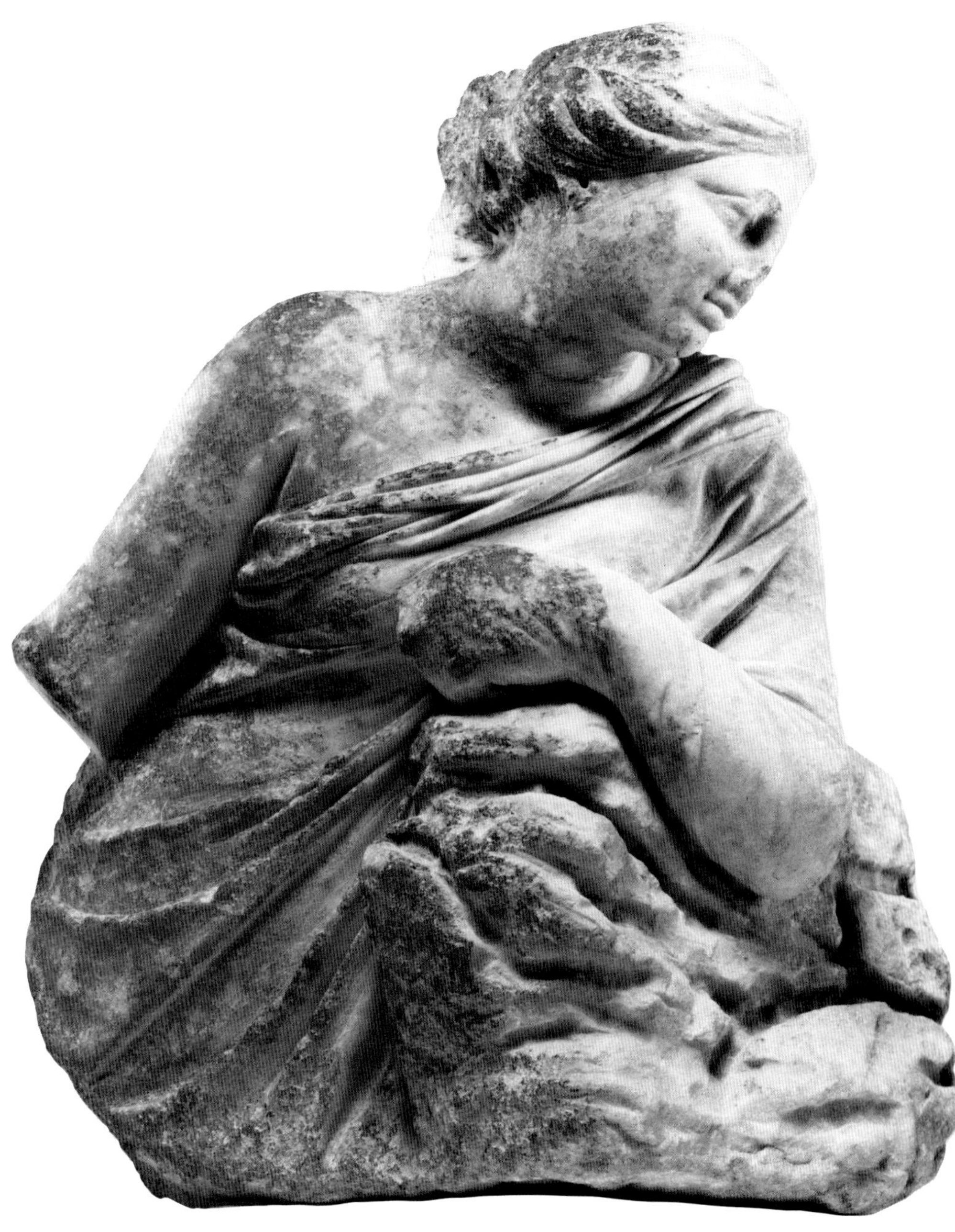

25.1

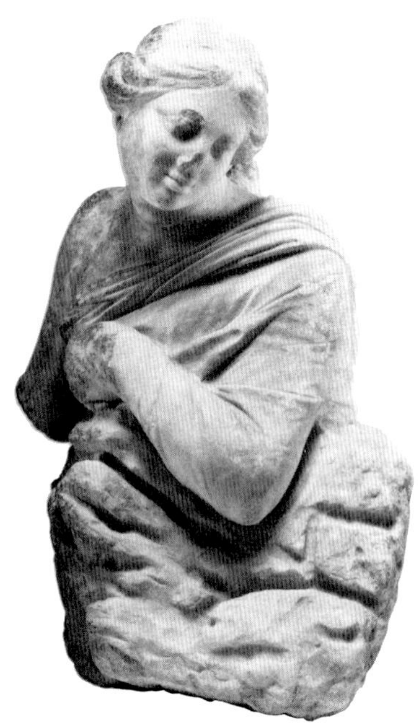

25.2

hymnia.[2] The draping of the mantle under the right arm finds a parallel both on the above-mentioned patrix, where the right shoulder is also completely exposed, and on both a terracotta from Tanagra of the third century and representations of Muses on the Archelaos Relief (ca. 220–150), where a chiton or peplos lies beneath the himation folds.[3] The uncomplicated system of drapery with its flat folds support a date for the Walters maiden in the third century.[4]

1. B. Neutsch, *Studien zur vortanagräisch-attischen Koroplastik,* *JdI-EH* 16 (1952) 17, 19, 25, pls. 12–13.
2. M. Bieber, *Ancient Copies* (New York, 1977), 249, pl. 154, fig. 885. Compare the figure leaning over a ledge on a grave relief from Smyrna of ca. 150 in E. Pfuhl and H. Möbius, *Die ostgriechischen Grabreliefs* (Mainz, 1977), I, 182–183, no. 646, pl. 98.
3. For the terracotta from Tanagra, see Higgins, *Tanagra,* pl. 8. For the Archelaos Relief, see D. Pinkwart, *Das Relief des Archelaos von Priene und die "Musen des Philiskos"* (Kallmünz, 1965).
4. Compare the more sharply angled head of a figure, also with her head turned to the side, on the frieze from Lagina, in A. Schober, *Der Fries des Hekateions von Lagina,* Istanbuler Forschungen 2 (Baden bei Wien, 1933), no. 202, pl. 28.

HEAD OF A HORSE
Third to second century

23.173. Marble. From Sardis. Purchased in 1929. Ht, 35.3 cm; D, base 22 cm; W, neck 16.5 cm; Depth, nose to mane 45.3 cm. Fragment of iron bit in left side of mouth; hole for bit pierced through right side of mouth. Underside smooth with dowel hole (4.5 x 3.5 cm) near front and shallow depression at back edge. Tips of ears broken off. Chips missing from mane, forelock, and left eyelid. Smaller chips missing over rest of surface.

The head and neck of a horse turn slightly to the animal's right with the mouth open and the nostrils flaring. The browband continues to the throatlatch with a disc in the center front and is also connected to the noseband by three straps: a bifurcated one down the nasal bone and two others incised only on the cheeks. Three locks of the mane are brushed to the left side, a forelock in front of the left ear, and two locks behind. The head and neck are very narrow, with greater plasticity and finer detail on the proper left side.

Exhibitions and Catalogues: *An Exhibition of Treasures from The Walters Art Gallery,* Wildenstein (New York, March 16–April 15, 1967), no. 76.

Publications: H. C. Butler, "Excavations at Sardes," *AJA* 18 (1914) 430 and 429, fig. 2; T. L. Shear, "Sixth Preliminary Report on the American Excavations at Sardes in Asia Minor," *AJA* 26 (1922) 391, fig. 1; H. C. Butler, *Sardis I: The Excavations, pt. 1, 1910–14* (Amsterdam, 1922), 154 and 153, fig. 173; T. L. Shear, "The Horse of Sardis," *ArtB* 10 (1927–28) 215–230 and 214, fig. 2; 218, fig. 4; 221, fig. 6; 228, fig. 19; D. K. Hill, "The Horse of Sardis Rediscovered," *ArtB* 24 (1942) 155–159, figs. 2, 3, 4; G. M. A. Hanfmann and N. Ramage, *Sculpture from Sardis: The Finds through 1975* (Cambridge, 1978), 169, no. 258, figs. 444–446.

This head was found at Sardis in 1914 on the last day of the excavations, which were thereafter suspended until 1921 when the disappearance of the piece was discovered. The head reemerged in 1929 when Henry Walters purchased it from an unknown dealer who provided a provenance of Egypt. Excavated with the head were a gilded marble sandal, three hands, and a statue base too small to have belonged with any of these other finds. From the same site were also recovered a marble head wearing a pilos, which Dorothy Hill associated with the horse head, the hands, and the sandal, suggesting that the Walters head and a hypothetical lost mate served as accompanying attributes and support to a statue group of the pilos-adorned Dioskouroi.[1] Although statues of this type are best known from the Roman period, a close parallel to the Walters horse exists in a fragmentary late Hellenistic statue base from Eleusis on which a similar conically necked horse protome adjoins a sandaled foot which surely belonged to a Dioskouros.[2] The Walters horse is clearly earlier than both this classicizing version and one found at Antikythera, because it displays the prominent brows and plastic locks of hair familiar from the horse of the Mausoleum of Halikarnassos.[3]

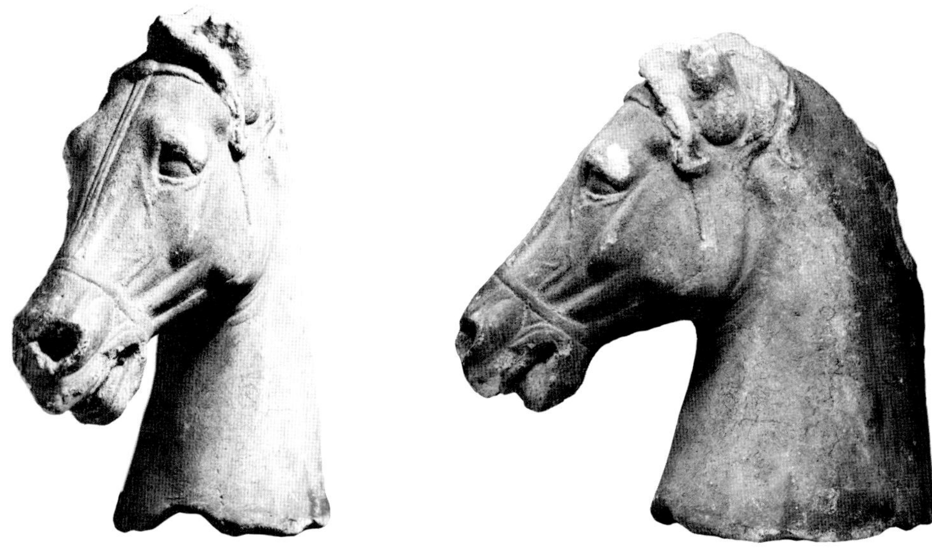

26.2

26.3

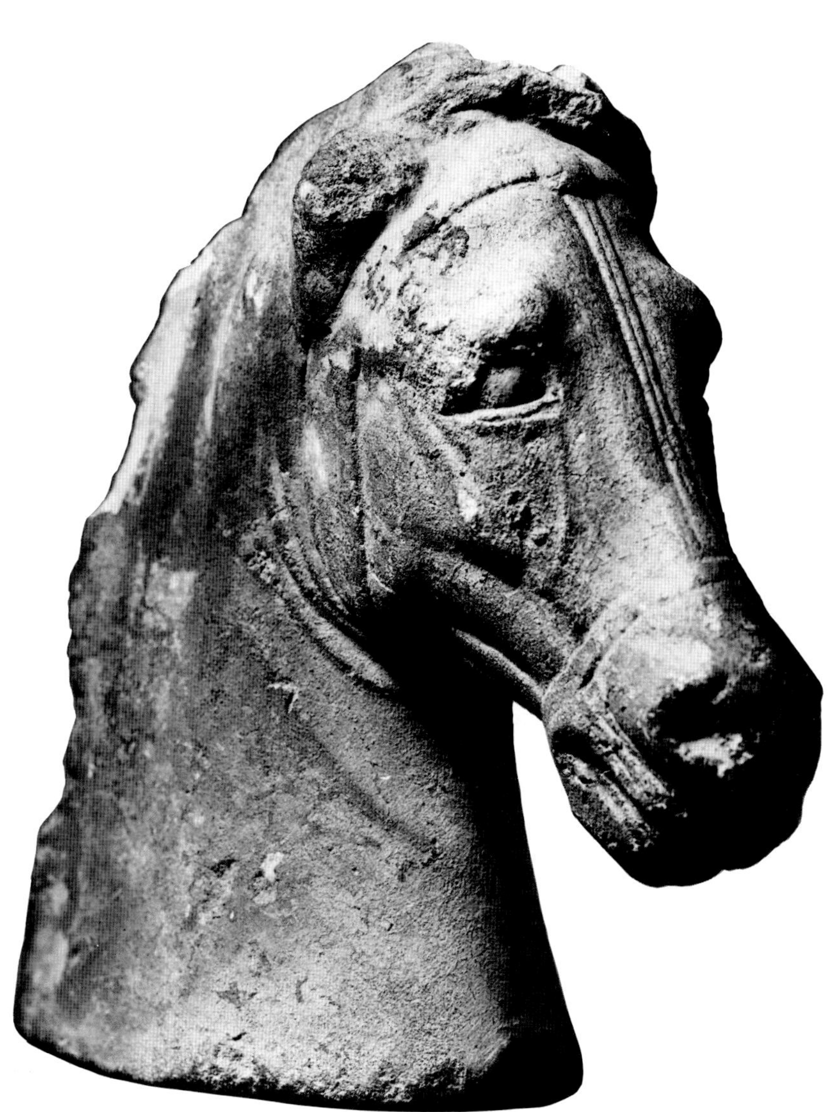

26.1

1. Hill, *ArtB* 24 (1942) 157–58. For further parallels, see G. M. A. Hanfmann and N. Ramage, *Sculpture from Sardis* (Cambridge, 1978), 169.
2. R. Schoder, *Masterpieces of Greek Art* (Greenwich, 1960), no. 73, dated first century.
3. For the Antikythera example see P. Bol, *Die Skulpturen des Schiffsfundes von Antikythera, AM-BH* 2 (1972) 84–85, no. 93a, pl. 51.3; G. B. Waywell, *The Free-Standing Sculptures of the Mausoleum at Halicarnassus in the British Museum* (London, 1978), pl. 5.

STATUETTE OF SATYR AND DIONYSOS
Late third or early second century

23.69. Marble. Purchased in 1920. Ht, 24.8 cm; W, 13.3 cm. Red pigment in hair of satyr. Rasping on front of body. Broken across satyr's waist, and his right arm is cut smooth below the right shoulder. Modern dowel hole on underside.

A nude male gazes upward behind his right shoulder. He has large eyes, an overhanging brow, open mouth, and his wavy hair extends to the nape. His right arm was extended; his left arm is bent at the elbow and the left hand supports the left leg of a boy who straddles the older male's left shoulder. The child rests both hands on the head of the other figure and turns his head to his right, following the other figure's gaze. The child wears a braid pulled back from the brow and short curls around the nape.

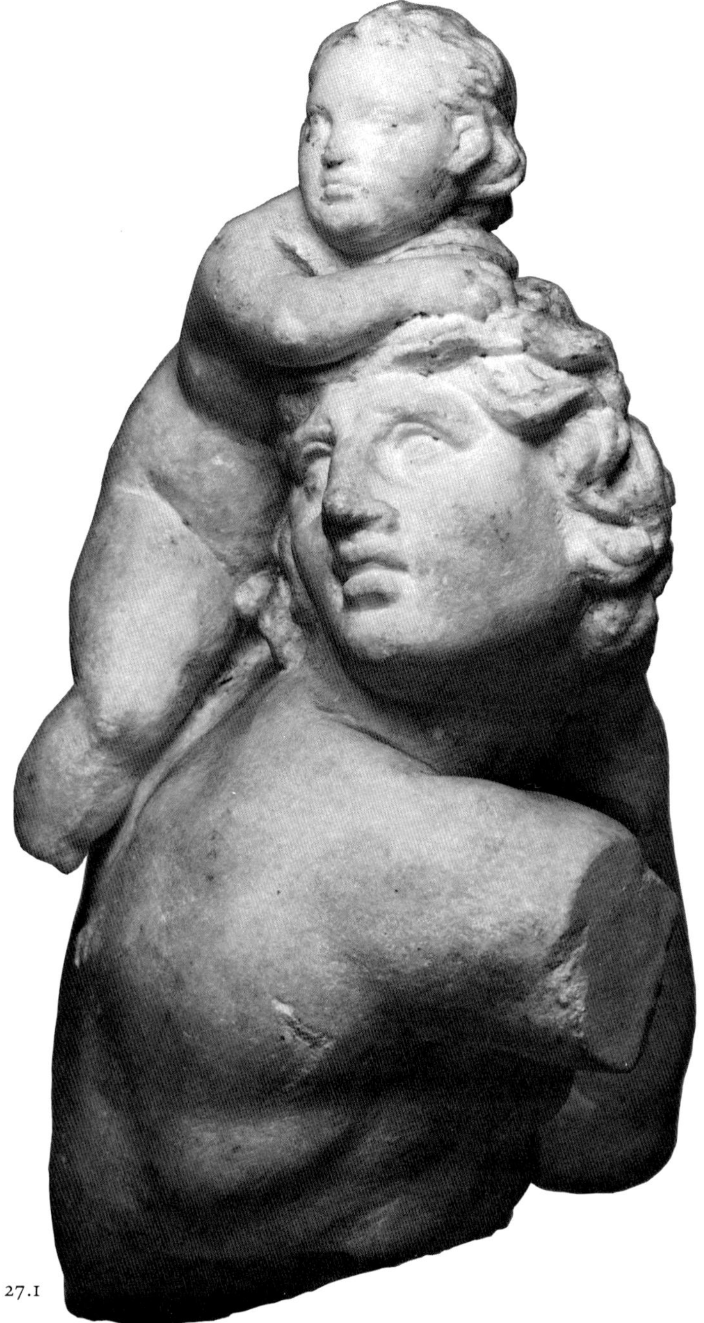

27.1

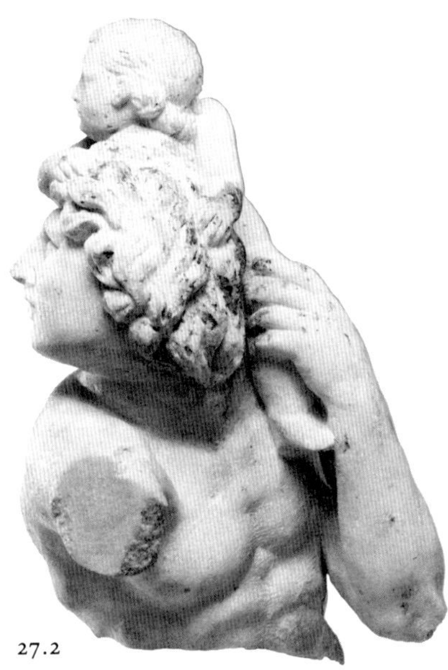

27.2

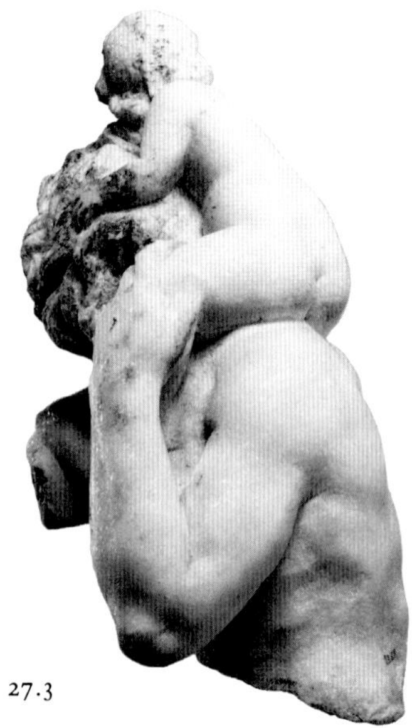

27.3

Exhibitions and Catalogues: *The Greek Tradition in Painting and the Minor Arts,* The Walters Art Gallery and the Baltimore Museum of Art (Baltimore, May 15–June 25, 1939), 62, no. 29.

Publications: Bieber, *Sculpture,* 139–140, fig. 571; *LIMC* III (1986) pt. 1, 480, no. 694, pt. 2, 379.

The animal skin seen on other examples of this type identifies the adult as a satyr, who traditionally carries on his arm the child Dionysos, identified by the cornucopia he may grasp.[1] On the Walters group the child is perched, not on the arm, but on the shoulder, a pose that can be traced back to fifth- and fourth-century depictions of Aphrodite and Eros.[2] The Walters group or its prototype should probably be assigned to the late third or second century, because the violent turn of the satyr's head brings to mind the statue of the Gaul and his wife, which has also been dated to this period.[3] The anatomical impossibility in the turn of the satyr's head coupled with the distinctive features of thick lips, protruding nose, and broad cheeks are suggestive of Alexandrian workmanship, with which the small size of the statuette as well as the simplified contours of the face are also compatible.[4] Probably of later date is a type that survives on several Roman copies; here Dionysos straddles the neck of the satyr who turns to gaze at a cluster of grapes held in the child's raised right hand.[5]

1. *LIMC* III (1986) pt. 1, 480, nos. 689–690, pt. 2, 379. Bieber, *Sculpture,* 140, fig. 570.
2. G. P. Carratelli, ed., *Megale Hellas* (Milan, 1983), 500, figs. 576–577.
3. Pollitt 85–86 and 87, fig. 86.
4. Compare a bronze figurine in K. A. Neugebauer, "Aus der Werkstatt eines griechischen Toreuten in Ägypten," *Schumacher-Festschrift* (Mainz, 1930), 233–237. See also a marble statuette of Herakles: J. Frel, "Ancient Repairs to Classical Sculpture at Malibu," *GettyMusJ* 12 (1984) 83, figs. 17–20.
5. *LIMC* III (1986) pt. 1, 480, no. 693, pt. 2, 379. This same work is Bieber, *Sculpture,* 139, fig. 569. Another example is Bol, *Liebieghaus,* 190, no. 58.

Head of Arsinoe III
217–206/5 or 204/3

23.6. Marble. Purchased in 1928. Nahman Collection. Ht, 13.5 cm; W, 8.3 cm; Depth, 8.3 cm. Traces of red on eyes, lips and hair. Back of head roughly worked. Hole in top of head. Broken off in back and across bottom, possibly from a relief.

A female gazing forward has a polished face and a Venus ring. Her hair is center-parted beneath a three-tiered mass of coiled ringlets. Around the head runs a depressed groove for the addition of a diadem. V-shaped neckline beneath.

Identifying this head as the portrait of a Ptolemaic queen is the Isis hairstyle coupled with the diadem, which was surmounted by a uraeus that fitted into the hole at the crown of the head. The closest parallels lie with a marble head in Cairo and a bronze head in Mantua, both of which have been identified as portraits of Arsinoe III, who also appears on the faience fragment, No. 104.[1] A head almost identical to the Walters example comes from ancient Thmuis and is now in Cairo.[2]

1. H. Kyrieleis, *Bildnisse der Ptolemäer* (Berlin, 1975), 104–105. For the head in Cairo, see 182, no. L 2, pls. 90–91. For the bronze head in Mantua, see 182, no. L 3, pls. 92–94. I thank Andrew Stewart for help with this identification.
2. G. Grimm, *Kunst der Ptolemäer und Römerzeit im Ägyptischen Museum Kairo* (Mainz, 1975), 18, no. 10, pl. 11.

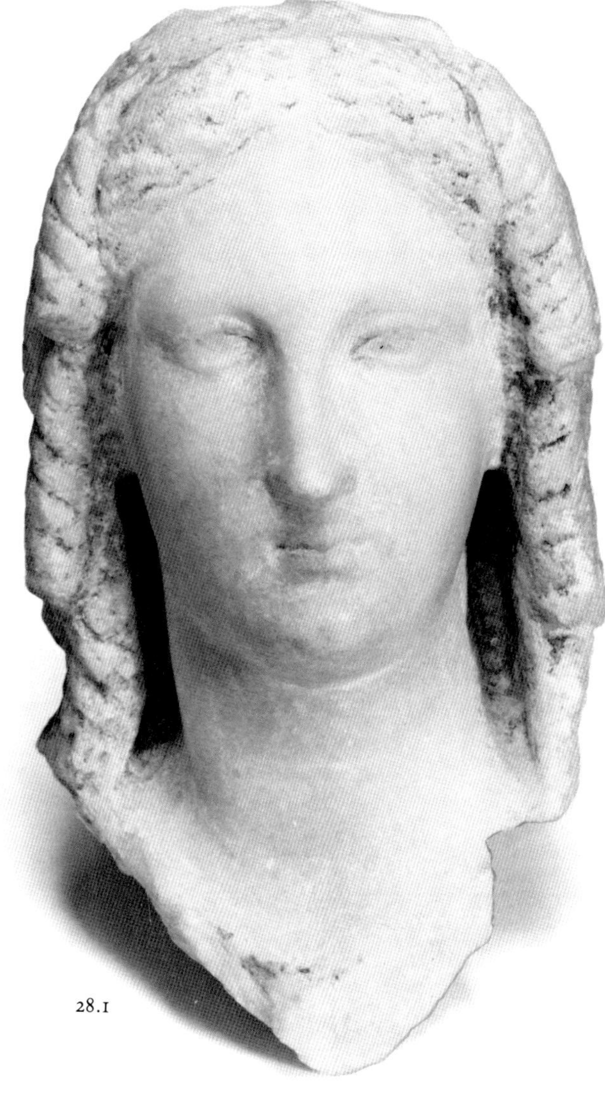

28.1

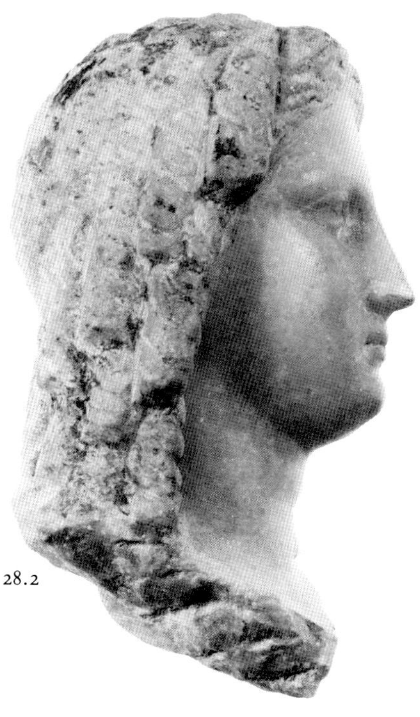

28.2

Head of Kleopatra II
or Kleopatra III
Ca. 175–107

22.407. Limestone. Purchased from Kelekian in 1928. Ht, 24.7 cm; W, 17.8 cm; Depth, 26 cm. Broken across neck. Uraeus broken off and nose chipped. Deep gash in front of right ear; smaller gashes and chips missing from entire surface.

A female head wears a diadem that has a uraeus at center front and is tied in a Herakles knot behind. Beneath the diadem are corkscrew locks in two rows across the brow and in staggered rows behind the head with the hair pulled back to what must have been a knot at the nape. The ears are exposed with two locks in front of the left ear, and probably originally the right ear as well. Above the diadem the hair is center-parted with the locks indicated by shallow, close-set, parallel grooves. The eyebrows are rendered by incision. The face is asymmetrical with the left ear protruding, and the left cheek, eyeball, and hair set lower and carved with less depth.

Exhibitions and Catalogues: *Pagan and Christian Egypt,* Brooklyn Museum (Brooklyn, January 23–March 9, 1941), 19, no. 17.

Publications: Steindorff 70, no. 226, pl. 39; B. V. Bothmer, *Egyptian Sculpture of the Late Period, 700 B.C.–100 A.D.* (Brooklyn, 1960), 170.

The diadem with uraeus and the Isis locks identify the maiden as a Ptolemaic queen.[1] The closest parallels to the treatment of her nose and mouth are found on a statuette in New York and a granite head in Alexandria, both of which have been

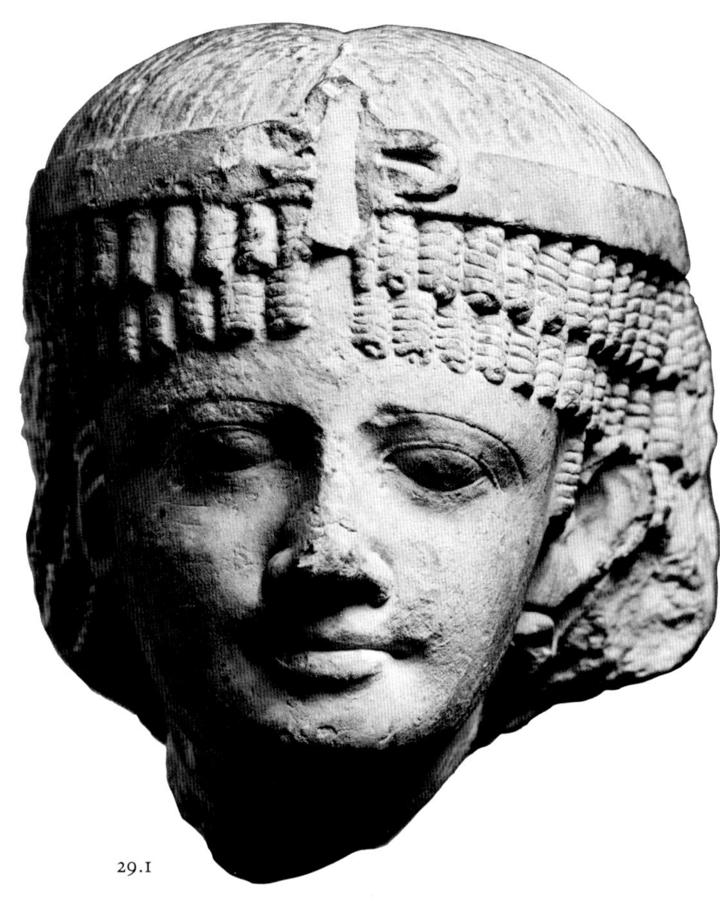

29.1

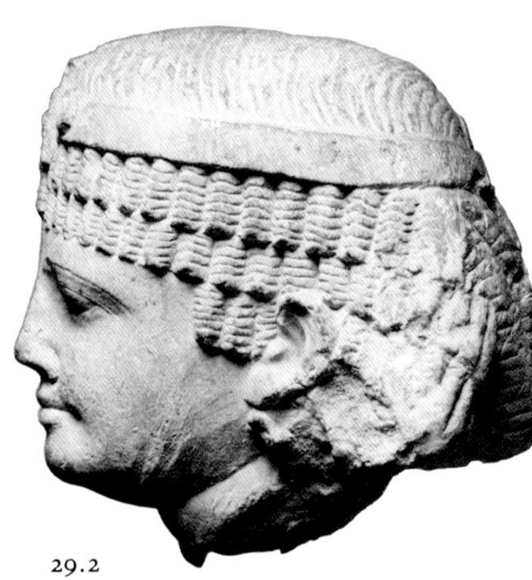

29.2

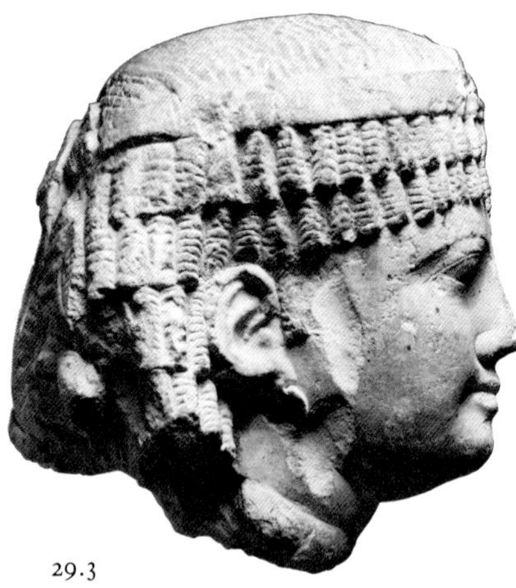

29.3

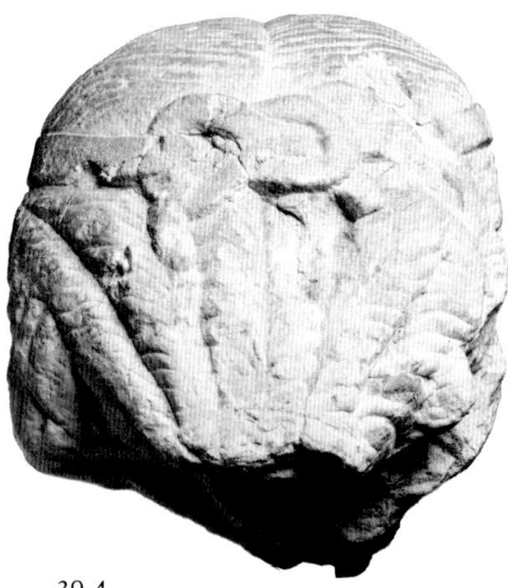

29.4

identified as Kleopatra II or III.[2] Kleopatra II is also depicted on the peridot, No. 141.

The lives of Kleopatra II and Kleopatra III constitute extreme examples of Ptolemaic dynastic complexities and turbulence. Kleopatra II (185 or 180–116/5) was the daughter of Ptolemy V and Kleopatra

I, and married her brother, Ptolemy VI in about 175/174. She became the wife of another brother, Ptolemy VIII, in 144. Her daughter by Ptolemy VI, known as Kleopatra III, married Ptolemy VIII two years after his marriage to her mother, and produced two sons: Ptolemy IX and Ptolemy X, who succeeded to the throne in 107.

1. The tight ringlets of the hairstyle can be traced back to representations of Libya on late fourth-century coins from Cyrene. See E. S. G. Robinson, *A Catalogue of the Greek Coins in the British Museum, Vol. XXIX: Catalogue of the Greek Coins of Cyrenaica* (repr. Bologna, 1965), 249.

2. H. Kyrieleis, *Bildnisse der Ptolemäer* (Berlin, 1975), 117–118. For the granite head, see 183, no. M 2, pl. 101.2. I thank Andrew Stewart for help with this identification.

HEAD OF A MAN

100–50

22.226. Diorite. "From Luxor." Purchased from Kelekian before 1931. Ht, 12.7 cm; W, between ears 9.5 cm; Depth, 12.1 cm. Hair unpolished; face highly polished. The stone beneath nape is rough-picked. Broken across neck; chipped on chin, cheeks, lips and right brow. Nose restored.

A male head with short curly hair, the locks of which are broader and wider at the sides and back.

Exhibitions and Catalogues: *Egyptian Sculpture of the Late Period,* Brooklyn Museum (Brooklyn, October 18, 1960–January 9, 1961), 155, no. 120, pl. 3, figs. 298–300.

Publications: J. Keith, "Notes on a Marble Head of a Youth in the Brooklyn Museum," *JARCE* 6 (1967) 159, n. 20, pl. 6; K. Michalowski, *Art of Ancient Egypt* (New York, 1969), 459, fig. 628; G. Grimm, *Die römischen Mumienmasken aus Ägypten* (Wiesbaden, 1974), 56, n. 112. A. Adriani, "Ritratti dell'Egitto greco-romano," *RM* 77 (1970) 87.

Although the Greek influence in this piece is substantial and unmistakable, distinctively Egyptian elements are also easily recognized: the narrow almond-shaped eye with the outer corners tapering upward, and the broad nose with a very narrow bridge that continues well above the inner corners of the eye. Especially noteworthy are the short wavy locks of hair, which are delineated with multiple parallel grooves and which increase in

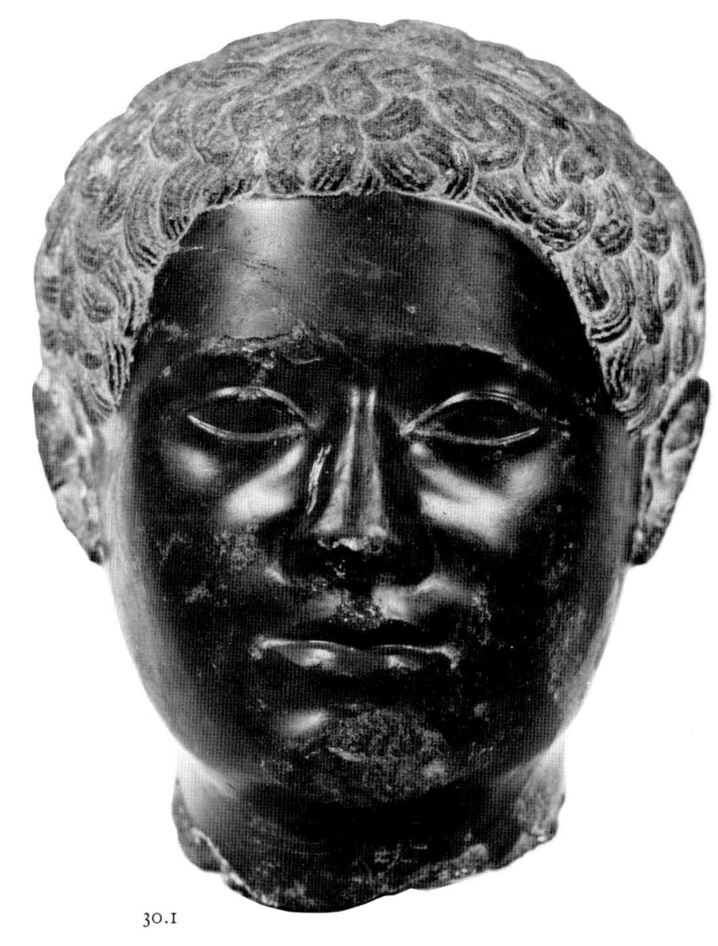

30.1

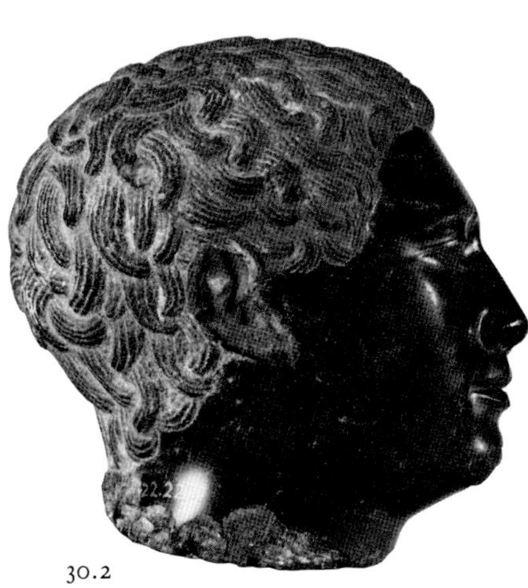

30.2

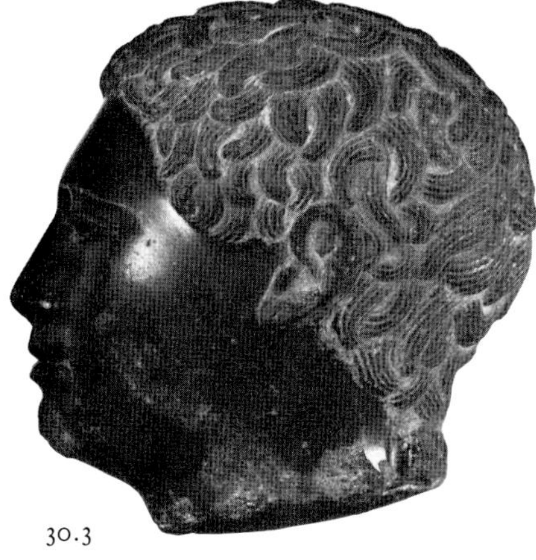

30.3

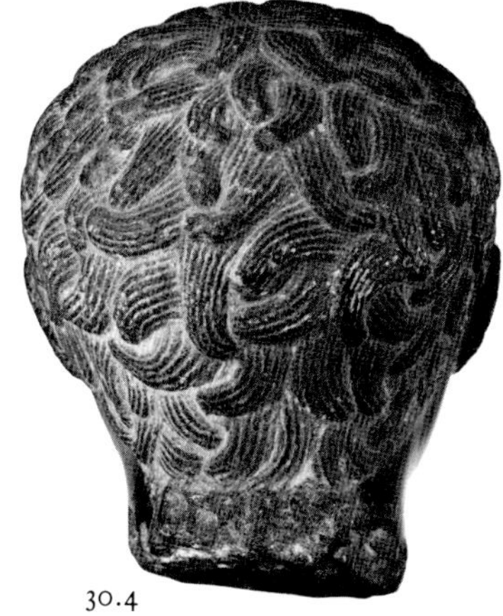

30.4

scale at the back of the head, forming a starlike pattern at the crown. A pronounced groove demarcates the hairline, and a strong textural contrast is established between the incised and unpolished locks of the hair and the smoothly polished surface of the face. Noteworthy in the profile view are the concavity of the area between eyelid and brow, the sloping forehead, projecting lips, spherical shape of the back of the head, and the anatomical inaccuracy of the ear. The head compares closely with a diorite head in the Brooklyn Museum and a head of green schist now in London. Features shared by all three examples are the handling of the eyebrow and forehead as a projecting ledge that continues across the bridge of the nose, the emphatic demarcation of the hairline, and the stylized patterns of the individual locks.[1]

1. For the head in the Brooklyn Museum, see Adriani, *RM* 77 (1970) 87, pl. 44.2, and J. Keith, *JARCE* 6 (1967) 157–162, pls. 1–3. For the head in London, see Adriani, 86–87, pls. 43.1 and 44.4.

STATUETTE OF A SATYR
*Possibly a Roman copy after
an original of ca. third century*

23.81. Marble. Purchased before 1931. Ht, 26.8 cm;
W, 12.9 cm. Missing both arms below shoulders,
left leg, right leg below knee. Iron dowel in right
leg is ancient repair. Hole, perhaps modern, behind
right shoulder; remains of square strut (?) beside left
hip. Encrustation over surface and discoloration
around dowel.

A striding satyr turns his torso and head to his right
toward an adjacent figure whom the satyr supported
with his outstretched right arm. The left arm and
hand of the missing figure rest behind the satyr's
neck and upon his left shoulder; the protrusion on
the satyr's right knee probably also belonged to this
adjacent figure. The satyr has pointed ears, short
curly hair, and a tail.

This fragment survives from a group that
represented an inebriated Dionysos supported by a satyr, who is here recognized
by his pointed ears.[1] The subject was a
popular one in Hellenistic art, partly
because the god's lack of control was an
extreme form of the anomalies of behavior
that fascinated the Hellenistic mind, and
partly because the Hellenistic artist was
drawn to the challenge of convincingly
representing two interlocked torsos.
Although the frequency with which this
subject was portrayed in Hellenistic art
would seem to presuppose a consistent
and derivative iconography, Willers
observed that Hellenistic artists either
adhered closely to the iconographies established independently for each medium, or
devised a fresh solution for every handling
of the subject.[2]

1. For the type, see *LIMC* III (1986) pt. 1, 448–450, nos.
   264–280, pt. 2, 324–326.
2. D. Willers, "Typus und Motif; Aus der hellenistischen
   Entwicklungsgeschichte einer Zweifigurengruppe," *AntK*
   29 (1986) 149.

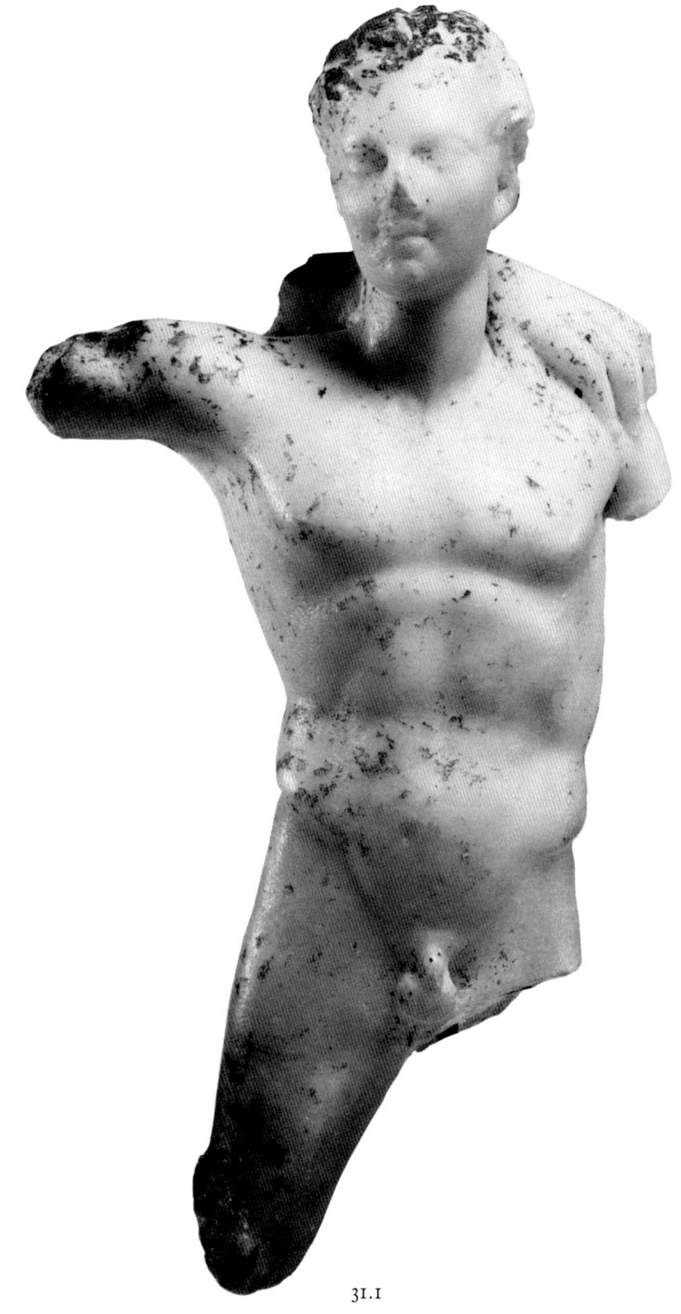

31.1

STATUETTE OF APHRODITE
*Possibly a Roman copy after
a type of ca. second century*

23.99. Marble. Purchased from Brummer in 1928.
Ht, 41 cm; W, 13.2 cm; Depth, base 10.7 cm. Pink
paint on drapery. Dowel hole in right upper arm.
Hole in each ear lobe. Broken across each upper arm
with section missing from drapery on left shoulder
and at left hip. Head and feet reattached.

A female stands on her right leg with the left leg
relaxed and the foot placed at the side. The ends of
her mantle lie upon her left shoulder; the rest of the
fabric is brought around her back and over the top of
her right thigh covering her legs and with the drapery's opposite ends anchored beneath her left elbow.
The rectangular base is carved in one piece with the
figure. Her hair is center-parted and drawn back
from the brow over her ears to the nape.

Exhibitions and Catalogues: *The Greek Tradition in
Painting and the Minor Arts,* The Walters Art Gallery
and the Baltimore Museum of Art (Baltimore, May
15–June 25, 1939), 66, no. 54.

This statuette represents a late Hellenistic
assimilation of several traditions. Reflecting influence from the type of the Aphrodite of Arles is the draping of the mantle
around the hips with the folds pressed
between the left elbow and hip.[1] Influenced by the type of the Aphrodite of
Miletos is the relaxation of the left leg
which results in a hipshot pose, although
in a departure from the type, the Walters
goddess does not rest her left elbow on a
pillar.[2] Unlike either above-mentioned
type are the drapery folds on the edge of
the left shoulder, the lowered position of
the right upper arm, and the position of
the head, which is turned to her right as
she gazes down, presumably at an object
she carried in her lowered right hand.

Most of the statues and statuettes
related to the Walters figure are dated to
the second and first centuries and have the
provenance of the eastern Mediterranean,
particularly Rhodes and Alexandria. In
style, the Walters maiden compares especially well with a fragment from Rhodes,
whose arms are raised in the Anadyomene
manner.[3] Like the Walters maiden the
piece exhibits the elongated torso, narrow
shoulders, and small, close-set round
breasts characteristic of the Rhodian
school which specialized in ornamental
domestic and garden statuary, of which
the Walters maiden may possibly be a
later copy.[4]

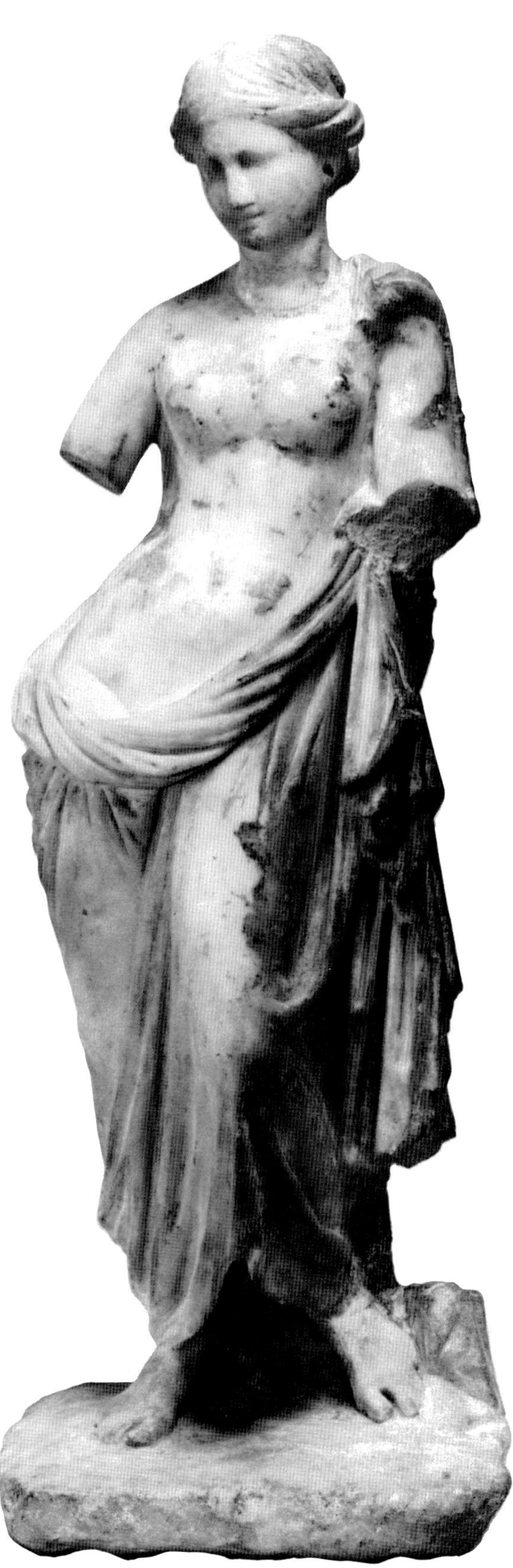

32.1

1. *LIMC* II (1984) pt. 1, 62 and 64, nos. 541, 542; 65, nos.
   543–544.
2. *LIMC* II(1984) pt. 1, 65, no. 551. See also 65, no. 552;
   67, nos. 571, 572, 576.
3. G. Merker, *The Hellenistic Sculpture of Rhodes,* 40 *SIMA*
   (Göteborg, 1973), 26, no. 4, pl.2. This piece is also cited
   in *LIMC* II (1984) pt. 1, 64, no. 542, dated late second
   century.
4. Merker (note 3) 7, 11–12.

STATUETTE OF APHRODITE
*Probably a Roman copy
after an early Hellenistic type*

23.86. Marble. "From Egypt." (sale catalogue, *Collections M. Jean P. Lambros d'Athènes et de M. Giovanni Dattari du Caire,* Paris, Hôtel Drouot, June 17–19, 1912, 40, no. 334, pl. 36). Purchased in 1912. Ht, 31.1 cm; W, 15.3 cm; Depth, 7.7 cm. Red paint on drapery. Finished completely in back. Head and feet broken off. Missing left forearm which was set into elbow, and end of drapery by right thigh. Scratches over chest.

A nude female with her weight on her right leg, her left knee bent, leans slightly forward. Her left arm was bent at the elbow with the forearm extended. Her right arm holds folds of her mantle in front of her body; the ends fly out behind her right thigh. The rest of the mantle conceals most of her right leg and passes behind her back with the ends draped over her left forearm.

Publications: Reinach, *Statuaire* 3 (1904) 256, no. 8; S. Reinach, "Statuette d'Aphrodite découverte dans la basse Égypte," *RA* ser. 4, 3 (1904) 374–381; H. Riemann, *Kerameikos II: Die Skulpturen* (Berlin, 1940), 121, no. 5; *LIMC* II (1984) pt. 1, 79, no. 700, pt. 2, no. 700, pl. 70, as late Hellenistic.

This statuette follows the type of the so-called Venus Felix that takes its name from a statue in the Vatican carrying a dedicatory inscription to that goddess and bearing the head of the younger Faustina.[1] The type is distinguished by the folds of drapery clasped by the right hand at the top of the right thigh and by the figure of Eros whose right arm is raised, in several instances grasping an alabastron which the goddess holds in her left hand. A late fourth-century or early Hellenistic date for the prototype is suggested by a fourth-century figurine vase of Aphrodite who is nude except for her mantle which is lightly draped around her hips; the terracotta departs from the type, however, in that the fabric covers both legs and the right arm hangs at her side.[2] The Walters example is noteworthy for the plastic and energetically rendered folds of the mantle which appear to be drawn around the body in haste, a logical extension of the scenario that is implied in the Aphrodite of Knidos and one, therefore, probably faithful to the prototype.

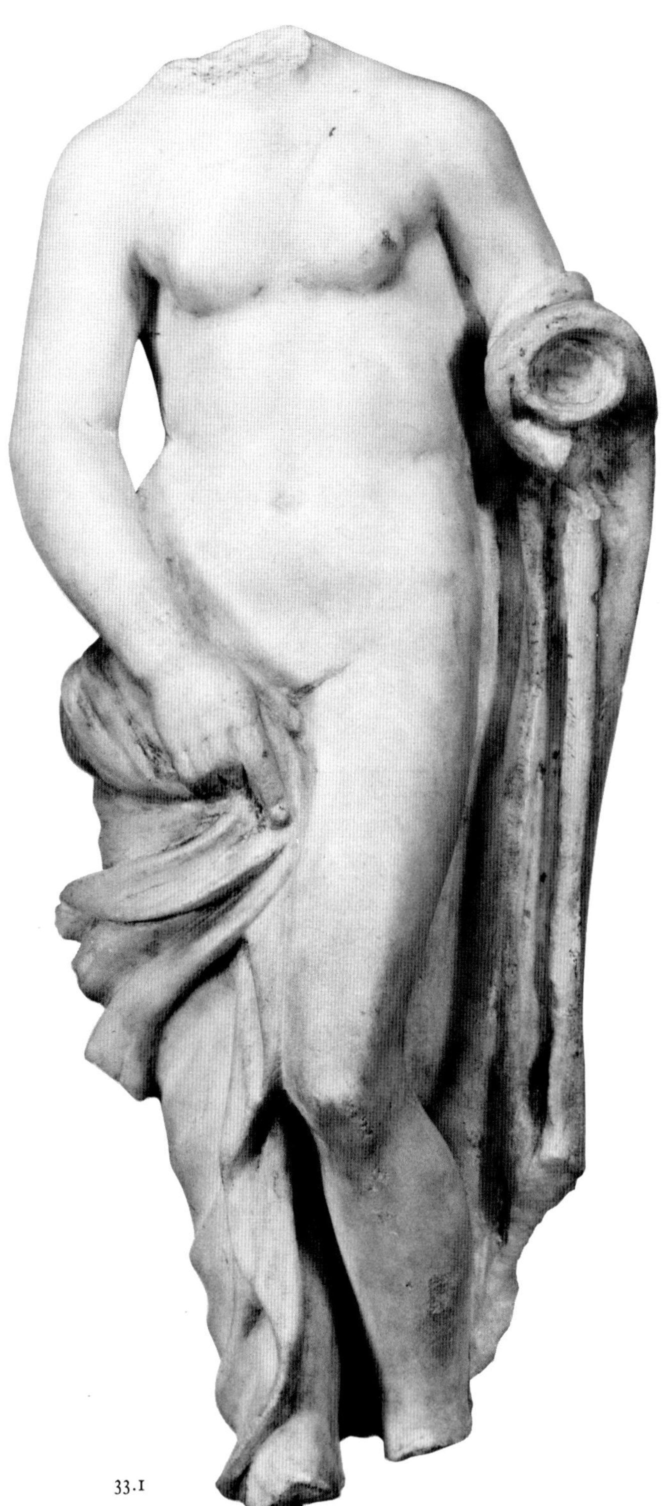

33.1

1. *LIMC* II (1984) pt. 1, 78; and 79, no. 696.
2. *LIMC* II (1984) pt. 1, 79, no. 704.

STATUE OF A WOMAN
First century

23.88. Marble. Massarenti Collection. Purchased in 1902. Ht, 2.0 m; L, base 70.4 cm; W, base 46 cm; Ht, base 7.6 cm. Clamp cutting in plinth beside her left foot. Vertical sides of plinth rough-picked. Broken across left forearm. Nose, chin, and parts of drapery chipped. Heavy brown encrustation.

A woman stands on her left leg with her right knee relaxed and her foot to one side. Her right elbow is bent with the raised right hand holding drapery folds by her throat. Her left upper arm rests by her side with the left forearm outstretched. She wears a chiton or peplos which falls to the ground revealing only the forepart of each foot. Her mantle, folded upon itself, is draped over her head, frames her shoulders, is brought forward over her right shoulder, and passes across her torso beneath her breasts to be wrapped counterclockwise completely around her left arm with the ends falling down her left side. The lower edge of the underlayer of the mantle passes from her right calf across her left thigh. Her right arm and hand are slipped beneath the upper layer which droops in soft folds over the abdomen. A separate garment whose rolled edge frames her face is placed directly on top of her head; the ends pass under her mantle at the shoulders. Her hair is center-parted, drawn back over her ears, and gathered in a knot protruding at the back of her head.

Publications: Esbroeck, pt. 2, 143, no. 16; D. K. Hill, "Three Portraits of the First Century B.C.," *AJA* 54 (1950) 264.

This statue is a late Hellenistic interpretation of traditions that originated in the fourth century, with the pose, gesture, and system of drapery closely related to the figure of a maiden on one of the latest Attic grave reliefs, executed before 317.[1] Noteworthy on the Walters version and indicative of a later Hellenistic date are the loop of drapery at the left hip, the almost horizontal roll of drapery at the left elbow, and the diaphanous rendering of the fabric over the right arm. Contrary to type, the relaxed and supporting legs are reversed, probably to increase the effectiveness of a group composition whose existence is established by the clamp cuttings on the left side of the plinth. The facial features compare with those on a head in Munich dated to the beginning of the third century, but the classicizing, almond shape of the eye, coupled with the small mouth, are closer to a head from the Heroon at Kalydon of the first century.[2]

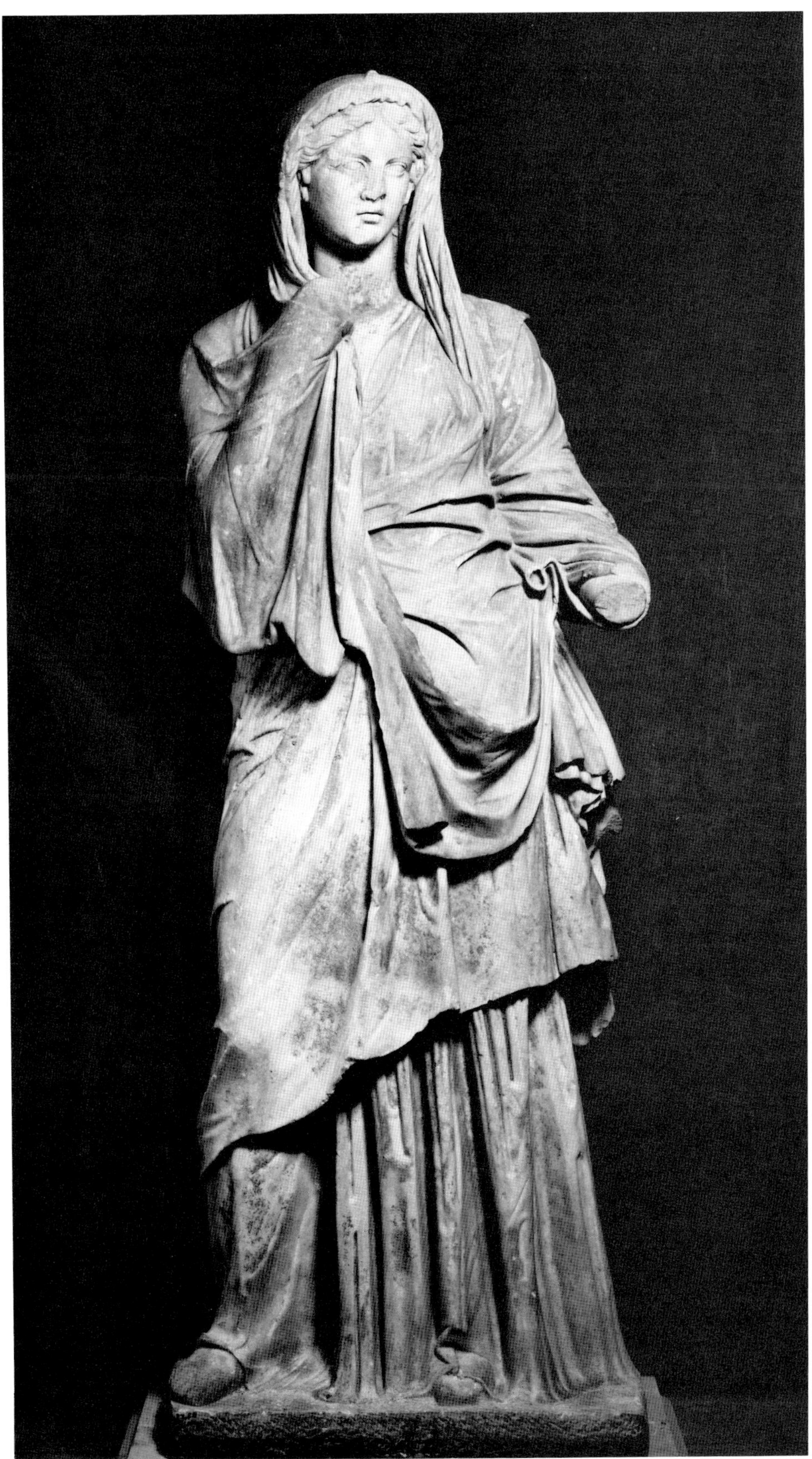

34.1

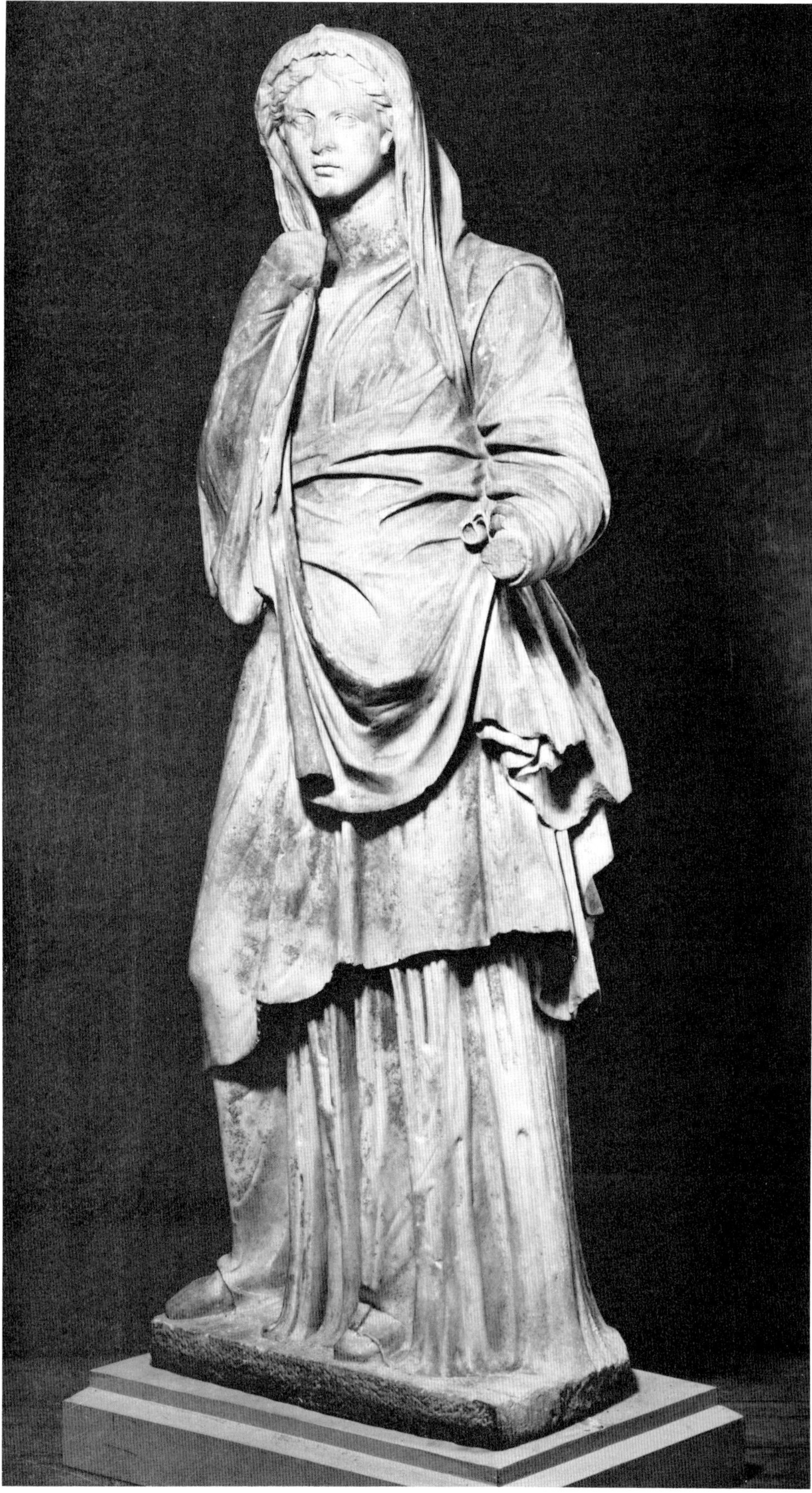

Parallels with statues of the family of L. Valerios Flaccos from Magnesia suggest that the Walters maiden was also carved in the first century as a public monument funded by, and depicting, a local benefactor, and made in a workshop that combined stock body types with heads influenced more by traditional formulae than by the individual features of the subject.[3] The Walters statue was probably made on the western coast of Anatolia and compares closely with a fragmentary Hellenistic statue from Rhodes which exhibits a similar hairstyle, draping of fabric over the head, downward directed gaze, and gesture of the right arm.[4]

1. B. Neutsch, *Studien zur vortanagräisch-attischen Koroplastik, JdI-EH* 16 (1952) 32, pl. 20.2.
2. For the Munich head, see D. Ohly, *The Munich Glyptothek: Greek and Roman Sculpture* (Munich, 1974), 39, pl. 12. For the head from Kalydon, see E. Dyggve, F. Poulsen, and K. Rhomaios, *Das Heroon von Kalydon* (Copenhagen, 1934), 366–367, no. 5, figs. 82–84. Compare also a head of the first century in Bol, *Liebieghaus,* 148, no. 43.
3. For statuary from Magnesia, see A. Linfert, *Kunstzentren hellenistischer Zeit* (Wiesbaden, 1973), 30–31, pl. 5, figs. 22–27; reviewed by D. Pinkwart in *Gnomon* 52 (1980) 47.
4. Rhodes Archaeological Museum 13636. G. Merker, *The Hellenistic Sculpture of Rhodes, SIMA* 40 (Göteborg, 1973), 34, no. 141, pl. 34; G. Jacopi, *Clara Rhodos* V: *Monumenti Scultura del Museo Archaeologico di Rodi II* (Rhodes, 1931–39) no. 3, figs. 13–14, pl. 3.

34.2

STATUETTE OF APHRODITE
BINDING HER HAIR
First century

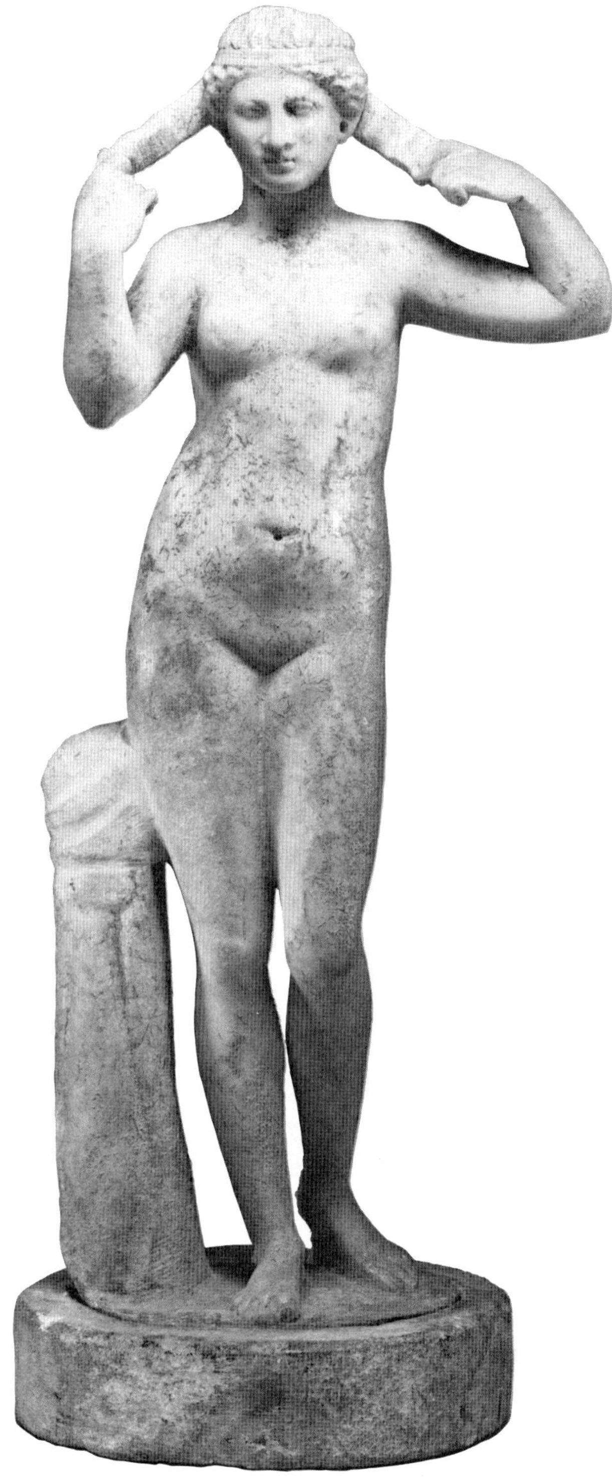

35.1

23.83. Marble. ''Found in 1884 at Panderma (Kyzi-kos).'' Collection of Mons. de Nelidow (sale catalogue, Paris, Galerie Georges Petit, May 23–24, 1911, no. 248, pls. II–IV). Purchased from Kelekian in 1911. Ht, 43.4 cm; W, 16.5 cm; Ht, base 3.8 cm; D, base 14.9 cm. Hole in each ear lobe. Body, strut, and base carved in one piece and set into larger round base. Encrustation over surface.

A nude maiden stands on her right leg with her left knee relaxed and her left foot placed slightly behind her right foot. Only the left heel is cut away from the stone base. A pillar covered with fabric is beside her right thigh. Her head is turned slightly to her right and inclined. Her wavy hair is brushed down from the crown, then center-parted above the forehead with the locks drawn back over the ears to a knot at the nape. Around the knot is a fillet, the ends of which she holds out to each side in the hands of her upraised arms.

Publications: A. Furtwängler, ''Aphrodite Diadumene und Anadyomene,'' *Monatsberichte über Kunstwissenschaft und Kunsthandel* (Munich, 1900–01), 177, pl. 1; Reinach, *Statuaire* 3 (1904) 106, no. 8; Bieber, *Sculpture,* 144, n. 69, pl. 605; N. Himmelmann-Wildschütz, ''Eine römische Bronze in Oxford,'' *MarbWPr* (1958) 4, pl. 2.4; D. K. Hill, ''The Beauty of Venus,'' *BWalt* 22 (1969) no. 2; B. Gassowska, *Polycharmos z Rodos Jako Twórca Pomnika Afrodyty Anadyomene* (Warsaw, 1971), fig. 16.

The nudity identifies this maiden as Aphrodite, but her gesture betrays the influence of the Diadoumenos by Polykleitos, a mid-fifth century statue of an athlete binding a fillet around his forehead.[1] The transposition of the gesture to Aphrodite was probably suggested by its similarity to the gesture of the Aphrodite Anadyomene, who holds a lock of hair in each raised hand, wringing out the water as she rises from the sea (see Nos. 71, 72).[2] In the Walters statuette the artist has retained from the Anadyomene iconography the position of the arms and turn of the head to the right, but has transformed the locks of hair into rather clumsy straps that are twice the width of the rest of the fillet. Another departure from the Anadyomene type is the relaxation of the left leg, which conforms instead to the Diadoumenos pose and not only precipitates the shift of the supporting element to the right side in the manner of the Diadoumenos, but also eliminates from the torso the sinuous curve characteristic of statues of the Anadyomene Aphrodite.

The allusion to a mid-fifth century statue, the Classical hairstyle with a knot at the nape, and the Classical features of the face assign the statuette to the classicizing phase of the late Hellenistic age. Supporting this attribution are the elongated proportions of the torso and the intermingling of male and female iconography, a phenomenon well illustrated in the work of the late Hellenistic sculptor Stephanos.[3] The allusions to monumental sculpture, one of which was of Classical date, suggests that the Walters statuette was made along the western coast of Asia Minor and was thence exported to nearby Kyzikos, an island in the Propontis (Sea of Marmara) off the Anatolian coast which enjoyed an extensive trade with Pergamon, and whose beauty and size reminded Strabo of Rhodes, Marseilles, and Carthage.[4]

1. M. Robertson, *A Shorter History of Greek Art* (Cambridge, 1981), 114, fig. 156.
2. *LIMC* II (1984) pt. 1, 54–57, nos. 423–455.
3. Pollitt 175–177, figs. 183, 185–186.
4. Strabo 12.8.11. Tarn 174.

Peplophoros Statue
First century

23.87. Large-grained marble. Hope Collection at Deepdene (sale catalogue, London, Christie, Manson and Woods, July 23–24, 1917, no. 234, pl. 12). Purchased from Kelekian in 1930. Ht, 121 cm; W, 55.8 cm; Ht, base 8.2 cm. Head missing with ancient and modern dowel holes in neck. Two pairs of holes at center front of waist for insertion of ornament. Two holes on top of each shoulder for peplos pins. Two holes on upper surface of each sandal: one outside small toe and the other flanking big toe. Hole in top of each foot. Right arm reattached above elbow. Restored are: right wrist and hand; outermost pleat down her left side at knee level; section in front of drapery at knee level. Smaller areas of restoration over surface. Chipped across and beneath buttocks; cracks across back of knees. Heavy brown encrustation.

A frontal maiden stands with her weight evenly distributed on both legs, her left foot slightly advanced and turned out to one side. The fingers of her left hand clasp the drapery at the side of her left thigh; her right elbow is bent with the forearm extended. She wears a belted peplos open on the right side, with an overfold that stops just above the waist. Beneath her sandals is a narrow trapezoidal base with smooth vertical sides.

Publications: A. Michaelis, *Ancient Marbles in Great Britain* (Cambridge, 1882), 285, no. 13; Reinach, *Statuaire* 5 (1924) 367, no. 6; A. Raubitschek, "Early Attic Votive Monuments," *BSA* 40 (1939–40) 36; E. Langlotz, "Bemerkungen zu einem Basaltkopf in München," *JdI* 61–62 (1946–47) 105, pl. 26.2; E. Paribeni, "Un torso di peplophoros da Piazza Barbarini," *ASAtene* n. s. 8–10, 24–26 (1946–48) 104–106, fig. 1 on 108; C. C. Vermeule, "Notes on a New Edition of Michaelis," *AJA* 59 (1955) 134; G. Bakalakis, *Proanaskaphikes ereunes ste thrake* (Thessaloniki, 1958), 25 and n. 5 on 34; L. Forti, *Le Danzatrici di Ercolano* (Naples, 1959), 24–25; H. Herdejürgen, "Athenakopf aus Ampurias," *MM* 9 (1968) 218, 220, pl. 65b; B. S. Ridgway, "Two Peplophoroi in the United States," *Hesperia* 38 (1969) 213–222, pls. 54–57; J. Dörig, "La Tête Webb, l'Harmodios d'Anténor et le problème des copies romaines d'après des chefs-d'oeuvre archaïques," *AntK* 12 (1969) n. 39 on 46; *Bertel Thorvaldsen,* Museen der Stadt Köln, G. Bott, ed. (Cologne, 1977), 186 ill.; Vermeule, *Sculpture,* 192, no. 158.

Although this sculpture has numerous restorations, the appearance of most of them has been dictated by the surrounding areas of pattern, and so is fairly reliable; one exception is the questionable restoration of the right wrist and hand. The piece entered the collection attached to head No. 37, which belongs to a different type.

Ridgway has convincingly set forth the features that identify this work as a neo-Attic creation of the first century.[1] Readily apparent is the fusion of Archaic and

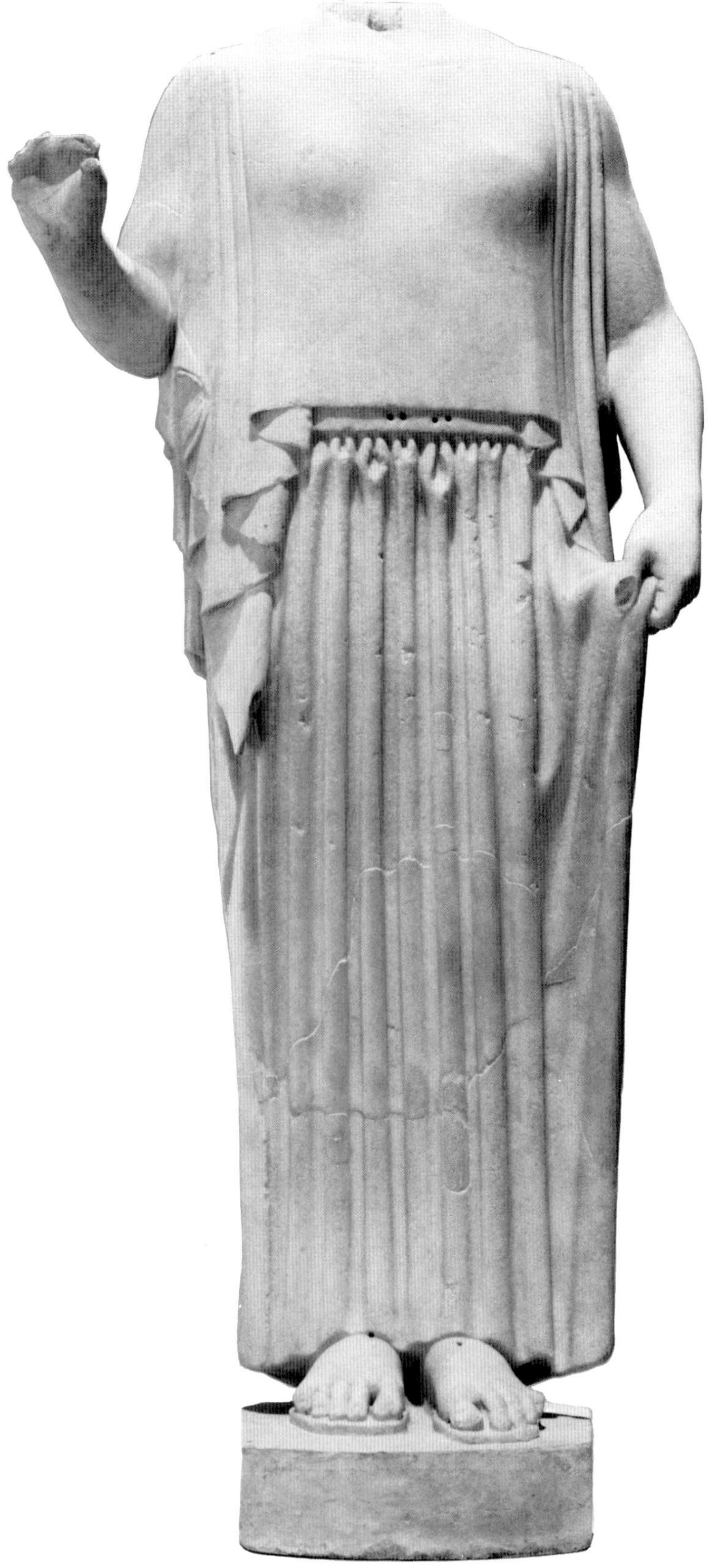

36.1

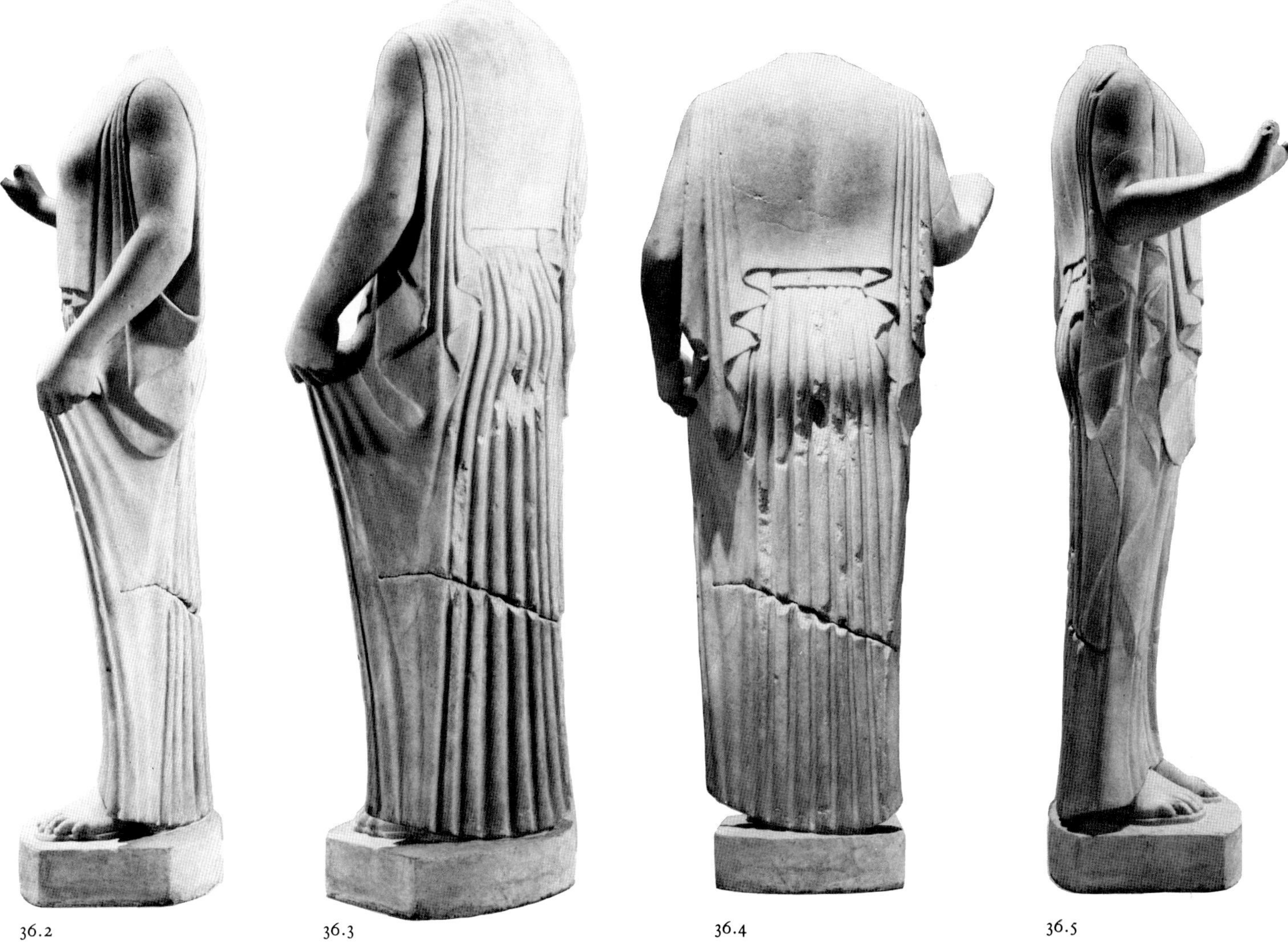

36.2   36.3   36.4   36.5

Severe style elements, specifically the Archaic gesture of the left hand coupled with the relentless corrugation of the peplos folds in a manner inspired by works of the Severe style. Particularly characteristic of late Hellenistic Archaizing sculpture is the tapering of the drapery folds to the ankles, especially visible in the left profile; also noteworthy are the way the fabric clings in back to the buttocks and the extra length at the back of the peplos which falls to the ground. Another Archaizing note is its modification of the typical Archaic stance; although the weight is evenly distributed on both legs following the Archaic manner, the foot of the advanced left leg is slightly angled.

In the handling of the peplos folds the Walters torso compares with the late Hellenistic peplophoros from the Antikythera shipwreck, which is now dated to the early first century.[2] Also related are statues of the Corinth-Moceniga type which surely goes back to a late Hellenistic prototype, the popularity of which is substantiated by the discovery of a plaster cast from one such statue among the finds from Baiae.[3]

1. Ridgway, *Hesperia* 38 (1969) 213–222.
2. J. N. Svoronos, *Die Funde von Antikythera* (Athens, 1903), 38–40, no. 17, pl. 6; P. Bol, *Die Skulpturen des Schiffs-fundes von Antikythera, AM-BH* 2 (1972) 17–18, pl. 5.
3. See C. von Hees, "Antike Gipsabgüsse antiker Statuen. Bericht über die Fragmente der Mantelfigur Korinth-Moceniga," *AntK* 21 (1978) 108–110, pl. 32.1; C. von Hees Landwehr, *Die antiken Gipsabgüsse aus Baiae*, Archäologische Forschungen 14 (Berlin, 1985), 47–60, pls. 12–25.

Archaistic Head of a Maiden

First century

23.241. Marble. Hope Collection at Deepdene (sale catalogue, London, Christie, Manson and Woods, July 23–24, 1917, no. 234, pl. 12). Purchased from Kelekian in 1930. Ht, 23.2 cm; W, 16.7 cm; Depth, 17.8 cm. Missing back of hair knot. Chipped on right eyeball and both cheeks. Nose, upper lip, and neck restored.

Face is framed by short tight curls separated by drillholes with the hair behind the ears pulled back to the nape. The wavy hair at the top and back of the head is rendered in low relief. She wears a wide diadem bearing a scalloped pattern in relief between rows of beading surmounted by radiating spikes. At the back of the head the diadem narrows to a strip that passes around the base of the skull.

Publications: See No. 36.

The head entered the collection attached to the Peplophoros No. 36 and belongs to a different, although approximately contemporary, tradition. The coupling of such archaizing features as the tight curls over the forehead, the wavy and almost incised locks on the back of the head, the soft smile and arched brows, with such Classical elements as the almond eyes produces an effect comparable to the head of an Archaistic Artemis from Pompeii, dated to the first century.[1] Pollitt has pointed out that the latter work served as a cult statue in a private shrine, and it is possible that the Walters head belonged to a statue with a similar function.

1. Pollitt 184, fig. 194.

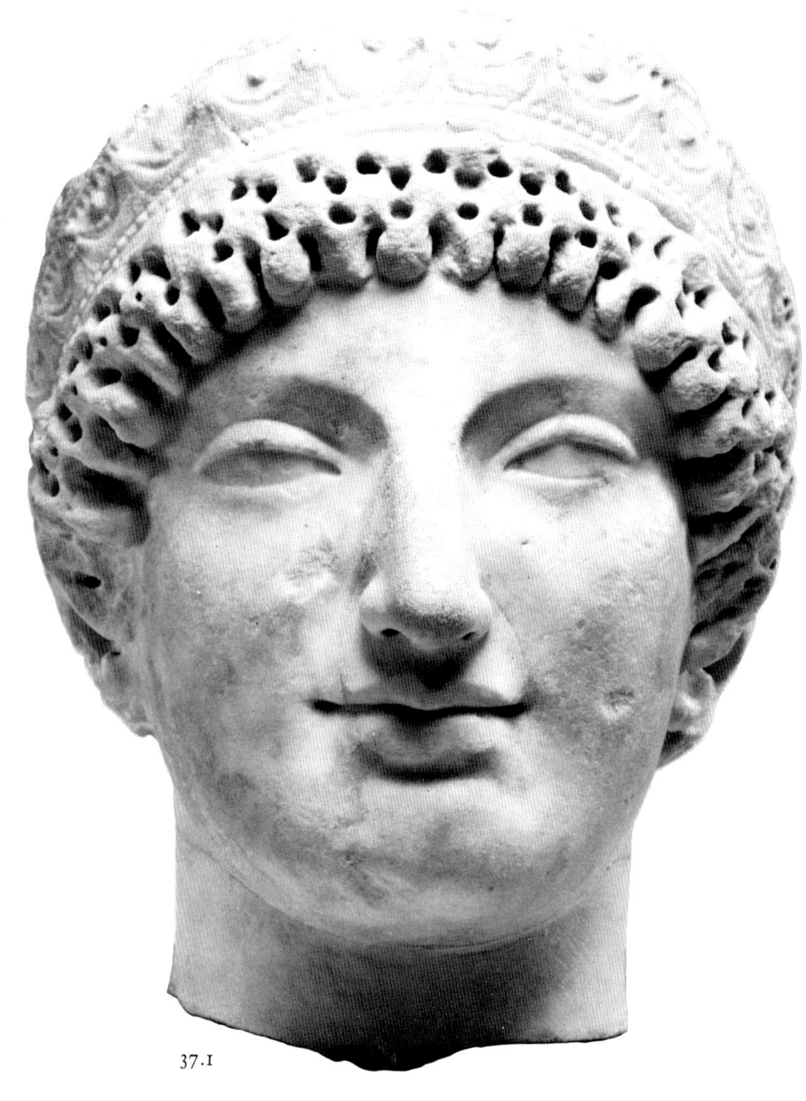

37.1

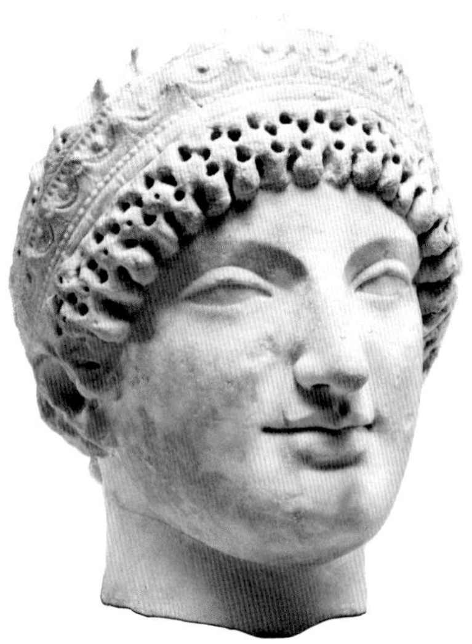

37.2

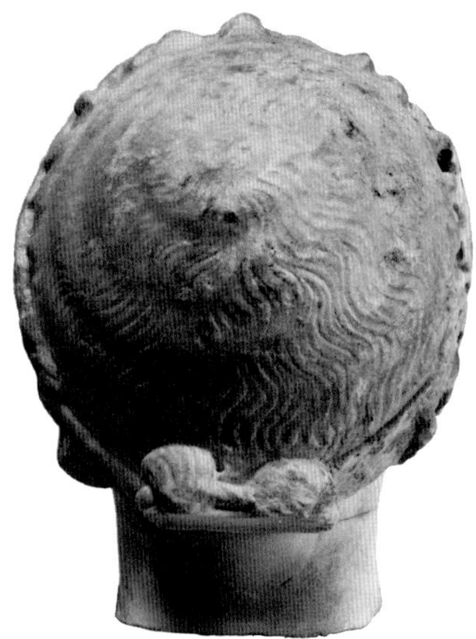

37.3

Relief with Procession of Twelve Deities
First century

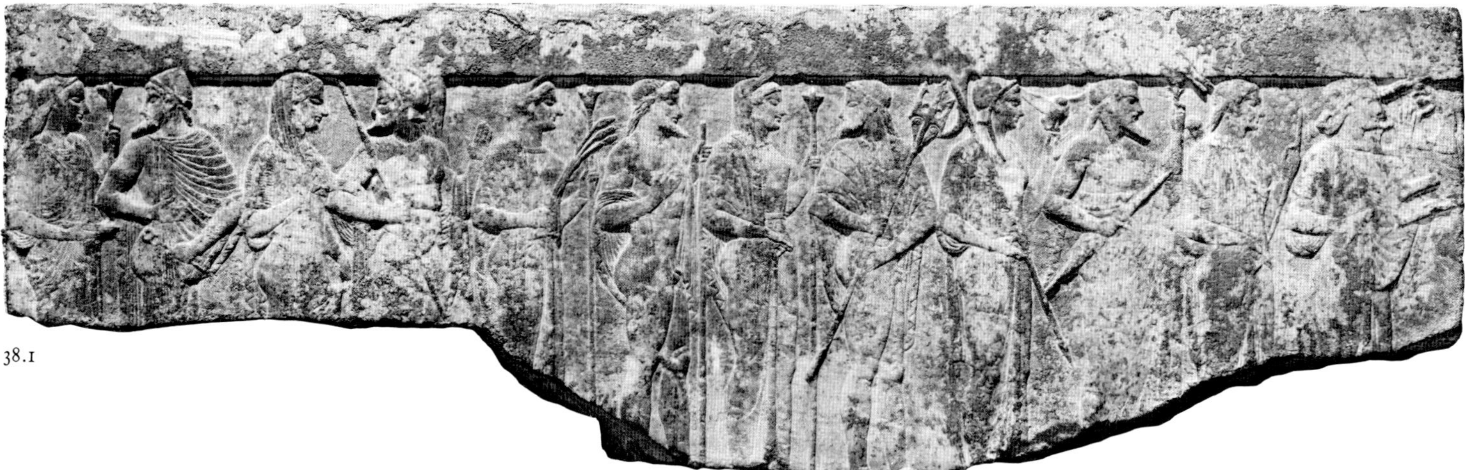

38.1

23.40. Pentelic marble. Purchased from Hirsch in 1913. L, 119.8 cm; Ht, 37.7 cm; Ht, flat molding 5.5 cm; Th, 6 cm. Carved in low relief. Sides and top smooth. Back is smooth below, with five clamp channels along left two-thirds. Lower edge broken along entire extent, removing lower parts of all figures.

Beneath a smooth fascia are twelve figures moving to their left, the left legs advanced, weight evenly distributed on both legs. All but figures nos. 5, 9, 11 are in three-quarters right profile with left upper arm obscured. Leading the procession, from the viewer's right, is a figure in a sleeved garment beneath a mantle which is draped across the front of his torso with the ends thrown over the right shoulder. In his right arm he holds a plektron; his left upraised hand supports a kithara, the upper part of which is rendered by a shallow groove in the upper molding. He wears a diadem over long locks of hair, which are pulled back at the nape and drawn up over the diadem. Behind him is a maiden in a chiton with paryphe beneath an himation whose ends fall on each side of her shoulder. The thumb and forefinger of her right hand clasp the folds of her garment at her hip; her upraised left hand holds a bow. Her hair is pulled back from her face and hangs down her back. The top of a quiver is seen behind her shoulder. Behind her is a bearded male, steadying in his upraised left hand a staff with floral tip surmounted by an eagle partially incised in the fascia. His right hand grasps a thunderbolt by his right hip. He wears a mantle which is draped over his left shoulder, under his right arm, and across his torso beneath the breasts; the ends of the mantle flare out behind his waist. He wears a diadem over his long hair, one coil of which is brought forward over his right shoulder. The fourth figure wears a chiton, himation, and aegis. The folds of her mantle hang down the front and back of her shoulder; the extended fingers of her right hand steady a spear which rests against her right shoulder. Her left forearm is raised with the fingers outstretched and with thumb and forefinger supporting an owl with open wings. She wears an

Attic crested helmet from beneath which a long coil of hair falls forward over her right shoulder. The top of the crest is interrupted by the fascia and must have been completed in paint.

Behind her is a bearded male whose head is seen in left profile and whose left arm is brought across to his right hip as he steadies a trident clasped in his right hand. He is nude except for a mantle which frames his back and is brought forward over each shoulder. Short snail curls lie across his forehead; long locks fall behind his shoulders beneath a diadem. His gaze is directed at the woman behind him who grasps a floral-tipped staff in her left hand while her right hand, held at her hips, plucks a fold of drapery with the thumb and forefinger. She wears a belted short-sleeved garment with an accentuated U-neckline and a mantle which is draped over her right shoulder and whose ends hang down in front and behind. A veil is draped over the back of her head behind a stephane. Her wavy hair is brushed back from her face above her ear.

Figure no. 7 is a bearded male who grasps a staff in his left hand; his right hand with fingers extended is held at chest level. He is nude except for his mantle which is draped behind his back with the ends falling forward over each elbow. Beneath a diadem his long hair is pulled back behind his shoulders. Behind him is a woman grasping a sheaf of wheat in her right hand while her left hand clasps a staff with floral tip. She wears a peplos with pronounced U-neckline and a mantle over her right shoulder and upper arm, the folds of which are visible at front and back. A veil lies over the back of her head behind a stephane. She is followed by a bearded male whose head is turned in left profile. The fingers of his upraised forearm are extended in a gesture of salutation, while his left hand, at waist height, steadies a spear which rests against his right shoulder. He wears a cuirass over a short pleated tunic and a short mantle which frames his back and is brought over each elbow. His crested helmet surmounts long locks of hair which fall behind his back. Behind him is a woman whose right hand fingers the drapery at her breast and whose left forefinger and thumb clasp the drapery at her left thigh. She wears a chiton with mantle which passes over her right shoulder and beneath her left breast, covering her torso, and falls down behind her right shoulder. A veil is brought across the back of her head; a narrow stephane rests atop wavy hair drawn back behind her ears.

The bearded male behind her turns his head in left profile. His left arm is brought across to his right hip and holds a kerykeion, while the right hand, fingers extended, rests against the waist. He is nude except for a pleated chlamys which is fastened on the right shoulder and which falls across his torso and left upper arm. A pilos rests upon the long locks which fall down behind his back. The last figure in the procession is a maiden who clasps a phiale in her right hand and a floral-tipped staff in her left. She wears a chiton beneath a mantle which is brought across her left shoulder and passes under her right breast with the lower edge passing from her left hip to the right thigh. She wears earrings and a diadem upon her long hair, which is pulled back at the nape.

Publications: E. Schmidt in Brunn-Bruckmann, *Denkmäler griechischer und römischer Skulptur* (Munich, 1912), 2–4, pl. 660; O. Weinreich, *Lykische Zwölfgötter-reliefs, Untersuchungen zur Geschichte des dreizehnten Göttes* (Heidelberg, 1913), 2, n. 2 and 59, n. 3; O. Weinreich, *Triskaidekadische Studien, Beitr. z. Geschichte der Zahlen* (Heidelberg, 1916), 23; H. Bulle, *Archaisierende griechische Rundplastik,* Abhandlungen der Königlich Bayerischen Akademie der Wissenschaften, philosophisch-philologische und historische Klasse 30 (Munich, 1922), II, 3, n. 1; E. Schmidt, *Archaistische Kunst in Griechenland und Rom* (Munich, 1922), 57; E. Pfuhl, "Bemerkungen zur archaischen Kunst," *AM* 48 (1923) 136, n. 1; O. Deubner, *Hellenistische Apollogestalten* (Athens, 1934), 69, no. 10; H. T. Bossert and W. Zschietzschmann, eds., *Hellas and Rome: The Civilization of Classical Antiquity* (New York, 1936), figs. 2 and 3; O. Weinreich and W. Roscher, eds., "Zwölf-götter," *Ausführliches Lexikon der griechischen und römischen Mythologie* 6 (1937) 791, pl. 2; B. Meissner and D. Opitz, "Die Heimkehr des Kriegers, ein nacharchaisches griechisches Relief," *Sitzungsberichte der Akademie der Wissenschaften, Berlin* 13 (1938) 143–144, pl. 2; E. Langlotz, *Die archaischen Marmorbildwerke der Akropolis* (Frankfurt, 1939), 10–11; A. Cook, *Zeus* (Cambridge, 1940), III, 1055 and 1057, fig. 851 on 1056; G. Becatti, "Lo stile arcaistico," *Critica d'Arte* 6 (1941) 42, no. 62; C.

Picard, *Manuel d'archéologie grecque* (Paris, 1948),
III.2, 860, fig. 386; M. Crosby, "The Altar of the
Twelve Gods in Athens," *Commemorative Studies in
Honor of Theodore Leslie Shear,* Hesperia Suppl. 8
(Baltimore, 1949), 96; G. Lippold, *Die griechische
Plastik,* Handbuch der Archäologie III.1, 5th ed., W.
Otto and R. Herbig, eds. (Munich, 1950), 126, n.
12; C. Picard, "Sur un 'naiskos' inédit de Cybèle, au
musée du Caire," *MonPiot* 49 (1957) 52; T. Kraus,
*Hekate. Studien zu Wesen und Bild der Göttin in Kleina-
sien und Griechenland* (Heidelberg, 1960), 115–116; C.
Havelock, "Archaistic Reliefs of the Hellenistic
Period," *AJA* 68 (1964) 47, n. 15 and 57, n. 48; F.
Brommer, *Der Gott Vulkan auf Provinzial römischen
Reliefs* (Cologne-Vienna, 1973), 49, nos. 62 and 65;
D. Willers, "Zu den Anfängen der archaistischen
Plastik in Griechenland," *AM-BH* 4 (1975) 22, 28,
31–32, 57, pl. 10, reviewed by E. B. Harrison in *Gno-
mon* 53 (1981) 496–498; C. Bowra, *Classical Greece*
(New York, 1977), 16–17; F. Brommer, *Hephaistos:
Der Schmiedegott in der antiken Kunst* (Mainz, 1978),
248, no. 8; W. T. Jewkes, *Man the Myth-Maker,* 2nd
ed. (New York, 1981), 70; *LIMC* II (1984) pt. 1, 125,
no. 1309, pt. 2, pl. 261, no. 868; pt. 1, 290, no. 868,
pt. 2, pl. 261, no. 868; pt. 1, 998 (no. 470), pt. 2, pl.
261, no. 868; *LIMC* III (1986) pt. 1, 651, no. 20, pt.
2, 512; C. Long, *The Twelve Gods of Greece and
Rome,* Etudes préliminaires aux religions orientales
dans l'empire romain 107 (Leiden, New York, 1987),
44–45, 182–185, no. 1; J. Sauser, "The Twelve Gods
Relief in The Walters Art Gallery," *JWalt* 45 (1987)
2–18.

Although peculiarities in style have pro-
voked a widely divergent assessment of
this relief over the past seventy-five years,
a recent study has persuasively argued that
the relief is an archaizing work of the first
century emulating with a high degree of
accuracy stylistic elements found in
Archaic and early fifth-century art.[1]
Although the identifications are not
entirely secure, the figures will be referred
to here as Hestia, Hermes, Aphrodite,
Ares, Demeter, Hephaestos, Hera,
Poseidon, Athena, Zeus, Artemis, and
Apollo.

Easily recognized as archaizing features
are: the mechanical reproduction of the
figural types, which share almost identical
body contours and are evenly separated;
the stylized zigzag borders of many of the
garments; the blunt end of Athena's mantle; and the thinness and swinging tips of
Zeus's mantle. In addition, the veils worn
by Hera, Aphrodite, and Demeter are not
unlike those seen in sculpture of the first
century (see No. 34). A fragmentary relief
in Athens replicates almost exactly the

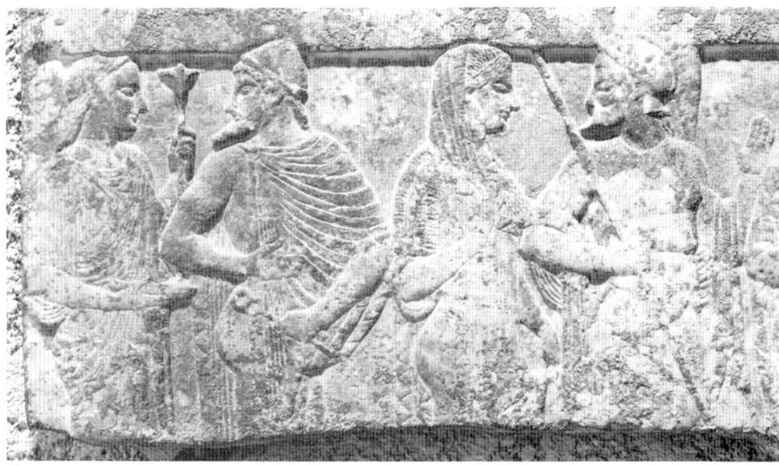

38.2

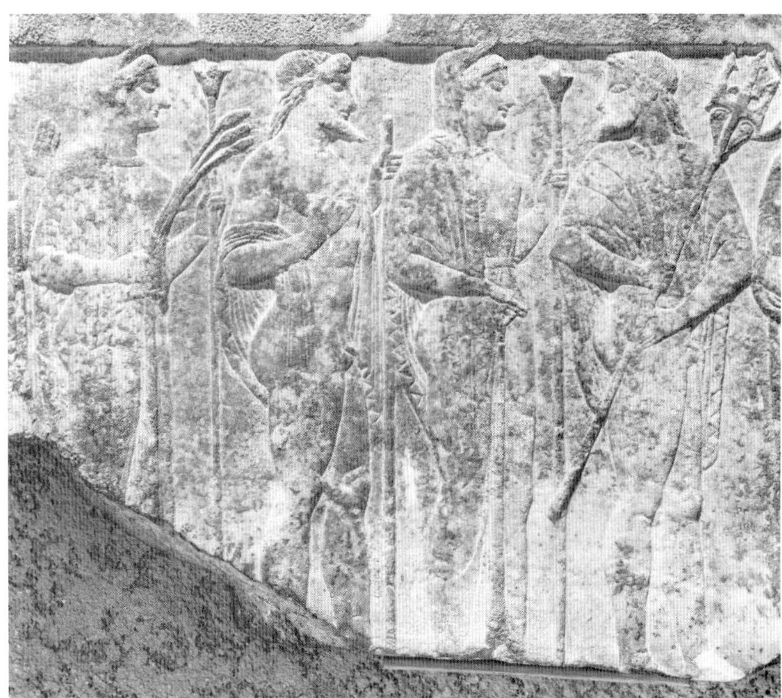

38.3

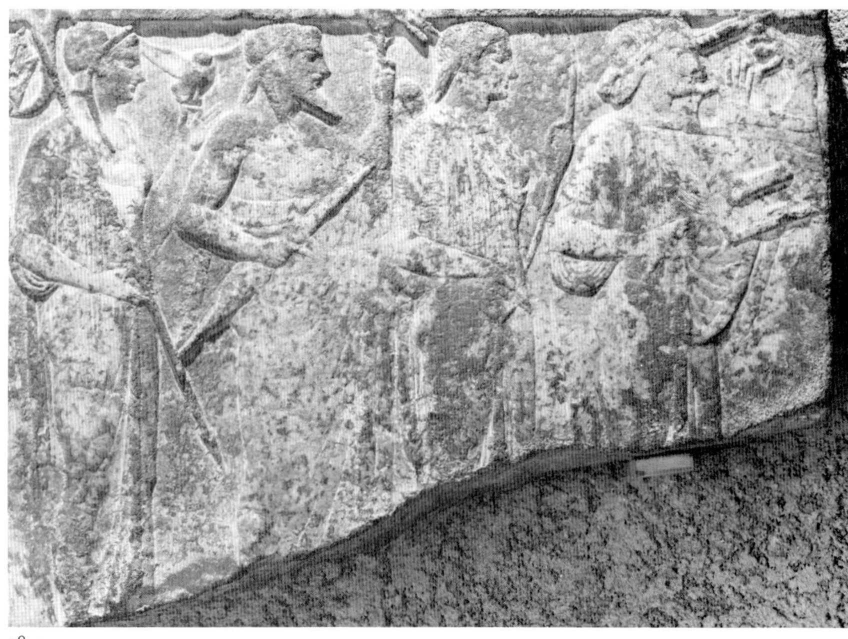

38.4

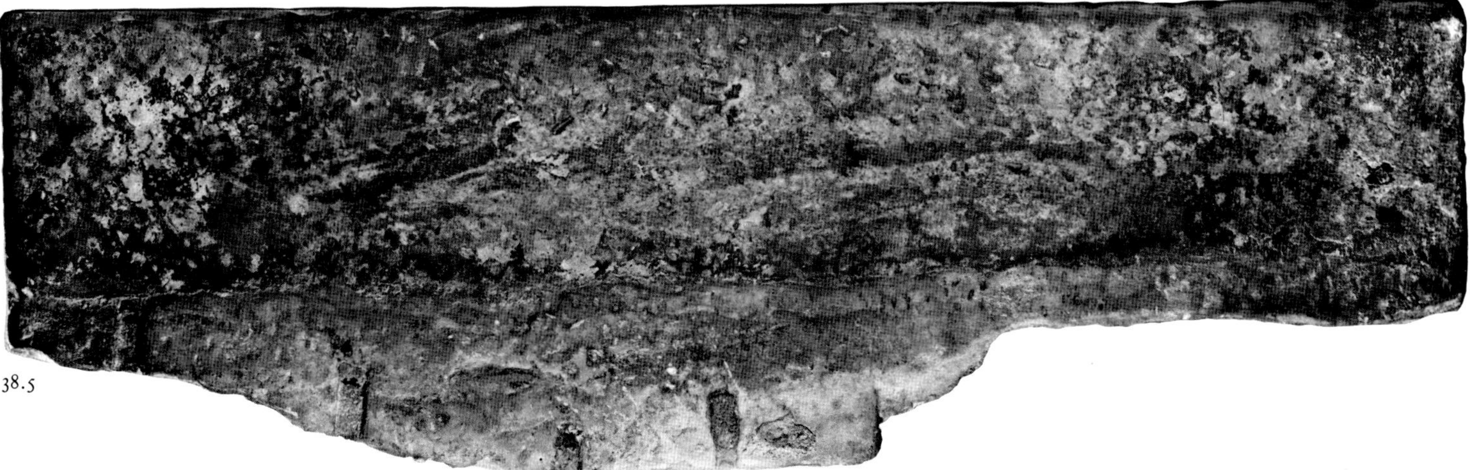

38.5

heads of Poseidon and Hera together with their attributes, and so suggests that other copies of this representation existed, a phenomenon characteristic of neo-Attic art.[2]

Coexisting with these indisputably archaizing traits are numerous elements that find parallels only in work of the Archaic and Severe styles: the frontal eyes that contrast with the more naturalistic faces of Archaistic figures; the static stances which differ markedly from the vigorous strides, often on tiptoe, of archaizing figures, whose legs are often rendered with plasticity and exaggerated muscular delineation; and the way Aphrodite and Hera hold their garments in front of their bodies, rather than behind in the archaizing manner. Other features consistent with Archaic use and antithetical to the archaizing style are the pilos worn by Hermes, Athena's Attic helmet without cheekpieces, the absence of flaring swallow tails in the drapery ends, and the similarity of the hairstyles to late Archaic and Severe fashion, particularly the manner in which Artemis and Hestia's hair is pulled back to the nape without locks in front of the shoulder. It should also be noted that the shawls of Ares and Hephaestos find parallels in Archaic art; Poseidon's mantle is seen also on fifth-century coins from Zankle; the capes with widely spaced folds worn by Demeter and Hera compare favorably with that worn by the late archaic Propylaea Kore; and the draping

of Hermes' chlamys on the right shoulder is compatible with early fifth-century usage.

There still remain puzzling elements in the scene for which analogies are not easily provided, such as the form of Zeus's thunderbolt, Apollo's combination of chlamys and chiton, the pairing of Demeter and Hephaestos, and the positions of Athena and Hera, which we would expect to be reversed. Also curious is the inconsistency in the treatment of the upper fascia where some details are incised, such as Apollo's kithara and Zeus's eagle, but others, both here and elsewhere on the scene, were left to be rendered in paint, e.g. Athena's crest, aegis scales, lance butt, and her owl's wings and its tips; the continuation of the scepter beneath Hestia's phiale; the kithara strings; and Ares' crest and spear butt. Also noteworthy is the unusual form of Ares' cuirass, the closest parallel to which is seen on the Città Castellana base, now dated to the third century.[3]

Isotopic analysis has identified the marble of the Walters relief as Pentelic.[4] This fact plus the Athenian provenance of the above-mentioned fragment representing Poseidon and Hera strengthens the sug-

gestion that the Walters relief was made in an Athenian workshop and then exported to Tarentum where it was reputedly found. Because of its close resemblance to works of Archaic date, it is not inconceivable that the Walters relief was intended to be viewed by its buyer as a genuinely Archaic work of art.

The piece has been cut down at the sides, eliminating part of Hestia's arm, and each end has been left rough-picked. If we restore the original relief with an extension on each side, the absence of clamps and dowel holes could be explained by the use of the relief as a table support, similar to one found on Delos.[5] A subsequent reuse in antiquity is indicated, not just by the recut ends, but also by the anathyrosis and the encrustation around the edges on the back; perhaps the recutting took place when the relief was mended, because the iron in the clamp holes appears to be ancient.

1. J. Sauser, *JWalt* 45 (1987) 2–18. I summarize here her arguments as well as observations in Long, *Twelve Gods*, 183–185.
2. J. N. Svoronos, *Das Athener Nationalmuseum* (Athens, 1903), 637, no. 360, pl. 141.
3. For the Città Castellana relief, see G. Hafner, "Zwei frühe römische Opferbilder," *Aachener Kunstblätter des Museumsvereins* 45 (1974) 17–31, and 17, fig. 1. See also Long, *Twelve Gods*, 184.
4. The only other marble source that matches the isotopic signature of the Walters relief is Iznik, a minor Roman Turkish quarry. I thank Norman Herz for his assistance. The letter, in the Walters files, is dated October 15, 1987.
5. I owe this suggestion to Evelyn B. Harrison. See J. Marcadé, "Trouvailles de la maison dite de L'Hermès," *BCH* 77 (1953) 576–579.

ARCHAISTIC RELIEF WITH
APOLLO AND ARTEMIS
Ca. 50

23.7. Marble. Purchased from Kelekian in 1925. Ht,
42.5 cm; W, 31.7 cm; Th, base 7.4 cm. Most of
back very smooth. Upper and lower edges smooth.
Two holes in top surface, each ca. 2 cm wide. In
lower edge are two pairs of modern holes; modern
iron dowels in one of these pairs. Chipped across
front of horizontal lower fascia.

Standing in left profile are two figures. In front is a
male with right leg advanced; his left arm is bent at
the elbow and his left hand holds a bow at his waist.
His right arm is bent at the elbow with the forearm
uplifted and the fingers outstretched, an arrow held
vertically between thumb and forefinger. A mantle
passes behind his back and falls to knee level at each
side with the ends flaring outwards. Beneath a diadem his wavy hair is drawn back at the nape with
two long spiral coils falling forward over the left
shoulder. Following behind him is a draped maiden
with her right leg advanced. The fingers of her left
hand grasp folds of her drapery behind her buttocks;
her right arm is bent at the elbow with the forearm
raised, the fingers extended and a torch steadied
between the thumb and forefinger of right hand. She
wears a short-sleeved pleated garment, the lower
edge of which is visible above her ankles. A mantle
passes from her right shoulder below her left arm,
leaving her right arm uncovered. The mantle has an
overfold which extends below her waist and zigzag
pleats along the entire right edge from beneath her
arm to her foot. Behind her right shoulder are a bow
and quiver. Beneath a diadem her hair is pulled back
to the nape with two long side coils falling forward
over the left shoulder.

Exhibitions and Catalogues: *The Ruins of Rome,*
University Museum (Philadelphia, December 15,
1960–February 15, 1961) and Detroit Institute of Arts
(Detroit, March 26–May 7, 1961), catalogue R. C.
Smith, no. 225.

Publications: Vermeule, *Sculpture,* 196, no. 162;
LIMC II (1984) pt. 1, 711, no. 1171.

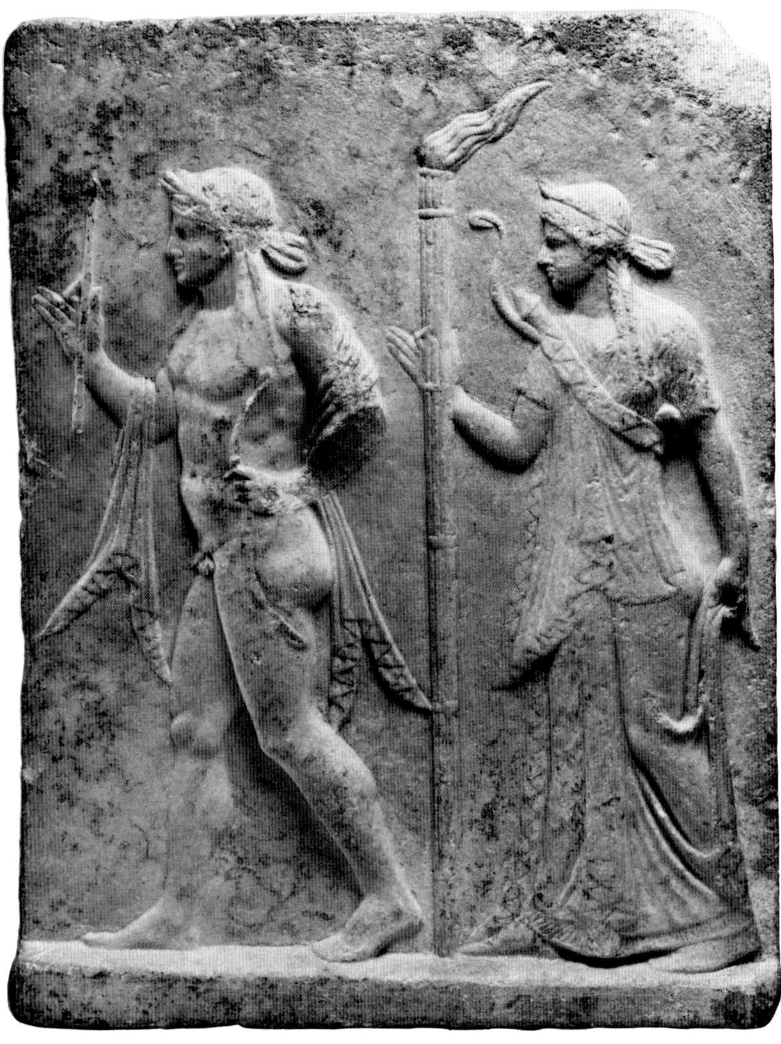

39.1

This piece can be grouped with several
other almost identical examples: a fragment in Athens and three reliefs in the
Piraeus, Delos, and the Villa Albani,
which preserve the full composition
where Apollo and Artemis are preceded
by Hermes and Athena.[1] The differences
are slight; an altar appears on the version
in the Villa Albani, and on the Delian
relief we find a frieze of garlands and
bukrania similar to those seen on Delian
altars. Harrison suggests that the prototypical work was Attic, an attribution
supported by the Attic findspot of two
examples, the similarity of Hermes to the
figure of this god on Attic nymph reliefs
of the fourth century, and the resemblance
of Apollo to the representation of that
deity on the Copenhagen copy of the
undoubtedly Attic Tripod Relief.[2] Further evidence for an Attic origin lies in the
dissimilarity of the work to other Hellenistic sculpture found on Delos, a fact
suggesting that an artist trained in Athens
executed a copy on Delos, while introducing the distinctive local feature of bukrania and garland frieze.[3] The particular
assemblage of deities, which pair Apollo
and Artemis, who were sacred to Delos,
with Athena and Hermes, god of commerce, suggested to Harrison that the
prototypical relief was a dedication on the
Athenian Acropolis made by Delian merchants in acknowledgment of the Athenian presence on the island in the later
second century. If this is the case, it
would be entirely appropriate for an
Athenian-trained artist to execute a local
replica on Delos and for other replicas to
be made in Athens over the following

decades, with the Walters example executed about the middle of the first century. The reliefs are a good illustration of
the mechanical nature of late-Hellenistic
neo-Attic manufacture. Not only was the
entire relief replicated with little change
and apparently in more than one sculptural center, but the figures of Apollo and
Artemis are themselves stock archaizing
types, with Artemis here rendered, apparently for no reason, in slightly smaller
scale. The continued survival of the type
and style into Roman times is attested by
the Piraeus relief, which was probably
made in the second century A.D.

1. *LIMC* II (1984) pt. 1, 711, nos. 1167–1171.
2. E. B. Harrison, *Archaic and Archaistic Sculpture,* The Athenian Agora 11 (Princeton, 1965), 81–83, no. 129, pl. 29.
3. J. Marcadé, *Au musée de Délos* (Paris, 1969), 292–293.

Head of Augustus
27 B.C.–14 A.D.

23.21. Marble. "From Egypt." Purchased from
Kelekian in 1913. Ht, 41.2 cm; W, 19.6 cm; Depth,
23.8 cm. Neck broken on left side, carved for insertion into statue. Top of head cut cleanly across
crown. Back of head cut off at angle with surface
rough. Sliced cleanly down left side. Hair carved
summarily behind the right ear. Clamp cutting
behind left temple is filled with stucco. Hair just
above nape chipped.

The frontal head and neck of a man who has short
wavy hair brushed forward over the forehead. The
pupils are indicated by indentations.

Exhibitions and Catalogues: *Bilder von Menschen in
der Kunst des Abendlandes,* Staatliche Museen Preussischer Kulturbesitz (Berlin, May 7–September 28,
1980), 76, no. 47. *The Taste of Maryland,* The Walters Art Gallery (Baltimore, May 17–August 28,
1984), 65, no. 132.

Publications: *Handbook of the Collection: The Walters
Art Gallery* (1936) 39; C. C. Vermeule, "Greek and
Roman Portraits in North American Collections
Open to the Public," *Proceedings of the American
Philosophical Society* 108 (1964) 101; D. K. Hill,
"Augustus as Emperor," *BWalt* 22 (1970), no. 7; P.
Zanker, *Studien zu den Augustus-Porträts I. Der Actium
Typus* (Göttingen, 1973), 44, fig. 34a; G. Grimm,
Römische Mummienmasken aus Ägypten (Wiesbaden,
1974), 110, no. 87; Vermeule, *Sculpture,* 283, no. 240;
Bol, *Liebieghaus,* 221.

Although not a Hellenistic work, this
piece is a forceful illustration of the impact
of Hellenic traditions upon the art of the
Roman Imperial era. The head exemplifies an Augustan portrait type familiar
from the Prima Porta statue but best represented by a head from Chiusi and the
togate statue from the Via Labicana.[1]
Zanker suggests that this type was created
shortly after 27, modifying the Actium
type of several years before by emulating
more explicitly a Polykleitan prototype in

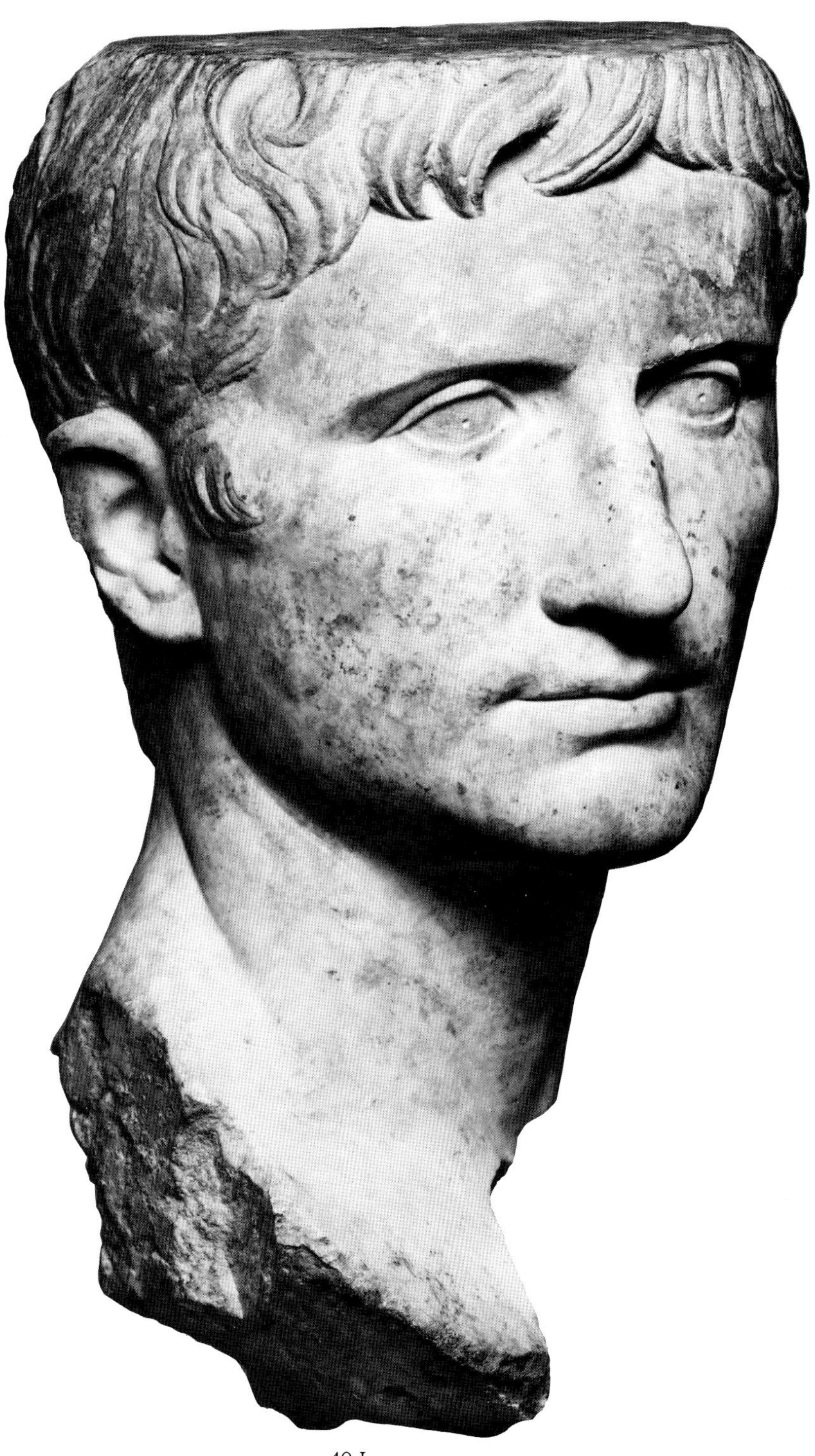

40.1

the hairstyle, the turn of the head, and the
wide, short neck. Even more than the
Actium type, heads of the Prima Porta
tradition illustrate how the classicizing
style of the late Hellenistic era was reinforced and refined under Augustus's influence. The eastern provenance of its closest
parallels suggested to Bol that the Walters
head was carved by an artist who was
trained in the eastern Mediterranean, but
who brought his skills to Italy to produce
a work that would serve the political
function of promoting the leader as a uni-
fying force and an embodiment of the
Roman spirit.[2] If the reputed provenance
is correct, the head was then sent, most
suitably, to Egypt, where the notion of
employing royal portraiture in the service
of the state was first conceived.

1. P. Zanker, *Augustus-Porträts*, 44–45.
2. Bol, *Liebieghaus*, 221.

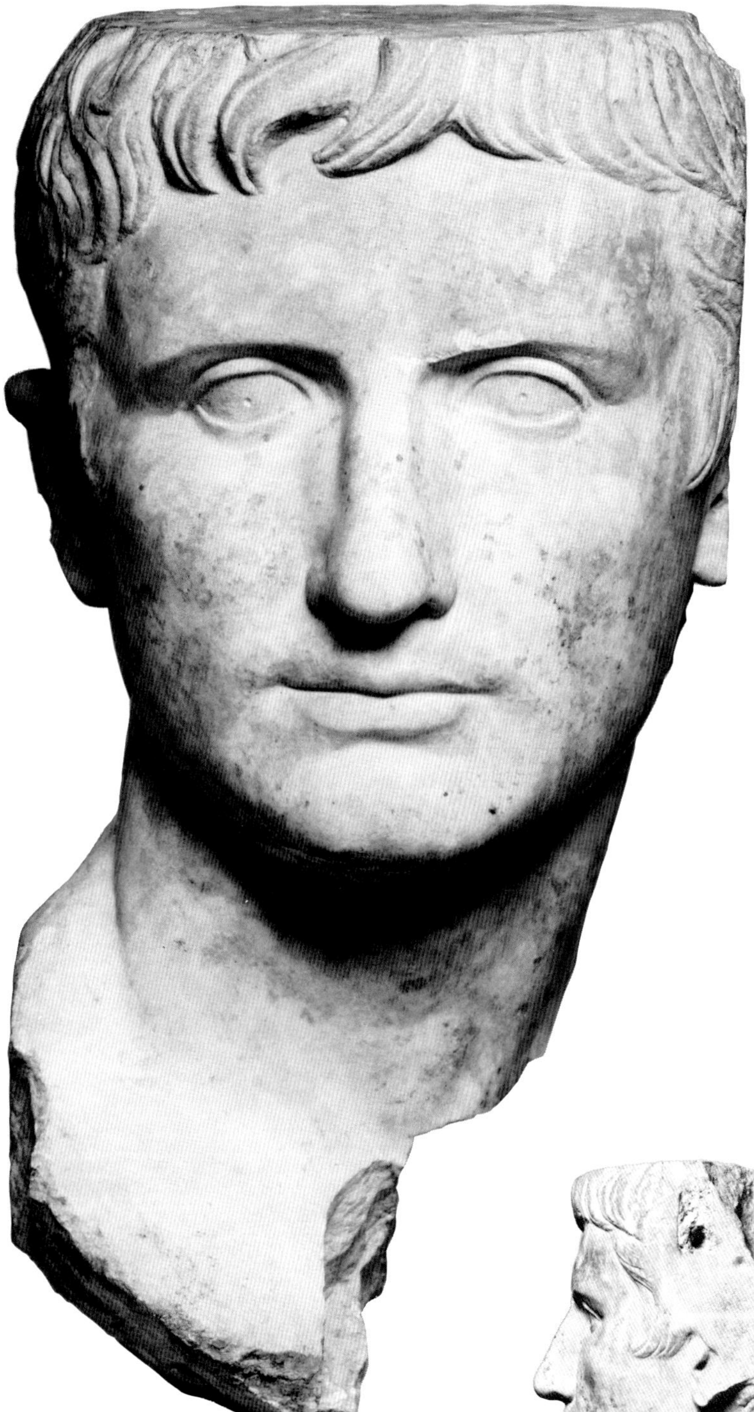

40.2

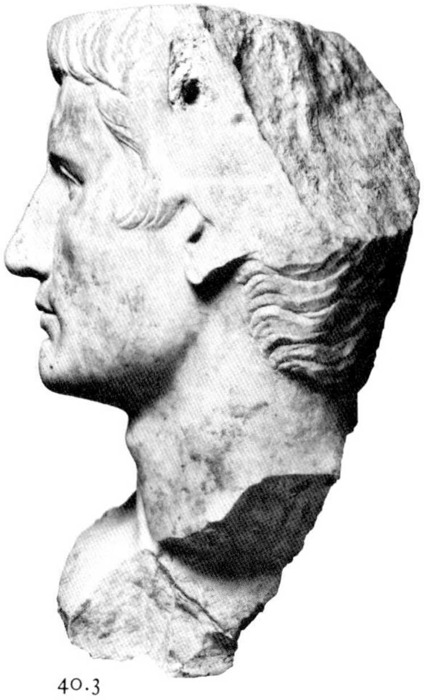

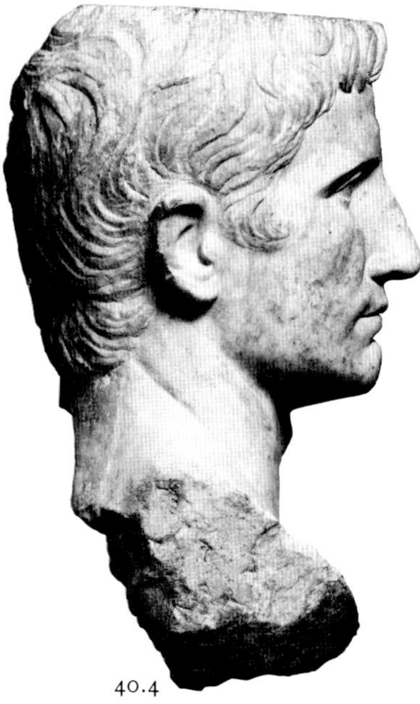

40.3

40.4

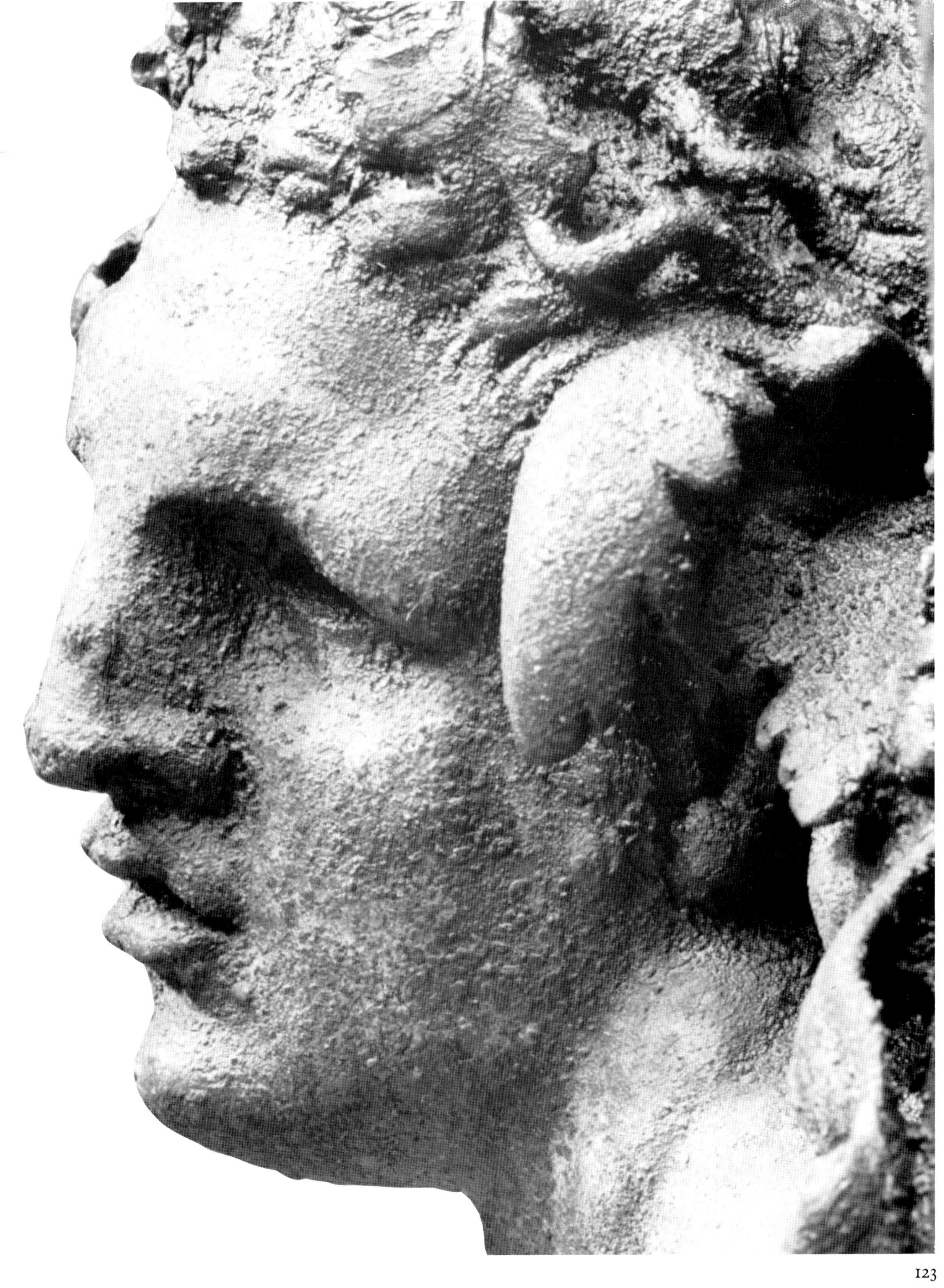

Footless Cup
300–250

Ladle
Late fourth to early third century

57.1843. Silver. Collection of N. Koutoulakis. Purchased from Galerie Segredakis in 1951. Ht, 5.1 cm; D, rim 8.6 cm. Two large sections missing from bowl.

A deep cup has an undecorated flaring neck and an everted rim. The ornament is hammered on the bowl in low relief. The undecorated center of the underside is encircled by tongues surmounted, on the shoulder, by a guilloche between hatched bands; above is a band of heart-and-dart.

Exhibitions and Catalogues: *Greek and Roman Metalware,* The Walters Art Gallery (Baltimore, February 14–April 14, 1976), catalogue D. K. Hill, no. 62.

Publications: D. K. Hill, "From Alexander to Augustus," *BWalt* 7 (1955) no. 5; D. K. Hill, "Silverware from Ancient Banquets," *BWalt* 12 (1960) no. 7; D. von Bothmer, *Ancient Art from New York Private Collections* (New York, 1960), 70; B. Sparkes and L. Talcott, *Black and Plain Pottery,* The Athenian Agora 12 (Princeton, 1970), pt. 1, 122, no. 58.

This vessel is a fine example of the calyx cup, which is distinguished by its concave upper wall, rounded bowl, and decorative scheme, consisting of a band of heart-and-dart above a band of guilloche or composite wreath around the shoulder, and tongues over the bowl. Occasionally there is a rosette on the underside with a plastically rendered head on the interior floor. The type of this vessel is Near Eastern in origin, but direct Persian forerunners from the early fourth century exhibit a squatter shape, a smooth body, and horizontal ribbing around the shoulder.[1] By the second quarter of the fourth century a Hellenized version of the Achaemenid type had been introduced in the West, presumably in metal, although only black-glaze examples have survived.[2] In the Greek world the greatest popularity of the type was achieved in Macedon where a number of silver examples similar to the Walters cup have been found in tombs in Nikesiani, Thessaly, Derveni, and Vergina, dating to the last half of the fourth and the beginning of the third century.[3] The prominence of the vessel in this part of the Greek world was probably a result of both increased Macedonian contact with the Near East and the traditional Macedonian predilection for silverplate. Not surprisingly, the interior medallions often feature Dionysiac subjects, but female heads are also known.[4]

1. Oliver, *Silver,* 40, no. 10.
2. Sparkes and Talcott, *Black and Plain Pottery,* 121–122, pl. 28, fig. 7.
3. For a discussion of these examples, see B. Barr-Sharrar, "Macedonian Metal Vases in Perspective: Some Observations on Context and Tradition," *Macedonia and Greece,* 131. The example from Stavroupolis is 132, fig. 17. See also M. Andronicos, *Vergina. The Royal Tombs and the Ancient City* (Athens, 1984), 150–151, figs. 112–113.
4. Barr-Sharrar (note 3) 132, fig. 18.

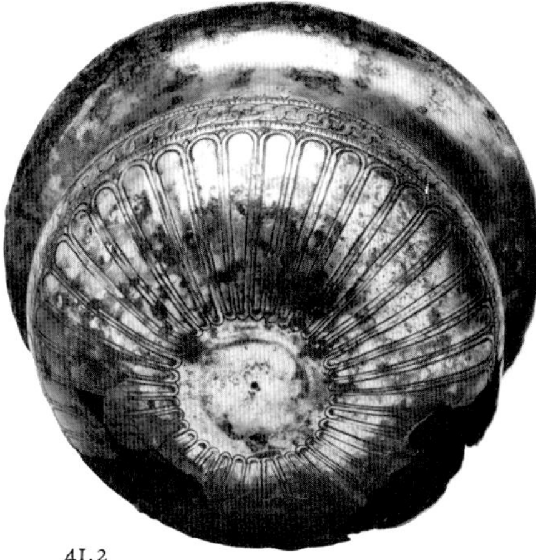

41.2

57.909. Silver. "From Kavalla, Thessaly." Purchased from Kelekian in 1911. L, 26.6 cm; D, bowl 6.7 cm.

The strap handle widens above and terminates in a duck neck and head; the other end has upward-curving tangs at the juncture with the shallow bowl.

Exhibitions and Catalogues: *Greek and Roman Metalware,* The Walters Art Gallery (Baltimore, February 14–April 14, 1976), catalogue D. K. Hill, no. 50. Oliver, *Silver,* 43, no. 13.

Publications: D. K. Hill, "Wine Ladles and Strainers from Ancient Times," *JWalt* 5 (1942) 40–55, fig. 1; M. Crosby, "A Silver Ladle and Strainer," *AJA* 47 (1943) 213; D. K. Hill, "Kitchen and Banquet: The History of Ancient Metalware," *CJ* 43 (1948) 452; D. E. Strong, *Greek and Roman Gold and Silver Plate* (London, 1966), 92.

Ladles, used for dipping wine, were usually paired with strainers, and this example was, in fact, said to have been found with the following entry (No. 43). The shallow bowl assigns the piece to an early Hellenistic date and links it with a number of other silver examples from northern Greece, northern Asia Minor, and southern Russia.[1]

1. Oliver, *Silver,* 43; 46, no. 15 from Akarnania; 63, no. 30 from Montefortino, Italy.

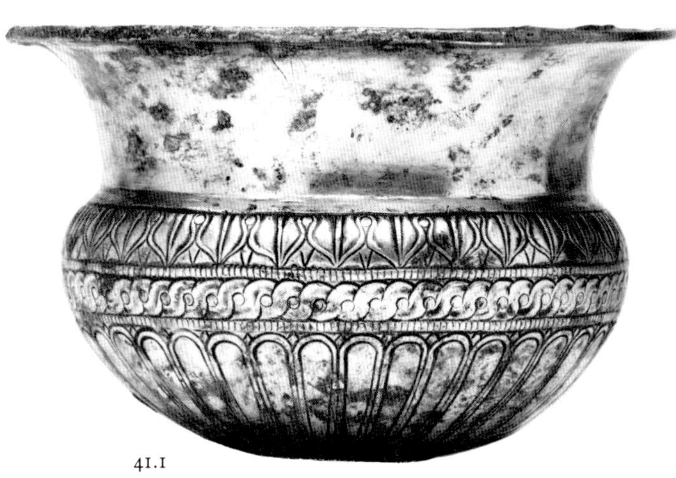

41.1

STRAINER
Late fourth to early third century

57.910. Silver. "From Kavalla, Thessaly." Purchased from Kelekian in 1911. L, 21.8 cm; D, bowl 11.8 cm.

The bowl has a flanged edge with lathe-cut grooves and a perforated design of a spiraling six-petal rosette within two concentric circles. Each of the two handles is composed of a flat plate that narrows to form a long, curved duck neck and head.

Exhibitions and Catalogues: *Greek and Roman Metalware,* The Walters Art Gallery (Baltimore, February 14–April 14, 1976), catalogue D. K. Hill, no. 50. Oliver, *Silver,* 44–45, no. 14.

Publications: D. K. Hill, "Wine Ladles and Strainers from Ancient Times," *JWalt* 5 (1942) 52, fig. 1; D. K. Hill, "Kitchen and Banquet: The History of Ancient Metalware," *CJ* 43 (1948) 454; B. Crewdson, "Silver Strainers," *The Connoisseur* 125 (1950) 106, fig. 1; D. E. Strong, *Greek and Roman Gold and Silver Plate* (London, 1966), 93, fig. 22 A.

A strainer, usually coupled with a ladle (No. 42), was used to eliminate sediment from wine; the flat handles enabled the strainer to rest on the rim of the wine vessel. Very similar examples have been found in Asia Minor, Thessaloniki, and in Meroe, Sudan, in a tomb of King Araka-kamani, who ruled from 315–297 B.C.[1] Two other very closely related strainers were recently recovered from the royal tombs at Vergina, which are dated to the late fourth century.[2]

1. Oliver, *Silver,* 45.
2. M. Andronicos, *Vergina. The Royal Tombs and The Ancient City* (Athens, 1984), 148, fig. 108, and 211, fig. 178.

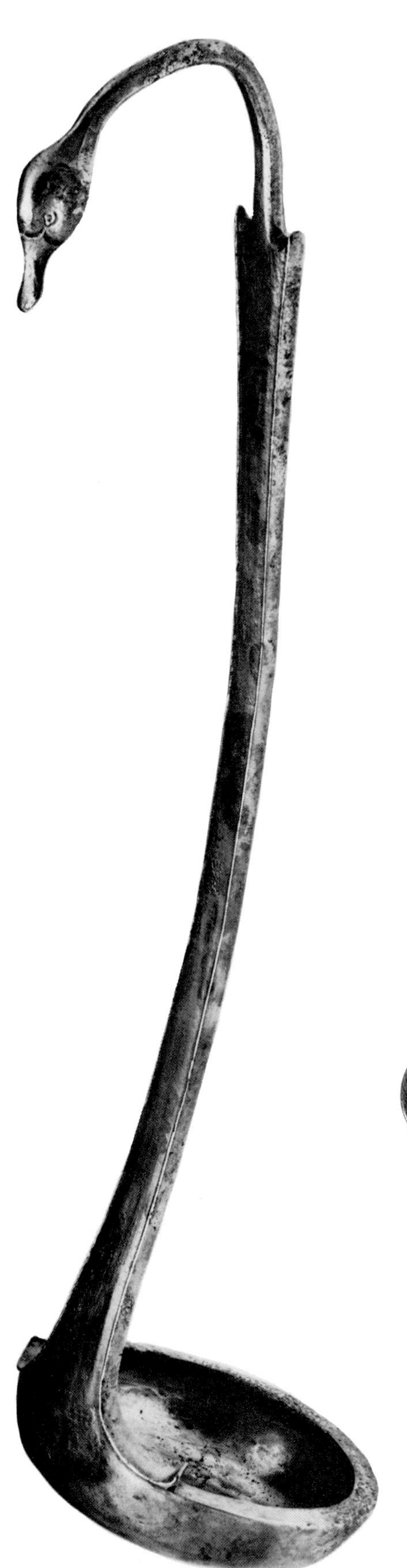

42.1

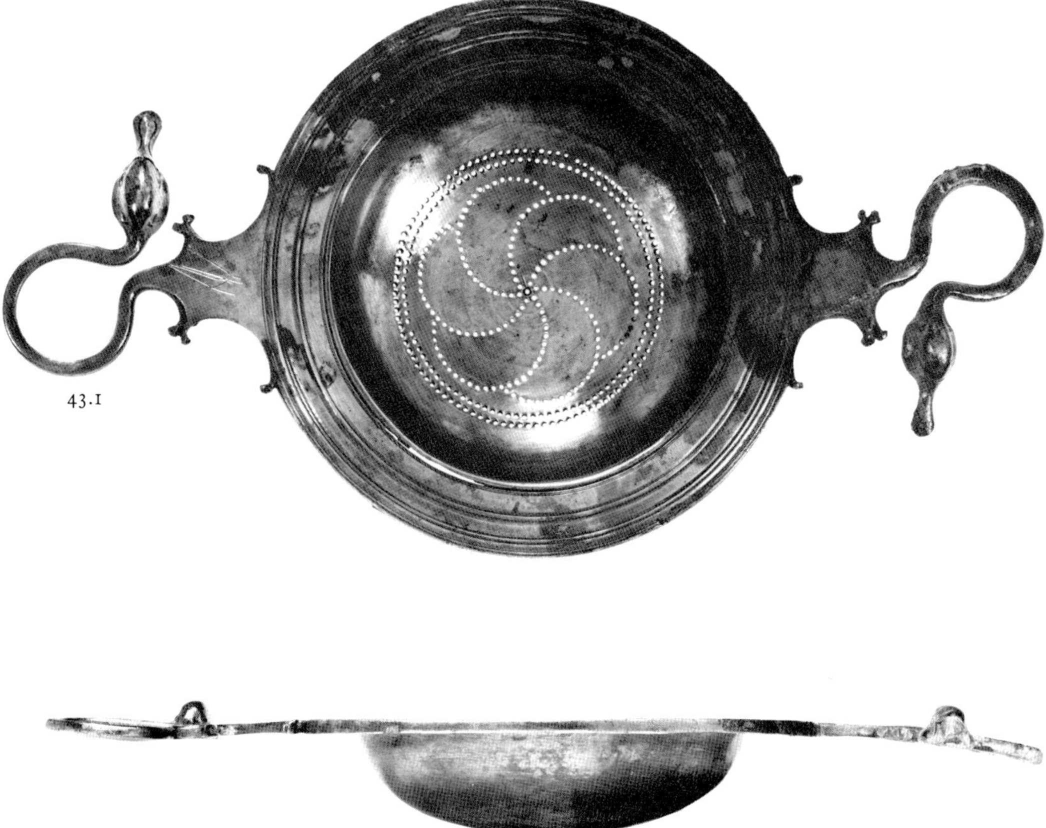

43.1

43.2

Statuette of the Weary Herakles
Early third century

54.1005. Bronze. "From Alexandria." Purchased from Kelekian in 1925. Ht, 15.6 cm; W, 5.8 cm; Depth, 2.6 cm. Missing thumb and forefinger from left hand; right foot; toes of left foot abraded; back of left thigh cracked.

A nude male stands with his weight on his right leg, his left leg relaxed with the foot in front of him. His right elbow is bent with his forearm resting behind his waist. His left arm hangs away from side. His head is turned slightly to his left and inclined; he has a mustache and beard; his pupils are indented. Upon his short curly hair he wears a tainia to which three clusters of fruit or flowers are attached; the ends of the tainia fall forward over each shoulder.

Exhibitions and Catalogues: *The Greek Tradition in Painting and the Minor Arts,* The Walters Art Gallery and the Baltimore Museum of Art (Baltimore, May 15–June 25, 1939), 58, no. 17 and 59, fig. 17. *Man in the Ancient World,* Queens College (New York, February 10–March 7, 1958), 21, no. 131 and 50, fig. 131.

Publications: B. Segall, "Realistic Portraiture in Greece and Egypt," *JWalt* 9 (1946) 66–67, 106, figs. 13, 15; Hill, *Bronzes,* 47, no. 97, pl. 24; Bieber, *Sculpture,* 99, fig. 98; D. K. Hill, "Masterpieces Continue," *BWalt* 9 (1957) no. 5; D. Pinkwart, "Drei späthellenistische Bronzen von Burgberg in Pergamon," *Pergamenische Forschungen I,* Pergamon gesammelte Aufsätze (Berlin, 1972), 119, no. 18; 121, n. 11 and n. 18; M. A. Chelotti, "Osservazioni sull'Ercole del tipo Farnese," *Annali della facoltà di lettere e filosofia Bari* 16 (1973) 185, no. 79; C. C. Vermeule, "The Weary Herakles of Lysippos," *AJA* 79 (1975) 325, no. 6; J. Inan, *Roman Sculpture in Side* (Ankara, 1975), 87, no. 421, 9.

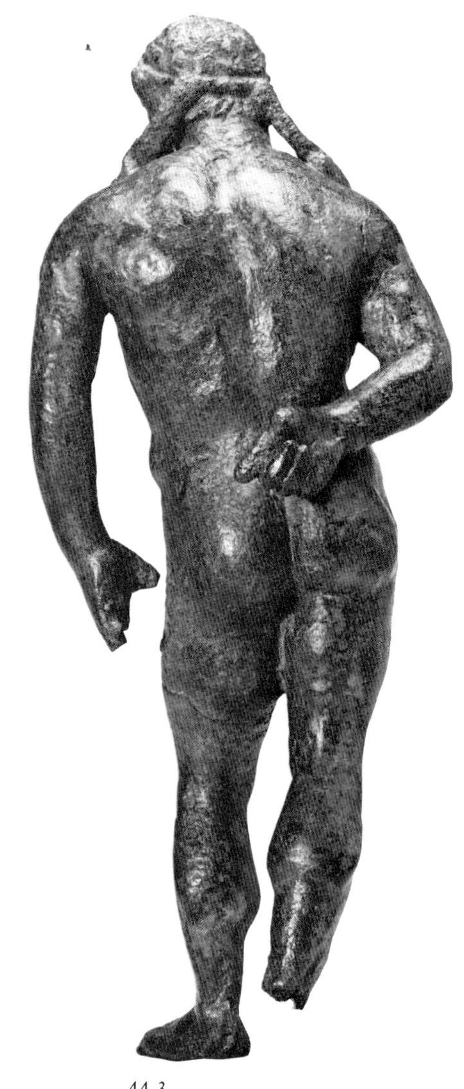

44.3

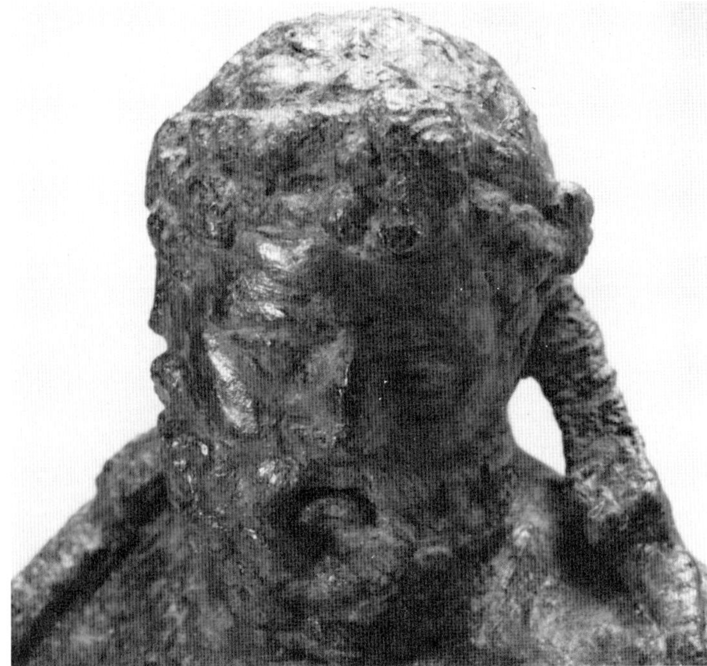

44.2

This statuette is one of the earliest known replicas of a type known either as the Weary Herakles or the Herakles Farnese, after a copy of the Roman period that was signed by the sculptor Glykon.[1] The original work is believed to have been a statue by Lysippos, whose name appears on another Roman version that is in the Pitti Palace. It has been postulated that the Lysippan statue was erected in Sikyon because the motif appears on Sikyonian coinage of the late fourth and early third centuries, and because Pausanias wrote that he had seen there a statue of Herakles executed by Lysippos.[2]

The multiple copies enable us to envision the original type. Herakles leans forward upon his club over which a lionskin is draped; in his right hand, behind his back, he clutches the apples of the Hesperides. The hero is exhausted, according to one version because he defeated the serpent that guarded the apple tree, or, following another tradition, because he had agreed to support the heavens on his shoulders while the giant Atlas traveled to the ends of the world to procure the fruit. A rock that possibly appeared beneath the club would have referred to this burden (see No. 45). The hero's fatigue is underlined by the contrast between his powerful physique and the manner in which his body is buttressed by his club, which, in its use here, recalls the staff conventionally associated with men of advanced age on fourth-century Attic grave reliefs.[3] Because the apples are obscured in the frontal view, and, consequently, the meaning of the statue is not self-evident without walking around it, Lysippos elicits from the viewer a physical exertion that the hero himself is seeking to avoid. The humor, the subtlety of the three-dimensional composition, and the emphasis upon antithetical contrasts, which looks forward to the Tyche of Antioch (No. 150), suggests that the Weary Herakles postdated the Apoxyomenos of ca. 330 and may have been executed after the death of Alexander, in about 320–310. In the light of Lysippos's close relationship with Alexander and Alexander's own indentification with Herakles, it is likely that the work was a reference to Alexander's accomplishments and to the rewards of peace and repose that ensued for the Greek world and for Alexander himself in death.[4] This sentiment is more explicitly expressed later in the Hellenistic period. In a painting from the Basilica at Herculaneum, which is probably based on a Pergamene original of the third or second century, Herakles, again in the Weary Herakles pose, is shown in the presence of Arcadia and his son Telephos.[5]

The Walters statuette is said to have been found in Alexandria, a provenance that is consistent with the quality of the work and the freshness of the surface. It is possible that the statuette was inspired by one of the large-scale copies of sculptural monuments that Ptolemy II is said to have set up in the Alexandrian gymnasium, and this setting would have been compatible with the athletic prowess of the subject as well as with the allusion to the Garden of the Hesperides.[6] Inscriptional evidence indicates that a garden of Herakles adjoined his sanctuary on Thasos, and it has been suggested that the original Lysippan work was erected within a garden sanctuary in Sikyon.[7]

Because of the exaggerated muscularity of the Farnese Herakles, it has often been assumed that the hero was rendered in this manner only in Imperial times. Fragments of a statue recovered from the Antikythera shipwreck (ca. 75–50), however, as well as an approximately contemporary bronze statuette from Pergamon tell us that this adaptation had already occurred by the late Hellenistic period.[8]

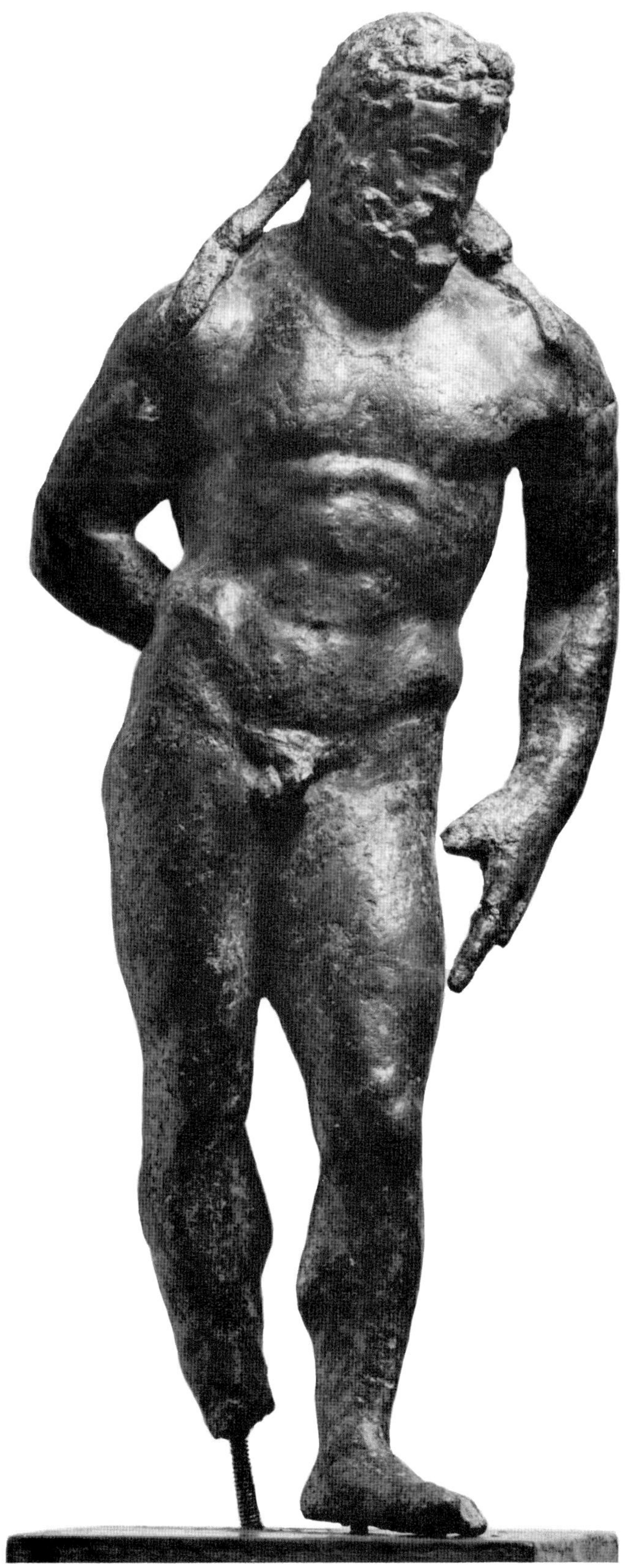

44.1

1. Pollitt 50 and 306, note 8; Ridgway 73; Robertson 467.
2. Pausanias, 2.9.8.
3. H. Diepolder, *Die attischen Grabreliefs* (Berlin, 1931), pls. 29, 30. For the pose, compare pls. 22, 23, 53.
4. For the introduction of Alexander's features into coin types of Herakles, surely seen on a tetradrachm issued by Alexander in Alexandria ca. 325, see Pollitt 26 and 25, fig. 13a. For Alexander, see Arrian 3.3–4.
5. Robertson 443, 544, 577–578, pl. 187d.
6. B. Segall, *JWalt* 9 (1946) 67.
7. B. Ridgway, "Greek Antecedents of Garden Sculpture," *Ancient Roman Gardens* (Washington, D.C., 1981), 25.
8. P. Bol, *Die Skulpturen des Schiffsfundes von Antikythera, AM-BH* 2 (1972) 48–49, no. 23, pl. 25; Ridgway 9; D. Pinkwart, *Pergamenische Forschungen,* 124.

Mirror with the Weary Herakles, Eros, and Nymph
Third century

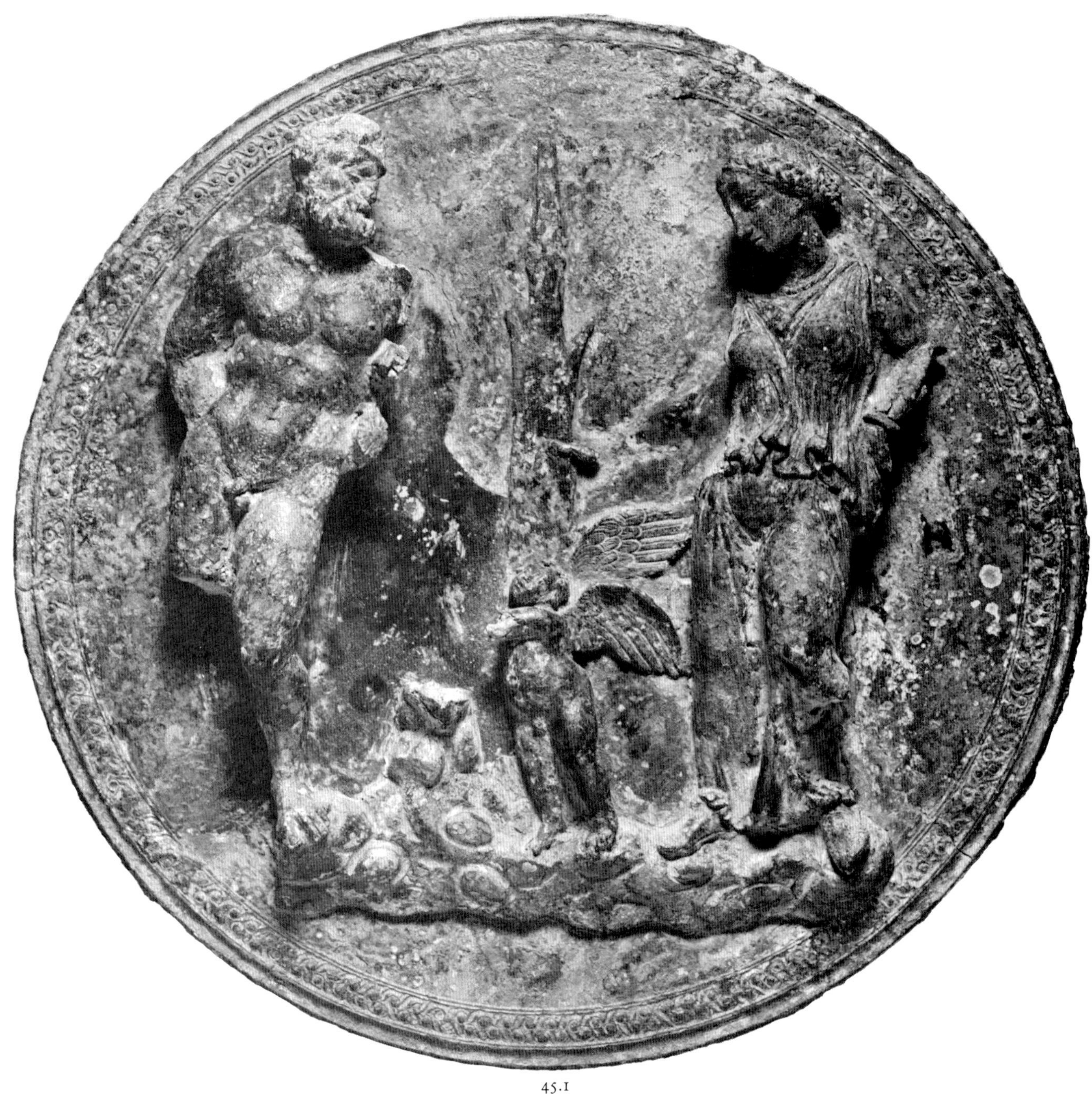

45.1

54.743. Bronze. Purchased from Sambon in 1926. D, mirror 19.2 cm; D, cover 19.4 cm; Ht, 1 cm. The mirror comprises a mirror proper and a lid with a separately applied repoussé relief; both the mirror proper and lid were cast and turned. Engraved on the underside of the lid is a twelve-point star within two concentric circles. On the underside of the mirror proper are four concentric circles; around the vertical edge are three pairs of ridges. On the top of the lid is a repoussé relief surrounded by a cast guilloche enclosed by concentric circles cut around the edge. The relief is worked from a single piece of bronze with the figures almost in the round. The lid was repaired in many places and the relief was reattached with plaster. Missing are the right leg of Herakles, the area to his left including his left arm and staff, both arms of Eros, the maiden's right arm except for the thumb, and her lower leg.

The repoussé relief on the cover shows three figures standing on rocky ground and flanking a central tree. At the viewer's left is a nude bearded Herakles who stands on his right leg, his left leg relaxed, the wrist of his right arm resting behind his waist. A quiver is visible at his left hip; its strap is brought over his right shoulder and breast. He gazes to his left at a maiden who stands with her weight on her right leg, her left leg relaxed with the foot to the side. The back of her left wrist rests against her left hip; her right arm was extended. She wears a peplos with overfold, necklace, and bracelet. Her head is inclined down, and her hair is arranged in a braid which is brought from the nape to her brow. Between the figures and in front of the tree is a

standing nude winged Eros who turns to his right, his left shoulder and upper arm extended and upraised, his head gazing up at Herakles in three-quarter left profile. In front of Eros is a pile of rocks, on which the club of Herakles may have rested; the figures stand on a rocky groundline.

Publications: D. K. Hill, ''Ancient Metal Reliefs,'' *Hesperia* 12 (1943) 106 and 108, fig. 10; D. K. Hill, ''Masterpieces Continue,'' *BWalt* 9 (1957) no. 5; F. Brommer, *Denkmälerlisten zur griechischen Heldensage I. Herakles* (Marburg, 1971), 60, no. 1.

Because such stylistic details as the deep V-neck of the maiden's garment suggest a date for the piece in the early third century, this mirror, like the bronze statuette No. 44, can be numbered among the earliest replicas of the Weary Herakles by Lysippos.[1] Herakles is seen here in the Garden of the Hesperides attended by one of its nymphs, who proffers to him an apple from the tree that stands between the figures; we are, therefore, to understand that Herakles has just defeated the serpent that stood guard in the garden. The artist has altered the original meaning of the statue by shifting Herakles' gaze from the ground to the maiden, and this adjustment undermines the weariness in his posture and suggests that it is not repose alone that will be the reward for the hero's efforts. The implication is made more explicit by the outstretched arms of the diminutive Eros, whose presence is very much in keeping with the romantic preoccupations of the Hellenistic age and brings to mind words of the contemporary (ca. 310) poet Menander: "Is not Eros the greatest of all the gods, and by far the most honored? For there is no man so miserly or inflexible that he does not share part of his property with this god."[2]

1. See Thompson, *Troy*, 35.
2. Menander, fragment 235k from ΘΗΣΑΤΡΟΣ.

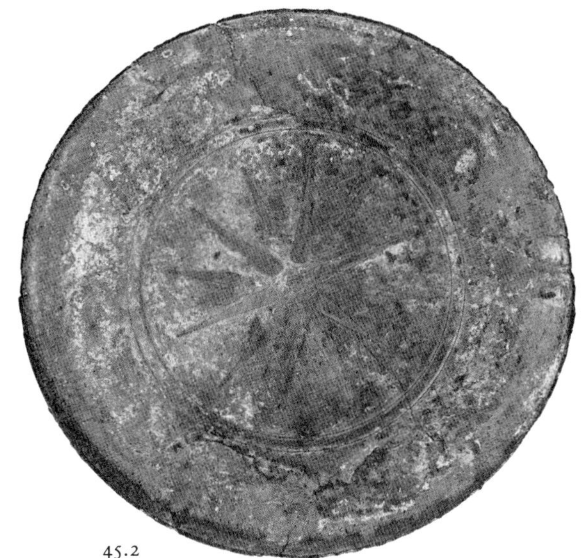

45.2

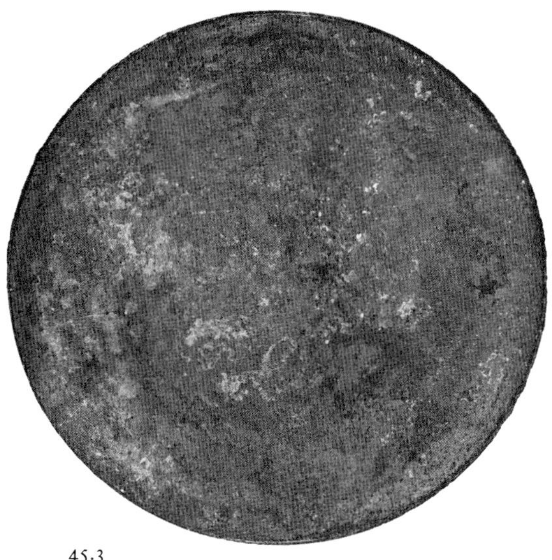

45.3

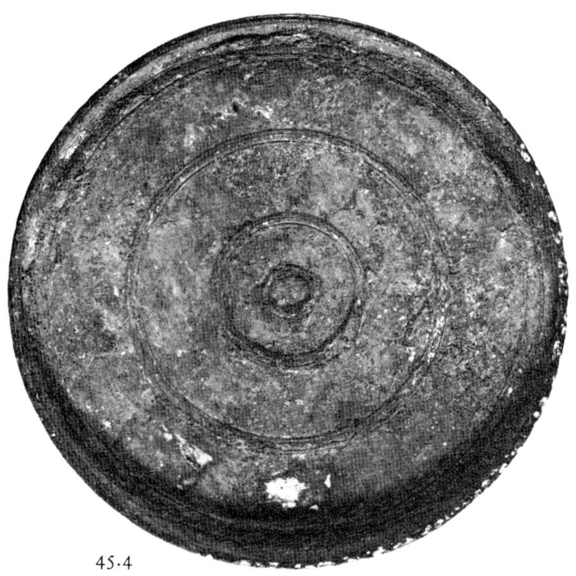

45.4

Mirror with Seated Figures
Third century

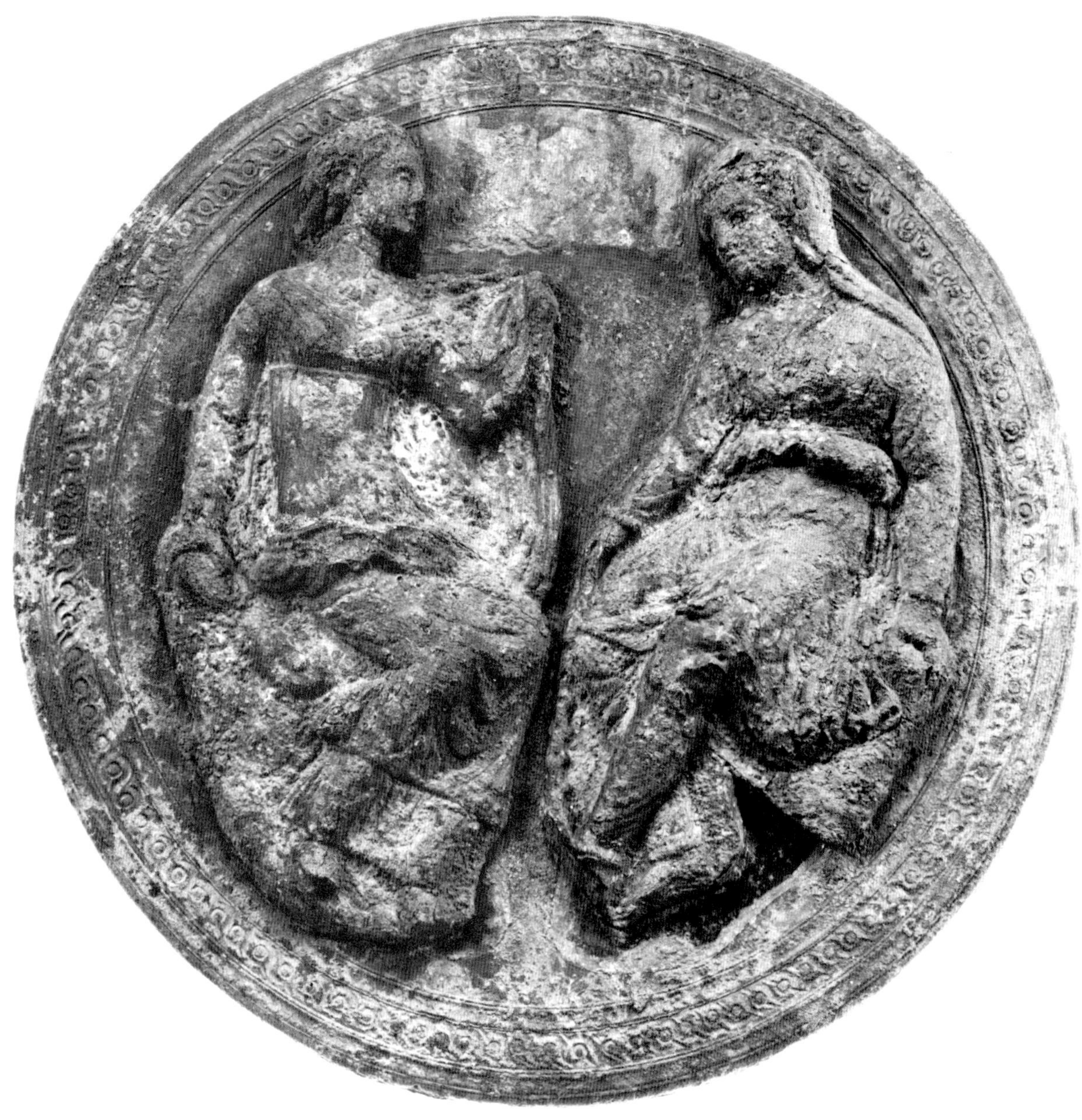

46.1

54.1170. Bronze. Purchased before 1931. D, 16.2 cm; Ht, left figure 12.1 cm; Ht, right figure 11.8 cm; Th, mirror 2.1 cm; Th, cover 1.7 cm. The lid may have a silvered surface. The mirror comprises a mirror proper and a lid which was decorated with separately applied repoussé reliefs; those presently in place are ancient but probably do not belong. The mirror and lid were cast, then turned on a lathe; a guilloche pattern was cast on the lid near the edge; concentric circles were cut on the undersides and edges of the mirror proper and the lid. Broken away is the left foot of the youth. Chips are missing from his left knee, the top of his head, and the mantle folds on the maiden's right thigh.

Two facing figures are seated on rocks. Seen in three-quarters left profile is a male figure with his legs crossed at the ankles, his right hand clasping the end of a club by his right thigh. His left arm is at his side with the hand resting on part of a rock by his left hip. He wears a long-sleeved, girded tunic extending to his knees above leggings; his head is inclined. Fabric is draped over the back of his head, with a lappet by his left ear, and hangs down behind his shoulders. Facing him with legs in three-quarters right profile, torso frontal and head in right profile, is a maiden whose right hand rests on the rock by her side and whose left hand is raised to hold the edge of her mantle at shoulder level. She wears a high-girded, V-necked chiton beneath a mantle, which she draws around her left shoulder and which passes behind her back and across her waist, covering her legs to mid-calf. The folds of her chiton emerge beneath and extend to her ankles. Her hair is drawn back from her face and is gathered at the nape.

Publications: D. K. Hill, ''Ancient Metal Reliefs,'' *Hesperia* 12 (1943) 102 and 106, fig. 9.

The youth's Phrygian cap suggests that the pair are Aphrodite and Adonis, but certainty is impossible. The ambiguity results not only from the absence of attributes and the conventionality of the three-quarter poses, but also from the additive character of the composition which is comprised of separately fabricated reliefs derived from independent traditions and conceivably from different ancient mirrors. The maiden is on a larger scale than the youth and her high V-necked garment follows a third-century style, in contrast with the attire of her companion which finds parallels in the later fourth century.[1] Another jarring note is the juxtaposition of her direct gaze and gesture with the withdrawn musing of her companion.

1. For the dress, see Thompson, *Troy*, 35.

MIRROR WITH NIKE
Late fourth to third century

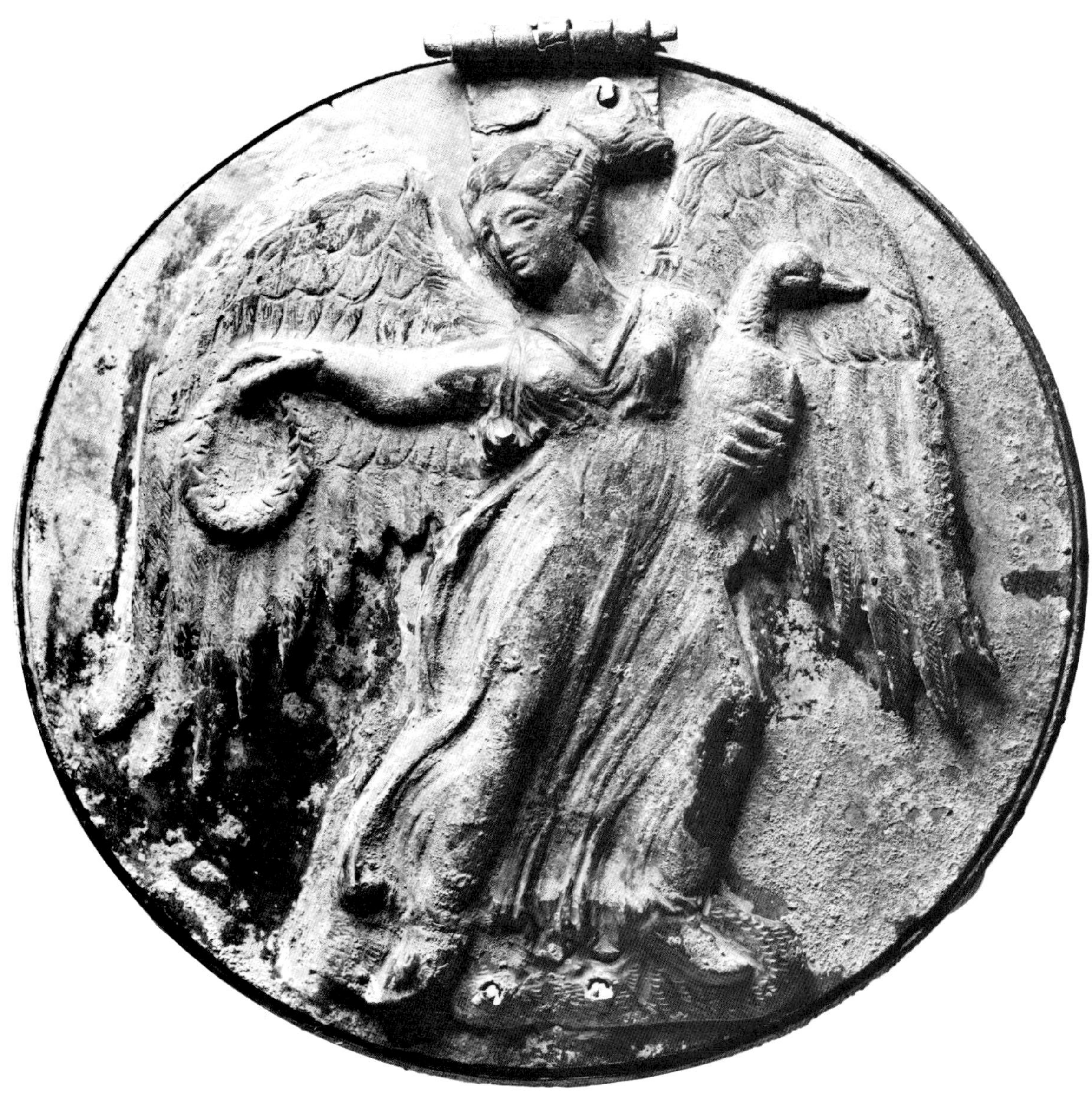

47.1

54.1160. Bronze. "From Greece." Purchased from Lambassis in 1929. D, mirror and lid 15.9 cm; Th, cover 1 cm; Th, mirror 2.1 cm. The mirror comprises a mirror proper with a polished surface and a lid decorated with a relief. The mirror proper is a round box, cast and turned; four concentric circles are cut on the inset underside, others on the vertical edge. The front of the mirror proper has a protruding ridge around the edge into which a convex hammered disc fitted as the cover. Attached to the disc is a repoussé relief. At the top of the relief is part of a hinge secured to the mirror by two pins, one of which passes through the woman's hair. On the opposite edge two pins for the attachment of a handle are pierced through both the disc and the relief. The relief has been reattached.

A winged maiden worked in repoussé strides upon rocky terrain to her left, her left leg in right profile, her right leg and torso frontal, her head turned back in three-quarters left profile. The fingers of her right, extended arm clasp a wreath at which she is gazing; her left hand clutches a long-necked bird to her side. She wears a V-necked peplos, girt beneath the breasts. Her hair is arranged in a melon hairstyle gathered in a knot behind the crown, with the ends falling free.

Publications: D. K. Hill, "Ancient Metal Reliefs," *Hesperia* 12 (1943) 102, and 104–105, figs. 7 and 8.

The deep V-neckline, high girding, and the melon hairstyle with a gathering of locks at the crown indicate that the Nike is an early Hellenistic, and probably provincial, interpretation of late fifth-century works, whose movement and spirit are better embodied by figurine vase No. 10 and the terracotta relief No. 12. The goose was a traditional love offering; the wreath was a grassy rope adorned with flowers of a type worn by terracotta figurines Nos. 76 and 85.

Mirror with Eros and Nymph
Third century

54.1169. Bronze. Purchased before 1931. D, of mirror and cover is 11.4 cm; Th, cover 1 cm; Th, mirror 2.3 cm. Wingspan of Eros is 8.9 cm. The mirror comprises a mirror proper with a polished surface and a lid decorated with a separately made repoussé relief. Both mirror and lid were cast and turned. There are concentric circles around the underside of the mirror proper and the vertical edges of the mirror proper and its lid. Incised circles also surround the repoussé relief on the lid. On the underside of the lid, incised circles enclose an engraved scene. Outermost band outside the scene and all the elements in the scene except the background are silvered. A section is missing from the edge of the lid. The right and most of the left leg of Eros are missing, as are the tips of both wings.

The repoussé relief on the cover shows a nude chubby boy with outspread wings moving to his left, his left leg advanced, his torso seen in three-quarters right profile, and his head in right profile. Both arms are bent at the elbow with the hands brought close to the body. His mantle falls over his left elbow, is brought behind his back, and flutters out between and behind his legs. He has short curly hair and his iris is incised. On the underside of the cover, within concentric circles, is a nude standing female seen from behind in three-quarters right profile, her weight on her right leg, her left knee bent with the toes of the left foot resting on the ground behind her. Her head is in right profile; her wavy hair flows back from her brow and is brushed up from her nape. Her right arm is extended towards a basin supported by a columnar shaft into which a jet of water is cascading. Her left arm is outstretched behind her and the extended fingers rest on a pile of rocks. The rocky setting is further indicated by irregular contours around the edge of the circular field and beneath her feet.

Publications: *LIMC* III (1986) pt. 1, 868.

This mirror presents a later version of a scene that appears on an early fourth-century mirror in Boston, where an adolescent Eros lounges on the back of a dolphin.[1] On the Walters example Eros is now a chubby boy with the truncated wings fashionable in Hellenistic times, and he is seated, probably sideways, on a dolphin which has not survived. The dolphin was a perennially popular animal in Greek culture and in time came to be associated with Eros, partly because of the

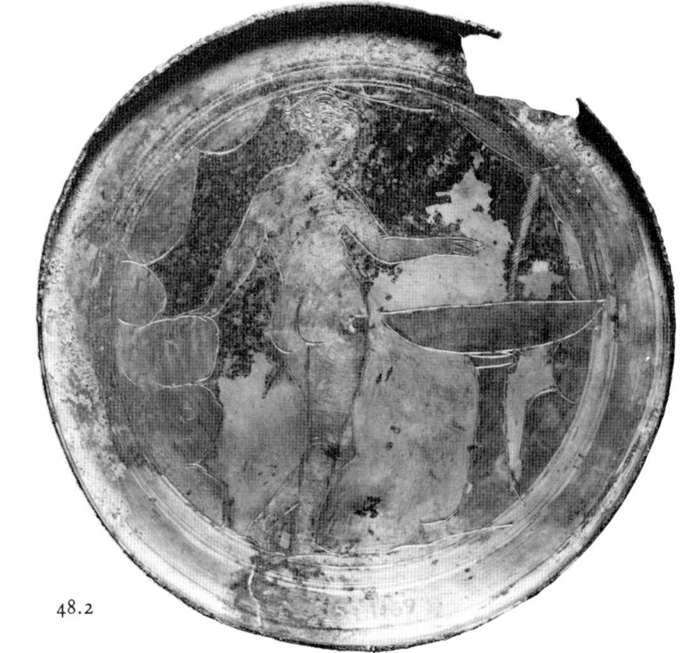

48.2

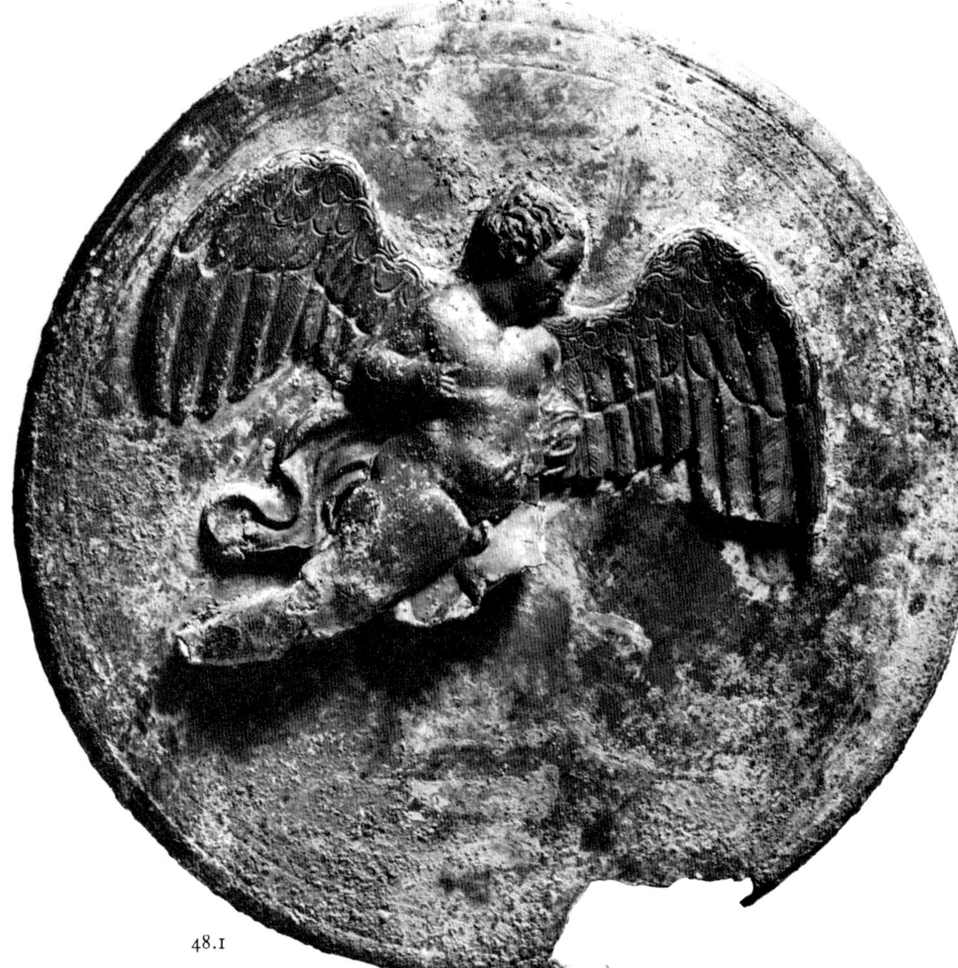

48.1

reputed birth from the sea of Aphrodite, Eros's mother, and partly because of the erotic connotations underlying the assistance dolphins offered to such mythical youths as Taras and Arion.[2] The billowing mantle folds of the Walters Eros, as well as his tightly bent right arm, convey an animation that contrasts markedly with the tranquility of the grotto scene on the interior, where a maiden, probably a Nymph, prepares to take her bath. Whereas the grace with which the nude female is presented demonstrates the broad acceptance that the motif had received by this date, the rustic setting, which identifies the maiden as a mythical personage and provides a motivation for her undress, reveals a lingering discomfiture with the portrayal of female nudity.

1. C. C. Vermeule and M. Comstock, *Greek, Etruscan, and Roman Bronzes in the Boston Museum of Fine Arts* (Greenwich, 1971), 250, no. 361; *LIMC* III (1986) pt. 1, 868, no. 172.
2. G. Grigson, *The Goddess of Love: The Birth, Death, and Return of Aphrodite* (New York, 1977), 137; S. Fasca, *Eros: La figura e il culto* (Genoa, 1977), 105, n. 124.

STATUETTE OF ALEXANDER KTISTES
Roman copy after an original of the late fourth century

54.1075. Bronze. "From Alexandria." Purchased from Kelekian in 1922. Ht, 11.2 cm; W, 6.75 cm. Missing attribute in right hand, which is reattached.

A youth stands with his weight on his right leg, his left leg relaxed with the foot behind him. His right arm is raised; his left arm is bent at the elbow with the forearm extended to clasp a rectangular object in his upturned left hand. He wears an aegis in the form of a chlamys which is fastened on his right shoulder, with the right side open. Scales are incised over the surface of the aegis, a Gorgoneion sits on his left breast, and the hem is perforated at regular intervals with small holes, some of which have broken through the edge. His short hair is center-parted with locks of hair framing his face beneath a headband. The irises are incised.

Exhibitions and Catalogues: *Search for Alexander,* Boston supplement 7, no. 9; Toronto supplement II, no. S–12.

Publications: Hill, *Bronzes,* 53, no. 109, pl. 28; A. Linfert, *Von Polyklet zu Lysipp* (Giessen, 1966), 68.I; G. Grimm, "Die Vergöttlichung Alexanders der Grossen in Ägypten und ihre Bedeutung für den ptolemäischen Königskult," H. Maehler and V. M. Strocka, eds., *Das ptolemäische Ägypten* (Mainz, 1978), 104, n. 12.

This Roman statuette, which exhibits the hairstyle traditionally associated with Alexander the Great, reproduces a type that survives in a number of other statuettes, most of which were found in Egypt.[1] The figure wears a garment draped like a Macedonian chlamys (cloak), and bears the incised scales and Gorgoneion of an aegis, which would have been further enhanced by snaky coils attached around the perforated hemline. The aegis and the spear, which is held in the right hand on many copies, belong to Zeus, for whom the aegis, usually rendered as a goatskin, was a principal attribute; Homer tells us it was shaken by the god to bring on a thunderstorm.[2] In the left hand the Walters statuette grasps a rectangular object, probably the base of a (now lost) Palladium which was a sacred image of Athena given by Zeus to Dardanos, the founder of Troy.[3] It was believed in ancient times that the well-being of that city depended upon the security of this image, which, tradition relates, was removed from Troy, with calamitous consequences, by both Diomedes and Aeneas.[4] The rendering of the aegis as a chlamys, the allusions to Zeus, the presence of the Palladium, and the Egyptian findspot of so many replicas indicate that the prototypical work represented Alexander Ktistes, the city founder of Alexandria, which ancient writers tell us was laid out in the shape of a chlamys.[5] The presence of the Palladium probably referred to a tradition that Alexander, following the precedent of mythical heroes, had procured the Palladium from Troy for his new city in Egypt.[6] Although it is not clear exactly where in the city the statue was located, the honoring of Alexander through a hero's cult with a cult statue would have conformed to a long-established Greek tradition, which was probably observed soon after the establishment of Alexandria in 332. The quantity of small-scale replicas suggests that an image of Alexander became a conventional fixture in Alexandrian household shrines.

1. G. Grimm, *Das ptolemäische Ägypten,* 103; P. Perdrizet, "Un type inédit de la plastique grecque," *MonPiot* 21 (1913) 59–71; E. Schwarzenberg, "The Portraiture of Alexander," *Alexandre le Grand,* 233–245; R. M. Errington, "Alexander in the Hellenistic World," *Alexandre le Grand,* 170–72.
2. Homer, *Iliad* 17.593–594.
3. On another image in Berlin and on a marble hand in Munich, the shaft or feet of the Palladium are preserved. For a complete representation of a Palladium on a cameo, see Schwarzenberg (note 1) 234, n. 3.
4. Vergil, *Aeneid* 2.162–179.
5. Strabo, 17.1.8; Diodoros, 17.52; Pliny, *NH* 5.11.62.
6. Schwarzenberg (note 1) 234–235.

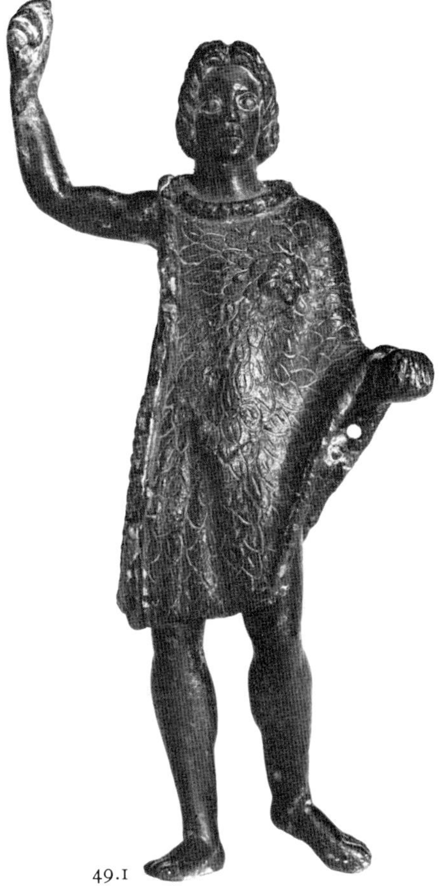

49.1

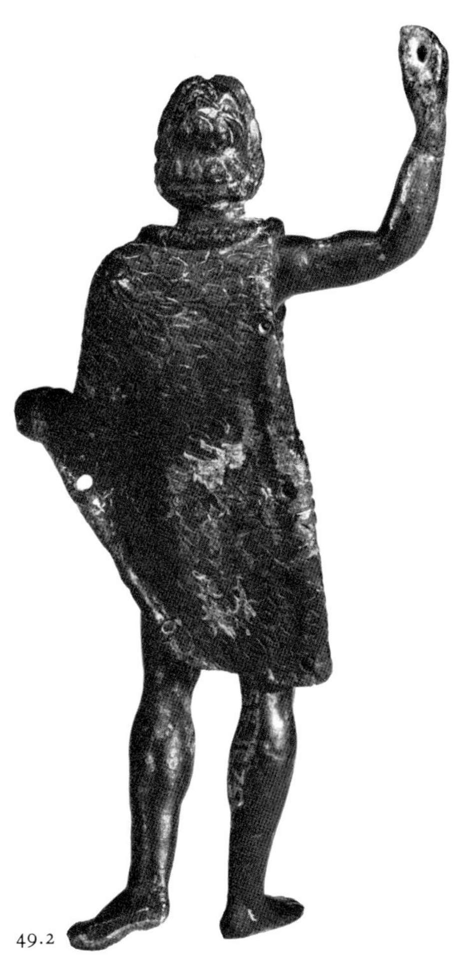

49.2

Appliqué Fulcrum Bust of a Ptolemaic King
Third century

54.598. Bronze. "From Tarentum." M. Jean P. Lambros Collection (sale catalogue, *Collections Jean P. Lambros d'Athènes et de M. Giovanni Dattari du Caire,* Paris, Hôtel Drouot, June 17–19, 1912, 30, no. 254, pl. 17). Purchased from Kelekian, in 1913 (?). Ht, 11.3 cm; W, 8.6 cm; Th, 4.2 cm. Back open and flat. Deposit over surface. Inlay missing from eyes. Cracked over surface.

A bust of a nude male consists of his left shoulder, chest, and head which is turned three-quarters to his left; his right shoulder was elevated above his left. On his short wavy hair he wears a wreath of vine leaves with the ribbon ends falling to each shoulder. He has deep-set eyes, a protruding fleshy area beneath his brows, a large, bumpy nose, and his mouth is open.

Publications: Reinach, *Statuaire* 5 (1924) 50, no. 5; B. Segall, "Realistic Portraiture in Greece and Egypt," *JWalt* 9 (1946) 52–55, 66–67, figs. 1, 2, 4; J. Tondriau, "La dynastie Ptolémaïque et la religion dionysiaque," *Chronique d'Egypte* 50 (1950) 283; B. Segall, "Alexandria und Tarent," *AA* (1965) cols. 555, 574–575, figs. 17–18 on cols. 579–580; H. Kyrieleis, *Bildnisse der Ptolemäer* (Berlin, 1975), 7, no. 16, pl. 7.1.2; H. Maehler and V. M. Strocka, eds., *Das ptolemäische Ägypten* (Mainz, 1978), 1–3, 109, no. 75, fig. 86; 132, no. 51; Reinsberg, *Toreutik,* 81–82, 91, 124–127; B. Barr-Sharrar, "The Anticythera Fulcrum Bust: A Portrait of Arsinoe III," *AJA* 89 (1985) 691; B. Barr-Sharrar, *The Hellenistic and Early Imperial Decorative Bust* (Mainz, 1987), 52, no. 3, pl. 26.

The deep-set eye with its overhanging brow, the flaring nose, and the projecting chin identify the subject as a Ptolemaic king, here wearing the ivy wreath of Dionysos who was more conventionally portrayed at this date with fleshier facial features and longer locks of hair.[1] The incorporation of divine attributes into a ruler's portrait follows a precedent that can be traced back to Alexander, whose image was assimilated with that of Herakles on coins issued in the monarch's own lifetime and whose posthumous coin portraits bore the lion scalp of Herakles and the horns of Zeus Ammon.[2] The Walters bust makes a further allusion to Alexander in the turn of the head, which is a deliberate echo of Lysippan portraits of that sovereign. Segall identified the Walters bust as that of Ptolemy I (367/6–283/2) both because of similarities to coin portraits and because a statue of Ptolemy I wearing Dionysos's ivy wreath was included in the procession of Ptolemy II Philadelphos during the 270s.[3] Indeed, a

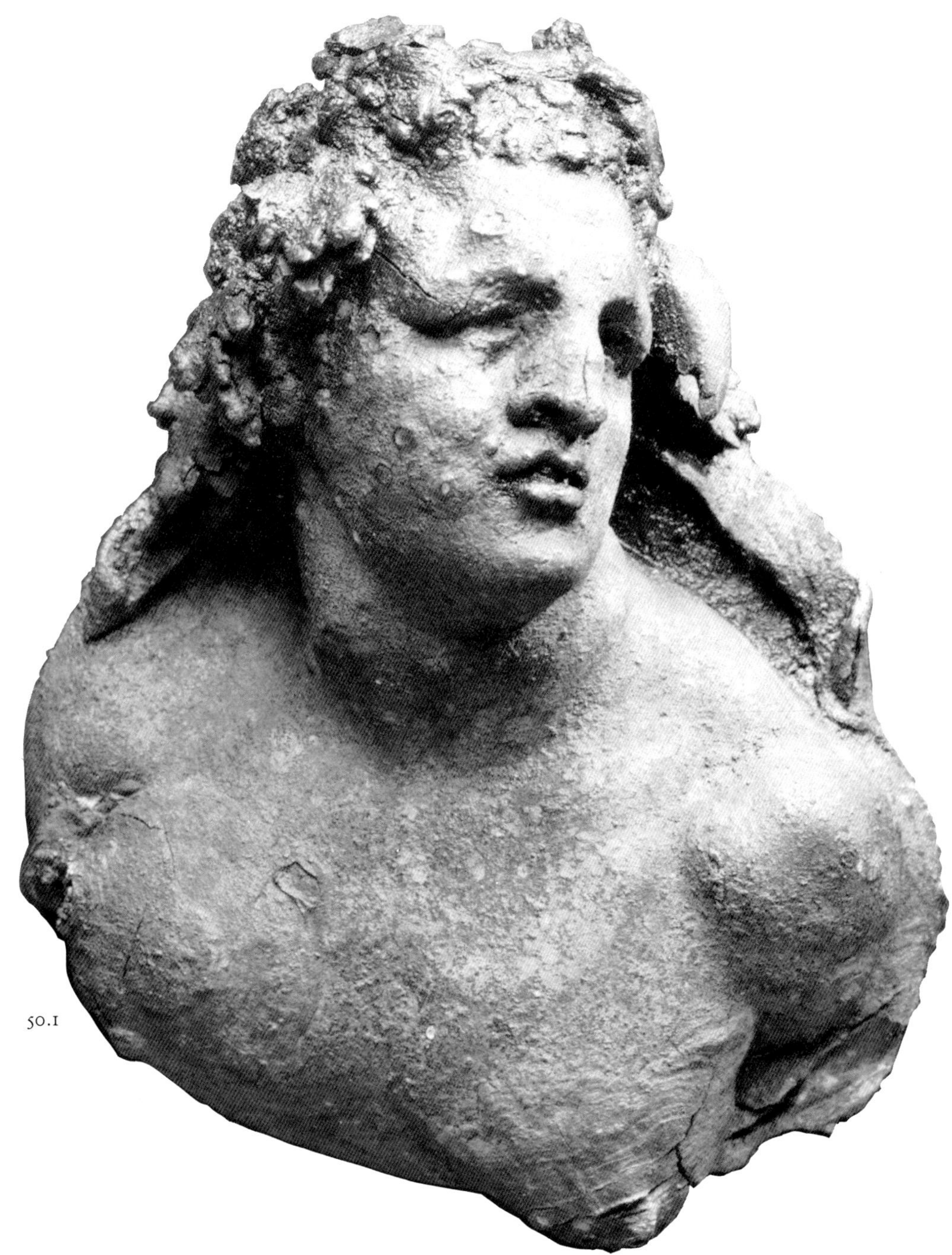

50.1

posthumous date for the bust and its
probable large-scale prototype is highly
likely given that Ptolemy I was deified
only after his death in 283 and that the
earliest examples of fulcrum (armrest)
attachments are not earlier than the second quarter of the third century.[4] The
baroque intensity of the expression is also
compatible with a later third-century date
and admits the possibility that the bust
could alternatively portray Ptolemy III
Euergetes (288/80–221).[5]

The Walters bust was said to have been
found in Tarentum together with the
Coppa Tarantino (now lost), a prometopidion in Basel, and six silver discs in Boston and Princeton, and it is possible that
all were buried together just before Tarentum was destroyed by the Romans in
207.[6] The integrity of the find is difficult
to substantiate because the works
appeared individually on the art market
between 1890 and the 1940s; even should
the objects have been found together, they
need not share the same provenance nor
be contemporary with each other,
although it is noteworthy that the Coppa
Tarantino, the prometopidion, and the
medallions are generally dated to 270–
260.[7] In addition to the Walters bust the
Coppa Tarantino is also thought to
exhibit Alexandrian qualities, thereby
providing further testimony for a vigorous trade between Alexandria and South
Italy during the third century.[8]

The appearance of small-scale busts on
the fulcra of beds (klinai) undoubtedly
echoes the existence of marble or bronze
busts in the major arts, examples of which
were found in the late Hellenistic Heroon
at Kalydon.[9] Portrait busts were also featured in the procession of Ptolemy II at
Alexandria and may have been fairly common in Egypt.[10] Miniature versions like
the Walters piece were intended for the
domestic environment and, like the Ptolemaic oinochoai (Nos. 113, 114), served as
an effective political tool by establishing a
personal link between ruler and ruled.

Ptolemy I (367/6–283/2) was one of
Alexander's most trusted generals and at
the latter's death in 323, he acquired
Egypt, to which he soon added Cyrenaica. In 304 he assumed the title of King
and Soter and, after he defeated Antigonos

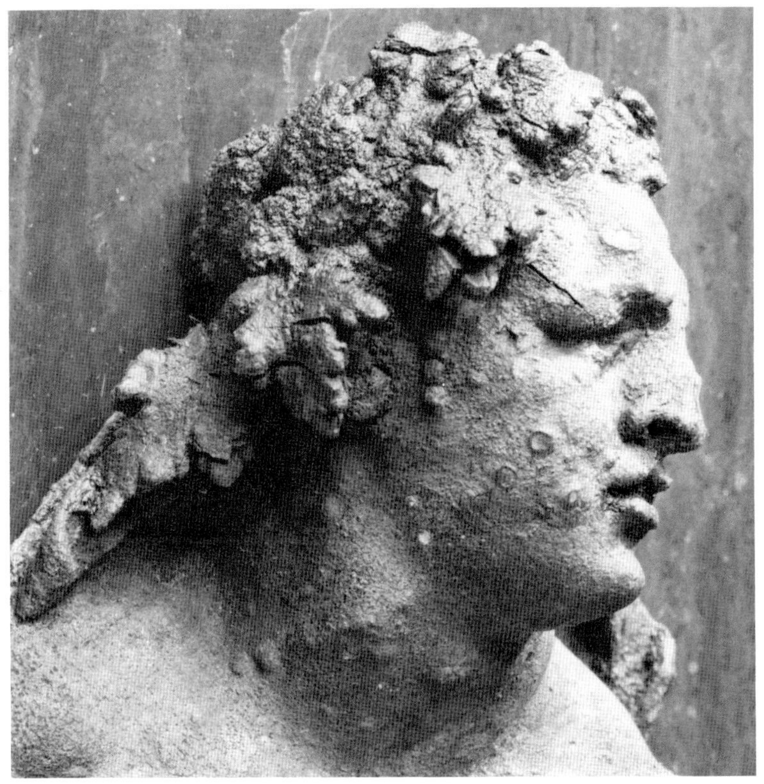

50.2

at Ipsos in 301, expanded his empire to
include Palestine and Cyprus. He was the
founder of the Library and Mouseion at
Alexandria and was deified at his death in
283, an honor that several years later was
also accorded his wife, Berenike I.

Ptolemy III Euergetes (288/80–221) was
the son of Ptolemy II and Arsinoe I.
Ascending the throne in 246, he soon
after married Berenike II, daughter of
King Magas of Cyrene. His success in the
Third Syrian War (246–241) secured additional territory in Syria and Anatolia,
which proved to be the last significant
expansion effected by the Ptolemaic
dynasty.

1. H. Kyrieleis, *Bildnisse,* 7–8.
2. Pollitt 26–28; 271–274.
3. Segall, *JWalt* 9 (1946) 66; Athenaeus, *Deipnosophistae,*
   5.201.
4. For the deification of Ptolemy I, see Pollitt 273. For fulcrum attachments see B. Barr-Sharrar, ''The Anticythera
   Fulcrum Bust: A Portrait of Arsinoe III,'' *AJA* 89 (1985)
   691.
5. Barr-Sharrar, *Decorative Bust,* 52, 96.
6. Segall, *AA* (1965) cols. 553–588; Segall, *JWalt* 9 (1946)
   53; Reinsberg, *Toreutik,* 91, 124–126.
7. Ibid., 124–25.
8. Ibid., 124, 127; Segall, *AA* (1965) col. 579.
9. Barr-Sharrar (note 4) 691.
10. Segall, *AA* (1965) col. 577.

Statuette of Papposilenos Playing the Flute

Ca. third to second century

54.1076. Bronze. "Found in South Italy." Warneck Collection (sale catalogue, Paris, Hôtel Drouot, June 13–16, 1905, 15, no. 90, pl. 5). Purchased before 1931. Ht, 10.7 cm; W, 5.1 cm. Flute restored.

A nude chubby male with fleshy breasts steps forward on his left leg with his weight evenly distributed over both legs. Each uplifted hand supports the shaft of a double-flute which is raised to his lips. He wears a beard and mustache. His hair is brushed forward onto his brow and is surmounted by a thick round cord to which three balls are attached, one above each bestial ear and at the crown; beneath the latter ball is a hole for the attachment of another object. The top of the head above the cord is smooth; the carefully delineated locks beneath it fall to his shoulders. Around each knee is a band of fur rendered by incisions.

Exhibitions and Catalogues: *The Greek Tradition in Painting and the Minor Arts,* The Walters Art Gallery and the Baltimore Museum of Art (Baltimore, May 15–June 25, 1939), 62, no. 33; *Musical Instruments and Their Portrayal in Art,* Baltimore Museum of Art (Baltimore, April 26–June 2, 1946), 8, no. 8.

Publications: Reinach, *Statuaire* 4 (1910) 35, no. 1; D. K. Hill, *The Dance in Classical Times* (Baltimore, 1945), 14, ill.; Hill, *Bronzes,* 41, no. 83, pl. 20.

The bald pate and incised fur on the thighs identify the figure as the Papposilenos, patriarch of the Silenoi. These semibestial beings were followers of the wine-god Dionysos whose festivities are recalled by this figure's wreath. During the Hellenistic period the appearance of the Papposilenos became so humanized that even his equine ears occasionally disappeared, leaving only his nudity and furry body to establish his bestial identity.[1]

Satyrs and Silenoi were traditionally associated with the flute, partly because of the exotic associations of the instrument's Asiatic origins and partly because the flute distorted the face when it was played. This unexpected consequence was said to have so displeased Athena that after inventing the flute she discarded it.[2] The satyr Marsyas thereupon retrieved the instrument, but was bested in a musical competition with Apollo, who triumphed because he was able to sing to his lyre's accompaniment. The traditionally inferior stature of the flute was observed in the early fifth century by Pratinas who proclaimed that the flute must dance behind like a servant; Aristotle echoed this sentiment when he complained that the lyre calmed the emotions and the flute excited them.[3] In the international atmosphere of the Hellenistic period, the flute grew in popularity and was appreciated for the very animation that Aristotle deplored, here convincingly embodied in the statuette's lively pose and twisting form.

1. See E. Reeder Williams, *The Archaeological Collection of the Johns Hopkins University* (Baltimore, 1984), 26–27, no. 14 and 103, no. 71. See also E. Reeder Williams, "A Roman Theater Relief at the Johns Hopkins University," *AntK* 21 (1978) 35–36.
2. Apollodoros, *Bibliotheke,* 1.4.1–2.
3. See J. Onians, *Art and Thought in the Hellenistic Age* (London, 1979), 66–67; Aristotle, *Pol.* 8.6.5.

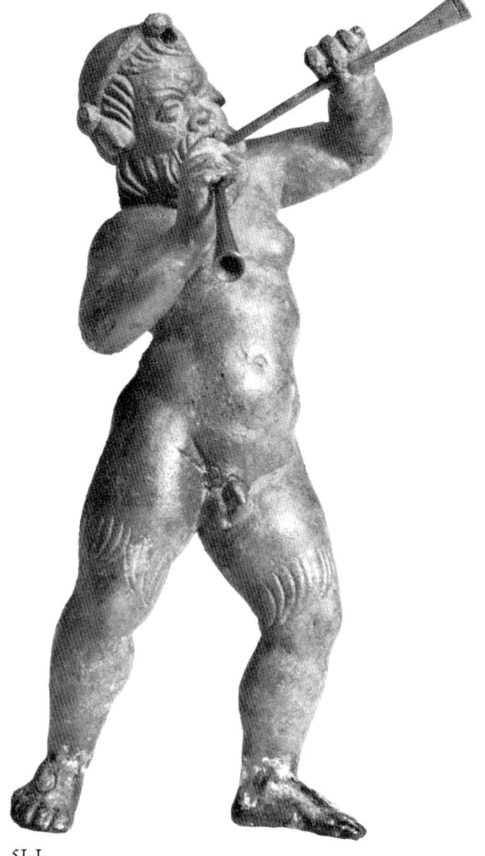

51.1

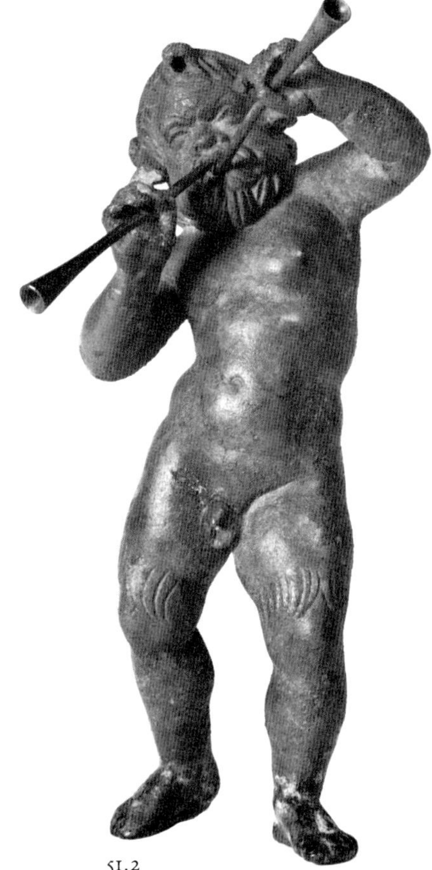

51.2

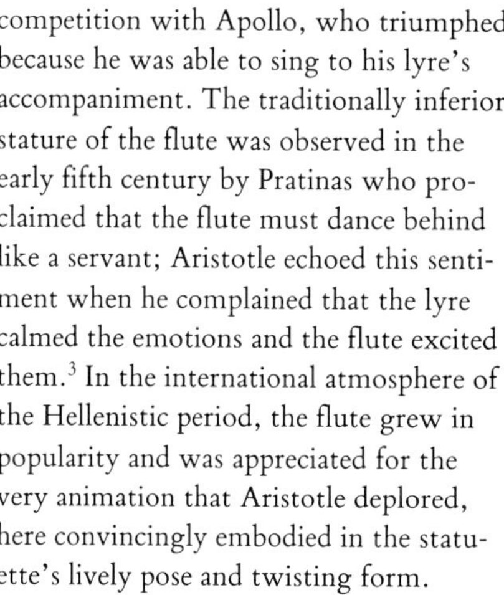

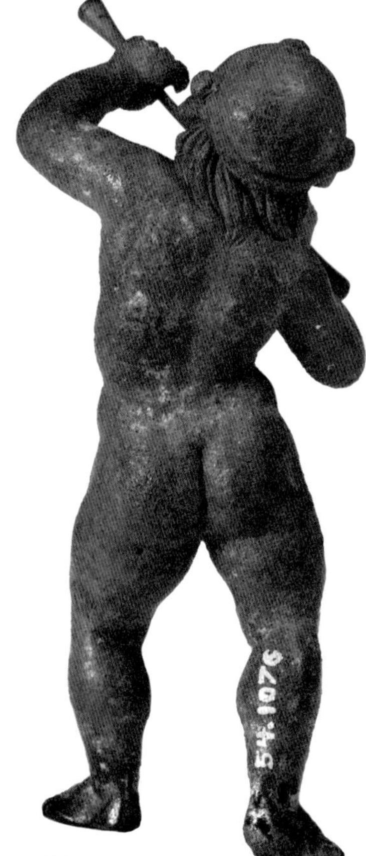

51.3

Statuette of a
Child Boxer
Third to second century

54.1001. Bronze. ''From Alexandria.'' Warneck
Collection (sale catalogue, Paris, Hôtel Drouot, June
13–16, 1905, 24, no. 152). Purchased from Kelekian
before 1931. Ht, 10.8 cm; Ht, figure alone 8.9 cm;
D, base 4.6 cm. Missing thumb and tip of index finger of left hand. Heavily corroded. Ancient base,
reattached by modern screw and nut, probably does
not belong.

A nude, muscular boy stands on his right leg with
his left leg relaxed and his foot at the side. Both arms
hang at his sides. Boxing gloves on each hand are
constructed of leather straps around wrist and
knuckles connected by thongs behind thumb and
cross straps over the back of the hand. His head
turns slightly to his left. His short curly hair is
wrapped around a band and gathered at the nape.

Publications: A. Thomas, ''La collection
Warneck,'' *Le Musée* 2 (1905) 131, fig. 6; Reinach,
Statuaire 4 (1910) 268, no. 7; D. K. Hill, ''Ancient
Representations of Herakles as a Baby,'' *GBA* 33
(1948) 196 and 195, figs. 3, 4; Hill, *Bronzes,* 74, no.
157, pl. 34.

The statuette can be dated through the
Hellenistic style of the boxing gloves,
which are recognized by the wad of hard
leather that protects the knuckles and is
secured by thongs to a padding of wool
over the back of the hand and a reinforce-
ment around the wrist.[1] The muscular
handling of the child's body, as well as
the contrapposto more usually associated
with an adult, suggests that the figure is
Herakles, who, Theokritos tells us,
learned boxing skills from the son of Hermes, Harpalykos of Phanote.[2] Both Theokritos's poem to the young hero and the
Walters statuette may be veiled allusions
to the Ptolemaic royal family, which, in
the tradition of Alexander the Great,
traced its descent from this hero.[3]

1. Hill, *GBA* 33 (1948) 197.
2. Theokritos, *Idyll* 24.
3. F. W. Walbank and A. E. Astin, eds., *The Cambridge
   Ancient History VII, pt. 1, The Hellenistic World,* 2nd ed.
   (Cambridge, 1984), 86; Theokritos, 17.26–27; R. M.
   Errington, ''Alexander in the Hellenistic World,'' *Alexandre le Grand,* 155–157; Tarn 51. For Alexander, see Arrian, 3.3–4.

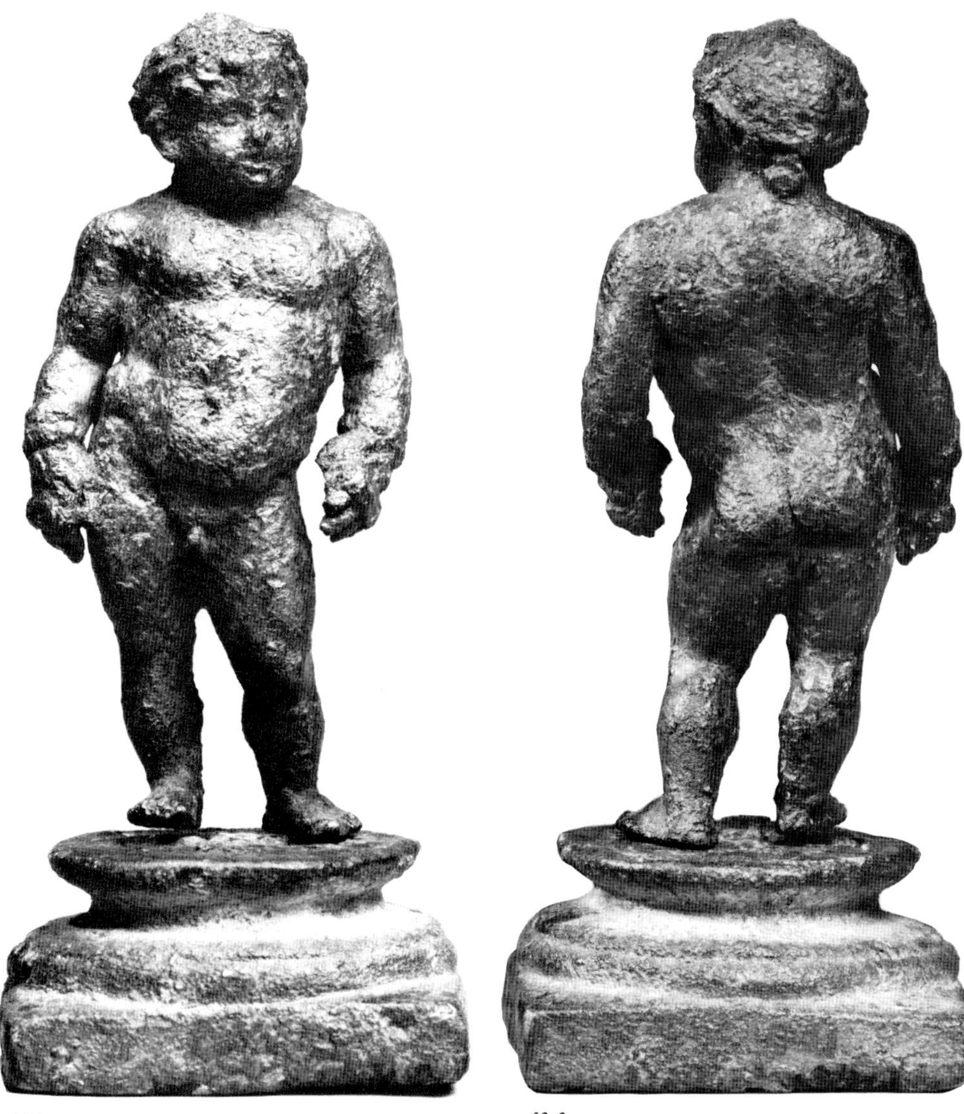

52.1 52.2

STATUETTE OF CROUCHING PAN
Third to second century

54.2380. Bronze. Purchased in 1953. Ht, 7.4 cm; W, 5.3 cm; Th, 3.5 cm. Underside has V-shaped notch for attachment. Missing right arm beneath elbow, attribute in left hand, both feet, tip of right horn.

A bearded figure sits on his buttocks with his knees bent and his lower legs drawn up. Both arms are bent at the elbow with the forearm extended, the fingers of his left hand closed. He wears an animal skin, which is draped behind his back with the paws knotted at his throat. His head is turned slightly to his right and is inclined; his pupils are indented. He has long pointed ears, a mustache, a long beard, and two pointed horns rising above the brow. His wavy hair lies closely upon the back of his head; across the forehead and nape the hair is wrapped in loose curls around a band. The hair on his legs is rendered by incisions.

Publications: D. K. Hill, ''Some Representations of the Greek Pan,'' *JWalt* 17 (1954) 61–69, figs. 3–5.

The coiled energy in Pan's twisting torso and the poised readiness of the crouching goat-legs and tensed arms anticipate a moment of action, possibly a dance inspired by music from the syrinx, which he may have grasped. His long face with its large nose, flaring nostrils, and pro-truding brow finds parallels in late Hellenistic metalwork, but antecedents for the image probably lie in later fifth and fourth century portrayals of barbarians.[1]

Pan was, however, no barbarian, but increasingly in the Hellenistic period the embodiment of the pleasures of rural life.[2]

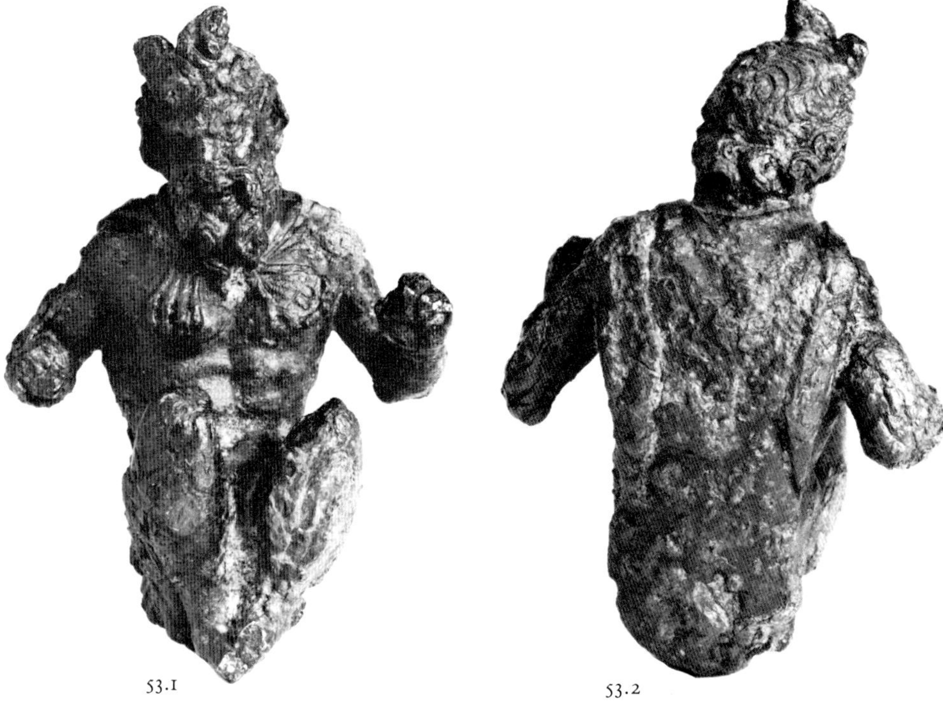

53.1 53.2

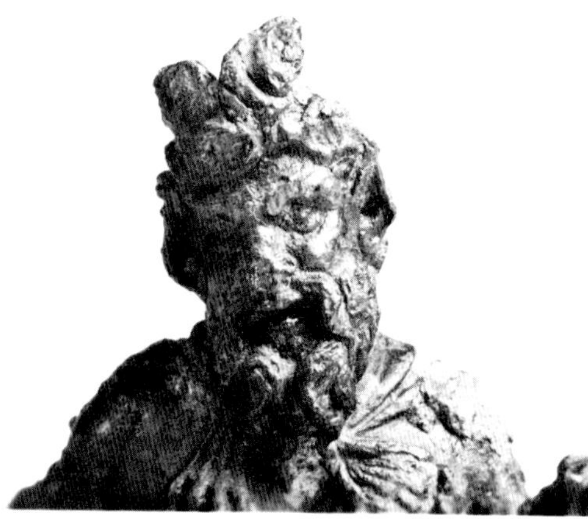

53.3

A nostalgic yearning for rustic haunts, particularly in Arkadia, was expressed as early as the late fourth century by the poetess Anyte: ''Why, rural Pan, thus seated in the dark and lonely wood do you sound the sweet-voiced reed pipe? So that the heifers may graze over these dewy mountains, cropping the luxuriant blades of grass.''[3] This ennobling assessment of the herdsman's existence probably explains in part the emphasis upon Pan in Macedonia during the Hellenistic period. Already by the early fourth century Zeuxis had dedicated an image of Pan to Archelaos, and recently recovered from Pella was a statuette of Alexander in the guise of Pan.[4] Coins issued by Antigonos Gonatas following the defeat of the Gauls in 277 bore the device of a Macedonian shield surmounted by a head of this god, who was said to have secured victory by spreading terror among the barbarians; on several of these coins, Pan is accorded the features and royal diadem of Antigonos.[5] Surely in keeping with these traditions was the helmet surmounted by goat horns that Pyrrhos wore into battle a century later.[6]

1. Compare the Stevensweert kantharos of the second century in A. Roes and W. Vollgraff, ''Le canthare de Stevensweert,'' *MonPiot* 46 (1952) pl. 8. For an image of a Scythian, see E. Reeder Williams, ''Ancient Clay Impressions from Greek Metal Reliefs,'' *Hesperia* 45 (1975) 53, no. 6, pl. 7.

2. J. Onians, *Art and Thought in the Hellenistic Age* (London, 1979), 66.

3. *Pal. Anthology* 16.231.

4. For Zeuxis, see Pliny, *NH* 35.62; for the statuette from Pella, see *Search for Alexander*, 179, no. 153. See also H. P. Laubscher, ''Hellenistische Herrscher und Pan,'' *AM* 100 (1985) 338–345.

5. C. Seltman, *Greek Coins,* 2nd ed. (London, 1955), 223; F. W. Walbank and A. E. Astin, eds., *The Cambridge Ancient History, VII, pt. 1, The Hellenistic World,* 2nd ed. (Cambridge, 1984), 85 and 86, n. 82.

6. Plutarch, *Pyrrhos* 11, 389.

STATUETTE OF A HUNCHBACK
Second century

54.744. Bronze. "From Cairo." Dattari Collection (sale catalogue, *Collections Jean P. Lambros d'Athènes et de M. Giovanni Dattari du Caire,* Paris, Hôtel Drouot, June 17–19, 1912, 51, no. 441). Purchased before 1931. Ht, 8.9 cm; W, 5.8 cm; Depth, 3 cm. Broken off across right wrist and above knees. Hole in center top of left thigh.

A standing male with a humped back wears a belted tunic and raises his right arm above his head; his left arm is bent at the elbow with the forearm upraised, the fingers closed over an indeterminate object. His head is inclined to his right; the pupils are indented. Above the ears are wavy locks rendered by incisions.

Publications: Hill, *Bronzes,* 72, no. 151, pl. 32, reviewed by F. Eichler in *Gnomon* 23 (1951) 61.

Although terracotta representations of grotesques and disfigured individuals are attested from Smyrna, the subject is particularly associated with Alexandria, as is the animation of this figure, whose momentary action has been captured as by a camera lens.[1] The tunic belongs to a slave or laborer who lifts his arms in what is probably a dancing gesture.[2]

1. For grotesques from Smyrna, see Leyenaar-Plaisier 235–249, nos. 605–655, pls. 86–91; V. Poulsen, *Catalogue des terres cuites grecques et romaines* (Copenhagen, 1949), 31, no. 55, pls. 36–37; Higgins, *Terracottas,* 112, pl. 52d.
2. Compare an example from Egypt in H. Philipp, *Terrakotten aus Ägypten im Ägyptischen Museum, Berlin* (Berlin, 1972), 20–21, no. 9, fig. 6, dated second century.

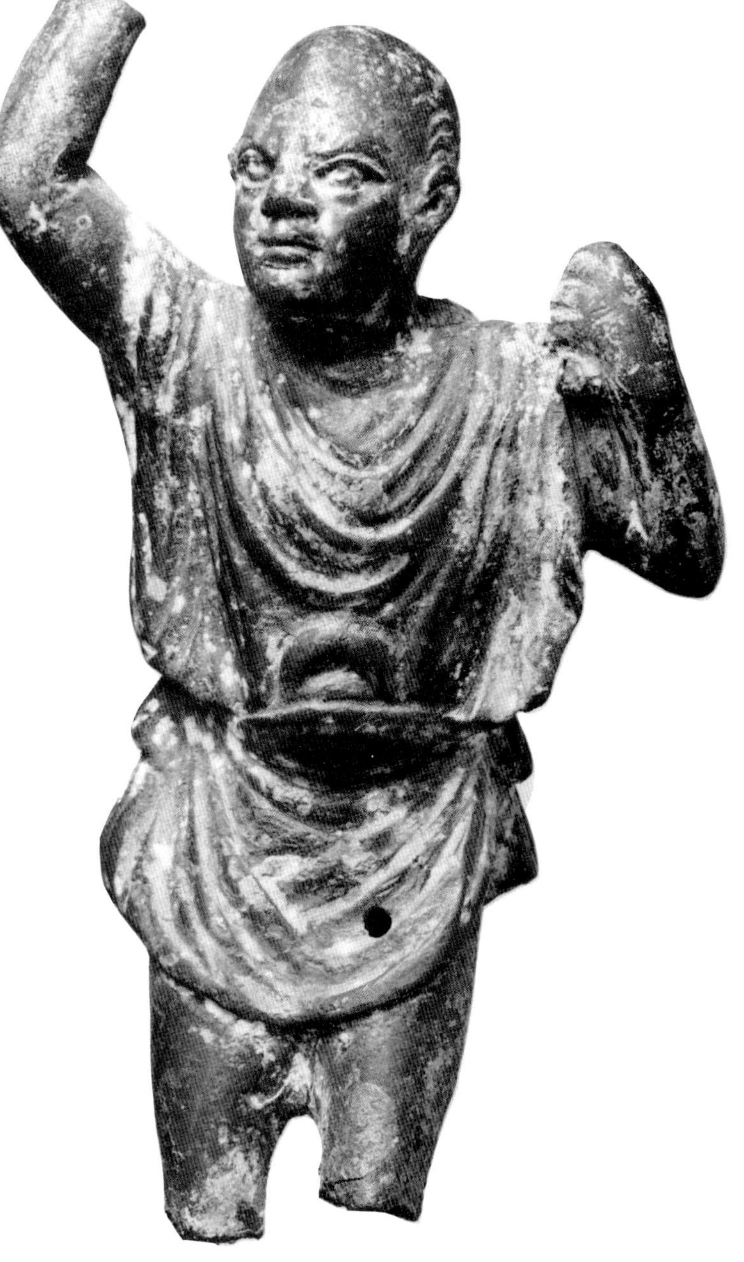

54.1

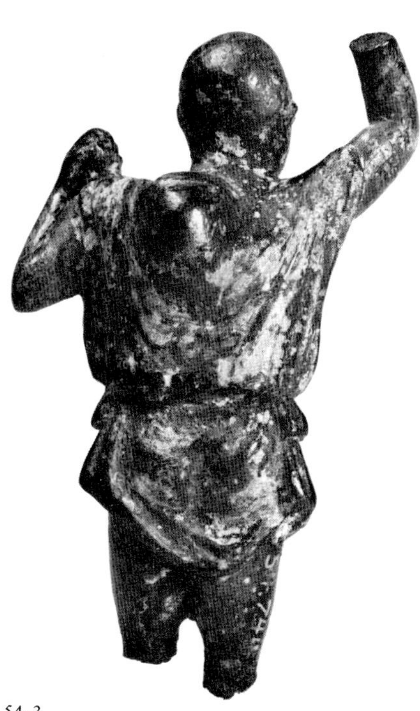

54.2

STATUETTE OF A DANCING DWARF
Ca. third century

54.1107. Bronze. Pozzi Collection (sale catalogue, *Catalogue des objets d'art antique. Collection de feu le Dr. Prof. S. Pozzi*, Paris, Galerie Georges Petit, June 25–27, 1919, 30, no. 420). Purchased before 1931. Ht, 10.2 cm; W, 4.4 cm. Right arm reattached above elbow.

A male dwarf in a loin cloth prances with his weight on his left leg, his right leg advanced, the foot resting only on the toes. The back of his left hand rests on his left hip; his right arm is raised above his head, the elbow bent, and the wrist cocked. His head is inclined and turned to his left. He has a short beard, indented pupils, a furrowed brow, and short curly hair beneath a peaked cap.

Publications: S. Reinach, ''Nouvelles archéologiques et correspondance,'' *RA* 10 (1919) 230–34, and 232, fig. 10; Reinach, *Statuaire* 5 (1924) 308, no. 6; D. K. Hill, *The Dance in Classical Times* (Baltimore, 1945), 14; Hill, *Bronzes*, 73, no. 154, pl. 33; A. Adriani, ''Microasiatici o alessandrini i grotteschi di Mahdia?'' *RM* 70 (1963) 85, pl. 36.4; L. Lawler, *The Dance in Ancient Greece* (London, 1964), 136, fig. 59.

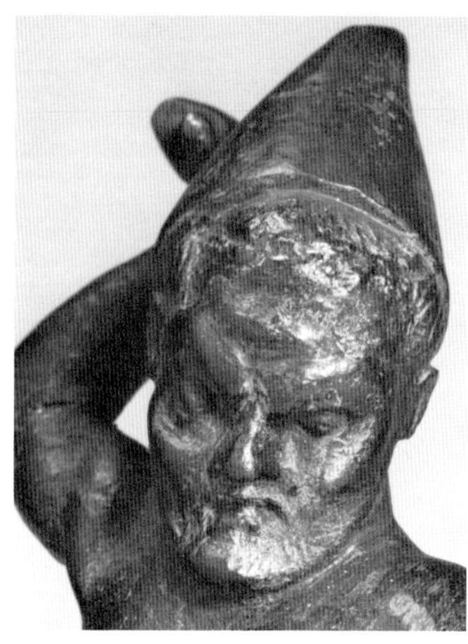

55.2

This figurine belongs to a group of bronze dancing dwarfs, most of whom are nude or wear only a loin cloth. The best-known examples were found in the Mahdia shipwreck and are dated to the second century, but the Walters example compares most closely with counterparts in Rome and Paris, each of which exhibits the identical garment, inclination of the head, and gesture, probably to be completed by restoring clappers in each hand.[1] The handling of the torso of the Walters dwarf compares well with those of a figurine in London and a second example in Paris.[2] The peaked cap, which appears on still another figurine in Paris, suggests that the dancers are mimes who wear the traditional headdress identified with the clown or buffoon.[3]

The reputed findspot of the Walters example and the Alexandrian provenance of a close parallel support an Egyptian origin for the dancing dwarfs, all of whom exhibit the achondroplasia that can be documented in Egypt from Predynastic times.[4] Despite or because of the deformity, dwarfs always enjoyed a respected position in Egyptian society. Not only were they entrusted with the care of jewelry, possibly because their physical activity could be easily curtailed, but they were also credited with magical powers and were often invoked in spells. Several inscriptions, one of which is Ptolemaic, refer to a dance performed by dwarfs, and the dancing dwarfs of the Walters type may in some way reflect this tradition.[5]

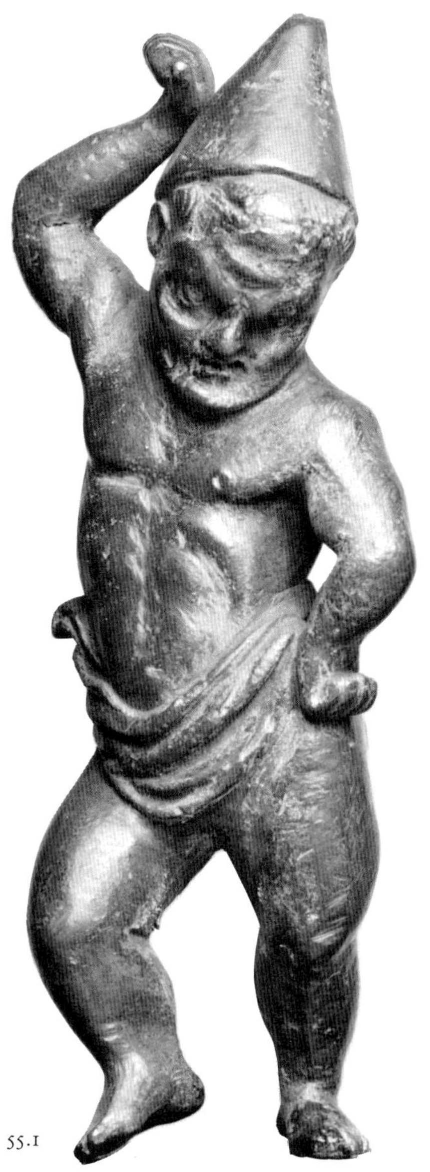

55.1

1. For the Mahdia examples, see A. Adriani, *RM* 70 (1963) 92. For the statuette in Rome see 85, pl. 37.4. For the statuette in Paris, see pl. 34.4. The same gesture is seen on a nude figurine in Hildesheim; see I. Noshy, *The Arts in Ptolemaic Egypt* (Oxford, 1937), 101, pl. 11.2.
2. For the example in London, see Adriani (note 1) pl. 36.1. For the example in Paris, see pl. 36.2.
3. J. Petit, *Bronzes antiques de la collection Dutuit, Paris. Palais des Beaux-Arts* (Paris, 1980), 105, no. 40. See also H. Goldman, ''Two Terracotta Figurines from Tarsus,'' *AJA* 47 (1943) 24.
4. W. R. Dawson, ''Pygmies and Dwarfs in Ancient Egypt,'' *JEA* 24 (1938) 186.
5. Ibid., 188–189.

STATUETTE OF A MALE DANCER
Third century

54.1053. Bronze. Purchased in 1929. Ht, 11.4 cm;
W, 4.9 cm; Depth, 2.5 cm. Missing left foot, left
arm above the elbow, and tip of phallus.

A nude male steps forward on his left leg, his right
knee bent with the lower leg lifted behind him. His
upper torso is turned to his left; his arms are raised
above his head, which is tilted to rest against his left
upper arm. His hair is stippled over the surface and
gathered into a knot at the crown of his head. He
has elongated proportions and large genitals.

Publications: Hill, *Bronzes,* 70, no. 148, pl. 32; L. B.
Lawler, *Terpsichore,* Dance Perspectives 13 (Brooklyn, 1962), 46.

Typically Alexandrian are the skill and
charm with which the moment's exuberance and energy have been captured, primarily through a closed silhouette that is
eloquent from every viewpoint. The
dancer is oblivious to the viewer and completely unself-conscious of his misshapen
body, which is even further distorted by
the intensity of the dance. Accentuating
his self-absorption are his downcast head
and the self-contained spin of his body. It
is this scrutiny of, and affection for, the
mundane that characterizes Alexandrian
art and enabled the Alexandrian artist to
evoke so successfully the spirit and cultural diversity of Ptolemaic Egypt.

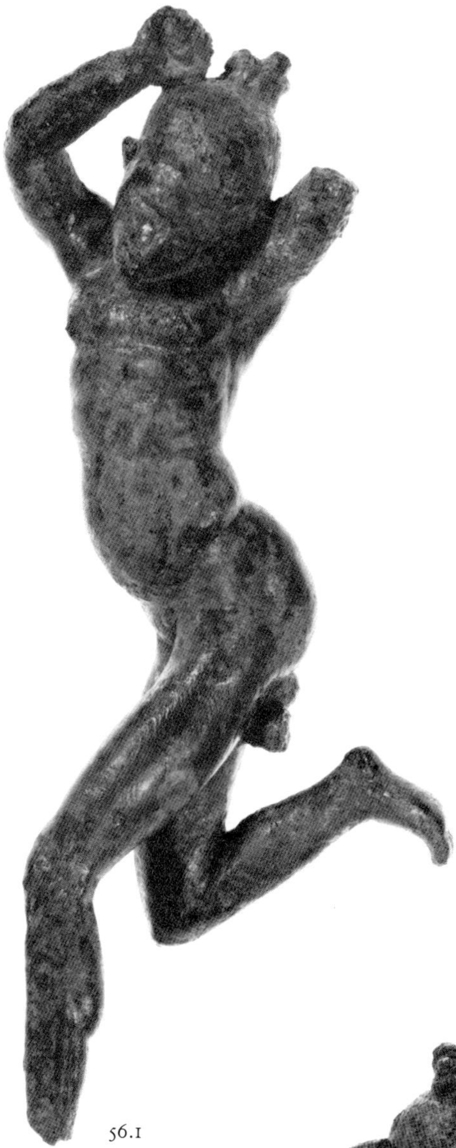

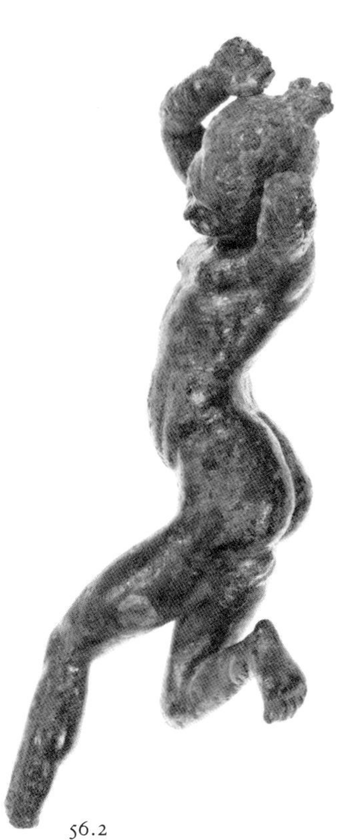

56.1

56.2

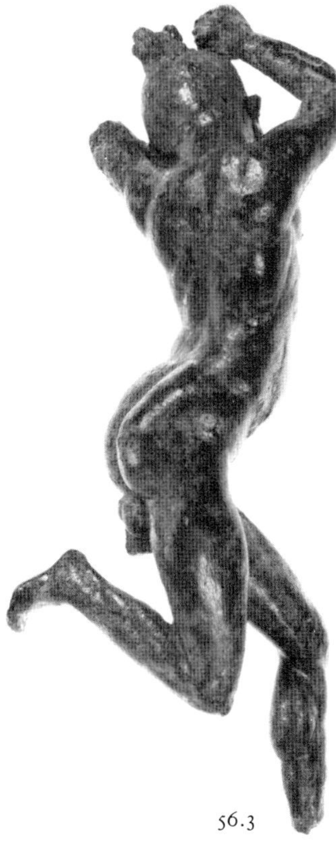

56.3

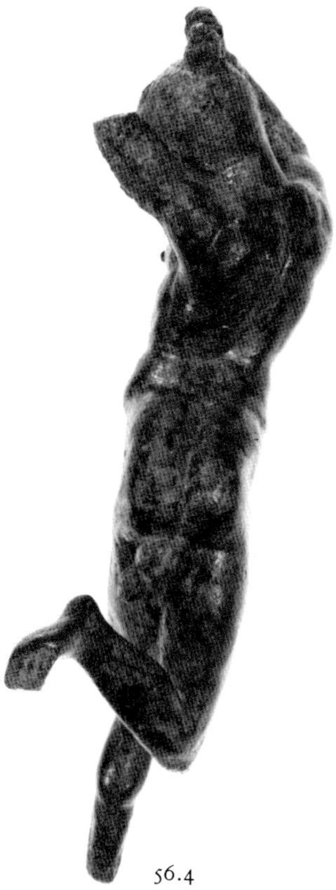

56.4

Statuette of a Dancing Black
Third to second century

54.702. Bronze. From Erment, Egypt. Possibly William A. Laffan Collection. Purchased before 1931. Ht, 9.2 cm; W, at elbow 3.2 cm; Depth, hand to buttocks 3.5 cm. Missing left foot.

A nude youth with a protruding belly steps forward on his left leg with the knee bent. His right leg, also with the knee bent, is behind him with the foot resting on its toes. His left arm is bent at the elbow with the forearm brought across to his right shoulder, the hand lifted and the fingers extended. The left arm, with elbow bent, is outstretched before him, the thumb extended, and the fingers lightly bent. He gazes upward and to his left and has thickened lips, a snub nose, and short hair arranged in thick clumps radiating outward from behind the crown.

Publications: O. Rubensohn, "Archäologische Funde im Jahre 1905," *AA* (1906) col. 139 and col. 141, fig. 9; Reinach, *Statuaire* 4 (1910) 354, no. 6; D. K. Hill, *The Dance in Classical Times* (Baltimore, 1945), 14; Hill, *Bronzes,* 71, no. 149, pl. 5; K. A. Neugebauer, *Katalog der statuarischen Bronzen im Antiquarium, II, Die griechische Bronzen der klassischen Zeit und des Hellenismus* (Berlin, 1951), 92. Review by D. K. Hill in *CP* 49 (1954) 125; D. K. Hill, "A Bronze Statuette of a Negro," *AJA* 57 (1953) 266 and n. 7; D. K. Hill, "From Alexander to Augustus," *BWalt* 7 (1955) no. 5; L. Lawler, *The Dance in Ancient Greece* (London, 1964), 137, fig. 60; F. M. Snowden, *Blacks in Antiquity* (Cambridge, 1970), 241, fig. 103; A. Adriani, "Lezioni 2 sull'arte Alessandrina," *Librarea scientifica* (1972) 67, 162, pl. 38.3 and 4; H. Kyrieleis, "ΚΑΘΑΠΕΡ ΕΡΜΗΣ ΚΑΙ ΩΡΟΣ," *AntP* 12 (1973) 138, note 29; D. K. Hill, "The Classical Collection and its Growth," *Apollo* 100 (1974) 357, pl. 8; F. M. Snowden, "Iconographical Evidence on the Black Populations in Greco-Roman Antiquity," *The Image of the Black in Western Art* (New York, 1976), I, 210, n. 207; A. Adriani, "Il negretto di Chalon-sur-Saône e la statuina Dimitrio," *AM* 93 (1978) 126, note 13, pl. 42; D. K. Hill, "The Bronze Negro from Erment," *Alessandria,* 182–184, pl. 34; N. Himmelmann-Wildschütz, *Alexandria und der Realismus in der griechischen Kunst* (Tübingen, 1983), 69.

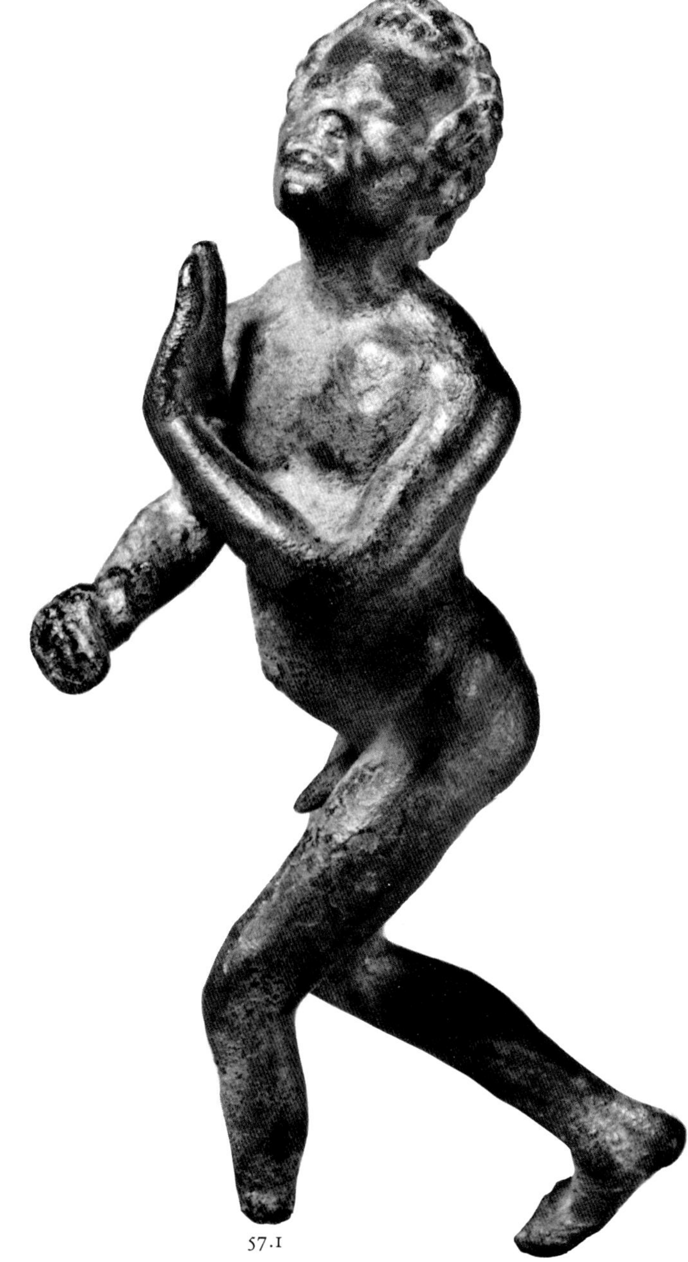

57.1

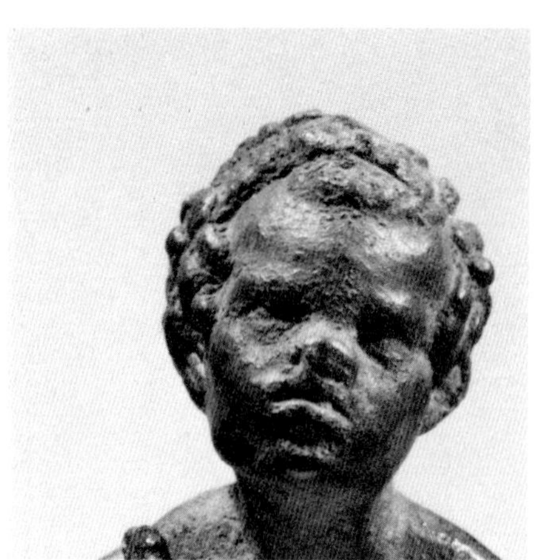

57.2

This figure was found in Erment, near Luxor, together with bronze figurines of a priest and an acrobat which are also in the Walters collection and were probably made in early Imperial times.[1] Also said to have been found with the objects were three small statuettes of Horos and a small nude Aphrodite, an assemblage that typifies the cultural diversity of Ptolemaic and Roman Egypt.[2] Characteristically Egyptian are the subject matter of a dancing black and the roughened, almost unfinished surface. Less easily paralleled are the pose and gesture. A notable contrast is offered by the well-known dancing black discovered near Chalon-sur-Saône and now in the Bibliothèque Nationale, dated to 200–180; this figure exhibits a hipshot stationary stance with the frontal upper torso twisted and the head tilted in the direction of the supporting leg.[3] Closely comparable to the Chalon youth are two statuettes from Egypt: a basalt example in Athens and a bronze figurine from Memphis, which is now in the Louvre.[4] In contrast to these three works, the Walters figurine displays both animation and torsion and is rendered with such three-dimensionality that a spirited and convincing image is achieved from every viewpoint. The conception compares closely with the Baker Dancer, which was probably made at the end of the third century, and a similar date for the Walters youth is supported by the figure's spontaneity and freshness, which argue for its origin still well within the Hellenistic period.[5]

1. For the acrobat, see Hill, *Bronzes*, 69, no. 144, pl. 5; D. K. Hill, ''Seventeen Little Acrobats,'' *Actes du IVe colloque international sur les bronzes antiques, 17–21 mai 1976*, Annales de l'université Jean Moulin (Lyon, 1977), 75–81, fig. 1. For the priest, see Hill, *Bronzes*, 64–65, no. 137, pl. 5. This piece is dated second to first century in C. Rolley, *Les bronzes grecs* (Fribourg, 1983), 209, fig. 189, but is considered Roman by D. K. Hill, *Alessandria*, 183.
2. See O. Rubensohn, ''Archäologische Funde im Jahre 1905,'' *AA* (1906) col. 141 and col. 139, fig. 9.
3. A. Adriani, *AM* 93 (1978) 119, 129.
4. For the example in Athens, see ibid., 129, pl. 37, dated ca. 190; for the statuette in the Louvre, see K. A. Neugebauer, ''Aus der Werkstatt eines griechischen Toreuten in Ägypten,'' *Schumacher-Festschrift* (Mainz, 1930), 235, fig. 2.
5. See Pollitt 270, fig. 290 and D. B. Thompson, ''A Bronze Dancer from Alexandria,'' *AJA* 54 (1950) 371–385.

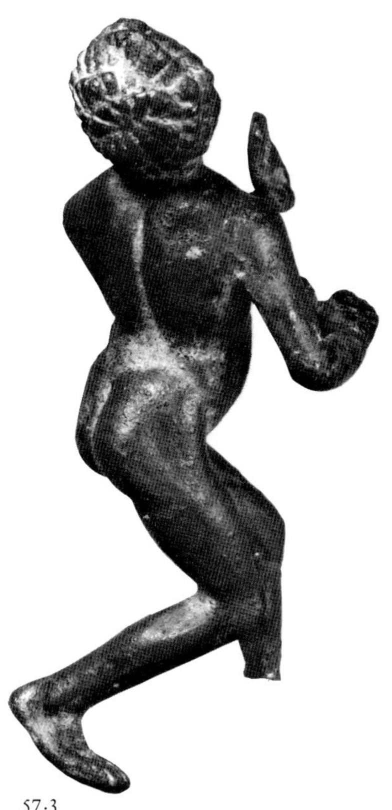

57·3

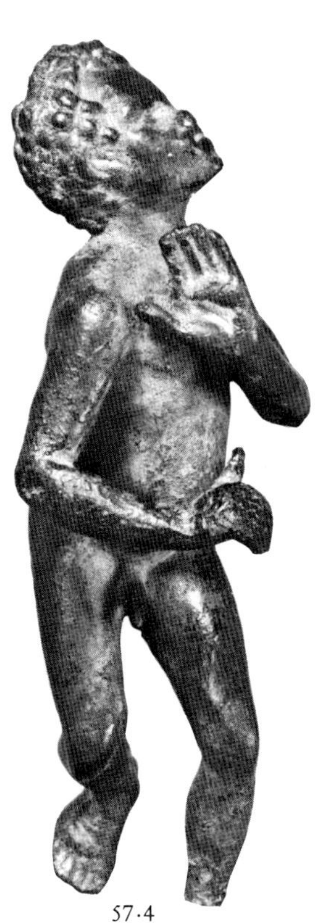

57·4

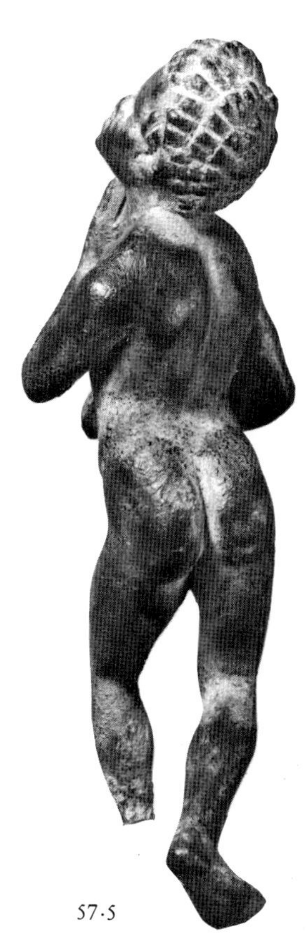

57·5

STATUETTE OF A BLACK SLAVE
Second to first century

54.2372. Bronze. Purchased in 1951. Ht, 10.1 cm; W, 8 cm; Depth, 3.8 cm. Both arms broken off. Repaired above right ankle.

A youth strides forward with his left leg advanced and both knees bent. He turns to his right, his head gazing back behind and above him. He wears a sleeved belted knee-length tunic and has short, woolly hair and a flat nose; the pupils of his large eyes are indented.

Publications: D. K. Hill, "A Bronze Statuette of a Negro," *AJA* 57 (1953) 265–267, pl. 75; Segall, "Tradition," 45–46, no. 173.

Struggling under the strain of the burden he pulls, this figure leans forward, his posture and the turn of his head masterfully calculated to create an elegant silhouette, while successfully avoiding a contrived effect. One might easily envision behind the figure a heavily laden cart or horse, certainly a substantial enough element that we can speak of the piece as belonging to a sculptural group. Perhaps it was the complexity of this entity in terms of balance or weight that motivated the solid casting of the figure. The work was certainly made in Egypt, an attribution indicated by the subject, the roughly finished surface, and the momentary action.[1]

Slavery was a long-established institution in Greek culture, with state-owned slaves used in industry and mining, and privately owned slaves employed in shops and as household servants.[2] Precise figures

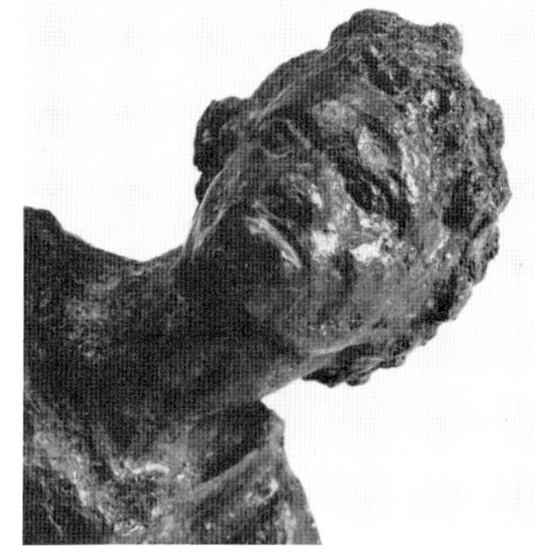

58.3

are difficult to calculate, but the number of slaves was substantial in Classical times and mushroomed during the Hellenistic period as trade and military triumphs increased the availability of African, Anatolian, Asian, and especially the coveted Syrian slaves.[3] By late Hellenistic times the Roman market had so elevated demand that ten thousand slaves could pass through the slave market at Delos daily.[4]

Enslavement was not restricted to non-Greek peoples; after the battle of Pydna (168) one hundred fifty thousand prisoners from Epirus were sold into slavery, and following the Roman general Mummius's destruction of Carthage, all of the women and children were sold as slaves.[5]

Although some slaves were undoubtedly poorly treated, there exists in Menander's works and elsewhere in Hellenistic literature a widespread sentiment that the mistreatment of slaves was morally reprehensible and pragmatically ill-advised.[6] In the *Oeconomica* of Aristotle, owners are urged to offer their slaves the opportunity to purchase their own freedom.[7]

1. Compare the similar dress of a terracotta figurine from Smyrna, dated first century, in D. Burr, *Terracottas from Myrina in the Museum of Fine Arts, Boston* (Vienna, 1934), 75–76, no. III, pl. 41. An image of a similar figure restraining a horse appears on a large relief in Athens, NM 4464, dated perhaps early 3rd century; see Pollitt 112 and fig. 116.
2. W. Westerman, *The Slave Systems of Greek and Roman Antiquity,* Memoirs of the American Philosophical Society 40 (Philadelphia, 1955), 10–13. For slavery in Egypt, see R. S. Bagnall and P. Derow, *Greek Historical Documents: The Hellenistic Period* (Ann Arbor, 1981), 196–198, nos. 118–121.
3. Westerman (note 2) 14. Athenaeus, *Deipnosophistae* 6.272.
4. Tarn 265; Austin, *Hellenistic World,* 282–283, no. 171; E. S. Gruen, *The Hellenistic World and the Coming of Rome* (Berkeley, 1984), 299.
5. See Austin (note 4) 147, n. 6 and 149, no. 82; Pausanias, 7.16.7–17.1.
6. Menander, fr. 370k from *The Slave* and fr. 110k from *The Superstitious Man.*
7. Aristotle, *Oeconomica* 1.5.6.

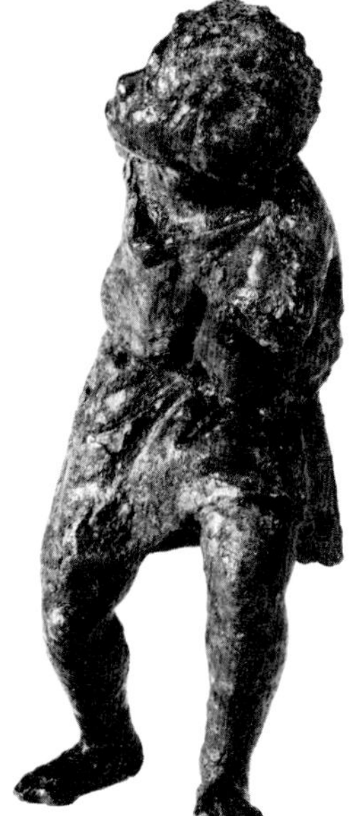

58.2

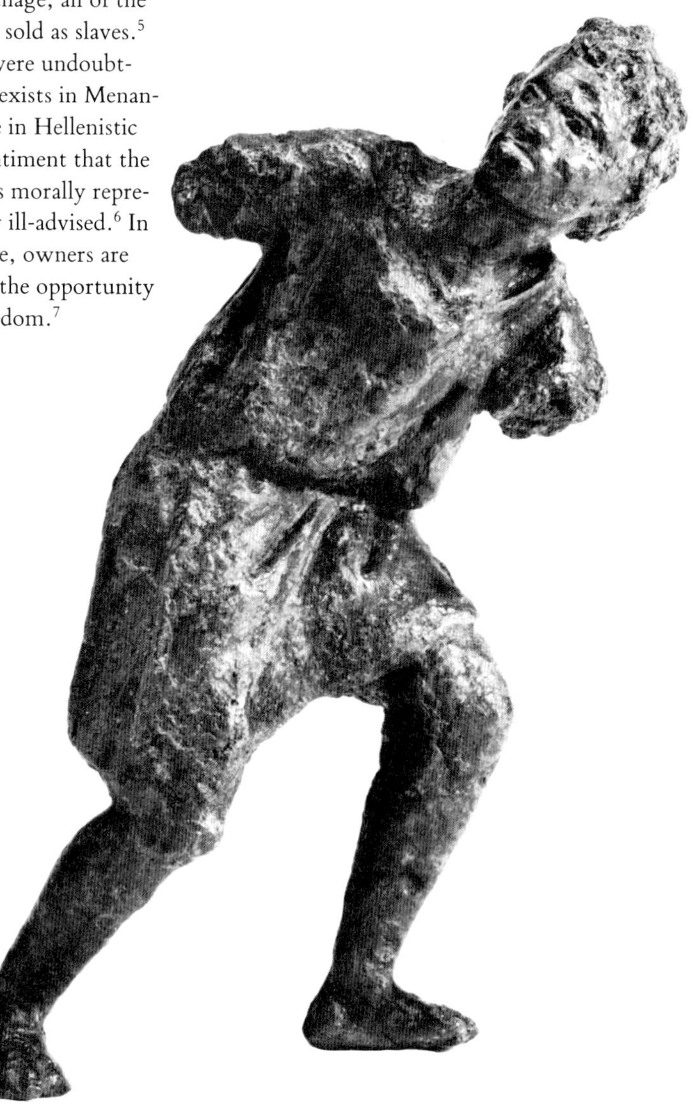

58.1

Grotesque
Third to second century

54.1103. Bronze. ''From Alexandria.'' Purchased
before 1931. Ht, 6.5 cm; W, 3.1 cm; Depth, 3.9 cm.
Cast in one piece with its base, which has a modern
(?) nail hole behind left foot.

A male figure with a large head kneels with his left
knee on a rock, the right knee bent with the lower
leg drawn back, a flat oval base beneath. Resting
upon his right thigh and supported by both hands is
his phallus toward which his large head is inclined.
He has short wavy hair, and a bunch of curls above
the center of his forehead. Falling down his back are
the ends of a ribbon, the rest of which is not indicated.

Publications: Hill, *Bronzes,* 72, no. 152, pl. 33.

The figure is reputedly from Alexandria,
an attribution buttressed by both the subject matter and the satirical tone, with
pose and tilted head testifying to a concentration traditionally associated with
grander endeavors. Typical of Alexandrian work are the diminutive size, the
rough, almost unfinished surface, and the
zestful gaiety of the subject.[1]

1. Compare a bronze dwarf with a large phallus, carrying an
   Amazon shield and with his right arm upraised for com-
   bat, surely also from Alexandria: P. Holtermüller and S.
   Wischhusen, eds., *Antiken aus rheinischen Privatbesitz*
   (Cologne, 1973), 141, no. 215, pl. 104.

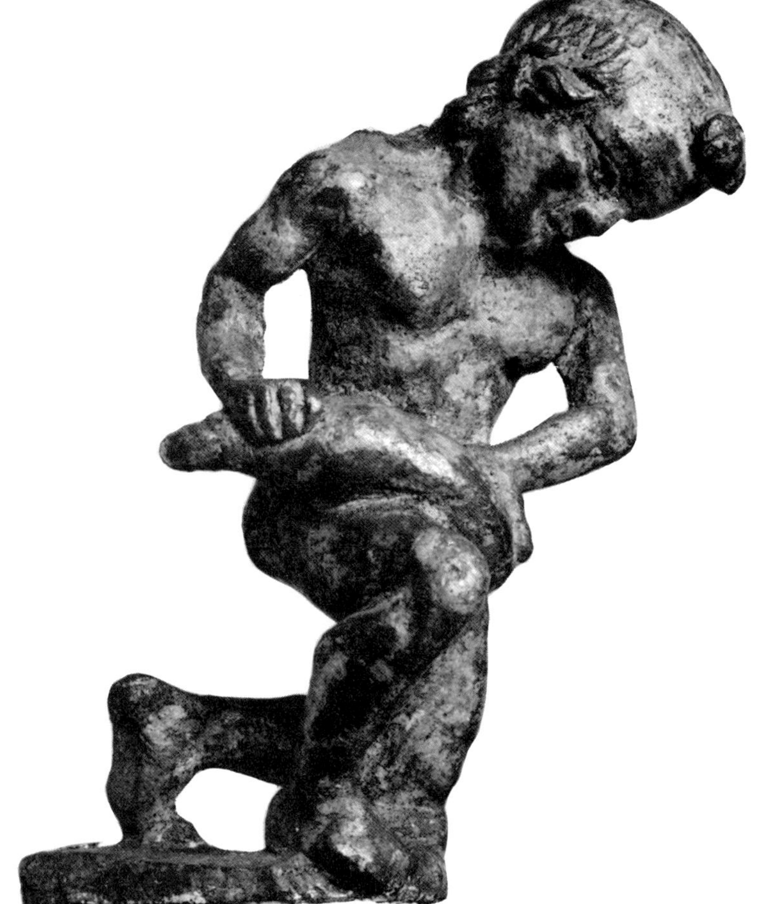

59.1

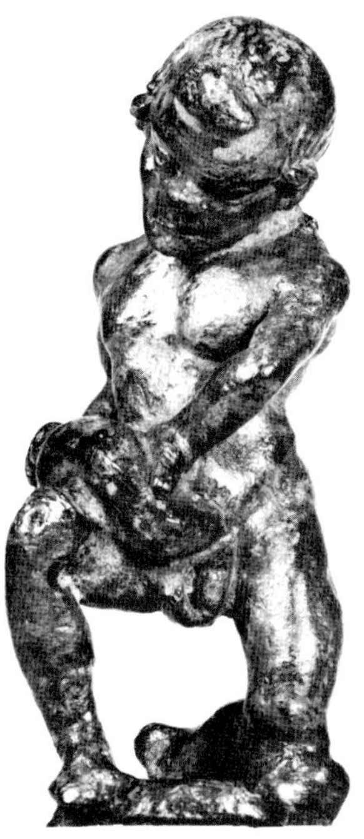

59.2

STATUETTE OF AN ACTOR
Ca. 150–100

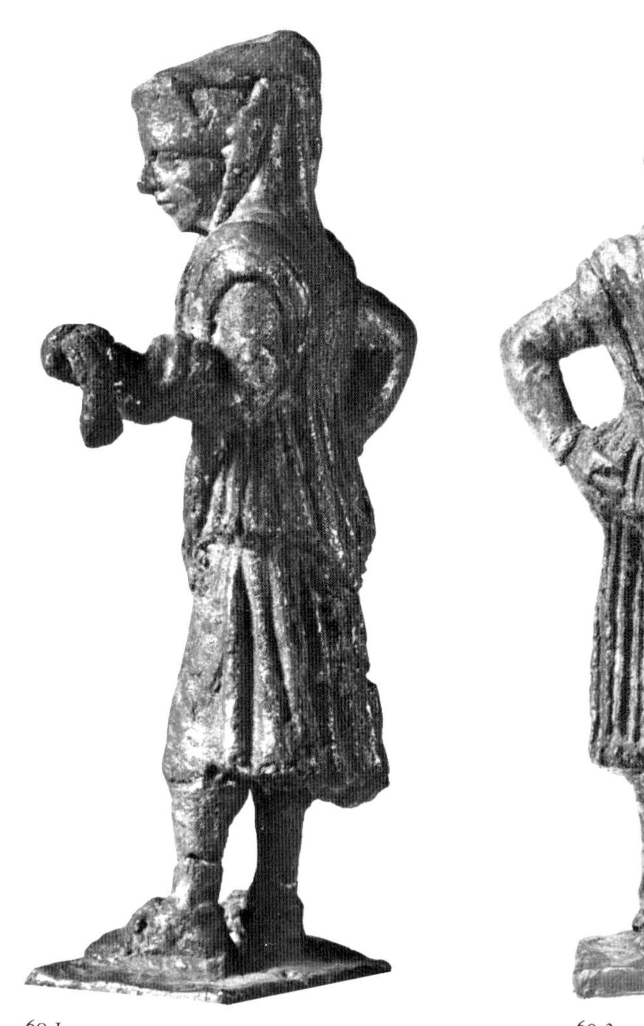

60.1

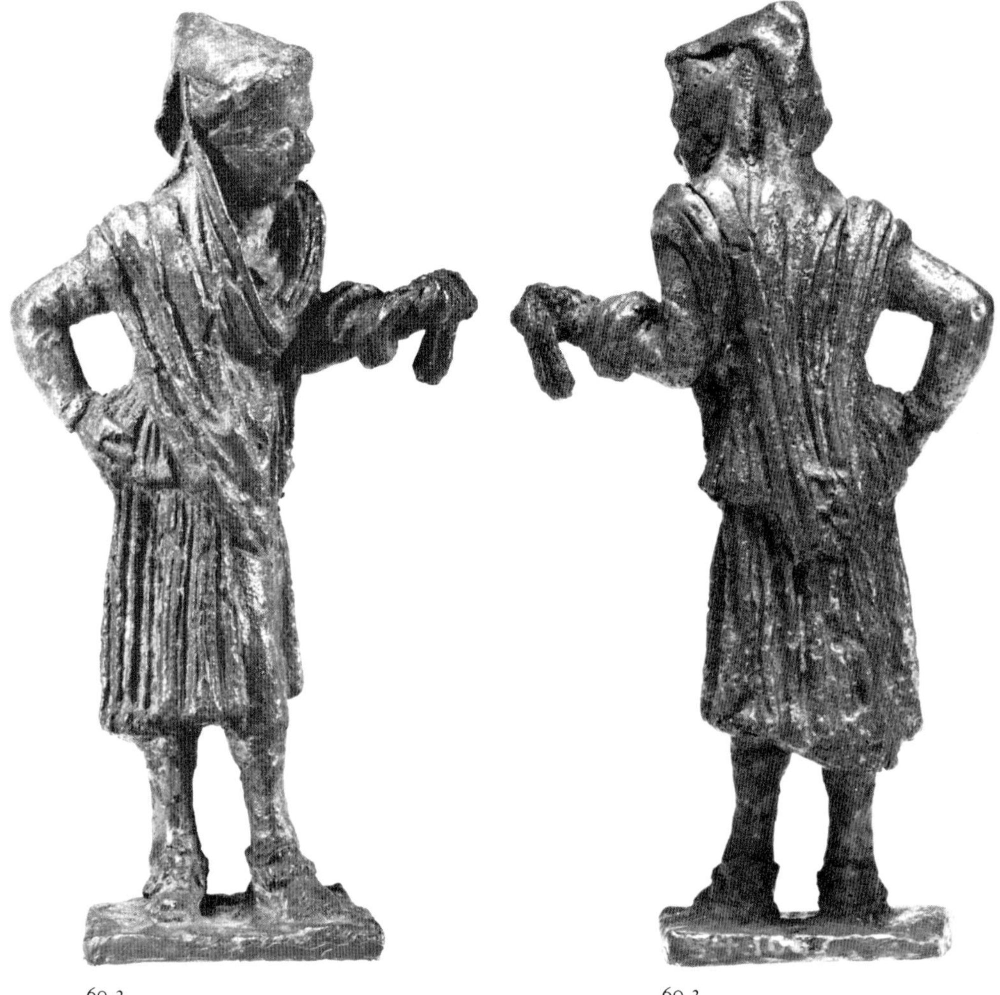

60.2

60.3

54.1067. Bronze. A. Kann Collection (sale catalogue, New York, American Art Galleries, January 6–8, 1927, no. 98). A. Sambon Collection (sale catalogue, Paris, Galerie Georges Petit, May 25–28, 1914, 20, no. 63, ill.). Purchased from Brummer in 1927. Ht, 9.8 cm; W, 5.1 cm; Depth, base 2.3 cm. Both legs reattached.

A male stands with his left leg advanced, his torso and head turned to his left, his right hand on his hip, his left elbow bent with the forearm extended. His long-sleeved garment, carefully rendered in closely set folds, is belted at the hips, with an overfold, and extends below his knees. His mantle is draped over a peaked hairstyle or cap, and a headband. The mantle then passes over both shoulders with one end wrapped around his left arm, another end hanging down the center of his back. A separate head-covering is brought from the nape over the crown of the head, covering the forehead and possibly the nose. He wears laced shoes that cover his ankles. The rectangular base was cast together with the statuette.

Publications: Reinach, *Statuaire* 5 (1924) 248, no. 6; Hill, *Bronzes*, 65, no. 139, pl. 33; N. Himmelmann-Wildschütz, *Alexandria und der Realismus in der griechischen Kunst* (Tübingen, 1983), 68–69, pl. 40.

The half-mask appears infrequently in Hellenistic art, in several instances on terracotta figurines with Dionysiac attributes that associate their wearers with the theatrical world.[1] A similarly masked terracotta head from Smyrna also carries a Dionysiac allusion in the satyr horns that underlie the head covering.[2]

Both the conical cap and the dress of the Walters figure find parallels on a bronze statuette in Cairo and a marble statue in Florence.[3] The latter work has the ringlets of the Isis hairstyle which, in combination with the conical cap usually worn by men, suggests that this figure is an actor; the Walters statuette must also surely be a theatrical performer.

1. P. Ghiron-Bistagne, "Les demi-masques," *RA* 2 (1970) 253–282.
2. Leyenaar-Plaisier, II, 340, no. 923; III, pl. 123; Ghiron-Bistagne (note 1) 269, figs. 21–24.
3. M. C. C. Edgar, *Greek Bronzes*, Catalogue général des antiquités égyptiennes du musée du Caire 19 (Cairo, 1904), 21, no. 27.710, pl. 5; Bieber, *Sculpture*, 90, fig. 333.

Statuette of
Alexander the Great
150–100

54.1045. Bronze. "From Egypt." Collections of Matossian, Lépine. Purchased from Maison Nadaud in 1930. Ht, 26.6 cm; W, 13.2 cm; Depth, 7.6 cm; Ht, to top of head 24.1 cm. Missing forefinger of right hand and object held in it; all except hilt of sword held in left hand; toes of right foot; left ankle and foot.

A nude male steps forward with his weight on his left leg, his right knee bent with the right foot behind him. His right lifted arm is bent at the elbow with the forearm upraised, thumb extended and fingers closed. His left arm is lowered with the forearm outstretched and the fingers closed over the hilt of a sword, the blade of which rests along the inside of his left forearm. Folds of his mantle rest on top of his left shoulder; the ends fall down behind his left arm and are brought under his left arm and over the forearm. His head is turned and lifted toward his right hand; his short curly hair is surmounted by a laurel wreath.

Exhibitions and Catalogues: Mitten, *Bronzes, 23,* 130, fig. 132; *Search for Alexander,* Boston supplement, 6, no. 8; San Francisco supplement, no. S–8; New Orleans supplement, no. S–5; Toronto supplement, 10–11, no. S–11.

Publications: Reinach, *Statuaire* 5 (1924) 311, nos. 5, 6; E. Langlotz, *Die Darstellung des Menschen in der griechischen Kunst* (Bonn, 1948), 24, fig. 16; Hill, *Bronzes,* 53, no. 110, pl. 27; E. Buschor, *Das hellenistische Bildnis* (Munich, 1949) 37, fig. 4, 2nd ed. (Munich, 1971), 38, 81, no. 149, fig. 2; J. Charbonneaux, "Un Poseidon hellénistique au musée du Louvre," *MonPiot* 46 (1952) 37; G. M. A. Hanfmann, "Acquisitions of the Fogg Art Museum: Sculpture and Figurines," *AJA* 58 (1954) 229, no. 39; M. Housen, "Master Bronzes from the Classical World," *Connoisseur* 167 (1968) 129, fig. 10; H.Oehler, *Untersuchungen zu den männlichen römischen Mantelstatuen* (Berlin, 1961), I, 34, no. 50; Reinsberg, *Toreutik,* 107, 108, 198 (no. 733), 199, 288.

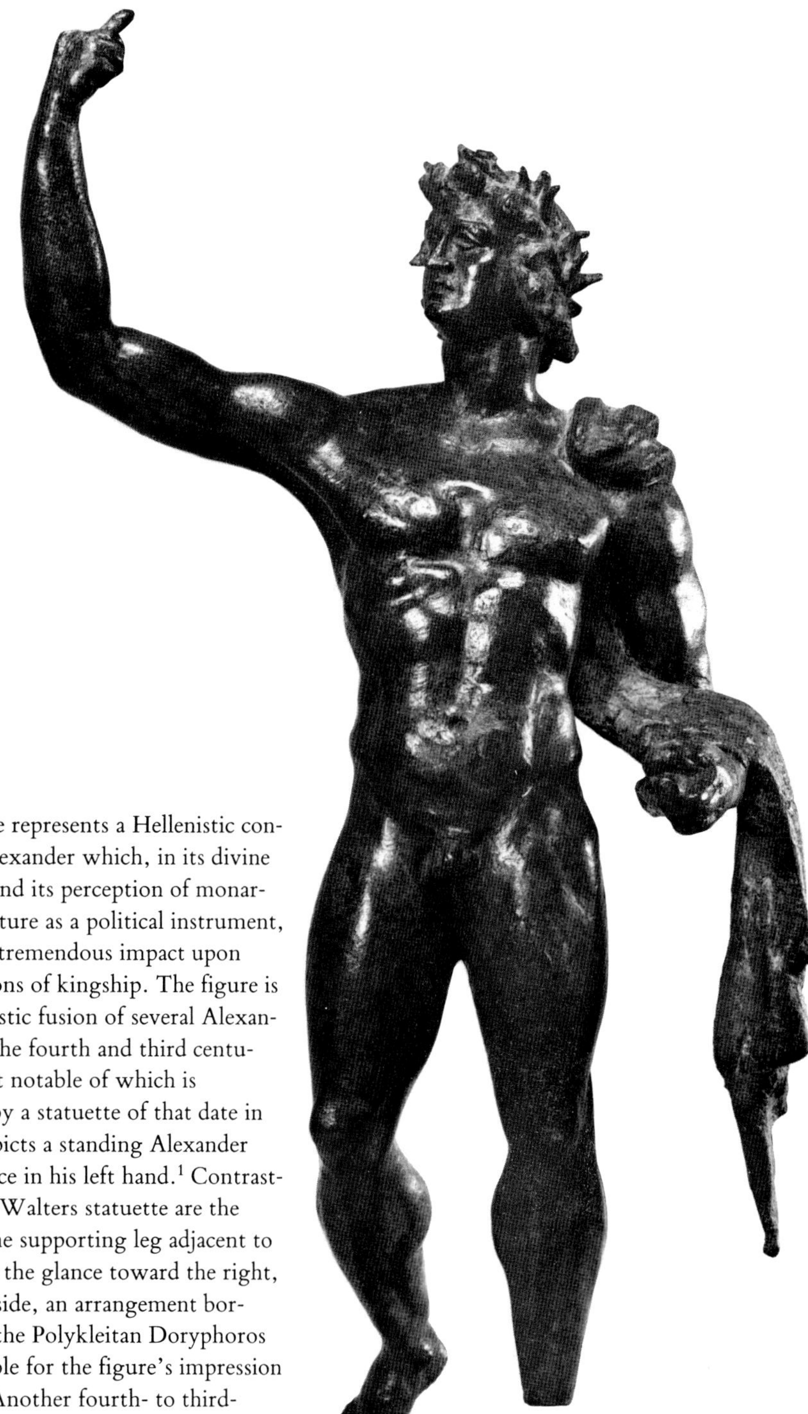

61.1

This statuette represents a Hellenistic conception of Alexander which, in its divine associations and its perception of monarchical portraiture as a political instrument, was to exert tremendous impact upon Roman notions of kingship. The figure is a late Hellenistic fusion of several Alexander types of the fourth and third centuries, the most notable of which is exemplified by a statuette of that date in Paris that depicts a standing Alexander holding a lance in his left hand.[1] Contrasting with the Walters statuette are the position of the supporting leg adjacent to the lance and the glance toward the right, or opposite, side, an arrangement borrowed from the Polykleitan Doryphoros and responsible for the figure's impression of stability. Another fourth- to third-century type of the standing Alexander survives on a gem in Leningrad; here Alexander's gaze is directed towards a thunderbolt in his extended right hand while in his lowered left hand he clasps the hilt of a sword, the blade of which is turned back over his arm and rests upon an aegis.[2] The eagle at his side reinforces the identification with Zeus to whom the wreath on the Walters statuette is also an allusion.

A later Hellenistic date for the Walters statuette is suggested by the instability of the pose, due to both the placement of the supporting leg opposite the lance in the manner of the Loeb Poseidon of ca. 150, and the widespread position of the legs,

which echoes the restlessness of the
Poseidon from Melos of the same date.[3]
Dissimilar is the upward turn of the head
of the Walters figurine, a feature borrowed from Lysippan portraits of Alexander.[4] In the Walters statuette, the
position of the head is motivated by the
focus of the gaze upon the lance tip, a
curious arrangement that has some of the
awkwardness seen in the mid or perhaps
late Hellenistic Pasquino group.[5] Certainly late Hellenistic is the rubbery and
inflated handling of the body.[6] Reinsberg
has noted that the muscularity of the
thighs and irregularity of the contours of
the Walters figurine so closely parallel the
handling of the Neoptolemos on a plaster
cast from Memphis that an Egyptian origin for the Walters Alexander is clearly
indicated.[7] Further support for this attribution lies in the irregular proportions,
particularly the long forearms, and the
awkward juncture of arms and shoulder,
evidence that the wax model from which
the statuette was cast had been assembled
from preexisting and incompatible piece-
molds, following a well-attested Egyptian
practice.[8]

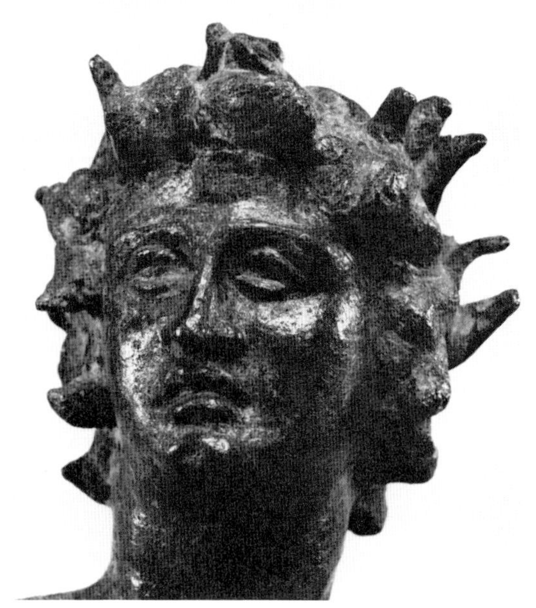

61.2

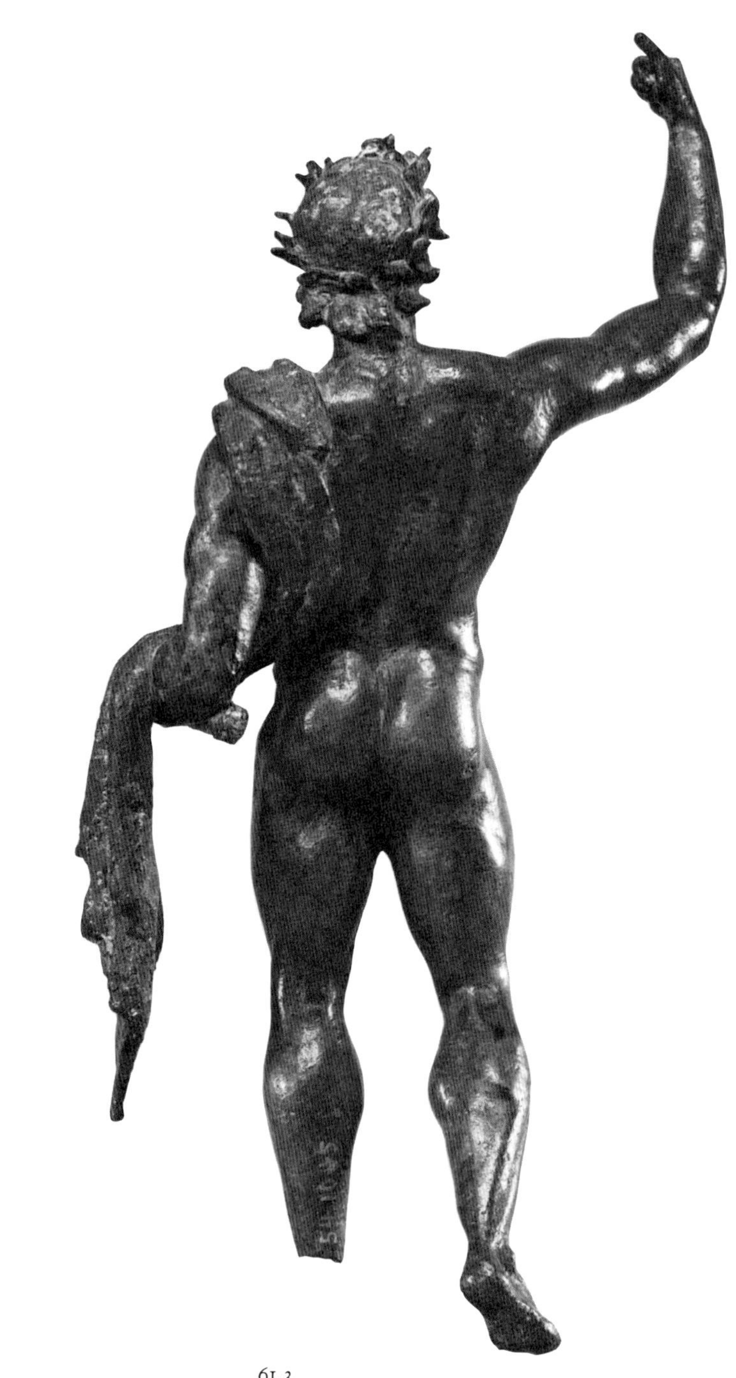

61.3

1. Pollitt 22, fig. 8, thought to be based on a statue of ca.
   330–25.
2. Ibid., 23, fig. 10.
3. For the Loeb Poseidon, see M. Maass, *Griechische und
   römische Bronzewerke der Antikensammlungen,* Bildhefte der
   Staatlichen Antikensammlungen und der Glyptothek
   München (Munich, 1979), 25, no. 9; Reinsberg, *Toreutik,*
   198–199; E. Buschor, *Bildnis,* 2nd ed., 39. For the
   Poseidon from Melos, see Pollitt 268, fig. 290; J. Schäfer,
   "Der Poseidon von Melos," *AntP* 8 (1968) 55–67.
4. For the Lysippan tradition of Alexandrian portraiture, see
   Pollitt 2–23, 29; Plutarch, *Alexander* 4.1; Plutarch, *De
   Alexandri Magni Fortuna aut Virtute* 2.2.3.
5. For the Pasquino group, also known as Menelaos and
   Patroklos, see Pollitt 118 and 117, fig. 119. For the dating,
   which ranges from the third to the first century, see 118
   and 310, note 8.
6. Reinsberg (note 3) 107.
7. Ibid., 195, 198, 288, no. 69, fig. 100.
8. E. Reeder Williams, *The Archaeological Collection of the
   Johns Hopkins University* (Baltimore, 1984), 95–96, no. 64.

Statuette of a Nude Warrior
Late third or second century

54.1046. Bronze. "From the Fayum." Purchased from Kelekian in 1913. Ht, 25.4 cm; W, 7.1 cm; Depth, toe to heel 9.8 cm. Core visible at right shoulder. Missing right arm from shoulder; most of right toes, left hand, front tip of crest.

A nude male strides forward on uneven ground, his left leg advanced with the knee slightly bent, his right foot and leg turned out to the side, the toes on lower terrain. His left arm is extended out to the side; his head is turned far to his right. He has short curly hair with wisps in front of each ear and wears a visored helmet with a crest. His irises are incised and his forehead grooved.

Publications: Reinach, *Statuaire* 4 (1910) 106, no. 2; O. Rubensohn, "Funde in Ägypten," *AA* (1907), cols. 357–360, figs. 1–2; Hill, *Bronzes,* 58, no. 118, pl. 27; G. M. A. Hanfmann, "Acquisitions of the Fogg Art Museum," *AJA* 58 (1954) 229, no. 39; H. Kyrieleis, "ΚΑΘΑΠΕΡ ΕΡΜΗΣ ΚΑΙ ΩΡΟΣ," *AntP* 12 (1973) 128, no. 28.

The dramatic posture and the exaggerated twist of the figure's neck are reminiscent of the figure of the Gaul in the group of the Gaul and his wife, whose prototype is placed by Pollitt in the later third century.[1] One can further compare the subject of a helmeted nude warrior with abruptly turned head and intense gaze with the Menelaos of the Pasquino group, which also goes back to an original of about the third century.[2] The Walters youth is certainly earlier than a bronze statuette of a satyr from Mahdia which is dated ca. 100.[3] This latter figure is captured in a similar moment of action, but his lack of torsion and greater stride forward result in a two-dimensional effect with the emphasis primarily on the silhouette.

The parallels between the Walters figure and monumental sculpture not only demonstrate a close affinity between large- and small-scale Hellenistic works of art, but also suggest that like his larger-scale counterparts, the Walters warrior belonged to an extended composition. One can perhaps imagine him as part of a montage analogous to the assemblages of Gauls set up by Attalos I in Pergamon and Athens.[4]

The Walters statuette was said to have been found in Egypt and exhibits the blue-green patina associated with pieces found in the Delta. Also conforming to our notions of Alexandrian art are the perfunctory modeling of the musculature, the unpolished surface, and the liveliness

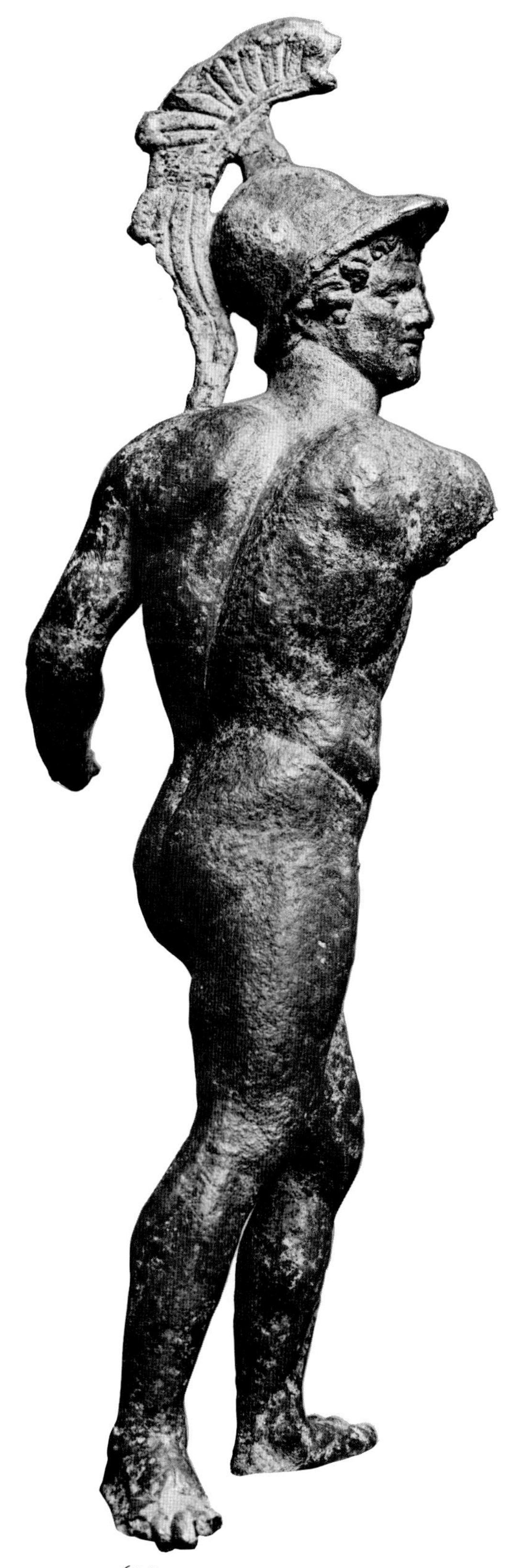

62.1

and immediacy of the action.[5] The similarities in pose and style between this apparently Egyptian figure and works linked with Pergamon are further testimony to the international character of Hellenistic art.[6]

Although this figure's nudity and his high-crested helmet evoke the age of Homeric heroes, the Hellenistic viewer would probably have associated the Walters warrior with contemporary soldiers, most of whom were mercenaries. Perpetual warfare, the large size of Hellenistic armies, and the promise of wealth and adventure attracted to this way of life men from all over the eastern Mediterranean and especially mainland Greece, where the lack of agricultural opportunity traditionally encouraged emigration.[7]

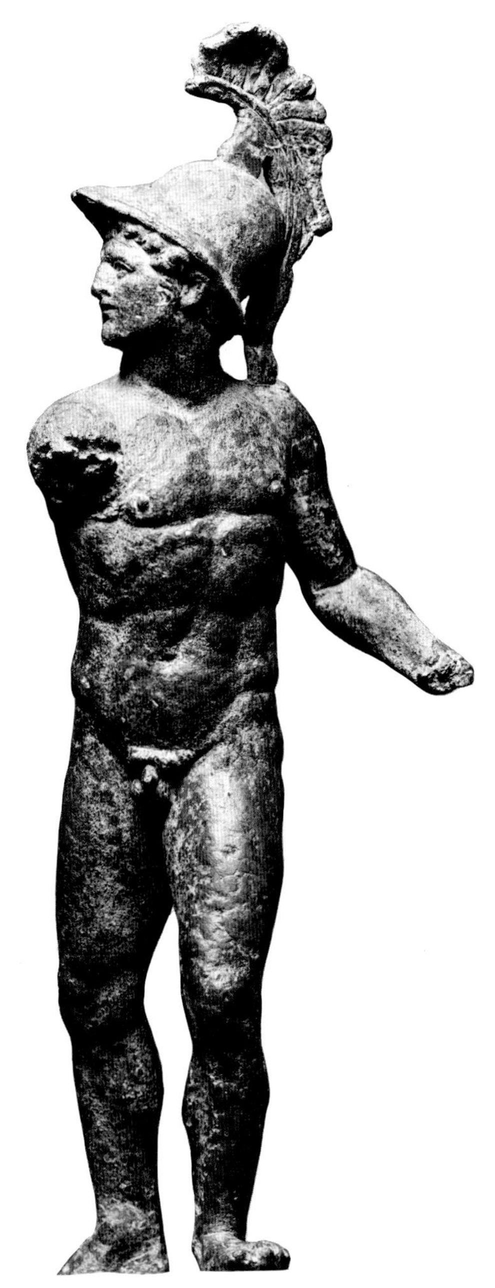

62.3

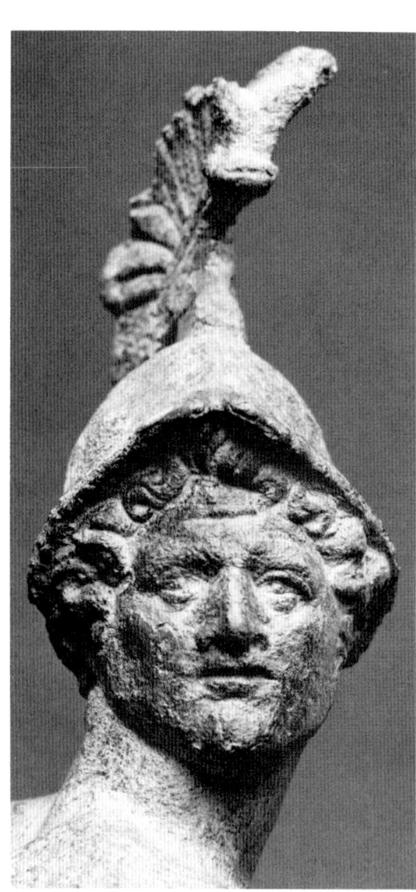

62.2

1. Pollitt 85–91, especially 87, fig. 86.

2. Ibid., 118 and 117, fig. 119.

3. C. Rolley, *Les bronzes grecs* (Fribourg, 1983), 242, fig. 297.

4. Pollitt 85–91.

5. See the comments in H. Kyrieleis, *AntP* 12 (1973) 128, n. 28.

6. Later, but with the same monumental quality, is a bronze figurine of a satyr from Pergamon dated to the middle of the first century. See D. Pinkwart, "Drei spräthellenistische Bronzen vom Burgberg in Pergamon," *Pergamenische Forschungen* 1, Pergamon gesammelte Aufsätze (Berlin, 1972), 124–131 and 125, figs. 10–13.

7. Tarn 101.

ALLEGORICAL GROUP OF
TRIUMPHANT PTOLEMY

150–100

54.1050. Bronze. "From Kharbia, Lower Egypt."
Purchased from Kelekian between 1910 and 1915. Ht,
19.7 cm; W, 10.7 cm; Depth, 9.8 cm. Left foot of
standing figure restored. Repaired on standing figure's left shoulder and behind his right shoulder;
other figure's right upper arm restored. Missing fingers of both hands and several toes of left foot of
kneeling figure. Cracks over surface. Modern base.

Two nude youths are locked in combat. The victor
lunges forward on his bent left leg, his left foot resting on his victim's left foot; his right leg, resting
only on the toes, is stretched out behind him. His
right arm is extended forward and is pressed over the
right ear of his crouching opponent while his left
hand, held at waist height, grasps the right forearm
of his victim. The victor's head is turned to his
right; he has wavy hair held back from the face by a
broad diadem, and four long curly locks which tum-
ble behind his shoulders; each eyeball is outlined by a
groove. The protrusion at his forehead is the remains
of a uraeus. His opponent crouches on his right knee
and toes; his left knee is bent with the foot placed
flat upon the ground. His body is further supported
by his left arm, whose palm lies flat on the ground.
His right arm is stretched violently out behind him;
his head is pressed to his left shoulder. His hair is
rendered as short, thick clumps; he has indented
pupils and his mouth is open.

Exhibitions and Catalogues: *The Greek Tradition in
Painting and the Minor Arts,* The Walters Art Gallery
and the Baltimore Museum of Art (Baltimore, May
15–June 25, 1939), 74, no. 83; *Small Sculptures in
Bronze from the Classical World,* The William H.
Ackland Memorial Art Center at the University of
North Carolina (Chapel Hill, March 7–April 18,
1976), no. 38.

Publications: D. K. Hill, "Some Bronze Statuettes
from Graeco-Roman Egypt," *Art in America* 31
(1943) 190–191, 194, and 187, fig. 3; Hill, *Bronzes,* 66,
no. 140, pl. 30; Bieber, *Sculpture,* 151, fig. 643; D. K.
Hill, "An Egypto-Roman Sculptural Type and Mass
Production of Bronze Statuettes," *Hesperia* 27 (1958)
311, 314; D. K. Hill, "Greek Sculpture Exhibition,"
BWalt 15 (1963) no. 6; E. Künzl, *Frühhellenistische
Gruppen* (diss. Cologne, 1968), 50, no. 4; H.
Kyrieleis, "ΚΑΘΑΠΕΡ ΕΡΜΗΣ ΚΑΙ ΩΡΟΣ,"
AntP 12 (1973) 134, no. 2, and 140–141, figs. 1–3, 10–
12, 14; H. Kyrieleis, *Bildnisse der Ptolemäer* (Berlin,
1975), 173, no. E7, pl. 43.2.5.6; B. Höfler, "Zur
Ringtechnik der ptolemäischen Ringergruppen,"
AA (1978) 551–553; A. Krug, "Die Bildnisse ptole-
maios IX, X, XI," H. Maehler, V. M. Strocka,
eds., *Das ptolemäische Ägypten* (Mainz, 1978), 15, no.
50; M. Poliakoff, *Combat Sports in the Ancient World*
(New Haven, 1987), 40, fig. 43; H. P. Laubscher,
"Ein ptolemäisches Gallierdenkmal," *AntK* 30
(1987) 148.

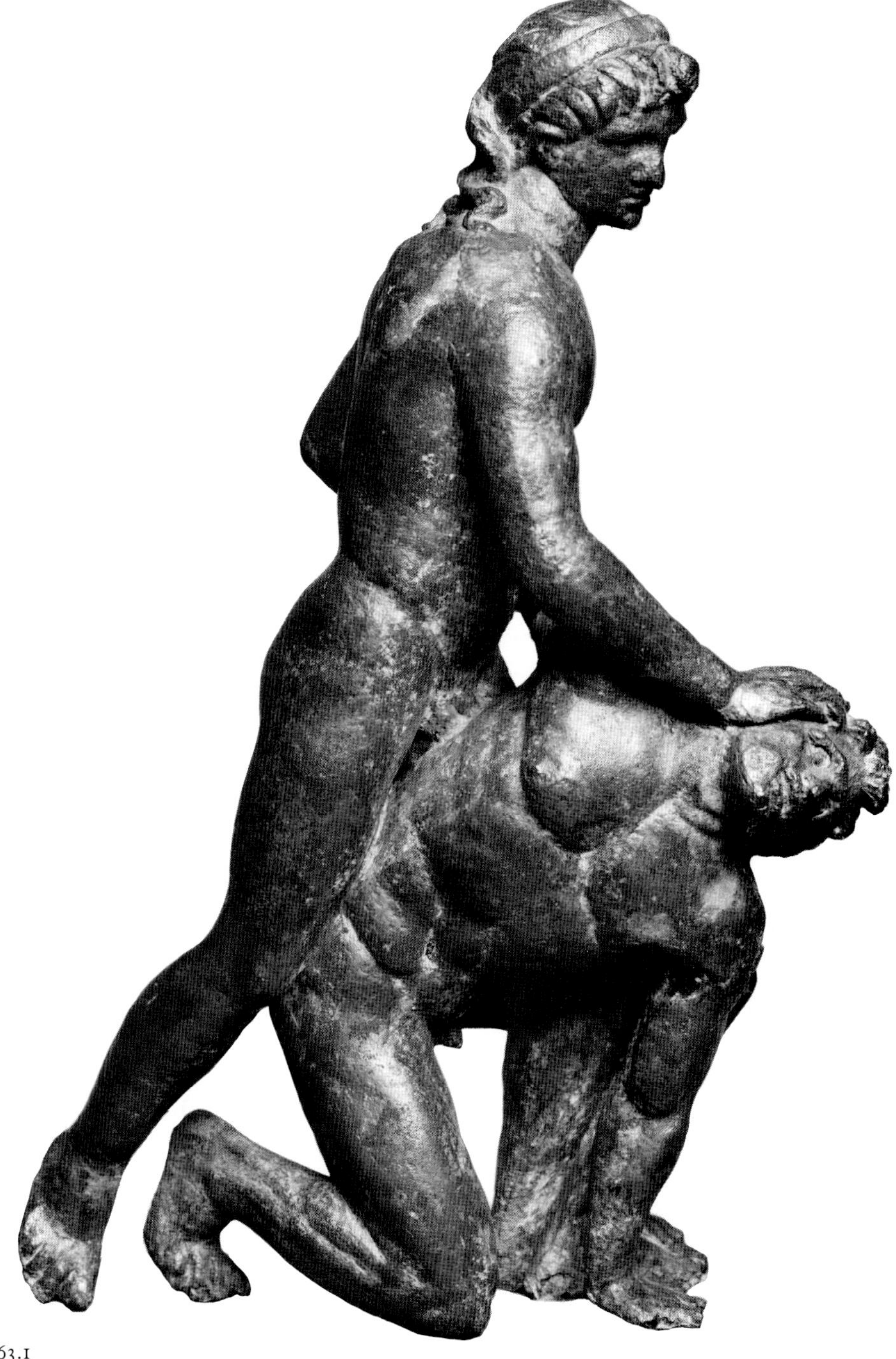

63.1

This group was solid cast from a wax
model which was assembled from a number of discrete elements whose joins are
still visible; one, for example, is seen at
the top of the victim's left leg. Typical of
bronzes from Ptolemaic Egypt are the
rough surface, which reproduces the
rough texture of the wax model, and the
absence of coldworking on the cast
bronze.

At least seven other groups similar to
the Walters example are known, five of
which were found in Egypt and one of
which, in London, wears an Egyptian
headdress, therewith unambiguously
establishing an Egyptian connection for
the type.[1] The Baltimore example is
unique in that the victor wears a diadem
and uraeus; like an example in Athens, he
also has long locks to his shoulder in the
tradition of the god Horos.[2] Noteworthy
are his youthful physique and face, which
deliberately contrast with the heavier-set
body and face of his opponent. Kyrieleis
argues that all these features as well as the
physiognomic resemblance of the victor to
portraits identified as Ptolemy V
Epiphanes establish the Walters youth as a
representation of that monarch.[3] Kyrieleis
further suggests that the Baltimore group

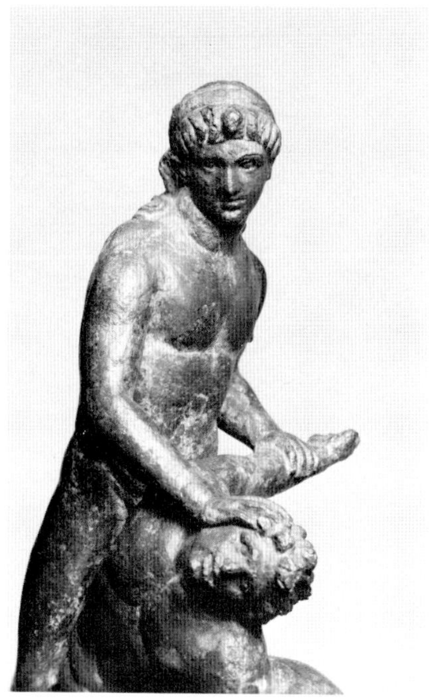

63.2

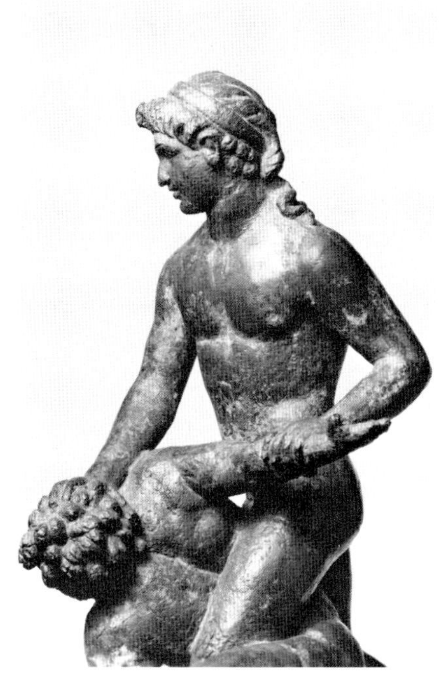

63.3

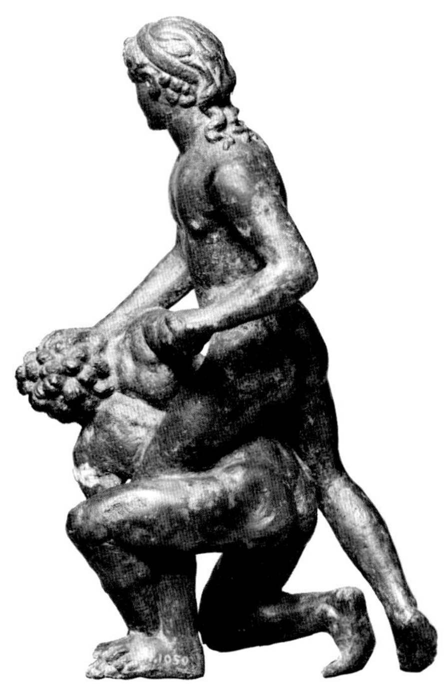

63.4

was made before 197 when Ptolemy was still young and when he was associated with Horos in such inscriptions as the Rosetta Stone, the only Ptolemaic king to be so openly acknowledged. The victim in the Baltimore group would then logically be identified with Seth with whom were associated the rebellions in upper Egypt that Ptolemy V had suppressed.

Although the Baltimore group may have been made in the years around 200, the prototype is probably earlier, partly because the pyramidal composition seems most suitable to the third century, contemporary, for example, with the Pasquino (Menelaos and Patroklos) group.[4] Because the winged headdress worn by the victor of a group in Istanbul identifies that youth as Hermes, with whom Ptolemy III Euergetes was closely linked, Kyrieleis contends that the original sculptural group was erected in the 240s fol-

lowing Ptolemy III Euergetes' victory at Laodike and that the defeated opponent in the prototypical work symbolized the Asian barbarians over whom the monarch's troops had triumphed.[5] The royal identities of the victorious youths in both groups underline the derivation of the composition from a traditional Egyptian motif in which a monarch stands over and pulls the hair of his opponent; at the same time, the piece introduces such specifically Greek elements as heroic nudity and, in the arm lock, an allusion to the Greek sport of wrestling.[6] This form of athletic contest became enormously popular in the Hellenistic period, and by Roman times victors vied for prizes worth six times the value of awards presented in the running and field events.[7]

The athletic theme of the Walters group suggests that the prototypical work was erected in a gymnasium and served as

a model for copies made for other sanctuaries following an attested Egyptian custom.[8] The small-scale copies follow a precedent familiar from the Ptolemaic faience oinochoai (No. 104) in that they replicate in reduced size the monumental portraiture of the monarch, a practice that was certainly politically motivated but that would not have been viable had the ruling family been less popular with at least certain segments of the population. Not all of the small bronze groups with this subject date from the Hellenistic age, and it is possible that well into Roman times groups like the Walters athletes were manufactured and even reworked to align the contestants with contemporary leaders.

1. For a discussion of groups of this type, see H. Kyrieleis, *AntP* 12 (1973) 135. The example in London is 133, no. 4.
2. For this example in Athens, see ibid., 139 and 133, no. 3.
3. Ibid., 140–42.
4. Pollitt 118 and 117, fig. 119.
5. Kyrieleis (note 1) 133, 141–142, 145.
6. For the traditional Egyptian motif, see ibid., 137. For holds in Greek wrestling, see M. Poliakoff, *Combat Sports,* 49 and 47, fig. 43.
7. R. Ling, ed., *The Cambridge Ancient History. Plates to Vol. VII, pt. 1, The Hellenistic World to the Coming of the Romans* (Cambridge, 1984), 134.
8. Kyrieleis (note 1), 144–145.

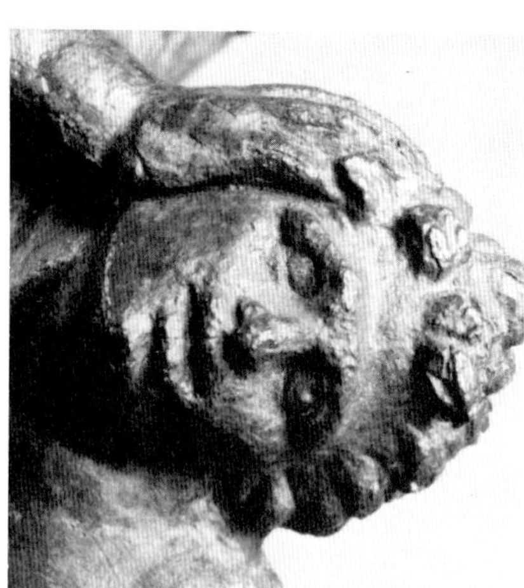

63.5

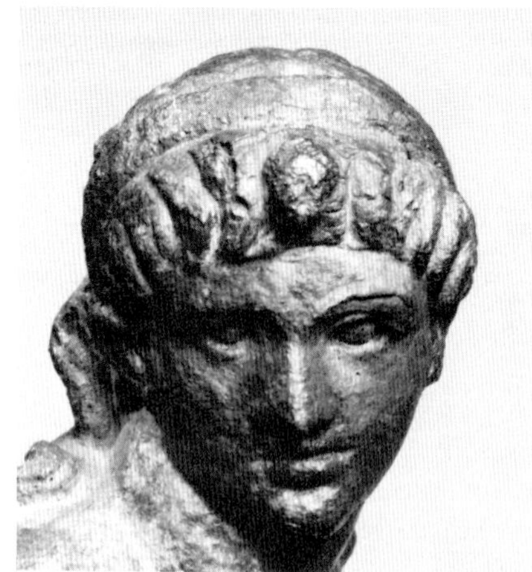

63.6

PAIR OF WRESTLERS
Second to first century

54.742. Bronze. Possibly purchased from Brummer in 1931. Ht, 15.2 cm; W, 7.4 cm; Depth, 8.2 cm. Left foot and part of right arm of standing figure restored.

A nude male steps forward on his right foot with his knee bent, his left leg behind him and resting on his toes. His head is inclined and turned to his right. Both hands are wrapped around the waist of a second figure who is held aloft by the grasp and whose back is pressed against the standing figure's left breast. The second figure is a nude youth, his knees bent with his right foot hanging free and his left foot pressed against the left knee of his opponent. Both forearms lie across his waist with his hands pressed against those of his opponent, which lie beneath; his head is directed down. The hair of both figures is gathered into knots at the back of the heads; the surface of the hair is stippled. Both figures have large ears and the mouth of the victor is drawn into a grimace.

Exhibitions and Catalogues: *The Greek Tradition in Painting and the Minor Arts,* The Walters Art Gallery and the Baltimore Museum of Art (Baltimore, May 15–June 25, 1939), 74, no. 86, and ill. on 69.

Publications: E. N. Gardiner, *Athletics of the Ancient World* (Oxford, 1930), 196, fig. 171; Hill, *Bronzes,* 67, no. 141, pl. 30; Bieber, *Sculpture,* 151, fig. 643; C. Rolley, *Greek Minor Arts I: The Bronzes,* Monumenta Graeca et Romana 5 (Leiden, 1967), 12, no. 122, and ill. on 41; F. Brommer, *Denkmälerlisten zur griechischen Heldensage I. Herakles* (Marburg, 1971), 25, no. 1 (as possibly Herakles and Antaios); C. Havelock, *Hellenistic Art,* 2nd ed. (New York, 1981), 147–148, no. 144; *LIMC* I (1981) pt. 1, 809, no. 77a, pt. 2, 657 (erroneous reference is to another bronze identified as possibly Herakles and Antaios); C. Rolley, *Les bronzes grecs* (Fribourg, 1983), 242, fig. 299; N. Himmelmann-Wildschütz, *Alexandria und der Realismus in der griechischen Kunst* (Tübingen, 1983), 69; M. Poliakoff, *Combat Sports in the Ancient World* (New Haven, 1987), 42, fig. 32.

An Egyptian origin for this piece is established by the Egyptian provenance of at least one similar group and by the presence on this example of such technical features associated with Egyptian manufacture as traces of the seams by which the wax model was assembled through the technique of piece-molds, and by the rough surface which, in the absence of coldworking, reproduces the irregularities of the wax model.[1] Several other types of wrestling groups are

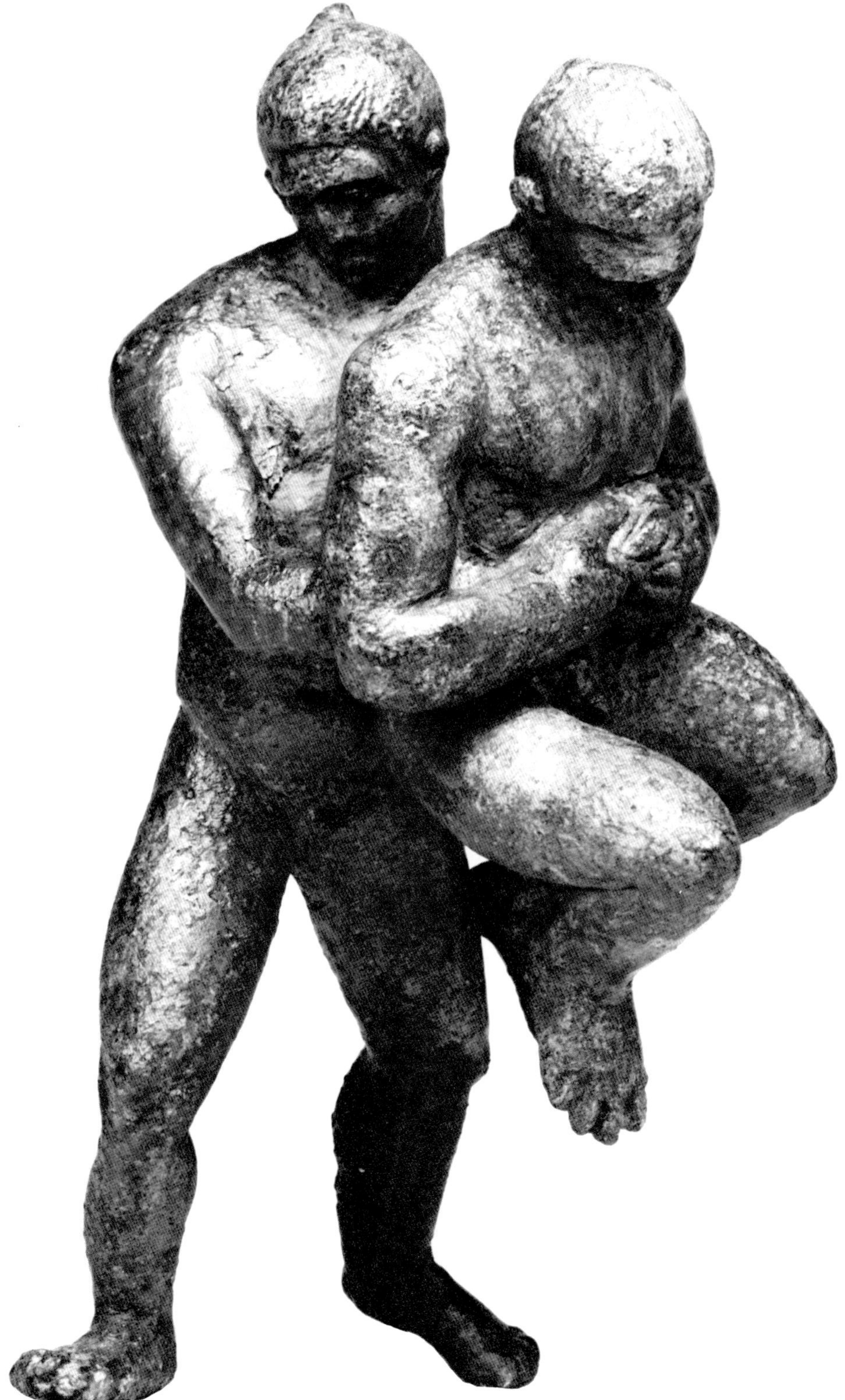

64.1

known, but many of these are Roman in
date; the type of the Walters group is
notable in that it can be traced back at
least to the fourth century when a terracotta version was placed in a south Russian burial.[2]

Wrestling was one of the most popular
of Greek sports and exemplified the Greek
preference for individual athletic contests
over team endeavors. Whereas striking
was prohibited, contestants were allowed
to break their opponents' bones in an
effort to achieve victory, which was
declared after three falls.[3] Competition
took place in the palaestra, an athletic
complex that included a sandy wrestling
area and dressing rooms where athletes
rubbed olive oil over their bodies before
exercising. Because of its relaxed atmosphere, the palaestra was a perennially
favorite social gathering-place of the
Greek male community.

The knotted hair worn by the Walters
athletes looks forward to the cirrus hairstyle of the Roman period and suggests
that the combatants are not mythological
heroes, but simply mortal athletes who
were able to take advantage of the proliferation of festivals in Hellenistic times to
exist as full-time, itinerant competitors.[4]
In wrestling groups of the Roman period,
the piece-mold process encouraged the
substitutions of such heads as those of
Herakles and Alexander, thereby transfer-
ring this Hellenistic genre subject to the
mythological arena.

1. For the Egyptian parallel, see D. K. Hill, "An Egypto-
Roman Sculptural Type and Mass Production of Bronze
Statuettes," *Hesperia* 27 (1958) 316, pl. 56. For the use of
piece-molds in Egyptian metalworking, see E. Reeder
Williams, "A Bronze Statuette of Isis-Aphrodite,"
JARCE 16 (1979) 94.
2. For Roman wrestling types, see *LIMC* I (1981) pt. 1, 809–
811, where the Walters group is incorrectly listed among
examples of Herakles and Antaios dated to the fourth century A.D. See also Hill (note 1) 311, pl. 55a.
3. M. Poliakoff, *Combat Sports,* 24–27. See also E. N. Gardiner, *Athletics,* 181. For the terracotta version, see A.
Peredol'skaia, "Attische Tonfiguren aus einem südrussischen Grab," *AntK* Beiheft 2 (1964) 6, 27–28,
pl. 13.
4. Poliakoff (note 4) 14–15, 18–19.

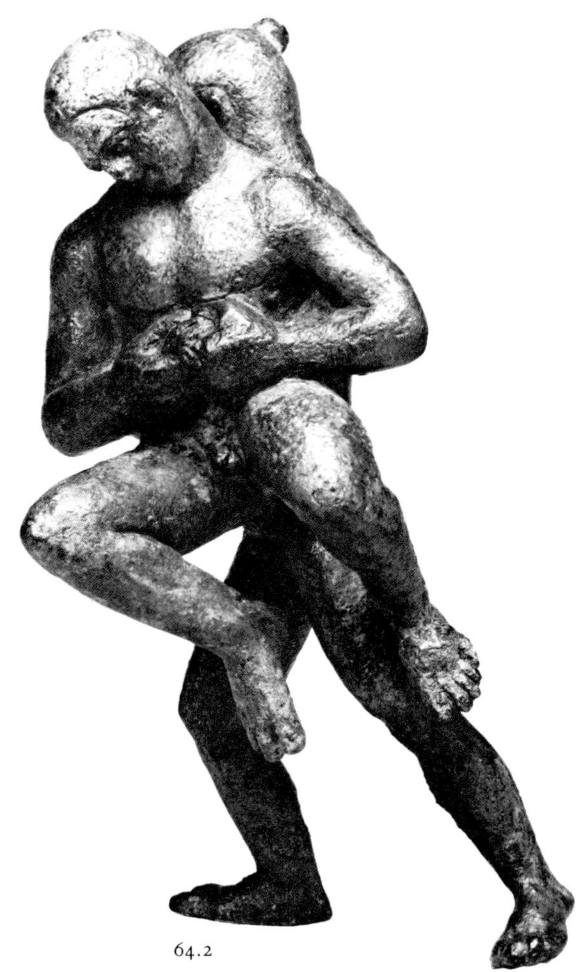

64.2

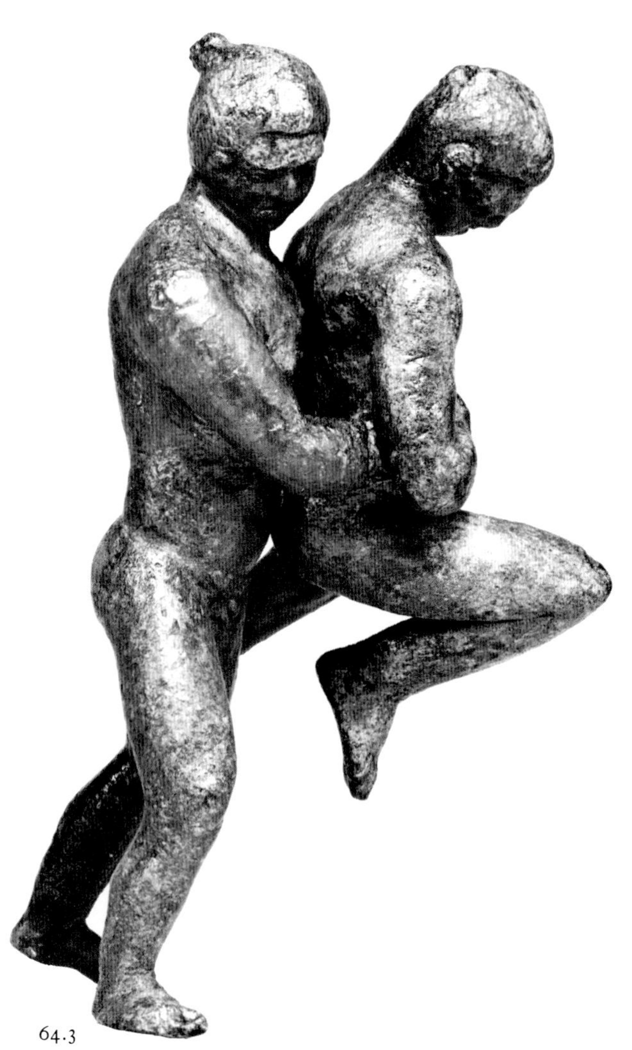

64.3

Statuette of Dionysos
First century

54.741. Bronze. "From Erment, Egypt." Purchased before 1931. Total Ht, 18.1 cm; Ht, to top of head 16.2 cm; W, 6.4 cm. Missing right leg and left arm. Shoulder has an unbroken bronze surface across the point of attachment.

A nude youth stands with his weight on his left leg, his right leg relaxed. His right arm is upraised with the elbow bent; the hand holds an upturned rhyton with a curving tip. His head is turned to his right; his wavy hair is pulled back from his face to a knot at the nape with one long wavy lock falling forward over each shoulder. A headband lies horizontally across his brow beneath a wreath of ivy leaves in high relief to which two large clusters of berries are attached above his forehead. He wears sandals, which are laced up to midcalf and secured by a cord.

Publications: Reinach, *Statuaire* 4 (1910) 62, no. 7; O. Rubensohn, "Archäologische Funde im Jahre 1905," *AA* (1906) cols. 142–143 and col. 140, fig. 12; F. Weege, "Der einschenkende Satyr aus Sammlung Mengarini," *BWPr* 89 (1929) 29, no.2; Hill, *Bronzes,* 23, no. 40, pl. 14; D. K. Hill, "Note on the Piecing of Bronze Statuettes," *Hesperia* 51 (1982) 279, and 281, no.A26, pl. 77a.

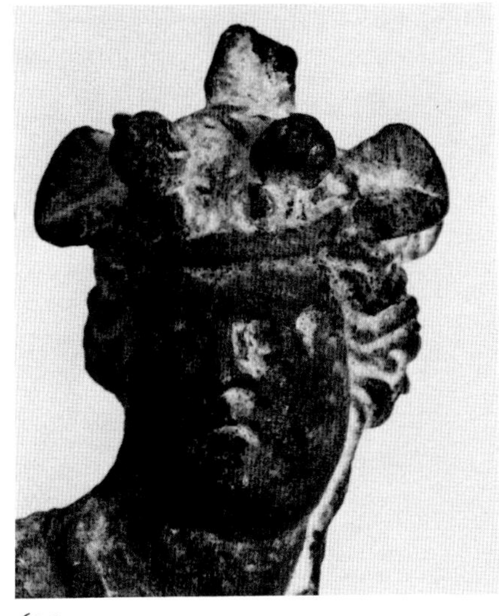

65.2

Rubensohn's 1906 archaeological report mentioned a right leg and a left arm wrapped in a mantle, but neither piece appears to have entered the Walters collection with this statuette. The figure was said to have been found in Erment, near Luxor, and an Egyptian provenance is further supported by a parallel in the Cairo Museum and another from Athribis that was formerly in the Fouquet collection.[1] The Walters figure shares with the latter example a typically Egyptian technique of manufacture whereby torso and arm were cast separately, after which the arm was attached to the closed socket of the torso by a practice known as cold piecing.[2] The system not only facilitated mass production through an assembly-line process of manufacture, but also encouraged a conflation of iconography and styles because the body extremities could be so easily interchanged. This method of fabrication may be responsible for the awkward angularity of the Walters figure which results from the combination of the sideways inclination of the frontal torso with the sharp turn of the head and raised right arm. The resulting restlessness seems at home in the late Hellenistic age and contrasts with the Praxitelean pose of the Cairo example. At the same time, the soft contours of the body, the boots, and the elaborate hairstyle with long locks to the shoulders look forward to a similarly fabricated statuette of Dionysos in the Walters, whose summary modeling and exaggerated facial features point to an early Imperial date.[3]

Dionysos, the god of the vine and the patron deity of theatrical performers, enjoyed an enormous popularity in Hellenistic times. Both the Attalids and the Ptolemies claimed descent from him, and, when promoted by Ptolemy IV who himself claimed to be a "New Dionysos," the god's cult garnered an extensive following in Italy during the early second century.[4]

1. For the Cairo example, see M. C. C. Edgar, *Greek Bronzes,* Catalogue général des antiquités égyptiennes du musée du Caire 19 (Cairo, 1904), 4, no. 27.643, pl. 1. For the example from Athribis, see P. Perdrizet, *Bronzes grecs d'Egypte de la collection Fouquet* (Paris, 1911), 13, no. 9, pl. 6.
2. See Hill, *Hesperia* 51 (1982) 278–279.
3. Hill, *Bronzes,* 24–25, no. 43, pl. 14.
4. Tarn 339, and see No. 135.

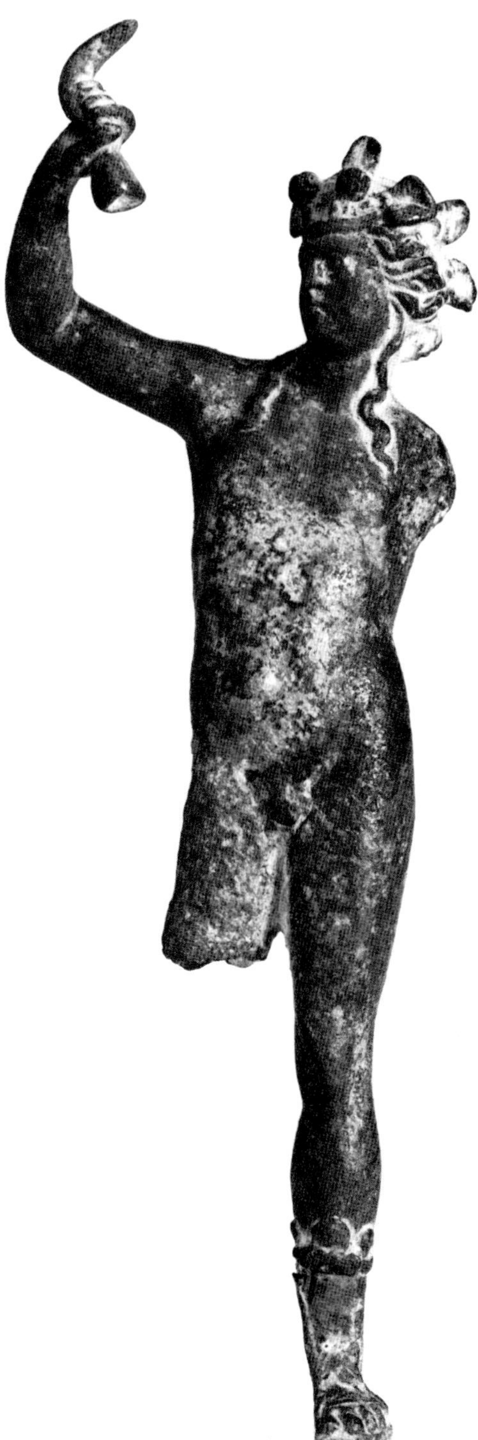

65.1

LAMPSTAND WITH BOXER
First century

54.1006. Bronze. Purchased from Brummer in 1924. Total Ht, 27 cm; Ht, figure alone 13.9 cm; max W, capital 9.8 cm. At each corner of the top of the capital are the remains of three iron pins for attachments. Figure missing tip of thumb and tips of fingers of right hand. Capital missing one blossom with the two leaves beneath.

A smooth column shaft terminates in a capital composed of three akanthos leaves separated by a flower above two leaves; the lower end of the shaft is transversed by a movable pin. On the narrow flat top of the capital stands a nude male, his weight on his right leg with his left leg to one side. He has a chunky, muscular body and a large head. His left arm is bent at the elbow; the forearm is outstretched and the fingers hold a sponge with a stippled surface. The right arm hangs at his side away from the body. Both hands wear boxing gloves consisting of a twisted and a plain strap over a leather strip secured around the forearm, a curved strap worn over a leather pad across the knuckles and through which the fingers are inserted, and two cross-thongs over the back of the hand. His head is turned to his left and the pupils are indented; he has a furrowed brow, and large eyes and nose. The beard and hair are rendered as broad, wavy clumps.

Exhibitions and Catalogues: Mitten, *Bronzes,* 133, no. 133, and ill. on 132; M. L. Hadzi, *Transformations in Hellenistic Art,* Mount Holyoke College (South Hadley, February 3–March 18, 1983), 14, no. 3 and ill. on 15.

Publications: D. K. Hill, "Ancient Representations of Herakles as a Baby," *GBA* 33 (1948) 196–197, figs. 5 a-b; Hill, *Bronzes,* 69, no. 146, pl. 31 and frontispiece; D. K. Hill, "From Alexander to Augustus," *BWalt* 7 (1955) no. 5; D. K. Hill, "The Spectacular in the Classical," *Apollo* 84 (1966) 453–454, no. 58, fig.1; E. Raftopoulou, "Remarques sur des bronzes provenant du sol grec," *Bronzes hellénistiques et romains; tradition et renouveau, Actes du Ve colloque international, mai 8–13, 1978* (Lausanne, 1979), 45, n. 45, pl. 19, fig. 21.

Chains suspended from each corner of the capital may have held lamps, in which case the piece would be a removable lampstand finial similar to examples which have been recovered from Pompeii.[1] The boxing gloves follow a style introduced in the fourth century and have their closest parallels in the late Hellenistic period both

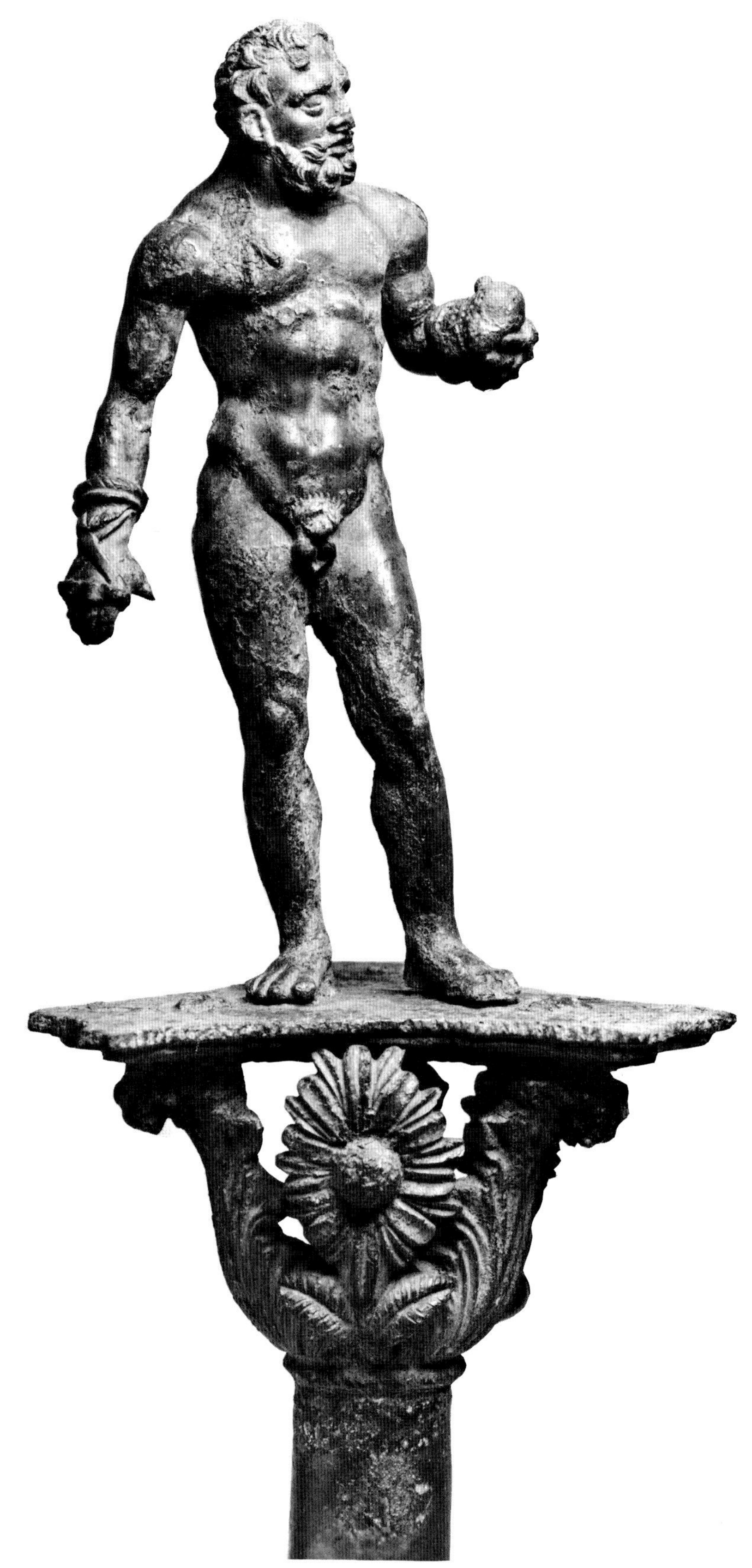

66.1

with those worn by the seated boxer by
Apollonios in the Terme and among the
finds from Antikythera.[2] Because professional boxers did not wear beards, it is
possible that the figure is Herakles, or
possibly Polydeukes, whose boxing match
with Amykos is described by Theokritos
with a plethora of lurid detail rarely
encountered in literature before the Hellenistic age.[3]

Boxing was a popular and often violent
contest to which almost any punch was
admitted, including eye-gouging and
blows to the groin. The competition proceeded without rounds until one opponent was knocked out or acknowledged
defeat by raising a finger.[4] Despite its
obvious physicality, the Greeks were cog-
nizant of the skills that success in this
sport entailed, and recognized Apollo as
boxing's patron god, in reference to the
deity's mythical defeat of Ares through a
triumph of intelligence and technique over
sheer brutality.

1. E. Pernice, *Die hellenistische Kunst in Pompeji IV. Gefässe
   und Geräte aus Bronze* (Berlin, 1925), 43–57. See also Hill,
   Apollo 84 (1966) 33.
2. M. Poliakoff, *Combat Sports in the Ancient World* (New
   Haven, 1987), 70–71. For the seated boxer, see Pollitt
   146–147 and 145, fig. 157, dated second or early first century. For the example from Antikythera, dated late Hellenistic, see P. Bol, *Die Skulpturen des Schiffsfundes von
   Antikythera*, AM-BH 2 (1972) 34–35, pl. 18, 1–2.
3. Theokritos, *Idyll* 22. 75–134. For Herakles, see Theokritos, *Idyll* 24.III.
4. Poliakoff (note 2) 80–85.

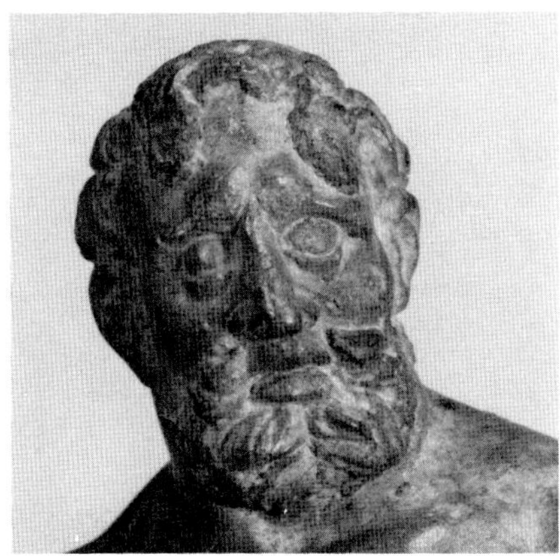

66.2

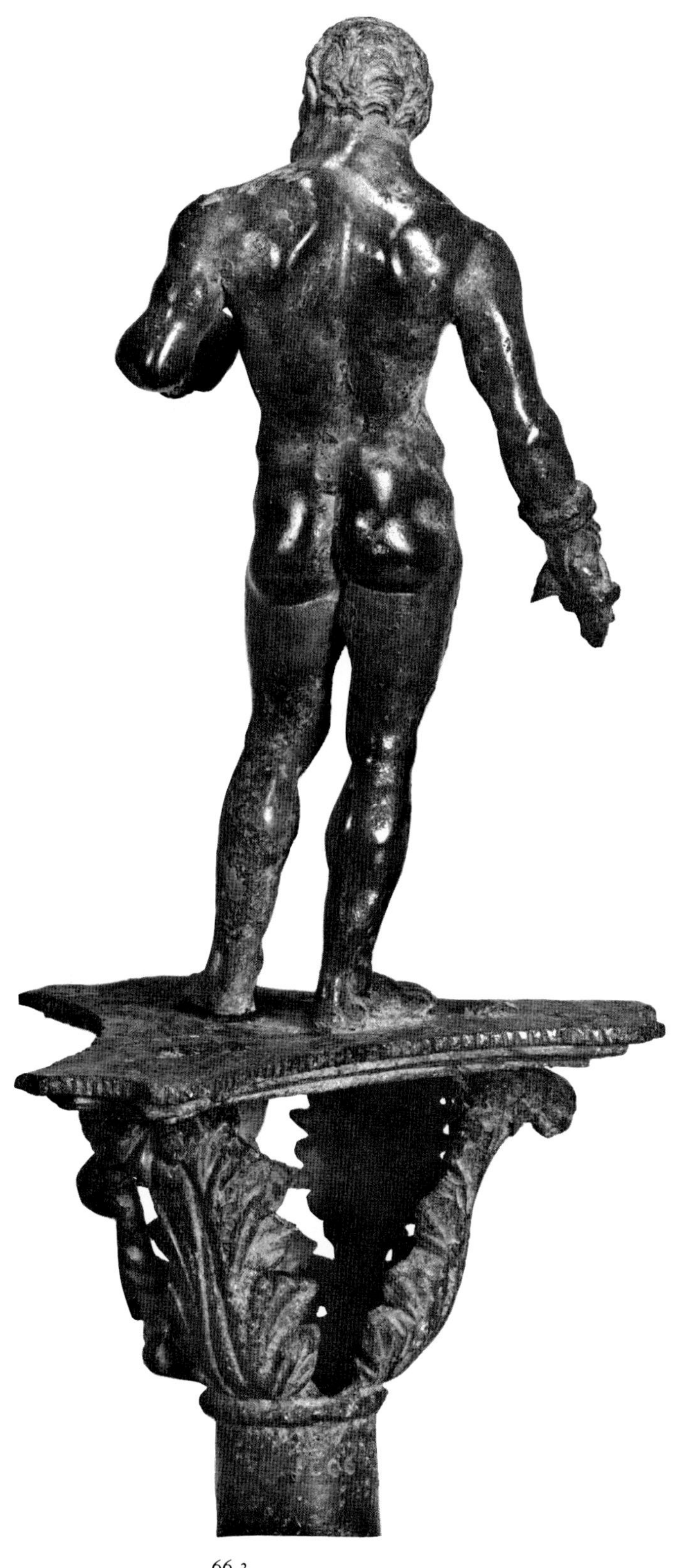

66.3

CUP WITH LEAF ORNAMENT
Ca. 250–100

57.911. Silver. "From Kavalla." Purchased from Kelekian in 1911. Ht, 6.9 cm; D, rim 7.8 cm. Upper part turned on lathe. Gilding on engraved shoulder and on akanthos, lilies, and central rosette. Small holes in sides. The hemispherical body has repoussé decoration.

In the center of the underside is an eight-petal rosette encircled by four akanthos leaves alternating with four lotus leaves. Above them is a larger band of similar ornament; the area between the leaf tips is filled with lilies and other blossoms, and the background is stippled. On the shoulder, between ridges, is a cyma reversa engraved with a band of leaf-and-dart. Above is a wide everted rim with two concentric circles incised on the horizontal surface.

Exhibitions and Catalogues: D. K. Hill, *Greek and Roman Metalware,* The Walters Art Gallery (Baltimore, February 14–April 14, 1976), no. 63; Oliver, *Silver,* 71, no. 35.

Publications: Segall, "Tradition," 14, fig. 5, reviewed by L. Byvanck-Quarles van Ufford in *BABesch* 42 (1967) 147; Reinsberg, *Toreutik,* 40, n. 143a, 45, n. 162.

Typically Hellenistic are both the individual motifs and the system of ornament defined by concentric circles of alternating leaves and flowers. Vessels like the Walters example served as prototypes for the familiar mass-produced Hellenistic ceramic moldmade bowls (Nos. 97–99), and the floral patterns developed on these metal examples surely inspired such other forms of contemporary metalwork as diadems (No. 127).[1] The plasticity and intense agitation of the leaves on the Walters cup support a mature Hellenistic date of the later third to second centuries.

1. See M. Vickers et al., *From Silver to Ceramic* (Oxford, 1986), pl. 26.

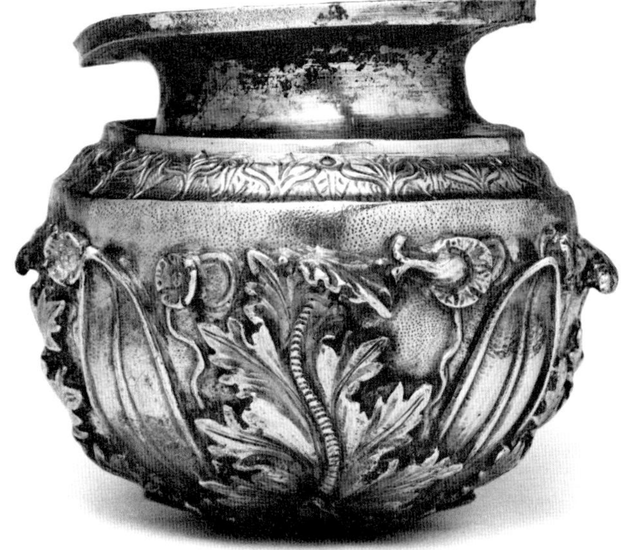

67.1

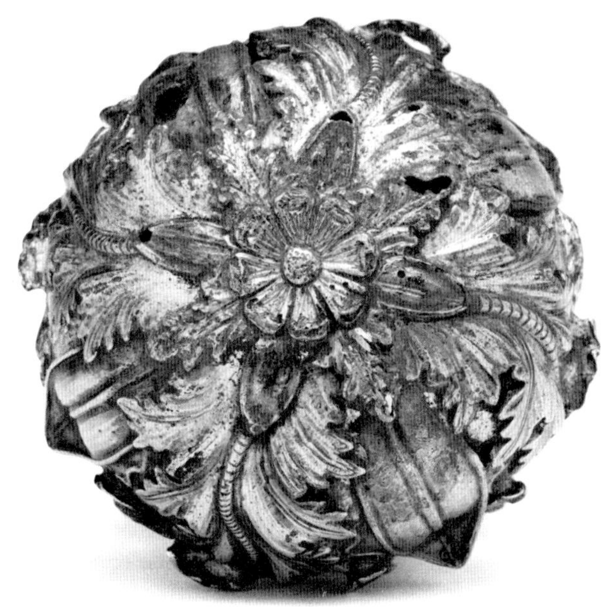

67.2

BED

100–50

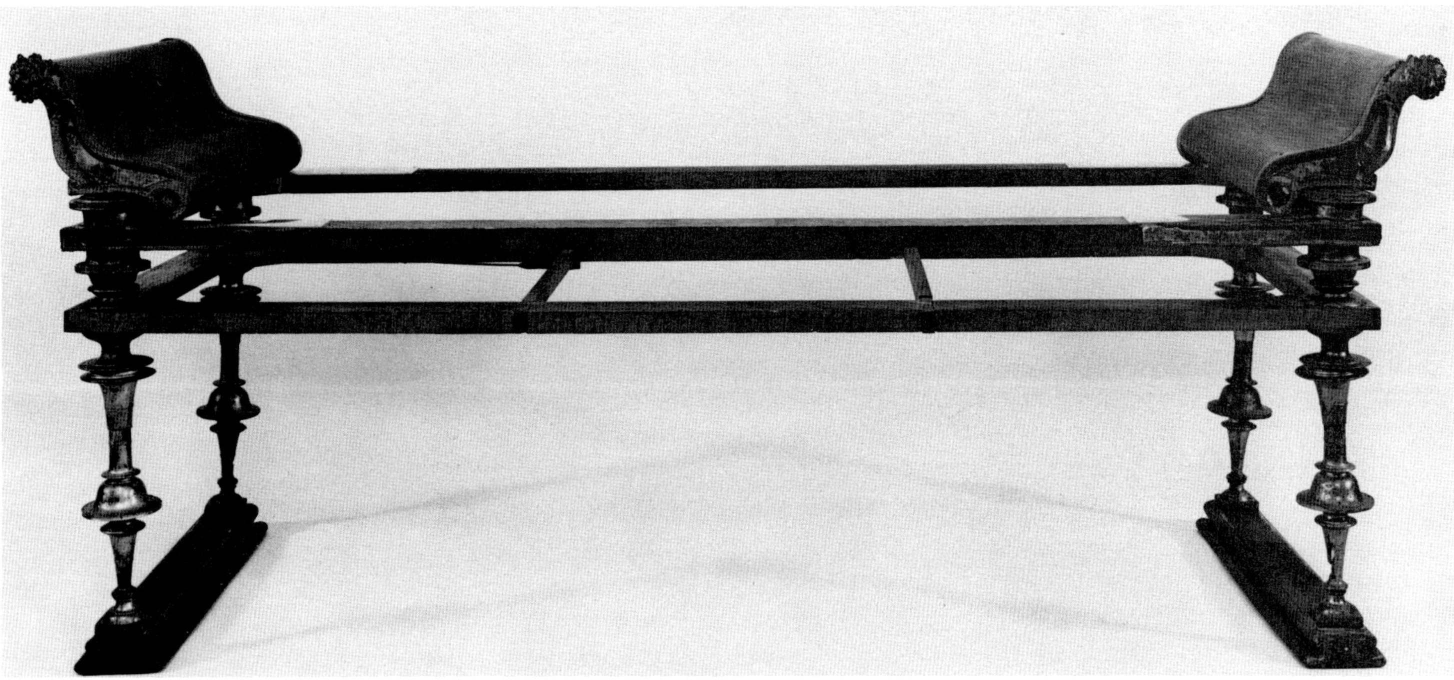

68.1

54.2365. Bronze. "From Canosan tomb in Apulia."
Collection of Arnold Ruesch of Zurich (sale catalogue, Lucerne, Galerie Fischer, September 1, 1936,
15, no. 135, pls. 28–29). Collection of W. R. Hearst,
New York; J. Brummer (sale catalogue, New York,
Parke-Bernet, June 8–9, 1949, pt. III, 8, no. 38).
Purchased in 1949. Ht, 81.5 cm; L, 188 cm (modern);
Depth, 69.2 cm; L, fulcrum 30.3 cm. Restored with
wood crosspieces from fifty-one bronze pieces. Fulcra medallions are missing.

Bed has turned legs. Fulcra at the head and foot on
one side terminate in duck heads; lion heads are in
the same position on the fulcra on the other side of
bed.

Publications: L. Pollak, "Arnold Ruesch," *Italien* 3
(1930) 175; A. Greifenhagen, "Bronzekline im Pariser Kunsthandel," *RM* 45 (1930) 137–146 and 146,
no. 53, pl. 47; W. Deonna, *Exploration archéologique
de Délos XVIII: Le mobilier délien* (Paris, 1938), 2, n.
13; D. K. Hill, "Catalogue of the Exhibition,
Recent Accessions," *BWalt* 2 (1949) no. 1; D. K.
Hill, "Life of the Romans," *BWalt* 5 (1953) no. 8;
D. K. Hill, "A Bronze Couch," *JWalt* 15–16 (1952–
53) 48–61; E. Packard, "The Cleaning of the Bronze
Couch," *JWalt* 15–16 (1952–53) 61–63; D. K. Hill,
"The Roman Collections of the Walters Art Gallery," *Archaeology* 10 (1957) 23; D. K. Hill, "Ivory
Ornaments of Hellenistic Couches," *Hesperia* 32
(1963) 294, pl. 79c; C. Boube-Piccot, "Les lits de
bronze de Maurétanie Tingitane," *Bulletin d'archéologie marocaine* 4 (1960) 277, no. 23; C. Boube-Piccot,
Les bronzes antiques du Maroc II. Le Mobilier, Etudes et
travaux d'archéologie marocaine 5 (Rabat, 1975), 14–
15, 364–365, no. 20; B. Barr-Sharrar, *The Hellenistic
and Early Imperial Decorative Bust* (Mainz, 1987), 63,
no. C118, pl. 37.

At the time of its acquisition this bed had
been restored as a bisellium, or chair. The
current reconstruction does not include all
of the parts that constituted that bisellium, a fact suggesting that the bisellium,
and also conceivably the present reconstruction, incorporated elements from
more than one ancient bed. Other aspects
of the restoration are also uncertain; the
bed should probably be longer to accommodate the full height of an adult, and the
modern wood stretcher should probably
be positioned lower, or halfway up the
leg. Because ancient beds with double sets
of fulcra (armrests) are documented in
vase painting, both of the pairs on the
Walters example may have belonged to
the same original piece of furniture; however, each end of a bed was probably decorated with matching fulcra, and so one
duck or lion head should be interchanged.[1]

The Walters bed belongs to a group of
Hellenistic bronze beds, the earliest of
which was found in the Taman peninsula,
along the shores of the Black Sea, together
with coins of the first half of the third
century.[2] Other Hellenistic examples with
dated contexts are rare; an example from
Pella has been placed between 300 and
168, and fulcrum parts were found in the
Antikythera and Mahdia shipwrecks
which are dated to the second quarter of
the first century and ca. 50, respectively.[3]
Two examples from Priene are thought to
have been made in the late third or early
second century, but have also been
assigned a first-century date.[4] The Wal

ters bed resembles all these examples in its
elegantly turned legs, and its elongated,
inclined, and narrow fulcra; its fulcrum
terminals compare especially well with
one recovered from Mahdia.

Supporting the bed's reputed provenance from a Canosan tomb are both the
staining and corrosion on the legs, which
could have resulted from the leakage that
commonly occurred in these tombs, and
the widespread and diverse use of these
beds in Hellenistic times. Although elaborate beds were known in the Greek world
before Alexander's conquests, their popularity was enormously enhanced with the
Eastern contact that followed Alexander's
death. In describing the symposium of
Ptolemy II, Athenaeus refers to a gold bed
couch whose form undoubtedly reflected
influence from the Persian world and
recalls an anecdote told of the fourth-
century Persian King Artaxerxes.[5] Doubtful of Greek ability to arrange a bed
properly, Artaxerxes sent attendants to
assist in preparing the bed of his guest
Timagoras.

The introduction of the bed into the
Roman world occurred relatively early.
Pliny tells us that Cn. Manlius Vulso
brought beds back to Italy in 187, and
three golden beds were included in Lucullus's triumphal procession that followed
the defeat of Mithradates VI in 63.[6] In
particular demand in the Roman world
were the so-called Delian beds, which
may have been distinctive for their bronze
fittings.[7] Less certain is the appearance of
the presumably contemporary "lecti

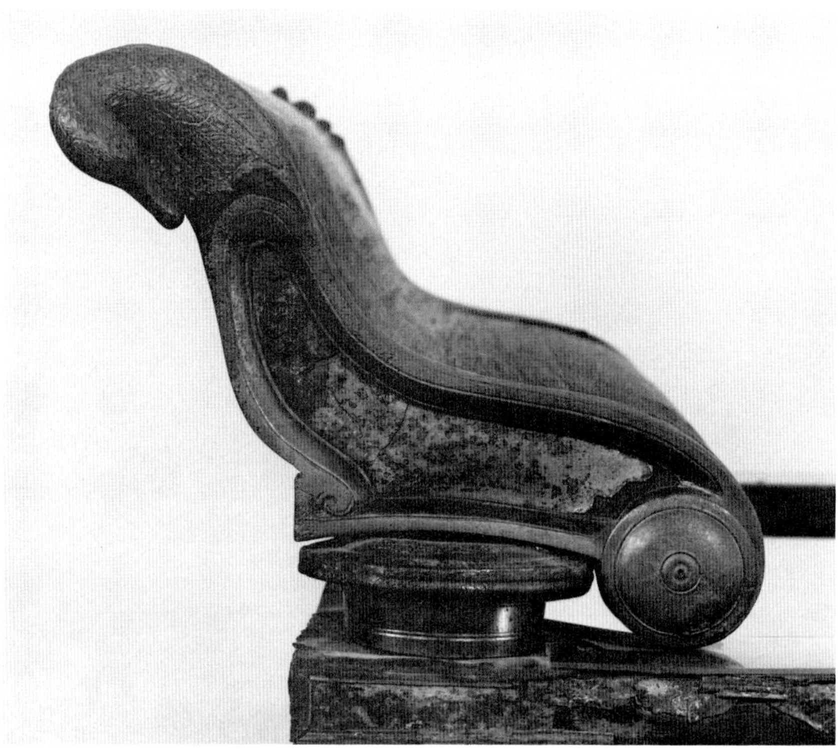

68.2

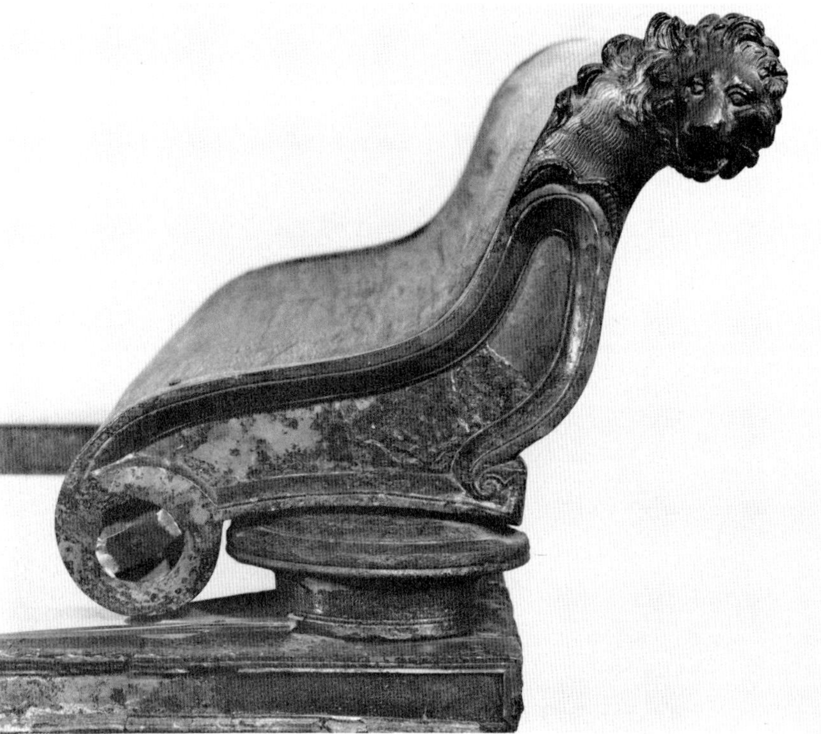

68.3

Boethiaci'' mentioned in literary sources.[8] It is quite possible, therefore, that the Walters example was locally fabricated in Italy during the first century, emulating a style that by this time had become widely disseminated throughout the Mediterranean world.

Bedsteads of the Hellenistic age were probably fitted with a lattice frame of leather or metal and a mattress of straw or wool. Coverlets were of brightly colored wool and were probably accompanied by several embroidered pillows. Only in Egypt were linen sheets common. Beds were used for dining, sleeping, and burial with no apparent distinction in style according to their intended function.[9] Fulcrum subjects for terminals included panthers (No. 69), horses, and swans, probably because of their long necks. Ivory appliqués are also known (No. 111). Rondels bore motifs appropriate to dining and sleeping, such as Eros, maenads, and satyrs, and, from the early third century, portraits in bronze (No. 50).

Beds of the Roman period are recognized by the shorter, thicker legs with fewer turned members. The fulcra are shorter and more upright, and do not usually bear a relief figure on the sloping surface, which may be open or decorated with inlaid ornament.[10]

1. See G. M. A. Richter, *Furniture of the Greeks, Romans and Etruscans* (London, 1966), 56, fig. 300; Barr-Sharrar, *Decorative Bust*, 4, 6.
2. C. Boube-Piccot, *Le mobilier,* 12, 359, no. 1. For a general discussion of Greek and Roman beds, see Richter (note 1) 52–58, and Barr-Sharrar (note 1) 7, 20–29.
3. For the Pella example, see Boube-Piccot (note 2) 14. For the Mahdia and Antikythera examples, see Boube-Piccot, 14, 363, nos. 13–17; W. Fuchs, *Der Schiffsfund von Mahdia JdI* Bilderhefte 2 (Tübingen, 1963) 31, no. 37, pl. 45. See also G. Seiterle and A. Mutz, ''Ein hellenistisches Bronzebett im Basler Antikenmuseum,'' *AntK* 25 (1982) 62–65. Barr-Sharrar (note 1) 22, dates the Antikythera fulcrum parts to the late third-early second century, and on 23–25 assigns the Mahdia examples to the last quarter of the second century.
4. For the Priene beds see Boube-Piccot (note 2) 13, 360; J. Raeder, *Priene. Funde aus einer griechischen Stadt* (Berlin, 1983), 21, fig. 8a; Barr-Sharrar (note 1) 21–22.
5. Athenaeus, *Deipnosophistae* 5.197a. For Artaxerxes, see Plutarch, *Artaxerxes,* 22.
6. Pliny *NH* 34.14. For Mithradates, see Pliny, *NH* 37.14.
7. Pliny *NH* 33.144; 34.9 and 14–15. See G. Siebert, ''Mobilier délien en bronze,'' *Etudes déliennes, BCH* Suppl. 1 (Athens, 1973) 555, 573.
8. Porphyry, *Ad Horat. epist.* 1.5.1.
9. E. Diehl, ''Bronzener Silenskopf von der Lehne eines römischen Bettes,'' *Jahrbuch des Römisch-Germanischen Zentralmuseums Mainz* 7 (1960) 208–213.
10. See Richter (note 1) 107.

Panther Fulcrum
Attachment from a Bed
Second to first century

57.710. Bronze. Purchased before 1931. Ht, 16.5 cm; W, 12.5 cm; Th, 6.1 cm. Head and top of neck worked in the round.

Panther head and left side of curving neck. The jaws are open with the tongue extended. The irises of the eyes are incised and the pupils indented. Short, incised lines indicate the fur. Around the neck is tied a cord to which ivy leaves are attached and from whose ends clumps and berries are suspended. The base of the neck has a curving edge on which leaves are incised.

Exhibitions: *Designed For Use: Ancient Tools,* The Walters Art Gallery (Baltimore, July 26–September 11, 1983).

Following conventional practice the panther head was cast separately from the rest of the fulcrum.[1] The degree of curvature in the neck, the shape of the lower border, the caliber of the execution, and the momentary quality of the expression compare well with two horse-head fulcrum attachments that are dated to the second and first centuries.[2] A less detailed rendering of a panther head set on a more tightly curved neck appears on a fulcrum attachment in Berlin assigned to the first century A.D.[3]

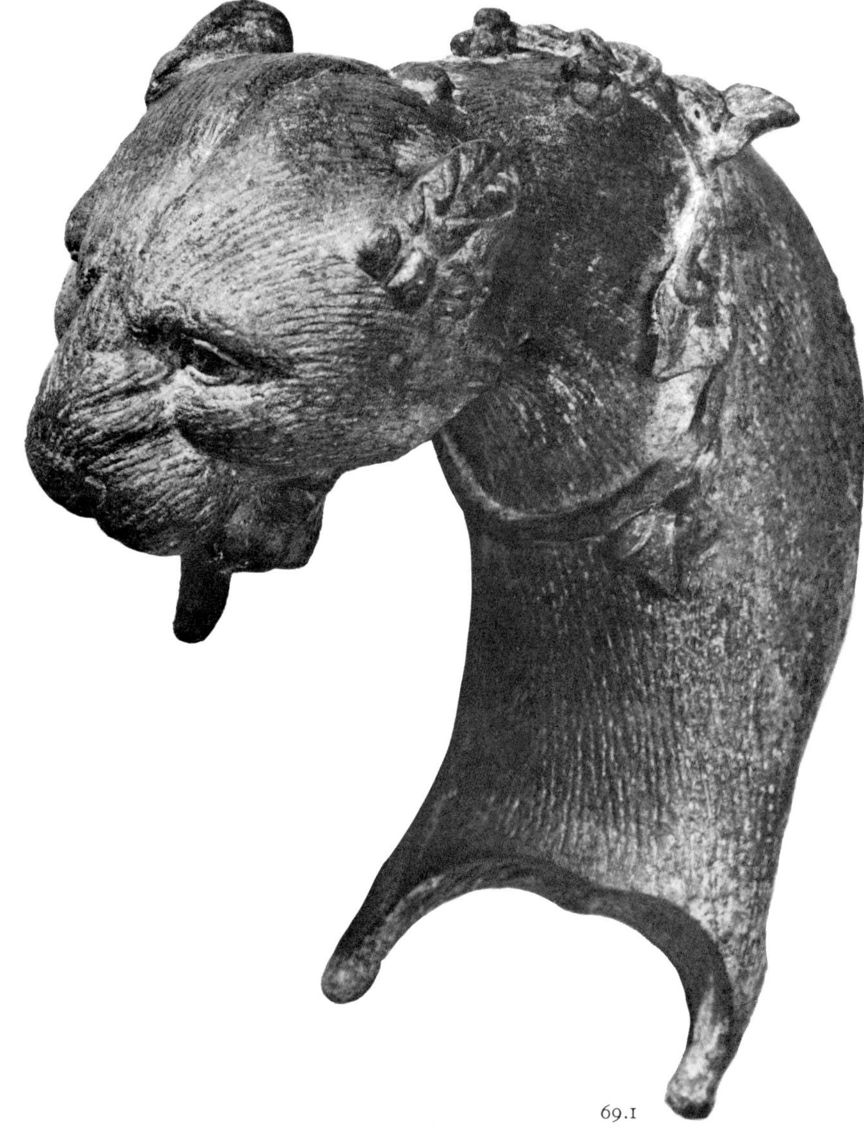

69.1

1. C. Boube-Piccot, "Les lits de bronze de Maurétanie Tingitane," *Bulletin d'archéologie marocaine* 4 (1960) 246–247.
2. C. Seiterle and A. Mutz, "Ein hellenistiches Bronzebett im Basler Antikenmuseum," *AntK* 25 (1982) 62–65. J. Petit, *Bronzes antiques de la collection Dutuit, Paris. Palais des Beaux-Arts* (Paris, 1980), 44–46, no. 7.
3. E. Diehl, "Bronzener Silenskopf von der Lehne eines römischen Bettes," *Jahrbuch des Römisch-Germanischen Zentralmuseums Mainz* 7 (1960) 213, pl. 34.3.

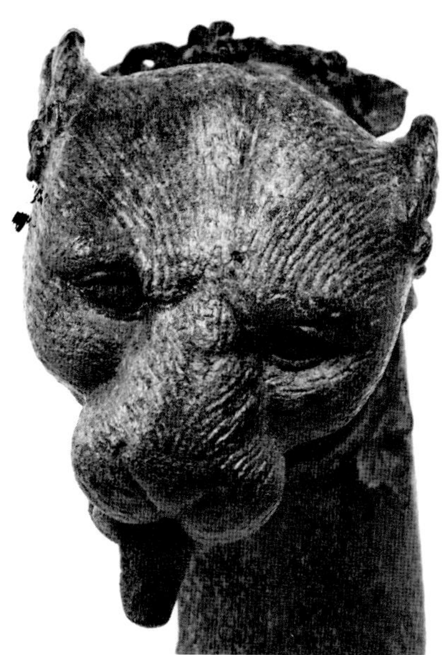

69.2

RING WITH BUST OF SARAPIS

Third to second century

54.1624. Bronze. Purchased before 1931. Ht, bust 4.3 cm; Th, bezel and bust 2.7 cm; Inner D, hoop 2.2 cm.

The vertical shoulder has an oval bezel on which is a high relief bust of Sarapis including his shoulders and part of his chest. He has a mustache and beard, and he wears a sleeved chiton; folds of his mantle lie on his left shoulder. His wavy hair is surmounted by a fillet and modios.

Publications: D. K. Hill, "Material on the Cult of Sarapis," *Hesperia* 15 (1946) 67, fig. 6.

The modios identifies the deity as Sarapis who is seen frequently on Hellenistic and Roman gold and gilded bronze rings, occasionally in combination with Isis.[1] Other variations are known; a similar image on a bronze ring in London wears a crown of feathers that identifies Sarapis with Zeus Ammon.[2] Although the origin of this type of ring is clearly Egyptian, rings with Sarapis busts were probably made in workshops around the eastern Mediterranean as the Sarapis cult spread in popularity.

1. For the type, see F. H. Marshall, *Catalogue of the Finger Rings, Greek, Etruscan, and Roman in the Department of Antiquities. British Museum* (London, 1907), 204, nos. 1298–1302, pl. 31. The example with Isis is 204, no. 1298, pl. 31. See also R. Winkes and T. Hackens, eds., *Love for Antiquity,* Archaeologia Transatlantica 7 (Louvain, 1985), 109, no. 83.
2. Marshall (note 1) 204, no. 1299, pl. 31.

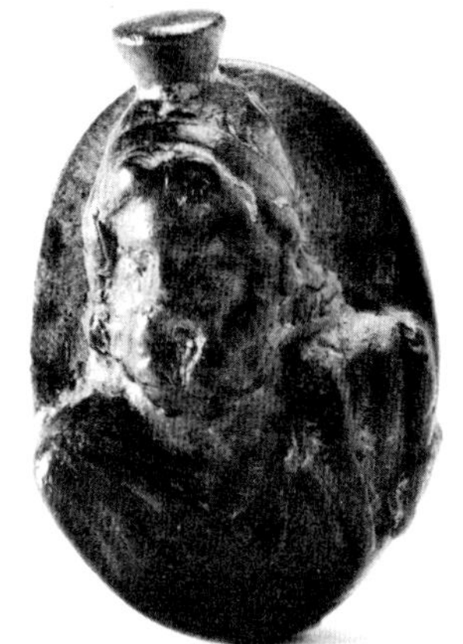

70.1

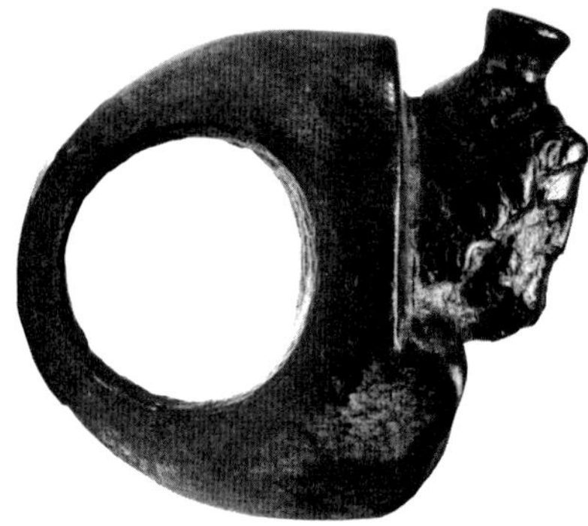

70.2

Statuette of Aphrodite Anadyomene
Late first century

54.948. Bronze. Possibly Hirsch Collection. Purchased from Kelekian in 1913. Ht, 21.9 cm; W, 8 cm; Depth, 4.6 cm. Repaired at left knee.

A nude maiden stands on her left leg with her right knee relaxed and her foot to one side. Her elbows are bent with the forearms uplifted. Her head is turned slightly to her right, and beneath a stephane her long center-parted hair is gathered in two locks, each of which is brought forward over the shoulder and held by her hand. Her pupils are indented.

Exhibitions and Catalogues: *Thou Shalt Have No Other Gods Before Me,* The Jewish Museum (New York, May 3–September 6, 1964), catalogue by A. Farkas with R. Arnold, no. 223, ill.

Publications: Hill, *Bronzes,* 92, no. 201, pl. 42; *LIMC* II (1984) pt. 1, 55, no. 430, pt. 2, 41, fig. 430.

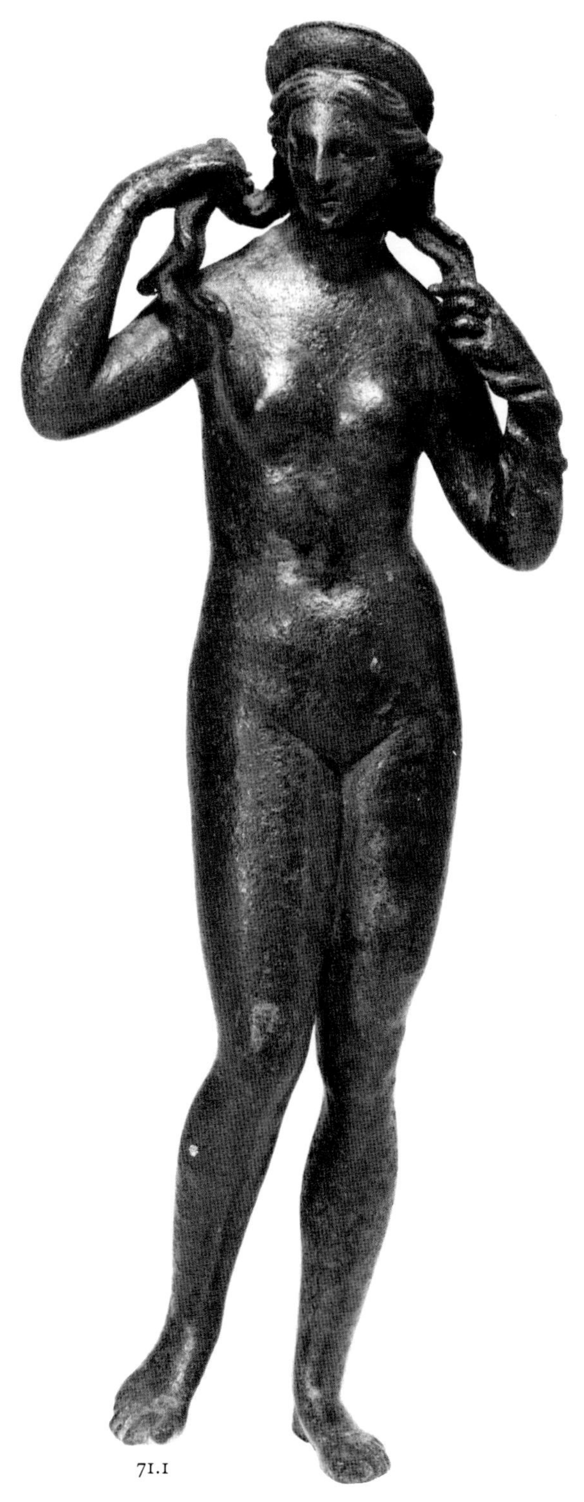

71.1

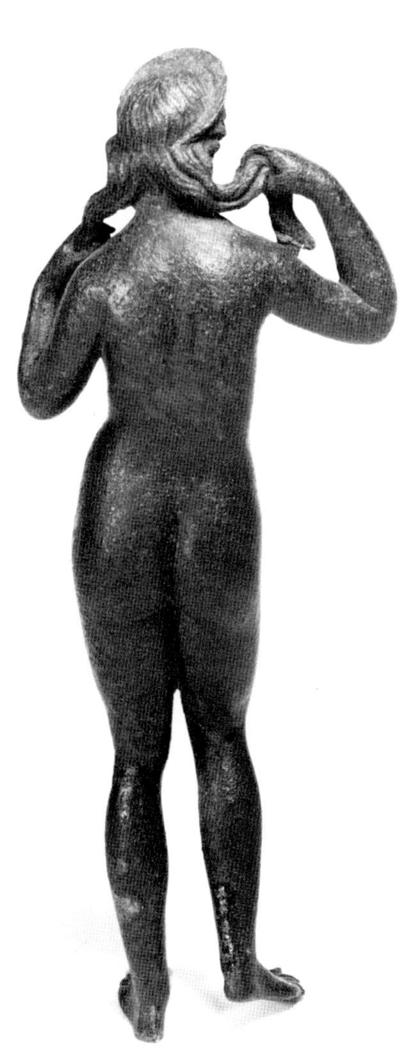

71.2

Statuette of Aphrodite Anadyomene
Late first century

54.954. Bronze. "From Greece." Purchased before 1931. Ht, 26.5 cm; W, 8.8 cm; Depth, 6.2 cm. Whites of eyes probably silvered. Missing are left forearm and the long locks of hair on each side of the face; stephane is chipped. Ancient base may not belong.

A female nude stands with her weight on her left leg, her right relaxed. The hands of her upraised arms held a lock of hair on each side of her head which is inclined to her right. She wears a stephane on her center-parted hair, and her pupils are indented.

Exhibitions and Catalogues: *The Greek Tradition in Painting and the Minor Arts,* The Walters Art Gallery and the Baltimore Museum of Art (Baltimore, May 15–June 25, 1939), 66, no. 53; *4000 Years of Modern Art,* Baltimore Museum of Art (Baltimore, November 27, 1956–January 13, 1957), 36, no. 10 and ill. on 8; *From the Shipwreck of Time: 100 Greek and Roman Antiquities,* Staten Island Museum (New York, February 14–March 28, 1965), no. 11, ill.

Publications: Hill, *Bronzes,* 91, no. 200, pl. 40; *LIMC* II (1984) pt. 1, 56, no. 447.

These two statuettes are testimony to both the popularity of the type of Aphrodite Anadyomene and the variant forms in which it could appear. Rising from the sea as she is born from the froth of the water's surface, Aphrodite wrings out her hair, grasping a long lock in each hand. The prototypical work has been identified as a painting by Apelles of the second half of the fourth century; if correct, then the goddess came to accept her nudity and even to revel in her sensuality not long after her self-conscious modesty in the statue of the Aphrodite of Knidos (Nos. 19, 20).[1] A late Hellenistic date for both Walters figurines is suggested by the soft handling of the torso, which exhibits a far more naturalistic rendering than was seen on the original Praxitelean figure of the Knidia.

1. *LIMC* II (1984) pt. 1, 55.

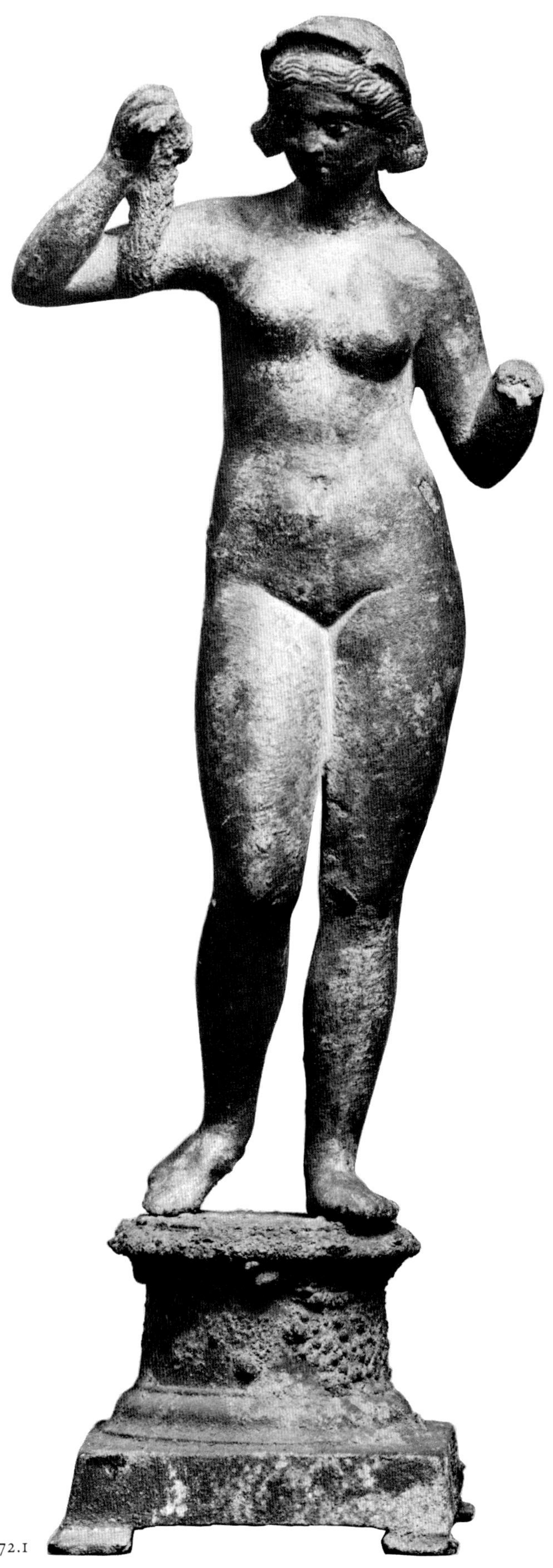

72.1

STATUETTE OF ISIS
Third to first century

54.2016. Bronze. Dattari Collection (sale catalogue, *Collections M. Jean P. Lambros d'Athènes et de M. Giovanni Dattari du Caire,* Paris, Hôtel Drouot, June 17–19, 1912, 48, no. 413, pl. 47). Purchased before 1931. Ht, 34 cm; Ht, to top of head 23.5 cm; W, 8.3 cm; Depth, 11.4 cm. Missing left arm above elbow and tips of wheat in headdress. Broken off at ankles. Right arm and headdress reattached with plaster.

A female stands with her weight evenly distributed on both legs, her left leg advanced. The left upper arm is at her side, the right arm is extended forward with the fingers grasping coils of a cobra whose head rises vertically and whose tail is coiled around her right forearm. She wears a chiton knotted between the breasts and a mantle, which is draped over her left shoulder, frames her right shoulder, and falls behind her back to the ground. She faces front to gaze at the cobra; her pupils are indented. Her hair or wig has short coiled locks across the forehead, and falls upon the front and back of her shoulders in horizontal rows of ringlets. Her headdress consists of a vulture cap beneath a polos surmounted by two stalks of wheat flanking attenuated horns. Between the horns are two plumes above a disc upon which a cobra is coiled.

Exhibitions and Catalogues: *Thou Shalt Have No Other Gods Before Me,* Jewish Museum (New York, May 3–September 6, 1964), catalogue by A. Farkas with R. Arnold, no. 171.

Publications: Steindorff III, no. 417, pl. 72.

Generally considered the most potent deity of the Hellenistic period, Isis was worshiped as a mother goddess and the consort of the immensely popular god Sarapis. Her epithet ''of the myriad names'' demonstrates both the extent of her authority and the monotheistic leanings of Hellenistic religious thought. The debt that Christianity owed to this age-old Egyptian goddess is revealed by the Roman tendency to rededicate many of her shrines to the Virgin Mary.

Comparisons with better-preserved examples indicate that the left arm was bent at the elbow and the forearm was raised, with an attribute grasped in the left hand.[1] Like the Hellenized Isis herself, the type is a curious blend of Egyptian and Greek features. The goddess wears the dress of the Hellenized Isis consisting of a pleated sheath, the ancestry of which lies in the New Kingdom, and a fringed mantle that frames the shoulders and back and is knotted between the breasts. In other,

probably more accurate, renderings of this garb, the mantle passes over the right and under the left shoulder, and the ends are knotted between the breasts.[2] This Hellenized dress with Isis knot is seen as early as 246–222 in faience portraits of Berenike II, where the garment is already a linear, stylized interpretation of its dynastic prototype.[3] The handling of the drapery on the Walters goddess has apparently also been influenced by Greek works in the archaizing style, because the paryphe, or central panel between the legs, is flanked by stacked pleats and concentric radiating folds.

We can assign the Walters figurine to the late Hellenistic period when a bronze parallel from Pompeii and a plaster piece-mold from Mit-Rahine can be dated with reasonable certainty.[4] The Walters goddess was surely also made by using plaster piece-molds to assemble a wax model that was then cast in one piece. This process of manufacture contrasts with that of such statuettes as the Dionysos from Erment (No. 65) whose left arm was soldered onto the torso after casting.

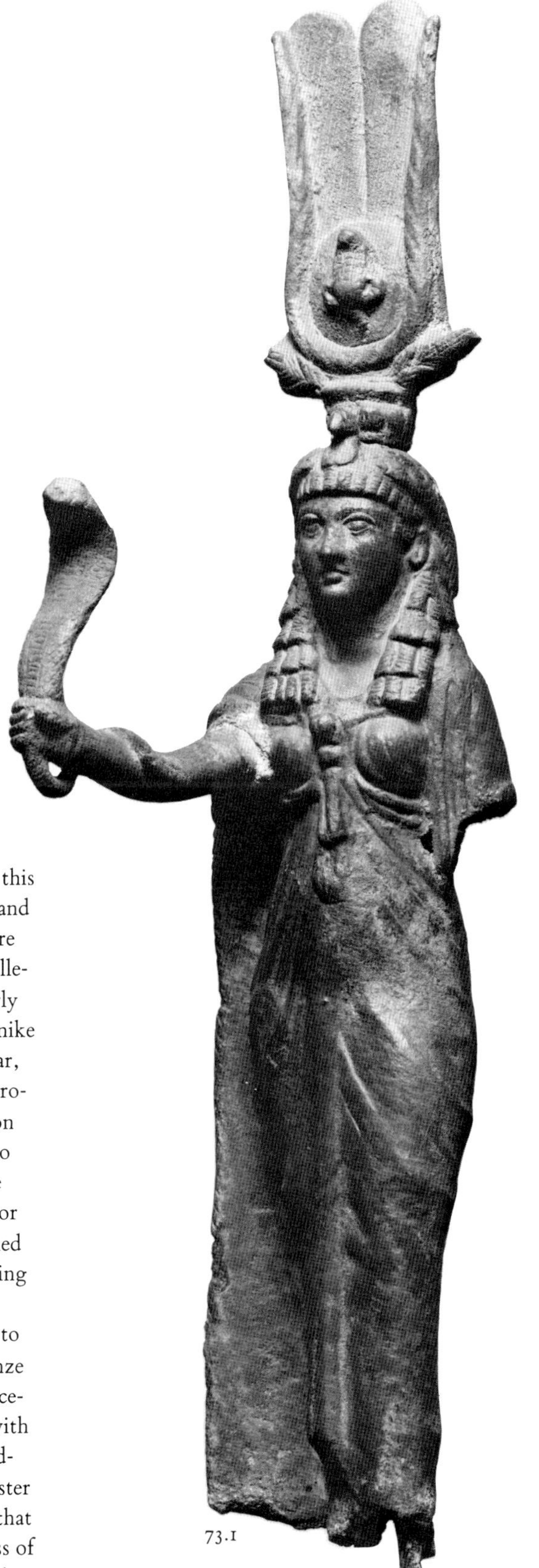

73.1

1. M. C. C. Edgar, *Greek Bronzes,* Catalogue général des antiquités égyptiennes du musée du Caire 19 (Cairo, 1904), 10, no. 27.669, pl. 4.
2. Thompson, *Oinochoai,* 30–31, 103.
3. Ibid., 122, 165, pl. 43.
4. For the example from Pompeii, see J. Petit, *Bronzes antiques de la collection Dutuit, Paris. Palais des Beaux-Arts* (Paris, 1980), 63–64, no. 16. For the mold from Mit-Rahine, see M. C. C. Edgar, *Greek Moulds,* Catalogue général des antiquités égyptiennes du musée du Caire 8 (Cairo, 1903), 15, no. 32.050, pl. 22.

STATUETTE OF A NUDE ATHLETE
First century

54.699. Bronze. "Probably from Egypt." Purchased from Kelekian in 1928. Ht, 17.8 cm; W, 7 cm; Depth, 4.2 cm. Thumb, fingertips and attribute missing from right hand; tip of left index finger broken away. Bottoms of feet have been filed.

A nude youth stands with his weight on his right leg, his left leg relaxed with the left foot to one side. His left arm, the fingers lightly closed, hangs at his side. His right forearm is extended from the hip with the palm upward, the fingers curled to clasp a missing object. He has a strongly modeled brow and turns his head to his left; his hair is rendered as a smooth cap.

Publications: Reinach, *Statuaire* 5 (1924) 291, no. 7; Hill, *Bronzes,* 82, no. 176, pl. 35, reviewed by F. Eichler, *Gnomon* 23 (1951) 61.

The long limbs and small head point to a late Hellenistic date, when elongation is frequently encountered in classicizing works of art. Also compatible with this date are the exaggerated breadth of the shoulders and backward curve of the torso, the stationary and presentational effect achieved by the placement of the relaxed leg to the side of the engaged leg, the position of the left arm almost at the side, and the downward-directed gaze.[1] The smooth cap of hair on the Walters athlete appears to derive directly from early Classical prototypes and compares favorably with the hair of a bronze statu-

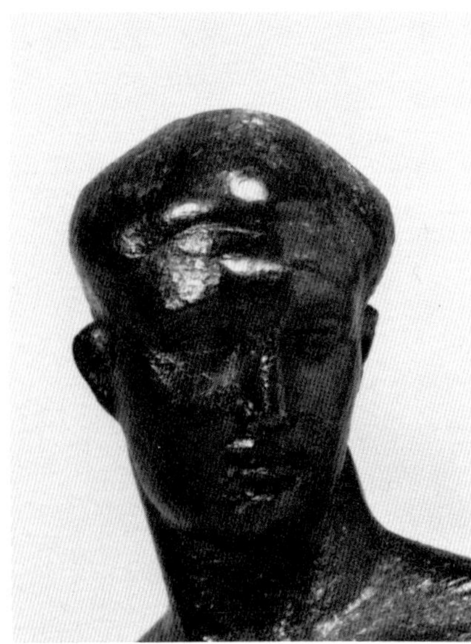

74.3

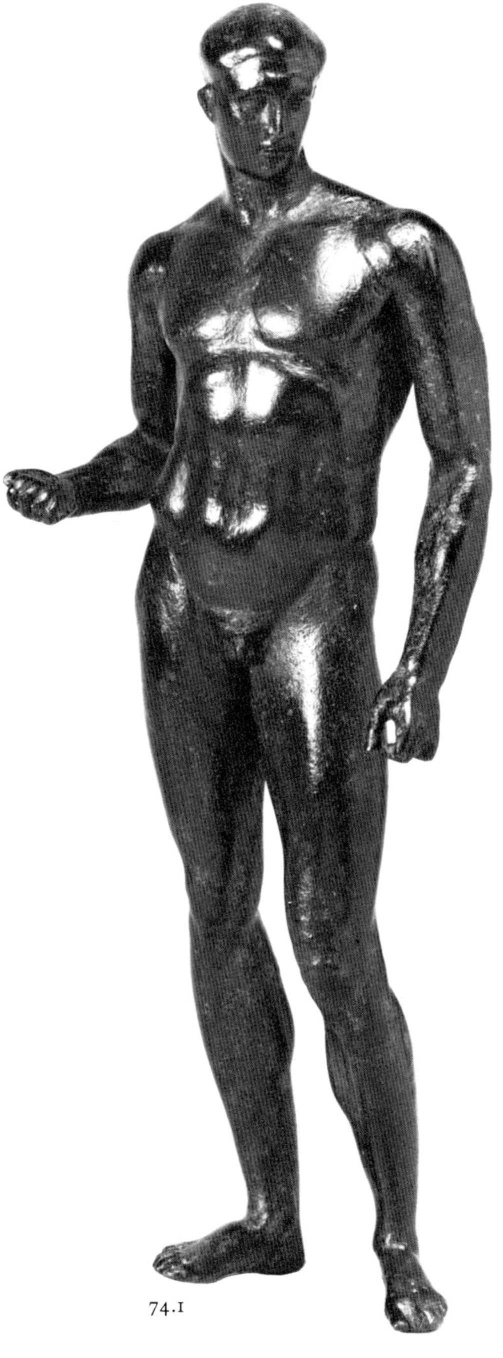

74.1

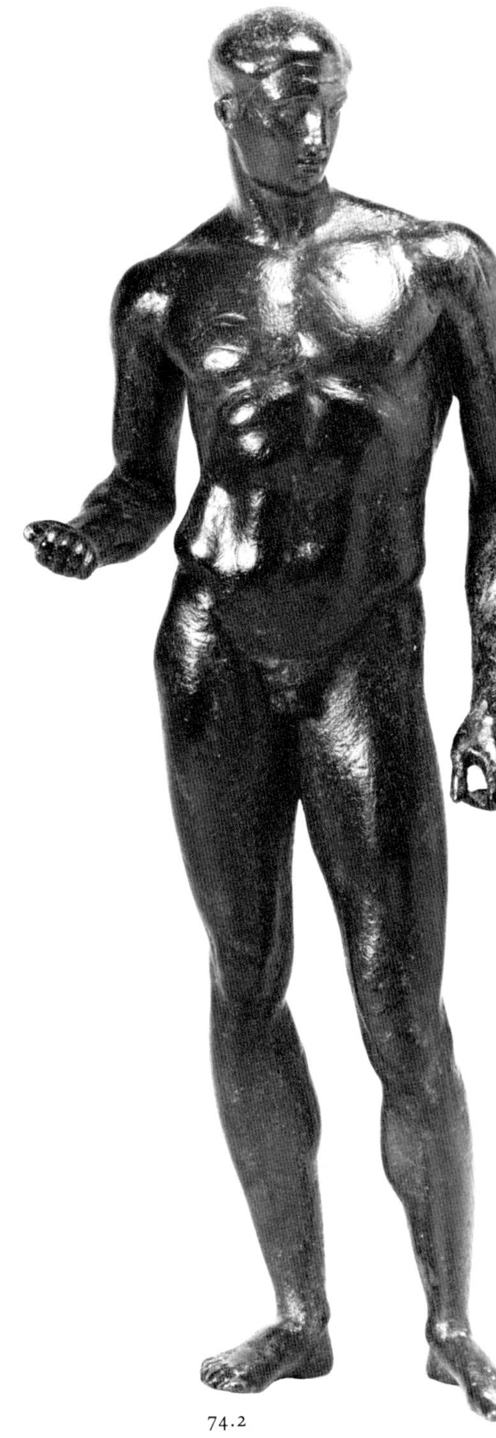

74.2

ette of a diskos thrower in New York.[2] The sway to the right of the upper torso of the Walters figure and the lightly closed fingers of the left hand convey a rhythm in keeping with Hill's suggestion that the athlete is a diskos player preparing for competition.

1. Compare the classicizing treatment and head angle of a bronze statuette in Paris: J. Petit, *Bronzes antiques de la collection Dutuit, Paris. Palais des Beaux-Arts* (Paris, 1980), 88, 92–93, no. 32.
2. See the bronze statuette, dated ca. 480, in G. M. A. Richter, *The Metropolitan Museum of Art: Greek, Etruscan and Roman Bronzes* (New York, 1915), 48–51, no. 78, acc. no. 07.286.87.

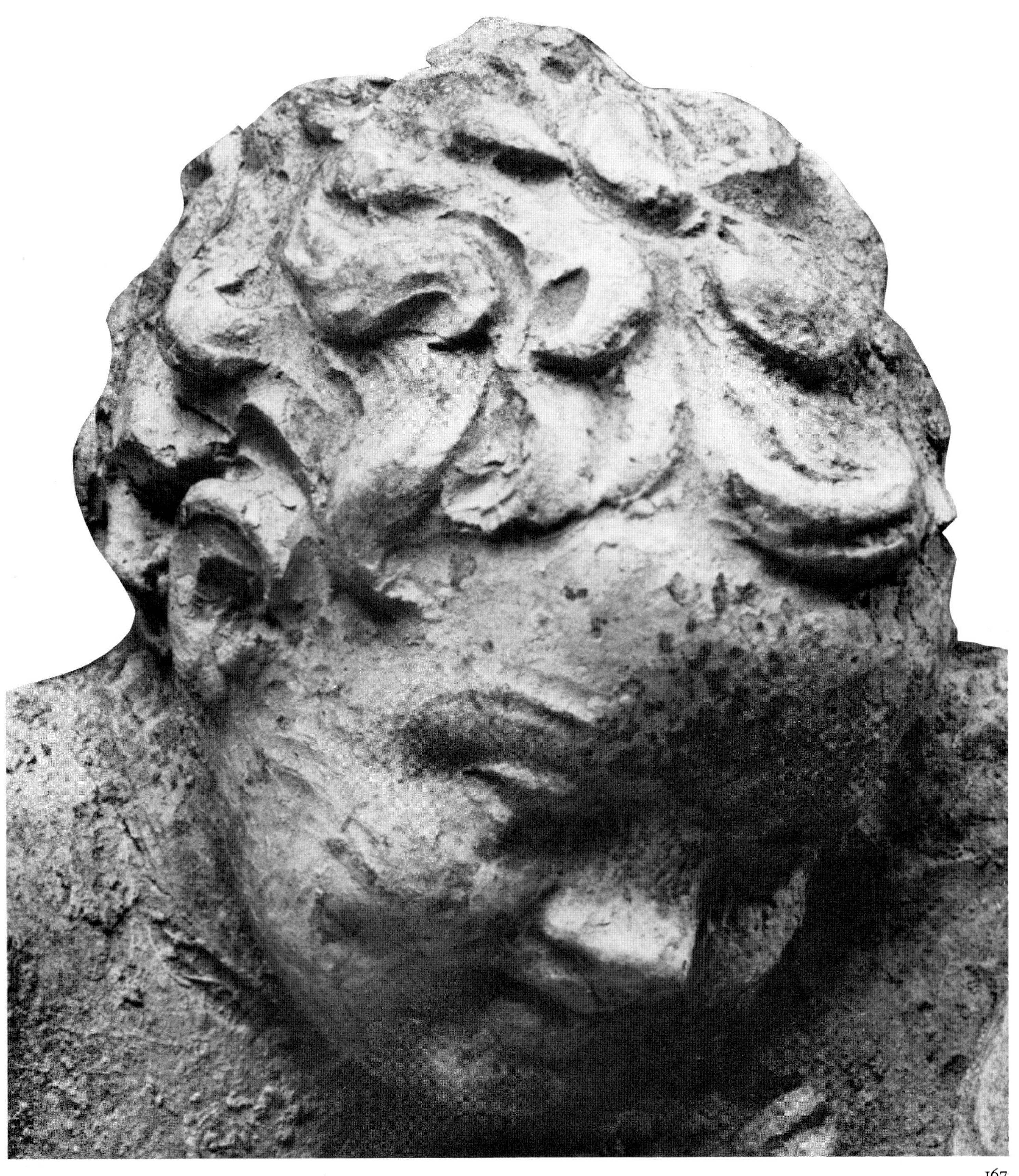

Figurine of a
Standing Maiden
Ca. 300

48.297. Terracotta. Purchased in 1925. Ht, 21.3 cm; Ht, vent hole 2.3 cm; L, vent hole 1.5 cm; L, base 8.2 cm; W, base 5.5 cm; Ht, base 0.6 cm. Rectangular vent hole at center back. White slip with traces of pink on drapery, red on hair and lips. Low, rectangular base reattached. Mended from several pieces. Restored areas include breasts, left forearm, right thigh, left thigh, and drapery behind left shoulder. Authenticity established by thermoluminescence.

A maiden stands on her right leg, her left leg to one side, her head turned to her right. Her left arm hangs at her side, its hand enveloped by the mantle folds. Her right arm is bent at the elbow with the forearm resting behind her right hip. Over a peplos or chiton, she wears a mantle which is draped completely around her torso above the knees with the ends wrapped around the left forearm. She has Venus rings, large round earrings, and her hair is arranged in a melon hairstyle with a knot at the nape.

Publications: D. K. Hill, *Ancient Greek Dress* (Baltimore, 1945), 11.

This maiden is an example of a Tanagra figurine, which take its name from a site in mainland Greece where large quantities of a distinctive type of terracotta figurine were discovered in the late nineteenth century.[1] Most of the figurines represent quietly standing draped women and children rendered with subtle charm. They were produced by means of front and back molds, and placed on low plaque bases, with a small vent hole in the back. Many of the figurines retain extensive areas of color which was applied after firing. In contrast with the predominantly votive or funerary use and religious iconography of terracotta figurines from the Archaic and Classical periods, Tanagra figurines served a primarily secular role as household decoration. The type originated in Athens about 330, and soon afterwards was manufactured in many centers around the eastern Mediterranean. The figurines continued to be made almost to the end of the Hellenistic age, although production ceased in Tanagra itself soon after 200. The popularity that the figurines enjoyed in the late nineteenth and early twentieth centuries stimulated a mass of forgeries which were often difficult to recognize, and the resulting confusion discouraged many scholars from carrying out research in this area. Only in recent years has it been possible to determine, almost unequivocally, the authenticity of a figurine through thermoluminescence testing.

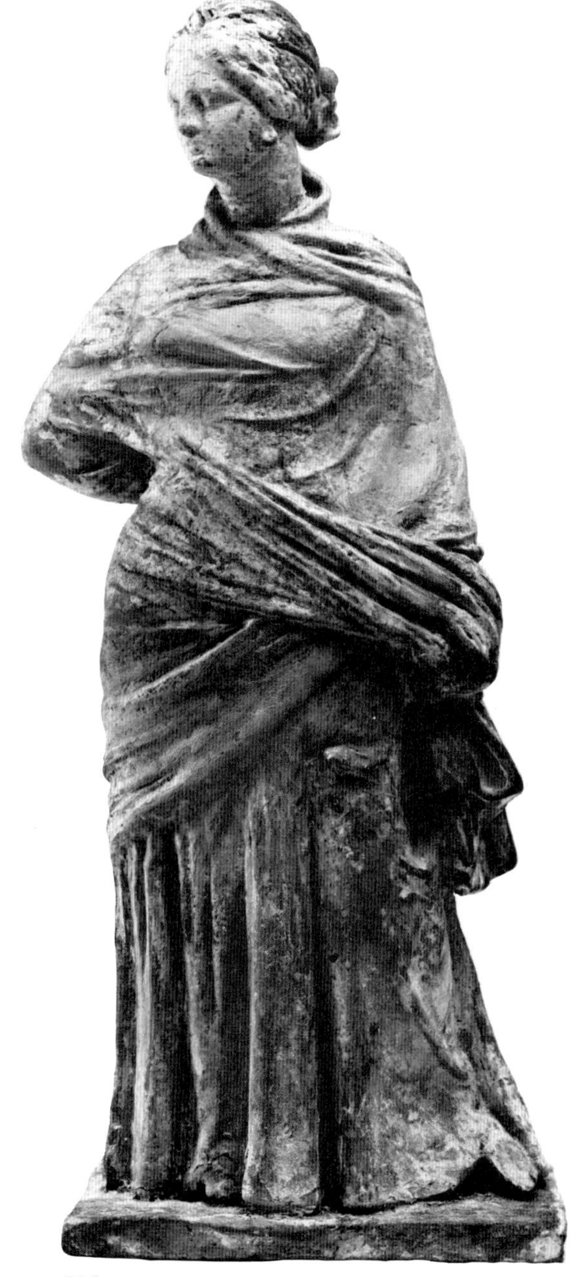

75.1

Tanagra figurines have a special appeal for the modern viewer because they gracefully evoke the elusive world of the ancient female. In Hellenistic times women's garments were made of linen or wool, in the latter case preferably of fabric loomed in the area around Miletos on the western coast of Asia Minor.[2] By the second century, silk cloth or thread was imported from China; silk cloth was also woven in Kos from thread obtained from the wild silkworm of western Asia. So expensive was silk thread that it was often combined with linen in a fabric woven with a linen warp and silk weft.[3] Garments were dyed bright colors, especially yellow, and probably carried extensive embroidered decoration.[4] Complementing this sartorial finery were elaborate hairstyles of the so-called melon type, in which broad sections of hair were brought back from the face to the back of the head. Cosmetics included face powder made of lead soaked in vinegar, rouge fashioned from seaweed or mulberries, and eyeshadow of lampblack or antimony.[5]

FIGURINE OF A STANDING BOY WITH SACK
Ca. 330–300

Balancing this elegant picture is the sobering and long-established practice of female infanticide which is thought to have continued through Hellenistic times. Widely documented are families consisting of many sons but only one daughter, and Polybios, living in the second century, stated that in his day parents refused to rear more than one child, who would almost certainly be male.[6]

The Walters example belongs to a well-known type that originated not long before 300 when the closest parallel, an example in Leiden, has been dated.[7] Both figurines display a crispness of detail that testifies to the freshness of the molds from which they were impressed. The development of the type can be followed through the third century in figurines that exhibit a progressive disintegration of the tautly defined patterns of drapery that demarcate the forms of the Walters maiden.[8] Heads of differing type inclined in both directions were regularly substituted; on the example in Leiden the mantle folds lie over the head, and other figurines wear kerchiefs.[9] The Boeotian clay of the Leiden example, the Tanagran provenance of a piece in the British Museum, and the Italian and Sicilian findspots of examples of third-century dates demonstrate how widely the type became diffused throughout the Hellenistic world.[10]

1. Higgins, *Tanagra,* 24, 42, 65–69, 119–120, 166; D. B. Thompson, ''The Origins of Tanagras,'' *AJA* 70 (1966), 51–63.
2. M. Johnson, ed., *Ancient Greek Dress* (Chicago, 1964), 97. For the ''Attalid brocade'' that was made in Pergamon and interwoven with gold threads, see Tarn 168.
3. Johnson (note 2) 99; E. Gullberg and P. Aström, *The Thread of Ariadne, SIMA* 21 (Göteborg, 1970), 1, 17; Tarn 256.
4. M. Davenport, *The Book of Costume* (New York, 1949), 73.
5. Johnson (note 2) 123.
6. Tarn 100, 102.
7. Leyenaar-Plaisier 105, no. 211, pl. 36.
8. Leyenaar-Plaisier 511, no. 1495, pl. 190; Higgins, *Tanagra,* 132–133, fig. 158, and 133, fig. 159; 134, fig. 160; Bell, *Morgantina,* 180, no. 404, pl. 86; 180, no. 405, pl. 86.
9. For the kerchief, see Higgins, *Terracottas,* 102, no. C311, pl. 44c. For the mantle folds, see ibid., 127, no. D120, pl. 60b.
10. For the figurine in Leiden, see Leyenaar-Plaisier 105, no. 211, pl. 36. For the piece in the British Museum, see Higgins, *Terracottas,* 102, no. C311, pl. 44c. For examples with Italian and Sicilian provenances, see Besques, *Italie,* 36, no. D3478, pl. 26c; 36, no. D3480, pl. 26e; 36, no. D3481, pl. 26f. See also Breitenstein 59, no. 548, pl. 67.

48.298. Terracotta. Purchased in 1925. Ht, 17.7 cm; Ht, vent hole 2 cm; L, vent hole 1.8 cm; L, base 5.8 cm; W, base 4 cm; Ht, base 0.5 cm. Rectangular vent hole at center back. White slip; traces of pink. Left hand and part of base broken away. Head reattached.

A boy stands with his weight on his right leg; he leans with his left elbow on a pillar and rests his left foot upon the pillar's base. His head is inclined down and to his right; his mantle is draped over his left shoulder and arm, is brought around his back, and falls down his right side over his right leg. His right arm hangs at his side, the hand clasping folds of the fabric. He holds a sack in his left hand and wears a wreath over short curly hair.

Among the most appealing of the Tanagra figurines are representations of children. Their youthful bodies are still imperfectly understood by the koroplasts who made them, but their charm and sweetness are captured with sympathy and affection. This boy leans against a pillar in a Praxitelean pose and clasps a bag that probably held astragaloi, or knucklebones, which were used in a game of love oracles. The stippling indicates that his thick wreath was made of flowers. On a figurine of the same type from Tanagra, the substitution of a different head gazing in the opposite direction illustrates the ease with which koroplasts interchanged heads and bodies to create fresh compositions.[1] That figurine was molded together with a spool base more typical of the early and middle fourth century, a feature which provides additional argument that the type dates from the beginning of the Hellenistic age.

In Hellenistic times both boys and girls learned to read and write in privately funded elementary schools. Education beyond this point was a male preserve, culminating at the age of nineteen or twenty with a year spent as an ephebe, an experience that combined athletic and military training, especially in the bow and javelin, with the study of literature and philosophy.[2]

1. Higgins, *Terracottas,* 151, fig. 183.
2. Tarn 96. See also Austin, *Hellenistic World,* 201–213, nos. 117–120; M. Hadas, *Hellenistic Culture* (New York, 1959), 65.

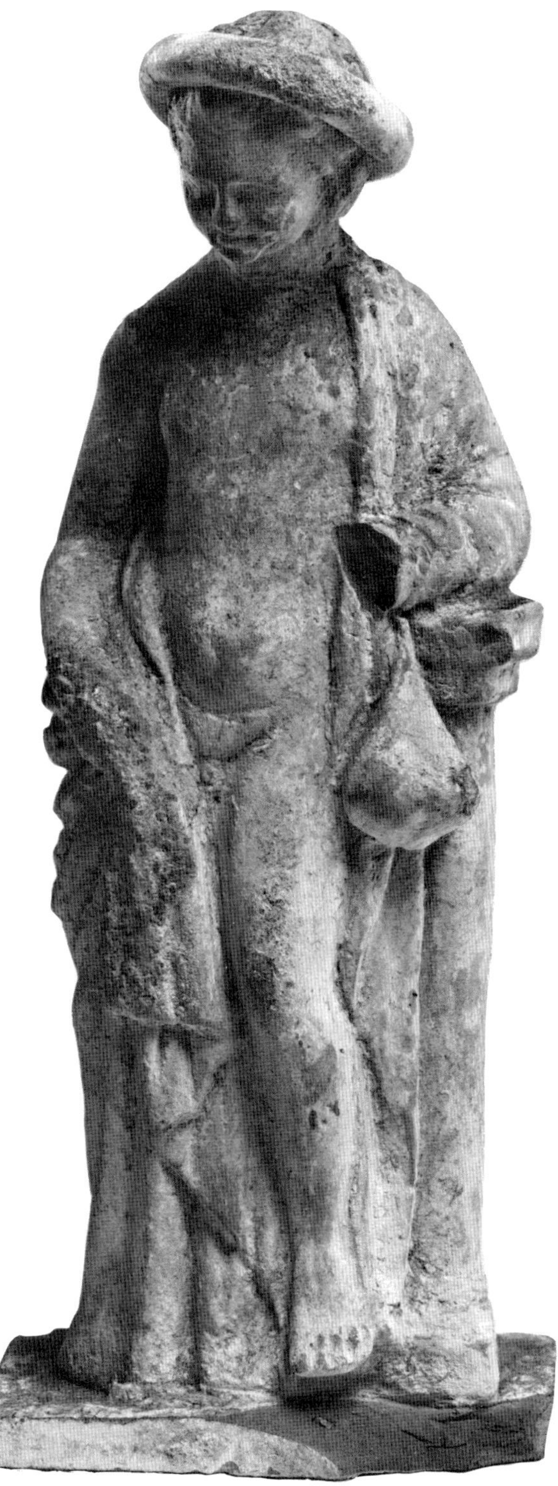

76.1

Figurine of a Standing Maiden with Clasped Hands
Ca. 300

48.285. Terracotta. Purchased from Brummer in 1927. Ht, 20.4 cm; Ht, vent hole 2.5 cm; W, vent hole 3 cm; L, base 4.7 cm; W, base 6.4 cm; Ht, base 0.7 cm. Large rectangular vent hole in back; heavy white slip. Gray deposit over surface. Base and head reattached; nose restored. Edge of vent hole broken away.

A maiden stands with her weight on her right leg, her left leg relaxed and to the side. Her right hand clasps her left wrist in front of her abdomen; her head is tilted slightly to her right. She wears a peplos or chiton which is visible only below the waist and which conceals her right foot. Her mantle is draped across her torso, covering both arms to the mid-forearm, and over her left leg to midcalf. The ends are thrown back over her left shoulder and hang down her left side. Her center-parted hair is gathered at the nape, and she wears ball earrings. The base of the statuette is low and rectangular.

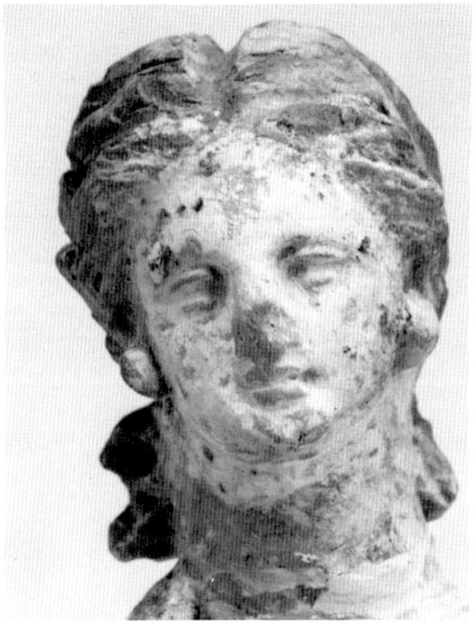

77.2

This figurine must surely reproduce a major original work of ca. 350–300, which was distinguished by the clasped hands in front of the abdomen and by the loops of drapery over the left shoulder, between the breasts and over the left upper arm, and from the waist across the left calf. The Walters figurine substitutes a frontal head for the inclined and leftward-turned head of the prototype, but remains otherwise faithful to the type, comparing well with terracotta versions from Tanagra in London and Copenhagen that have been dated about 300.[1]

1. Breitenstein 58, no. 543, pl. 66; Higgins, *Tanagra,* 136 and 138, fig. 166.

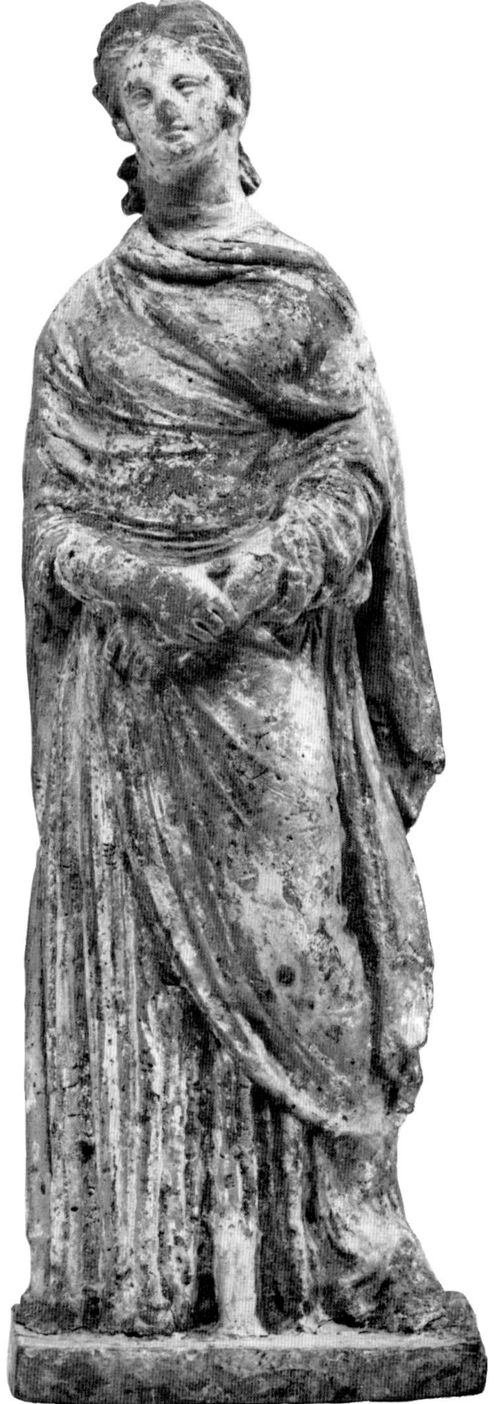

77.1

Figurine of a Maiden Playing Knucklebones

Late fourth or early third century

48.303. Terracotta. "From Tarentum." Hirsch Collection (sale catalogue, Paris, Hôtel Drouot, June 30–July 2, 1921, 19, no. 132, pl. 3). Purchased, possibly from Sambon, in 1924 together with No. 79. Ht, 15.2 cm; W, 6.3 cm; Depth, 10.8 cm. Open beneath. Back roughly worked. Traces of white slip; red paint on hair. Right arm broken above elbow. Missing fingertips of left hand and edge of wreath; hole in back of head.

A maiden crouches with both knees bent, her right thigh lowered with the toes resting on the ground behind her, her left lower leg drawn up with the foot flat on the ground beneath her. Her left elbow is bent with the forearm pressed against her left knee and the fingers of her left hand extended. She wears a peplos girt beneath the breasts, and shoes. Her center-parted hair forms a knot at the crown and is gathered back at the nape; she wears a tainia, the ends of which fall forward over each shoulder. She also has large round earrings and Venus ring.

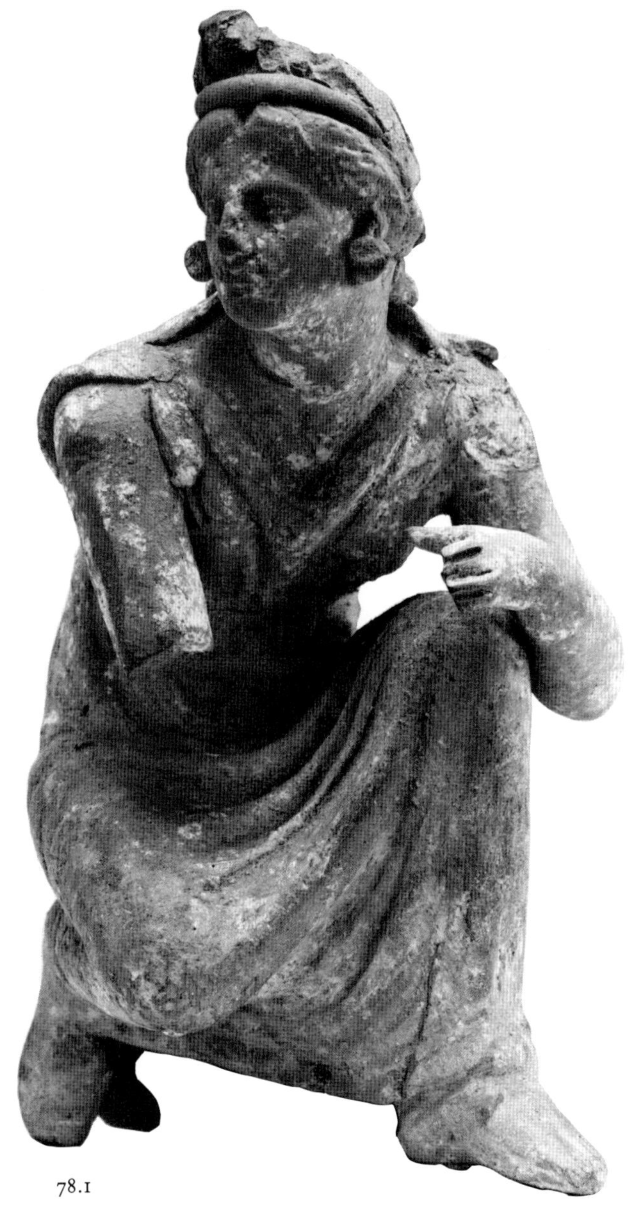

78.1

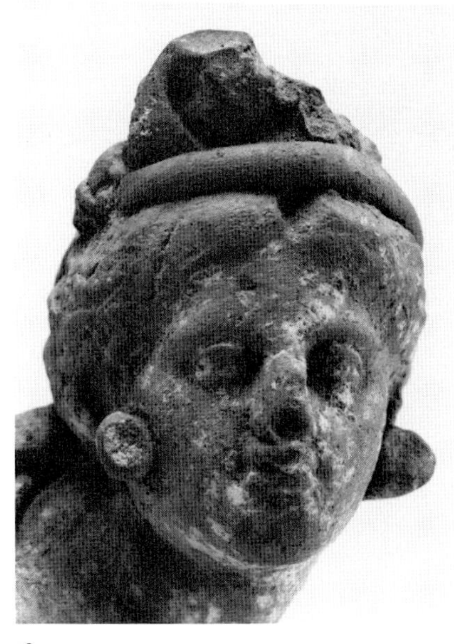

78.2

FIGURINE OF A MAIDEN
PLAYING KNUCKLEBONES
Late fourth or early third century

48.304. Terracotta. "From Tarentum." Hirsch Collection (sale catalogue, Paris, Hôtel Drouot, June 30–July 2, 1921, 19, no. 132, pl. 3). Purchased, possibly from Sambon, in 1924 together with no. 78. Ht, 14.9 cm; W, 6.6 cm; Depth, 11.2 cm. Open beneath. White slip. Red on hair. Right arm broken at shoulder; left arm broken across elbow. Missing right earring.

A maiden gazing to her left crouches with both knees bent, right thigh lowered with the toes resting on the ground behind her. Her left lower leg is drawn up with the foot flat on the ground beneath her. The upper torso leans forward with the left elbow resting on the left knee. She wears a peplos girt beneath the breasts, and shoes. Her hair is arranged in a melon hairstyle with the ends coiled at the back of her head; she also wears ball earrings.

In the ancient game of knucklebones, popularly known as astragaloi or pentelithoi (literally "five stones"), five bones from the ankle joints of sheep or goats were tossed in the air and caught on the back of the hand.[1] The game was popularly associated with romantic predictions and, for this reason, came to be linked with Eros. In a fragmentary text by Kallimachos written in the middle of the third century, Aphrodite promises her son five new knucklebones from a Libyan gazelle.[2] The first representation of the subject in terracotta dates from the middle of the fourth century, together with other representations in terracotta of a crouching or kneeling figure with the foot of the relaxed leg flat on the ground.[3] The type does not remain exclusively in the preserve of astragalos players; examples from Myrina of the second century represent both nude and draped maidens arranging their hair in the tradition of the Doidalsas Aphrodite.[4]

The deep V-neckline of the garments worn by the Walters maidens suggests a late fourth- or early third-century date which is consistent with the circlet worn by one maiden and the large disc of braids seen on her companion.[5] A very close parallel in Copenhagen, which exhibits the identical corrugated drapery folds, is also said to be from Italy and so reinforces the likelihood that the Walters maidens were indeed made in Tarentum.[6] The identical

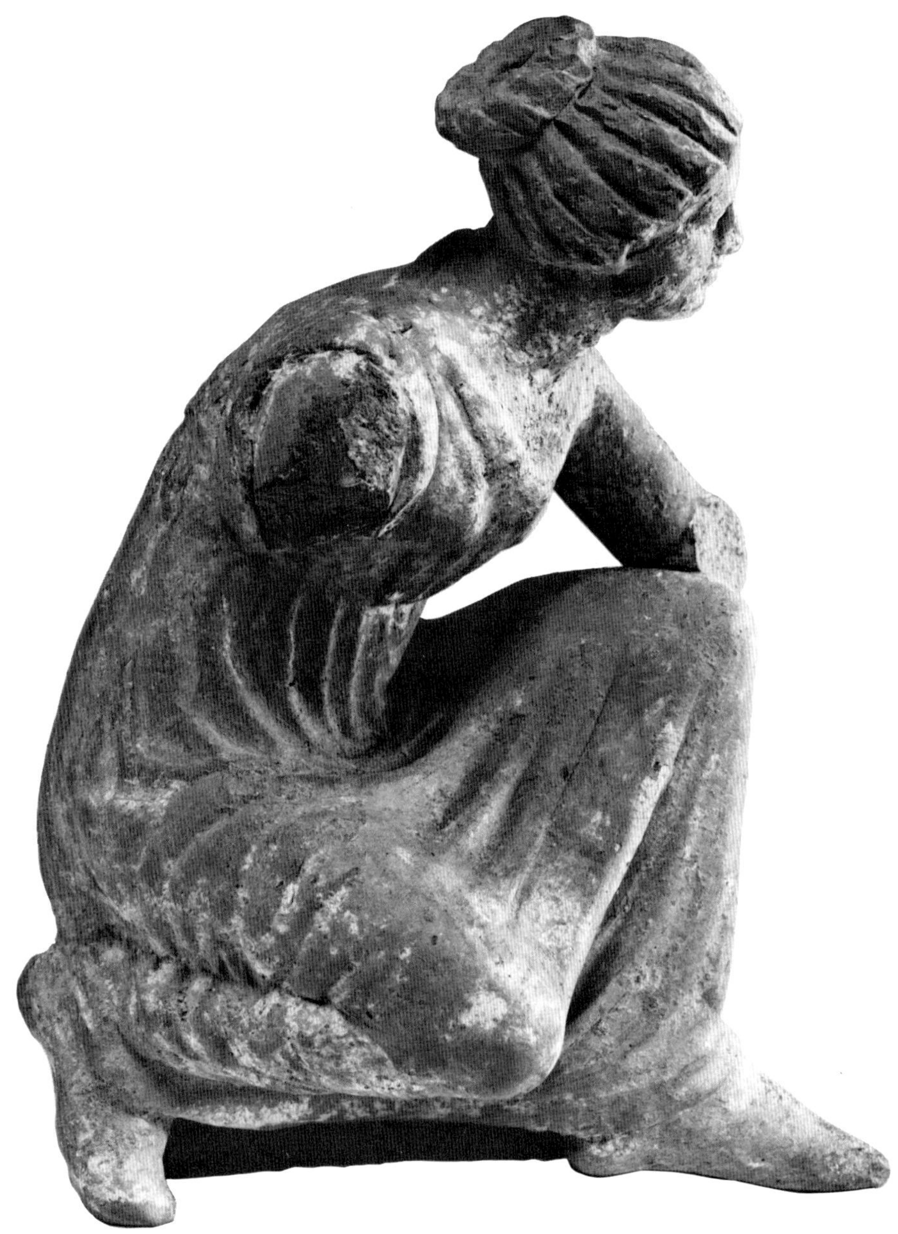

79.1

provenances of the two figurines, their close similarity in style, and the logical presentation of the figures as competitors argue that the two maidens were made as a pair; they thus serve as further evidence for the existence of Hellenistic sculptural groups in which figures were juxtaposed, but not contiguous. Additional examples of this type of composition are the black slave, No. 58, and the nude warrior, No. 62.

1. Higgins, *Terracottas,* 143.
2. Kallimachos, fr. 677.
3. Higgins (note 1) 145, fig. 175 (dated 330–300) and 129, pl. 61a (dated ca. 330). See also Besques, *Grèce,* 30, no. D160, pl. 36c, dated ca. 300.
4. Mollard-Besques, *Myrina,* 19, no. Myr. 18, pl. 18a-e, dated 150–100; Leyenaar-Plaisier 259, no. 681, pl. 96 from Myrina, dated 200–150.
5. Thompson, *Troy,* 35, 40, 44.
6. V. Poulsen, *Catalogue des terres cuites grecques et romaines* (Copenhagen, 1949), 43, no. 89, pl. 48.

FIGURINE OF A YOUTH
WITH WREATH
Early third century

48.278. Terracotta. Purchased from Brummer in 1925. Ht, 16.2 cm; Ht, vent hole 2.1 cm; W, vent hole 1.7 cm; L, base 5.6 cm; W, base 4 cm; Ht, base 0.7 cm. Small rectangular vent hole in center of back. Repaired from several pieces. Base broken and reattached, with right front corner broken away.

A youth stands with his weight on his left leg, his right leg relaxed with the foot to one side. His left hand is at his left hip with the fingers closed over a bird (?); his right arm, completely enveloped by his mantle, is bent at the elbow and brought to his chest. His mantle is draped over his left shoulder and arm, brought around his back, and crosses in front of his body with the edge falling over his left wrist; heavy folds fall to his ankles. His head faces forward and is downturned; his wavy hair is brushed back from his face and is surmounted by a broad stippled wreath. His sandaled feet rest on a low rectangular base.

This youth's quiet frontal pose, inclined gaze, and soft smile epitomize the musing figurines of the Tanagra type. He drapes about himself a mantle, which falls to the ground following youthful convention, and he sports a thick floral wreath made of a grass rope around which have been wrapped blossoms, here rendered by stippling. Dated to the early third century is a similar example in the Louvre, who holds a theatrical mask in his left hand.[1]

With the proliferation of festivals and the increased Egyptian contact of the Hellenistic age, wreaths became extremely popular and were often made with helichrysos, a flower which was said to resemble the Egyptian lotus.[2]

1. Besques, *Grèce,* 32, no. D170, pl. 39a.
2. Thompson, *Troy,* 44–46; Athenaeus, *Deipnosophistae* 15.680.

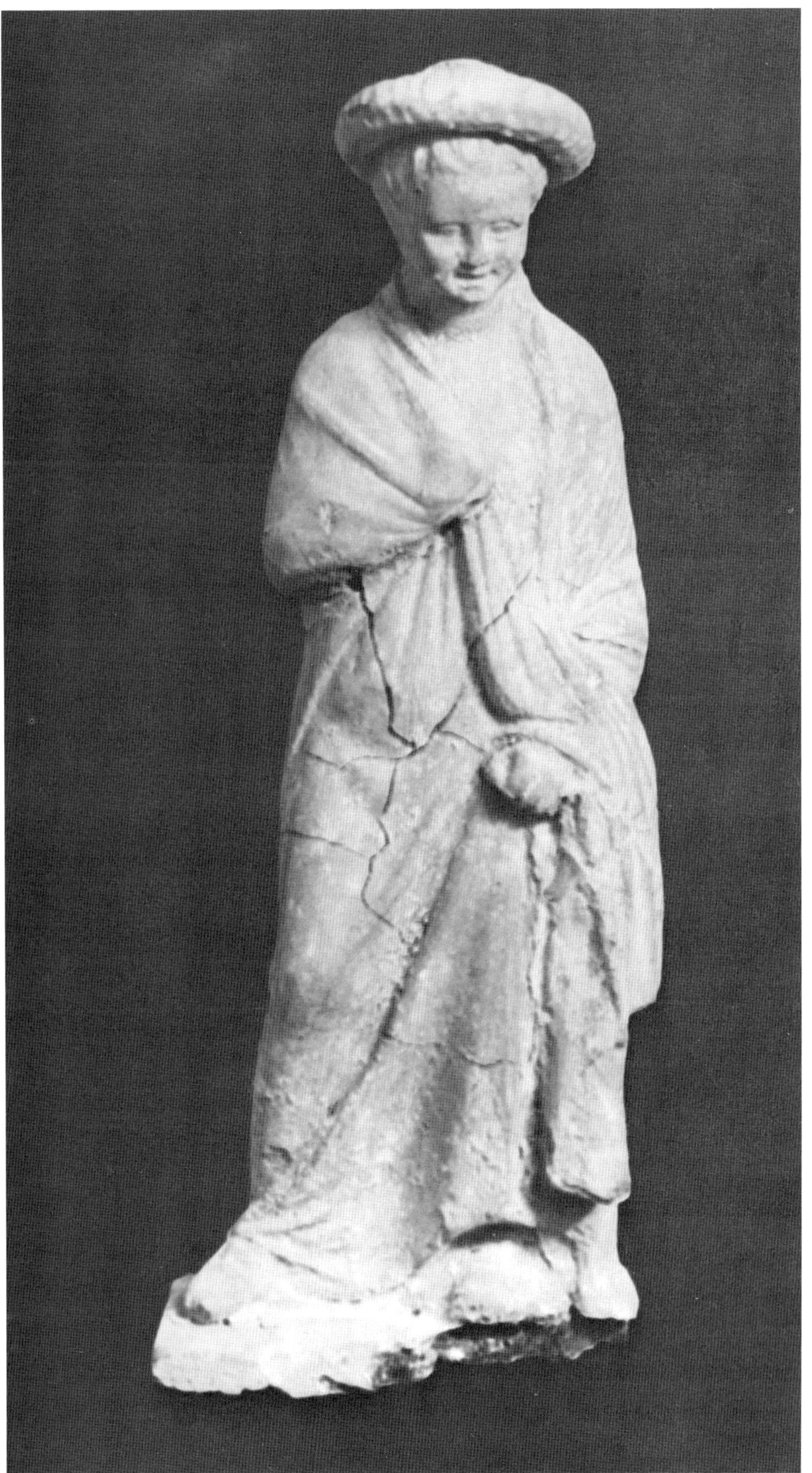

80.1

Figurine of a Standing Maiden with Kerchief

300–275

48.296. Terracotta. Purchased in 1925. Ht, 24.9 cm; Ht, vent hole 2.8 cm; W, vent hole 2.6 cm; L, base 8.5 cm; W, base 7.3 cm; Ht, base 0.5 cm. Rectangular vent hole in back. White slip over surface.

A maiden stands on her left leg with her right knee relaxed and her foot to one side. Her left arm is bent at the elbow with the forearm extended. Her head is inclined towards her left hand which is concealed by her drapery; her right arm, also concealed by drapery, hangs by her side. She wears a short-sleeved garment, which is girt beneath the breasts. Her mantle passes over her left upper arm, frames her back, and is brought across the body between the waist and mid-calf. She has Venus rings and round earrings. Her center-parted, stippled hair is gathered at the nape beneath a kerchief that covers the top of her head. She wears shoes and stands on a low rectangular base.

Publications: D. K. Hill, *Ancient Greek Dress* (Baltimore, 1945), 11.

Her high-girt garment, short sleeves, and crinkled horizontal neckline suggest a date for this figurine in the early third century.[1] The type is probably derived from an image representing a maiden who gazes at an object in her undraped left hand, but the reworking of the type has accentuated the way the underlying forms of the body are revealed by the tightly wrapped folds of drapery.

1. Compare Higgins, *Tanagra*, 173, fig. 213, from Tanagra, dated 300–275.

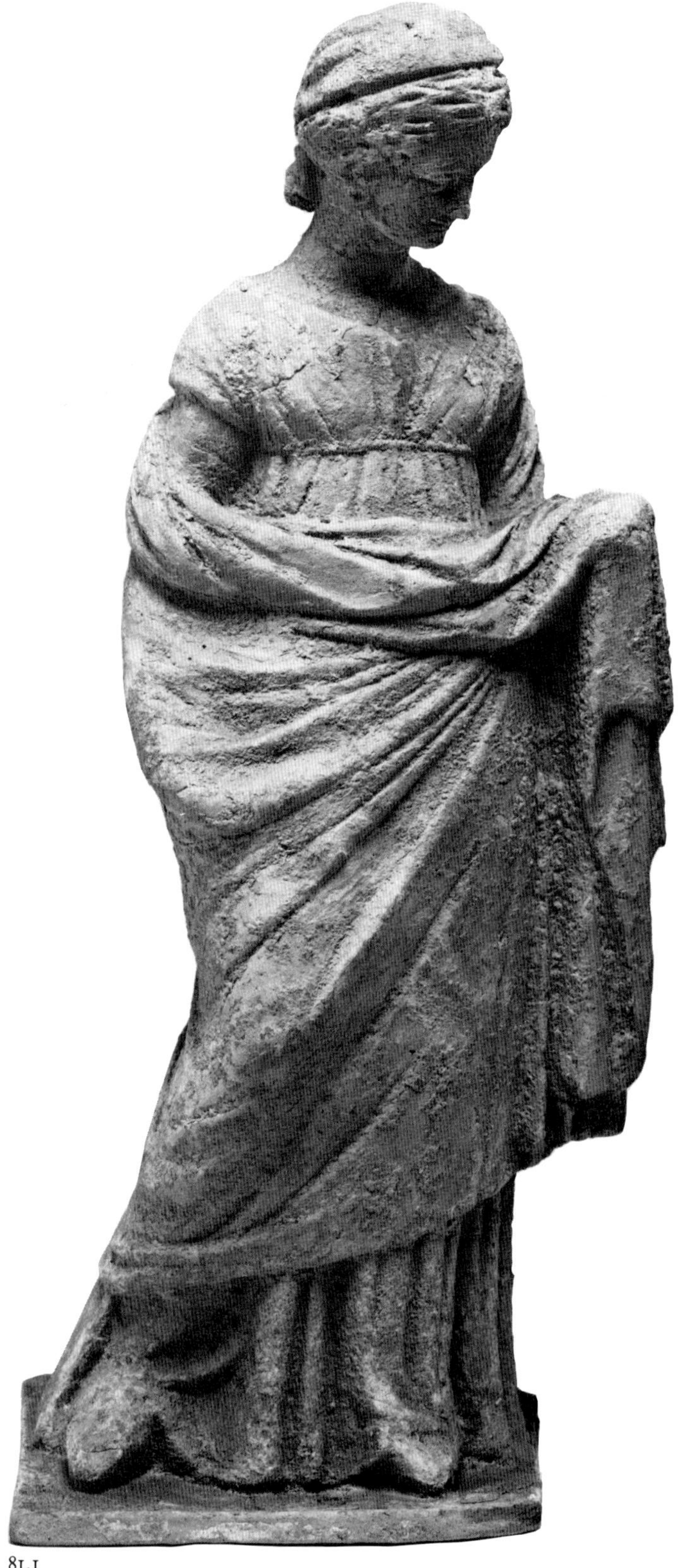

81.1

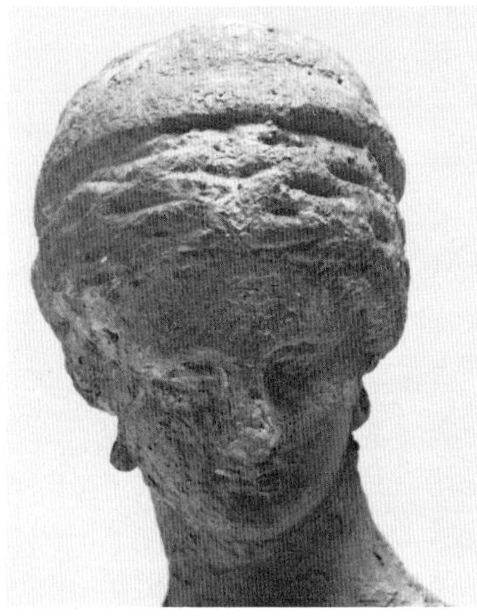

81.2

Figurine of a Maiden Stepping Forward
Late fourth–early third century

48.289. Terracotta. Purchased from Brummer in 1927. Ht, 19.1 cm; Ht, vent hole 1.9 cm; L, vent hole 1.9 cm; L, base 5.7 cm; W, base 6.3 cm; Ht, base 0.8 cm. Rectangular vent hole in back. Head worked completely only in back. Slip over surface. Hole in top of left hand for object. Base repaired from two pieces with edge of base in front of left foot broken away. Head reattached.

A maiden steps forward on her right foot, her forearms at waist level, her head turned slightly to her right. Over her undergarment, which is visible only at the ankles, she wears a mantle which is draped entirely around her body with an overfold extending to the waist, under which her left hand emerges to grasp an object, which may have been a fan. Her hair is arranged in a melon hairstyle which is gathered into a coil at the back of the head. She wears small round earrings.

This charming figure is draped entirely from neck to ankles. Her short proportions and thick drapery date her near the beginning of the Tanagra series, at the end of the fourth or beginning of the third century. Closely comparable are a figurine from Tanagra in Berlin and another said to be from Boeotia, formerly in the Loeb Collection.[1]

1. Berlin, Kaiserliche Museen, *Griechische Terrakotten aus Tanagra und Ephesos im Berliner Museum* (Berlin, 1878), pl. 20; J. Sieveking, *Die Terrakotten der Sammlung Loeb* (Munich, 1916), I, 33–34, pl. 48.

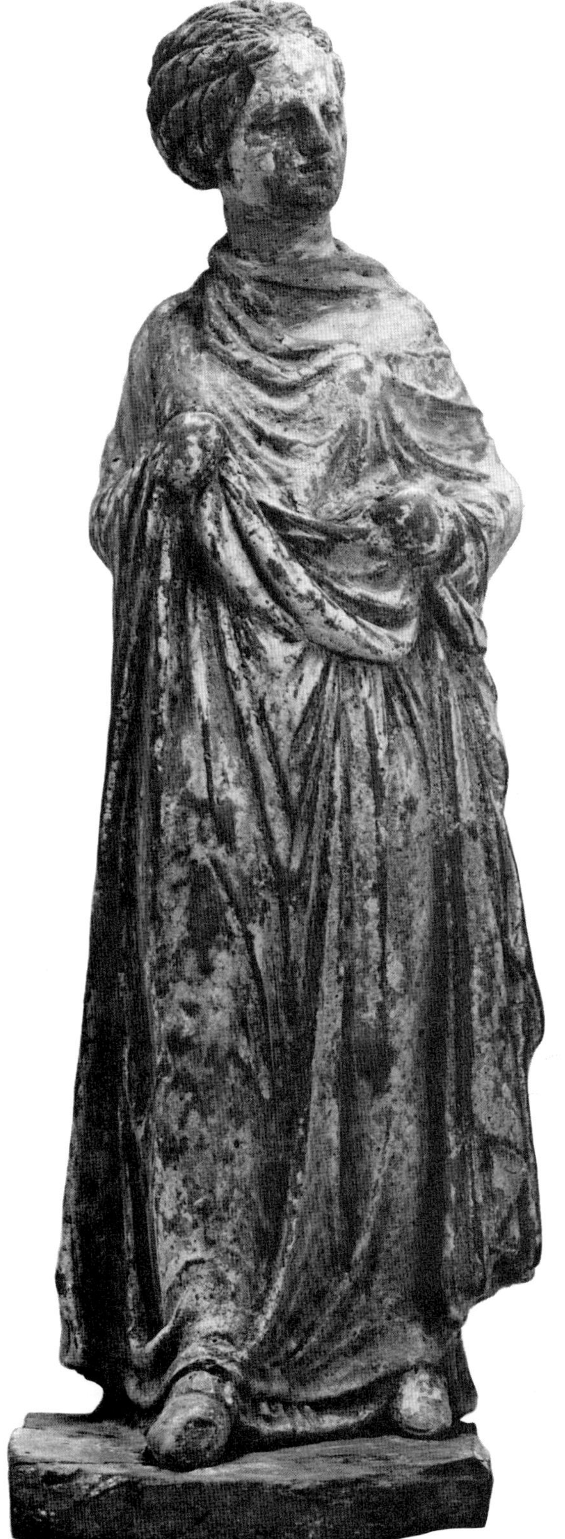

82.1

FIGURINE OF A SEATED MAIDEN
Ca. 230

48.290. Terracotta. Purchased from Brummer in 1927. Ht, 22 cm; Ht, vent hole 3.7 cm; L, vent hole 5.3 cm; L, base 12.9 cm; W, base 8.8 cm; Ht, base 0.4 cm. Large rectangular vent hole in back of rocky seat. White slip over surface; red in hair. Base repaired from several pieces.

A maiden sits on a rocky mound, her legs in three-quarters left profile, her right foot resting on the ground. Her left arm rests on the rock by her side; her right arm is bent at the elbow with the hand raised to her throat. Her head is inclined towards her left hand. She wears a peplos, the folds of which are visible only above the ankles, and a mantle, which is draped completely around her body and arms. The mantle's lower hem passes from her right ankle below the left knee, and the ends are wrapped around her left forearm and hand. She wears a melon hairstyle with stippled curls at the nape. The mound and foot rest on a low rectangular base.

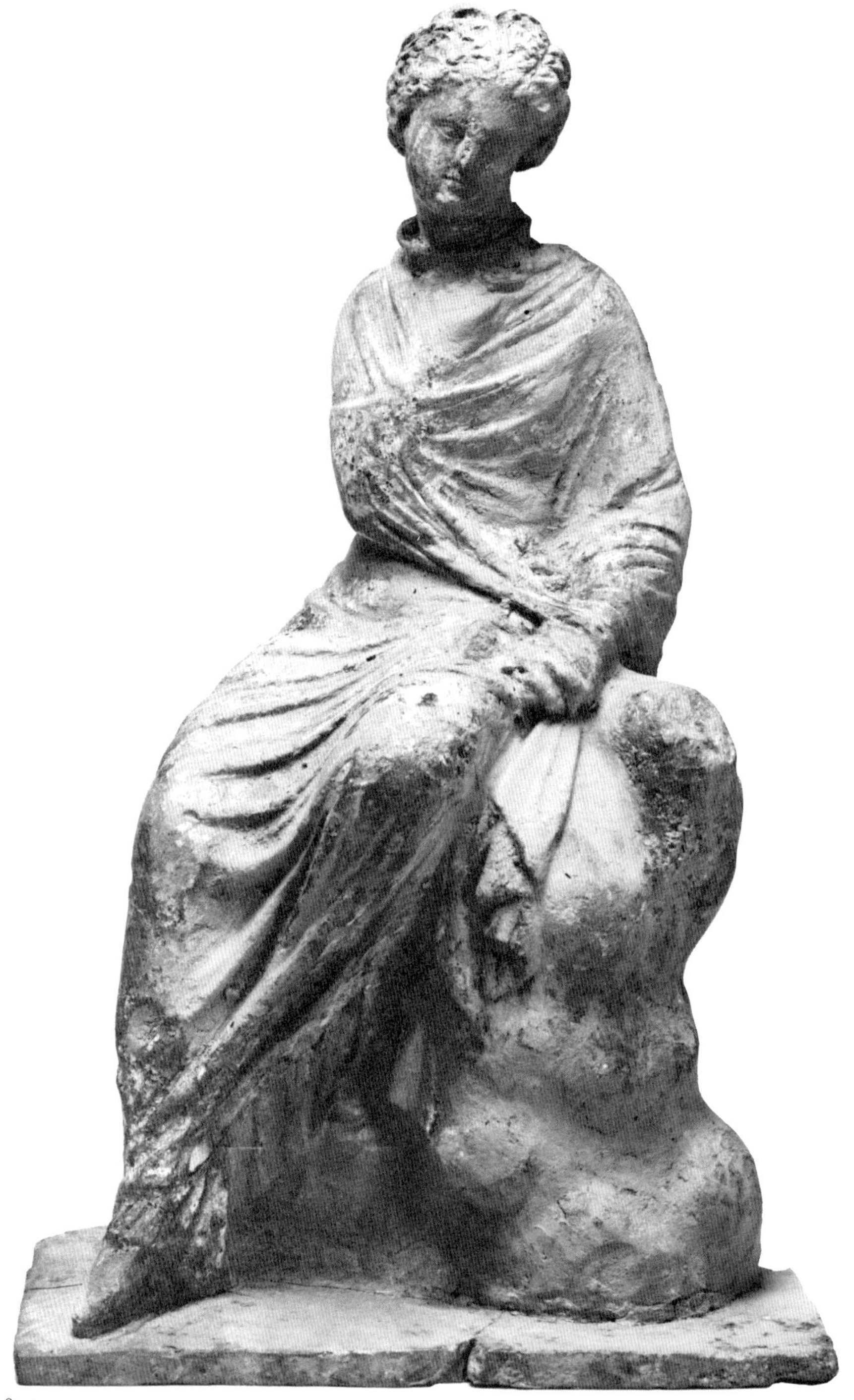

83.1

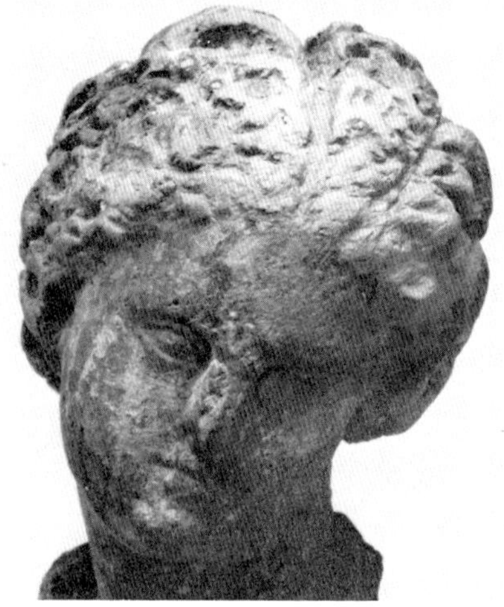

83.2

In this example a gesture familiar from standing figurines has been combined with a seated pose to result in a type that is not common among figurines of the Tanagra type. The few extant seated figures are usually shown on a klismos denoting a domestic milieu, but the rocky setting of this example coupled with the pensive gesture and inclination of the head are best compared with the withdrawn, contemplative Muses of the Mantinea base of ca. 330.[1] Dating the Walters example somewhat later are the handling of the melon hairstyle and the subtle torsion of the form.

1. For examples with a klismos, see B. Neutsch, *Studien zur vortanagräisch attischen Koroplastik, JdI-EH* 17 (1952) pl. 9.2. For the Mantinea base, see Robertson 395, 408, 480, 536, pl. 128a-c; and compare another seated maiden on a rock (Higgins, *Tanagra,* 143 and 144, fig. 174, dated 230–200).

Figurine of a Standing Maiden with Sunhat
Ca. 250

48.294. Terracotta. Purchased in 1925. Ht, 26.3 cm; Ht, vent hole 3.5 cm; L, vent hole 3 cm; L, base 9 cm; W, base 6.4 cm; Ht, base 0.8 cm. Rectangular vent hole in back. White slip, traces of blue paint. Mended from several pieces. Cracks over surface.

A maiden stands on her right leg with her left leg slightly behind her. Her left hand hangs at her side; her right arm is bent at the elbow with the wrist placed behind her right hip; her head is turned to her left. She wears a peplos or chiton with deep V-neck that is girt beneath the breasts and falls to the ground over her right foot. Her mantle is draped over her head and is brought over each shoulder with the ends wrapped around each arm concealing the hand. She has Venus rings and wears a sunhat over her mantle. She stands on a low rectangular base.

Publications: D. K. Hill, *Ancient Greek Dress* (Baltimore, 1945), II.

Because this piece has been extensively radiographed in the past, thermoluminescence testing could not verify its antiquity, but did establish the probable association of the figure with the hat. The type is distinguished by the position of the right hand on the hip and the folds of drapery that envelop the left arm hanging at the side. A close parallel from Myrina is dated to the second half of the third century, when the deep V-neckline of the high-girt garment was common.[1] The conical straw hat, or tholia, was often worn on top of the mantle folds; not enough of a clear join remains to indicate precisely its original angle.[2]

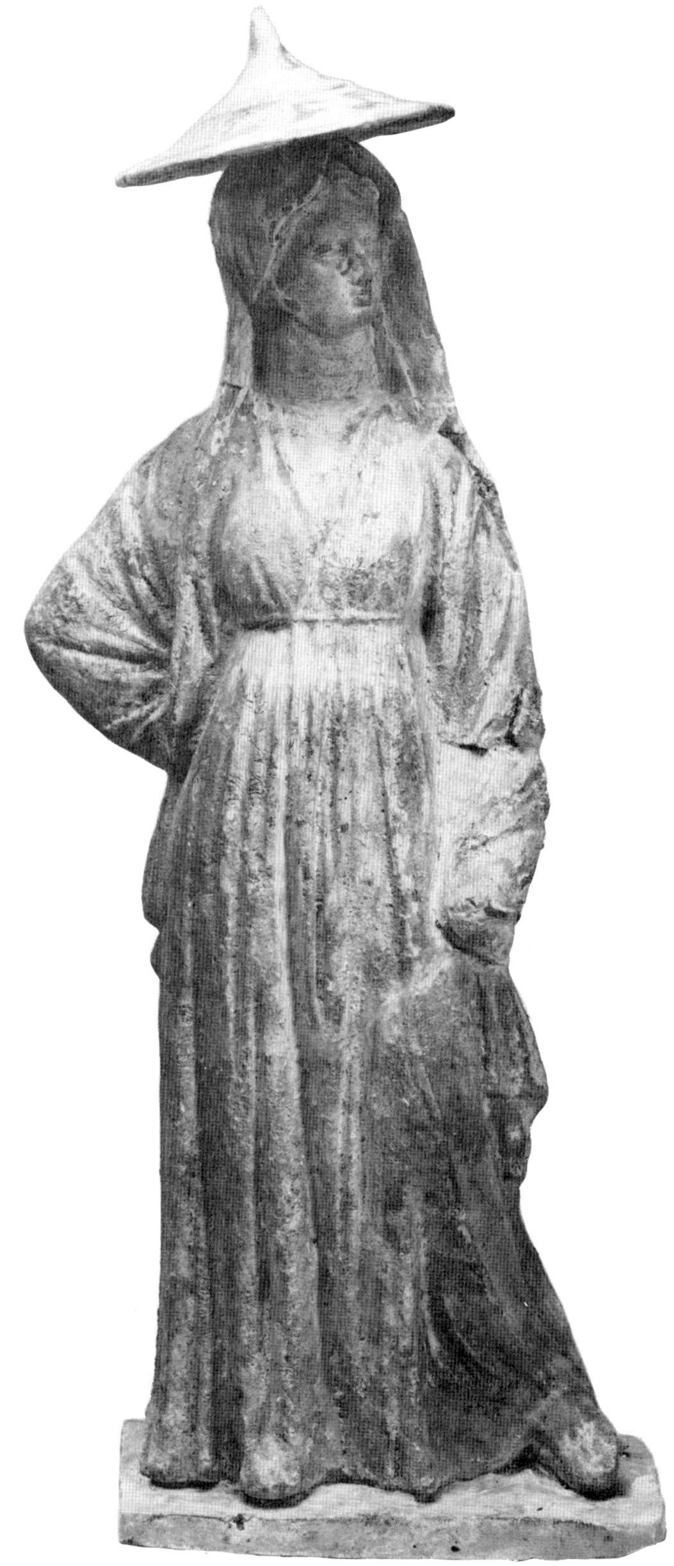

84.1

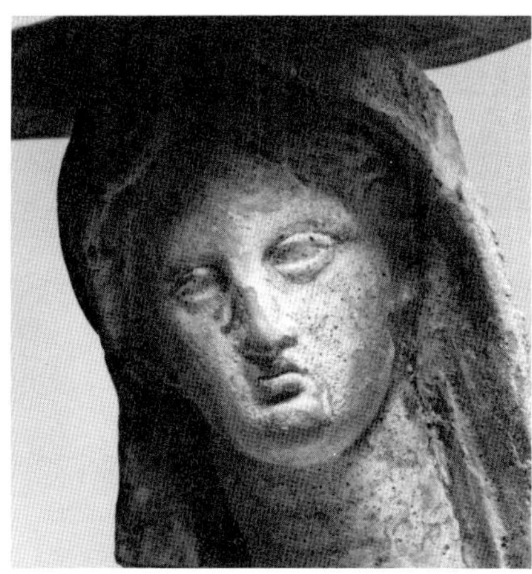

84.2

1. Mollard-Besques, *Myrina*, 100, no. Myr. 240, pl. 117,a. Compare also the drapery on a bust dated 275–250 in Bell, *Morgantina*, 147, no. 146, pl. 39.
2. Besques, *Grèce*, 31, no. D142, pl. 31 (250–225); 16, no. D62, pl. 14d (320–300); 17, no. D67, pl. 15d (mid-third century); Higgins, *Tanagra*, 124, fig. 145 (330–300); Higgins, *Terracottas*, 102, no. C312, pl. 42a-b (330–200); J. Chesterman, *Classical Terracotta Figurines* (Woodstock, 1974), 61, fig. 62 (330–200).

Figurine of a Maiden with Wreath
Ca. 250

48.277. Terracotta. "From Athens." Purchased from Brummer in 1925. Ht, 16.8 cm; W, 6.2 cm; Depth, 5.6 cm; each side of triangular vent hole is 2.4 cm. Bottom open. Back smooth. Traces of slip. Pitted over surface. Missing left foot. Neck broken and repaired twice.

A maiden stands on her right foot, her left leg relaxed with her foot behind her and at her side. Her left hand, enveloped by her mantle, hangs at her side; her right elbow is bent and the back of her hand rests on her right hip. She wears a chiton or peplos girt beneath the breasts and a mantle which is draped behind her back with one end wrapped counterclockwise around her left forearm and hand. The other end is brought forward over her right upper arm and is then wrapped around her right forearm and hand. She gazes slightly to her left and her neck has Venus rings; her hair is pulled back from her face beneath a smooth round wreath which has a round knob at the center above her forehead. Two large leaves are attached to the wreath: beneath it above her left ear and above it over her right ear.

The high girding, V-neckline, and softly crinkled folds indicate a third-century date for this figurine, which belongs to a type distinguished by the quiet frontal pose and the wrapping of the himation around the arms, one of which is akimbo, the other hanging at her side. The thick wreath is of a type woven from grass and flowers and is decorated with leaves and a large blossom above the brow.

1. Compare the handling of the drapery on Besques, *Grèce,* 25, no. D123, pl. 27e, dated 275–250; and 24, no. D121, pl. 27d, dated 275–250; Mollard-Besques, *Myrina,* 96, no. Myr. 648, pl. 113a, and 96, no. Myr. 649, pl. 113c, both dated to the end of the third century.

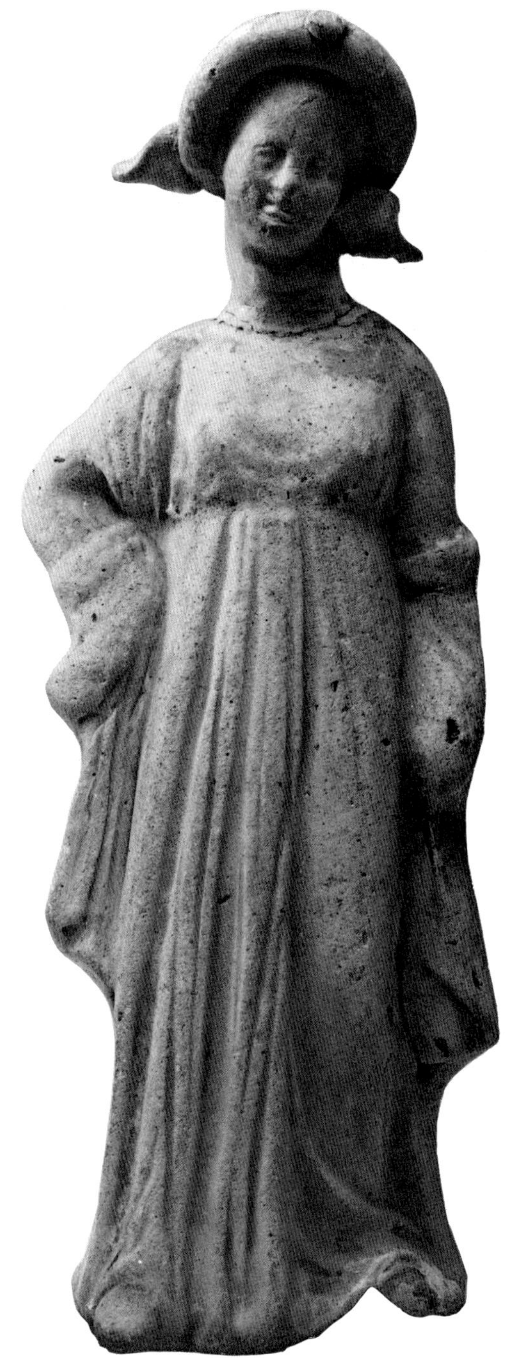

85.1

Figurine of a Standing Maiden
Third century

48.288. Terracotta. "From Tarentum." Purchased from Kelekian possibly in 1914. Ht, 45.7 cm; W, 14.6 cm; Depth, 16.2 cm; Ht, vent hole 6.3 cm; L, vent hole 3.9 cm. Back slightly modeled with large rectangular vent hole. Open beneath. White slip over surface. Pink on most of mantle; purple on mantle edges and on undergarment. Gold on diadem, on mantle edges at her right side and in band across the skirt at knee level; red pigment in hair. Edges of mantle over head broken away.

A maiden stands on her left leg, her right leg relaxed and the foot advanced. Her right arm lies close to her side with the hand resting on the front of her right thigh; her left arm is bent at the elbow with the back of her wrist placed on the left hip. Over a chiton or peplos she wears a mantle that is wrapped around her torso, its lower hem extending from the left hip to the middle of the right thigh, and its ends, which are colored as if part of her undergarment, bunched inside her left elbow and hanging down her left side. Both arms and hands are concealed by the fabric. Her head is tilted and turned slightly to her right. Beneath a diadem, her center-parted hair is gathered into a wrapped knot at the back of her head and the folds of her mantle are drawn up over the knot to frame her neck.

Publications: Bieber, *Sculpture,* 143, fig. 600.

Typically South Italian are the willowy elongation of the body and its subtle S-curve which extends from the inclination of the head to the advanced right foot.[1] Also characteristic is the draping of fabric on top of a high melon hairstyle, which has a bunch of curls at the crown.[2] Although the pose and gestures find parallels in terracottas of the previous century, the adjustment in torso and proportions has resulted in what is essentially a new type.

1. G. P. Carratelli, ed., *Megale Hellas* (Milan, 1983), 668–669, figs. 689–692.
2. Compare Bell, *Morgantina,* 66, and 196, no. 561, pl. 100, dated 250–200.

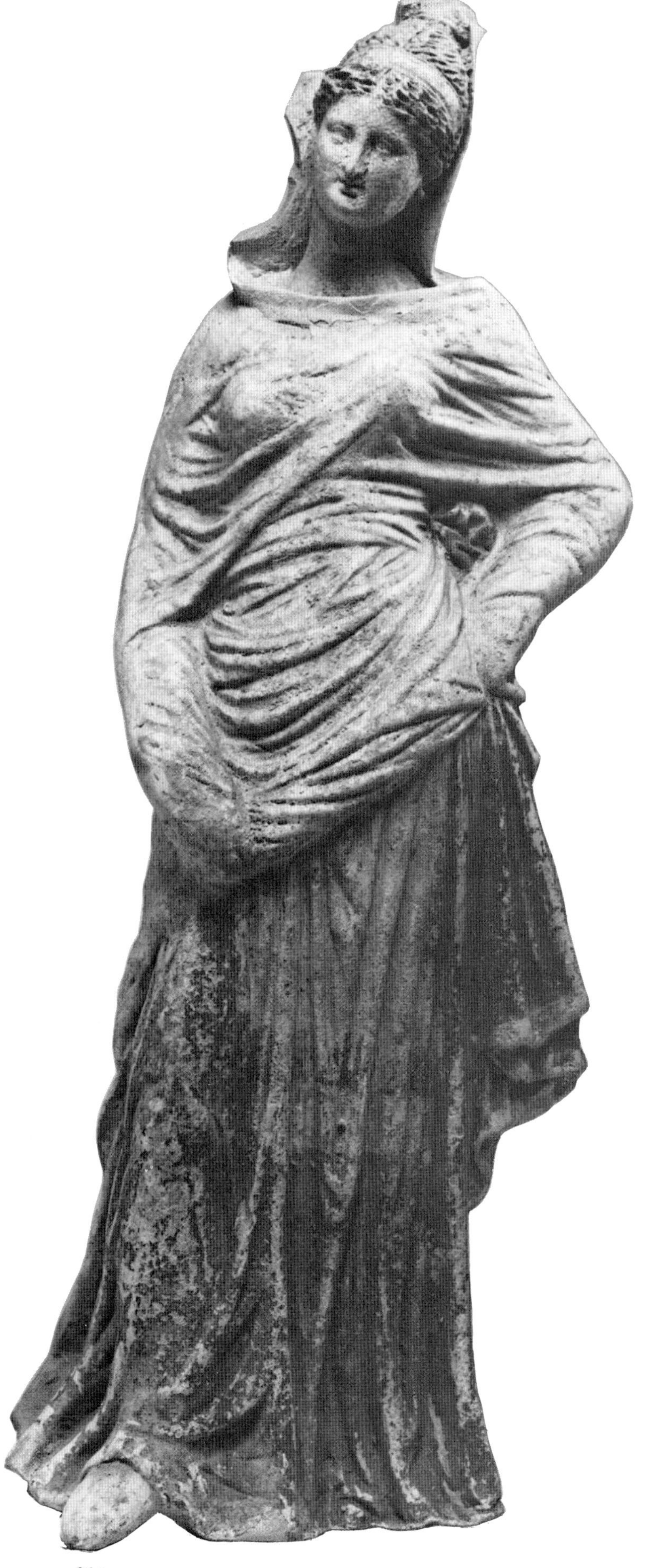

86.1

INCENSE BURNER IN THE FORM OF A FEMALE HEAD
Third century

48.2525. Terracotta. Gift of Frederick G. Stern, 1985. Total Ht, 17.3 cm; D, bowl 9.5 cm; L, base 10.3 cm; W, base 10 cm; Ht, base 3.2 cm; D, vent hole 1.9 cm. Open beneath; round vent hole in back of head. Back is painted but barely modeled without a leaf under the back of the bowl. White slip over surface. Interior of bowl reserved. A dark red pigment in the hair; a lighter red pigment picks out the balls attached to the wreath, the earring, the upper eyelid, the lips, and the necklace. Half of each leaf beneath the bowl is painted pink and half is blue. Blue pigment is also on the front of the wreath. The back of the base is black; the sides and top of the base are edged in black. The rest of the top is pink and the rest of the sides is white. The headdress is missing several leaves. The back of the base is chipped.

A frontal female head on long, flaring neck rests on a high square base; her neck has Venus rings. Supported by her head is a kalyx of three akanthos leaves beneath a low bowl with an everted lip. Her center-parted hair is pulled back at the nape beneath a wreath around which a ribbon is wrapped and to which leaves and berry clusters are attached. She wears disc and pendant earrings.

Incense burners in the form of female heads supporting shallow bowls are a distinctively South Italian, and specifically, Canosan, form of ceramic and are closely related to the oinochoai that take the form of female heads surmounted by other heads or by complete figurines.[1] Most incense burners apparently come from tombs where they were placed as grave gifts, a function which the absence of burning on the bowl of the Walters example supports. The maiden is surely to be identified as Persephone, following the long tradition in South Italian and Sicilian painting and terracotta of female heads and busts associated with this deity and her mother, Demeter.[2]

1. For other incense burners, see G. P. Carratelli, ed., *Megale Hellas* (Milan, 1983), 500, fig. 578; *Egyptian, Classical and Near Eastern Antiquities,* New York, Sotheby's, June 10–11, 1983, no. 104. For oinochoai in the shape of female heads, see No. 88.
2. Bell, *Morgantina,* 27–33.

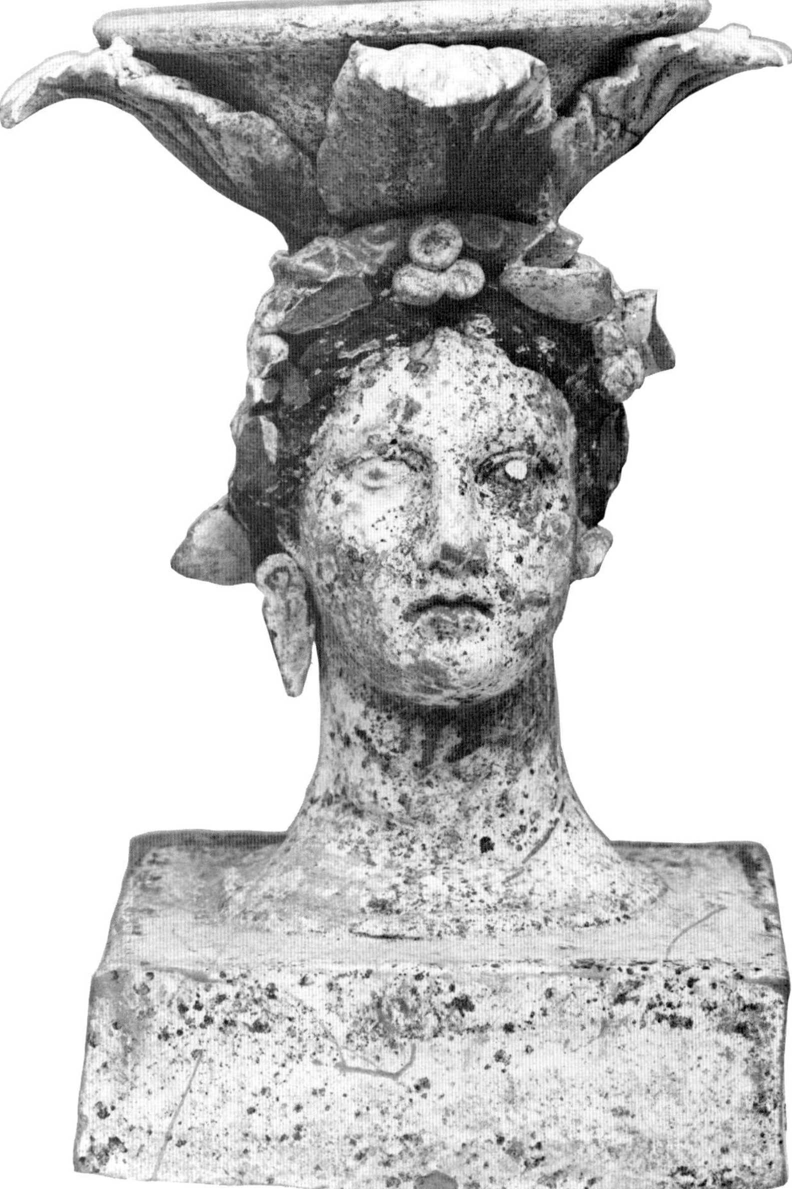

87.1

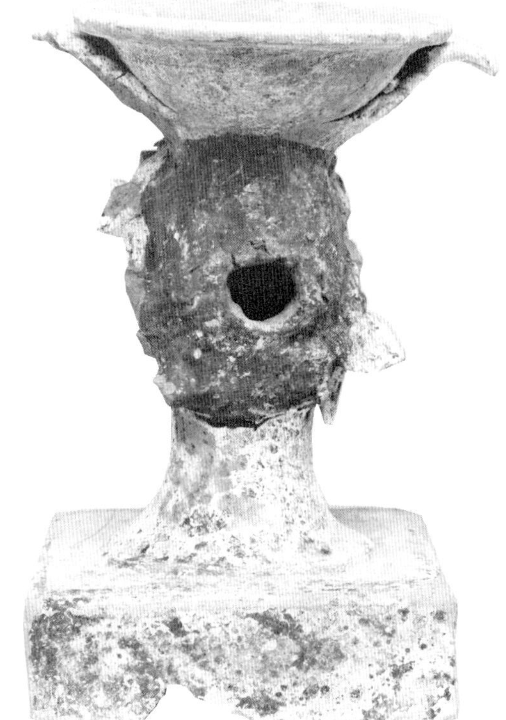

87.2

Female Figurine from a Vessel
Third century

48.2528. Terracotta. Gift of Frederick G. Stern, 1985. Ht, 46.4 cm; Ht, figurine alone 40.8 cm; W, 14.9 cm; Depth, 16 cm; D, vent hole 3 cm. Open beneath. Unmodeled back, round vent hole in center. Ribbed strap handle rises vertically from back of shoulder; above head is handle ring. Small holes are drilled in right and left hip, right and left shoulder. Head is reattached, right arm broken across elbow. Missing tip of vessel in left hand. Authenticity established through thermoluminescence.

A female, head frontal, stands with her weight on her right leg, left leg relaxed with the foot to one side. Her left elbow is bent and the forearm is extended with the fingers wrapped around a narrow jug. Her right upper arm lies close to her body. She wears a peplos beneath a mantle, which is draped in a roll across the torso from beneath the left breast to the right side of the waist with the fabric covering the thighs. The folds are brought over the left shoulder and wrapped around the left elbow with the ends falling down her left side. Over her center-parted, stippled hair she wears a thick ribbon-wrapped wreath with leaves and clumps of round fruits. She wears disc and pendant earrings.

This figure and the handle strap behind it were the surmounting elements to a type of vase made in the area around Canosa in the late fourth to early third century destined primarily for the grave. Most of the vases have a body in the form of a female head, but examples with the traditional shape of an oinochoe or prochous also exist.[1] The majority of the figurines are maidens, although at least one Nike is known, and occasionally such other plastic elements as birds were added to reinforce the funereal connotations. This type of ware can be compared with other pottery from South Italy that bears separately molded figurines and, in its plastic decoration and love of polychromy, is related to the approximately contemporary Centuripe vases of Sicily.[2] The Walters maiden exhibits the heavy jaw and prominently lidded eyes that are distinctive of South Italian work and displays a pose and system of drapery that find parallels in terracottas of third-century date.

1. For examples having the form of a female head, see Besques, *Italie*, 137, 141–142, pls. 150–151; *Antiquities and Islamic Art*, New York, Sotheby's, March 1–2, 1984, nos. 88, 90–91; De Juliis, *Taranto*, 429, no. 524. For examples with the conventional oinochoe form, see *Indiana University. Guide to the Collections* (Bloomington, 1980), 52; *Italische Keramik*. Münzen und Medaillen (Basel, 1984), 63, no. 114.
2. For other ware with plastic ornament, see Besques, *Italie*, 137–139, pls. 133–139; *Indiana University* (note 1) 52.

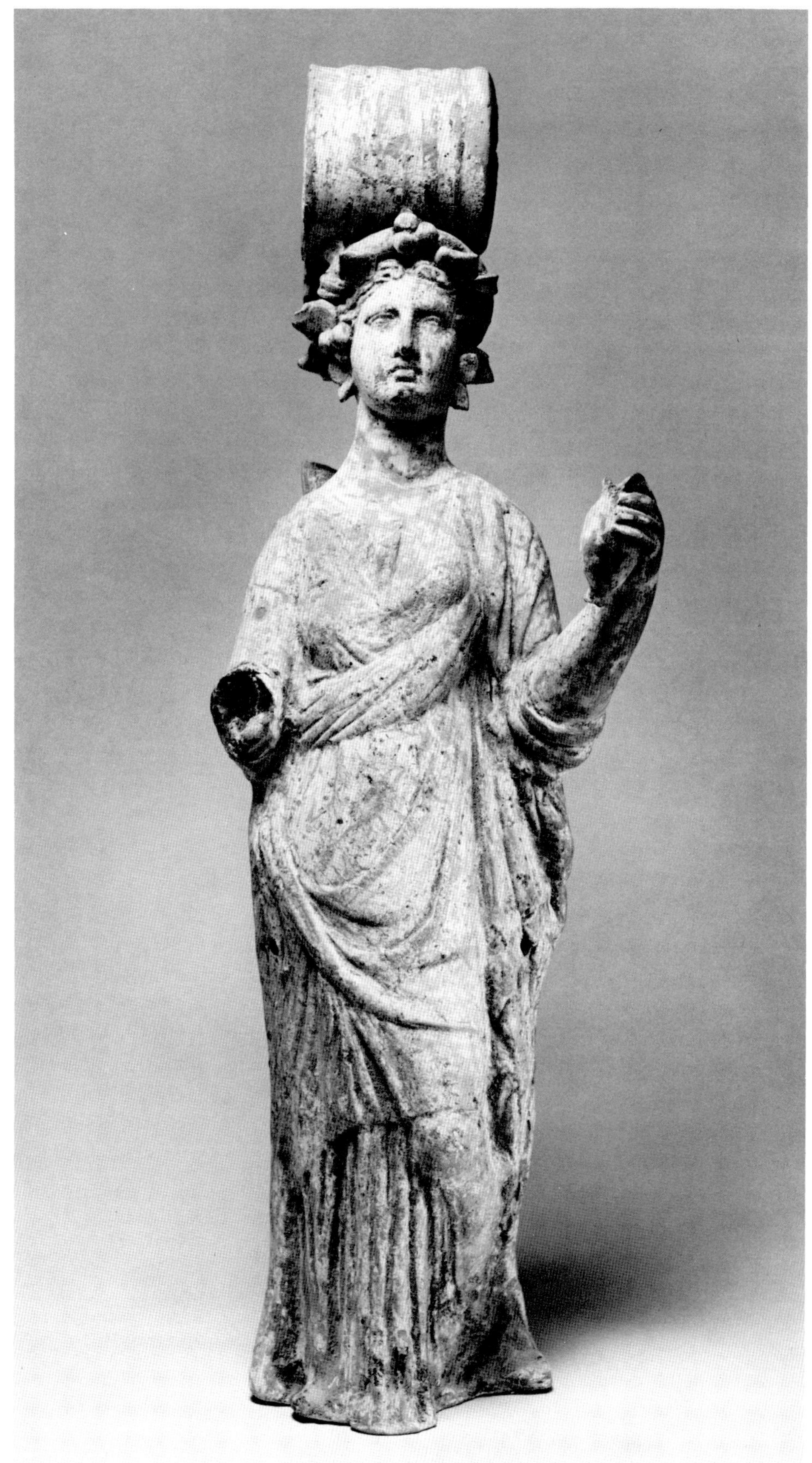

88.1

FIGURINE OF EROS
Third century

48.2527. Terracotta. Gift of Frederick G. Stern, 1985. Ht, 25.4 cm; W, wingspan 12.4 cm; Depth, 7.55 cm. Back partly modeled. White slip over surface; green, pink, and yellow on drapery; pink and blue on wings; red-brown on hair. Two holes in each side above waist; another hole between shoulder blades below neck; two more holes on either side of neck.

A nude winged boy steps forward on his left leg; his left hand at his side holds an omphalos phiale with a wavy contour. His right arm is bent at the elbow with the forearm upraised and the fingers holding a jug with a vertically ribbed body. His mantle is draped behind his back with the ends falling forward over his right shoulder and wrapped twice counterclockwise around his left upper arm and elbow. His head is slightly tilted and turned to the right. His center-parted hair is pulled back from his face beneath a narrow headband and diadem, the ribbon ends of which fall forward over each shoulder. He wears ball earrings. His wings have long primaries, short rounded binaries, and stubby tertiaries. Thin boots cover his feet to the ankles.

The popularity of children, especially Erotes, in Hellenistic art led to a more accurate rendering of children's bodies, as the miniature adult of the Classical era yielded by the third century to the pudgy and even shapeless form typified by this example.[1] The phiale and jug are appropriate to libation and surely carry with them funereal connotations appropriate to a grave offering. A number of Erotes similar to the Walters example have been found in South Italy and also exhibit the thick white slip characteristic of the region.

1. Compare Higgins, *Terracottas,* 155 and 156, fig. 191, dated 250–200.

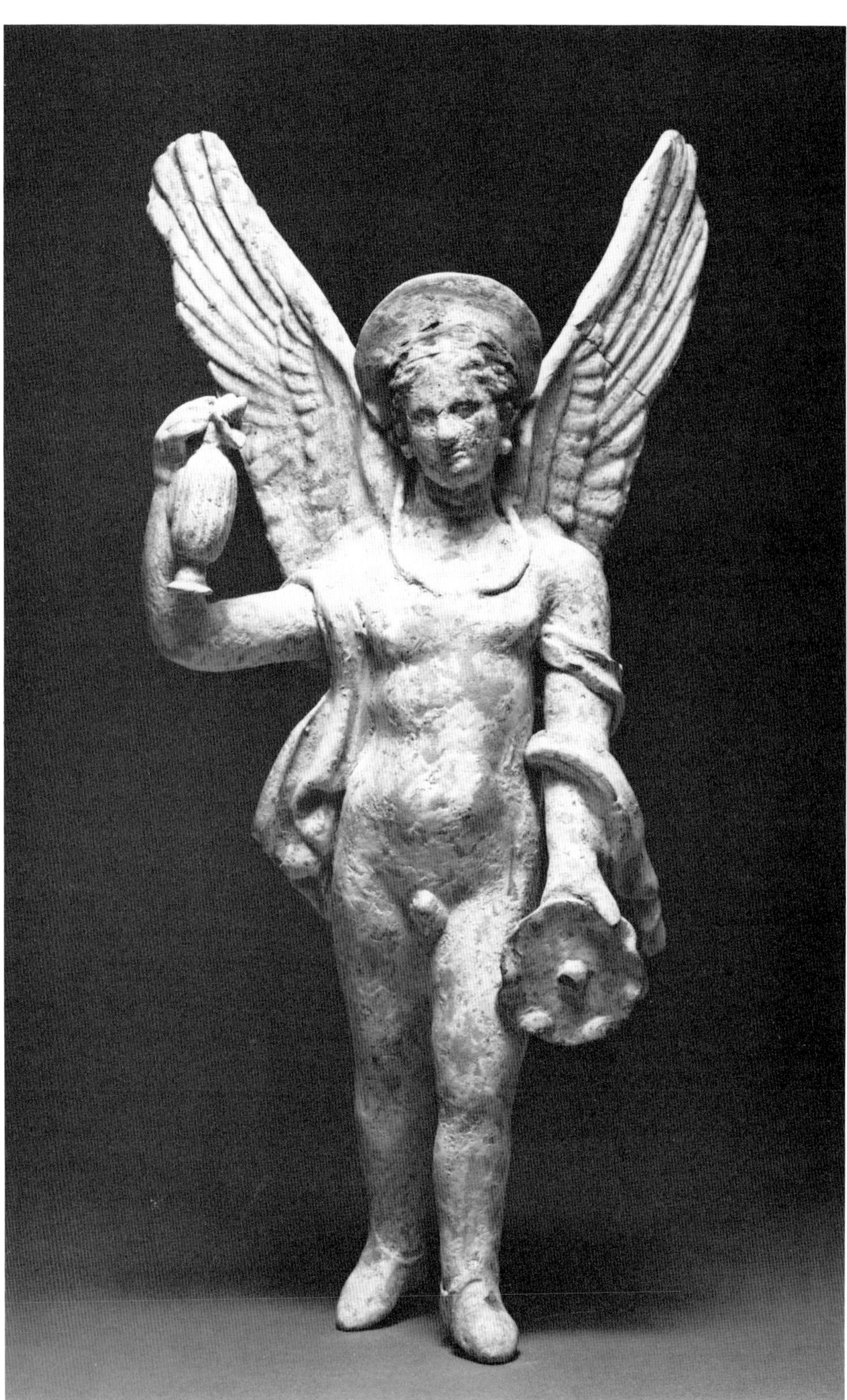

89.1

Group of Children at a Cockfight
Second-first century

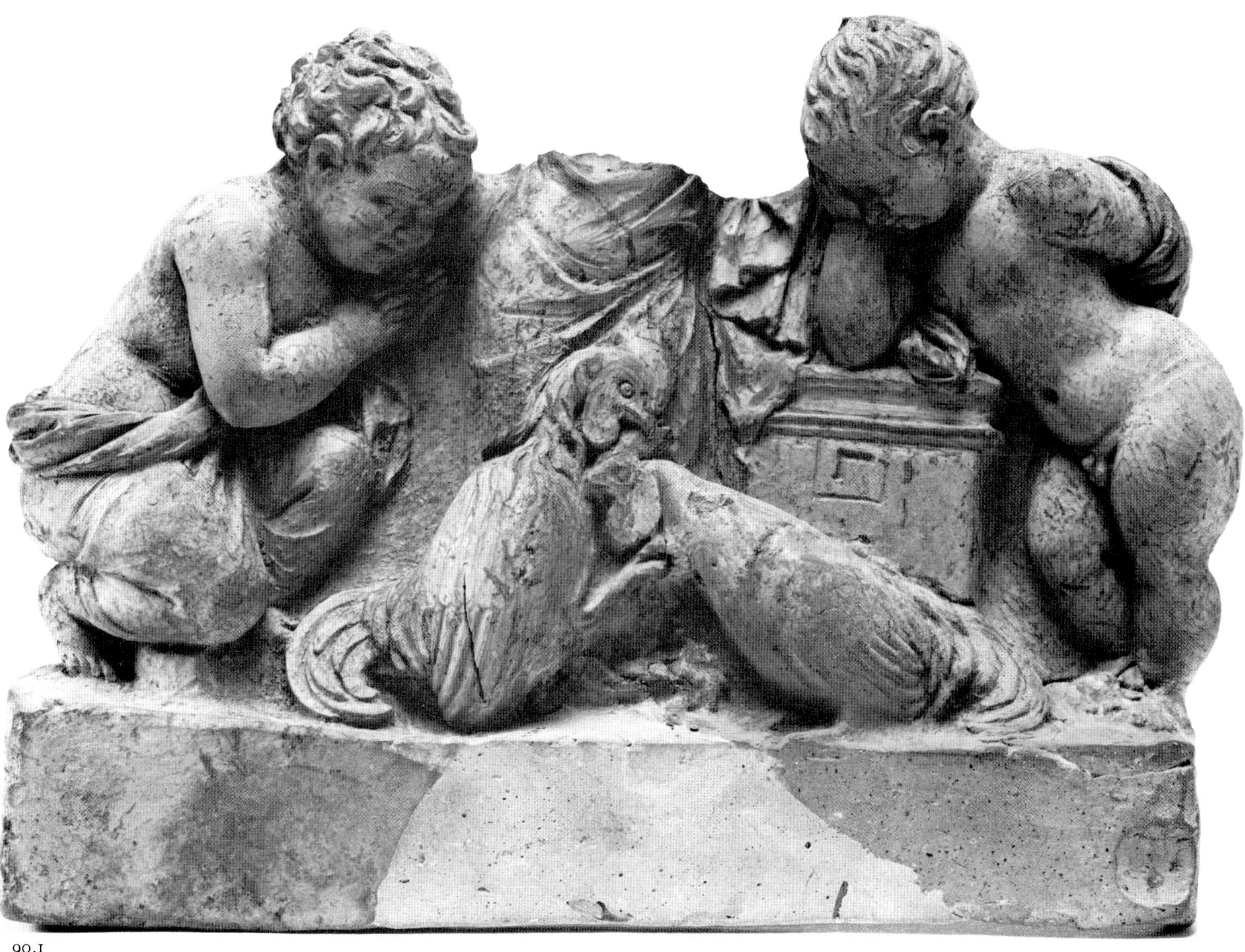

90.1

48.1714. Terracotta. "Found in Samsun in 1912." Purchased from Kelekian in 1913. W, at base 14 cm; Ht, 10.9 cm; Ht, base 2.3 cm. Molded in one piece with base. Open beneath. Children's bodies completely modeled in back with area between them smooth. Many details reworked by hand. Mended from several pieces. Much of back broken away; missing woman's body above waist. Midsection of base and upper torso of defeated cock restored.

Two boys flanking a woman observe a cockfight. A cock seen in right profile presses his right claw against the throat of a slumping opponent shown in left profile. Behind the triumphant cock is a boy crouching in right profile, right thigh lowered with toes resting on the ground, his left lower leg drawn back beneath him. He claps his hands at chest level and gazes down at his champion. His mantle is draped over his hips and lower legs with the ends brought forward over his left shoulder. He has short curly hair. Across from him is a nude boy in left profile standing on his left leg, the relaxed knee of his right leg advanced. He leans with his right elbow upon a rectangular altar and supports the right side of his head upon the palm and outstretched fingers of his right hand. His left arm is bent at the elbow with the forearm resting behind his back. His mantle is draped around his left elbow and forearm, and is brought around his back with the ends resting on

the altar. His short wavy hair is brushed forward upon his face. The altar has an incised meander on the front beneath moldings. On the other side of the altar stands a maiden facing front with her weight on her right leg, her left leg relaxed with the knee advanced. Her mantle is draped around her torso with the ends falling down her left side and over the altar, terminating in a tassel. A high base is beneath.

Publications: J. Sieveking, "Erwerbungen der Antiken-Sammlungen Münchens 1912," *AA* (1913) col. 441 and ill. in cols. 439–440; D. K. Hill, "Greek Cock Fighting," *BWalt* 2 (1949) no. 3; Bieber, *Sculpture*, 137, fig. 540; J. Sieveking, "Berichte der staatliche und städtischen Sammlungen und der Kunstwissenschaftlichen Gesellschaft in München, Königliche Antiquarium," *MüJb* 8 (1913) 76; P. Bruneau, "Le motif des coqs affrontés dans l'imagerie antique," *BCH* 89 (1965) 104, fig. 14; S. Barr, *The Mask of Jove* (New York, 1966), pl. I; *Jean-Léon Gérôme (1824–1904)*, G. M. Ackermann, ed., Exhibition catalogue (Dayton, 1972), 30 and 31, fig. 1–1; Pollitt 128.

This group has the reputed provenance of ancient Amisos, or modern Samsun, a city in northern Anatolia along the Black Sea coast. Also found in Samsun were several other terracottas of closely related type: a figural group in the Louvre that depicts two small boys at a cockfight; two terracotta groups in Munich showing a boy and a girl with a young animal; and a figurine, also in Munich, representing a boy leaning on a chest, his form and pose identical to those of his counterpart in the Walters.[1] The Munich and Walters pieces compare especially well in the form of the base, the handling of drapery folds, the rendering of the faces, and the careful reworking of the hair and parts of the drapery. The similarity among these terracottas from Samsun argues for their local manufacture, as does the fact that the two groups in Munich obviously came from the same mold.[2] At the same time, a close correspondence with sculptural and koroplastic workshops around Smyrna is demonstrated by the quality of the execution, the similarity of the woman to those seen in east Greek grave reliefs from the region around Smyrna, and the other allusions to the major arts, discussed below.[3] Because terracotta compositions with the complexity of the Walters group are rare, the Walters piece is important testimony to a highly sophisticated level of koroplastic expression. On the basis of its frontality and symmetry, it should be dated to the second or early first century.

Although it is not before the middle of the Hellenistic period that we encounter a figure who leans with the full weight of the upper body against a pillar, the pose of the downcast child is ultimately derived from that of the Weary Herakles of the fourth century (see Nos. 44, 45).[4] There is a double parody to the allusion, not only in the substitution of a pudgy boy for a muscular hero, but also in the contrast between a spectator's dejected languor brought on by the defeat of a pet bird, and Herakles' pensive exhaustion following the completion of his monumental labors.[5]

Cockfighting was a popular pastime among the ancient Greeks who admired the way the birds fought courageously to their deaths. A cockfighting contest took place every year in the Theater of Dionysos, probably in commemoration of the incident that was said to have occurred during the Persian wars, when, leading his men to battle, Themistokles passed a cockfight and exhorted his troops to emulate the bird's valiant spirit.[6] Not surprisingly the cock gradually came to symbolize victory and often appeared on Panathenaic prize amphorae and in representations that coupled the cock with the palm of triumph. By Roman times the cock came to signify immortality, and in the Christian world the bird symbolized resurrection.[7]

Cockfighting had other connotations as well, because the cock was the preferred love gift of an older man to a young boy.[8] These erotic associations may well be suggested in this scene, because the chubby boys compare very closely with Hellenistic depictions of Erotes. (See No. 89.)

1. For the example in the Louvre, see Besques, *Grèce*, 79, no. D466, pl. 103f; for the terracottas from Samsun, see J. Sieveking, *MüJb* 8 (1913), 76; inv. nos. 5424, 5444, 5445.

2. For the local fabric, see Higgins, *Terracottas*, 122.

3. For parallels among grave reliefs, see E. Pfuhl and H. Möbius, *Die ostgriechischen Grabreliefs* (Mainz, 1977), fig. 890, pl. 132; fig. 882, pl. 130; fig. 437, pl. 73; 229, fig. 441, pl. 74. For terracottas from Smyrna and their relation to the major arts, see Higgins, *Terracottas*, 110, 112; A. Laumonier, *Exploration archéologique de Délos XXIII: Les figurines de terre cuite* (Paris, 1956), 133–134, no. 357, pl. 38.

4. For the leaning pose, see Mollard-Besques, *Myrina*, 116, no. 926, pl. 140c; and no. 1176, pl. 140a of the second half of the second century.

5. For the Pan and Daphnis group as a parody, see Pollitt 130. For Eros as Herakles, see D. Burr, *Terracottas from Myrina in the Museum of Fine Arts, Boston* (Vienna, 1934), 38, no. 17, pl. 7.

6. See Bruneau, *BCH* 89 (1965) 106; Aelian, *var. hist.* 2.281. Pliny, *NH* 10.24.47.

7. Bruneau (note 6) 115.

8. Ibid., 97.

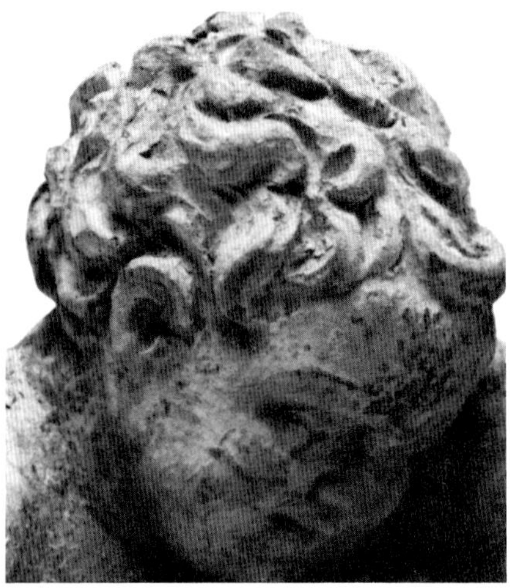

90.2

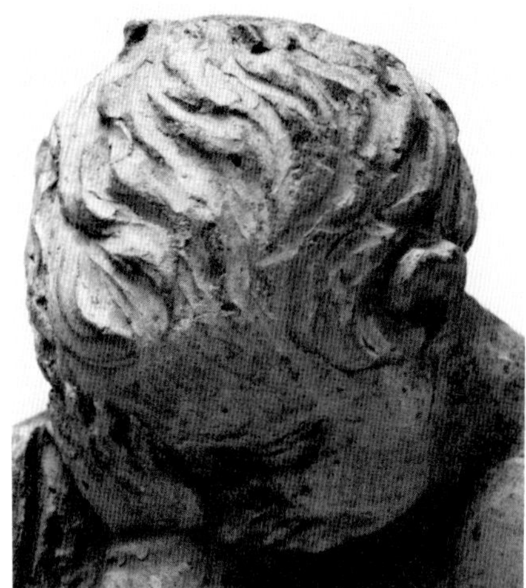

90.3

GROUP OF PEDAGOGUE
WITH YOUTH
Third or second century

48.1934. Terracotta. Gift of Charles William Lewis, Jr., 1946. Ht, 15.6 cm; Ht, vent hole 3.4 cm; L, vent hole 1.8 cm; L, base 3.5 cm; W, base 6.6 cm; Ht, base 3 cm. White slip over surface. Large oval vent hole in back. Open beneath. Three small holes in surface. Authenticity established through thermoluminescence.

A male stands frontally, his weight evenly distributed on both legs. He bends forward from the waist and his head is inclined; he has a bulbous nose, furrowed brow, and wears a cap. He wears a short-sleeved tunic beneath a mantle, which is thrown over his left shoulder and brought across the body from waist to mid-calf with the ends falling over his left arm. His left arm is bent at the elbow with the left hand at the waist. The right arm hangs at his side and clasps the left wrist of a boy who stands beside him, his right knee relaxed, his right elbow held close to his side with the forearm close to his chest. The boy's body and arms are enveloped in a long mantle which is draped over his head and around his body to his ankles with the ends falling forward over his left shoulder. The figures stand on a high rectangular base.

The aged pedagogue takes the hand of his youthful charge, the stooped form of the older figure forming a marked contrast with the tiny boy whose body is enveloped in a child's long mantle. The pedagogue, an adult male who supervised the moral and social education of a young boy, had a long history in Greek civilization, and the affection which developed between child and adult was legendary.[1] In the later Hellenistic period, Roman leaders sought out prominent Greek scholars to come to Italy to educate their children, and the genuine empathy for Greek culture felt by such Roman generals as Scipio Aemilianus was the result of an indoctrination into Greek culture which educators had instilled in their pupils from earliest childhood.

Not many Hellenistic terracotta groups of pedagogue and pupil are known. On an example in Paris from Myrina, a boy clutching a diptych stands beside a seated, bearded man who clasps an edge of the exercise tablet.[2] Another bearded pedagogue in Cairo, whose features have been influenced by depictions of Socrates and the Papposilenos, rests his right hand on the head of a small boy.[3]

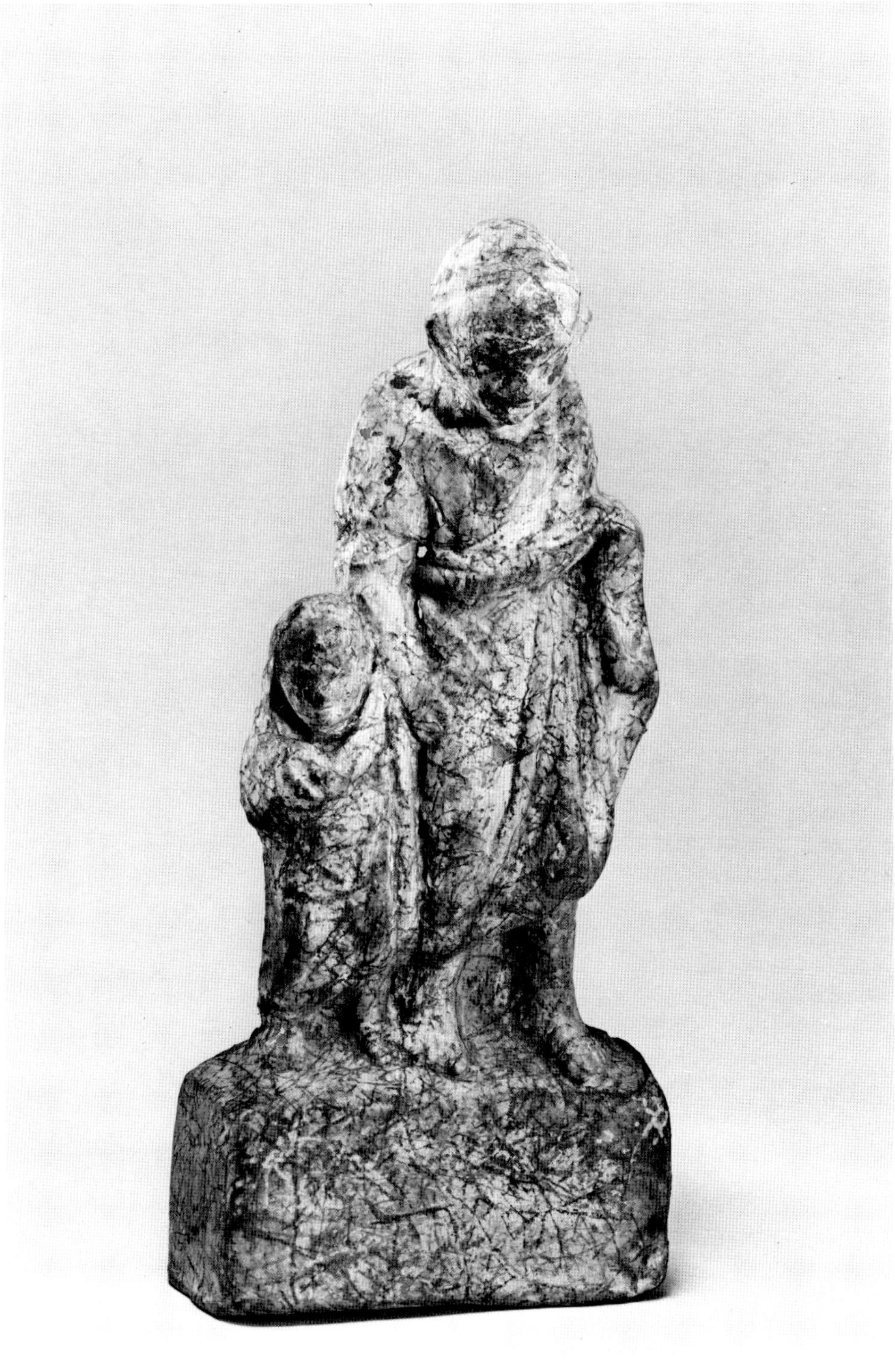

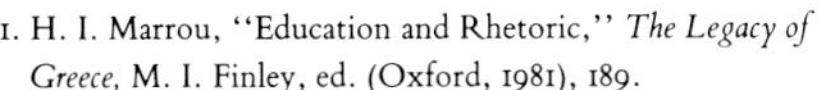

91.1

1. H. I. Marrou, "Education and Rhetoric," *The Legacy of Greece,* M. I. Finley, ed. (Oxford, 1981), 189.
2. M. Rostovtzeff, *The Social and Economic History of the Hellenistic World* (Oxford, 1941), I, 212, pl. 30.1.
3. Ibid., 416, pl. 50.1.

Group of Aphrodite with Eros
Second century

48.1946. Terracotta. Gift of David Rosen, 1947. Ht, 27.6 cm; W, 10.2 cm; Ht, base 5.1 cm; W, base 7.9 cm. Back was made by attaching a smooth, slightly curving slab of clay to the moldmade relief; round vent hole in center. Base rounded in back. Traces of white slip on the figures and red on base. Restorations beneath her right breast, at the top of both thighs, at base of drapery and feet of Eros. Hole in left cheek; chips missing from base.

A nude female wearing only ankle bracelets stands frontally on a high base with sloping top, her weight on her left leg, her right leg relaxed with the knee advanced. Each raised hand holds a thick lock of hair above her shoulders. Her head is inclined and turned slightly to her right; her center-parted hair is fashioned into a loose melon hairstyle with two locks gathered on top of the head behind the crown and two thick locks grasped in each hand and brought forward from the nape. Two other groups of locks, shorter and thinner, lie upon each shoulder flanking her neck, which has Venus rings. Beside her left thigh is a pedestal on which fabric is draped. Beside her right thigh and standing on a narrow groundline is a frontal Eros holding a quiver over his head with both hands. His mantle or skin is knotted at his throat and blows out behind him.

Publications: *LIMC* II (1984) pt. 1, 55, no. 431, pt. 2, 41, fig.431; D. Brinkerhoff, *Hellenistic Statues of Aphrodite* (New York, 1978), 62, pl. 49.

This figure follows the well-known type of the Aphrodite Anadyomene (see Nos. 71, 72), which is recognized by the raised hands clasping masses of hair on either side of the face in reference to the reputed birth of the goddess from the sea. The prototypical work has not been identified, but its suggested date ranges from the fourth to early second century.[1] The artist of the Walters terracotta enriched the composition with a small Eros whose raised hands grasp a quiver or strophion.

The piece is notable from a technical standpoint because the koroplast created the Anadyomene figure by adding heavy locks of hair to a head which originally had only two short slender locks on each shoulder. Her raised arms probably also result from combining a different set of piece-molds with a torso which was not originally of the Anadyomene type. This process of adaptation can be followed well into the Roman period when we find a terracotta figurine of the Anadyomene type whose hands clasp thick locks of hair, but accompanying her are two Erotes who hold over her head the Egyptian crown of the syncretic deity Isis-Aphrodite.[2]

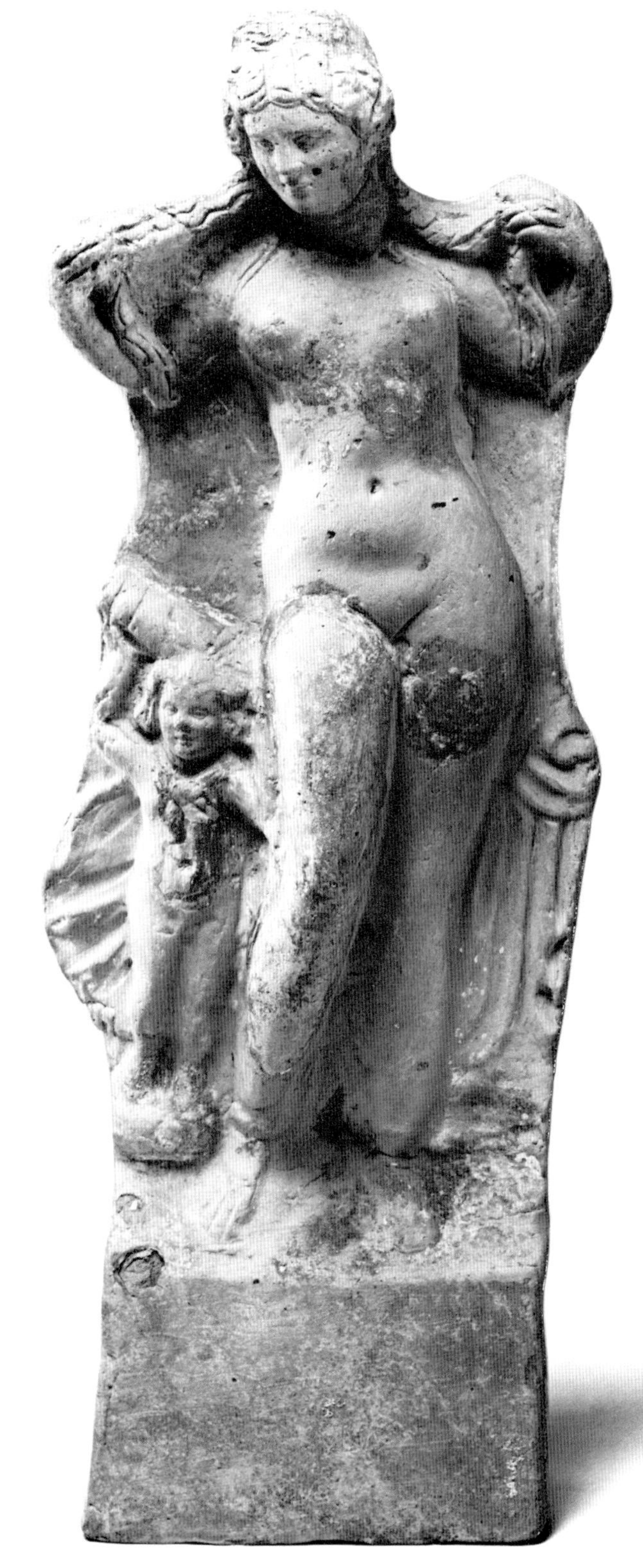

92.1

1. *LIMC* II, pt. 1, 55.
2. G. Schneider-Herrmann, "About the Significance of Alexandrian Terracottas," *Alessandria*, 305, 308, pl. 55.4.

Figurine of a Maiden with Pillar
Second century

48.272. Terracotta. Purchased from Brummer in 1925. Ht, 20.2 cm; W, 10.5 cm; Depth, 4.9 cm. Open beneath. Back was made by attaching smooth, flat slab to moldmade relief. Round vent hole in center. White slip on drapery and hair; red near waist. Cracked over surface; left hand and most of wreath missing.

A maiden stands on her right leg with her left knee bent and the calf crossing in front of the right leg so that the left foot rests lightly on the toes. Her right elbow is bent with the hand lying flat upon the right hip; her left elbow is supported by a pillar and her forearm is raised at an angle from it. She wears a peplos girt beneath the breasts and a mantle, which frames her back and is brought from her right hip across to the left side of her waist with the ends falling down her left side. The mantle's folds cover her legs to midcalf. A roll of drapery is brought over her right shoulder and passes between the breasts. Her head faces front and is inclined, and her curly hair was surmounted by a wreath. The pillar has a rectangular base with moldings at each end of the shaft. She stands on a low rectangular base.

Figurines with the same pose and gesture but with different heads and details of dress were made in Myrina in about the second century, and the type probably did not originate much before this date.[1] Although the relaxation of the leg nearest the support and the crossed legs can be traced back to Praxitelean statues and to the Ilissos stele of the fourth century, the combination is a late-Hellenistic phenomenon, as is the affected casualness of the gesture which in spirit compares well with that of the Boy from Tralles.[2] Also suggesting a late Hellenistic date are the frontal stance, the high waist with broad hips, the thick arms, and small head. The roll of drapery between the breasts finds a parallel on a terracotta figurine possibly of third century date.[3]

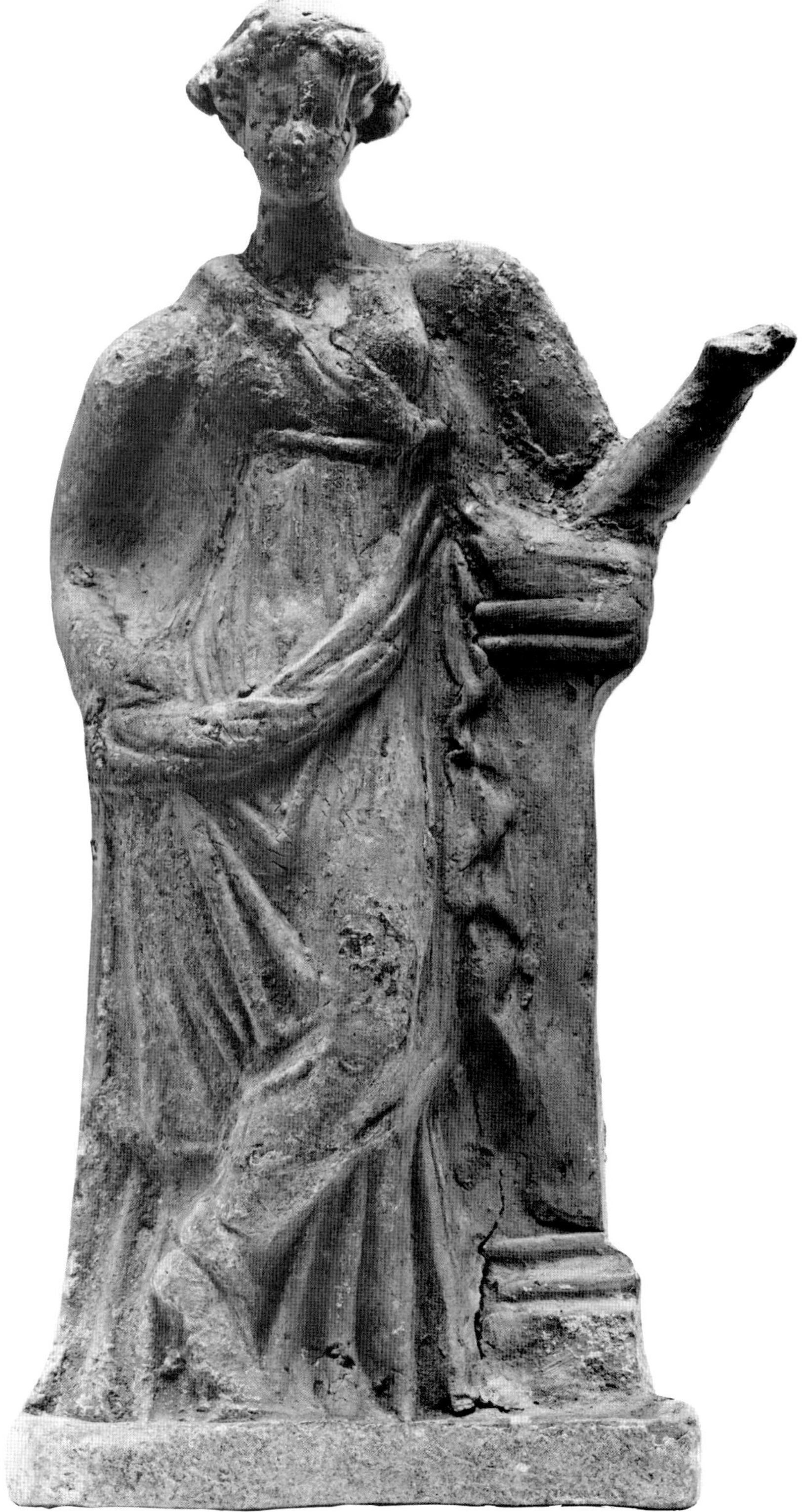

93.1

1. Mollard-Besques, *Myrina*, 24, no. LY1606, pl. 25a.
2. For the crossed legs, compare Mollard-Besques (note 1) 24, no. LY1606, pl. 25a; 24, no. LY1639, pl. 25b; and 24, no. Myr. 629, pl. 25e; Higgins, *Tanagra*, 144–145, fig. 177, dated ca. 230. For the Boy from Tralles, see Robertson 524, pl. 173b and 718, note 55.
3. J. Chesterman, *Classical Terracotta Figurines* (Woodstock, 1974), 64, fig. 70.

Figurine of Nike from Myrina
Second century

48.295. Terracotta. Purchased from Brummer in 1925. Ht, 26.7 cm; W, 13.5 cm; Depth, 11.8 cm; Ht, vent hole 4.3 cm; W, vent hole 2.5 cm. Back almost smooth with triangular vent hole in center. White slip over front. Small hole between shoulders; behind each arm is slit for wing. Two parallel grooves across crown are for addition of a headband. Broken across left ankle; left foot reattached. Missing are fingers of left hand, and tips of thumb and fingers of right hand. Cracked across right thigh; right big toe reattached.

A maiden advances on her left leg, the toes of both feet slightly pointed. Her left arm with elbow slightly bent is held to the side with the palm down, extended fingers drooping. Her right arm is stretched out to one side and bent at the elbow with the hand lifted, and the palm facing inward. Her head turns to gaze at her right hand. She wears a thin peplos, which has large round clasps on each shoulder, and is girt beneath the breasts with an overfold extending to the tops of the thighs. Her extended right leg is completely exposed; the left leg is concealed by drapery folds which billow out behind her. Her sandals have thick soles with the toe-loops protruding on either side of the foot. Her center-parted hair is arranged in a melon hairstyle gathered in a bun at the nape. A headband was fitted into a groove around her head. She wears ball earrings.

Exhibitions and Catalogues: *The Taste of Maryland,* The Walters Art Gallery (Baltimore, May 17– August 28, 1984), 64, no. 130.

Publications: R. Shoolman and C. Slatkin, *The Enjoyment of Art in America* (New York, 1942), 50, pl. 43; D. K. Hill, ''Mass Production in Antiquity,'' *GBA* 25 (1944) 75; D. K. Hill, *The Dance in Classical Times* (Baltimore, 1945), 12; D. K. Hill, ''Dance for Victory,'' *CJ* 42 (1947) 444 and frontispiece; L. Lawler, *The Dance in Ancient Greece* (London, 1964), 103, fig. 39; L. Lawler, *Terpsichore,* Dance Perspectives 13 (Brooklyn, 1962), 44.

Closely parallel figurines attributed to the workshop of Grave 112 B at Myrina of the late third and early second centuries have similar slits for wings which have also broken away. Like the Walters example as well is the suspension hole above the vent hole.[1] Following the analogy of better-preserved examples, the Walters figurine probably held a rhyton in the hand of her raised right arm.[2] The great variety of heads within the series, differing in hairstyle, headdress, and angle of inclination, demonstrate how often and how easily koroplasts altered a basic type through the use of piece-molds. The subtle torsion within the frontal pose and the agitation of the windblown garment look forward to the Nike of Samothrace of ca. 160 and remind us that baroque elements were very much present in Hellenistic sculpture by the end of the third century.

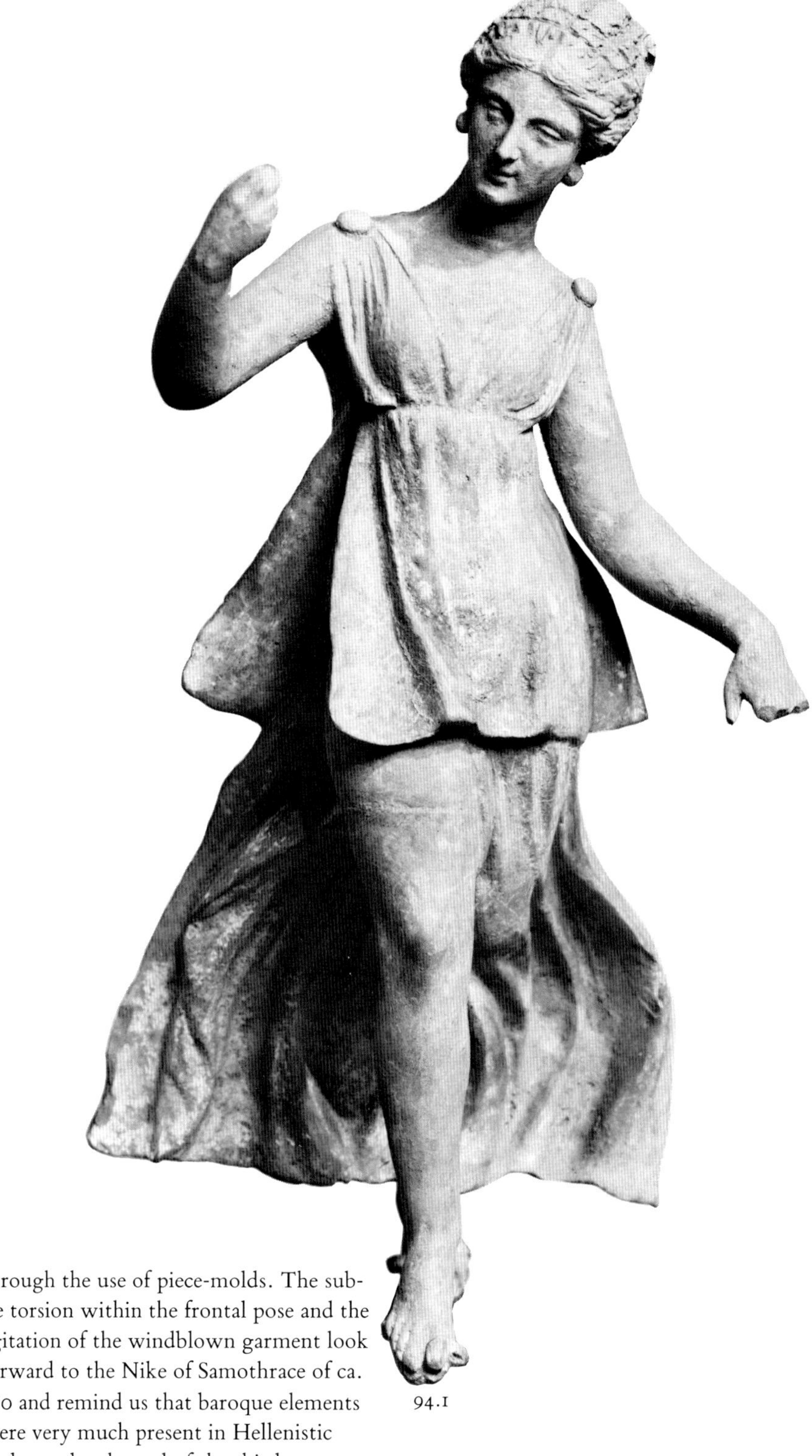

94.1

1. D. Burr, *Terracottas from Myrina in the Museum of Fine Arts, Boston* (Vienna, 1934), 59–60, no. 69, pl. 28; Mollard-Besques, *Myrina,* 66, no. Myr. 641, pl. 81c; 65, no. Myr. 169, pl. 80f; 65, no. Myr. 170, pl. 80e; B. Kingsley, ''A Myrina Figure in Malibu,'' *AJA* 76 (1972) 81–82.
2. See Leyenaar-Plaisier 257, no. 677, pl. 95, surely also from the same workshop.

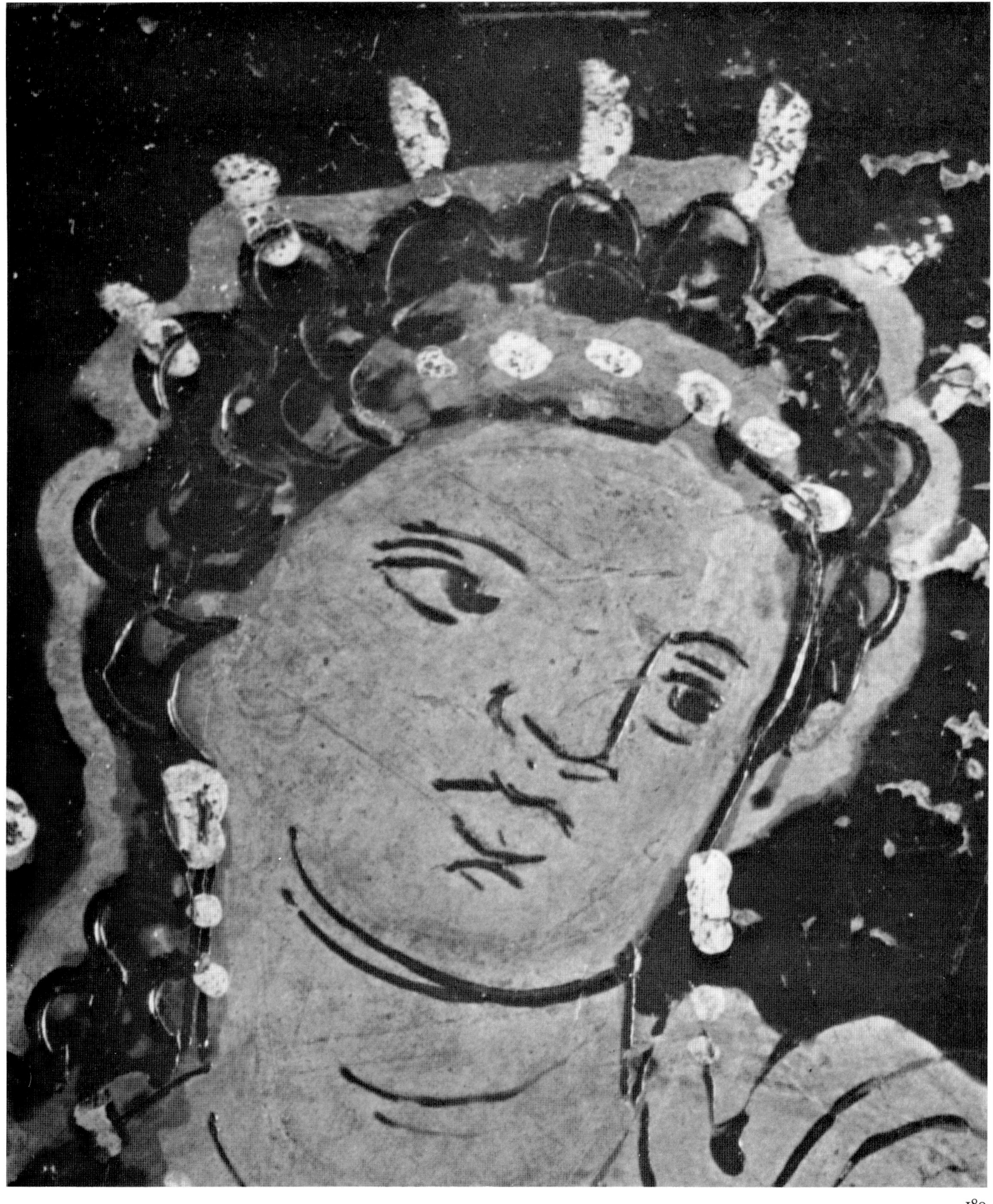

APULIAN VOLUTE KRATER
BY THE BALTIMORE PAINTER
320–310

48.86. Clay. Purchased from Brummer in 1925. Ht, 99 cm; Ht, with handles 112.7 cm; D, 48.7 cm; D, stand 29 cm. One duck head broken and repaired.

On the high foot, between a lower border of black waves and an upper border of egg-and-dot pattern is a figural scene showing Eros seated to his right and holding a box amid a spreading vine in which are tendrils, lilies, vases, and a bird. White with yellow highlights is used for many of the details. In the lower border of the body are black waves beneath rosettes with white centers alternating with pairs of white lotuses; a dotted-egg pattern is above. On the shoulder, a dotted-egg pattern is surmounted by a palmette-and-lotus frieze on the obverse, and a tongue pattern on the reverse. Under the handles are palmettes. The volute handles end in duck heads and have female masks in the volutes. White is used for the faces, yellow for some of the hair and features. Around the rim is a dotted-egg pattern.

On the neck of the obverse is a female head in three-quarter view set amidst florals; white and yellow are used for details. Above this are white waves, then rosettes with white centers alternating with clusters of dots. In the figural scene on the neck are a maiden and youth in a four-horse chariot with a winged figure in front. The group is flanked by two Erotes, one of whom is about to crown the first horse with a wreath. White with yellow highlights is used for details of the scene.

On the body of the obverse, Hermes and a seated woman are shown within a columned building depicted in perspective. On one side are a seated woman with parasol, a woman holding a mirror who leans forward, and a seated youth with a pilos, spear, and cuirass. On the other side are a seated youth with right arm on his cuirass, a woman with a fan, and a seated youth with a spear and a shield. Five seated youths are below; white, with yellow highlights, appears on many of the details, and the groundline is indicated by white dots.

On the neck of the reverse, above the figure scene is a central rosette; on either side is a laurel decorated with white dots. Above are white bead-and-reel, and reserved waves and dots. The figural scene shows Eros sitting on a campanula flower amidst vines; white with yellow highlights is used for details.

On the body of the reverse, an Oscan warrior with spear and shield is seated in a naiskos which is flanked by a seated woman, a seated youth, and a woman bending forward. White with yellow highlights is used for various details.

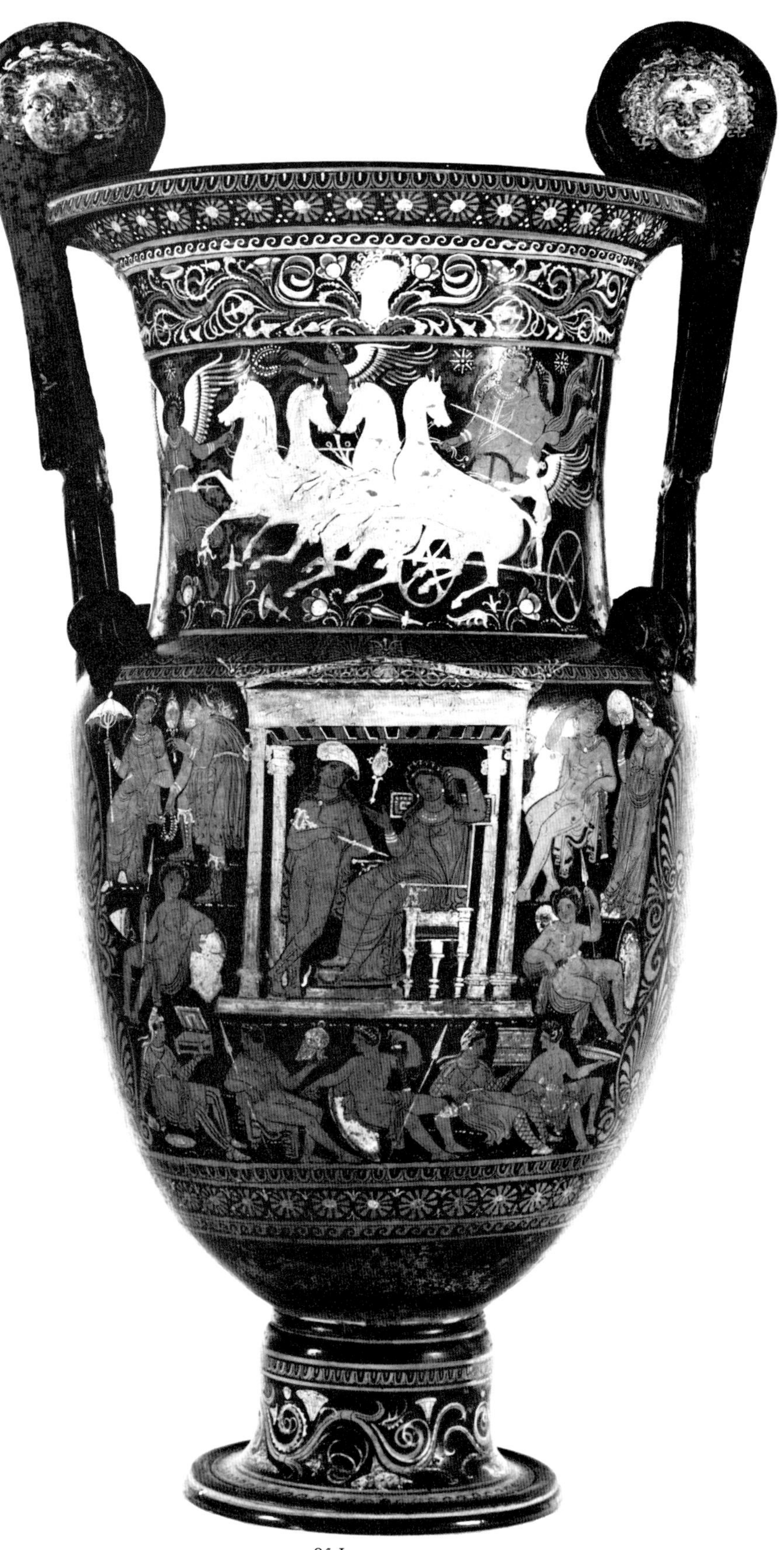

95.1

Exhibitions and Catalogues: *The Art of South Italy. Vases from Magna Graecia,* Virginia Museum of Fine Arts (Richmond, May 12–August 8, 1982); Philbrook Art Center (Tulsa, November 20, 1982–January 9, 1983); Detroit Institute of Arts (Detroit, February 7–April 10, 1983); catalogue M. E. Mayo, ed., 174–176, no. 71.

Publications: D. K. Hill, ''The Parasol,'' *BWalt* 6 (1954) no. 8; K. Schauenburg, ''Ganymed in der unteritalischen Vasenmalerei,'' *Opus Nobile; Festschrift Ulf Jantzen* (Wiesbaden, 1969), 136, no. 51, pl.21.3; M. Schmidt, *Eine Gruppe apulischer Grabvasen in Basel* (Basel, 1976), 54–55, 57 n. 171, 58, n. 175, 62–63, n. 196 and pl. 34a; H. R. Smith, *Funerary Symbolism in Apulian Vase Painting,* University of California Publications in Classical Studies 12 (Berkeley, 1976), 274–275; A. D. Trendall and A. Cambitoglou, *The Red-figured Vases of Apulia. Vol. 2. Late Apulia* (Oxford, 1982), 864, no. 21, pl. 324.1; *LIMC* II (1984) pt. 1, 149, no. 1556, pt. 2, 151.

This krater was painted by an artist who takes his name from this very piece and who worked in the ornate Apulian style during the last third of the fourth century.[1] Over thirty-five hundred vases, including thirty volute kraters, have been attributed to him, testifying to a large workshop of prodigious output.[2] A contemporary of the Darius and Underworld Painters of Tarentum, the Baltimore Painter appears to have worked in the area around Canosa where many of the vases painted by him and by the artists associated with him (the Arpi painter and the White Sakkos Painter) have been found. The mature phase of his career, as represented by the Walters krater, dates to 320–310, but, under the leadership of his followers, the Capodimonte painter and artists of the White Sakkos group, the workshop remained active until the demise of red-figure vase painting at the end of the fourth century.

The Baltimore Painter worked in the baroque style of late Apulian vase painting, which is recognized by flowery vines, elaborately patterned drapery, and extensive use of added color. Other typical features are the interest in foreshortening, visible in the parasol and naiskos roof, and the conventional and often repeated figural types. Distinctive features of the Baltimore Painter's own style are the naiskos scenes with mythological sub-

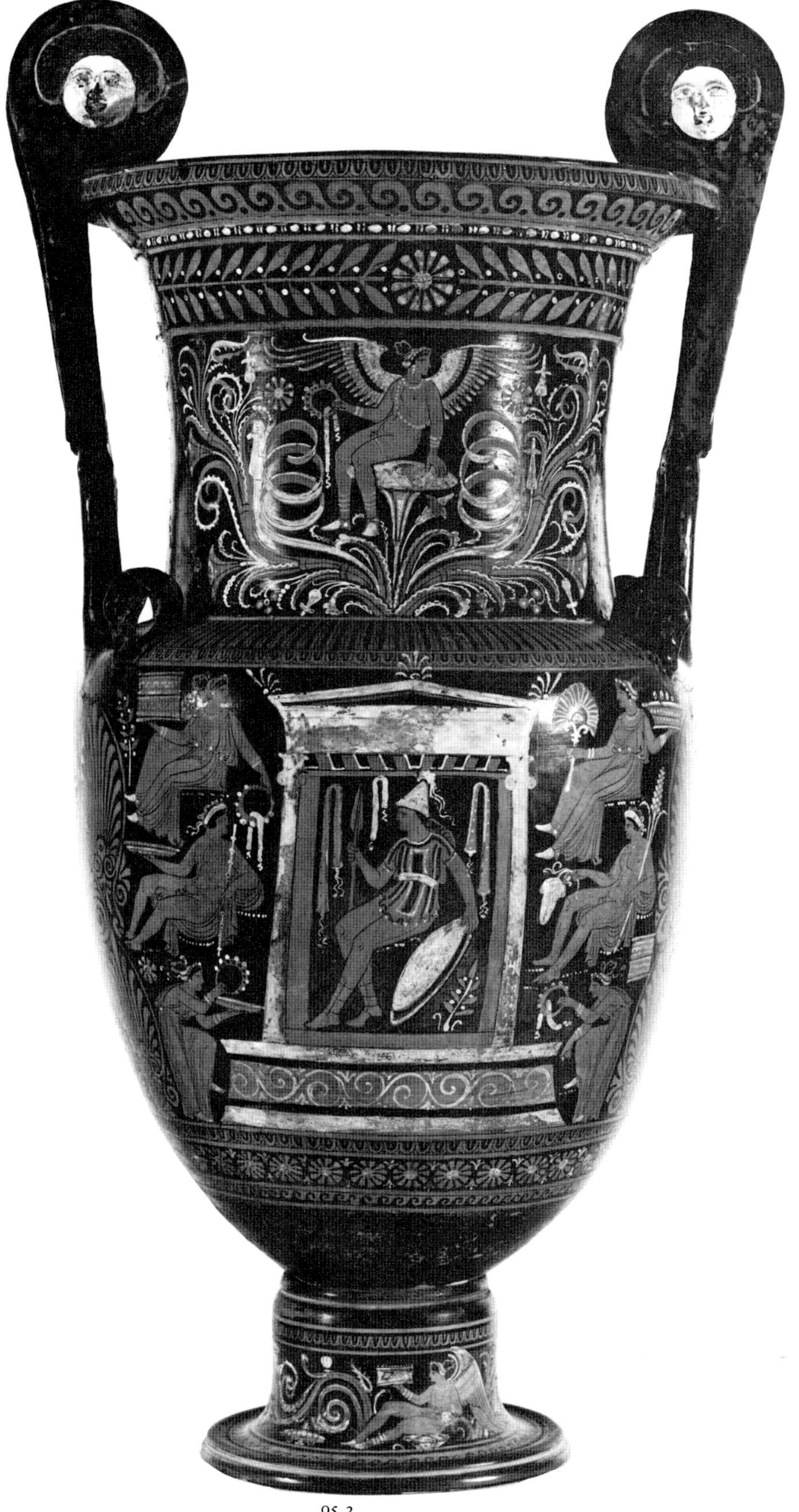

95.2

ject matter, the inclusion of armor and plants, the three-quarter or frontal faces with broad noses, the relief line running vertically between the breasts in the garments of the women, and the use of orange, red, and brown for the drapery of the naiskos figures.

The Baltimore krater probably functioned as a grave monument, a use to which the funereal subject matter is appropriate. The naiskos figures on the obverse have been identified as Persephone and Hermes, or Aphrodite and Adonis; the warrior on the reverse may possibly be the deceased or another deity. The multiplicity of attributes including parasol, mirrors, fans, caskets, and armor are an important source of information for the material culture of South Italy in early Hellenistic times.

1. Trendall and Cambitoglou, *Apulia,* 856–860; M. E. Mayo, ed., *The Art of South Italy* (Richmond, 1982), 78–81, 175–176.
2. See the catalogue that accompanied an exhibition at the André Emmerich Gallery (New York, May 1–30, 1986), *Ancient Vases from Magna Graecia,* nos. 10–13, 16. See also O. Cavalier, "Un ensemble de vases apuliens du IVe siècle av. J.C.," *La Revue du Louvre et des musées de France* 4/5 (1986) 247–250.

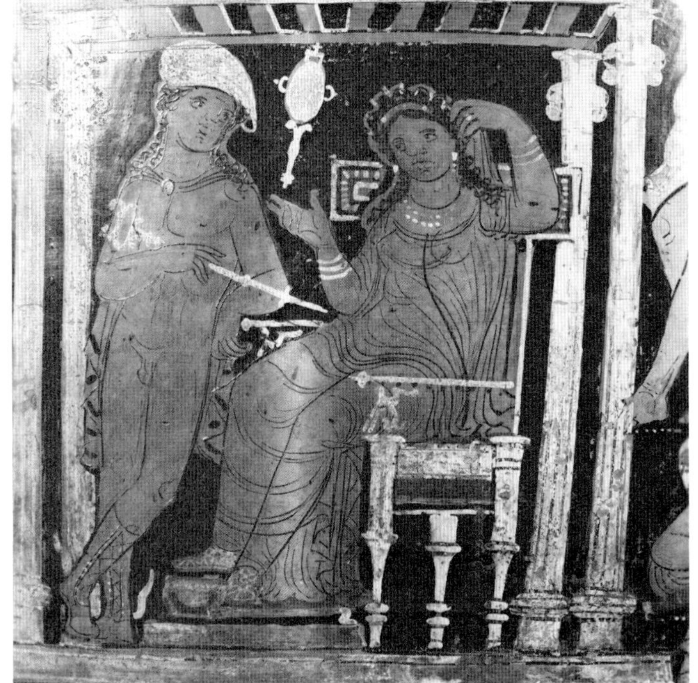

95.3

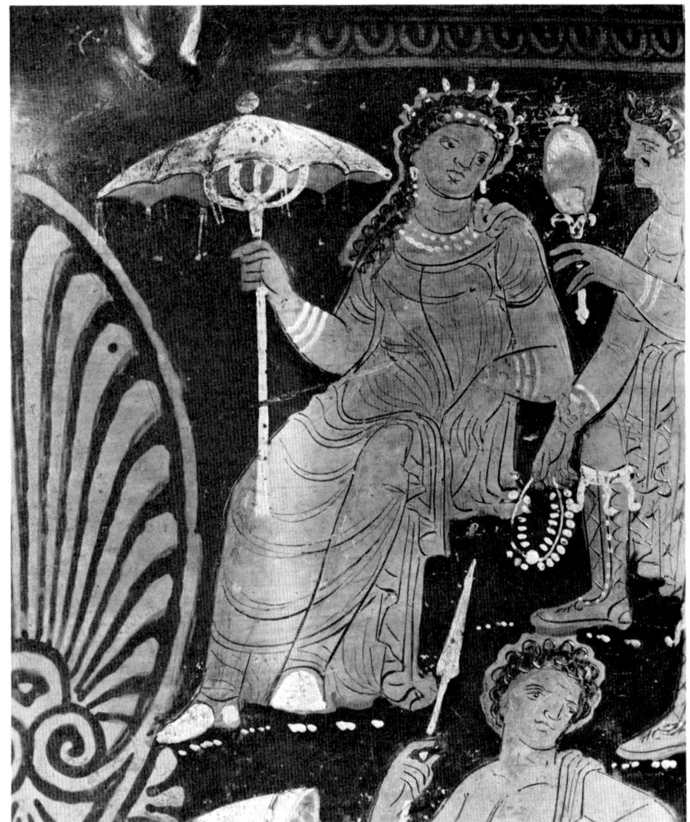

95.4

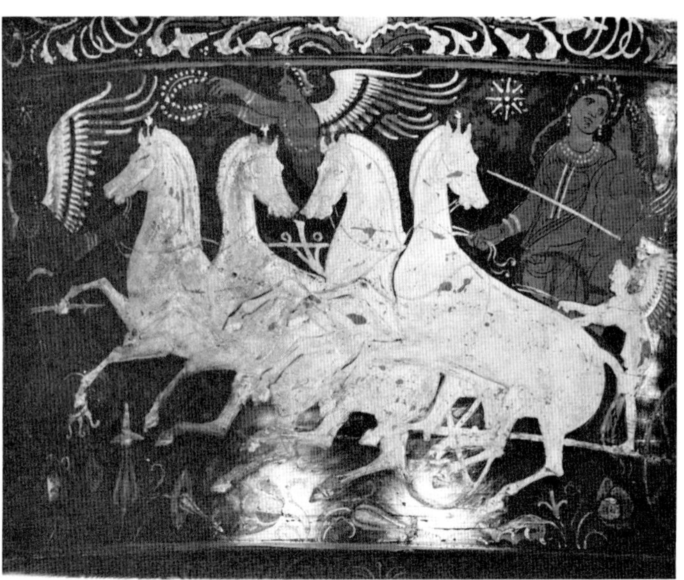

95.5

Relief Amphora with Bacchic Erotes
225–200

48.117. Clay. "From Tarentum." Massarenti Collection. Purchased in 1902. Total Ht, without lid 40.4 cm; W, between handles 24.1 cm; D, rim 11.2 cm; D, base 12.4 cm; D, base of lid 10.2 cm. Back is undecorated except for ridge at base of neck. White slip over surface. Gilding on horizontal ridges enclosing Erotes, ridge at top of shoulder, and modern? gilding on garland around neck. Pink on cover; pink on relief figures and background, and on leaves beneath body. Handles reattached. Foot has been reattached with a long dowel around which plaster has been poured. Repairs, retouching, and cracks over surface. Authenticity established through thermoluminescence.

The amphora has a flaring base beneath a turned stem supporting a kalyx of three akanthos leaves in which the body rests. The body of the amphora has, on one side, a figural frieze in relief around the mid-section enclosed by tongue patterns above and beneath. Five nude Erotes run to their left, their right legs outstretched. Their leader grasps a pair of flutes; the figure behind him carries a club (?) over his left shoulder and a torch in his right arm. The third figure clasps a pail in the left hand, and a torch in his right. Following him is an Eros plucking a kithara, and the last figure, who turns his head back in three-quarters left profile, carries a club (?) over his left shoulder and a torch in his right hand. On the front of the amphora's neck is a garland of rosettes from which seven pendants are suspended. The ribbed, upturned handles have leaves around the point of attachment. The convex cover is surmounted by a kalyx of akanthos leaves beneath a stalk with floral finial.

Publications: Esbroeck, pt. 2, 55, no. 246; D.K. Hill, "Bacchic Erotes at Tarentum," *Hesperia* 16 (1947) 248–249, pl. 67.1; P. Mingazzini, "Tre brevi note di ceramica ellenistica," *ArchCl* 10 (1958) 219, pl. 74.4; F. Matz, *Ein römisches Meisterwerk; der Jahreszeiten Sarkophag Badminton-New York* (Berlin, 1958), 59; 76, n. 140, no. 3; 80, n. 161; M. Borda, *Ceramiche apule* (Bergamo, 1966), 61, pl. 22.

This vase belongs with a small group of relief amphorae, two of which were found in Tarentum, where the Walters example was also reputedly discovered.[1] The piece is distinctive in being moldmade and adorned with separately molded elements, including the relief figures around the

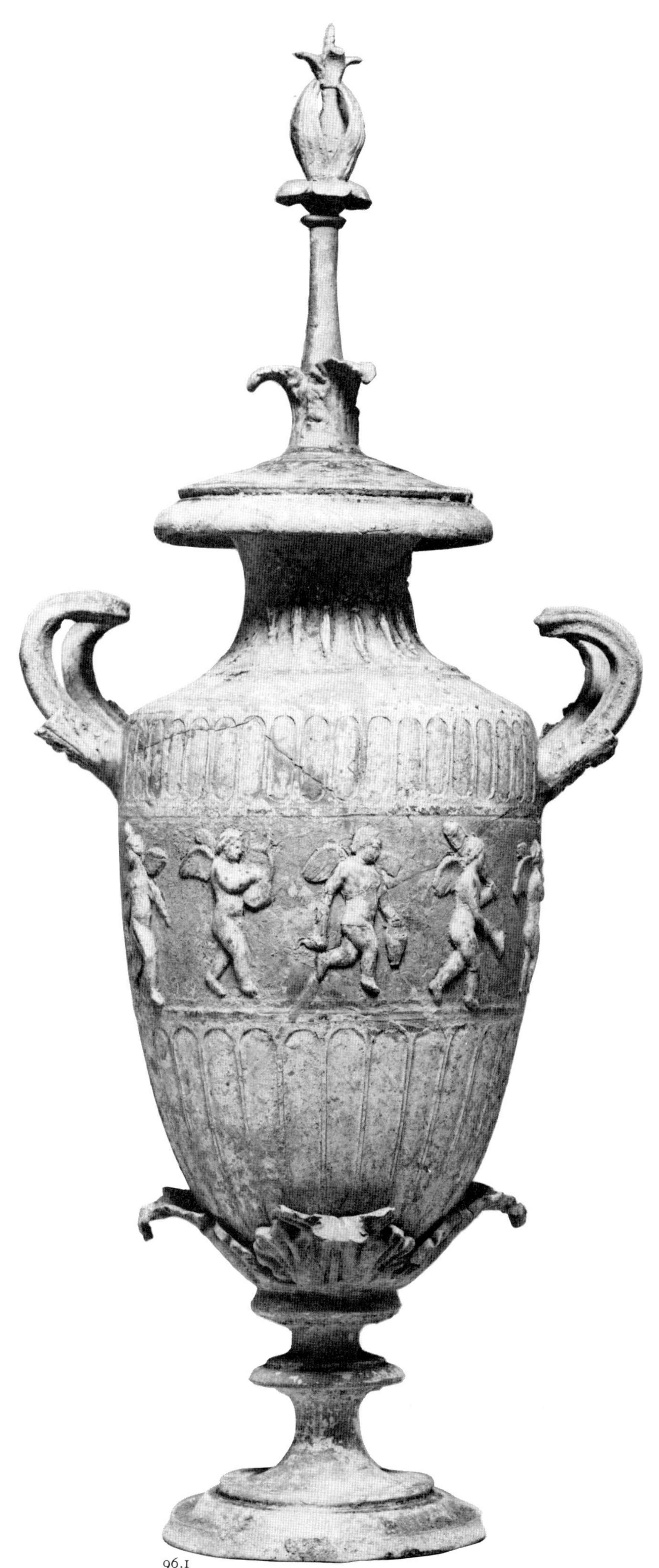

96.1

body, a pendant garland around the neck,
and akanthos leaves crowning the foot
and the base of the handles. Other pronounced features are the high turned base
with multiple windings, and the elongated finial with leafy tips. The largely
undecorated reverse indicates that the
amphora was intended as a display piece to
be exhibited in a niche. In the application
of individually fabricated reliefs the vessel
can be compared with other types of such
ware from South Italy, particularly relief
oinochoai and pyxides from Canosa dated
to the third century.[2] The prototype for
vessels of the Walters type is almost certainly metal, perhaps of the last quarter of
the third century, because a silver krateriskos of that date exhibits a similarily
turned base and elongated body with relief
tongues.[3] The Erotes in the figural frieze
carry the atributes, not of Aphrodite, but
rather of the Dionysiac realm, with which
Eros became increasingly associated in
Hellenistic times.[4]

Extensive thermoluminescence testing
verified the authenticity of this piece and
also established the modern date of
another vase of this type in the Walters
collection.[5]

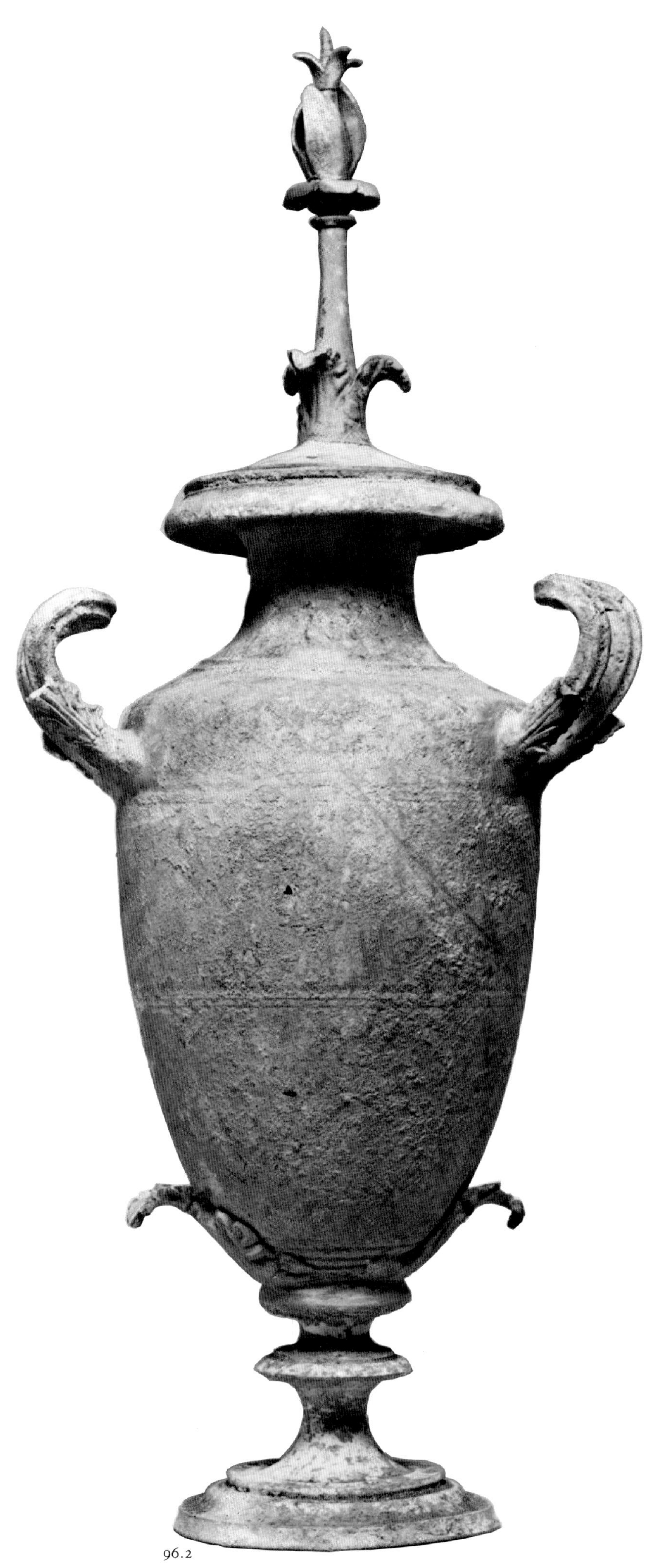

96.2

1. For the *Taranto* vases: De Juliis, *Taranto,* 280, fig. 324
   (inv. no. 22.796). The same piece appears in *Ori di
   Taranto,* 457, no. 17. For the mate (inv. no. 22.795), see
   Ori di Taranto, 457, no. 16 which also appears in G. P.
   Carratelli, ed., *Megale Hellas* (Milan, 1983), 649, no. 663.
   A second pair is in the Metropolitan Museum: inv. no.
   96.19.2 (GR 1016) and 96.19.3 (GR 1018) and appeared in
   J. de Witte and F. Lenormant, "Notes archéologiques sur
   Tarente," *GazArch* 7 (1881–82) 179–180, pl. 26, where
   they were said to have been found in Tarentum in a con-
   text ca. 250. The stand and lid of 96.19.2 are modern.
2. For relief oinochoai, see *Art of the Ancient World* IV,
   Royal-Athena Galleries (New York, 1985), 51, no. 165,
   dated to the third century. For pyxides, see W. Hornbostel, *Aus Gräbern und Heiligtümern, Museum für Kunst und
   Gewerbe Hamburg* (Mainz, 1980), 215–216, no. 123; F. L.
   Bastet, "Zwei Neuerwerbungen des Rijksmuseum van
   Oudheden in Leiden," *BABesch* 57 (1982) 155–158.
3. B. Barr-Sharrar, "Macedonian Metal Vases in Perspective:
   Some Observations on Context and Tradition," *Macedonia and Greece,* 126, fig. 7 from Tarentum.
4. Hill, *Hesperia* 16 (1947) 254–255. See also B. Segall, "Tradition," 22.
5. Inv. no. 48.1942. The piece has appeared in several publications: D. K. Hill (note 4) 249–253, pl. 67.2; F. Matz,
   *Ein römisches Meisterwerk; der Jahreszeitensarkophag
   Badminton-New York* (Berlin, 1958), 80, n. 161; 59, n. 63;
   and 76, n. 140, no. 3; R. Stuveras, *Le putto dans l'art
   romain,* CollLatomus 99 (Brussels, 1969), pl. 56, fig. 126.
   A fragmentary counterpart purchased shortly before 1900
   by The Metropolitan Museum of Art (96.19.4 [GR 1017])
   displays an almost identical frieze of Erotes. Unequivocably identified as modern on that piece are the necklace,
   foot, and some of the leaves.

MOLDMADE RELIEF BOWL
225–150

48.128. Clay. ''From Kyzikos.'' Purchased from
Kelekian before 1931. Ht, 7.6 cm; D, 12.8 cm.
Chipped around rim. Reddish glaze survives over
most of surface with half of upper surface blackened.

Hemispherical bowl with flaring rim. At center of
underside within a ridge border is a rosette, from
which radiate four akanthos leaves alternating with
four lotus leaves, all surmounted by palmettes.
Between the stems are small blossoms; above these
are palmettes, some of which are surmounted by
frontal heads, others by flying figures or Erotes.
Above is a ridge border; the neck is plain.

Perhaps no category of object, in its origin, manufacture, and use, more accu-
rately epitomizes Hellenistic culture than
does the so-called Megarian or Hellenistic
moldmade ceramic relief bowl. These vessels were fashioned in molds that were
made by pressing individual stamps into
the mold's surface, an assembly-line
process of manufacture which looks forward to the Arretine ware of the Augustan age.[1] The prototype of the vases lies in
a metal relief vessel, whose Egyptian
motifs indicate an Alexandrian origin;
however, the shape of that vessel was ultimately derived from the Persian kondu, a
hemispherical bowl used for libations.[2]
The Hellenistic moldmade bowl originated in Attic workshops sometime
around 225, possibly in direct imitation of
Alexandrian metal examples paraded at
the Ptolemaia, an athletic festival insti-
tuted in Athens in honor of the Egyptian
monarch Ptolemy III.[3] Soon after their
introduction, the bowls became popular
and immensely widespread; examples have
been found in a number of sites around
the eastern Mediterranean, and multiple
local manufacturing centers arose, many
of which have not yet been identified.
Until the end of the Hellenistic age the
moldmade bowl remained the conventional drinking vessel of the middle and
upper classes and was used primarily to
hold wine. The Walters example represents the floral style of moldmade bowl,
recognized by the rosette on its medallion
and the alternating lotus and akanthos
leaves. Its place of manufacture is uncertain, although parallels can be cited
among examples from Attika and Tarsos.
The Walters piece is probably approximately contemporary with its Attic counterparts, which have been dated to the last
quarter of the third century and first half
of the second century.[4]

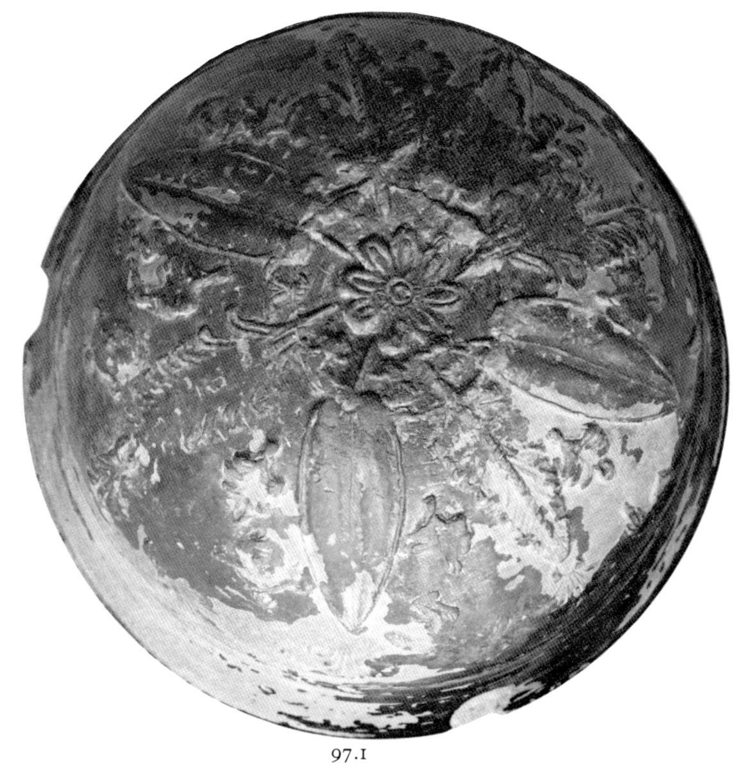

97.1

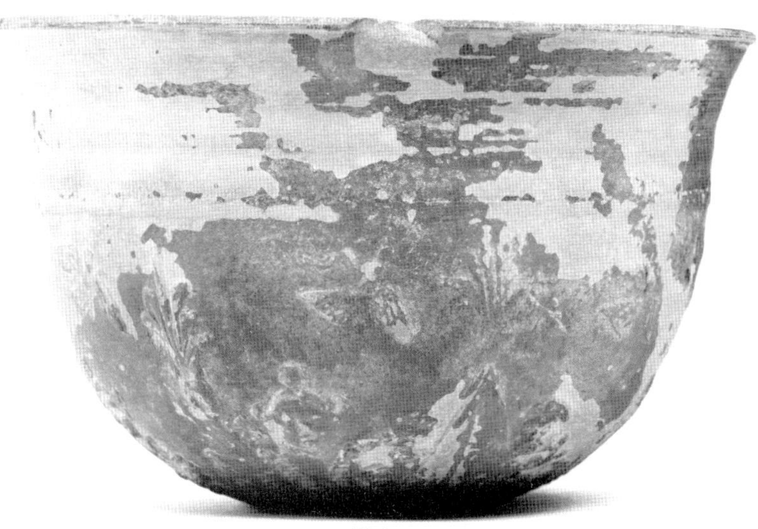

97.2

1. S. I. Rotroff, *Hellenistic Pottery. Athenian and Imported
   Moldmade Bowls,* The Athenian Agora 22 (Princeton,
   1982), 4–5.
2. Ibid., 3, 7–8. See also a silver bowl from Città Castellana
   in D. Strong, *Greek and Roman Gold and Silver Plate* (London, 1966), 109, pl. 31a, dated ca. second century; a silver
   bowl in Toledo in Oliver, *Silver,* 79, no. 43, dated 150–
   100; and a silver bowl dated 300–250 in G. Grimm, *Kunst
   der Ptolemäer und Römerzeit im Ägyptischen Museum, Kairo*
   (Mainz, 1975), 26, no. 58. pl. 98.
3. Rotroff (note 1) 11–12.
4. For the Tarsos examples, see Goldman, *Tarsus,* 235, nos.
   305–307. For the examples in Athens, see Rotroff (note 1)
   18, especially 51, no. 58, pl. 10 and 51, no. 59, pl. 10.

Moldmade Bowl of "Delian" type
169–69

48.130. Clay. "From Kyzikos." Purchased from Kelekian before 1931. D, 12.8 cm; Ht, 6 cm. Intact.

Bowl has ornament of moldmade relief. A rosette at the center of the underside is set within a ridged border, which is encircled by six akanthos leaves with curving tips alternating with six pyramidal leaves. Above is a raised band serving as a groundline for a frieze of paired running nude Erotes. A figure in right profile playing the flutes alternates with one in left profile waving clappers above and behind the head. Above is an egg-and-dart pattern between raised borders. The rim is smooth and carinated.

Exhibitions and Catalogues: *The Greek Tradition in Painting and the Minor Arts,* The Walters Art Gallery and the Baltimore Museum of Art (Baltimore, May 15–June 25, 1939), 68, no. 62.

Publications: D. K. Hill, "Mass Production in Antiquity," *GBA* 25 (1944) 67, and fig. 2 on 71; Goldman, *Tarsus,* 222, no. 148; G. Siebert, *Recherches sur les ateliers de bols à reliefs du Péloponnèse à l'époque hellénistique,* BEFAR 233 (1978), 32, pl. 16.

This bowl belongs to the so-called Delian group of moldmade bowls, now recognized as ware produced in Ionian workshops and widely exported, exerting influence on such local versions as that of the Demetrias-Iason workshop in Argos.[1] Bowls of the Delian type are dated by context to ca. 169–69 and are distinguished by their bands of ornament which often feature a leafy kalyx beneath figural friezes of Erotes. The appearance of Eros in Hellenistic pottery, further illustrated by the Tarentine relief amphora (No. 96), is not attested before the third quarter of the third century.[2]

1. G. Siebert, *Recherches,* 32; S. I. Rotroff, *Hellenistic Pottery. Athenian and Imported Moldmade Bowls,* The Athenian Agora 22 (Princeton, 1982), 7, note 8.
2. R. Horn, *Hellenistische Bildwerke auf Samos,* Samos 12 (Bonn, 1972), 207.

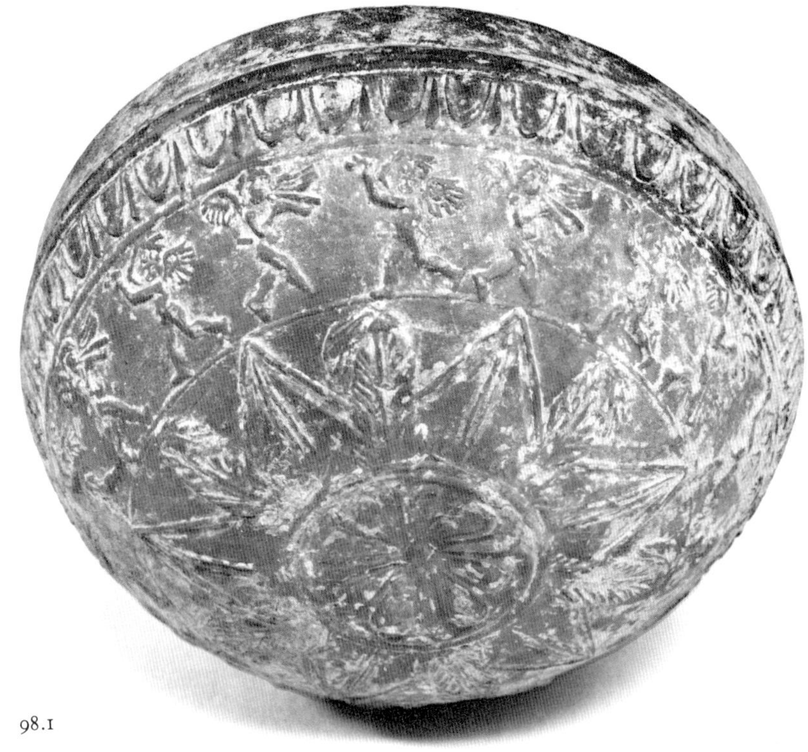

98.1

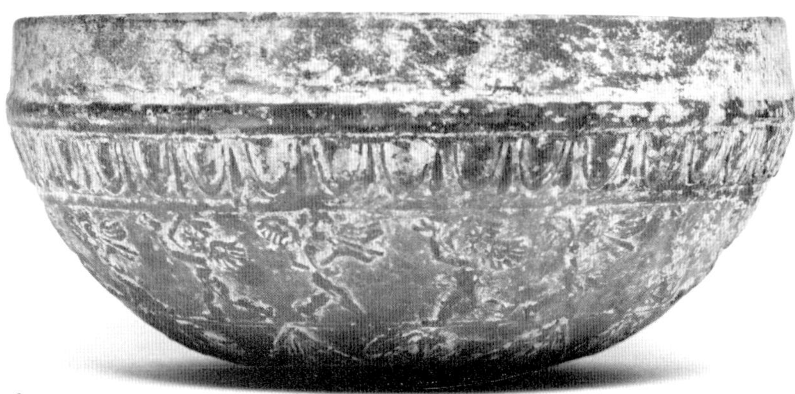

98.2

MOLDMADE BOWL OF
LONG-PETALED TYPE
150–first century

48.129. Clay. "From Kyzikos." Purchased from Kelekian before 1931. D, 11.2 cm; Ht, 6.4 cm. Chipped over surface.

Around the underside of the foot, in raised lettering, is the name: ΔΗΜΗΤΡΙΟϒ. Around the bowl are molded tongues separated by vertical rows of raised dots. Above is a band of egg-and-dart between ridges; the carinated rim has a raised ridge around its midsection.

Publications: G. Siebert, *Recherches sur les ateliers de bols à reliefs du Péloponnèse à l'époque hellénistique,* BEFAR 233 (1978), 30, no. DI 132, 31, no. 5, pl. 21.

The long-petaled style of the Hellenistic moldmade relief bowl was derived from Egyptian and Achaemenid metal proto-types and was apparently invented in Ath-ens about 150.[1] It rapidly became the most widespread variety of moldmade bowl and was manufactured in a number of centers, almost to the end of the first century. Variations in ornament included the jew-eling, or dotting, between the petals, as seen on this example. Although the Wal-ters bowl compares closely with the Attic versions, it represents a local imitation that was made in Kerch (Panticipaeon) on the Black Sea coast. Unlike the Attic ver-sions, which often have undecorated medallions, the medallion on the Walters bowl bears the name of the potter Deme-trios, whose ware has occasionally been confused both with vases from Delos and with bowls from the Demetrios-Iason workshop in Argos.[2]

1. S. I. Rotroff, *Hellenistic Pottery. Athenian and Imported Moldmade Bowls,* The Athenian Agora 22 (Princeton, 1982), 34.
2. G. Siebert, *Recherches,* 31.

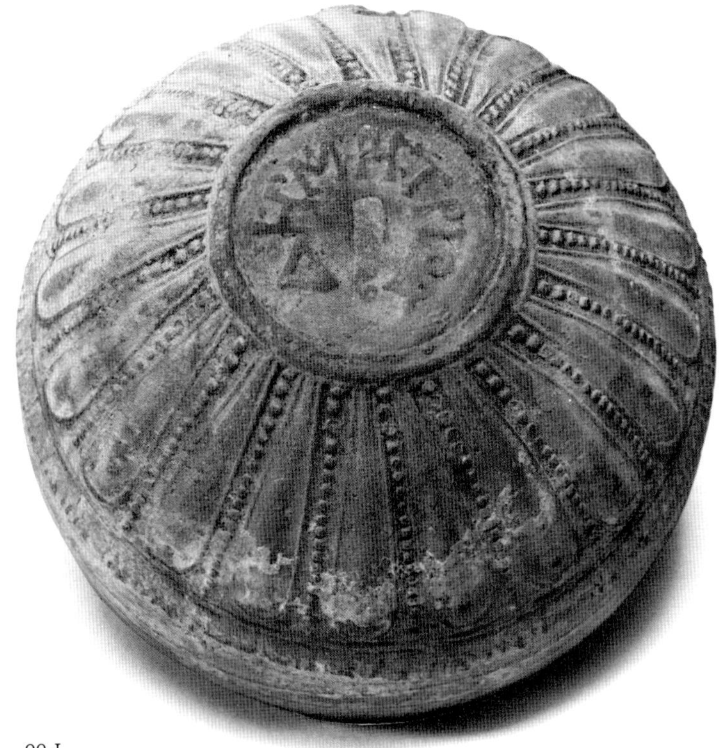

99.1

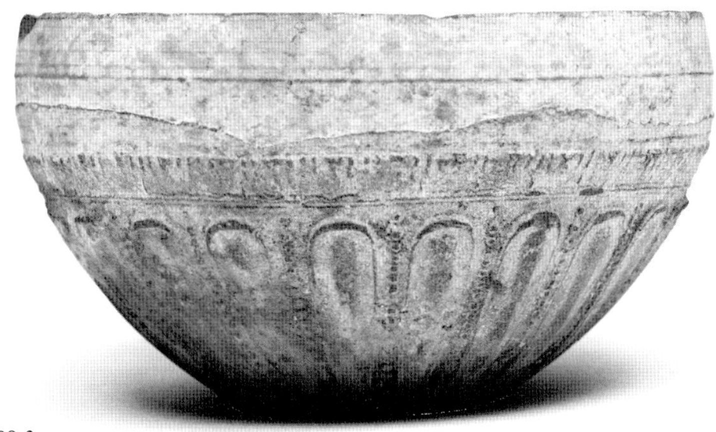

99.2

Hadra Hydria
Ca. 230

48.1916. Clay. Gift of David Rosen, 1945. Ht, 37.2 cm; D, base 11.6 cm; D, mouth 13.3 cm. Broken and mended from many pieces.

The hydria has a horizontal shoulder and flaring lip. Its decoration is in black glaze. On the raised center of the handle is a vertical leafy band. A wave pattern encircles the lip, and around the neck is a laurel band with a clump of berries at center front. A black line marks the transition from neck to shoulder. Around the top of the shoulder is a band of tongues separated by circles, which had white dotted centers and wavy stems. Between the handles is a band defined above and below by three black lines, the middle line in the upper border being especially thick. Within the band is a tainia, draped as a festoon with hanging ends, rendered in black pigment with incised contours. Incised inside the upper and lower edges of the tainia is a band of wave pattern. In the center of the tainia are two facing hippocamps with forelegs upraised, each followed by two leaping dolphins shown in profile. The frieze continues around the back as angled palmettes enclosed by scrolls.

This type of vase takes its name from the cemetery in Alexandria where a number of examples of this type of ware was discovered in 1883–84.[1] Subsequently, many more hydriai were recovered from other necropoli in Alexandria and still more were found in Cyprus, Rhodes, and Crete, areas closely allied with Ptolemaic interests in Hellenistic times. The hydriai functioned primarily as funerary ash urns, and some examples even have a dropped foot to expand the capacity of the container.[2] The mouths were usually closed with plaster or clay stoppers, and the vessels were placed in simple holes sunk into the rock or sand. Inscriptional evidence, as well as the resemblance of the shape and laurel band to those of metal hydriai with gold leaf wreaths from Macedon, suggest that the Hadra hydriai were introduced and primarily used by Greek officials and mercenary soldiers employed by the Ptolemies.[3] Judging by context and by the few extant inscriptions, the ware did not appear before about 260 and fell out of use about 180, probably because the indigenous Egyptian element reasserted itself following the successful use of native troops in Ptolemy IV's defeat of Antiochos III at Raphia in 217.[4] The Walters hydria can be attributed to the Painter of

the "Coureurs," whose best-known work is a vase in Brussels which was found on Cyprus and which exhibits the same leafy wreath around the neck and, on the body, a garlanded panel bearing representations of sea horses and dolphins.[5] Enklaar dates this period of the painter's career to about 230 and suggests that he continued to be active down to about 200.

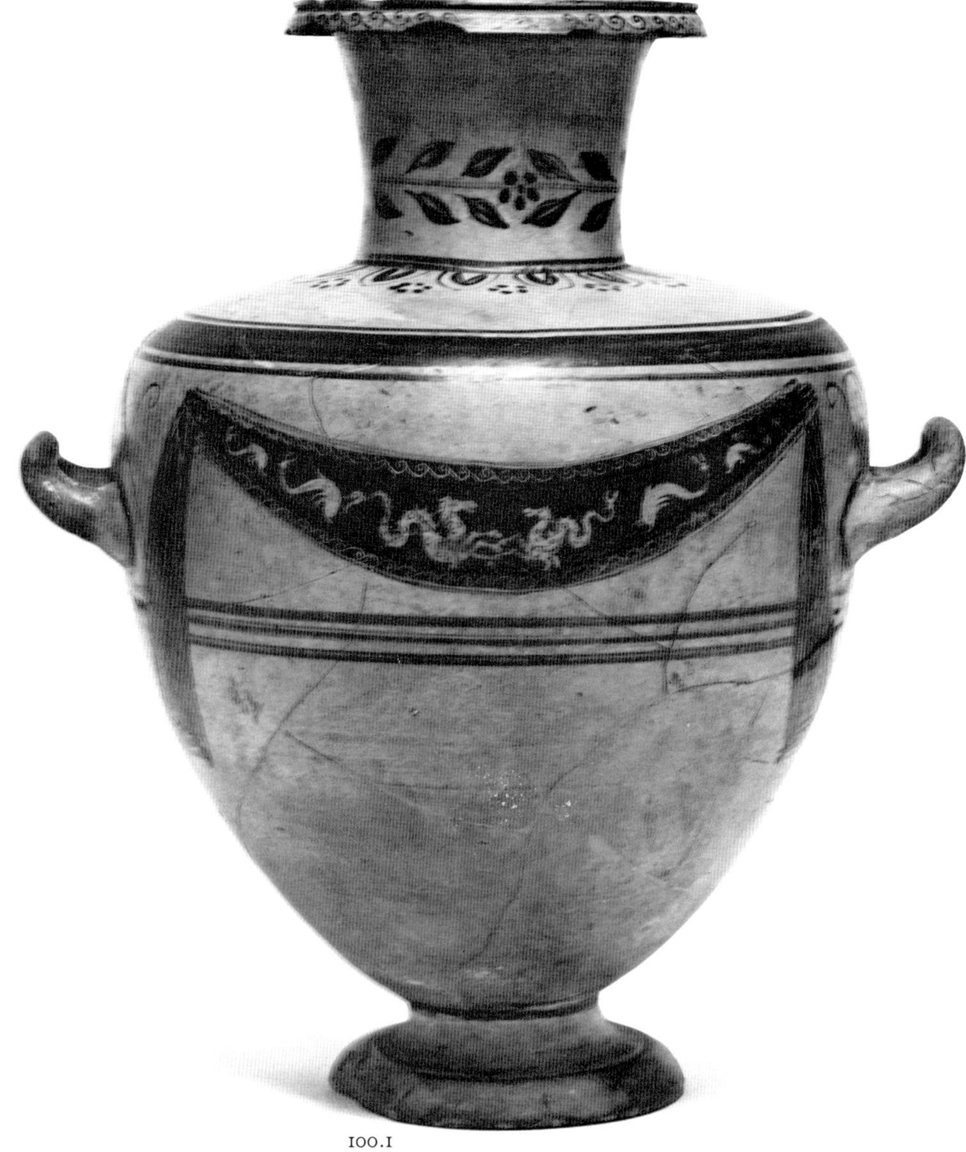

100.1

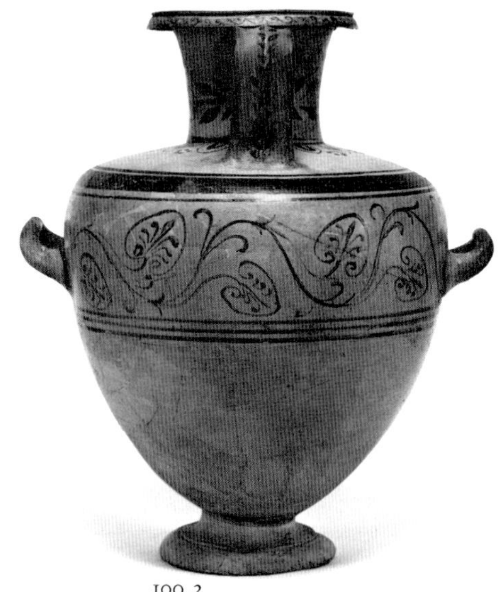

100.2

1. B. F. Cook, *Inscribed Hadra Vases in the Metropolitan Museum of Art* (New York, 1966), 7.
2. Ibid., 9.
3. A. Enklaar, "Chronologie et peintres des hydries de Hadra," *BABesch* 60 (1965) 110; W. Hornbostel, *Aus Gräbern und Heiligtümern, Museum für Kunst und Gewerbe, Hamburg* (Mainz, 1980), 19, no. 15. For a metal counterpart from Macedon, see M. Andronicos, *Vergina. The Royal Tombs and the Ancient City* (Athens, 1984), 212 and 214, fig. 183.
4. Enklaar (note 3) 110, 116.
5. Ibid., 140–141. See also L. Forti, "Appunti sulla ceramica di Hadra," *Alessandria*, 232–233.

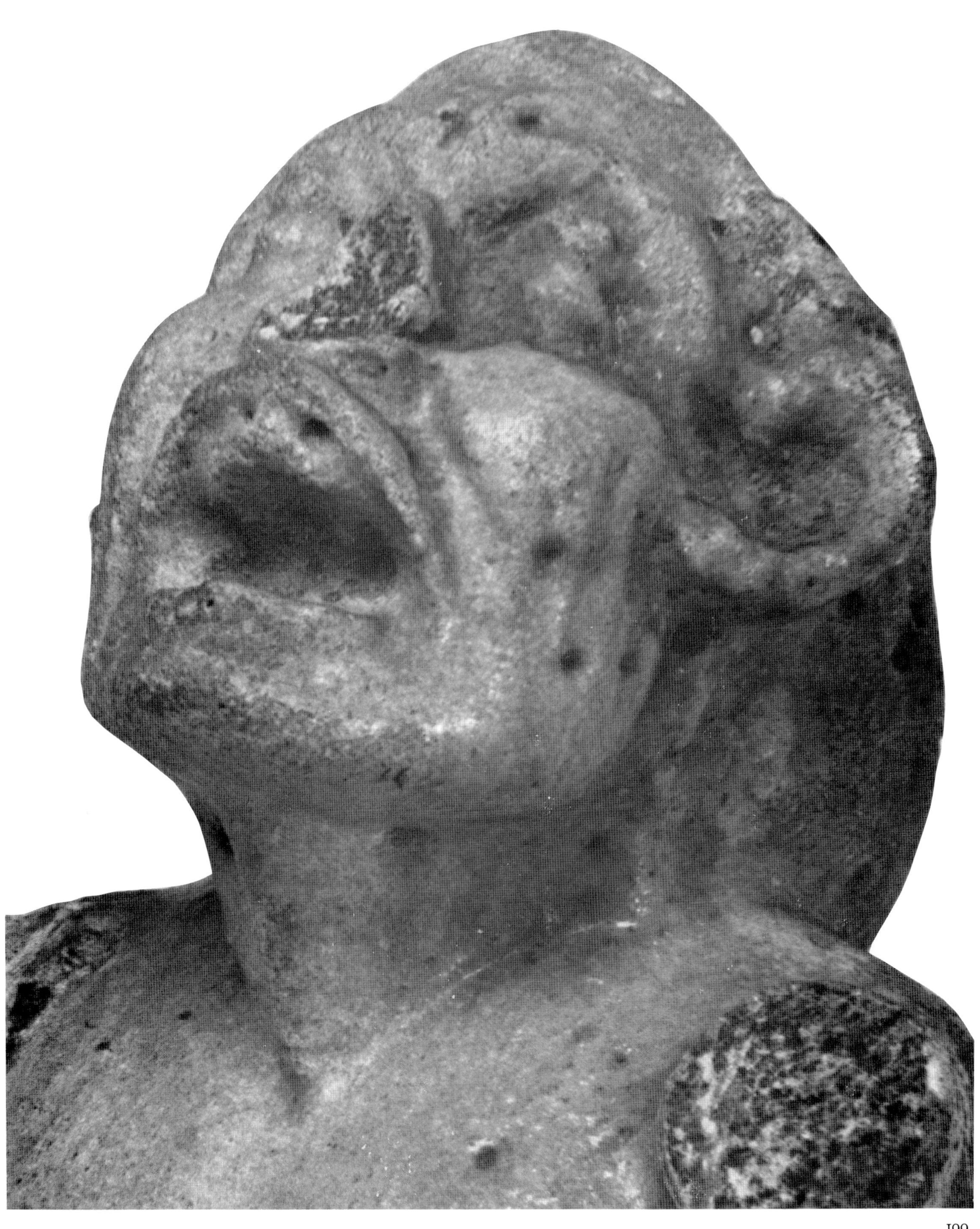

Faience Grotesque
Second century

48.1748. Faience. Purchased before 1931. Ht, 6.2 cm; W, 4 cm. Both legs missing below thighs.

A nude male has a chubby body and a large phallus and head. His left thigh is upraised; his upper torso twists to his right with his head pressed against his right shoulder. His right hand grasps his right buttock; his left hand is brought to his mouth. He has a snub nose, grooved brow, and wears a tainia, beneath which coiled locks are visible.

Publications: G. Grimm, ''Orient und Okzident in der Kunst Alexandriens,'' *Alexandrien,* N. Hinske, ed., Aegyptiaca Treverensia I (Mainz, 1981), 19, pl. 19c.

Faience is made by combining ground quartz with natron, which is a natural mixture of sodium carbonate and sodium bicarbonate. Copper oxide added to the paste results, through a self-glazing process, in a blue or blue-green color which can be intensified by brushing glaze over the object after molding and before firing. Occasionally encountered is faience with a brilliant deep green or peacock blue color obtained by firing the piece at a higher than normal (950° centigrade) temperature.[1] Although faience was made in Egypt from early times, the Alexandrian workshops of the Hellenistic age used the medium in innovative ways that reflect influence from both the Greek and Oriental worlds.

This piece is particularly illuminating because it constitutes a bridge between traditional Egyptian art and the Hellenizing character of Alexandrian workshops. The figure's stylized countenance compares closely with conventional depictions of the Egyptian deity Bes, but the momentary action of the twisted form, as well as the coarse features, which seem directly inspired by a living subject, call to mind the animated bronze grotesques and dwarfs (Nos. 55, 56) which are a more familiar legacy of Ptolemaic Egypt.[2]

1. Thompson, *Oinochoai,* 7–11.
2. Compare an image of Bes on an example of Naukratis ware in Grimm, *Alexandrien,* pl. 17a.

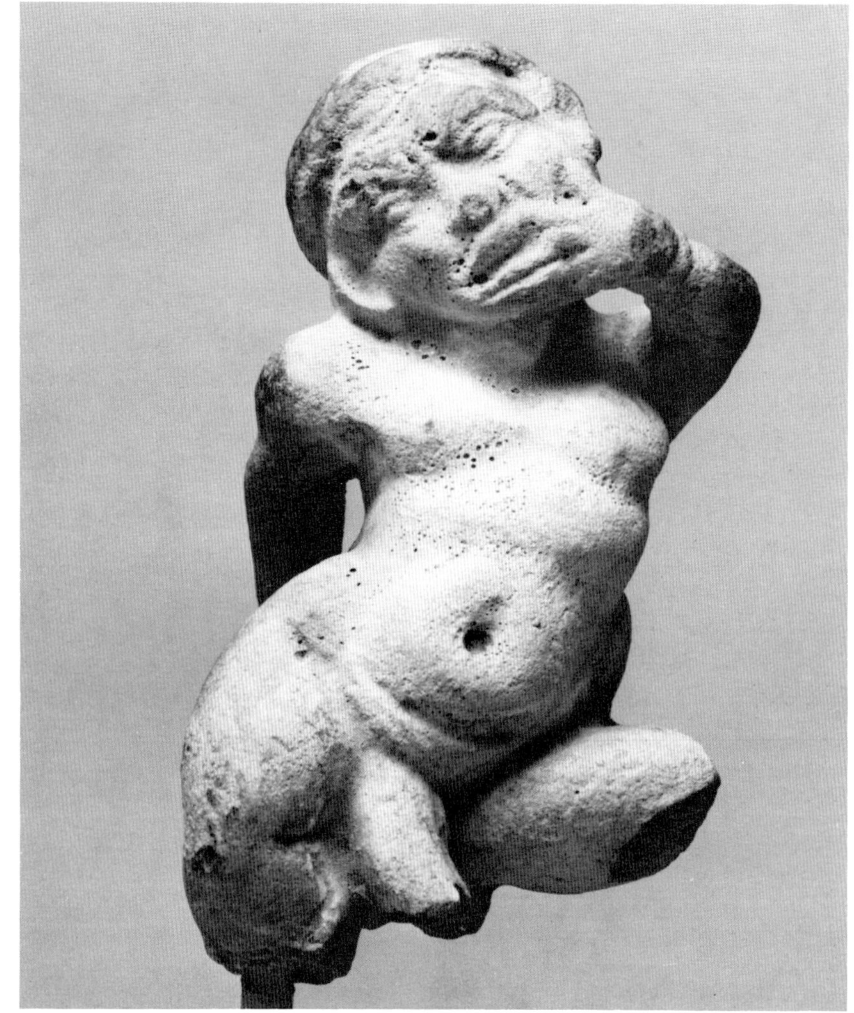

101.1

Figurine of a Dwarf
Third to second century

48.491. Faience. MacGregor Collection (sale catalogue, London, Sotheby, Wilkinson and Hodge, June 26–30, July 3–6, 1922, 46, no. 328. Purchased in 1923. Ht, 7.4 cm; W, 4.1 cm; Th, 3.8 cm. Both arms and legs broken off.

A male figure with fleshy, protruding belly and carefully delineated curved spinal column throws his head back, his large mouth open with the upper teeth visible. His cheeks and neck are vertically lined, his brow is furrowed, and his ears are very large. The top of his head is bald; the rest of his hair falls behind his ears to his shoulders.

Dwarfs were not uncommon among the Egyptian population and appeared in Egyptian art from very early times. This piece offers a harsher, more realistic treatment of physical abnormality than do the preceding example and the bronze dancing dwarf (No. 55). On those figures the stylized rendering creates a gently humorous and sympathetic effect which is probably due to a greater infusion of Greek influence than is apparent in this raw view of human incongruity.

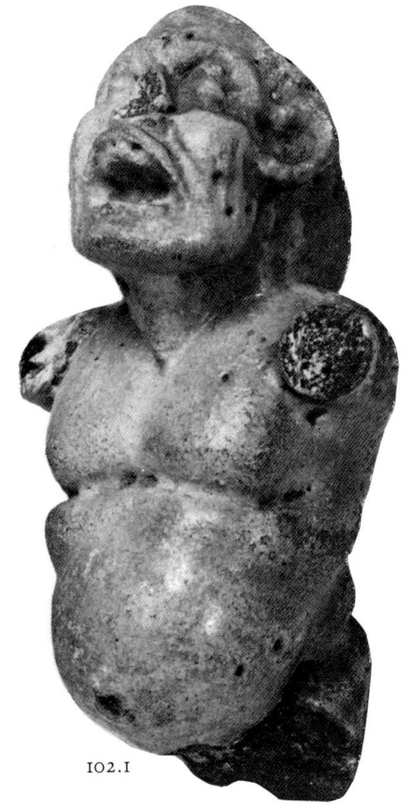

102.1

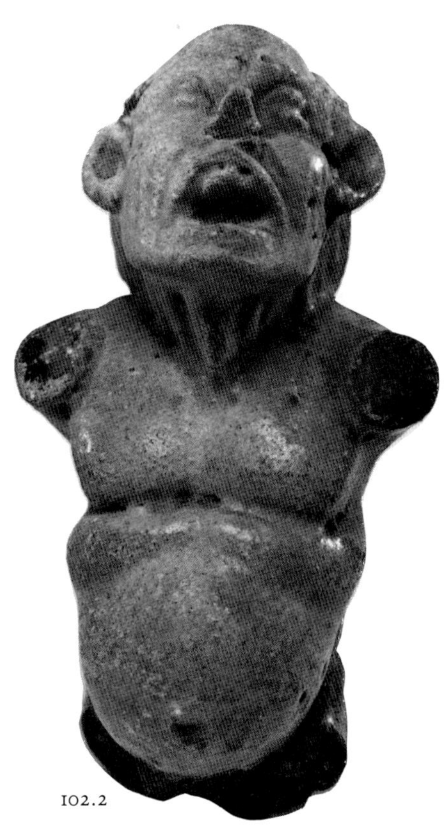

102.2

FRAGMENT OF AN
OINOCHOE WITH ARSINOE II
Ca. 267

48.315. Faience. Purchased before 1931. Ht, 7 cm; W, 5.1 cm; Th, 1.6 cm. Greenish glaze on both sides. Black paint on hair, eyebrow, pupil. Broken all around; remaining is the frontal torso of a woman preserved to below the waist. Black stains over surface.

Remaining are the head to waist and left arm of a woman with her torso frontal, her head in left profile. The fingers of her left hand support a double cornucopia with a ribbed tip which rests in the crook of her left arm. A stalk of wheat and several pieces of fruit emerge from each horn. She wears a peplos beneath an himation which is rolled across her torso beneath her breasts and wrapped around the left elbow and forearm with a knot of folds beside her left breast. She has Venus rings and wears hoop earrings. Her hair is arranged in a melon hairstyle beneath a wide headband; a braid coiled at the back of her head is wrapped in a fillet.

Publications: D. K. Hill, "Four Fragments of Ptolemaic High-Relief Faience," *RA* ser 6, 43–44 (1954) no. 1, 44–46 and 45, fig. 1; Thompson, *Oinochoai,* 127, no. 5 and pl. IV; E. LaRocca, *L'età d'oro di Cleopatra* (Rome, 1984), 43, fig. 42b.

This relief belongs to a type of Ptolemaic faience jug that was made in Alexandria and was used to pour libations at small temporary altars which were erected during festivals, therewith echoing an age-old Egyptian custom of exchanging faience gifts in celebration of the Egyptian New Year.[1] Although no metallic prototype is known, these vases were almost certainly inexpensive reproductions of counterparts in precious metal used by the upper classes.

The subject of this relief is Arsinoe II, who was married first to Lysimachos of Thrace, then to Ptolemy Keraunos, and finally (276/275) to Ptolemy II Philadelphos. In 267, only three years after her death in 270, the festival of the Arsinoeia was inaugurated in her honor, and it was probably on this occasion that faience oinochoai of this type were produced for the first time.[2] The Walters relief is one of the earliest examples of these vases and can probably be dated soon after 267, although vases with Arsinoe's portrait continued to be made down to about

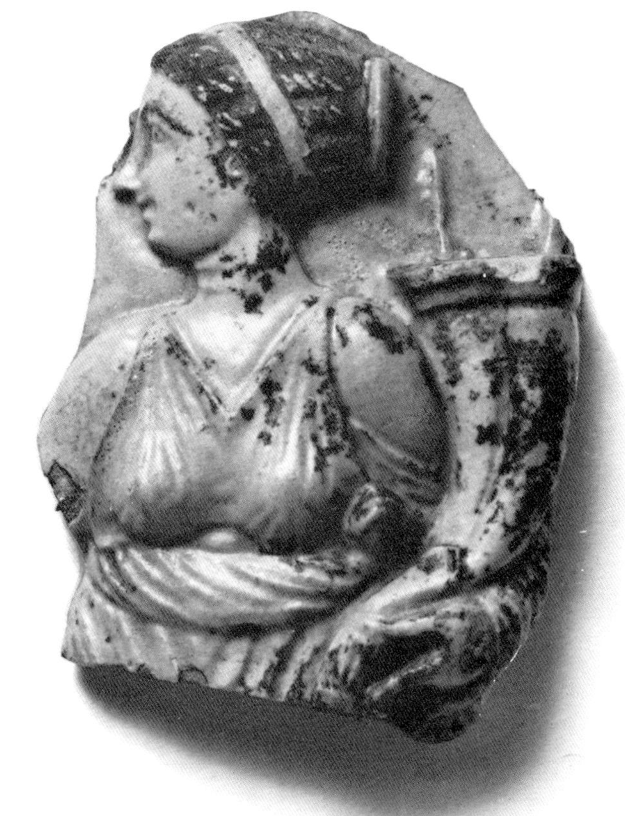

103.1

240.[3] The double cornucopia was introduced under Ptolemy II in allusion to the double or divine nature of Ptolemy and Arsinoe, who were worshiped as deities in their lifetimes.[4] The sheaves of wheat refer to the queen's identity as Isis, and the pyramidal cakes of wheat and honey seen in other examples of this type are associated with Demeter. Because Athenaeus mentions a statue of Arsinoe holding a cornucopia, it is possible that the Walters relief reproduces a statue erected to Ptolemy II and Arsinoe II upon their return from the First Syrian War (276–271).[5]

The relief exhibits a curious blend of Greek and native Egyptian stylistic elements. The roll of drapery is Greek, as is the shape of the vessel, but the frontality and linearity are Egyptian and may be either the inadvertent contribution of an Egyptian craftsman, or a deliberate attempt to fashion an image acceptable to both the Greek and the Egyptian populations.

1. Thompson, *Oinochoai,* 116, 122.
2. Ibid., 71, 120.
3. Ibid., 47.
4. Ibid., 33.
5. Ibid., 83; Athenaeus, *Deipnosophistae* 2.497b–c.

FRAGMENT OF AN
OINOCHOE WITH ARSINOE III
Ca. 217

48.309. ''From Lower Egypt.'' Purchased from
Kelekian between 1910 and 1915. Ht, 14.9 cm; W,
9.2 cm; Th, 4.2 cm. Blue glaze fading to white over
large areas. Incompletely glazed over interior. Broken all around. Missing are the right elbow and
lower arm, and both lower legs of the figure, and a
section from the mouth of the cornucopia. Chips are
missing from the jaw, nose, mantle, and cornucopia.

A woman stands frontally with her weight on her
right leg, her left knee bent. Her right forearm is
extended to one side, and her hand held a staff, the
remains of which survive along the edge of the
break. Her left arm cradles a cornucopia in the crook
of her elbow with her fingers supporting its tip. She
wears a peplos beneath a mantle which is brought
under the right breast, and over the left shoulder
with the ends hanging behind the left arm; the mantle folds cover the body to the knees. Her head is
turned in three-quarters right profile and her hair is
arranged in a melon hairstyle beneath a headband;
the ends are coiled at the back of her head.

Publications: D. K. Hill, ''Some Late Egyptian
Ceramics in the Walters Art Gallery,'' *GBA* 30
(1946) 195 and 195, fig.2; D. K. Hill, ''Four Fragments of Ptolemaic High-Relief Faience,'' *RA* ser.
6, 43–44 (1954) 46–48, no. 2 and 47, fig. 2; Thompson, *Oinochoai*, 26, 112, 160, no. 109, pls. D, 38;
H. Kyrieleis, *Bildnisse der Ptolemäer* (Berlin, 1975),
104, no. 420; A. Linfert, *Kunstzentren hellenistischer
Zeit* (Weisbaden, 1976), 21, no. 37b, 103, no. 372c;
S. Besques, ''Deux portraits d'Arsinoé III Philopator?'' *RA* n.s. 2 (1981) 235 and 238, fig. 17.

The staff, possibly with a lotus tip, links
the maiden with similar images identified
on coins as Arsinoe III and distinguishes
this figure from the libation-pouring types
typically seen on Ptolemaic oinochoai.[1] It
is likely that the figure on this fragment,
as well as a statuette in Crete depicting
the same figure in mirror image, is based
upon a statue of the queen addressing the
troops during the battle at Raphia in 217.[2]
The three flat waves of the melon hairstyle as well as the disc knot indicate that
this is one of the earliest types of Arsinoe
III to appear on the faience jugs.[3]

Arsinoe III was the wife and sister of
Ptolemy IV Philopator, who is best
remembered for his victory over Antiochos III at Raphia in 217. Almost twenty
thousand native troops were used in this
battle, the success of which strengthened
the voice of the native population, and
precipitated outbursts of domestic violence for years afterwards.[4] Arsinoe conspired with her son, Ptolemy V, to
murder her husband, but either before or
after the latter's death in 205, she died
herself under mysterious circumstances in
a palace fire. Despite her machinations,
Arsinoe III enjoyed the deep affection of
her subjects who, according to Polybios,
greatly lamented her death.[5]

1. Thompson, *Oinochoai*, 160.
2. Ibid., 26, 89, 112.
3. Ibid., 160.
4. Polybios 5.107.1–3 and 14.12.3–4. See Austin, *Hellenistic
   World*, 371–372, no. 225.
5. Polybios 15.25.8–10.

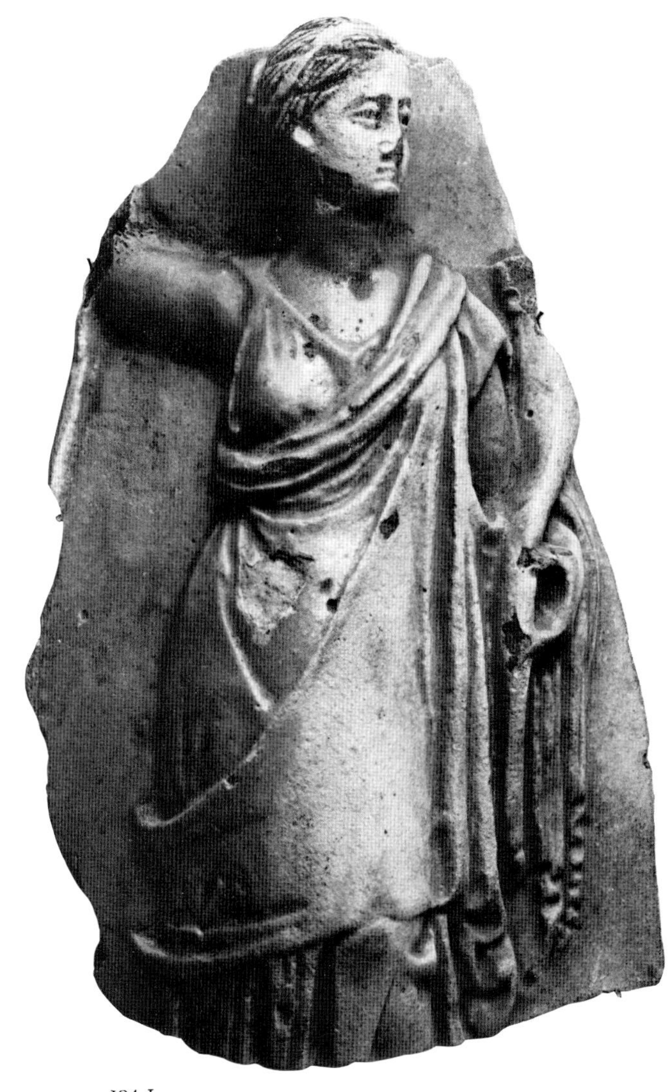

104.1

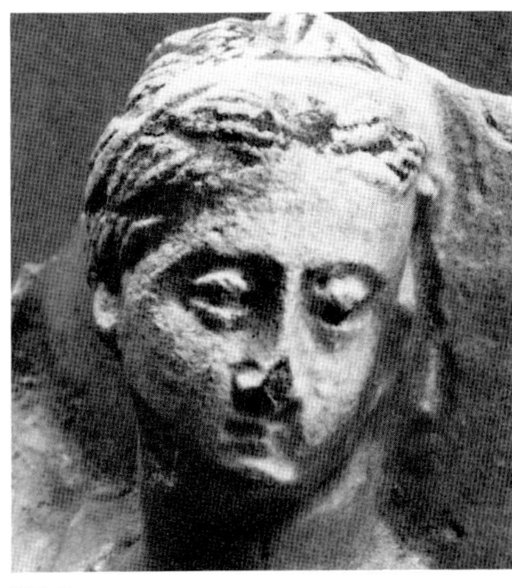

104.2

Rhyton
Third to second century

48.368. Faience. MacGregor Collection (sale catalogue, London, Sotheby, Wilkinson and Hodge, June 26–30, July 3–6, 1922, 29, no. 212). Purchased from Kelekian in 1923. L, 22.5 cm; D, mouth 9.5 cm. Chipped around rim. Lower third restored.

Surviving is the upper part of a rhyton with a flaring rim. Its ornament in low relief is arranged in registers. From the rim are two ridged bands above egg-and-dart, then bands of guilloche and rosettes separated by smooth bands. Beneath is a wave ornament above a frieze of three six-petal palmettes alternating with winged griffins seen in profile, their near front paws upraised. Beneath are bands of volute and guilloche separated by smooth bands, then a garland outlined by dots with the ribbon ends suspended from the points of attachment.

Publications: Burlington Fine Arts Club, *Illustrated Catalogue of Ancient Egyptian Art* (London, 1922), 13, pl. 46; D. K. Hill, ''Some Late Egyptian Ceramics in the Walters Art Gallery,'' *GBA* 30 (1946) 195, and 196, fig. 3.

This faience vessel is an example of so-called Naukratis ware, which takes its name from the Egyptian site where most pieces have been recovered. Characteristic features are the representations in low relief and the bicolor, or sgraffito, effect caused by brushing over the surface a glaze which settled into the depressed areas and fired a darker color than did the raised portions.[1] The ware was made in a variety of shapes from the early Hellenistic period well into the Roman era and was exported widely over the Mediterranean from workshops probably located in such centers as Alexandria and Memphis. Typical of the ware is the organization of the decoration into a series of friezes, which in this case rise above a garland which has been worked in the traditional Egyptian sunk relief and which has, consequently, fired darker than the raised background. Enough survives of the original vessel to recognize the curving walls of a rhyton, which is a shape of Near Eastern origin, as are many of the motifs, including the rosettes and the palmette flanked by griffins. Parallels to these devices as well as to the braid, wave, and scroll motifs are frequently seen on other examples of the fabric.[2]

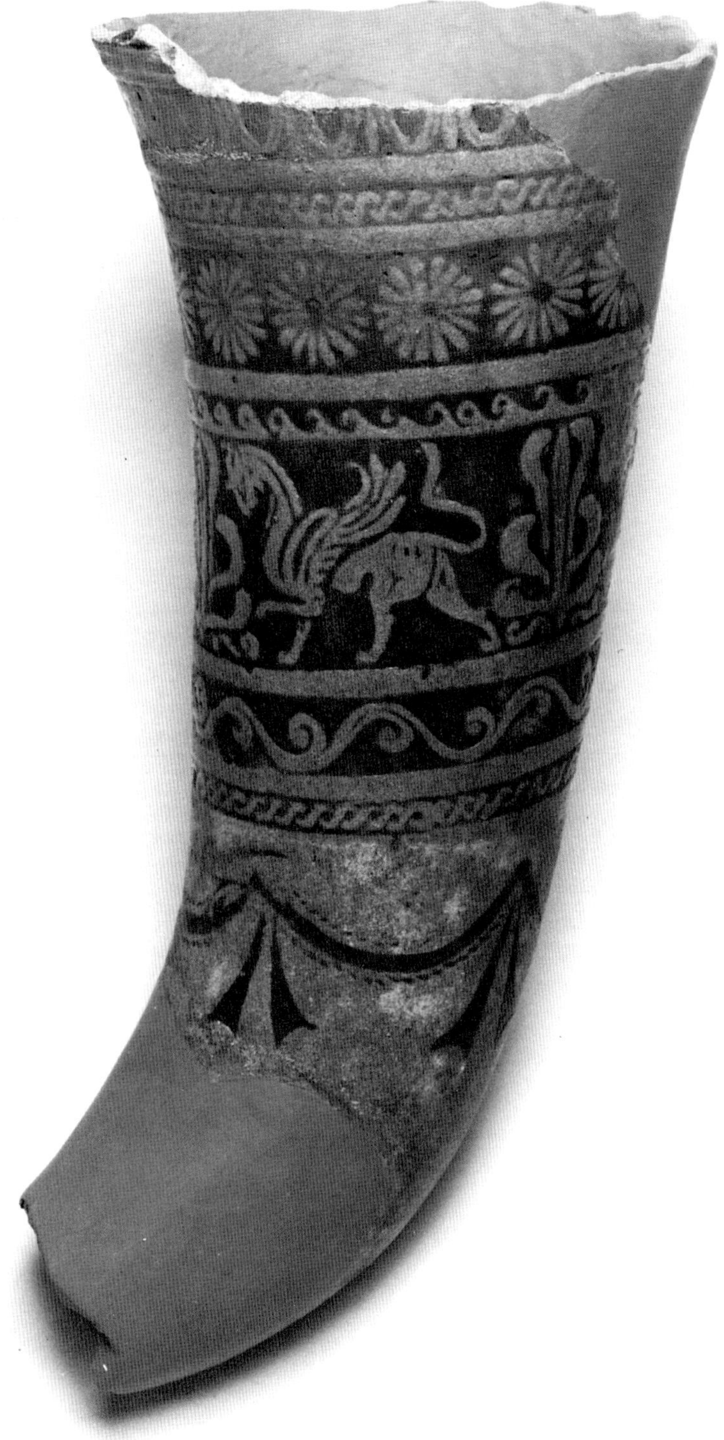

105.1

1. Thompson, *Oinochoai*, 12; Hill, *GBA* 30 (1946) 195.
2. G. Grimm, ''Orient und Okzident in der Kunst Alexandriens,'' *Alexandrien,* N. Hinske, ed., Aegyptiaca Treverensia 1 (Mainz, 1981), 19, pl. 17a, b. K. Parlasca, ''Zur Verbreitung ptolemäischer Fayencekeramik ausserhalb Ägyptens,'' *JdI* 91 (1976) 139 and 140, fig. 3 from Kition; 142, fig. 8 from Corinth; 143, fig. 9 from Thessaloniki; 151, fig. 23, probably from Italy.

TAPERED FLASK
Third to second century

48.370. Faience. Purchased from Kelekian in 1924. Ht, 17.1 cm; D, mouth 3.2 cm; D, base 3 cm. Chipped at base, around rim, and on shoulder.

A narrow vessel swells to its widest point one third the distance up the side, then gently tapers to a ridge beneath its high flaring mouth. Its ornament in low relief is organized in registers separated by smooth, narrow bands. Around the base are lotus leaves surmounted by a narrow register with a wavy line. Above is a frieze of short, frontal figures, moving to their left with their legs widespread, their heads in right profile and their hands linked. Each wears a dotted tunic over the upper torso and a short kilt with the drapery ends falling between the legs. Above is a frieze consisting of two birds in left profile with outstretched wings, separated by floral ornament. At the top of the shoulder is a register with a wavy line, beneath another with an egg-and-dart pattern.

Publications: D. K. Hill, ''Some Late Egyptian Ceramics in the Walters Art Gallery,'' *GBA* 30 (1946) 197 and 196, fig. 4.

Typical of Naukratis ware are the alternation of broad figural bands with narrow ornamental borders, and, in the lowest register, a cluster of lotus and palmette leaves. Subjects are typically drawn from the worlds of the hunt and banquet; on this example, the frieze of dancing men can be compared with a similar frieze on an alabastron in the Louvre.[1] Also typical of Naukratis ware are the non-Hellenic shapes, which were probably inspired by traditional Egyptian pottery. The closest parallels to the shape of this example are a vessel in Cairo and one that was formerly in the MacGregor collection.[2]

1. Segall, ''Tradition,'' 24 and 18, fig. 6.
2. G. Grimm, *Götter Pharaonen* (Mainz, 1978), no. 122, from Memphis, dated third century; H. Wallis, *Egyptian Ceramic Art. The MacGregor Collection* (London, 1898), 85.

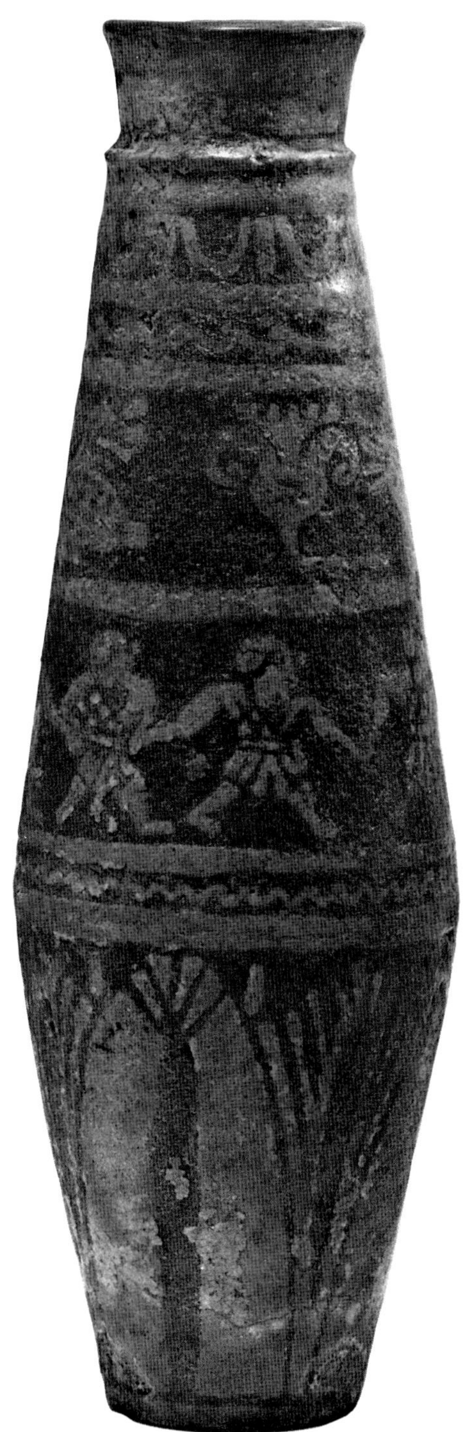

106.1

Bowl
Third to second century

48.364. Faience with light green lustrous glaze inside and out. Purchased from Kelekian in 1922. D, 14.6 cm; Ht, 9.5 cm. Laurel band impressed around the inside of rim. Mended from several pieces.

A round-bottom bowl bears ornament in low relief arranged in registers separated by smooth bands. On the underside is a rosette. Above is a band with pairs of vertical bars. Around the center of the body is a band in which winged griffins alternate with panels bearing either checkerboard or diamond patterns. A wave pattern appears above.

The similarity of the form to that of Megarian bowls suggests that both metal and clay prototypes can be claimed for Naukratis ware.[1] Typical of the ware is the alternation of hybrid beings and decorative panels which find parallels on an example in the Louvre.[2]

1. For other bowls in Naukratis ware, see K. Parlasca, "Neues zur ptolemäischen Fayencekeramik," *Alessandria,* 302, pl. 54.
2. Segall, "Tradition," 24 and 18, fig. 6. Compare also two fragments in H. Wallis, *Egyptian Ceramic Art. The Mac-Gregor Collection* (London, 1898), figs. 186–187.

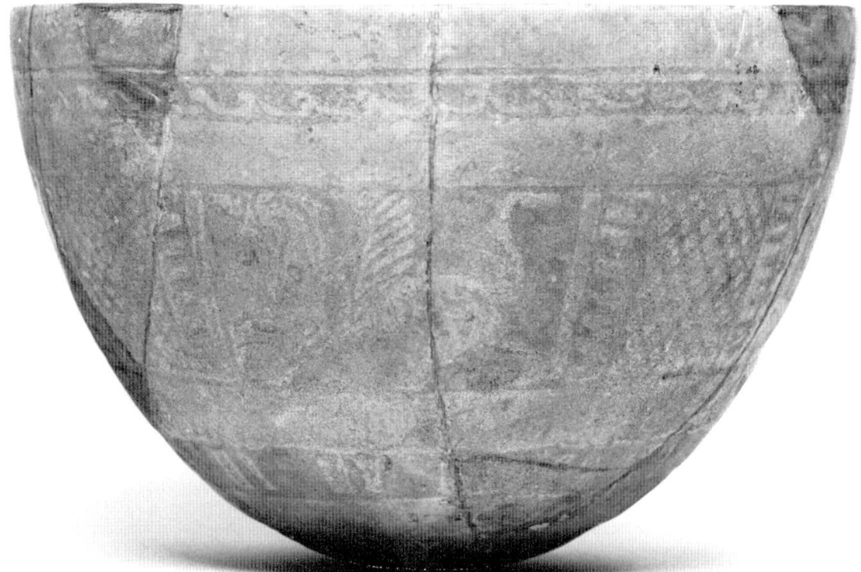

107.1

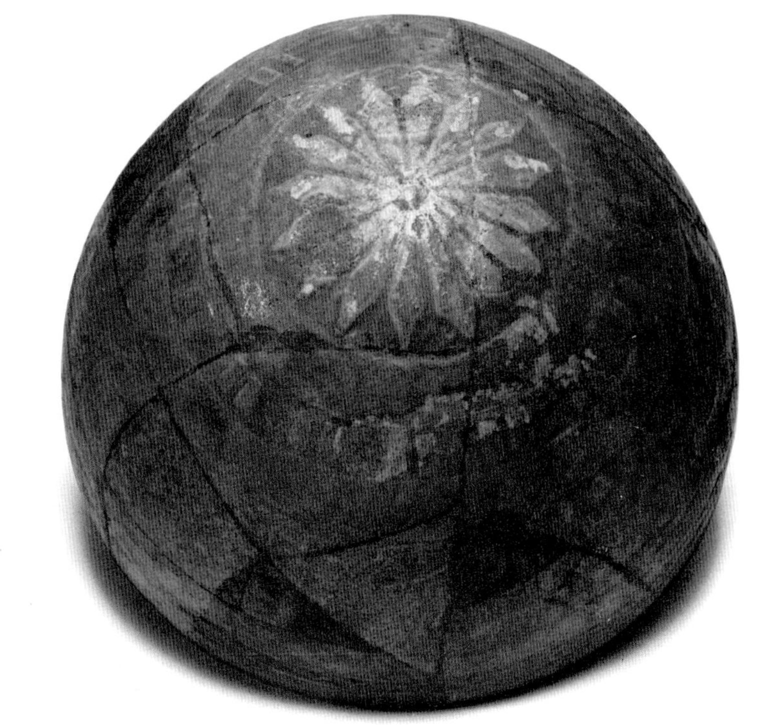

107.2

Bowl with Lotus Ornament

Third century

48.366. Faience. MacGregor Collection (sale catalogue, London, Sotheby, Wilkinson and Hodge, June 26–29, July 3–6, 1922, 33, no. 241). Probably purchased from Kelekian in 1923. Ht, 8.9 cm; D, 14 cm. Mended from several pieces.

A round-bottom bowl with gently flaring sides has an everted rim and bears moldmade relief ornament. There is a double rosette in high relief on the underside and a frieze of overlapping lotus leaves around the sides.

Publications: Goldman, *Tarsus,* 225, fig. 170–A (erroneously numbered 48.266).

Moldmade faience bowls of this type have principally been found in Egypt, where they were undoubtedly made, but have also been recovered from Crete, and in a third-century context from Tarsos.[1] The ware was probably partially inspired by the silver bowls found in Egypt which bear chased decoration comprised of superimposed rosettes surrounded by lotus petals.[2]

Both the elaborate treatment of the rosette ornament and the uneasiness with which the bowl rests on its underside indicate that when not in use, the vessel was stored upside down. Supporting this hypothesis are the ease with which the palm of the hand fits over the bowl, and the presence of knobs in the form of theatrical masks on a pair of silver buckets in New York.[3] When those vessels are inverted, the masks are viewed right side up and constitute the primary decoration of the buckets' exterior. What appear to be inverted bowls are seen on a grave relief from Smyrna of ca. 150.[4]

1. K. Parlasca, "Zur Verbreitung ptolemäischer Fayencekeramik ausserhalb Ägyptens," *JdI* 91 (1976) 144, figs. 11, 12; Goldman, *Tarsus,* 225, no. 183, fig. 132.
2. Oliver, *Silver,* 41, no. 11, of the early third century.
3. D. von Bothmer, *A Greek and Roman Treasury,* Bulletin of the Metropolitan Museum of Art 42 (New York, 1984), 59, nos. 105–106, from Magna Graecia.
4. G. M. A. Richter, *Furniture of the Greeks, Romans and Etruscans* (London, 1966), fig. 416.

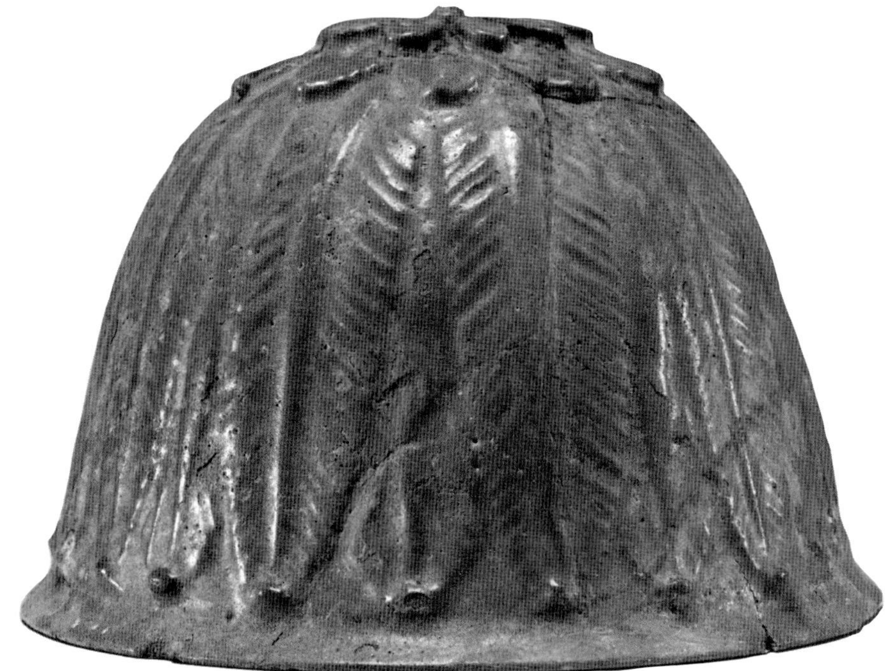

108.1

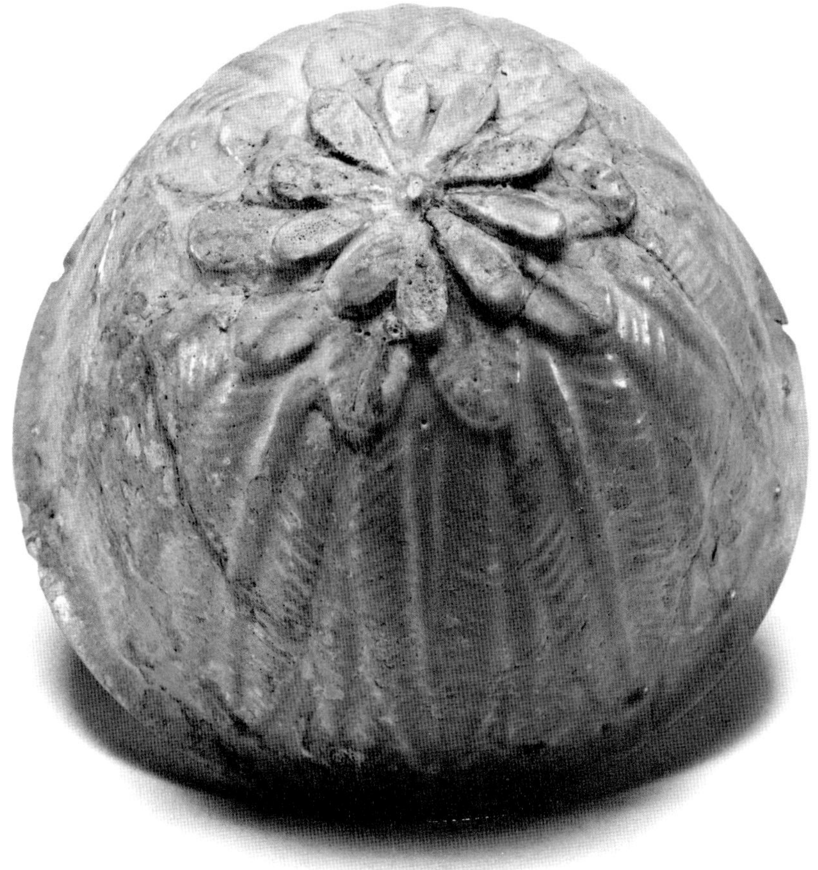

108.2

Duck
Third to second century

48.421. Faience. Purchased from Kelekian in 1926. L, 18.1 cm; W, 7.5 cm; Ht, 8.3 cm. Moldmade together with handle; raised dots over body; parts of feathers in the round. Blue-gray glaze on top of head, top of wings; yellow, brown, blue, and white glaze on long wing and tail feathers. White strip between brown bands down middle of back. Cheeks white, bill brown, stripes of yellow, brown, green, and blue on chest. Belly is white with blue dots; feet brown with blue tips; brown palmette behind and below wings on each side. Blue glass ball in right eye; hole in back between wing tips. Remains of ring handle on left side. Left eye missing. Neck and bill restored. Wings chipped.

A duck crouches on webbed feet with his wings folded. His down is rendered as tiny bumps. A ring handle was beside his left wing.

Publications: D. K. Hill, "Some Late Egyptian Ceramics in the Walters Art Gallery," *GBA* 30 (1946) 197–198, and 197, fig. 5; D. K. Hill, "What's in a Duck?" *BWalt* 1 (1949) no. 8; K. Parlasca, "Zur Verbreitung ptolemäischer Fayencekeramik ausserhalb Ägyptens," *JdI* 91 (1976) 141, no. 42.

Few parallels to this piece are known: an example in Athens with wings raised above the body; and an askos with Eros as rider from a grave in Tanagra, which yielded a vessel of Naukratis ware having close parallels in ceramic pottery of the third century.[1] The example from Tanagra resembles the Walters bird in the position of the ring handle and the pattern of the tail feathers; dissimilar is the rendering of the shorter feathers as half-brown and half-white oval units, a treatment which was probably inspired by the red-figure duck vases of Etruria and South Italy, which date from the fifth and fourth centuries.[2]

1. For the example in Athens, see H. Wallis, *Egyptian Ceramic Art. The MacGregor Collection* (London, 1898), 81–82. For the duck from Tanagra, see Higgins, *Tanagra,* 58, and 59, fig. 60, which was found with a two-handled cup (60, fig. 61) dated ca. 275. See also K. Parlasca, *JdI* 91 (1976) 141, fig. 4 and 152, who dates both pieces from Tanagra to the third century.
2. E. Reeder Williams, *The Archaeological Collection of the Johns Hopkins University* (Baltimore, 1984), 197–198, no. 128.

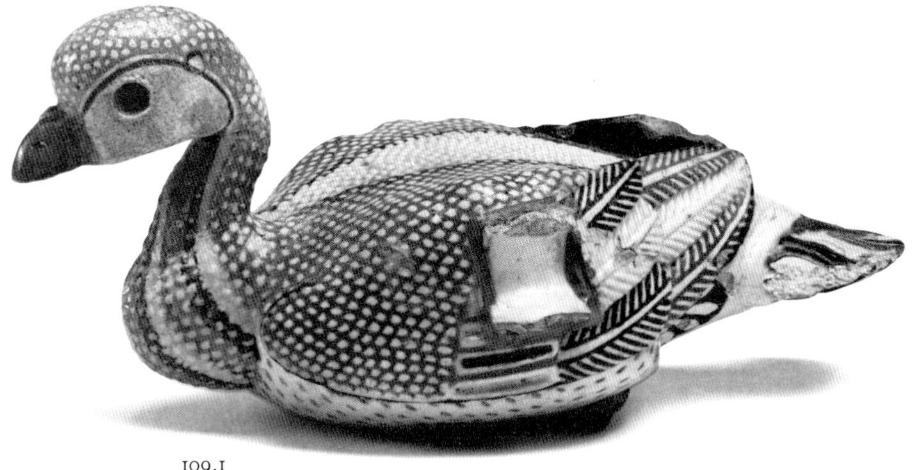

109.1

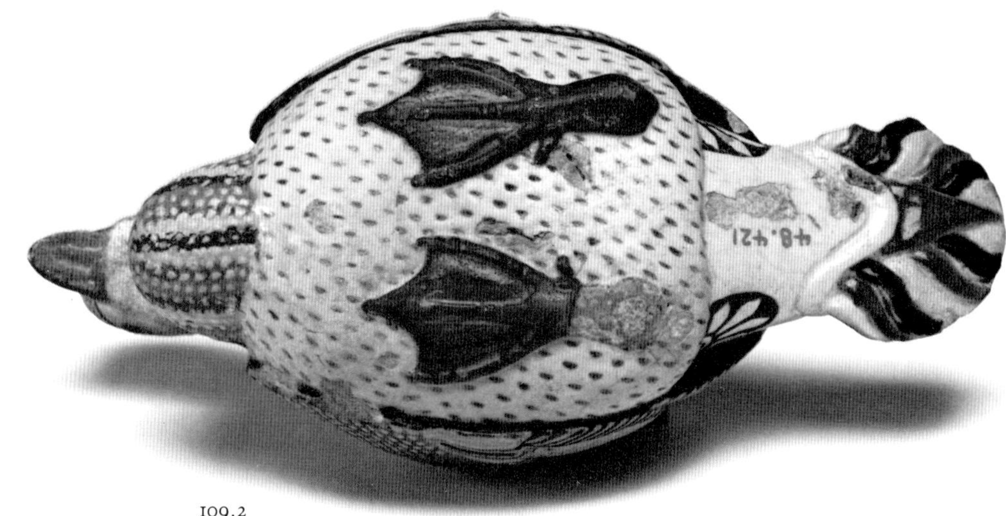

109.2

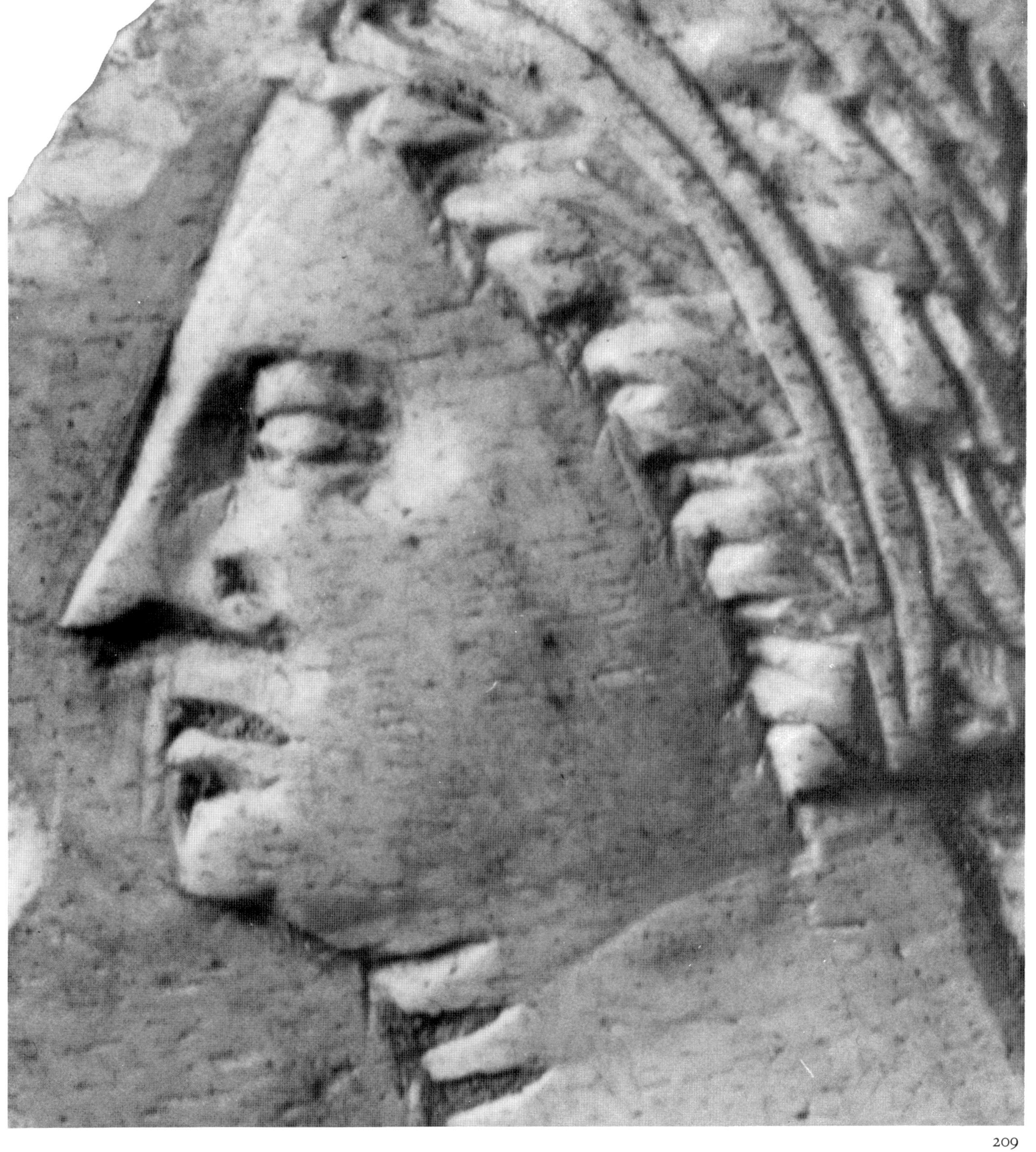

Appliqué Bust of Alexander
Third century

71.493. Ivory. ''From Alexandria.'' Purchased from Kelekian in 1924. Ht, 8.6 cm; W, 5.6 cm; Th, 3.7 cm. Top of head flattened, with a wood pin in the square depression at the crown. Cut off flat behind head and again behind chest. Groove for attachment down center of back. Left shoulder and upper arm broken away; chipped around bottom. Mended from two pieces. Left side of face very worn.

Head and upper chest of a male who gazes upward and to his left. The iris of his right eye is incised and the pupil is indented. He has a furrowed brow, very large eyes, and his wavy hair surmounted by a head-band extends below his ears.

Publications: *Ivory,* 64, no. 60, and ill. on 65.

This head belongs to a type of furniture appliqué that is especially familiar from examples found in the royal tomb at Vergina, dated ca. 320–300.[1] Like the Walters bust, the latter heads have individual features suggesting specific personalities, but the Walters example differs from these in that the head is almost in the round, the bust includes parts of the shoulder and chest, and the upward gaze and wavy locks of hair are clearly in the tradition of portraits of Alexander. In these respects the Walters head compares most closely with a series of bronze fulcrum appliqués which are believed to have originated in the second quarter of the third century. Like the Ptolemaic bronze bust, No. 50, the Walters ivory bust was probably made in the third century when there arose a fashion for portrait appliqués of deceased monarchs. Less clear is the precise use of the head; the bust may have functioned as a fulcrum medallion or, as is suggested by the flat cutting at the crown, may have been placed under the horizontal element beneath the mattress in a manner similar to the proposed use of the Vergina heads.[2]

1. *Search for Alexander,* 36, nos. 13–17 and M. Andronicos, *Vergina. The Royal Tombs and the Ancient City* (Athens, 1984), 123–130.
2. Ibid., 122–126 and 122, fig. 75.

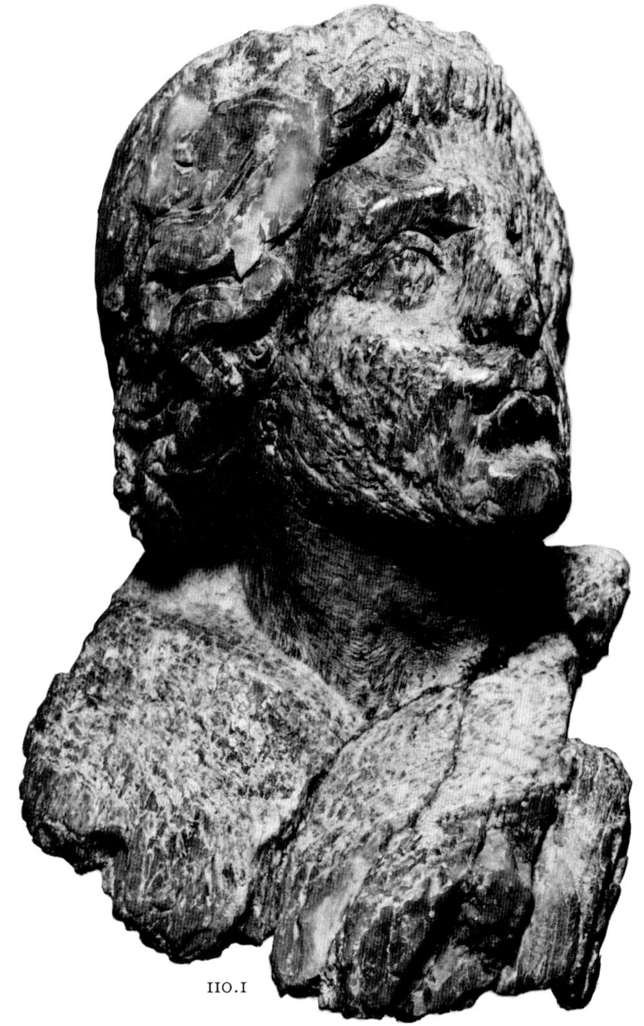

110.1

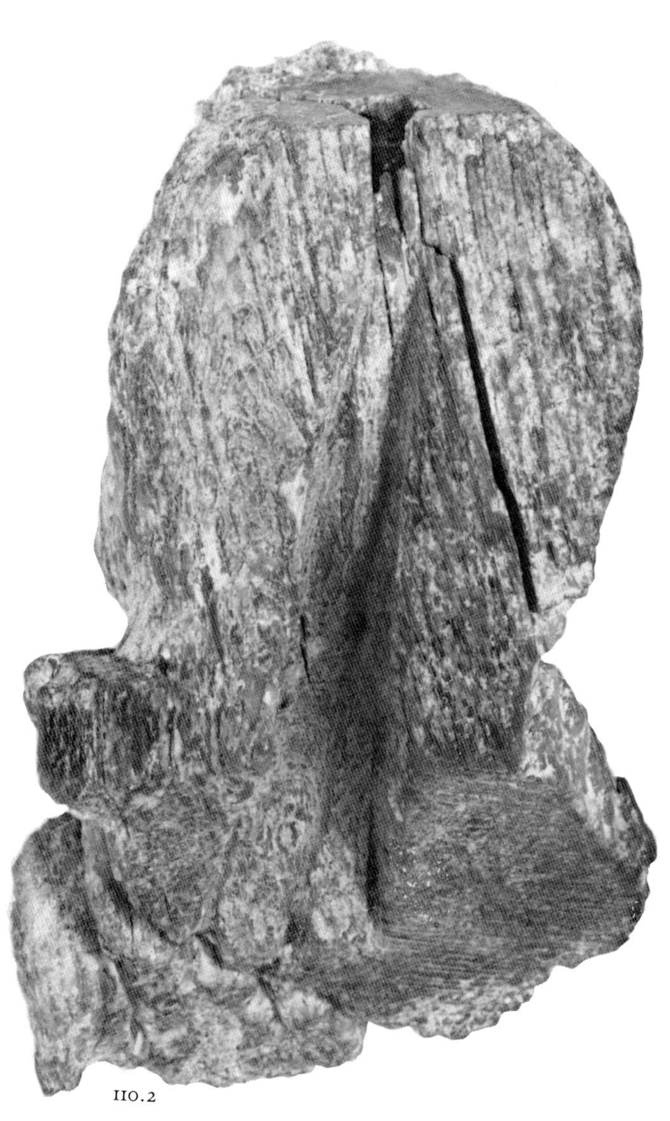

110.2

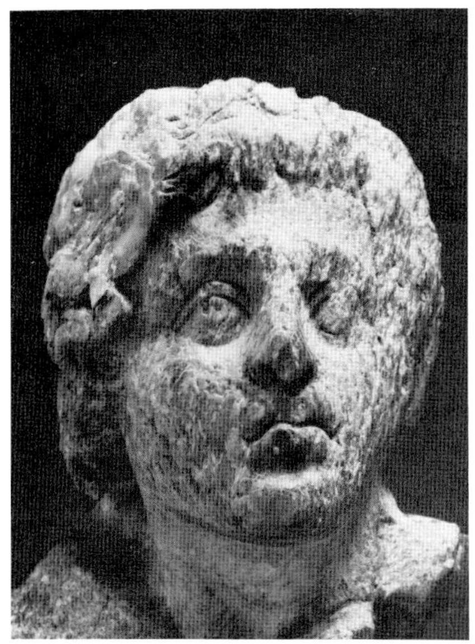

110.3

Appliqué Relief of a Satyr Head
Second century

71.616. Ivory. Purchased in 1929. Ht, 9.4 cm; W, 5.1 cm; Th, 1 cm. Flat, scored back. Relief has parabolic shape with edge by right cheek strongly cut in and lower border smooth and curved. Iron nail at the left corner of his mouth has stained the adjacent area.

In low relief is the frontal head of a satyr, with a furrowed brow, grooves across the bridge of his snub nose, and bulging eyes with indented pupils; his left ear is pointed. He has a mustache, a long wavy beard, and a bald pate upon which he wears a wreath of two rows of ivy leaves with two clusters of berries at the center front.

Publications: D. K. Hill, "Ivory Ornaments of Hellenistic Couches," *Hesperia* 32 (1963) 295, pl. 78a; G. M. A. Richter, *Furniture of the Greeks, Romans and Etruscans* (London, 1966), 108, fig. 541; *Ivory,* 64, no. 61, fig. p. 65.

Identifying the relief as part of a decorative attachment for a bed's fulcrum are the molding beneath the beard, the rounded upper surface, and the cutting away of his right cheek. Although beds inlaid with ivory are attested before Alexander, the earliest known fulcrum attachments in ivory date only from the third century and probably reflect the heightened popularity of beds in Hellenistic times and the increased availability of ivory which followed intensified trading activity with Asia and Africa.[1] The similarity of the Walters head to an ivory satyr head appliqué from a second-century context in the Athenian Agora suggests a date for this example in the late Hellenistic period, when depictions of Silenoi had been so extensively assimilated to the portrait tradition of Sokrates that only the bestial ear identified the subject.[2]

1. G. M. A. Richter, *Furniture,* 4. See Demosthenes, *Against Aphobus,* I.10 and I.30.
2. D. K. Hill, *Hesperia* 32 (1963) 295, pl. 78a.

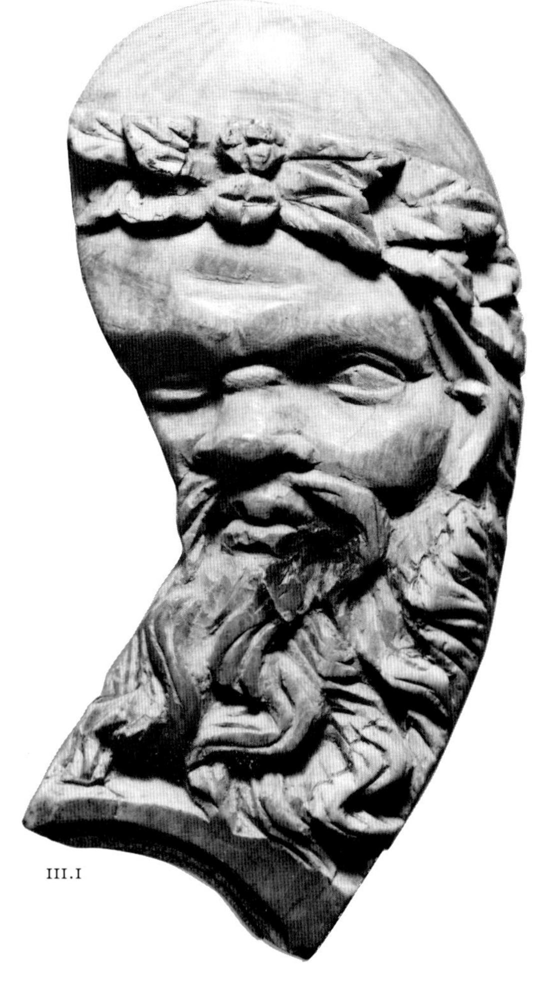

III.1

APPLIQUÉ RELIEF OF EROS WITH AMPHORA
Third to second century

71.18. Ivory. Purchased before 1931. Ht, 7.1 cm; W, 3.3 cm; Th, 1.7 cm. Flat back. Hole behind head completely pierces ivory; hole beneath and hole behind groin are not seen from front. Back is inset behind right arm with two additional holes, also not visible from front. Tip of right hand, left foot, and tip of right foot broken away.

A nude baby boy moves to his left with his left leg outstretched, and with legs, torso, and head in three-quarters right profile. Against his left shoulder he supports an amphora, the tip of which is clasped by his left hand near his waist, while his upraised right hand supports the vessel at the handles. An animal skin is draped over his left shoulder with the head hanging beneath his left hand; the folds blow out behind his right buttock. He wears a bracelet on his right ankle and right wrist, and over his short curly hair he wears a fillet.

Publications: *Ivory,* 66, no. 64, and ill. on 67.

The amphora and animal skin remove the figure from the world of Aphrodite and suggest that Eros is here associated with either Dionysos or Herakles, affiliations that are elsewhere attested: with Dionysos on a clay relief vase from Tarentum (No. 96); and with Herakles in the familiar painting of Herakles and Auge from Pompeii, which can surely claim Hellenistic ancestry.[1] Decorative ivory reliefs of Hellenistic date do not survive in number, but we can probably envision their use and appearance through comparison with the gilded terracotta reliefs from Tarentum that functioned as furniture appliqués.[2]

1. J. Charbonneaux, R. Martin, F. Villard, *Hellenistic Art* (London, 1973), 152, fig. 152.
2. *Ori di Taranto,* 393–395, nos. 26–39.

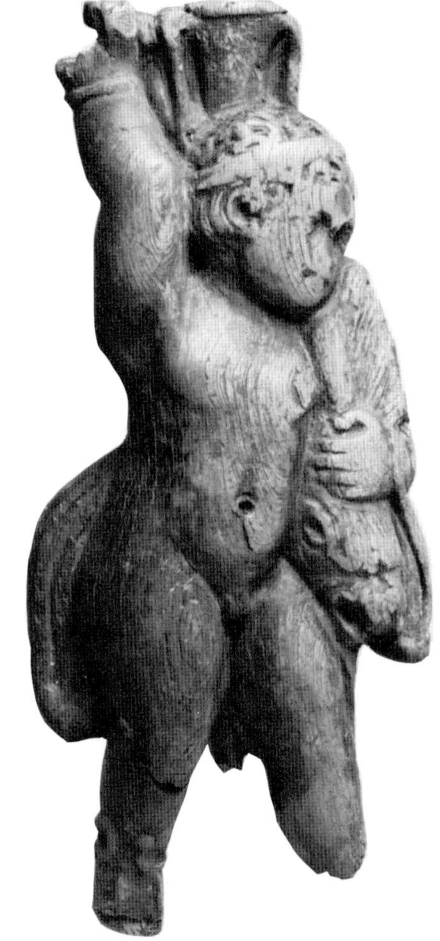

II2.I

Ring with Ptolemaic Portrait
First century

71.608. Bone. "Lower Egypt." Purchased in 1914. D, bezel 3 cm. Shank repaired.

Flat hoop carved in one piece with a circular bezel bearing in relief the left profile of a female head, neck, and part of shoulder. Venus rings are indicated on the neck. She wears a melon hairstyle beneath a fillet; the knot at the back of her head is bound by a double fillet, and the ends of her locks hang free. Part of the garment's folds can be seen at the edge of her neck.

Publications: L. Marangou, "Ptolemäische Fingerringe aus Bein," *AM* 86 (1971) 164, no. 13; E. Alföldi-Rosenbaum, "Ruler Portraits on Roman Game Counters from Alexandria," *Eikones, Festschrift Hans Jucker, AntK* Beiheft 12 (1980) 30–31, no. 28, pl. 11:5; *Ivory,* 66, no. 63.

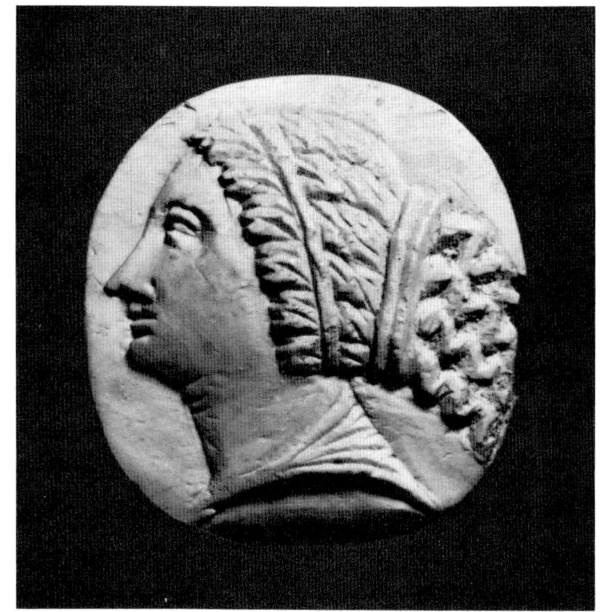

113.1

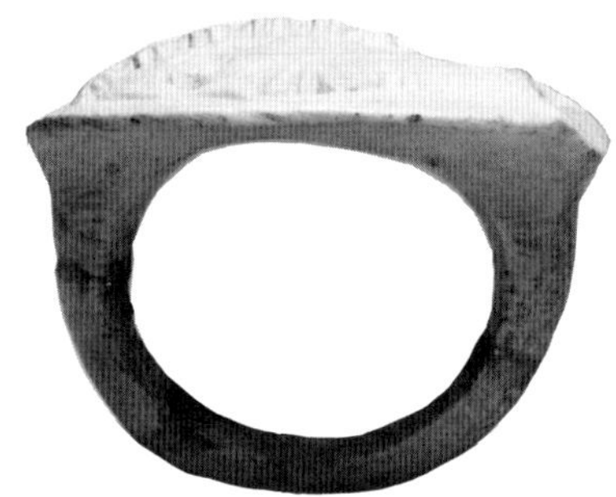

113.2

Ring with Ptolemaic Portrait
First century

71.609. Bone. "Lower Egypt." Purchased in 1914.
D, bezel 3 cm. Shank broken away; bezel chipped.

In relief on a nearly round bezel is the left profile of a female head, neck, and part of the shoulder. Three Venus rings are indicated on the neck; a groove demarcates the drapery edge at the shoulder. Her hair is drawn back from the face in a melon hairstyle surmounted by a double fillet. Behind the head is a braided coil bound by a double fillet.

Publications: L. Marangou, "Ptolemäische Fingerringe aus Bein," *AM* 86 (1971) 164, no. 14; E. Alföldi-Rosenbaum, "Ruler Portraits on Roman Game Counters from Alexandria," *Eikones, Festschrift Hans Jucker, AntK* Beiheft 12 (1980) 30, no. 27, pl. 11:4; *Ivory,* 66, no. 26.

About twenty examples of these rings are known, all having the same form and all bearing on the bezel in high relief the left profile of a female head.[1] Those on the Walters rings compare favorably with portraits of Arsinoe II (276/5–270), but were possibly fashioned long after her death.[2] In form and subject matter the rings are related to a group of bone game counters; some of the heads on these counters are reminiscent of Ptolemaic portraits, but others are specific portraits of Roman emperors of the first century A.D.[3] It is likely that the ornament on both rings and game counters was motivated by a late Hellenistic nostalgic allusion to a past that was rapidly vanishing under Roman intervention. The topographical allusions in the iconography of the game counters establish their place of manufacture, and by extension that of the rings, as Alexandria, where they were probably made as a spontaneous expression of affection for the ruling house.[4] As such, the rings and counters serve as further confirmation of the popular acceptance both of the Ptolemies and of the Ptolemaic policy of using royal portraiture as the embodiment of the state.

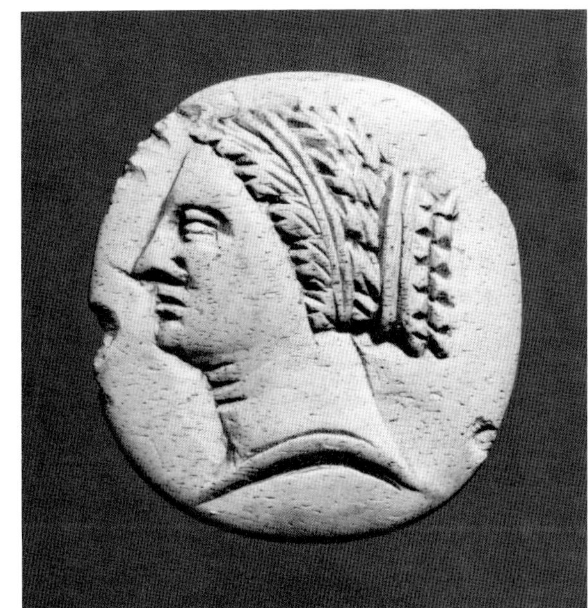

114.1

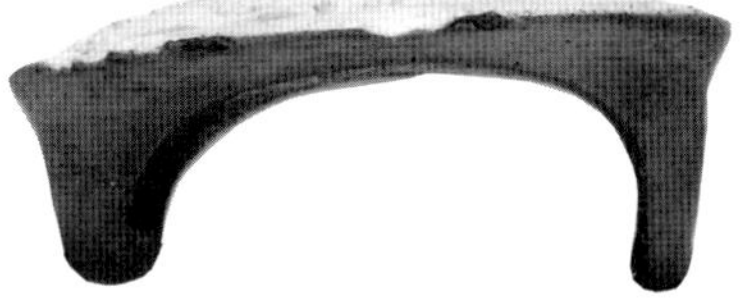

114.2

1. Alföldi-Rosenbaum, *Festschrift,* 30; Marangou, 164–165.
2. Alföldi-Rosenbaum (note 1) 37–38.
3. Ibid., 35.
4. Ibid., 38.

APPLIQUÉ RELIEF OF A SATYR
Second century

71.557. Ivory. Found in Sicily in the late nineteenth century. Collection of A. Sambon. Purchased before 1931. Ht, 22.8 cm; W, 15.5 cm; Th, 0.8 cm. Flat reverse. A nail hole is in the skirt at the groin; another pierces the edge of his animal skin above his right breast: a third is in drapery above left elbow. Missing drapery behind shoulder. Restored are: right arm; section of drapery beside knot; left forearm with contiguous section of club; right foot from instep; left leg from calf.

A satyr strides to his right, his legs in left profile, his weight on his right leg, his torso turned three-quarters to his left. His right arm is extended. Resting in the crook of his left arm and supported by his left hand is a knobbed club with curving tip. Knotted at his throat are the hoofed feet of a deerskin which flared out behind his shoulders. He wears a short skirt with a wide waistband above five rows of furrowed leaves. He has pointed ears, short wavy locks brushed back from his face and curled up at the nape, and a leafy wreath.

Publications: A. Sambon, "Jeune satyre, figurine découpée en ivoire," *Le Musée* 4 (1907) 176, ill.; Reinach, *Statuaire* 4 (1910) 74, no. 5; *Ivory,* 70, no. 79, and ill. on 71.

Particularly noteworthy is the perizoma, or skirt, of leaves which is worn by satyrs on the Altar of Dionysos erected on Delos during the first half of the second century and by terracotta satyrs from the Athenian Agora and Priene.[1] Marcadé has argued convincingly that the motif resulted from the transposition of a similar treatment of the being's hairy skin found in such Hellenistic renderings as a plaster mold in Cairo impressed from a metal relief, and that the translation of fur to leaves of ivy was suggested by the ivy leaf wreaths that Silenoi and satyrs wear in reference to Dionysos.[2]

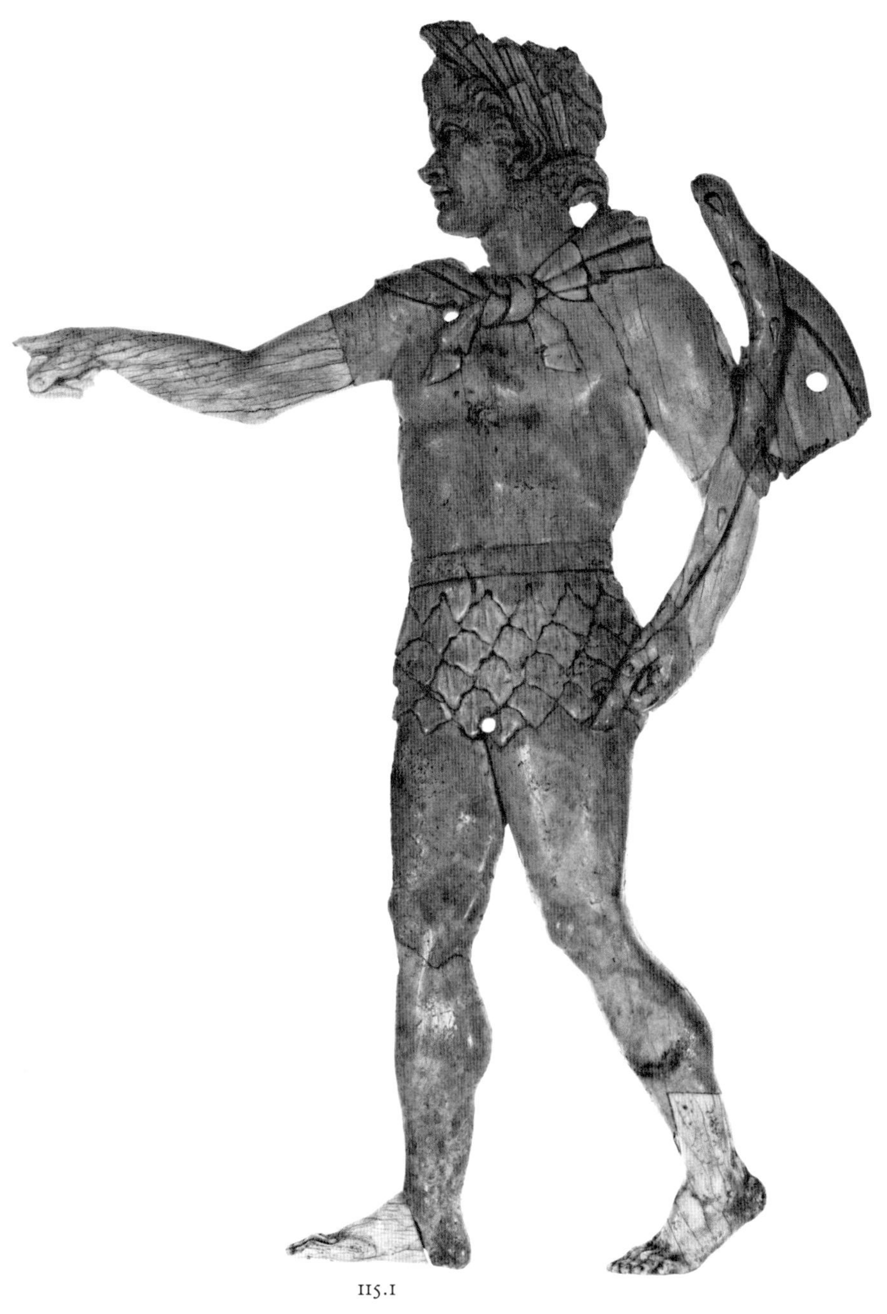

II5.I

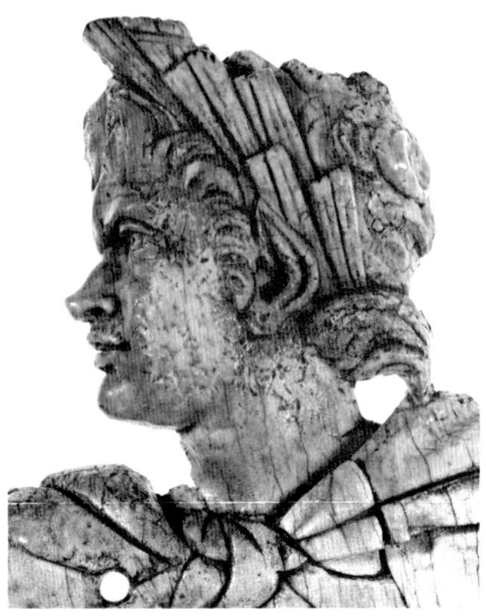

II5.2

The appearance of the leafy skirt on both satyrs and tritons is apparently a later Hellenistic innovation, and certainly the classicizing treatment of the Walters satyr would point to a date in the second or first century. Its western Greek provenance is supported by the similarity of his facial features and knotted deerskin to those seen on terracotta statuettes of satyrs from Tarentum.[3] The surface to which the relief belonged must have been fairly large, not only because of the height of the relief, but also because the subject and pose presuppose either a counterpart or a more extensive composition. The Walters relief would then follow the tradition represented by the gilded terracotta appliqués from Tarentum and by the ivory relief appliqués recovered from the royal tomb at Vergina.[4]

1. J. Marcadé, *Au musée de Délos* (Paris, 1969), 137; E. Reeder Williams, "Figurine Vases from the Athenian Agora," *Hesperia* 47 (1978) 366–367, no. 59; J. Raeder, *Priene. Funde aus einer griechischen Stadt* (Berlin, 1983), 36, no. 39, pl. 13b.
2. Marcadé (note 1) 448–449; A. Adriani, *Divagazioni intorno ad una coppa Paesistica del museo di Alessandria* (Rome, 1959), 22, and 68, note 115 no. 84, pl. 28. Compare also the leafy skirt of a triton in Frankfurt dated 125–100, in Bol, *Liebieghaus,* 145, no. 41.
3. *Ori di Taranto,* 479, nos. 22–25.
4. For the terracotta appliqués of mythological beings, including griffins, Scylla, and a Gorgoneion, see *Ori di Taranto,* 394–395, nos. 27–38. For the ivory shield from Macedon, see M. Andronicos, *Vergina. The Royal Tombs and the Ancient City* (Athens, 1984), 206–207, fig. 207; 135, fig. 93; 132–133, figs. 88, 90. Compare the more rugged handling of the satyr's face on 133, fig. 90.

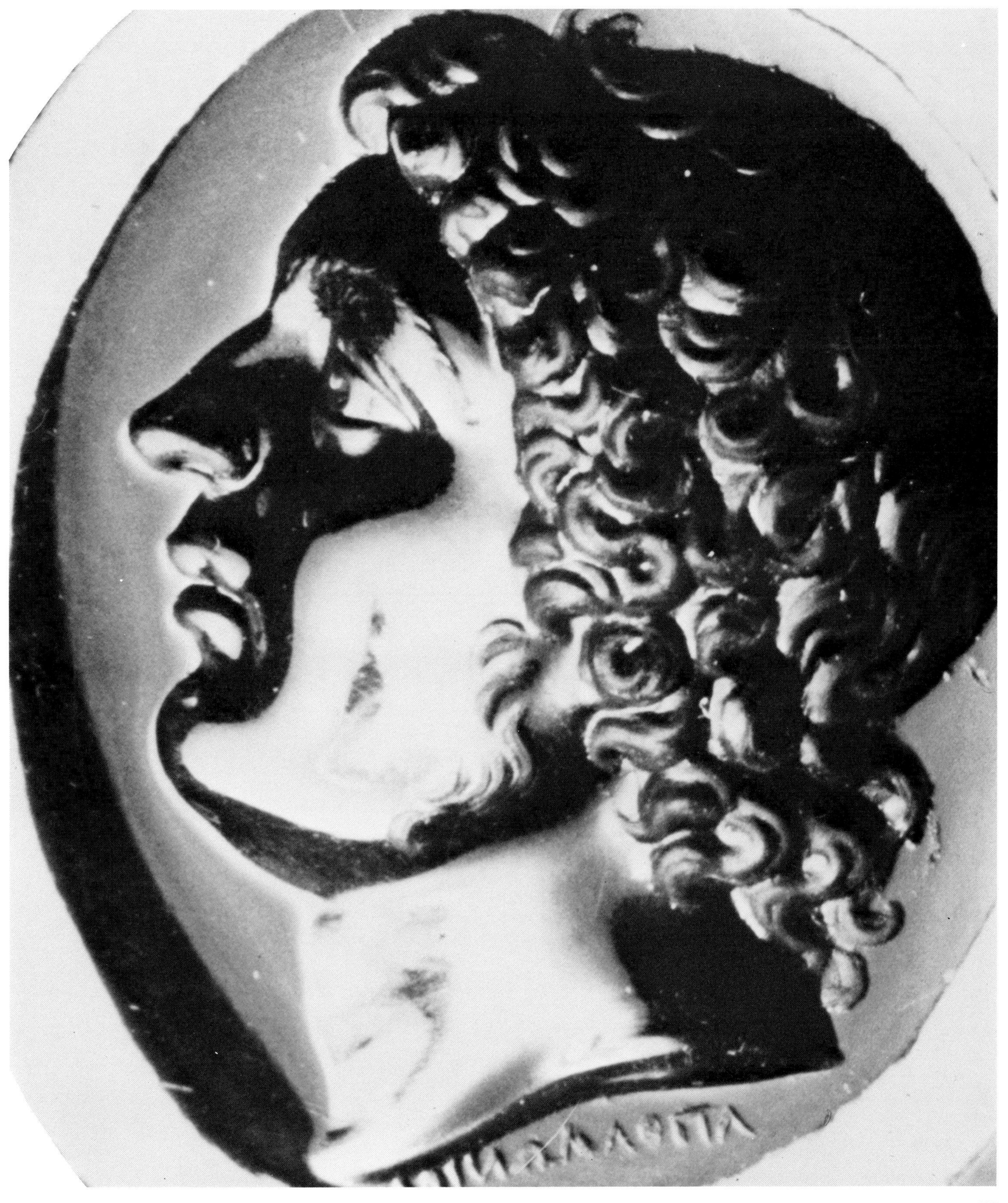

Pair of Bracelets with Antelope Heads
Late fourth century

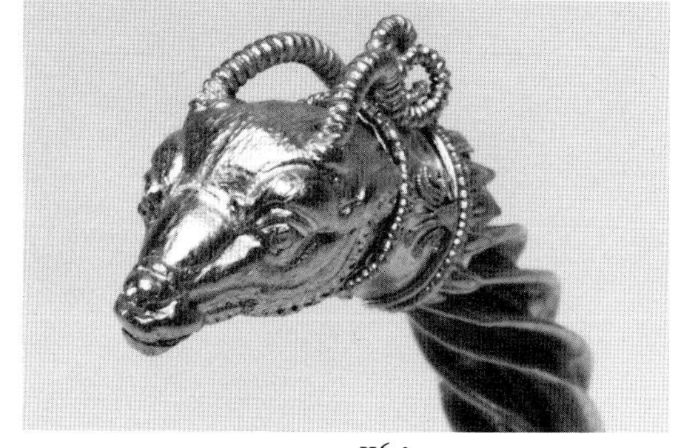

116.3

57.2021 and 57.2022. Gold. "From Anatolia." Collections of Joseph Brummer, Åke Wibert of Apertin, Sweden. Purchased in 1973 from Christie, Manson and Woods (sale catalogue, *Antiquities and Primitive Art,* London, December 5, 1973, 34–35, nos. 140 and 141, pl. 6). D, 8.1 cm and 7.5 cm; L, antelope head and collar 2.9 cm. One head flattened and reattached. Coils of one bracelet flattened.

Each bracelet is constructed of a gold tube pinched into six flanges with a beaded wire placed in each groove. The tube was then twisted and curved. At each end is a collar, from which triangular leaves are suspended, having three seven-petal palmettes worked in filigree; above and below is a twisted wire between two smooth ones. Detachable terminals are in the form of antelope heads. Each has ribbed horns with spiral tips. Beneath the jaw is a row of stylized locks; the hair is finely incised around the neck.

Exhibitions and Catalogues: Hoffmann-Davidson 160–161, no. 57 and 161, fig. 57a; *Jewelry,* 89, no. 267; *Objects of Adornment,* 65–66, no. 49.

Publications: P. Amandry, "Orfèvrerie achéménide," *AntK* 1 (1958) 15, no. 51 and pl. 12, fig. 34; Review of Hoffmann-Davidson by P. Amandry in *AJA* 71 (1967) 203, no. 5; D. K. Hill, "Greek Gold Bracelets," *BWalt* 26 (1974) no. 7; D. Stronach, *Pasargadae* (Oxford, 1978), 174, nos. 10–11; Deppert-Lippitz 232, pl. 19.

These bracelets belong to a type of hoop bracelet with animal-head terminals that is familiar from Achaemenid art, where the terminals usually take the form of lion or lion-griffin heads. Achaemenid examples of the late fifth and early fourth centuries include a bracelet from Vouni and another in Pforzheim.[1] Each is made from a single piece of gold and is distinguished by the oval shape of the hoop and the depression in the hoop opposite the terminals, probably intended to secure the bracelet tightly on the wrist in the manner of a cuff. The heads of the terminals are boxy, with a prominent eye, protruding eyebrow, and minimal modeling of the facial planes. A more direct Achaemenid predecessor to the Walters pair was found in Pasargadae and is dated by Stronach to the first half of the fourth century; here the hoop is twisted, the finials separately made, and an elaborate collar lies behind each head.[2] Most closely comparable to the Walters bracelets are examples from the Greek sites of Mottola and Pangaion, each with horned animal heads and dated to the third century.[3] Now the hoop is semicir-

cular and is rendered as a twist of hammered flanges; the head is elongated with a delicate modulation of facial planes, and the tips of the horns curve into an elegant spiral.

Representations in Achaemenid art suggest that bracelets of this form were worn by men, a custom later taken over by at least some Greek leaders, because Delian inventories list bracelets belonging to Demetrios Poliorketes.[4] Most Greek examples, however, were probably worn by women because they are usually found together with other jewelry that was clearly for female use. Indeed, the Walters pair was said to have been found in Anatolia together with other items of distinctively female jewelry now in New York.[5] These include the centerpiece from a diadem and a pair of earrings so thoroughly Greek in style that the inclusion of the

Walters bracelets in this context underlines the integration of Achaemenid forms into the mainstream of early Hellenistic jewelry design. This rapid synthesis of Hellenic and Oriental traditions is not difficult to comprehend. With Alexander's defeat of the Persian empire, craftsmen formerly employed by Persians, and probably themselves Greek, became available for commissions from such Greek patrons as Demetrios Poliorketes, an avowed enthusiast of Persian culture. Almost certainly a principal center of Hellenistic goldsmithing was the Seleukid capital of Antioch which must have exerted a stimulating effect on craftsmen of the eastern Mediterranean.

The hoop bracelet with animal terminals remained popular throughout the Hellenistic period. The third century saw the introduction of such varied motifs as hound and lynx heads.[6]

1. For the Vouni example, see P. Amandry, *AntK* 1 (1958) 14, 20, pl. 12.27–9. For the Pforzheim example, see B. Segall, *Zur griechischen Goldschmiedekunst des vierten Jahrhunderts v. Chr.* (Wiesbaden, 1966), 16, pls. 10–11.
2. D. Stronach, *Pasargadae,* 168, 174–175, 201, pl. 147a.
3. For the Mottola example, see Deppert-Lippitz 232–233, fig. 168; Hoffmann-Davidson 162, fig. 57b; *Ori di Taranto,* 243–245, no. 167. For the Pangaion example, see Greifenhagen, *Schmuckarbeiten I,* 33, pl. 12; A. Greifenhagen, "Goldschmuck-Verluste. Antiquarium, Berlin," *AA* (1946–47) cols. 108, 111 and col. 114, fig. 52.
4. See G. Macurdy, "A Note on the Jewellery of Demetrius the Besieger," *AJA* 36 (1932) 27–28.
5. P. Amandry, *AJA* 71 (1967) 202–205; Hoffmann-Davidson 64–65, no. 5; 152–155, no. 54; 155, fig. 54i.
6. Deppert-Lippitz 207.

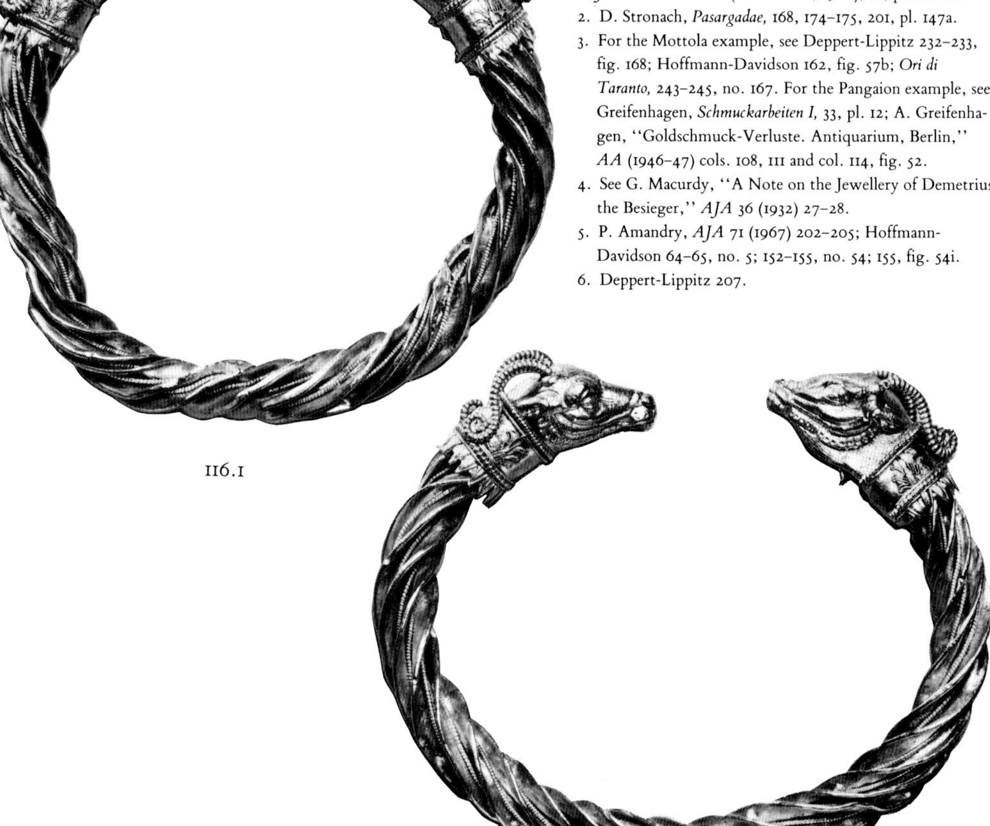

116.1

116.2

Boat-type Earring with Sphinx

Ca. 350–325

57.1733. Gold with blue enamel. Collection of Henry Walters before 1931. Collection of Mrs. Henry Walters (sale catalogue, *Art Collection of Mrs. Henry Walters,* New York, Parke-Bernet, December 2, 1943, 91, no. 524). Purchased in 1943. Ht, 3 cm; L, 2.2 cm; Th, 1.1 cm. Blue enamel remains in some of the ivy leaves.

A boat shape was formed by wrapping two crescent sheets over a core. Each horn of the crescent has a circle of twisted wire beneath five spool-shaped discs with the edges hammered to resemble twisted wire; each disc is separated by a strip of metal. The join along the outside perimeter is concealed by a narrow gold strip to which is attached a granule surmounted by a second granule. Worked in filigree on one side of the crescent is a Herakles knot set amidst a row of ivy leaves from which shoots and korymboi extend. On the other side is an inverted eleven-petal palmette suspended from each horn; between and beneath are volutes, linked by narrow bands, to which clusters of granules are attached. Over the concave join between the crescents are two curved sheets supporting a sphinx, each half worked in repoussé. The leg and wing on each side are worked in a separate sheet. Still another separate sheet between the wings is ornamented with a filigree leaf. The wire for attachment has a duck head at one end and terminates in a disc upon which are circles of smooth and twisted wire.

Exhibitions and Catalogues: *Jewelry,* 75, no. 237.

Publications: B. Segall, ''The Problem of Phoenician Artisans in Egypt, An Early Hellenistic Earring,'' *JWalt* 9 (1946) 97–101; D. K. Hill, ''From Alexander to Augustus,'' *BWalt* 7 (1955) no. 5; S. Miller, *Two Groups of Thessalian Gold,* University of California Publications in Classical Studies 18 (Berkeley, 1979), 9, 18, no. 107, pl. 3g (not 3f as referred to in text); Hackens-Winkes, *Louvain,* 57.

The boat, or leech, type of earring probably originated in Anatolia sometime during the second millennium and was popular in the Greek world through the end of the fourth century.[1] The Walters example belongs to a variation that is recognized by the filigree and granulation on the boat and by the fantastic creature that surmounts it. In earlier versions the granules are arranged in orderly rows; on our example the patterning of the granules, the globules outlining the contours, and the crude workmanship of the animal find their closest parallels on an example from a grave in Homolion, dated 375–325.[2] One might also compare both the turnings at each end of the boat, substituting for the conventional lion head, and the treatment of the palmettes with similar terminals on an example in Williams College.[3]

The sphinx is just one of several mythological beings found on boat-type earrings; other motifs, most of which are suggestive of the afterlife, are a hippocamp on the Homolion earring, and a gorgon and a harpy on examples in Boston and London, respectively.[4] Contemporary or slightly later boat-type earrings from Tarentum, Madytos, and Kul Oba carry multiple pendants and are occasionally suspended from discs.[5]

1. S. Miller, *Thessalian Gold,* 7.
2. For the sixth-century versions, see Miller (note 1) 8, pl. 3c from Spata in Attika. For the Homolion example, see ibid., 7, pls. 2–3 and dating, on 24.
3. Hackens-Winkes, *Louvain,* 56–57, no. 10.
4. See note 2 and Miller (note 1) 8, pl. 3d and e.
5. For the example from Tarentum, see *Ori di Taranto,* 154–155, 157, no. 68. For the Madytos earring in New York, see B. Segall, *JWalt* 9 (1946) 99, fig. 7. For Kul Oba, see B. Segall, *Zur griechischer Goldschmiedekunst des vierten Jahrhunderts v. Chr.* (Wiesbaden, 1966), pl. 21b in the Hermitage.

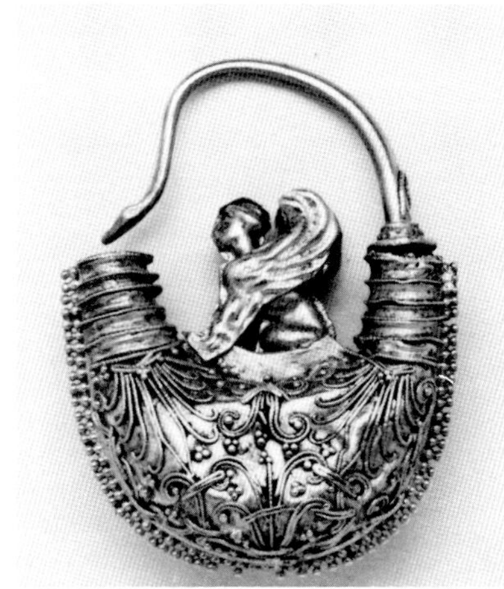

117.1

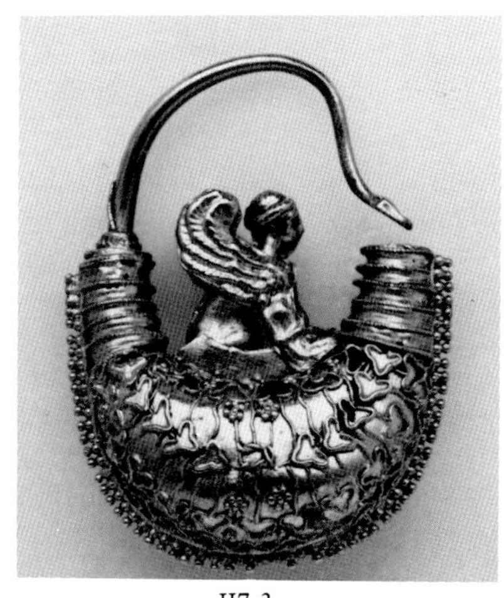

117.2

Disc and Pendant
Earring with Eros
Fourth to third century

57.1496. Gold. Purchased before 1931. Ht, 3.2 cm.

A nude boy, solid cast, alights on his left leg with his right knee bent and his foot slightly raised behind him. His right arm is extended with a torch in his hand. His left upper arm is outstretched to his side with the elbow bent; his forearm and hand are held horizontally at chest height. His head is frontal with short curly hair. A separate sheet for each wing is incised with a feather pattern on the front. Another sheet is used for the mantle which frames his back, with the ends brought forward over the left shoulder and right forearm. A loop behind his head interlocks with a loop suspended from a disc, the upturned edges of which are overlaid with twisted wire. Inserted in the cavity is a five-petal rosette surrounded by three double spirals. Behind the disc is an ear wire.

Exhibitions and Catalogues: *Jewelry,* 78, no. 241.

The earliest example of the disc earring with Eros pendant was found in a grave of the second half of the fourth century in the Athenian Agora; another example was recovered from a late fourth century grave in Thebes.[1] Characteristic of examples of this date, to which a pair of earrings in Kassel should also be assigned, are the filigree spirals surrounding the central leaf, which is almost three-dimensional.[2] In examples of the later third and second centuries, as seen in an example from Kerch (Panticipaeon), the central blossom has become more stylized and is surrounded by circles worked in wire.[3] At about this same time the center of the leaf is often replaced by a garnet.[4] On other examples of this type of earring, Eros carries a phiale or a mask, in allusion to his theatrical affiliations.[5]

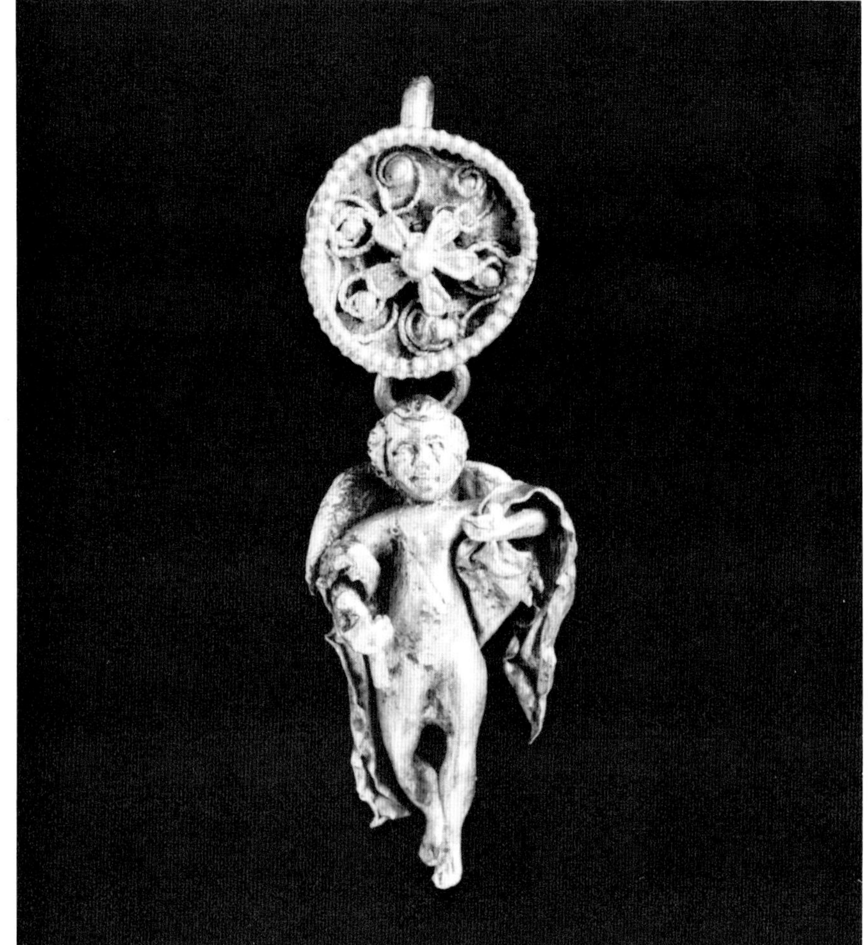

118.1

1. See Deppert-Lippitz 230.

2. For the example from Kassel, see F. Naumann, *Antiker Schmuck. Staatliche Kunstsammlungen Kassel* (Kassel, 1980), 22, no. 9, pl. 3. Compare also Davidson-Oliver, *Brooklyn,* 68, no. 66; Hoffmann-Davidson 94, no. 18, fig. 18b in the Hermitage; S. Murray, *Collecting the Classical Past; Antiquities from the Joseph Veach Noble Collection* (Tampa, 1985), 34, no. 143.

3. Compare an example from Kerch in Kassel in Naumann (note 2) 40, no. 69, pl. 15, dated to the second century; examples in Taranto in *Ori di Taranto,* 175–176, nos. 95, 96; a pair in Houston in Deppert-Lippitz 230, no. 166, fig. 166 of the late third and early second century.

4. M. Brouskari, *The Paul and Alexandra Canellopoulos Museum* (Athens, 1985), 35.

5. For the phiale, see *Ori di Taranto,* 175, no. 95. For the decorative mask, see Naumann (note 2) 22, no. 9, pl. 3.

PENDANT EARRINGS WITH EROTES
Late fourth to early third century

57.1498 and 57.1499. Gold with enamel. Purchased from Michel Abemayor in 1929. Ht, 5.8 cm. Traces of blue or green enamel remain in the akanthos leaves and blossoms, and in the rosette on one earring, the medallion bandolier on the other. Incrustation on parts of one earring.

The two earrings are mirror reversals and identical in detail. Affixed to the earwire is a seven-petal palmette above an akanthos leaf, set between two blossoms. Beneath is a disc edged by plain and twisted wire and by tongue ornament, within which is a rosette with two tiers of leaves with dog-toothed edges. Suspended beneath are two ivy leaves above a standing Eros, wings spread. He wears a bandolier with a medallion and tassels between the breasts, and he carries a torch and mussel shell. The base beneath has flanges above and below.

Exhibitions and Catalogues: *Jewelry,* 78, no. 242.

A single earring in Mainz has been attributed by Deppert-Lippitz to the same workshop.[1] Similar to the Walters pair is the palmette above the disc, the tongue border and beaded wire encircling it, the ivy leaves beneath, and the flanged base, in this case supporting a winged siren grasping flutes and staff.[2] An even closer parallel to the Walters earrings is a pair formerly in the Guilhou collection which shares such further details with the Mainz example as the round petals of the flower within the disc and the lowered eyelids of the winged Erotes.[2] The existence of the Mainz parallel dispels any lingering doubt about the authenticity of the Walters and Guilhou examples and supplements our documentation for pendant earrings with a flanged base, a further example of which is the sphinx earring, No. 126.

1. Mainz, Römisch-Germanische Zentralmuseum, inv. O-21651. I thank B. Deppert-Lippitz for this parallel.
2. For the Guilhou pair, see R. Zahn, ''Zur hellenistischen Schmuckkunst,'' *Schumacher-Festschrift* (Mainz, 1930), 202–06, pl. 22.1–2. For the subsequent history of the pair, see *Jewelry,* 78, no. 242.

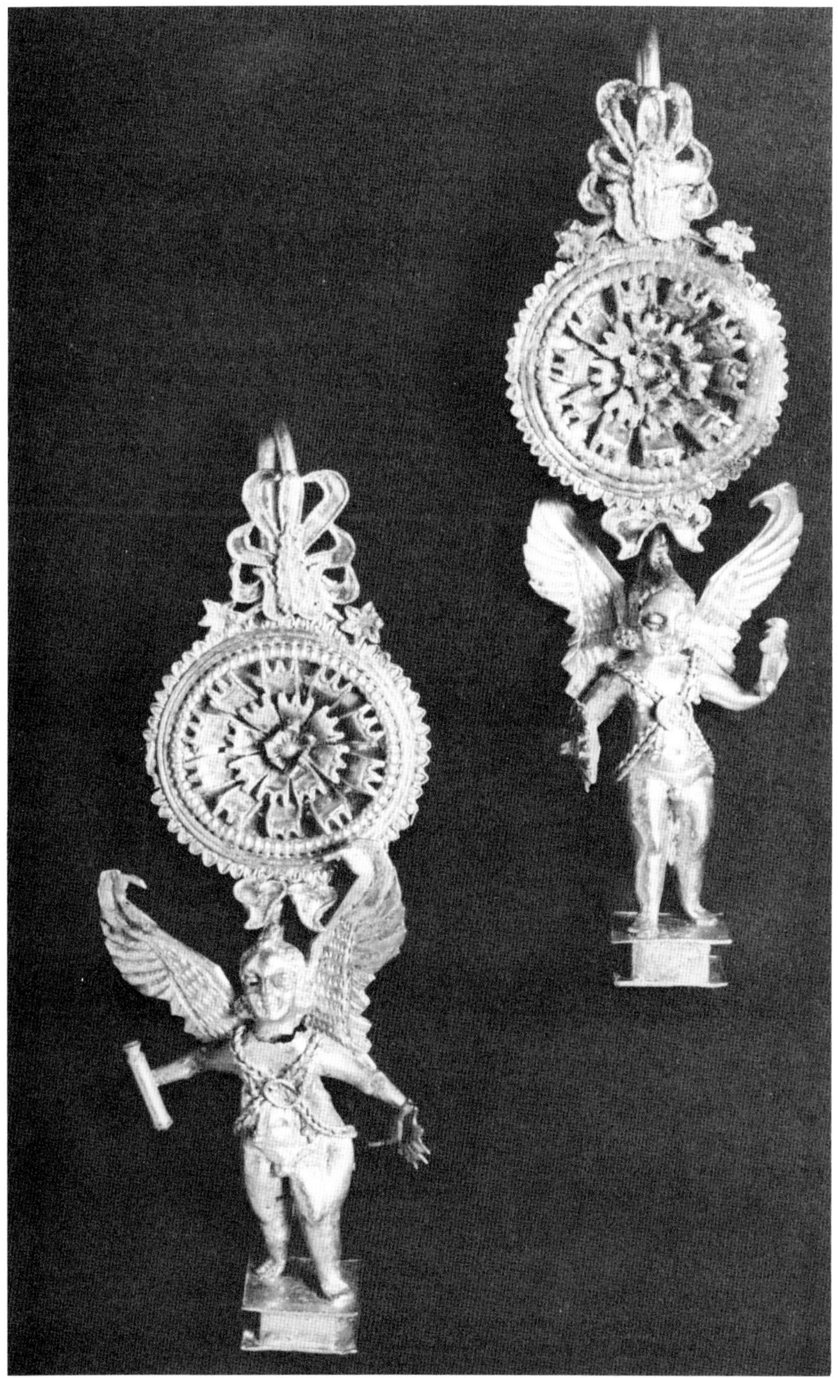

119.1

Disc and Pyramid Pendant Earrings
Second century

57.1671 and 57.1672. Gold and garnet. Collection of Henry Walters before 1931. Collection of Mrs. Henry Walters. Purchased from J. Brummer in 1941. Ht, 4 cm. One earring is a replacement mate of the other, incorporating a chain from its prototype and reproducing it.

The prototype consists of a disc from which an inverted pyramid is suspended. The disc is made of two sheets, the front having two hammered grooves, in the outermost of which a twisted wire is laid. In the innermost groove is a circle of granules surrounding a round garnet. On the back of the disc near the edge is a loop joined to a short chain of figure-eight loops, alternating with four cylindrical gold beads. On the opposite edge of the disc is a hole, probably for the attachment of a similar chain. In the center back of the disc is a wire with one end hooked for insertion in the earlobe; the other end is twisted into a loop which is slipped through another loop attached to an inverted hollow pyramid which has granulated triangles along the three edges of the top and on all three sides of the opposite apex. On the imitation earring, which approximates the prototype's decoration, the disc's grooves are inlaid with twisted wire; the back of the disc is a smooth, convex surface; the triangles on the pyramids are hammered projections or bosses without granulation; and the chain attached behind the disc possibly belonged originally to its prototype.

Exhibitions and Catalogues: *Jewelry,* 77, no. 239.

The type of this earring, of which the Walters example is a later variation, dates from the third century and is characterized by gold discs from which gold pyramids, often flanked by pendants, are suspended.[1] In the second century the discs bear a large round garnet and the pyramids become simplified. The prototypical earring of the Walters pair was probably made in Tarentum where the closest parallels were found.[2] The scratch-free surface of the garnet on its mate may indicate that this piece was made in recent times.

1. Deppert-Lippitz 231–232, fig. 167.
2. *Ori di Taranto,* 164, no. 78; 175, no. 94 of the second century.

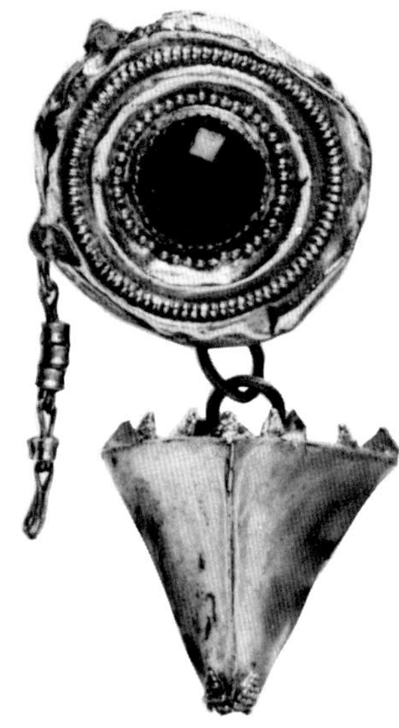
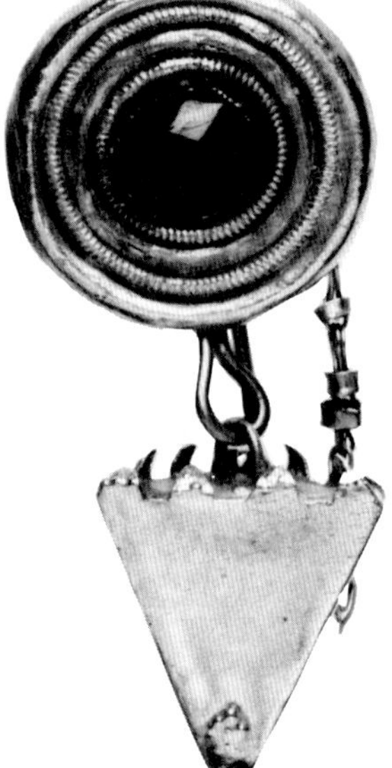

120.1

DISC AND AMPHORA PENDANT EARRINGS
Second to first century

57.610 and 57.611. Gold and garnet. Acquired before 1931. Ht, each earring 3.6 cm. Hook missing from each.

In the center of a round gold disc is a round garnet edged with twisted wire. Beneath is a coiled wire that interlocks with a loop above the rim of an amphora pendant that has a garnet body, gold wires for handles, and granulated detail around the shoulder and base. Above the disc is a suspension loop.

Exhibitions and Catalogues: *Jewelry,* 77, no. 240.

One late Hellenistic version of the disc and pendant earring introduces the motif of an amphora suspended from a disc, which is often set with a garnet. On some examples the amphora is flanked by pendants, and on several earrings an Isis crown surmounts the disc.[1] The similarity of the elongated amphora to shapes in Hellenistic pottery, and the existence on other earrings of pendant amphorae made entirely of gold, remind us that earrings of this type surely imitate actual vessels made of gold and colored stones.[2] The Isis motif seen on other examples of this type is so prevalent in late Hellenistic jewelry that its presence probably carries no specific religious meaning but simply testifies to the wide diffusion of Egyptian styles and motifs that had occurred by this date.

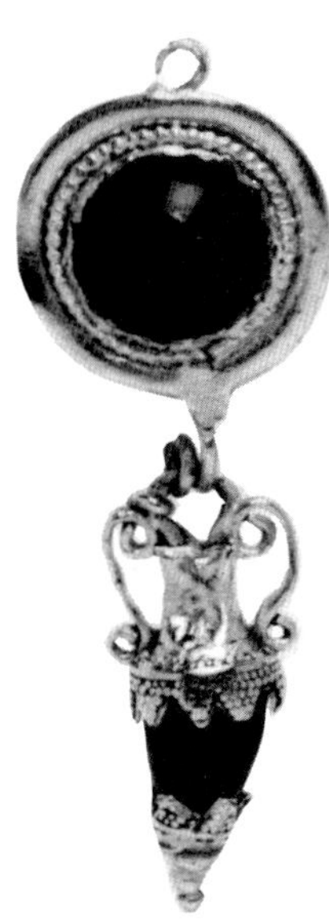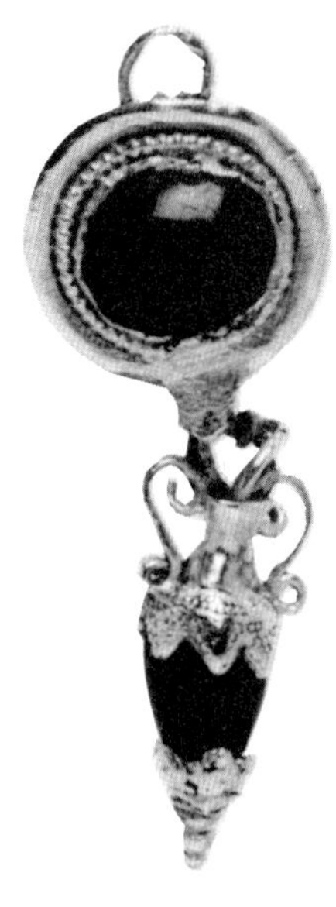

121.1

1. Deppert-Lippitz 261, pl. 31 from Tarentum in London, dated mid-second to first century; the same piece is Marshall, *BMCJ,* 274, no. 2331, pl. 51. See also *Ori di Taranto,* 166, no. 80b, dated to the second century. Especially close to the discs of the Walters pair are Greifenhagen, *Schmuckarbeiten II,* 48, no. 11, pl. 39, dated to the first century. See R. Higgins, *Greek and Roman Jewellery,* 2nd ed. (London, 1980), 163.
2. For earrings with gold amphorae, see A. Greifenhagen, *Schmuck der alten Welt* (Berlin, 1974), 44, dated to the second century; Greifenhagen, *Schmuckarbeiten I,* 35, no. 10, pl. 13, of the second century; *Ori di Taranto,* 166, no. 81, dated to the second century.

Hoop Earrings with Lion Heads
Third century

57.581 and 57.582. Gold. Purchased before 1931. Max D, 1.9 cm. Hole in center of one lion's mouth.

Each earring consists of four hollow wires twisted in a spiral and hammered together at one end into a single narrow wire. The other end is fitted into a collar of seven leaves beneath a band of smooth wire, surmounted by two twisted wires, then bands of smooth and twisted wire. Each lion head, worked in repoussé, has deep-set eyes, and the mane is rendered as broad clumps.

Exhibitions and Catalogues: *Jewelry,* 80, no. 246; *Objects of Adornment,* 62–63, no. 44.

Publications: Davidson-Oliver, *Brooklyn,* 42.

Although a form of lion hoop earring appeared in Etruscan art of the fifth century, the type is not known in the Greek world until the fourth century when we find examples from Macedonia, South Italy, and Sicily.[1] Because the type is especially common in Cyprus, Phoenicia, Egypt, and Syria, the lion hoop earring probably originated in the eastern Mediterranean and grew to popularity with the conquests of Alexander the Great.[2] In the beginning of the third century heads of other animals such as an antelope, lynx, and gazelle were introduced.[3] The type remained popular into the first century.

1. P. Amandry, review of Hoffmann-Davidson, in *AJA* 71 (1967) 204; Deppert-Lippitz 222–224. See also Davidson-Oliver, *Brooklyn,* 42, no. 36.
2. Amandry (note 1) 204. R. Higgins, *Greek and Roman Jewellery,* 2nd ed. (London, 1980), 159.
3. Deppert-Lippitz 224; 225, fig. 159.

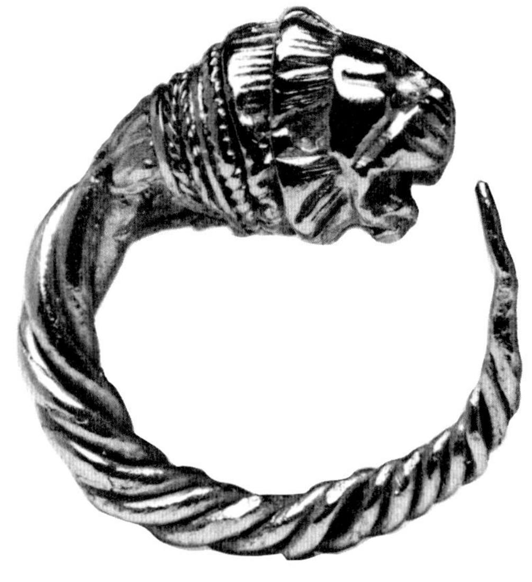

122.1

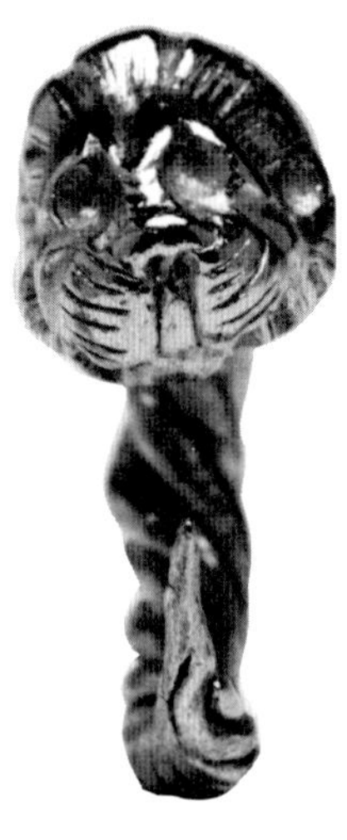

122.2

Hoop Earring with Lion-Griffin Head
Third century

57.1732. Gold. Collection of Henry Walters before 1931. Collection of Mrs. Henry Walters (sale catalogue, *Art Collection of Mrs. Henry Walters,* New York, Parke-Bernet, December 2, 1943, 91, no. 524). Purchased in 1943. D, 2.5 cm. Missing horns, which were inserted separately.

A hollow tapering cylinder was hammered into spiral flanges with twisted wire laid in the grooves. The small end is wrapped with a gold sheet beneath a circle of twisted and smooth wire surmounted by a conical cap. At the opposite end is a band of thirteen leaves edged with twisted wire. Above, and between twisted and smooth wires, is a band of granule clusters and double spirals worked in twisted wire. The lion-griffin head was executed in repoussé with ears, teeth, horns, and crest made separately.

Exhibitions and Catalogues: *Jewelry,* 81, no. 248.

This variation on the lion-head hoop earring was made by adding a crest and horns to the lion head; a further variation, seen on other examples, is a smaller lion head at the tapering end of the hoop. These refinements are apparently South Italian and find parallels in examples of the fourth and third centuries from Tarentum, Capua, Cumae, and Ithaka.[1] Also distinctively South Italian are the exaggerated transitions in the planes of the lion's face.

1. A. P. Kozloff, ed., *Animals in Ancient Art from the Leo Mildenburg Collection* (Cleveland, 1981), 160–161, no. 141, dated 325–300; Deppert-Lippitz 225, fig. 160, dated late third century; De Juliis, *Taranto,* 303, no. 349, from Tarentum; Davidson-Oliver, *Brooklyn,* 41, no. 35.

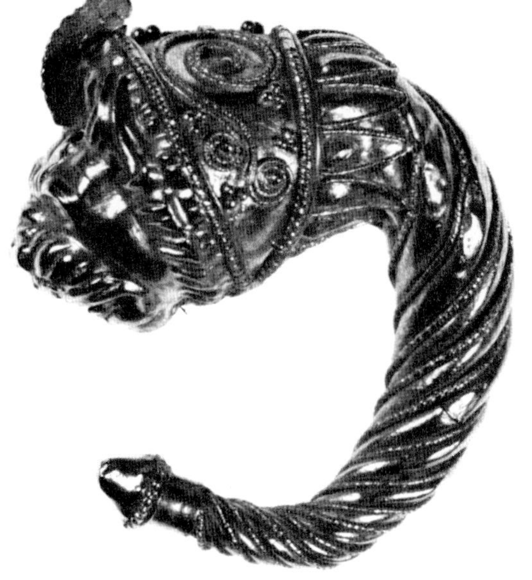

123.1

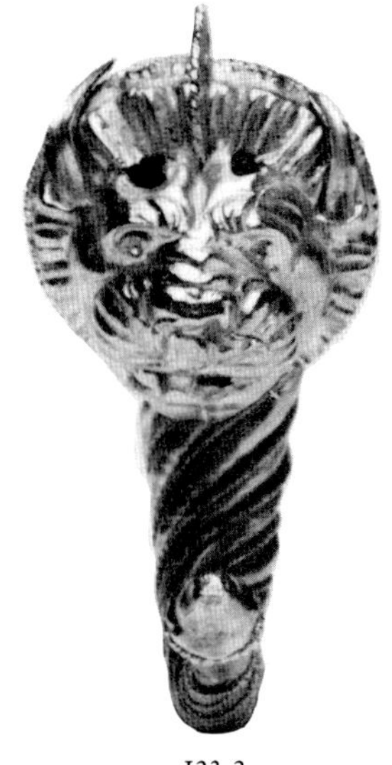

123.2

Hoop Earrings with Bull Heads
Second to first century

57.1730 and 57.1731. Gold and garnet. Collection of Henry Walters before 1931. Collection of Mrs. Henry Walters (sale catalogue, *Art Collection of Mrs. Henry Walters,* New York, Parke-Bernet, December 2, 1943, 90, no. 522). Purchased in 1943. Max D, 3.5 cm.

Each earring consists of two slightly convex, twisted strips and two pairs of twisted wires, tapering to a wire at one end. The other end is fitted into a collar made of nine-and-a-half long leaves outlined in twisted wire, beneath bands of smooth and twisted wire surmounted by another band of leaves. Above is a hollow bead encircled around its midsection by twisted wire and surmounted by a band of leaves edged in wire and by bands of smooth and twisted wire. The bull's head is worked separately in re-poussé; at the center of the brow is an oval garnet in a setting edged by granulation. Above and below are two pairs of discs, each encircled by granulation. Beneath the bull's chin is a loop, plain on one earring, twisted on its mate.

Exhibitions and Catalogues: *Jewelry,* 82, no. 252; *Objects of Adornment,* 63, no. 46.

Publications: Davidson-Oliver, *Brooklyn,* 59; Hackens-Winkes, *Louvain,* 80.

The hoop earring with bull heads appeared in Cyprus during the fourth century and remained popular through Hellenistic times in Cyprus, Egypt, and Syria.[1] Glass and stone inlay does not appear to have been introduced before the second century.[2]

1. Davidson-Oliver, *Brooklyn,* 53, no. 48; Hackens-Winkes, *Louvain,* 79, no. 17; R. Higgins, *Greek and Roman Jewellery,* 2nd ed. (London, 1980), 159–160.
2. Davidson-Oliver, *Brooklyn,* 58–59, no. 55.

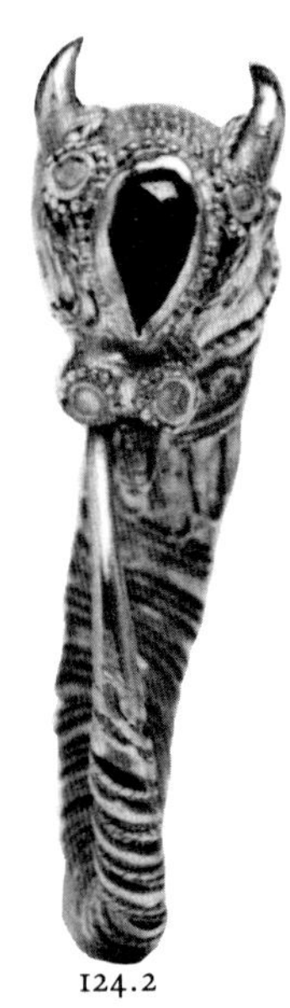

124.2

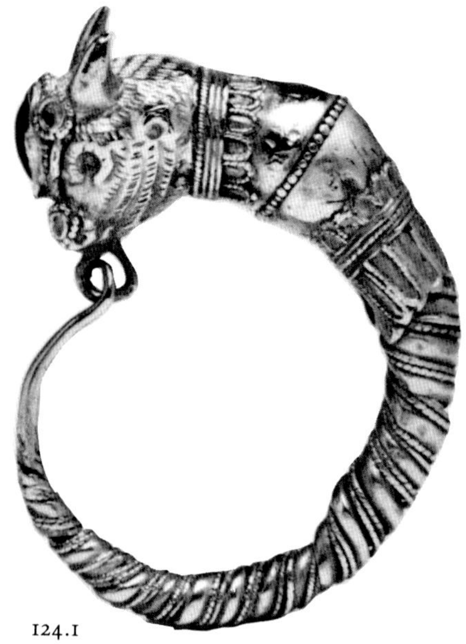

124.1

LYNX EARRING
Second century

57.2073. ''Asia Minor.'' Gold, banded agate, emerald. Gift of Cynthia and Lee Alderdice, 1982. Max D, 2.5 cm. One bead missing.

The forepart of a lynx with upright pointed ears and outstretched forelegs is separated by a collar from two spherical beads of emerald and banded agate; a third bead which originally separated the two has now disintegrated. A wire is wound around most of the rest of the hoop, which tapers to a smooth tip. The beads are separated by hoops of granules flanked by granulated triangles.

Publications: J. Ogden, *Jewellery of the Ancient World* (London, 1982), pl. 29.

The hoop earring partly strung with beads does not seem to be earlier than the second century, when we find hoop earrings with gold beads or discs alternating with pearls, glass balls, and beads made of such stones as sardonyx.[1] The pearls on earrings of this type have often partly disintegrated, and hence a single pearl is probably to be restored in the gap between the two beads on the Walters example. The terminals often take the form of such animals as dolphins or rams, but protomes are also known; a harpy torso is seen on an earring from Amphipolis of the second century and a goat protome appears on a late Hellenistic example in Switzerland.[2] A particularly close parallel to the Walters earring is an example in a private collection which features the protome of a lynx surmounted by an Isis crown with cabochon garnet.[3] The glass, which is used for the beads, appears on other earrings of this type and is also used for the inlay in the bull hoop earrings, No. 124.

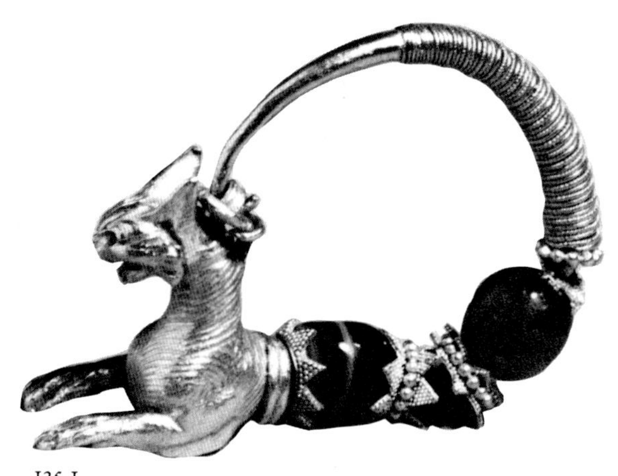

125.1

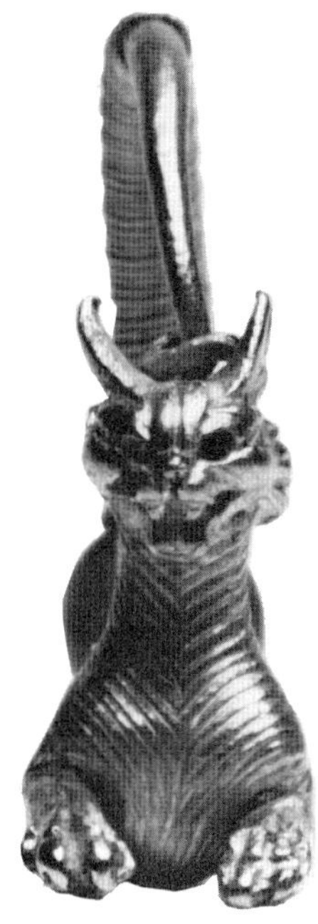

125.2

1. R. Higgins, *Greek and Roman Jewellery,* 2nd ed., (London, 1980), 160–61.
2. For the dolphin terminal, see Greifenhagen, *Schmuckarbeiten I,* 45, no. 6, pl. 22, dated to the second century and *II,* 56, no. 1, pl. 45, of late Hellenistic date. For ram heads, see Greifenhagen, *Schmuckarbeiten II,* 56, no. 4. For a lynx head, see Greifenhagen, *Schmuckarbeiten II,* 56, no. 6. For the harpy torso, see Greifenhagen, *Schmuckarbeiten I,* 34, no. 8, pl. 13, dated first century B.C.–A.D. and for the goat torso, see Hoffmann-Davidson 108, no. 29, dated late Hellenistic.
3. Hoffmann-Davidson 109, no. 30.

Sphinx Earring
Second to first century

57.1490. Gold and garnet. Purchased before 1931. Ht, 4.8 cm; W, 1.1 cm; Depth, 1.3 cm. Missing stone in left shoulder, several round stones in the headdress, and stones or enamel in the wings and Isis crown.

A trapezoidal base is composed of three separate sheets of gold for the top, bottom, and sides, with smooth and twisted wire over the joins and with colonnettes dividing the sides into square sections. Above is a hollow crouching sphinx, worked in repoussé, with a necklace, crossed straps between the breasts, and circles around the nipples worked in smooth wire to which clusters of granules are attached. An oval garnet survives on her right shoulder. Her legs are rendered by strips of metal, separately applied; between them is a rectangular garnet in a box setting. Each wing is made separately and connected with the other by a tubular strut. Each wing comprises separate sheets of gold with raised edges that functioned as settings for garnet or enamel to suggest feathers. The headdress consists of a round raised setting, the stone missing, with two round garnets beneath and two similar settings above. Above this is a round garnet beneath a setting worked in the shape of an Isis crown, with a circular hoop above.

Exhibitions and Catalogues: *Jewelry,* 79, no. 245. *Objects of Adornment,* 62, no. 43.

Publications: D. K. Hill, "From Alexander to Augustus," *BWalt* 7 (1955) no. 5; Davidson-Oliver, *Brooklyn,* 70.

The ancestry of the Walters example is represented by an earring that was discovered in a barrow near Kerch in 1965 and is dated to the second half of the fourth century. On that piece a sphinx, rendered in Classical style and without inlay, is perched on a base and surmounted by a rosette from which the ear wire rises vertically.[1] Assigning the Walters earring to a later date are the Isis headdress, which is not seen in Hellenistic jewelry before the first half of the second century, the extensive use of garnet inlay, and the handling of the base which can be compared with that supporting a biga on a hoop earring from Pelinna dated to the first half of the second century.[2] The disc surmounting the sphinx's head recalls earrings of the disc and pendant type exemplified by No. 121, and is particularly comparable to an example from Tarentum in which a disc, also surmounted by an Isis crown, is seen above an amphora resting on a base. The artist of the Walters earring has simply substituted the sphinx for the amphora and directly juxtaposed disc and sphinx.

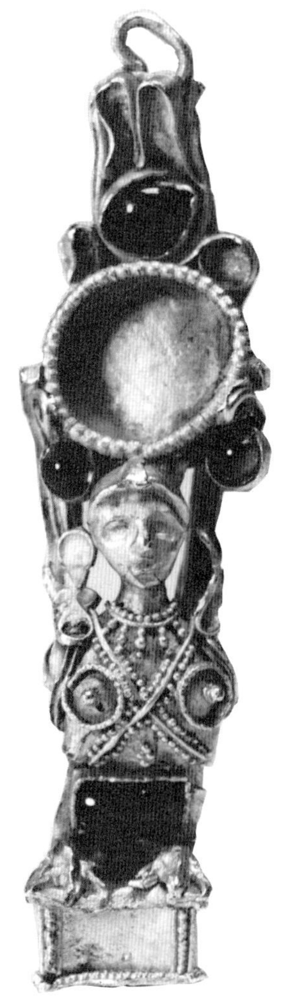

126.1

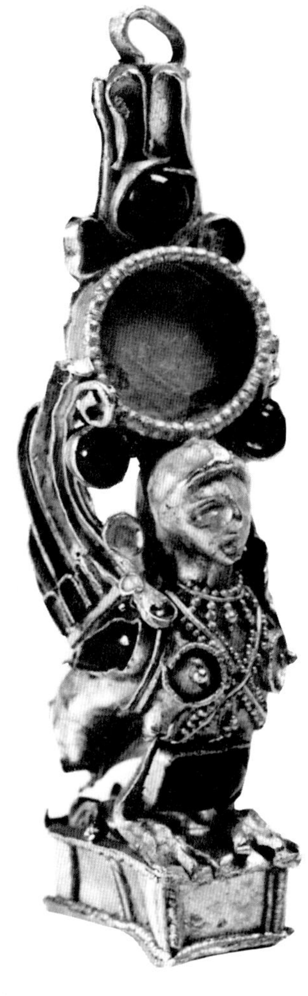

126.2

1. G. Sokolov, *Antique Art on the Northern Black Sea Coast* (Leningrad, 1975), 45, no. 26.
2. For the earliest appearance of the Isis crown in Hellenistic jewelry, see Davidson-Oliver, *Brooklyn,* 70–71. Oliver points out that the application of the crown to a wide variety of earrings featuring Erotes, amphorae, birds, and bigae indicates that the motif had entered a general decorative vocabulary and was probably without specific religious significance. For the biga earring from Pelinna, see S. Miller, *Two Groups of Thessalian Gold,* University of California Publications in Classical Studies 18 (Berkeley, 1979), 42–44, 61–62, pl. 24.
3. Deppert-Lippitz 261, pl. 31 in London (Marshall, *BMCJ* 2331) of the mid-second century. Compare also *Ori di Taranto,* 166, no. 80b.

Diadem
Third to second century

57.1541. Gold with garnet and enamel. "Found in Macedonia." Canessa Collection (sale catalogue, *Collection d'antiquités grècques et romaines,* Paris, Hôtel Drouot, May 11–14, 1903, 68, no. 259, pl. 9). Collection of M. Guilhou (sale catalogue, Paris, Hôtel Drouot, March 16–18, 1905, 16–17, no. 82, pl. 8). Acquired before 1931. L, 45.1 cm; L, central unit 3.9 cm; Ht, without pendants 2 cm.

A Herakles knot is set between openwork straps and is connected to them by hinges. The knot consists of sheet gold whose upturned sides are edged with twisted and smooth wire. Set within the cavities are ten garnets separated by twelve rosettes, of which four were probably inlaid. At each corner of the knot are gold spirals terminating in snake heads. Between the knot and the hinges is a row of pointed leaves and rows of smooth and twisted wire. The end of each strap adjacent to the hinge has a row of green enamel filigree tongues. The rest of each strap

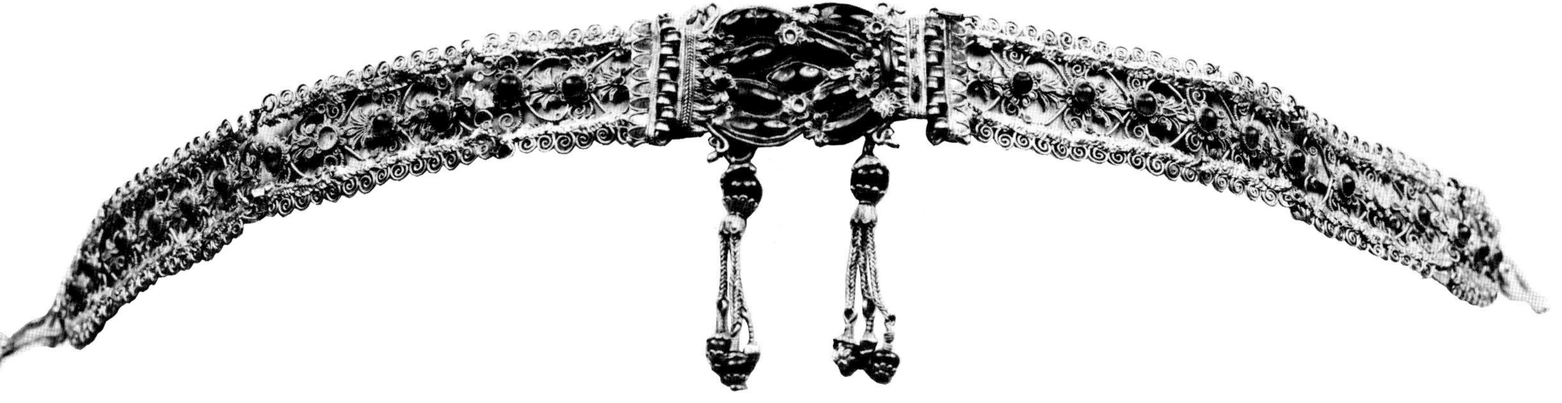

127.1

consists of three parallel gold strips terminating in a loop at the end opposite the hinge; there is a rosette at each end of the loop. The central strip is decorated with a row of palmettes and scrolls, aligned end-to-end and inlaid with green and blue enamel. At the base of each palmette is a garnet within a rosette. On the flanking strips is a row of spirals enclosing a row of rosettes and leaves. Another rosette is on each loop. Suspended from the Herakles knot are two pendants, each composed of a garnet ball set between half-rosettes; beneath is an inverted half-rosette from which are hung three chains, two of which terminate in a garnet ball between half rosettes, the third in a gold bead above a square.

Exhibitions and Catalogues: *Jewelry,* 87, no. 265, and ill. on 84.

Publications: B. Segall, "Realistic Portraiture in Greece and Egypt," *JWalt* 9 (1946) 65 and fig. 12 on 65; R. H. Randall, Jr. "Jewellery through the Ages," *Apollo* 84 (1966) 495, fig. 3; D. Scarisbrick, "Ma nessuno era bravo come gli etruschi," *Bolaffi-Gioielli* 7 (1980) 9; J. Ogden, *Jewellery of the Ancient World* (New York, 1982), pl. 17.

The patterns and craftsmanship of the strap's openwork find a parallel in a diadem from the Stathatos Collection, which is dated to the late third century.[1] Garnets are, however, more commonly found in later Hellenistic jewelry, and one might compare the garnet knot in a diadem in the Benaki Museum of the second century, and another from Kerch, also with ball and tassel pendants, which has been dated between 200 and 150.[2]

Diadems with Herakles knots were a favorite form of Hellenistic jewelry and have been found in South Russia, South Italy, and northern Greece.[3] Their popularity can be traced back to Alexander who brought this form of jewelry into fashion when he adopted the Persian diadem as a symbol of his own kingship. When Alexander, followed by the Ptolemies, claimed descent from Herakles, the monarch came to be identified with the double knot by which Herakles secured the Nemean lionskin at his throat. In its affiliation with Herakles, the knot connoted the mythical hero's strength as well as his fecundity in producing seventy children, and for this reason the double knot was traditionally used in the marriage belt. The motif was also associated with the love affair between Herakles and Deianira, unfortunate though the outcome was, and so it was a popular device in women's jewelry, appearing on Hellenistic thigh ornaments, necklaces, finger rings, and bracelets. As early as the later fourth century the motif forms the centerpiece of a gold diadem which was included in the gold larnax found in the antechamber of the royal tomb at Vergina.[5]

The snaky coils on the corners of the Walters knot refer to a different artistic motif into which the Herakles knot became assimilated. The device of two entwined snakes originated in Egypt or Mesopotamia at an early date. Its apotropaic and fertility connotations were retained in the Greek adaptation of the motif seen in the Gorgon's buckle on the pediment of the Temple of Artemis at Corfu and in the interwoven coils of Hermes' kerykeion.[6] The fusion of the Herakles knot with the entwined snakes may have been prompted by Alexander's association with snakes through his affiliation with Zeus Ammon.[7]

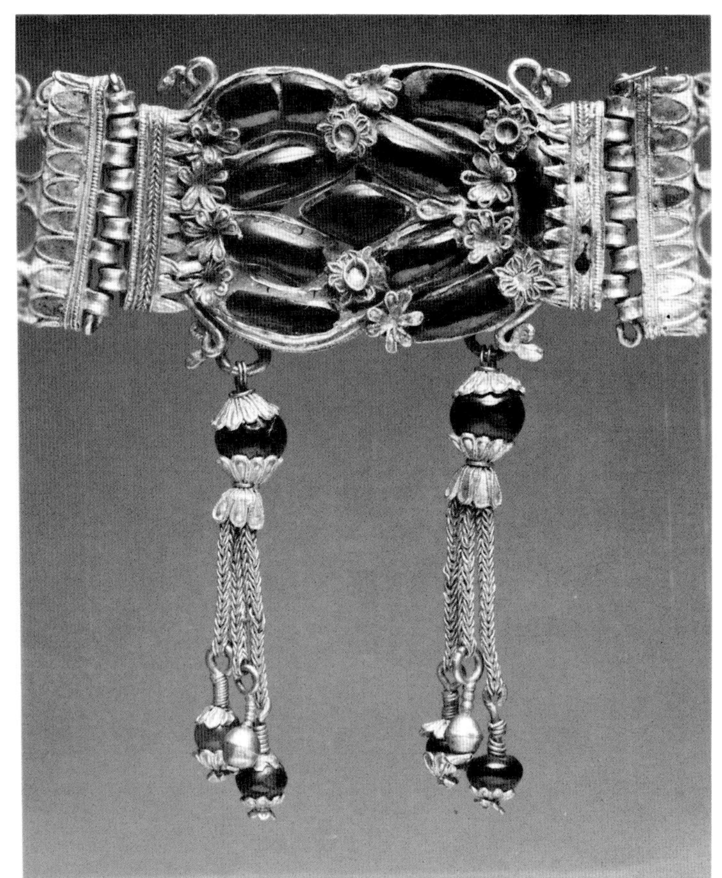

127.2

1. Hoffmann-Davidson 60–62, fig. 3b.

2. For the Benaki example, see R. Higgins, ''Macedonian Royal Jewelry,'' *Macedonia and Greece,* 147, fig. 13. For the Kerch example, see Deppert-Lippitz 256, pls. 28–29, and 275, fig. 212. Compare also a garnet Herakles knot in the British Museum in J. Ogden, *Jewellery of the Ancient World* (New York, 1982), pl. 20.

3. *Ori di Taranto,* 121–122, no. 52. Greifenhagen, *Schmuckarbeiten I,* 1, pl. 12; Deppert-Lippitz 215, fig. 152.

4. Thompson, *Troy,* 42; Hackens-Winkes, *Louvain,* where the knot's probable association with the Gordion knot is discussed.

5. M. Andronicos, *Vergina. The Royal Tombs and the Ancient City* (Athens, 1984), 196, fig. 159.

6. A. N. Zadoks and J. Jitta, ''Intertwined Snakes,'' *BABesch* 57 (1982) 1–2.

7. For the two snakes that led Alexander's army to the oracle of Zeus Ammon, see Arrian 3.3–4.

GOLD AND GARNET NECKLACE
Third to second century

57.1540. Gold, glass and garnet. ''From Pontos.'' Purchased in 1911. L, 42 cm.

A double loop chain threaded with sixteen garnet beads alternating with nineteen hollow gold beads is edged at each end with twisted wire. Each finial takes the form of a lion-griffin head with a collar of smooth, turned wire. Behind is a truncated cylindrical purple glass bead encapsulated in gold at the opposite end. The animal's mouth holds the hook or loop for fastening. The horns and crest were added separately.

Exhibitions and Catalogues: *Jewelry,* 84, no. 258.

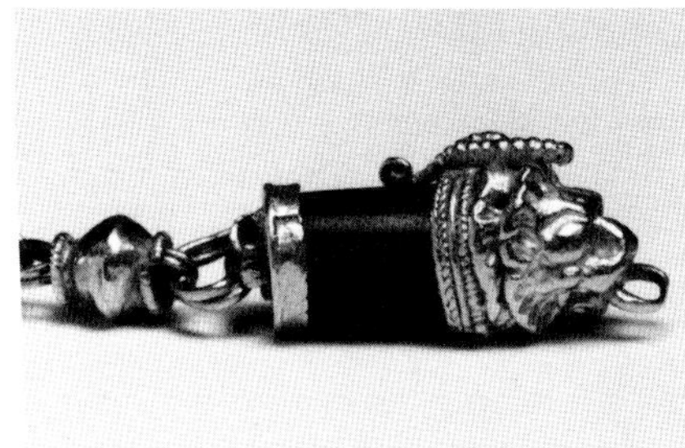

128.2

Distinctively Hellenistic are the lion-griffin finial and the collar in the form of a cylindrical bead.[1] Variations in the finials include the heads of a lion, antelope, and bull.[2] Carnelian as well as garnet beads were also occasionally used in alternation with gold beads.[3]

1. Greifenhagen, *Schmuckarbeiten II,* 20, pls. 9.9 and 10.9; 19, pls. 9.2 and 10.2; 19, pls. 9.4 and 10.4; Deppert-Lippitz 247, 251 dates the type to the third or second century.
2. Greifenhagen, *Schmuckarbeiten II,* 19, pls. 9.1 and 10.1 (lion head); 19–20, pls. 9.5 and 10.5 (antelope); 19–20, pl. 9.6 (bovine head).
3. Ibid., 19–20, pl. 9.6; 20, pls. 9.7 and 10.7; 20, pls. 9.8 and 10.8.

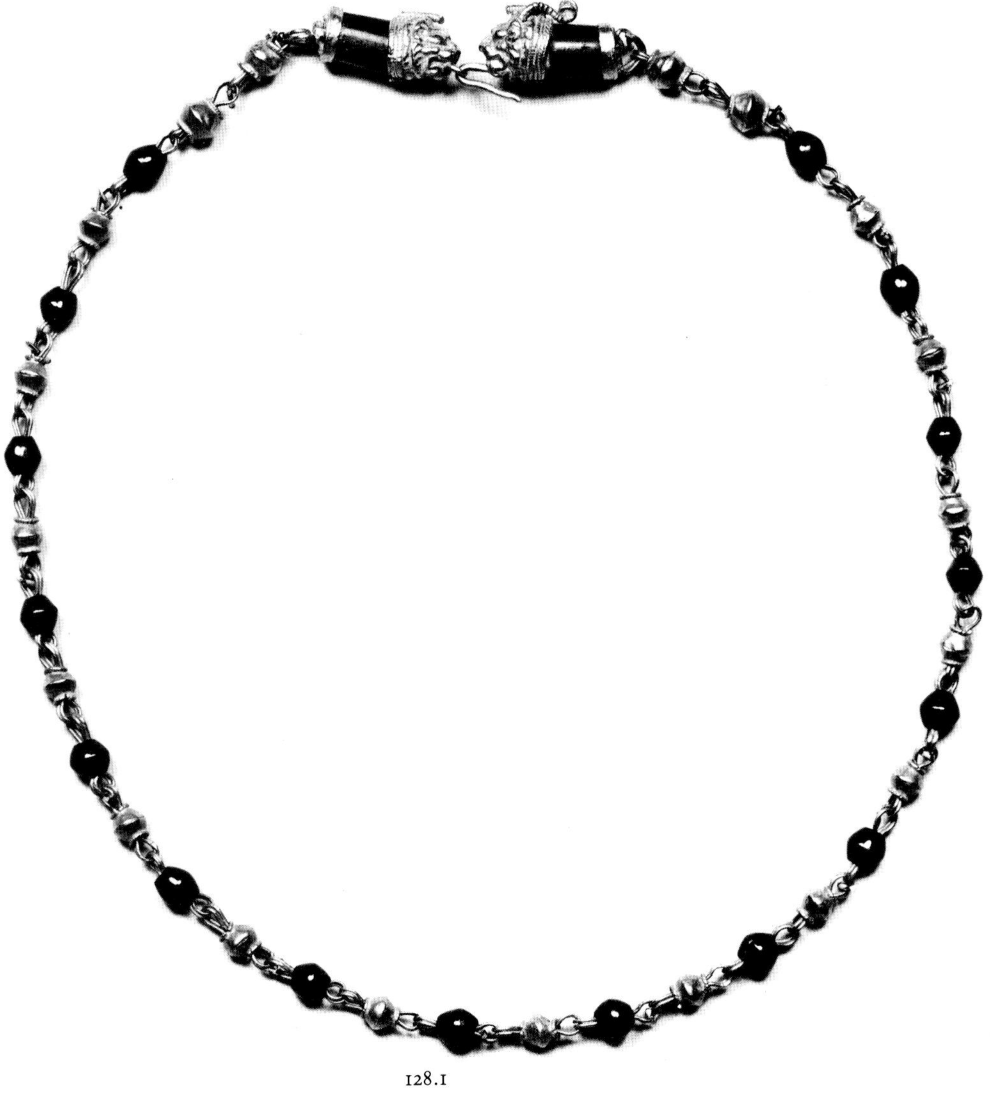

128.1

GOLD BEAD NECKLACE WITH GARNETS
Ca. third century

57.598. Gold and garnet. Dattari Collection (sale catalogue, *Collections de M. Jean P. Lambros d'Athènes et de M. Giovanni Dattari du Caire,* Paris, Hôtel Drouot, June 17–19, 1912, 62, no. 572). Purchased in 1912. L, 49 cm; L, of each finial, 1.9 cm. Inlay missing from eyes.

A chain of double loops is threaded with eighty-five hollow gold beads. Each finial is composed of a bull head with a collar consisting of a garnet bead flanked by rows of tongues inside a smooth and twisted wire. A gold cone forms the transition from collar to chain. The bull mouths hold the ring and loop for fastening.

Exhibitions and Catalogues: *Jewelry,* 84, no. 257; *Objects of Adornment,* 64, no. 47.

Popular in Hellenistic times was a necklace of gold balls terminating in garnet collars with animal-head finials. Garnets were imported from India and were also found in the Balkan area.

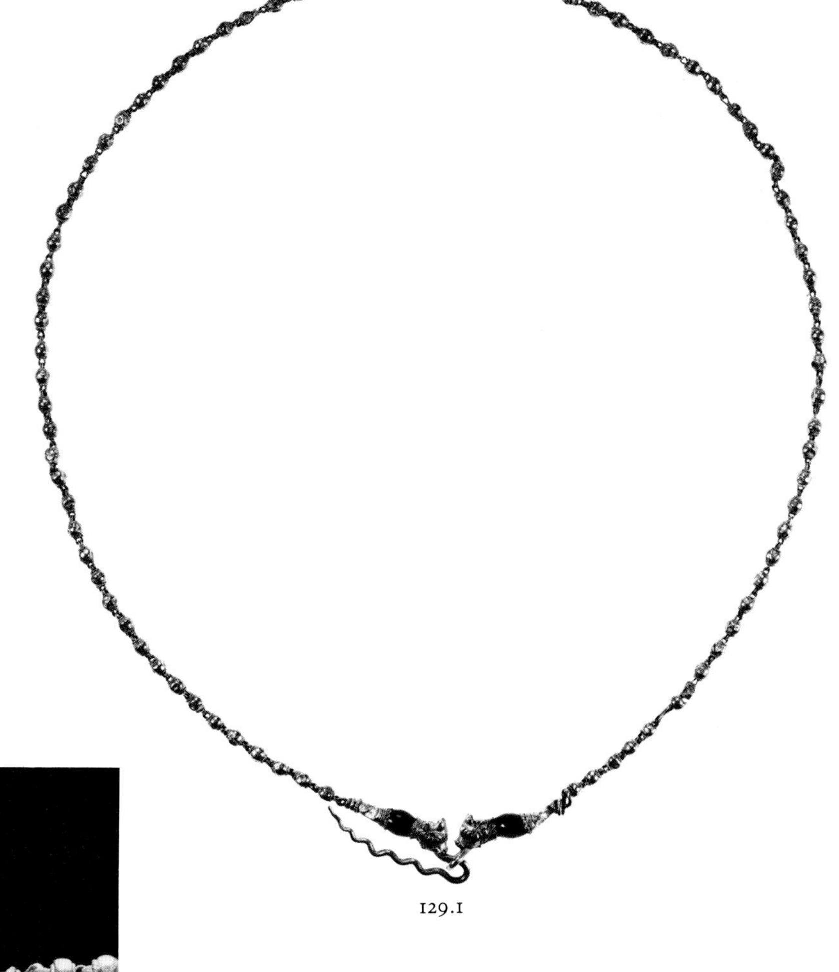

129.1

129.2

Pendant with Bust of Sarapis
Second to first century

57.1524. Gold. Purchased before 1931. D, 4.4 cm.

A disc bears a relief bust of Sarapis, which includes the upper shoulders and chest. He has a beard and mustache, wavy hair that falls to his shoulders, and a modios ornamented with wheat sheaves flanking a circular ornament. He wears a tunic, and the folds of his mantle lie on his left shoulder. The disc is encircled by a thick hoop terminating in globules beneath. Attached to the hoop above the bust is a corrugated, transverse tube with a pellet in the center front.

Exhibitions and Catalogues: *Pagan and Christian Egypt,* The Brooklyn Museum (Brooklyn, January 23–March 9, 1941), no. 129; *Jewelry,* III, no. 309.

The circular frame terminating in two contiguous balls is surely descended from a type of ancient Near Eastern amulet that was of crescent form with globular tips. A vestige of that type is seen on two medallions from Delos dated to the second century; here a crescent with spherical finials is superimposed onto a circular disc which, in one example, bears a red stone in the center, and, on the second medallion, carries a representation in relief of Aphrodite on a goat.[1] Also comparable is a necklace, dated to the third century, which bears a pendant of circular form with two directly adjacent balls; within the open center is suspended an emerald.[2] On the Walters piece, the association of a Near Eastern amuletic type with the bust of a deity having Egyptian roots and a cult influenced by Greek culture epitomizes the international flavor of the Hellenistic era, when the same amuletic frame can enclose a representation of Sarapis or the Greek goddess Aphrodite. The similarity between the ribbed tube on the Walters pendant and those on the Delian examples suggests that all three medallions are approximately contemporary.

1. E. Lévy, "Nouveaux bijoux à Délos," *BCH* 92 (1968) 533–535 and 534, fig. 9; E. Lévy, "Trésor hellénistique trouvé à Délos," *BCH* 89 (1965) 565–566 and 565, fig. 23.
2. *Antiken aus dem östlichen Mittelmeerraum,* Galerie Heidi Vollmoeller (Zurich, 1986), no. 33.

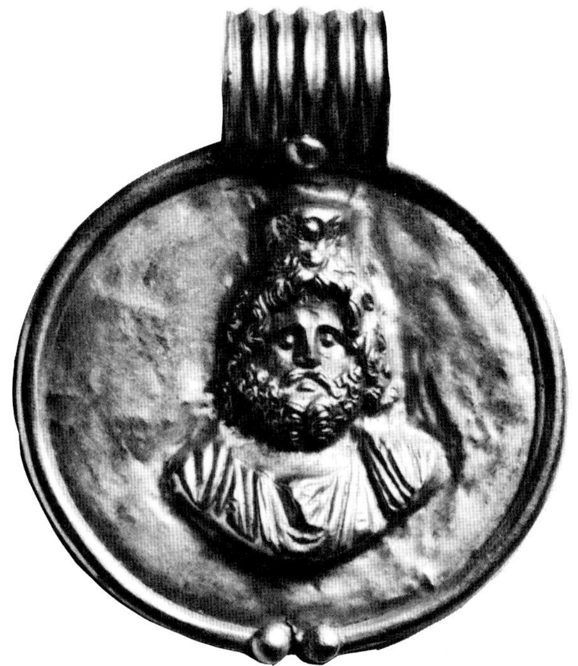

130.1

Pair of Bracelets from Olbia
Late second century

57.375 and 57.376. Gold, garnet, amethyst, emerald, chrysoprase, pearl, white and blue glass, and red, blue, green, and turquoise enamel. "From a tomb near Olbia." Collection of Peter Mavrogordato, acquired in 1913. Collection of F. L. von Gans in Frankfurt. Purchased from the Galerie Bachstitz in 1921–1931. D, 7.9 cm and 7.3 cm; Ht, 5.2 cm; W, central unit 3.1 cm. Many of the stones are modern replacements.

Each bracelet is composed of a central unit set between two curved arms and attached to them by hinges. The clasp consists of a pin that slipped through intermeshing loops. The backing is a gold sheet folded up at the sides. Beading articulates the edges and the divisions between the decorative elements. The rectangular center section has an oval box setting for a garnet, which is flanked at each end by a granulated blossom and leaves in green enamel. At each end of the curved sections are rectangular crosspieces set with oval or square emeralds flanking oval garnets separated by pairs of gold rosettes. Between the crosspieces is a wide horizontal band bearing an amethyst between leaves worked in granulation; those in one of the bracelets are carved in intaglio. Above and below is a row of pearls strung upon a wire. The two outer registers are rectangular crosspieces set with oval glass stones flanking a round chrysoprase, one of which has been replaced by glass.

Exhibitions and Catalogues: *The Dark Ages. A Loan Exhibition of Pagan and Christian Art in the Latin West and Byzantine East,* Worcester Art Museum (Worcester, February 20–March 21, 1937), 33, no. 68, ill.; *Russian Art,* The Walters Art Gallery (Baltimore, November 9, 1959–January 3, 1960), catalogue P. Verdier, no. 1; *An Exhibition of Treasures of the Walters Art Gallery,* Wildenstein (New York, March 15–April 15, 1967), no. 79; *Jewelry,* 97, no. 238 and 94, color; *Objects of Adornment,* 72, no. 54.

Publications: R. Zahn, *Galerie Bachstitz, s'Gravenhage II, Antike byzantinische islamische Arbeiten der Kleinkunst und des Kunstgewerbes, Antike Skulpturen* (Berlin, 1921), 27–28, 32–33, pl. 24; C. R. Morey, "Art of the Dark Ages, A Unique Show," *The Art News* (February 20, 1937), 13, ill.; P. Cowles, "Jewelry," *BWalt* 5 (1953) no. 4; M. C. Ross, *Arts of the*

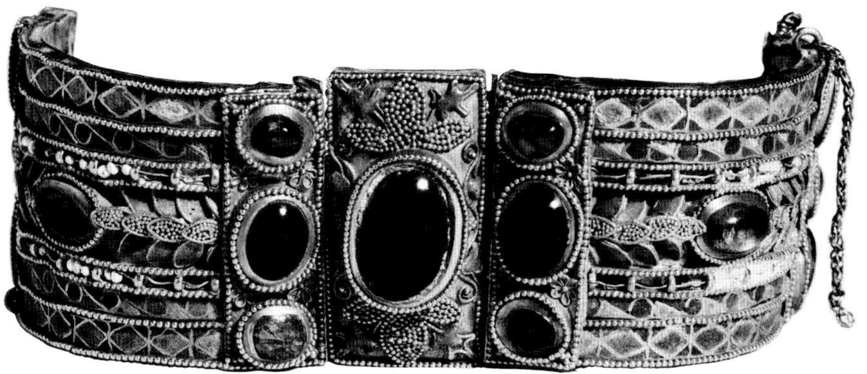

131.1

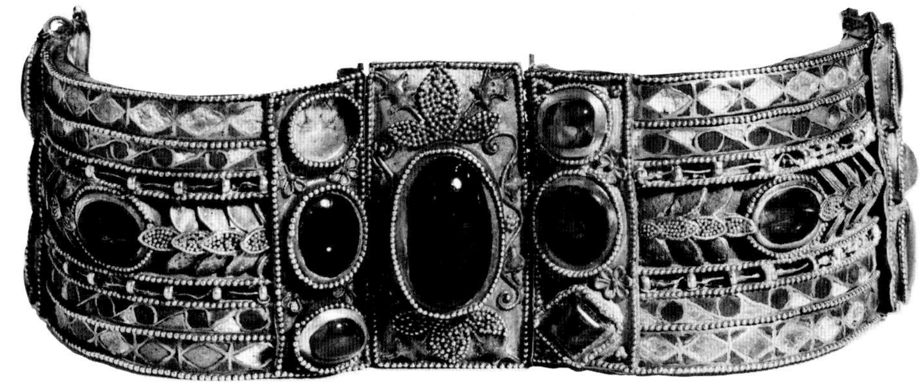

131.2

Migration Period in the Walters Art Gallery (Baltimore, 1961), 21; R. H. Randall, Jr., "Jewellery Through the Ages," *Apollo* 84 (1966) 497, fig. 8; B. Pfeiler-Lippitz, "Späthellenistische Goldschmiedearbeiten," *AntK* 15 (1972) 109, 110, 116, 117, pl. 33,1; D. Scarisbrick, "Ma nessuno era bravo come gli etruschi," *Bolaffi-Gioielli* 7 (1980) 10; M.-L. d'Otrange-Mastai, *Jewelry* (Washington, D.C., 1981), 34, pl. 7; M. A. McCrory, "Objects of Adornment: Five Thousand Years of Jewelry from the Walters Art Gallery, Baltimore," *Archaeology* 37 (1984) 54–57 and cover; Deppert-Lippitz 292 and 295, fig. 224.

This pair of bracelets was reputedly found in Olbia in the late nineteenth or early twentieth century, but not necessarily together with the butterfly necklace (No. 132) or the pendant necklace (No. 133) with which the bracelets are often grouped.[1] Although parallels to the bracelet type are few, individual elements find counterparts in jewelry of the late Hellenistic age. Most noticeable is the lavish use of colored stones which almost eclipses the goldwork and follows a fashion that becomes prominent during the second century.[2] This emphasis on polychromy was an indirect result of Alexander's conquests, which released Persian treasures of precious gems, opened up trade routes to the East, and introduced Greeks to the traditional Oriental taste for colored gemstones.[2]

Other late Hellenistic features on the bracelets are the stylization of the centerpiece, the combination of oval and square elements, the presence of pearls, and the wreath of pointed leaves.[3] The hinged clasp appears on bracelets only in the Hellenistic period, some of which resemble the Walters examples in having a fixed element opposite the clasp.[4] A particularly close parallel for the form and the use of cloisonné in the Walters pair is a bracelet from Palaiokastron which is dated to the first century.[5]

Olbia was a city along the north shore of the Black Sea which was colonized by Miletos in the seventh century and grew to prosperity in the sixth and fifth centuries as a commercial emporium through which passed amber, slaves, and grain from Scythian lands. In Hellenistic times the city safeguarded its welfare by making large payments to neighboring chieftains, but, nonetheless, suffered repeated raids by the Scythians and, in the mid-first century, by the Getae. Despite the city's reduced fortune, epigraphical evidence confirms the enormous wealth garnered by at least a few families, whose taste, as the size and lavish ornamentation on these bracelets suggest, was probably flavored by contact with non-Hellenic peoples.[6] The city was rediscovered in 1851, but systematic excavations were initiated only in this century.

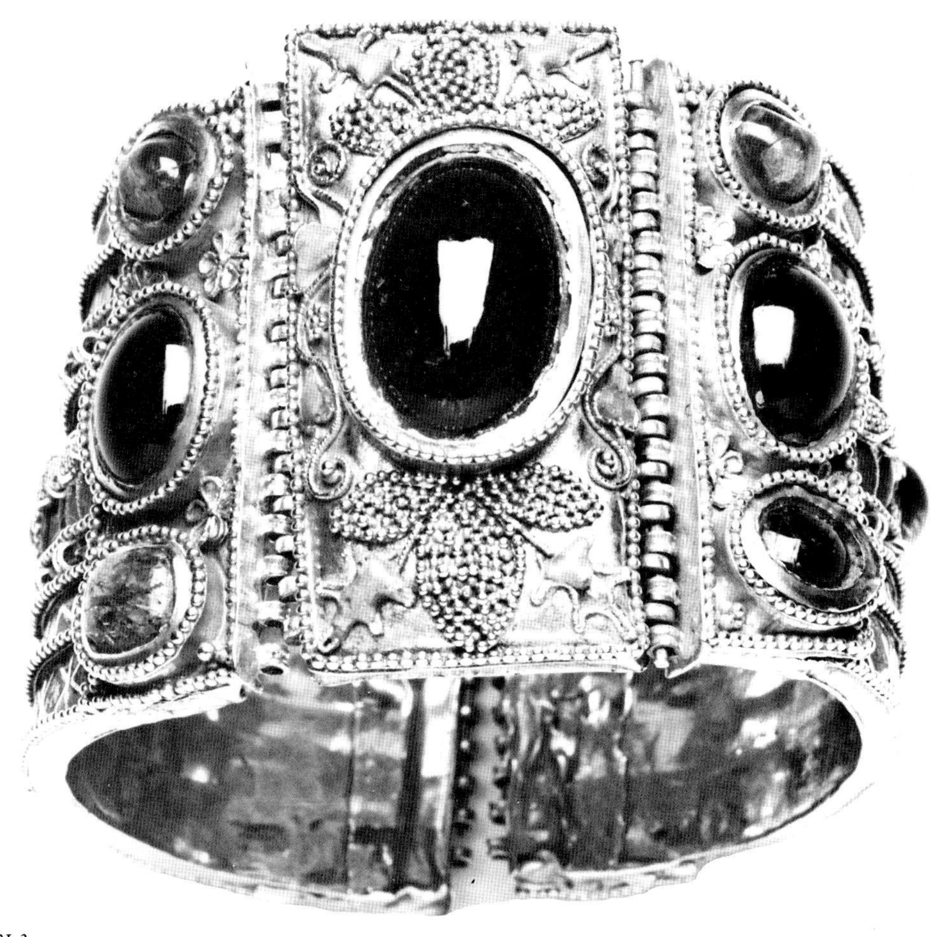

131.3

1. For the full history of the Olbia treasure, see *Jewelry*, 95.
2. B. Pfeiler-Lippitz, *AntK* 15 (1972) 114–115, 116, 118.
3. Ibid., 117. For the leafy garland, see E. Reeder Williams, *The Archaeological Collection of the Johns Hopkins University* (Baltimore, 1984), 74 and 76, note 3.
4. Compare a bracelet from Izmir of the early third century (Deppert-Lippitz 235–236 and 237, fig. 173); and an armband from western Syria in the Oriental Institute in Chicago (Deppert-Lippitz 271 and 270, fig. 204), which she implies is third to second century. This piece is also discussed in Hoffmann-Davidson 159–160, no. 56.
5. Pfeiler-Lippitz (note 2) 107, 109, pl. 33.2–3; Deppert-Lippitz 292, and 295, fig. 225.
6. See Austin, *Hellenistic World*, 170–174, no. 97.

NECKLACE WITH
BUTTERFLY PENDANT
FROM OLBIA
Late second century

57.386. Gold, amethyst, emerald, rock crystal, pearl, and blue-green, blue, brown, red, and white glass. "From a tomb at Parutino near Olbia in 1891." Collection of Postnikov ca. 1900. Possibly thereafter at Spink, London. Acquired in 1913 by Peter Mavrogordato. Collection of F. L. van Gans. Purchased from the Galerie Bachstitz in the Hague between 1921 and 1931. L, 32.7 cm; Ht, butterfly pendant 2.5 cm; W, butterfly pendant 3.6 cm. Central oval stone and oval stones of pendants are modern.

The central section of the necklace comprises five stones, alternating ovals and squares. All are blue-green glass except for the central amethyst which replaces the original blue-green stone which existed in the nineteenth century; beneath the central stone a pearl and emerald ball are suspended. The borders of the settings bear granulated triangles, round stones of brown glass, and gold blossoms. Beneath the square stones flanking the central one are two pendants, each consisting of an oval emerald above a teardrop-shaped garnet in a granulated setting from which a rock crystal ball and an emerald ball are suspended. Gold chains link the pendants and the side oval stones. Suspended from the pendants and hanging between them is a butterfly which has a round emerald for the head, a blue glass stone for the body, and gold feet and antennae. Each wing is inset with an emerald and two white or blue round glass cabochons. The braided chain terminates in two gold lynx heads with rock crystal necks that are connected to the stones by hinges.

Exhibitions and Catalogues: *Jewelry,* 96, no. 281.

Publications: A. V. Oreshnikov, "Remarks on Antiquities Found at Parutino in 1891," *Drevnosti* 15:2 (1894) 1–13, pl. 1:2; E. H. Minns, *Scythians and Greeks* (Cambridge, 1913), 406; R. Zahn, *Galerie Bachstitz, s'Gravenhage II, Antike byzantinische islamische Arbeiten der Kleinkunst und des Kunstgewerbes, Antiken Skulpturen* (Berlin, 1921), 28–29, 32, pl. 25; P. Cowles, "Jewelry," *BWalt* 5 (1953) no. 4; B. Pfeiler-Lippitz, "Späthellenistische Goldschmiedearbeiten," *AntK* 15 (1972) 108, 116, pl. 31; D. Scarisbrick, "Schmetterling, Mariposa, Butterfly, Papillon . . . Farfalla," *Bolaffi-Gioielli* 4 (1981) 49, no.11; Deppert-Lippitz 284, 286, and 283, fig. 215; Hackens-Winkes, *Louvain,* 67–82, 62, fig. 5.

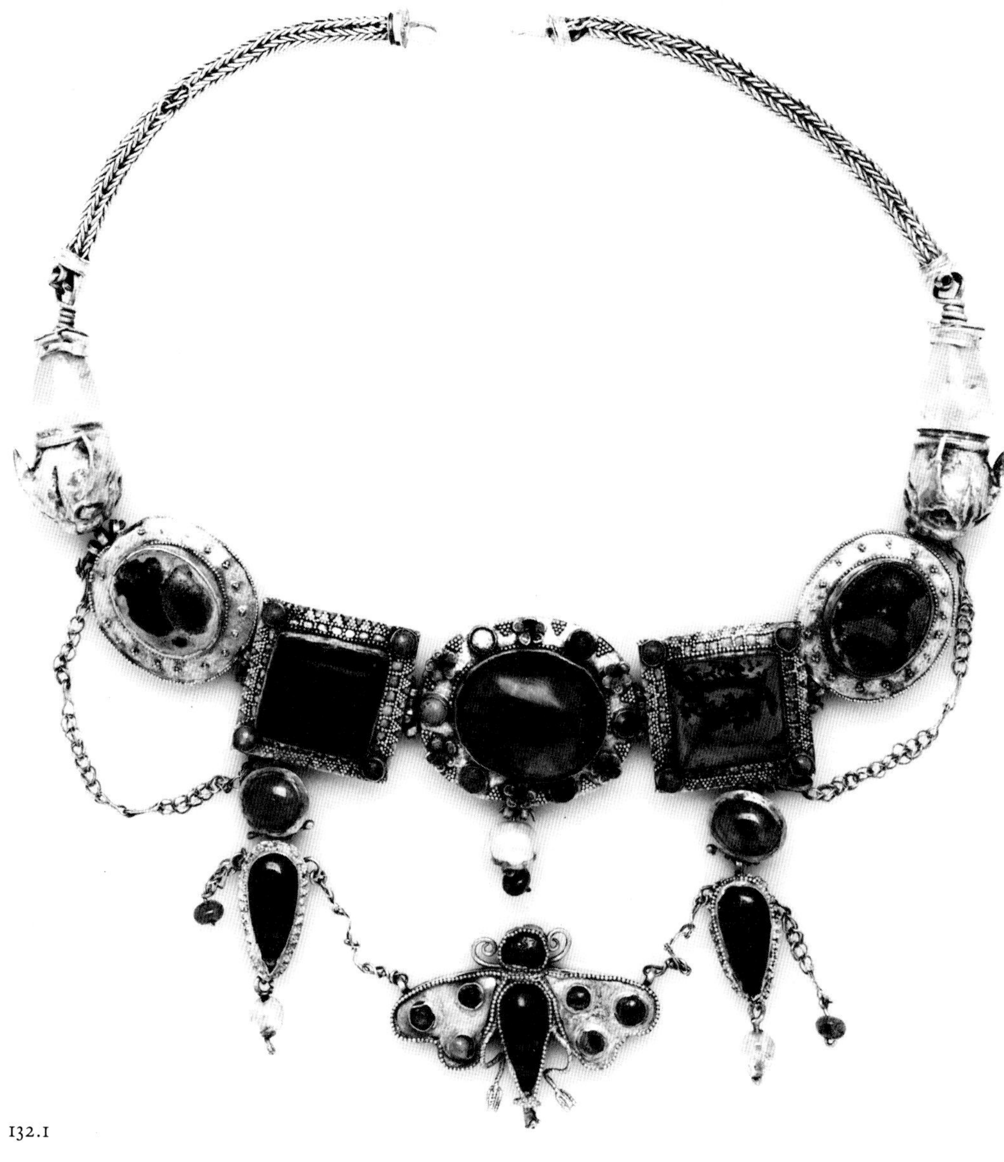

132.1

This necklace was reportedly found around the neck of a female skeleton and was accompanied by earrings, a small gold vessel, silver cups, a ladle, distaff, and pitcher, now divided among the Walters, the Wadsworth Atheneum in Hartford, and The Metropolitan Museum of Art in New York.[1] The necklace is generally thought to date from the late second century, both because the gold vessel found with it has parallels from mid-second century contexts and because the Walters necklace is similar to one from Palaiokastron, also dated to the late second to first centuries, which exhibits both the same lavish use of colored stones in alternating round and square shapes and a similar design of a central and flanking pendants.[2] Also comparable are the lynx heads on the terminals of the adjoining chain; however, the chain on the Walters necklace may not originally have been part of the same necklace, although both pieces were reputedly found together. Other typically late Hellenistic features on the Walters necklace are the triangular clusters of granulation, and the ball and teardrop form of the pendants which recall late Hellenistic pendant earrings that take the form of amphorae fashioned in garnet (No. 121).[3]

Several other necklaces with butterfly pendants are known. Slightly earlier is an example in a private collection which exhibits a more naturalistic butterfly.[4] Necklaces with more simply mounted stones and with more stylized butterflies include an example discovered in the

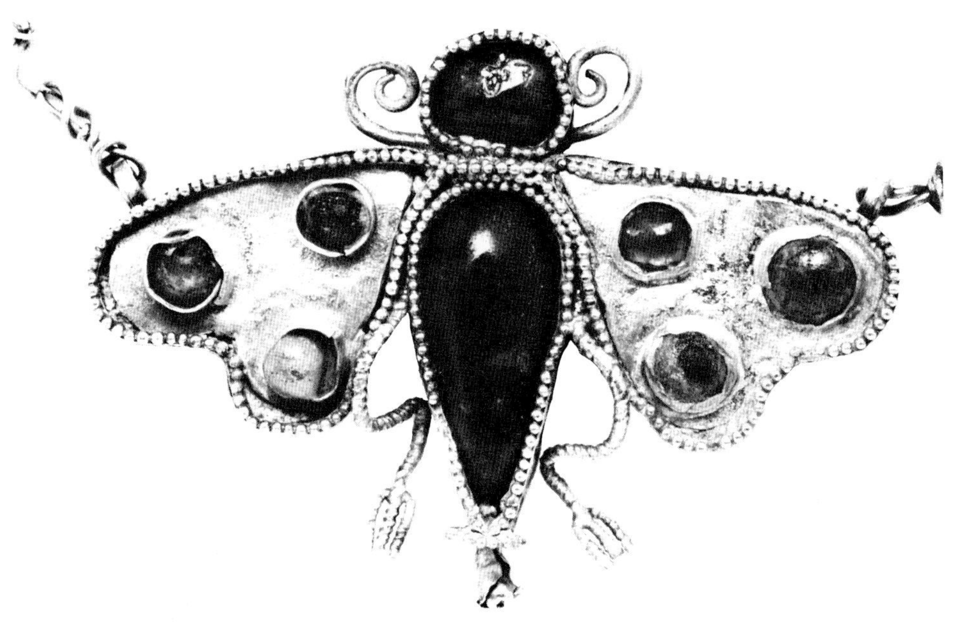

132.2

Chersonnesus in 1896; a second one found in 1898 together with a coin of Domitian; and an example in London said to have come from Rome and thought to be of the first century A.D.[5] Although the butterfly pendant necklace is unknown before late Hellenistic times, the butterfly motif is not uncommon on Hellenistic gems. Seen in the hands of Eros, the butterfly undoubtedly represented the soul, or Psyche, the erotic overtones of whose relationship with Eros were expressed in both Hellenistic art and literature.[6] Other distinctively Hellenistic features on the Walters necklace are the lavish use of glass and the presence of emeralds, which were imported at great expense from India or the Ural mountains.[7]

1. For a full discussion of the find, see *Jewelry*, 95.
2. For the Palaiokastron necklace, see Deppert-Lippitz 283–284 and 282, fig. 214, where she suggests that the central pendant may not belong; B. Pfeiler-Lippitz, *AntK* 15 (1972) 108, pl. 30.1.
3. See ibid., 117.
4. Hoffmann-Davidson 143, fig. 51, dated late third to early second century.
5. The necklace found in the Chersonnesus in 1896 is in G. Sokolov, *Antique Art on the Northern Black Sea Coast* (Leningrad, 1975), 138, no. 148. The example found in 1898 is discussed in G. Charrière, *Die Kunst der Scythen* (Paris, 1971), no. 335. Both are discussed by E. Minns, *Scythians and Greeks* (Cambridge, 1913), nos. 407–408. For the example in the British Museum, see *Jewellery through 7000 Years* (London, 1976), 115, no. 162; see also Marshall, *BMCJ* 320, no. 2746; Deppert-Lippitz 285, fig. 216.
6. E. Brandt and E. Schmidt, *Antike Gemmen in deutschen Sammlungen. Bd 1. Staatliche Münzsammlung Munich*, pt. 2 (Munich, 1970), 81, 103–104, no. 1188, pl. 127. See also B. Barr-Sharrar, *The Hellenistic and Early Imperial Decorative Bust* (Mainz, 1987), 162; G. Hanfmann, "Notes on the Mosaics from Antioch," *AJA* 43 (1939) 241–242.
7. Pliny, *NH* 37.20.77.

Pendant Necklace
from Olbia
Late second century

57.385. Gold, chalcedony, emerald, garnet, pearl, and rock crystal. ''Found in a tomb in South Russia.'' Collections of P. Mavrogordato (1913) and of F. L. von Gans of Frankfurt. Purchased from Galerie Bachstitz in the Hague between 1921 and 1931. L, 39.6 cm. The necklace on which the centerpiece is set is ancient but probably does not belong.

The centerpiece is composed of a large oval chalcedony flanked by two emeralds, all in box settings separated by hinges with toggle pins. Attached beneath the central stone, and also in box settings, is a unit comprised of five stones: two round emeralds, attached by chains held by crystal-capped pins to the emeralds above, flank a round garnet above and a teardrop-shaped one below. All the box settings are edged with beaded wire. The rest of the necklace consists of garnets, pearls, and natural crystal emeralds on looped wire.

Exhibitions and Catalogues: *Jewelry*, 97, no. 282; *Objects of Adornment*, 71, no. 53.

Publications: R. Zahn, *Galerie Bachstitz, s'Gravenhage II, Antike byzantinische islamische Arbeiten der Kleinkunst und der Kunstgewerbes, Antike Skulpturen* (Berlin, 1921), 29, 33, pl. 26; B. Pfeiler-Lippitz, ''Späthellenistische Goldschmiedearbeiten,'' *AntK* 15 (1972) 108, 116, pl. 31; Deppert-Lippitz 284, 286, and 283, fig. 215.

Although it is not absolutely clear that the central unit of this piece was found with the butterfly necklace, both are probably contemporary.[1] The use of large cabochon stones finds parallels in the Palaiokastron necklace of the second to first century and in a necklace from Artjukhov's barrow (near Kerch), dated to the second century.[2] The shapes of the stones in the Walters necklace also compare with those of the glass cabochons in a diadem reputedly found in the eastern Mediterranean together with an aureus of Mark Antony which can be dated about 34.[3]

1. For the history of the piece see *Jewelry*, 95 and 97, no. 282.
2. For the Palaiokastron necklace, see Deppert-Lippitz 283–284 and 282, fig. 214, dated late second to first century. She suggests the central pendants may not be original to the piece; Pfeiler-Lippitz, *AntK* 15 (1972) 107–108, pl. 30.1, and dated to the first century on 116. For the necklace from Artjukhov's barrow, see E. Minns, *Scythians and Greeks* (Cambridge, 1913), 406, 431, fig. 321; Pfeiler-Lippitz 107.
3. A. Oliver, ''A Set of Ancient Silverware in The Getty Museum,'' *GettyMusJ* 8 (1980) 155, 165–166, and 160–161, figs. 10–12.

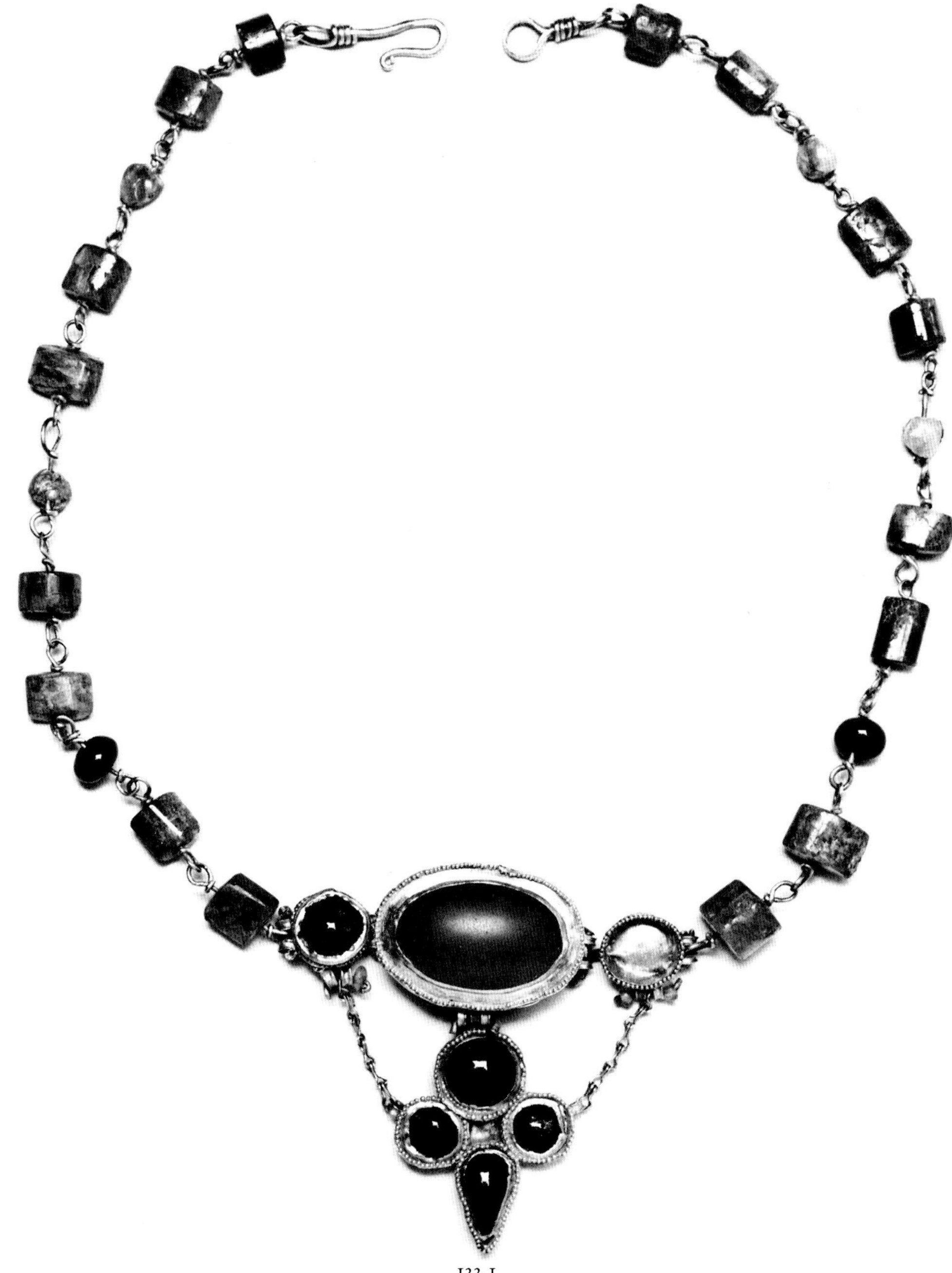

133.1

RING WITH HEAD OF
ATHENA
Third century

57.1027. Gold. Robinson Collection. Wyndham
Cook Collection. Purchased from Kelekian in 1926.
L, bezel 2.5 cm; W, bezel 2.2 cm; Th, bezel 0.6 cm;
Inner D, 1.8 cm. Hoop ring has a flat oval bezel to
which is attached a separately made relief with the
face of Athena, slightly flattened.

A woman turns her head slightly to her left; she has
indented pupils, and her hair is brushed back from
her face and falls to her shoulders with locks of hair
fluttering out to each side. Pushed back from her
brow is a triple-crested helmet. A tubular necklace is
visible above the beginnings of a chiton under her
aegis.

Exhibitions and Catalogues: *Jewelry,* 92, no. 277.

Publications: C. H. Smith and C. A. Hutton, *Catalogue of the Antiquities in the Collection of Wyndham
Francis Cook* (London, 1908) II, 5, no. 1, pl. 1.

The frontal head of a helmeted Athena
was a popular motif in Hellenistic jewelry, and the motif also appears elsewhere
in the minor arts, particularly on clay
vases, which probably reflect counterparts
in bronze, gold, and silver.[1] The flat surface of the bezel in the Walters ring and
the high relief of the representation find a
parallel in an early third-century ring from
Gela, and details in the handling of
Athena's helmet compare with a ring
from Kerch which has also been dated to
the third century and on which a carved
garnet forms the face of the goddess.[2]
Athena's popularity in the Hellenistic
period may be due to her association with
Athens and Pergamon, artistic centers of
the Classical and Hellenistic periods,
respectively, as well as with her identity as
patroness of craftsmanship and the martial
arts.

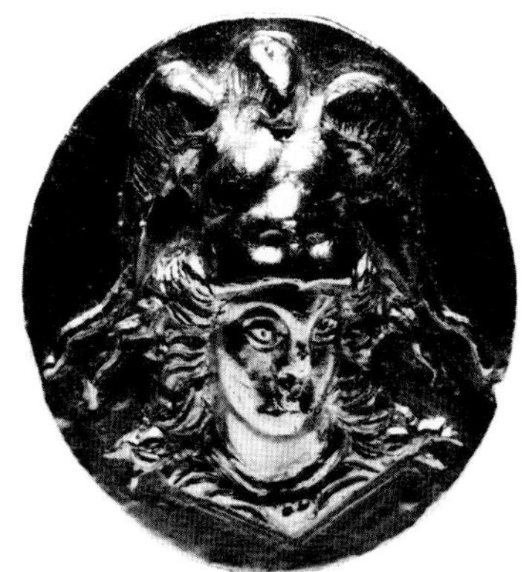

134.1

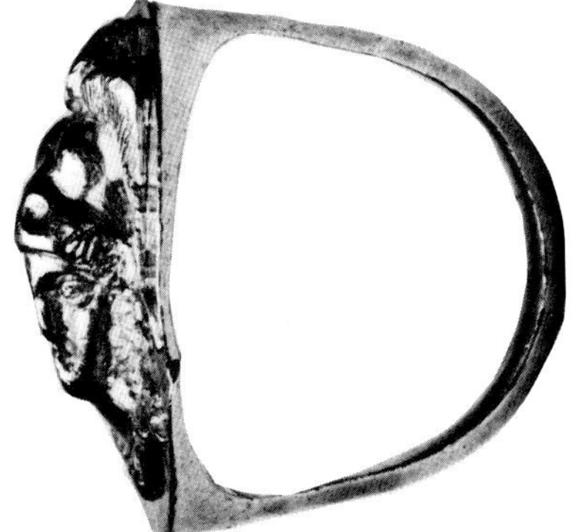

134.2

1. For Athena busts and heads in Hellenistic jewelry, see S.
   Miller, *Two Groups of Thessalian Gold,* University of California Publications in Classical Studies 18 (Berkeley, 1979),
   12–13, pls. 6–7. She discusses Calenian gutti on 12–13, pl.
   6d.
2. For the Gela find, see Deppert-Lippitz 211, fig. 148, found
   with coins of 280. For the gold and garnet ring, see G.
   Sokolov, *Antique Art on the Northern Black Sea Coast* (Leningrad, 1975), 54, no. 39. See also a Hellenistic gold
   medallion from Delos with the bust of a draped goddess
   whose face is carved from an inset garnet, in
   P. Zaphiropoulou, *Delos: Monuments and Museum* (Athens,
   1983), 59.

Garnet Ring with Bust of Ptolemy IV as Dionysos
Third century

57.1699. Convex garnet set in gold ring. Collection of Alfred Morrison (sale catalogue, London, Christie, Manson and Woods, June 29, 1898, 32, no. 255, pl. 2). Collections of E. Guilhou and Sir Arthur Evans. Purchased from Jacob Hirsch in 1942. L, bezel 3 cm; W, bezel 2.5 cm; Inner D, hoop, 2.1 cm. The convex bezel of a heavy gold ring is carved in intaglio. The bezel is oval and has a wide border, a vertical shoulder, and thick hoop.

The cast shows the right profile of a male head and neck with drapery below. His neck is grooved, his iris is incised, and his pupil is indented. Wispy locks are brushed forward to his face and fall below his ear. He wears a wreath of ivy leaves with a bunch of berries above his forehead; the ends hang from his nape.

Exhibitions and Catalogues: *Jewelry,* 92, no. 279; *Objects of Adornment,* 67, no. 52.

Publications: S. de Ricci, *Catalogue of a Collection of Ancient Rings Formed by the Late E. Guilhou* (Paris, 1912), 40, no. 268, pl.V; A. Evans, *An Illustrative Selection of Greek and Greco-Roman Gems* (Oxford, 1938), 18, no. 76; Furtwängler, *AG* III, 167, fig. 117; D. K. Hill, ''Some Hellenistic Carved Gems,'' *JWalt* 6 (1943) 66, fig. 2 on p. 61 and fig. 4 on p. 63; M. L. Vollenweider, ''Das Bildnis der Scipio Africanus,'' *MusHelv* 15, fasc. 1 (1958) 30, no. 4; D. K. Hill, ''Gem Engraving in Greece and Rome,'' *BWalt* 13 (1961) no. 4; Vollenweider-Boardman, *Oxford,* 98, no. 336.

This ring, which was owned by several prominent gem collectors of the eighteenth and nineteenth centuries, retains its original heavy gold setting, which, like the large, oval convex garnet within it, is characteristic of rings connected with the Ptolemaic court.[1] The ivy leaf crown identifies the subject as Dionysos, but the large eye, fleshy cheeks and chin, and soft flowing strands of hair that extend to the base of his neck suggest that the representation is a Ptolemaic portrait. Vollenweider contends that numismatic parallels identify the subject as Ptolemy IV Philopator, who assumed the epithet Neos Dionysos and who was depicted as Dionysos on coins as well as gems.[2] So popular was this revitalized cult of Dionysos throughout the Mediterranean that in 186 a Roman senatus consultum banned its observance in Italy.

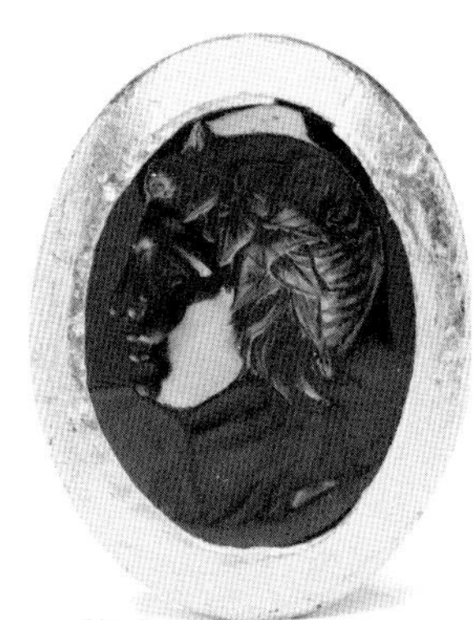

135.1

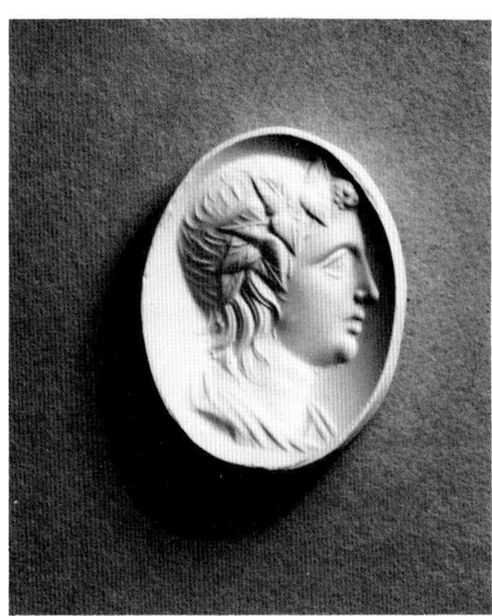

135.2

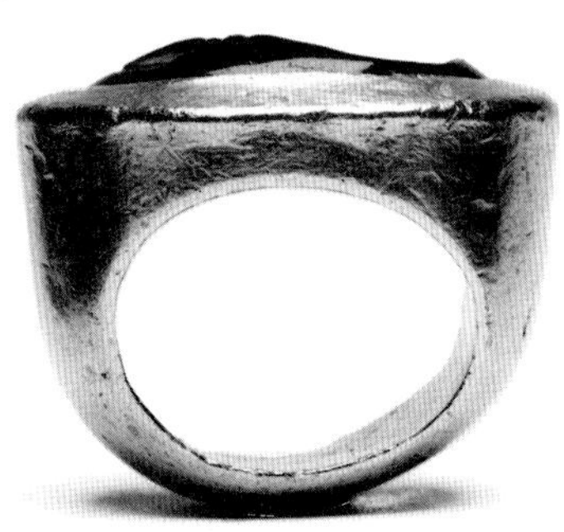

135.3

It is believed that rings with Ptolemaic portraits were exchanged as gifts, possibly with a distinction in metal or type of gem according to class or rank.[3] Plutarch tells us that in the first century the Roman general Lucullus received from Ptolemy X an emerald that was set in gold and carved with the monarch's image.[4] The practice of bestowing such rings upon court favorites renders plausible the reputed findspot of the Walters example in Tarsos, which lay under Ptolemaic control until the end of the third century.

In 221, Ptolemy IV Philopator conspired with his mother, Berenike II, to murder his father, Ptolemy III Euergetes, after which he ruled jointly with his mother until he engineered her murder a few months later. In 217, he married his sister Arsinoe III, but she fell out of favor with him and in about 206–203 died in a palace fire that had been deliberately set.

Intensified trade with India during Hellenistic times increased the availability of garnets, which enjoyed enormous popularity in the second and first centuries, and were also imported from the Balkan area (Czechoslovakia), and possibly Libya and Ethiopia.[5]

1. Compare Vollenweider, *Deliciae Leonis* (Mainz, 1984), 42–43, no. 57, dated ca. 200, identified as a Hellenistic prince portrayed as Hermes; M. L. Vollenweider, *MusHelv* 15 (1958) 31, 44. See also Vollenweider-Boardman, *Oxford,* 98, no. 336.
2. Vollenweider, *MusHelv* 15 (1958) 30; Vollenweider-Boardman, *Oxford,* 84, no. 295. See also Vollenweider, *Geneva,* 50, no. 47, pl. 22.1.
3. Ibid., 31.
4. Plut. *Lucullus,* 3.
5. See Theophrastos, *De Lapidibus,* 3.18. Vollenweider-Boardman, *Oxford,* 70; G. M. A. Richter, *Engraved Gems of the Greeks and the Etruscans* (London, 1968), 134; Hackens-Winkes, *Louvain,* 67.

Garnet Ring signed by Apollonios
Ca. 220

57.1698. Garnet set in ancient gold swivel ring. Collection of Alfred Morrison (sale catalogue, London, Christie, Manson and Woods, June 29, 1898, 33, lot 261, pl. 2); E.Guilhou Collection. Collection of Sir Arthur Evans. Purchased from Jacob Hirsch in 1942. L, bezel 2.75 cm; W, bezel 2.3 cm; Inner D, hoop, 2 cm. Oval, slightly convex stone carved in intaglio and set in gold with gold moldings at points of attachment to hoop.

Bezel cast shows the right profile of a male head and neck. Short curly locks frame his face and a wisp trails before his ear. Signed beneath neck:
ΑΠΟΛΛΩΝΙΟΥ

Exhibitions and Catalogues: *Jewelry,* 93, no. 280; *Objects of Adornment,* 67, no. 52.

Publications: A. Furtwängler, *AG* I, no. 37, pl. 63; II, 285–286, no. 36; III, 163; S. de Ricci, *Catalogue of a Collection of Ancient Rings Formed by the Late E. Guilhou* (Paris, 1912), 32, no. 202, pl. 4; A. Evans, *An Illustrative Selection of Greek and Greco-Roman Gems* (Oxford, 1938), 15–16, no. 65, pl. 4; D. K. Hill, "Some Hellenistic Carved Gems," *JWalt* 6 (1943) 62, figs. 2 and 3; D. K. Hill, "About Faces," *BWalt* 4 (1952) no. 8; D. K. Hill, "Gem Engraving in Greece and Rome," *BWalt* 13 (1961) no. 4; D. K. Hill, "Gem Pictures," *Archaeology* 15 (1962) 124, fig. 6 and p. 125; G. M. A. Richter, *Engraved Gems of the Greeks and the Etruscans* (London, 1968), 168, no. 677, fig. 677; M. L. Vollenweider, "Deux portraits inconnus de la dynastie du Pont et les graveurs Nikias, Zoilos et Apollonios," *AntK* 23 (1980) 151–152, pl. 40.3; P. Zazoff, *Die antiken Gemmen,* Handbuch der Archäologie (Munich, 1983), 207, n. 85, pl. 54.1.

This garnet is signed by an artist whose name appears on only one other gem, a garnet in the Numismatic Museum in Athens which is inscribed "Apollonios." That gem bears a portrait of the Seleukid king Antiochos III, who is identified through comparison with that monarch's coins, particularly an example which was issued at the mint at Nisibis and signed "Apo," presumably the same Apollonios.[1] Both the coin and the garnet in Athens depict Antiochos III as a youth, probably soon after he came to the throne in 220 at the age of eighteen, following the murder of his predecessor, Seleukos III. Certainly also contemporary is the Walters garnet, which compares closely with the Athenian garnet in the treatment of the jaw, lips, nose contour, and the

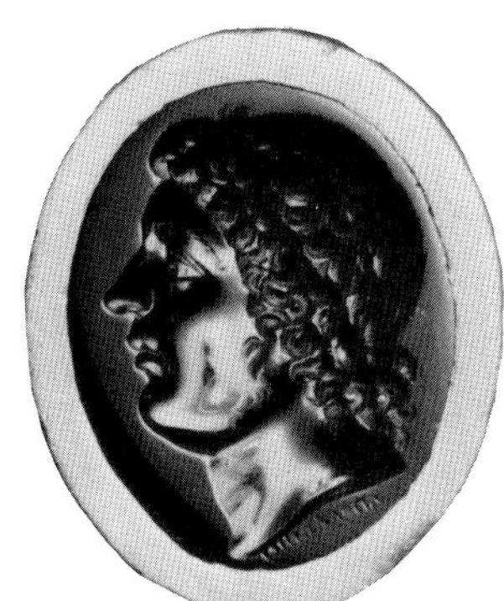

136.1

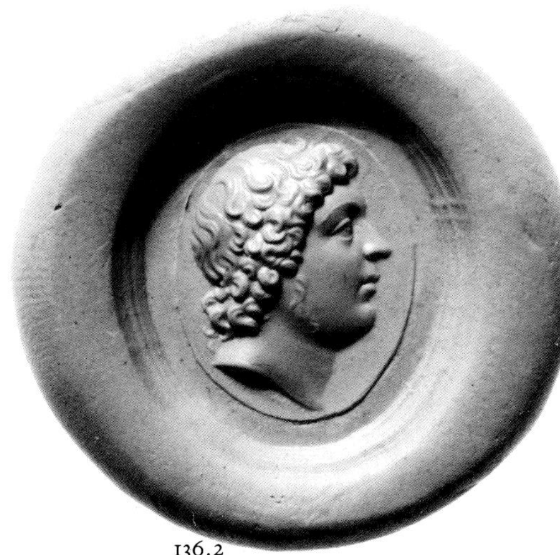

136.2

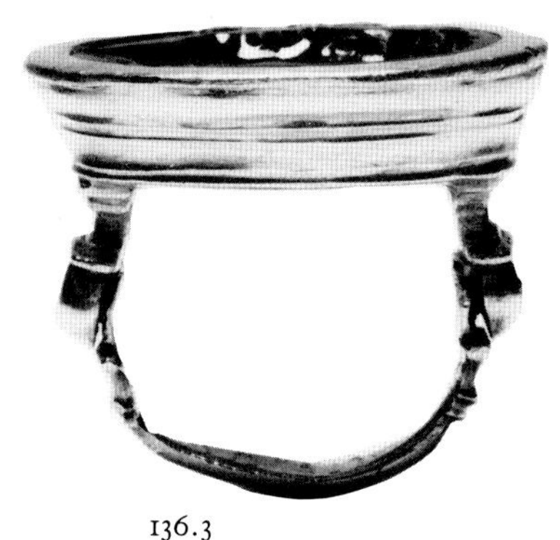

136.3

handling of the open eye with the lids at the edge of the iris. Vollenweider suggests that the subject of the Walters gem is a prominent individual in the Seleukid court, possibly Hermias, the trusted and powerful associate of Seleukos III.[2]

The handling of the alpha in the signature of Apollonios links him with several other gem engravers of the third and second centuries: Nikandros, Lykomedes, and finally Nikias, who signed a tetradrachm of Antiochos III issued at Tyre or Tarsos between ca. 197 and 187.[3] Nikias's career exemplifies the international circles in which Hellenistic gem engravers operated. Employed by Perseus of Macedon in about 170, Nikias also executed a gem which compares closely with coins of Mithridates IV of Pontos (169–50), whose brother Pharnakes I married the granddaughter of Antiochos III.[4] Such itinerancy certainly contributed to the uniformity of style and lettering among Hellenistic gem-carvers, a phenomenon that was influenced by other factors as well: dynastic marriages between royal courts, the versatility of artists who functioned as both gem- and die-engravers, the mobility of patrons, and the portability of the gems themselves, as attested by the reputed findspot of the Walters garnet in Kerch. The Walters gem also demonstrates the skill that was attained by the very finest Hellenistic gem-engravers, who became such masters of the drill that they were able to execute representations in deep intaglio with the most delicate modulation of planes. Several other hinged rings are known, most of them dated to the second century or later, and some of them with bezels of even more elaborate design.[5]

1. For the garnet in Athens, see G. M. A. Richter, *Engraved Gems,* 168, no. 678; Zazoff, pl. 54.2. For the coin, see M. L. Vollenweider, *AntK* 23 (1980) 151, pl. 39.3a.
2. Vollenweider (note 1) 152, n. 33.
3. Ibid., 151.
4. Ibid., 147–148, 152.
5. S. Miller, *Two Groups of Thessalian Gold,* University of California Publications in Classical Studies 18 (Berkeley, 1979) 40–41, pl. 26.

GARNET RING WITH EROS
Fourth to third century

57.1021. Gold and garnet. Purchased in 1911. L,
bezel 1.9 cm; W, bezel 1.6 cm; L, garnet 1.1 cm;
W, garnet 0.9 cm; Inner D, 1.9 cm. Convex oval
garnet set in a gold ring which has a square shoulder
and oval bezel with scroll pattern between the
ridges. Hoop is flat inside, rounded outside.

Seen in the cast is a nude Eros moving to his right on
a narrow groundline, his left leg advanced and
upraised. His right hand at his side holds a torch. His
left arm is upraised and outstretched; fabric, draped
over both upper arms, flares out on each side.

Exhibitions and Catalogues: *Jewelry,* 92, no. 275.

The oval shape, with vertical shoulder and
ornamental bezel, compares favorably
with similar examples found in burials at
Kerch and dated to the fourth and third
centuries.[1] In the following century rings
were distinguished by a more accentuated
stepped setting.[2] The rinceau pattern of
this example compares with an example in
Taranto of the late fourth century; the
still-Classical handling of the Eros looks
forward to a more animated version of
this figure on a sardonyx ring of the late
first century.[3]

1. R. Higgins, *Greek and Roman Jewellery,* 2nd ed. (London,
   1980), 169, pl. 53a. Deppert-Lippitz 238, fig. 174a.
2. Ibid., 238, fig. 176 and 273, fig. 203. M. L. Vollenweider, *Deliciae Leonis* (Mainz, 1984), 42, no. 57.
3. *Ori di Taranto,* 294–295, no. 223. Vollenweider (note 2)
   68–69, no. 100.

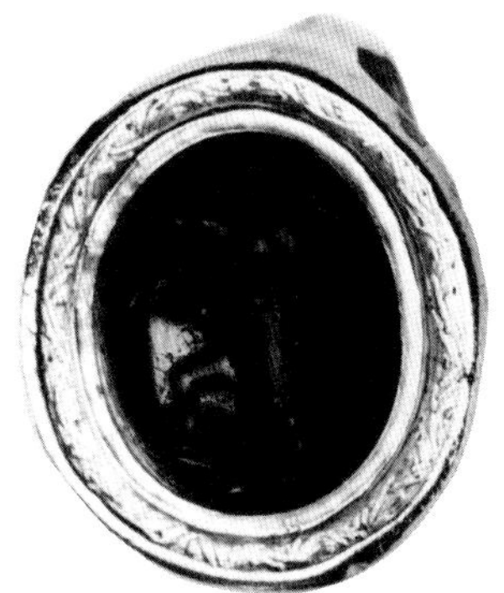

137.1

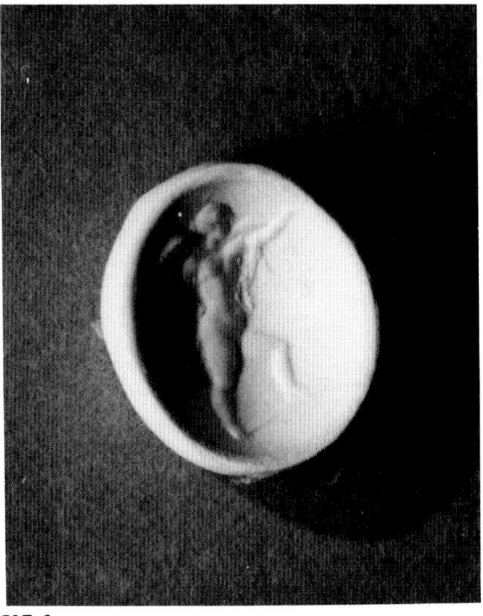

137.2

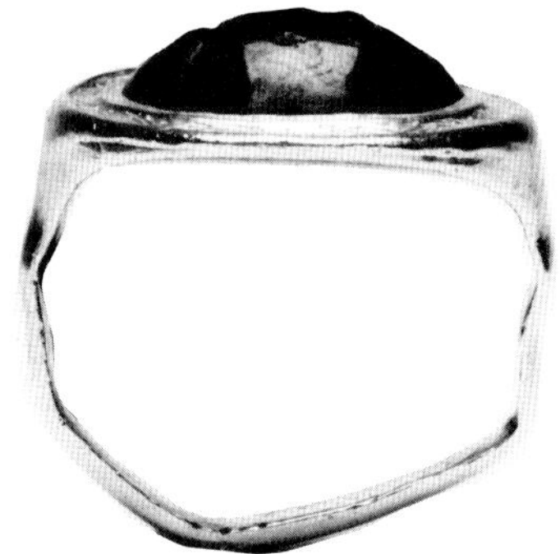

137.3

Carnelian Ring with Eros on a Swan

Fourth to third century

42.856. Gold and carnelian. Collection of Henry Walters. Collection of Mrs. Henry Walters. Purchased in 1942. L, bezel 1.9 cm; Inner D, hoop 1.8 cm. Oval, convex carnelian set in a gold ring which has a square shoulder and a stepped bezel in two stages, with a flat outer border beneath an inner convex band engraved with heart-and-dart.

Seen in the cast is a nude Eros in right profile, seated astride a swan, holding a rein in the hand of his extended right arm.

Exhibitions and Catalogues: *Jewelry,* 92, no. 276.

The elaborate bezel with engraved decoration dates the ring to the fourth or third centuries and finds parallels among gold and garnet rings in the British Museum.[1]

1. Compare F. H. Marshall, *Catalogue of the Finger Rings, Greek, Etruscan, and Roman in the Department of Antiquities, British Museum* (London, 1907), 18, no. 19, pl. 4; 66, no. 362, pl. 11; 118, no. 707, pl. 18; Greifenhagen, *Schmuckarbeiten I,* pl. 13.3–5; J. Ogden, *Jewellery of the Ancient World* (New York, 1982), pl. 20.

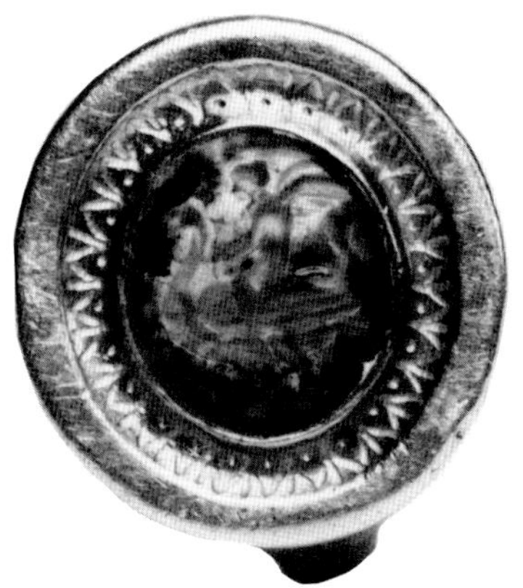

138.1

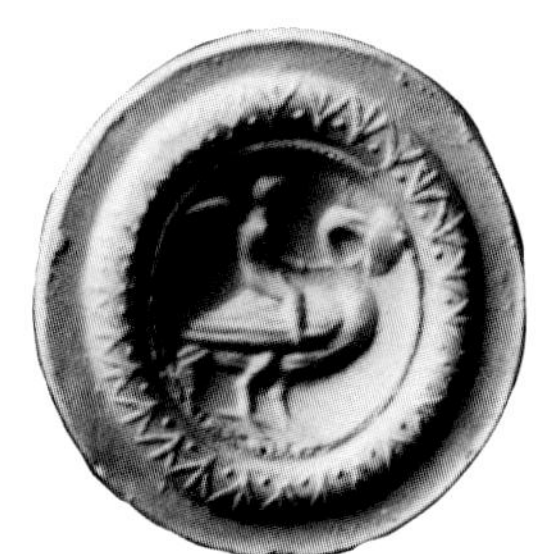

138.2

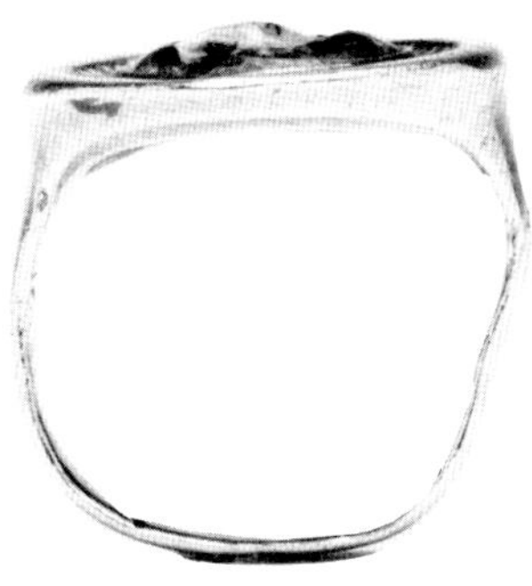

138.3

Amethyst Head of Arsinoe II
Ca. 270

42.190. Amethyst set in modern gold mount. Carmichael Collection (sale catalogue, London, Sotheby's, June 8, 1926, 42, no. 375). Purchased from Brummer in 1927. Ht, 2.2 cm; W, 1.4 cm; Depth, 1.3 cm.

Front half of a female head has center-parted hair pulled back from her face beneath a diadem. She has incised irises and indented pupils.

Exhibitions and Catalogues: *Pompeiana,* Smith College Museum of Art (Northampton, November 18–December 15, 1948), catalogue E. Schenck, ed., no. 33.

Publications: M. L. Vollenweider, *Die Steinschneidekunst und ihre Künstler in spätrepublikanischer und augusteischer Zeit* (Baden-Baden, 1966), 13–16, nos. 6–8, pl. 4; Vollenweider, *Geneva,* 65–66, no. 61, pl. 26.

Three other amethyst busts of similar size and equally high relief exist in Cleveland, the Cabinet des Médailles, and Florence, and agate versions are also known.[1] Common to all these busts are the broad cheek, continuous line from forehead to nose, and receding chin recognized in portraits of Arsinoe II on coins struck at Ephesos between about 288 and 280.[2] Vollenweider argues that the mantles seen on the amethyst busts identify Arsinoe as Hera, the divinity with whom the Ptolemaic queen was linked in her lifetime, and an affiliation lauded by Theokritos in an ode comparing Ptolemy II and Arsinoe II with Zeus and Hera.[3] The identification of Arsinoe as Hera would date the busts between the time of her marriage (276–275) and her death in 270, after which she was more closely linked with Isis. Vollenweider believes that the gems were forehead jewels worn by priests and priestesses in the goddess's cult and hypothesizes that the agate examples were sold in her sanctuaries together with inexpensive statuettes.[4]

Pliny tells us that amethysts were imported from Arabia, Egypt, and especially India, and that the purple color of the Indian amethyst was emulated by Tyrian factories producing the famous purple dye from the murex snail.[5] A facile and incorrect reading of the word amethyst to mean ''not drunk'' probably gave rise to the ancient tradition that the gem could ensure the sobriety of the wearer. The stone's connotations of succour were also familiar to the Zoroastrian priests of Persia known as the magi, who believed that an amethyst could assist an individual who approached a monarch as suppliant.[6]

1. M. L. Vollenweider, *Steinschneidekunst,* 12–13; Vollenweider, *Geneva,* 44–45, no. 41, pl. 19. For a garnet profile bust identified as Berenike II and now in the Getty Museum, see J. Boardman, *Intaglios and Rings* (London, 1975), 92, no. 59.
2. Vollenweider, *Steinschneidekunst,* 15.
3. Ibid., 14, 16; Theokritos, *Idyll,* 17.132.
4. Vollenweider, *Steinschneidekunst,* 14. Priestesses in the cult of Laodike, wife of Antiochos III, wore crowns with Laodike's portrait. See Austin, *Hellenistic World,* 262, no. 158. See also Vollenweider, *Geneva,* 65–66, no. 61, pl. 26 for a glass cameo of Arsinoe II.
5. Pliny, *NH* 37.40.121–22.
6. Ibid., 37.40.124.

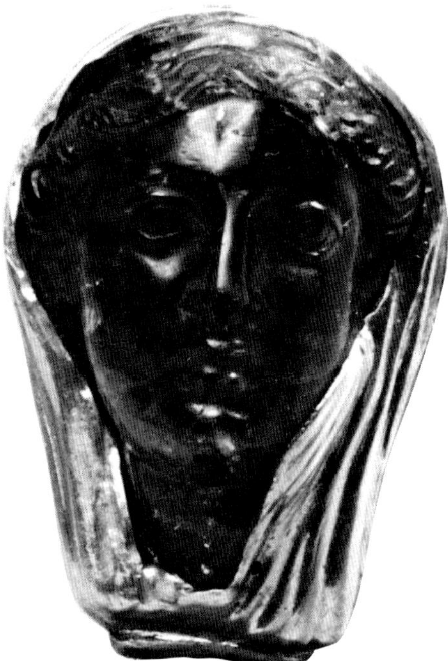

139.1

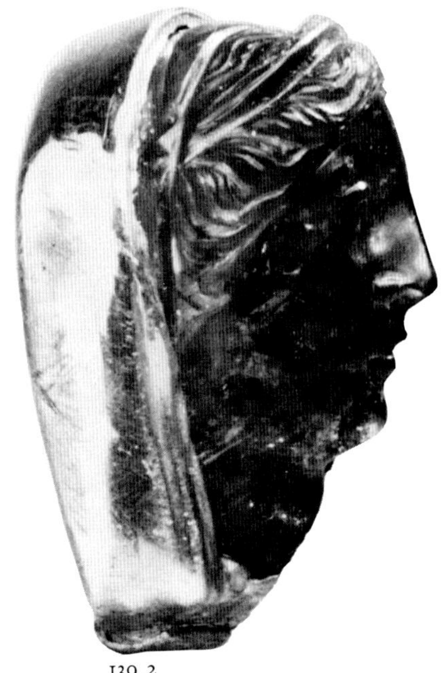

139.2

GARNET WITH PORTRAIT OF BERENIKE II
Ca. 246–22

42.1339. Garnet in modern gold mount. Collections of Deringh, Horcasita, Marlborough (sale catalogue, *The Marlborough Gems,* London, Christie, Manson and Woods, June 28, 1875, 70, no. 447). Collection of David Bromilow (sale catalogue, *The Marlborough Gems,* London, Christie, Manson and Woods, June 26, 1899, 79, no. 447). Collection of Sir Arthur Evans. Purchased from Hirsch in 1942. L, 2.4 cm; W, 2.5 cm; Th, 1 cm. Oval convex bezel carved in intaglio. Upper part missing. Signed behind nape (reading from cast): ΝΙΚΑΝΔΡΟ·C ϹΠ·ϹΙ

Seen in the cast is a female head in right profile, her bust turned almost three quarters to the right. She wears a sleeved garment which has a clasp at her shoulder and a U-neckline; mantle folds frame her shoulders. She has a beaded necklace and Venus ring. Her hair is arranged in a melon hairstyle; there is a braided coil at the back of the head and tendrils around the nape and in front of the ear. A bifurcated headband passes around her head behind the ear.

Publications: M. H. N. Story-Maskelyne, *The Marlborough Gems* (London, 1870), xv, 75, no. 447; C. W. King, *Handbook of Engraved Gems* (London, 1885), 254; A. Furtwängler, "Gemmen mit Künstlerinschriften," *JdI* 3 (1888) 210–211, no. 14, pl. 8; H. Brunn, *Geschichte der griechischen Künstler,* 2nd ed. (Stuttgart, 1889), I, 353–354; J. H. Middleton, *The Engraved Gems of Classical Times* (Cambridge, 1891), 74; E. Babelon, *La gravure en pierres fines* (Paris, 1894), 132–133; Furtwängler, *AG* I, pl. 32.30; II, 159; A. Evans, *An Illustrative Selection of Greek and Greco-Roman Gems* (Oxford, 1938), 15, no. 64, pl. 4; D. K. Hill, "Some Hellenistic Carved Gems," *JWalt* 6 (1943) 60 and 64, fig. 1; M. L. Vollenweider, "Das Bildnis des Scipio Africanus," *MusHelv* 15 (1958) 28, no. 17; A. Stazio, "Nikandros," *Enciclopedia dell'arte antica* 5 (1963) 460; G. M. A. Richter, *Engraved Gems of the Greeks and the Etruscans* (London, 1968), 160, no. 636, fig. 636; P. Zazoff, *Die antike Gemmen.* Handbuch der Archäologie (Munich, 1983), 195, n. 10; 206, pl. 53.2.

This gem has had a long and distinguished history of ownership, forming part of a number of major private collections, including that of the Dukes of Marlborough and, finally, Sir Arthur Evans. By the early twentieth century the gem was restored with the head and hair of Julia Titus, but Evans identified the portrait as Berenike II, and certainly the treatment of the neck, neckline, and necklace accords well with coins bearing images of that Ptolemaic queen.[1] Also suggesting a third-century date is the lettering of the inscription. The rendering of the omicron as a point and the form of the alpha com-

pare favorably with signatures of several other gem carvers believed to be active in the second half of the third and early second century: Lykomedes, Nikias, and Apollonios (see No. 136).[2] Typical of Hellenistic court jewelry are the large size of the stone and the strongly convex shape.

Berenike II (ca. 273–221) was the granddaughter of Berenike I, wife of Ptolemy I of Egypt, and the daughter of Magas, King of Cyrene, which she inherited. She was married to Ptolemy III Euergetes in 247 just before his ascension to the throne and is best remembered for the lock of hair that she dedicated at her husband's departure for the Third Syrian War (246–241). The astronomer Konon declared that the lock had been transformed into a constellation, a pronouncement which became the subject of a bantering poem by Kallimachos. A much later parody of this work is the famous *Rape of the Lock* by Sir Alexander Pope.

Berenike II was the mother of both Arsinoe III and Ptolemy IV Philopator, who became husband and wife. In 221 she conspired with him to assassinate her husband Ptolemy III, after which she ruled for a few months as regent of Egypt until her son engineered her assassination.

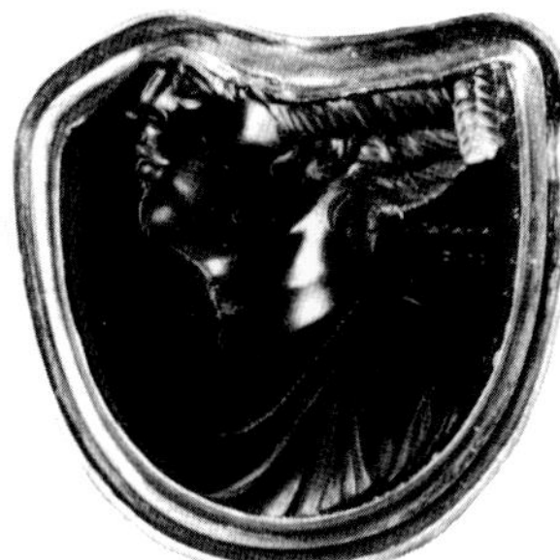

140.1

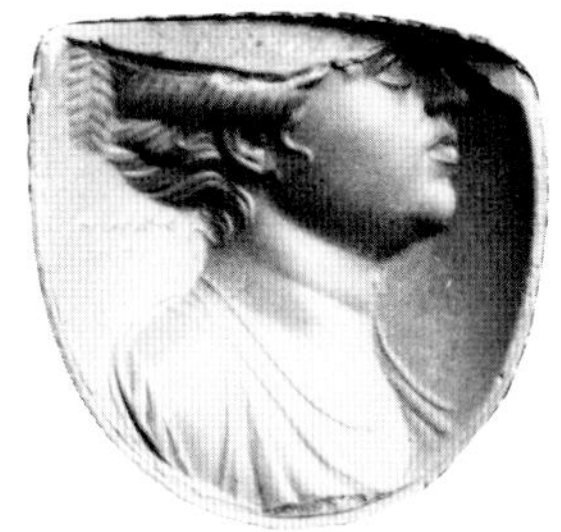

140.2

1. Bieber, *Sculpture,* 91, fig. 344. See especially E. T. Newell, *Royal Greek Portrait Coins* (New York, 1937), 86–87, pl. 15, fig. 5 and R. S. Poole, *A Catalogue of the Greek Coins in the British Museum. The Ptolemies, Kings of Egypt* (London, 1882), VI, 61, pl. 13.9. Compare a sard, identified as Berenike II, in the Ashmolean Museum (Zazoff, 195, pl. 46.2). Compare also the handling of necklace and garment on coins of Arsinoe III; H. Kyrieleis, *Bildnisse der Ptolemäer* (Berlin, 1975), pl. 88.
2. Vollenweider, *MusHelv* 15 (1958) 28, n. 17.

Peridot with Portrait of Kleopatra II
Ca. 175/4–116/5

42.1319. Olivine (peridot). Collection of Henry Walters. Purchased from Brummer in 1942. L, 2.8 cm; W, 2.2 cm; Th, 1.3 cm. Oval peridot is convex on both sides. Face worn.

Seen in the cast is the right profile of a female head, neck, and part of a shoulder on which a sleeveless garment is fastened with a clasp. A fringe edges her forehead; the rest of her hair is brought down from the crown in six coiled ringlets, the longest of which fall to her shoulders. Over her hair she wears a diadem surmounted by the solar disc and horns; the ends of the diadem blow out behind her.

Publications: Vollenweider-Boardman, *Oxford,* 82.

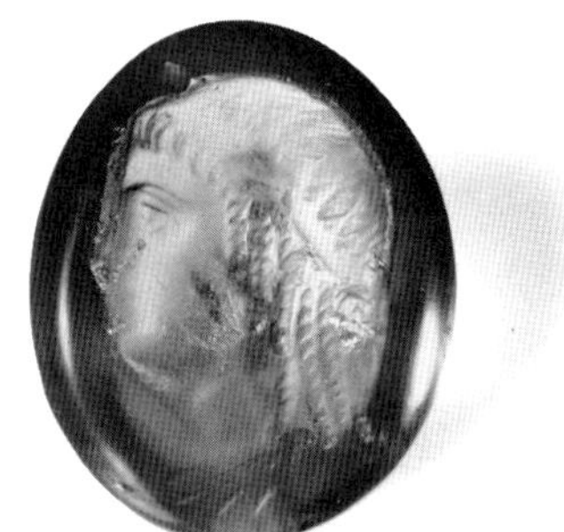

141.1

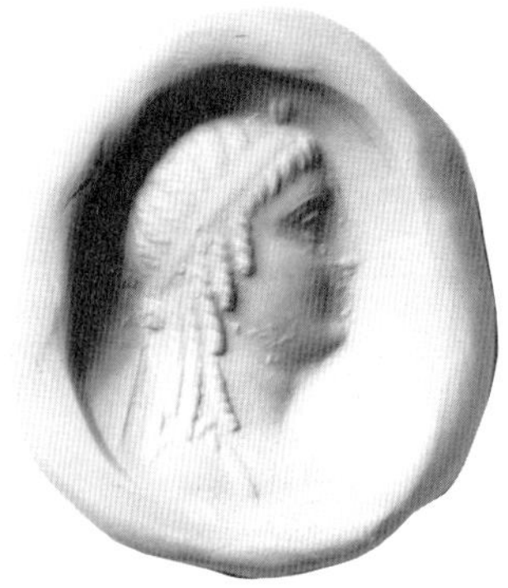

141.2

The tight ringlets, first worn by Libya on late fourth-century coins from Cyrene, rapidly became identified with the Hellenized Isis.[1] On a number of Hellenistic gems and glass intaglios, this goddess can be recognized both from the hairstyle and the lotus flower which often adorns her diadem; in many cases the individualized features suggest that the representations are portraits of Ptolemaic queens, who had identified themselves with Isis at least since the time of Arsinoe II.[2] The Walters gem is probably a portrait of Kleopatra II, because the fleshy cheeks and neck compare well with a chalcedony in Boston signed by Lykomedes and identified by Kyrieleis as Kleopatra II.[3] Both gems are quite large, and the engraved side is strongly convex. A later example of the type is the following entry (No. 142), and another portrait of Kleopatra II is possibly seen in No. 29.

In ancient times peridot was called *topazion,* after its source, an island in the Red Sea named Topazios (modern Zebirget). In the eighteenth century, for unknown reasons, the name topaz was given to another stone and the gem variety of olivine was henceforth known as peridot.[4]

1. For Libyan coins, see E. S. G. Robinson, *A Catalogue of the Greek Coins in the British Museum. Vol. 29. Catalogue of the Greek Coins of Cyrenaica* (repr. Bologna, 1965), 249.
2. See Thompson, *Oinochoai,* 58–59. Thompson points out that not until the Pithom stele of 264/263 is Arsinoe II depicted in full Egyptian dress, completely assimilated to Isis.
3. H. Kyrieleis, *Bildnisse der Ptolemäer* (Berlin, 1975), 117, no. 460, pl. 100.2; P. Zazoff, *Die antike Gemmen.* Handbuch der Archäologie (Munich, 1983), 206, no. 77, pl. 53.4.
4. C. Hurlbut, Jr., and G. Switzer, *Gemology* (New York, 1979), 161–162.

Garnet Ring with Portrait of a Ptolemaic Queen as Isis
Second century

57.1022. Garnet set in gold ring. Purchased from Kelekian in 1911. L, bezel 1.7 cm; W, bezel 1.2 cm; Inner D, hoop 1.1 cm. Hoop has square shoulders. Oval flat bezel carved in intaglio.

Seen in the cast is a female head and neck, broadening at the base, in right profile. Her hair is brushed down from the crown and rolled back from the brow. A ringlet extending to the jaw frames her face; behind are three ringlets which fall to the shoulder. She wears a bifurcated diadem surmounted by a lotus flower or leaves above the brow. The ends hang down from the nape. The beginning of drapery appears below.

Exhibitions and Catalogues: *Jewelry,* 92, no. 278.

This garnet represents a more summary handling of the type seen on the previous example, but is possibly contemporary with it. At the same time, the treatment of the eye, mouth, and chin compare well with a portrait on a gem in Oxford that has been identified as Kleopatra I (ca. 180).[1] This Ptolemaic queen was a Seleukid princess who married Ptolemy V Epiphanes in 193 and was widowed in 180 when her son Ptolemy VI Philometor was only five years old. From that year until her death in 176, Kleopatra I ruled Egypt jointly with her son, enjoying a preeminence that was reflected in the large number of images created of her, many of which, not surprisingly, associate her with the mother deity Isis.

1. Vollenweider-Boardman, *Oxford,* 82, no. 290, pl. 18. See also a brown glass intaglio with the portrait of Kleopatra I in Vollenweider, *Geneva,* 67, no. 63, pl. 26.

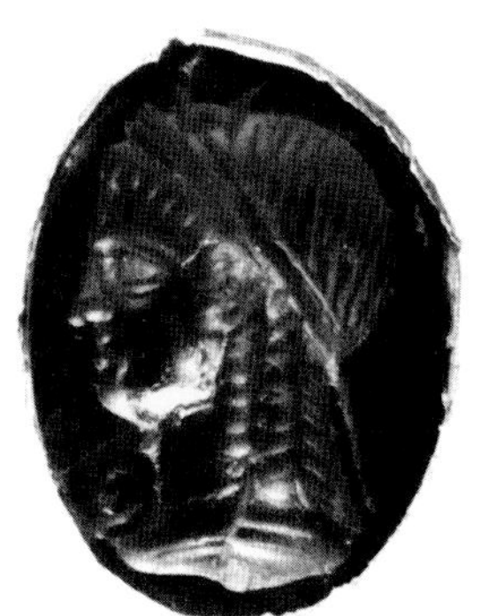

142.1

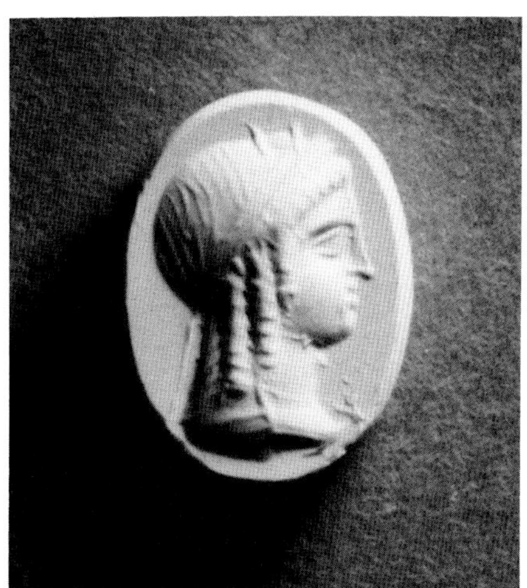

142.2

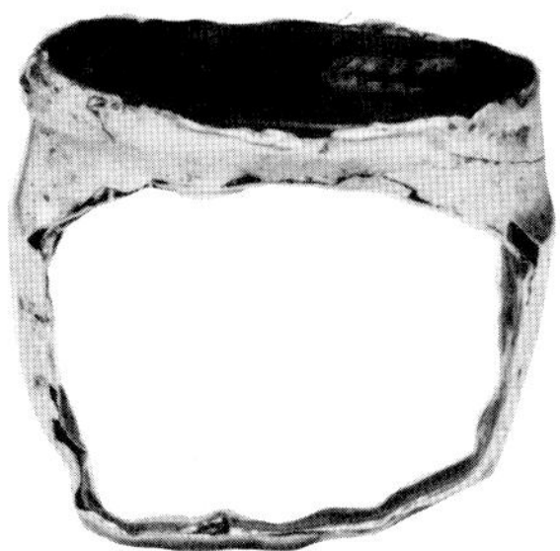

142.3

GARNET WITH HERMES
Second or first century

42.103. Garnet in modern gold ring. Newton-Robinson Collection (sale catalogue, London, Christie, Manson and Woods, June 22, 1909, 16, no. 56). Purchased in 1909. L, gem 2.5 cm; W, 1.6 cm; Th, 0.5 cm. Oval gem has a convex bezel and a flat back.

Seen in the cast is a nude Hermes wearing a petasos and sandals and standing on a short groundline with his weight on his right leg, his left leg relaxed. A chlamys is draped over his left shoulder and arm. His left hand holds a kerykeion at his side; in his extended right hand he holds a cornucopia.

Exhibitions and Catalogues: *Burlington Fine Arts Club Illustrated Catalogue of Ancient Greek Art* (London, 1904), pt. V, 217, no. 160, pl. 110.

Publications: A Furtwängler, *AG* I, no. 8, pl. 65; II, 298.

Assigning this gem to the Hellenistic period and possibly to an Alexandrian workshop are the oval shape with convex engraved surface and flat back. Also distinctive are the slightly three-quarters pose, the elongation of the body, the delicate modulation of planes, and the cursory treatment of the attributes.[1] Vollenweider compares the Walters ring to a garnet representing Hermes in chlamys and petasos, and suggests that both gems belonged to a Hellenistic prince or king who claimed a close association with that god.[2]

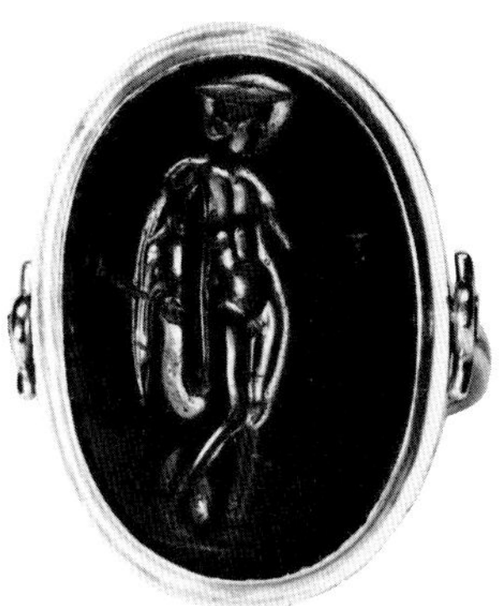

143.1

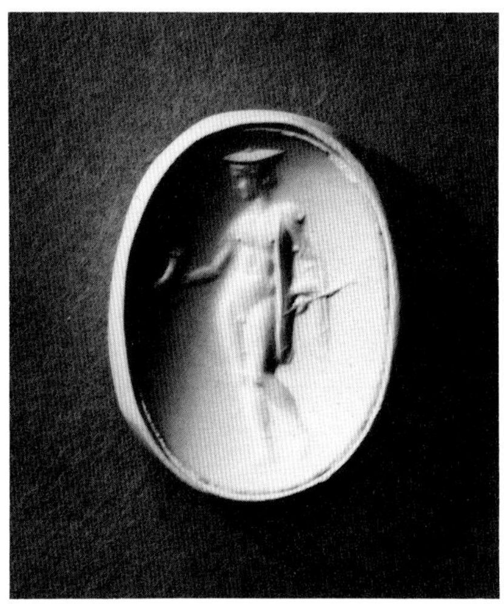

143.2

1. J. Boardman, *Engraved Gems. The Ionides Collection* (London, 1968), 21, 93, no. 14.
2. M. L. Vollenweider, *Deliciae Leonis* (Mainz, 1984), 42–43, no. 57, dated third to second century and attributed to Alexandria.

Carnelian with
Priestess
Second to first century

42.110. Carnelian set in modern? gold ring. "From Rhodes." Newton-Robinson Collection (sale catalogue, London, Christie, Manson and Woods, June 22, 1909, 10, no. 9). Purchased in 1909. L, 2.2 cm; W, 1.6 cm; Th, 2.3 cm; Inner D, hoop 1.7 cm. An oval carnelian has a convex bezel which is pierced through the upper part of the underside.

Seen in the cast is a female striding forward in right profile with right foot advanced and holding a torch in her extended right hand. She wears a belted garment which has vertical folds over the hip. Between and behind her legs a bunch of stacked folds falls vertically. Her hair is drawn back beneath a headband to the nape, with long coiled locks falling in front and back of her shoulder.

Suggesting a Hellenistic date are the convexity of the engraved surface, the elongation of the figure, and the archaizing style, which is recognized by the long coiled locks of hair and the stacked pleats which fall between and behind the legs. A close parallel is a carnelian in Berlin which also represents a maiden in archaizing dress holding a torch, but with a cornucopia in the other hand which suggests she is a goddess; the Walters figure could equally well be a priestess.[1]

1. For the Berlin carnelian, see Furtwängler, *AG* I, no. 10, pl. 39; II, 187.

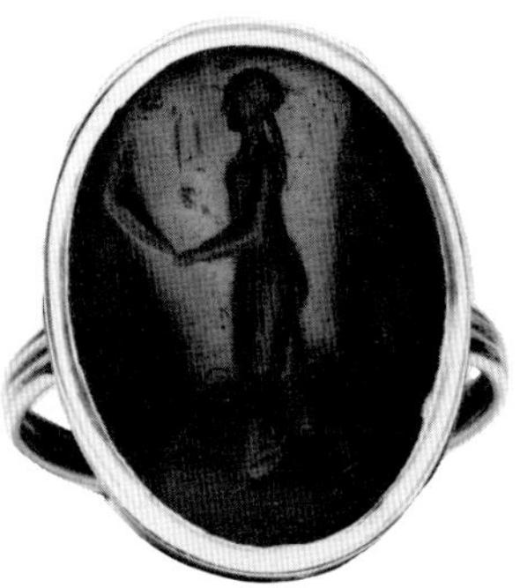

144.1

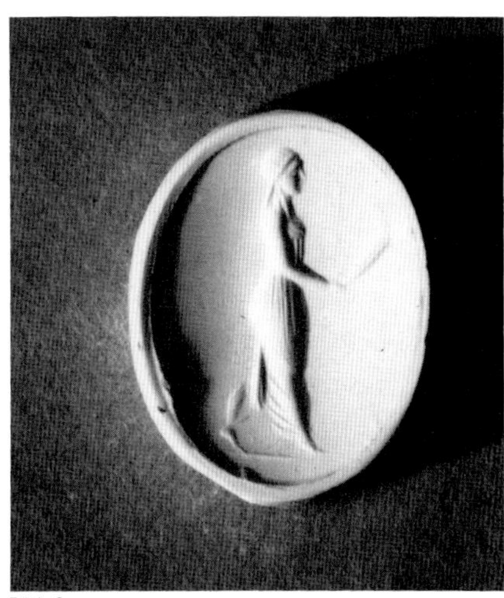

144.2

GARNET WITH HEAD OF DIONYSOS
Second to first century

42.934. Garnet. Purchased from Brummer in 1942. L, 1.7 cm; W, 0.7 cm; Th, 0.4 cm. Flat bezel carved in intaglio; convex back.

Seen in the cast is a bearded head in right profile with folds of drapery at the neck. His beard is formed of six vertical corkscrew locks with wisps in front of his ear; the tip of his long mustache curves upward. A wavy roll of hair is brought across the forehead and passes over his ears to the nape. Beneath a bifurcated fillet the rest of his hair falls straight down at the sides. Two corkscrew locks fall behind his nape.

Publications: D. K. Hill, ''Some Hellenistic Carved Gems,'' *JWalt* 6 (1943) 68 and 69, fig. 8; D. K. Hill, ''Gem Engraving in Greece and Rome,'' *BWalt* 13 (1961) no. 4.

Despite its small size, this gem is one of the finest examples known of an archaizing head of Dionysos. It is carved in a combination of earlier styles: archaizing features include the rendering of the hair as individual metal-like strands brought down from the crown beneath a fillet, the wavy coils of hair framing the face, and the corkscew locks of beard and hair that alternate thick and narrow turnings. Classicizing features are the open mouth, the pronounced lower eyelid, and the rendering of the eyebrow as a sharp ridge which extends beyond the eye's outer corner. Close parallels for the rendering of the beard can be found on a garnet from Cairo in the Ashmolean Museum, dated to the first half of the first century, which depicts a theatrical mask of a Silen.[1] Another archaizing head of Dionysos is seen on a carnelian in the Thorvaldsen Museum in Copenhagen.[2]

1. Vollenweider-Boardman, *Oxford,* 105, no. 360, pl. 60.
2. P. Fossing, *The Thorvaldsen Museum. Catalogue of the Antique Engraved Gems and Cameos* (Copenhagen, 1929), 167, no. 1090, pl. 13. Compare a similar treatment on an agate, dated Roman Imperial, in the Cabinet des Médailles, Paris: G. M. A. Richter, *Engraved Gems of the Romans* (London, 1971), 44, no. 173.

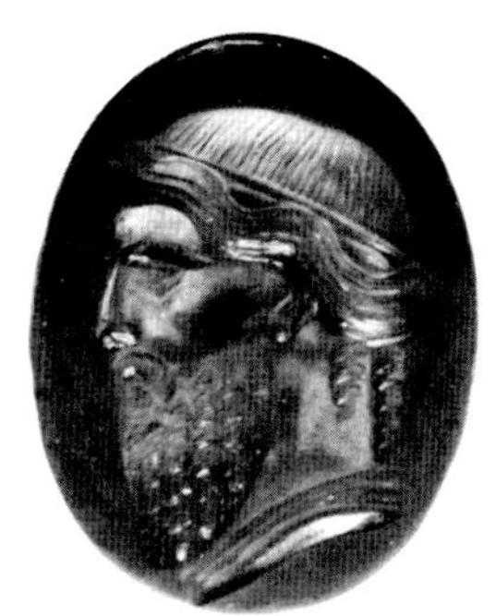

145.1

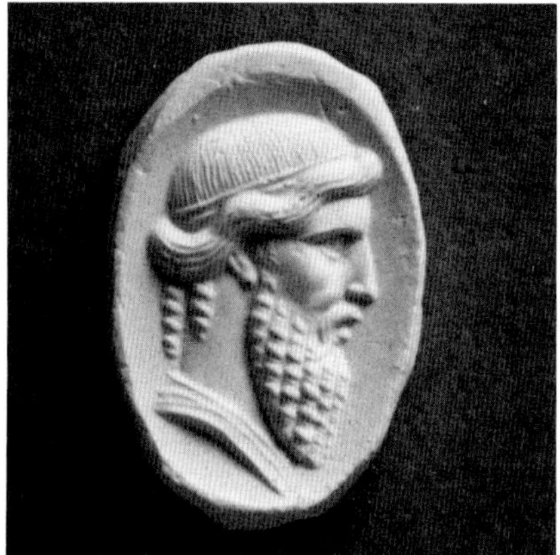

145.2

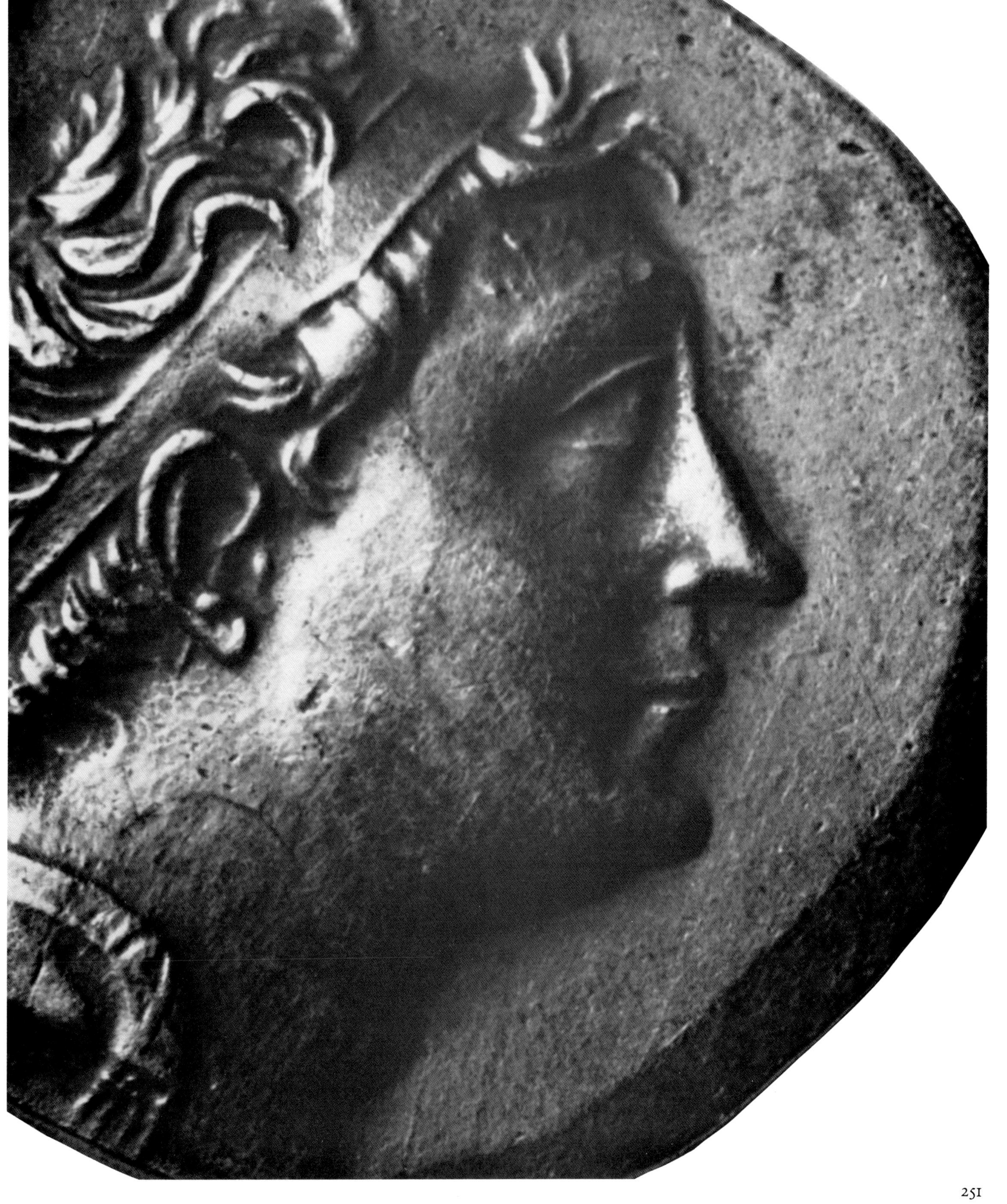

SILVER TETRADRACHM OF
DEMETRIOS POLIORKETES
291–288

59.526. Silver. Purchased before 1931. D, 2.7 cm.

On the obverse within a circular dotted frame, a male head appears in right profile with short curly hair, a fleshy neck, and prominent Adam's apple. Behind his temples are bull horns with curving tips. He wears a tainia whose ends flutter at the nape. On the reverse, a nude male leans forward onto his right leg with his foot on a rock. His legs are in left profile; his torso is almost frontal with the right elbow resting on the right thigh, and the left forearm lifted with the fingers clasping a trident. His head is in left profile and gazes forward. The lettering in vertical columns in front and behind him reads ΒΑΣΙΛΕΩΣ ΔΗΜΗΤΡΙΟΥ and the mintmarks:

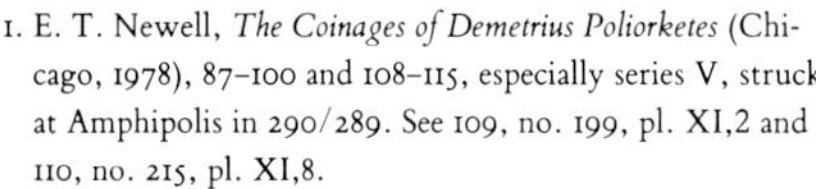

One of the most colorful and bellicose leaders of the early Hellenistic age was Demetrios Poliorketes, under whose tenure as king of Macedon coins of this type were struck at Pella and Amphipolis between 291 and 288.[1] In these years Demetrios was still at the height of his power, although his major naval victory over Ptolemy I off Cyprus in 306 had been followed by an unsuccessful siege of Rhodes in 305/304, where he received the epithet Poliorketes in reference to his extensive use of siege machinery. A major defeat followed at Ipsos in 301 at the hands of Seleukos I and Lysimachos, but by 294/293, Demetrios had assumed the throne of Macedon where he remained in power until 288. Captured by Seleukos in about 285, he died two years later in captivity at Apamea.

Demetrios's powers of endurance owed no small debt to a charisma that is communicated by the coin's obverse, although this idealizing type surely cannot be a very accurate rendering of the monarch's appearance at the age of about forty-six when the coin was struck. Ancient writers tell us that Demetrios was outstandingly handsome and that he was admired both for his stature and his gentle temperament, which were combined with a recklessness and daring that accounted for both his vacillating fortunes and his amazing resiliency.[2] Described by Plutarch as a king suited to a tragic stage, Demetrios eagerly embraced Persian dress and

bedecked himself with necklaces and bracelets for arms and legs, and also commissioned a gold and purple mantle so lavish that none of his successors dared to wear it.[3] The coins of Demetrios mark the first time that the portrait of a living man had been seen on a European coin and find precedent only in those he issued at Ephesos between 301–295, and in the coins struck by Ptolemy I at Alexandria in 306.[4]

The diadem which Demetrios wears on the obverse was taken over from the Persian kings by Alexander. The bull horns are probably a reference to Poseidon and were inspired by the naval victory over Ptolemy I in 306, which Demetrios commemorated with a coin featuring a standing Poseidon holding a trident.[5] The horns are also intended to recall the ram horns which identified Alexander as the son of Ammon and which appeared on coins issued after Alexander's death. Because Demetrios was still living when coins of the Walters type were issued, the obverse constitutes the first time the portrait of a living man on a coin was seen with the attributes of a god.

The figure of Poseidon on the reverse is based upon a type known as the Lateran Poseidon, the original of which was surely made by Lysippos for Corinth.[6] It has been suggested that an adaptation of that statue portraying Demetrios may have been executed in Pella by Teisikrates of Sikyon in allusion to the naval victory of 306, and that this adaptation is reproduced in a bronze statuette from Herculaneum.[7] It has also been argued that the bull horns on the Herculaneum portrait, as well as the horns on the coin's obverse, are an allusion to Dionysos and to Demetrios's attested affiliation with that god.[8]

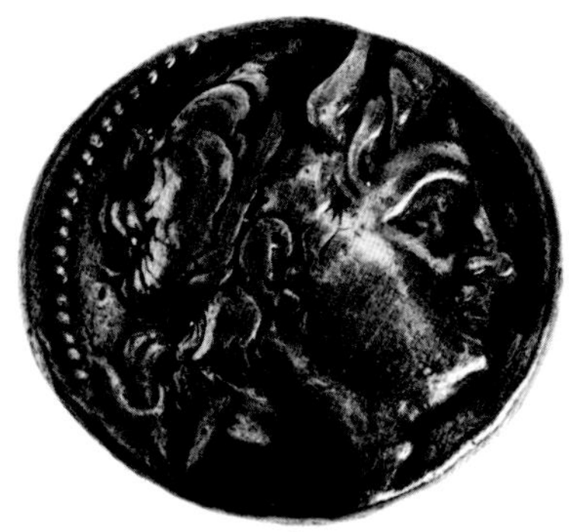

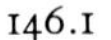

146.1

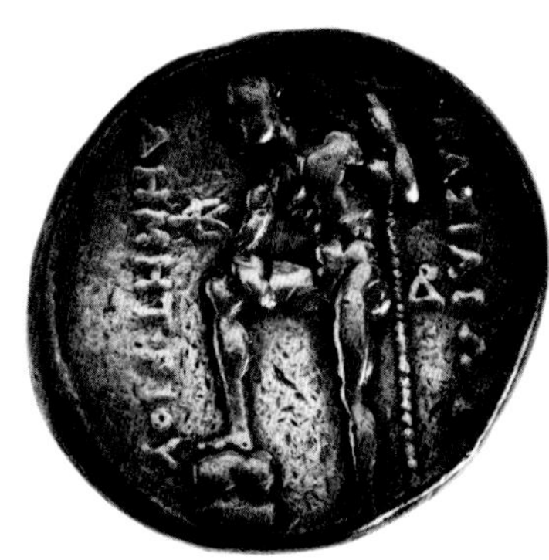

146.2

1. E. T. Newell, *The Coinages of Demetrius Poliorketes* (Chicago, 1978), 87–100 and 108–115, especially series V, struck at Amphipolis in 290/289. See 109, no. 199, pl. XI,2 and 110, no. 215, pl. XI,8.
2. Plutarch, *Demetrius* 11.2; Diodoros 19.81.1–5; 20.92.2–3.
3. G. Macurdy, ''A Note on The Jewellery of Demetrius the Besieger,'' *AJA* 36 (1932) 27–28; Plutarch, *Demetrius* 41.
4. Newell (note 1) 65–73; C. Seltman, *Greek Coins*, 2nd ed. (London, 1955), 222.
5. Pollitt 31–32, fig. 20.
6. Robertson 516.
7. See P. W. Lehmann, ''A New Portrait of Demetrios Poliorketes?'' *GettyMusJ* 8 (1980) 113. See also H. P. Laubscher, ''Hellenistische Herrscher und Pan,'' *AM* 100 (1985) 338, who identifies the horns as those of Pan.
8. Diodoros 20.92.4; Plutarch, *Demetrius*, 11.3; Lehmann (note 7) 110.

SILVER DRACHM OF
PHILIP V OF MACEDON
221–179

59.527. Silver. Purchased before 1931. D, 1.7 cm.

On the obverse is a male head in right profile with a mustache, stubby beard, and short curly locks beneath a fillet whose ends hang from the nape. On the reverse is a club within an oak wreath. Flanking the club within the wreath is the inscription: ΒΑΣΙΛΕΩΣ ΦΙΛΙΓΓΟΥ and the mintmarks:

The rule of Philip V was characterized by almost endless warfare, commencing with the Social Wars against Aetolia in 220–217. Initial victories in the First Macedonian War resulted in a favorable Peace of Phoenice in 205, but Philip's ill-fated treaty with Hannibal against Rome resulted in a crushing defeat at Cynoscephalae in 197. It was in this battle that Roman troops led by T. Quinctius Flamininus proved decisively the superiority of the Roman maniple and Roman battle tactics over the long-piked sarissa of the Macedonian army. Following this defeat, Philip was dispossessed of all lands beyond Macedonia, and spent his remaining years ineffectually plotting to avenge his loss. His son Perseus met with no greater success than his father, for his massive defeat at Pydna in 168 led to the annexation of Macedonia as a Roman province in 146.

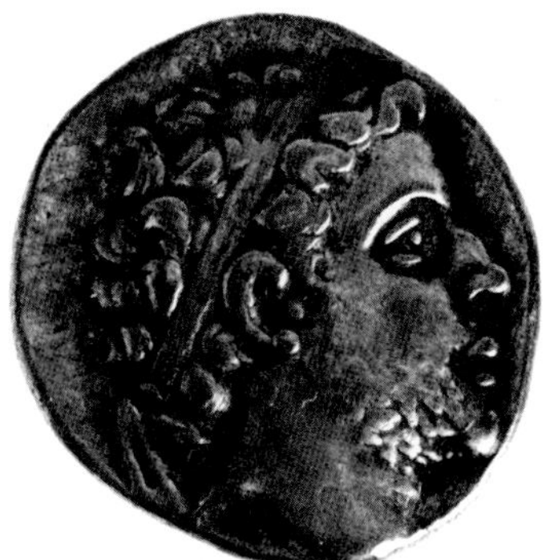

147.1

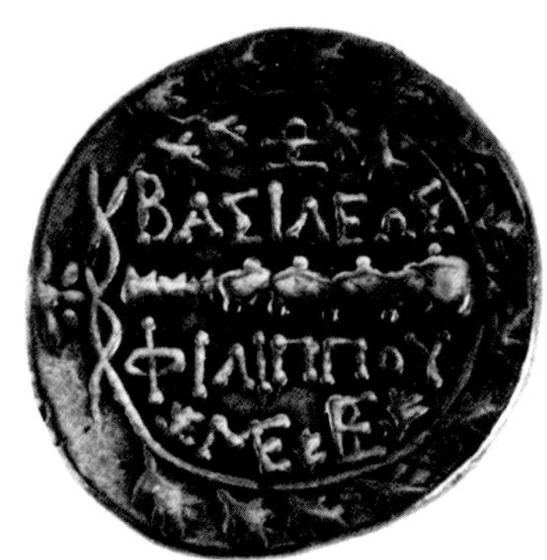

147.2

SILVER TETRADRACHM OF ANTIOCHOS IX OF SYRIA
113–95

59.530. Silver. Purchased before 1931. D, 2.7 cm.

The obverse shows within a circular frame formed of an elongated bead-and-reel pattern a male head in right profile with a short curly beard. His wavy locks are brushed forward onto his forehead and fall behind the nape in three twisted coils. He wears a broad diadem, the ends of which hang from the nape. On the reverse is shown a high base ornamented in relief with a garland between bukrania draped with fillets; there is a molding above and below. Above the base is a pediment supporting a basin and enclosing a representation of a figure standing on a lion. The lettering in vertical rows to the viewer's right reads: ΒΑΣΙΛΕΩΣ ΑΝΤΙΟΧΟΥ. On the other side the letters read ΦΙΛΟΠΑΤΟΡΟΣ. Beside them are the mintmarks:

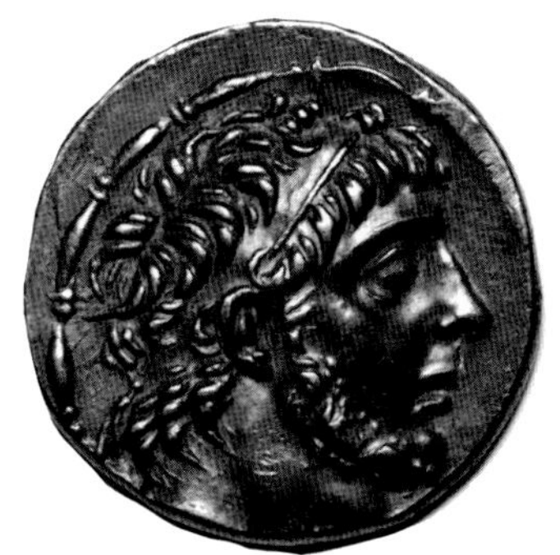

148.1

The fortunes of Antiochos IX dramatize the instability of the Seleukid dynasty in the late second century. Antiochos IX Kyzikenos came to the throne in 114/13 when he revolted against his half-brother Antiochos VIII Grypos, but by 108 his dominion had been reduced to the lands bordering the Mediterranean coast. After Grypos's murder in 96, Antiochos IX married his brother's widow, but was soon after assassinated by Grypos's son, who was named Seleukos VI.

The motif on the coin's reverse is a forceful reminder of the survival through the Hellenistic age of deeply rooted indigenous cults and artistic forms. Depicted is a monument dedicated to Sandon, a local deity of the Cilician pantheon whose roots can be traced back to the second millennium, and whom the Greeks later associated with Herakles. The motif appears on

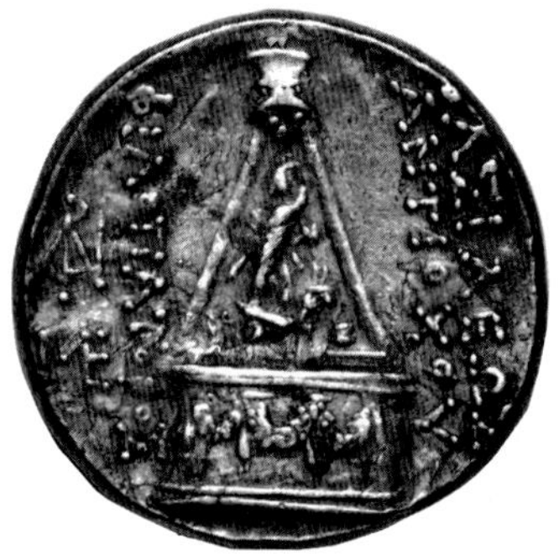

148.2

many terracotta reliefs found in second-century contexts in Tarsos, a phenomenon which suggests that the monument was also executed at about this date. Goldman believed that the pediment's steep sides and the absence of a doorway indicate a rockcut relief comprised of a wall beneath a pediment enclosing a figure of the god. With a quiver and bow, or sword, behind his back, he stood in right profile with right hand raised, and carried a double ax in his right hand, a stylized wreath in his left. Beneath his feet, following traditional representations of Anatolian deities, stood a horned lion with folded wings, the front legs rendered as paws, the hind legs with vulture talons.[1]

1. H. Goldman, "The Sandon Monument of Tarsus," *JAOS* 60 (1940) 544–553.

Silver Tetradrachm of Nikomedes II of Bithynia
Ca. 131

59.723. Silver. Purchased from Hesperia Art (*Bulletin* 37, no. 30) in 1966. D, 3.3 cm.

The obverse shows a male head in right profile with small bull horns above the forehead and short wavy hair brushed forward over the brow. He wears a broad diadem, the long ends of which fall below the nape. One end is brought forward over the right shoulder. On the reverse, a bearded standing male turns to his right, his left leg relaxed with the foot resting only on the toes. His right arm is extended and upraised, with a wreath in the hand. His left arm is bent at the elbow with the upraised hand clasping a staff. His mantle is draped around his hips and legs with the ends thrown back over his left shoulder. His hair is rolled across his brow and around the nape, and hangs behind his left shoulder. There is a short ridge for the groundline. Beside his right hip is an eagle in left profile. The lettering is arranged in vertical columns: to his left ΒΑΣΙΛΕΩΣ, to his right ΕΠΙΦΑΝΟΥΣ ΝΙΚΟΜΗΔΟΥ. Beneath the eagle are the mint marks:

✳ ϹΡ

Publications: D. K. Hill, ''Greek Heads,'' *BWalt* 19 (1967) no. 5.

Bithynia was a kingdom in northwestern Anatolia that successfully resisted first Persian, then Macedonian, rule, partly by assimilating many of the Gauls who in the third century threatened Greece and Thrace. A plot in collusion with the Pergamene king Attalos II resulted in the assassination of King Prusias in 149, and the ascent of his son Nikomedes to the throne. The latter's coinage retains the reverse image employed by his predecessors but introduces on the obverse a sensitive and convincingly individualized

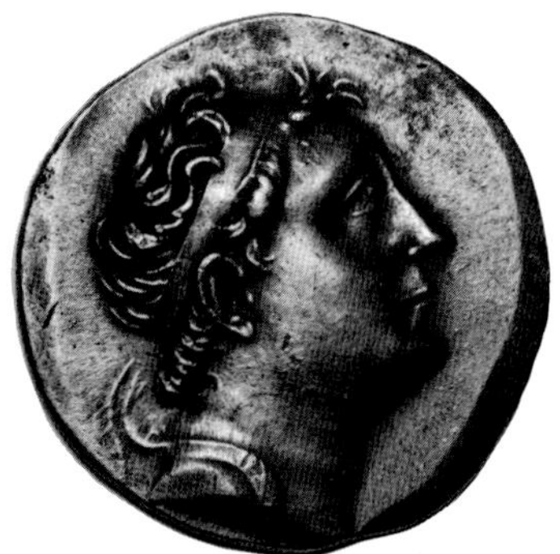

149.1

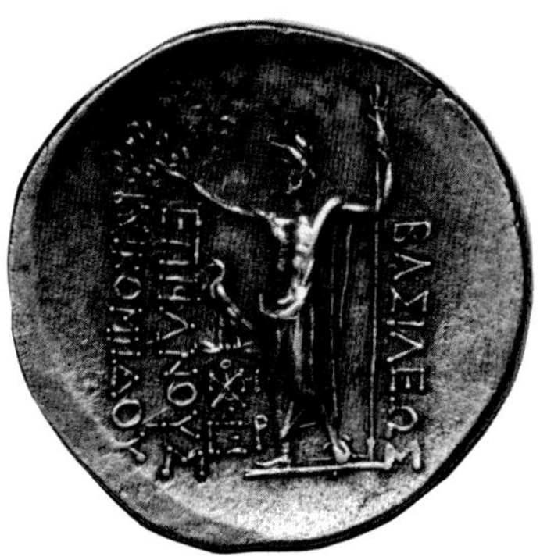

149.2

portrait, which was retained by his successors. The epithet Epiphanes was probably borrowed from the Seleukid monarchs, but in contrast to Seleukid usage, is here applied before the name as an attribute of the title itself.[1] With the issue of Nikomedes, the coins of Bithynia were henceforth dated from the foundation of the dynasty in 297; the mintmark on this coin, therefore, indicates the one hundred and sixty-sixth year, or 131.[2]

1. The translation of the epithet Epiphanes can range in meaning from ''god made manifest'' (when applied to deities and deified rulers) to ''distinguished'' (when used of men); this ambiguity was exploited by Hellenistic rulers. See A. Nock, ''Notes on Ruler-Cult, I–IV,'' *JHS* 48 (1928) 38–41.
2. W. Wroth, *British Museum Department of Coins and Medals. A Catalogue of the Greek Coins in the British Museum Vol. 12: Pontus, Paphlagonia, Bithynia* (London, 1889), 213–214 and pl. 38.

SILVER TETRADRACHM
TIGRANES I OF ARMENIA
83–69

59.531. Silver. Purchased before 1931. Max D, 2.7 cm.

The obverse shows within an elongated bead-and-reel frame a male head in right profile. He wears a headdress consisting of a high polos with a lappet falling to the shoulders. The polos is decorated by an eight-ray star flanked by two birds. The ends of a tainia? blow out behind the nape. On the reverse is a representation of the Tyche of Antioch in right profile. The vertical lettering in front of her reads ΒΑΣΙΛΕΩΣ; adjacent are the mintmarks: ⳨ Ρ The lettering behind her reads ΤΙΓΡΑΝΟΥ. Part of an encircling wreath is above her.

Tigranes I of Armenia was a Parthian vassal who in 83 was offered the Seleukid throne by inhabitants of Antioch seeking respite from the tumultuous upheavals of the Seleukid fraternal wars. Syria prospered under Tigranes's leadership, but his reign extended only until 69 when Rome triumphed over Tigranes's ally, Mithradates VI of Pontos. The Romans then returned to the throne in Antioch the last of the Seleukid kings, Antiochos XIII, whose power evaporated in 64 when Syria was named a Roman province.

The obverse of this coin bears a portrait of Tigranes wearing the high Armenian tiara adorned with two eagles flanking a rayed sun. The reverse bears the earliest representation of the famous Tyche of Antioch, which was executed by Eutychides in about 295–292 for the newly established Seleukid capital on the Orontes.[1] The work is generally agreed to epitomize the many directions that Hellenistic art would explore in the following centuries, such as compositions incorporating more than one figure and inviting multiple viewpoints, and the personification of abstract forces. In this instance, divine providence is presented as the city's guardian spirit, although the mercurial nature of Tyche, meaning ''fortune,'' or ''chance,'' was the subject of much reflection in Hellenistic times. Theophrastos was convinced that chance governed human experience, and a character in Menander proclaims that human will offers ineffectual resistance to Tyche's onslaught.[2]

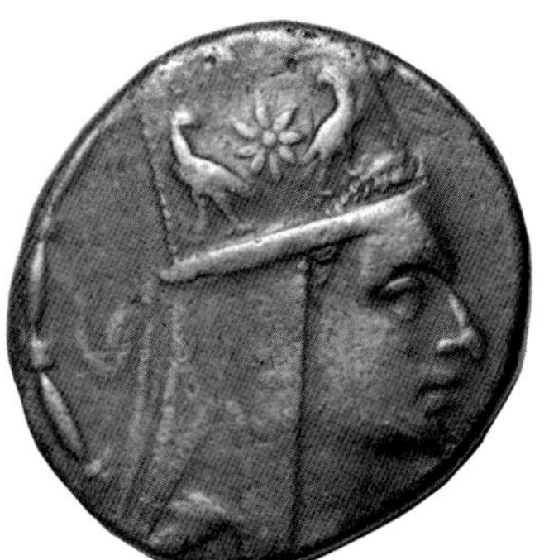

150.1

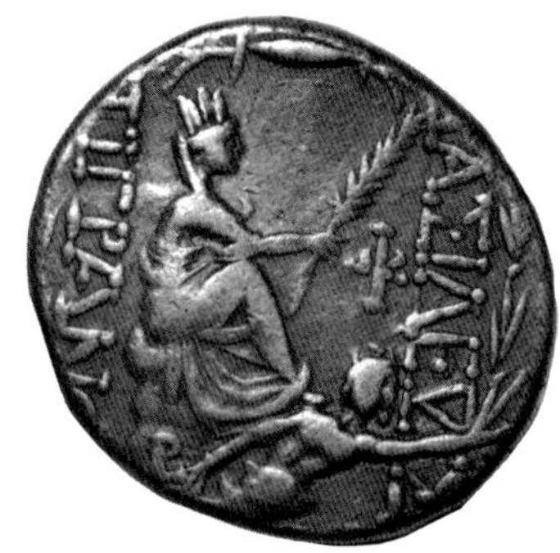

150.2

1. Robertson 470–471 and 704, notes 61, 62.
2. See J. Ferguson, *The Heritage of Hellenism* (New York, 1973), 73. See also the comments by Demetrios of Phaleron in his *Treatise on Fortune*: Polybios 29.21.1–6, Austin, *Hellenistic World,* 37–38, no. 20.

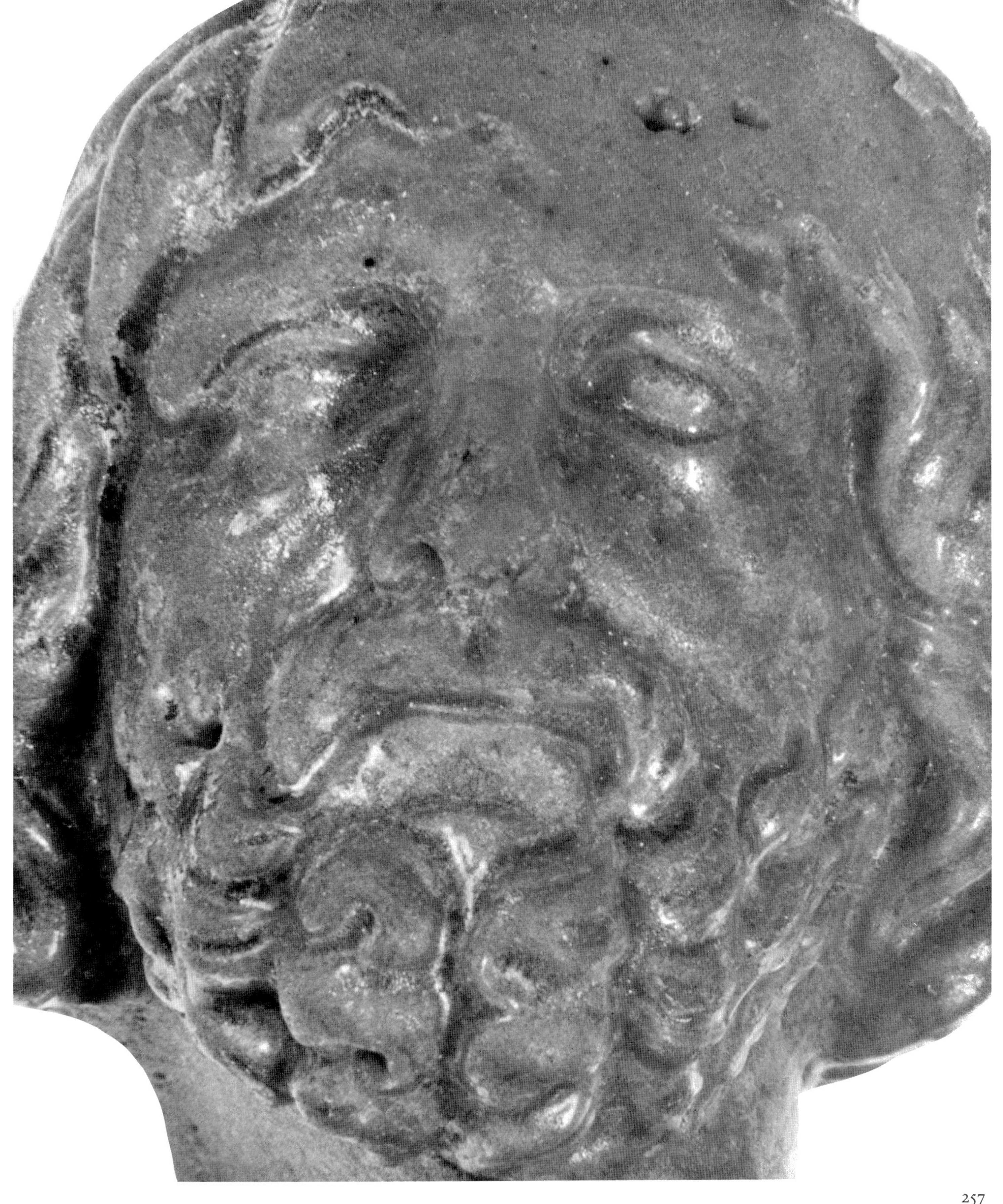

Core-Formed Glass
Amphoriskos
300–150

47.87. Dark blue glass with opaque white trails. "Found near Aleppo." Purchased from Kelekian in 1913. Ht, 14 cm; W, 7 cm; D, rim 3 cm. Iridescence.

A core-formed amphoriskos has an elongated body and an end knob. A white trail dropped on the side of the rim disc winds spirally down the neck and shoulder, then forms feather and festoon patterns on the body. Simple spirals appear again near the bottom of the body.

Exhibitions and Catalogues: *Three Thousand Years in Glass. Treasures from the Walters Art Gallery* (Baltimore, May 15–September 15, 1982).

This vessel was made by the core-formed technique wherein a core of clay was wrapped around a metal rod and then dipped into molten glass. The vessel was rolled, or marvered, on a flat surface, and decoration was added by winding around the surface glass threads, which were then combed into feather and festoon patterns. The rim and base were then shaped, and the handles added separately. After the glass had cooled, the core was scraped away.[1] The industry of core-formed glass prospered in Egypt from the fifteenth to the twelfth centuries and again during the eighth to sixth centuries, primarily in Mesopotamia and Asia Minor. During the Hellenistic period core-formed glass regained popularity, first in Alexandria to the end of the third century, then during the first half of the second century in Phoenician and Rhodian workshops. Core-formed vessels continued to be made in Syria and Cyprus to the end of the first century.[2]

This particular example is an amphoriskos, or perfume container, and belongs to Harden's type iii, the most common shape of Hellenistic core-formed amphoriskoi, recognized by the elongated body and end knob.[3] The Walters example is most similar to examples of the third and early second centuries, which are characterized by the upright festoon and feather patterns, the use of dark blue and clear glass in the

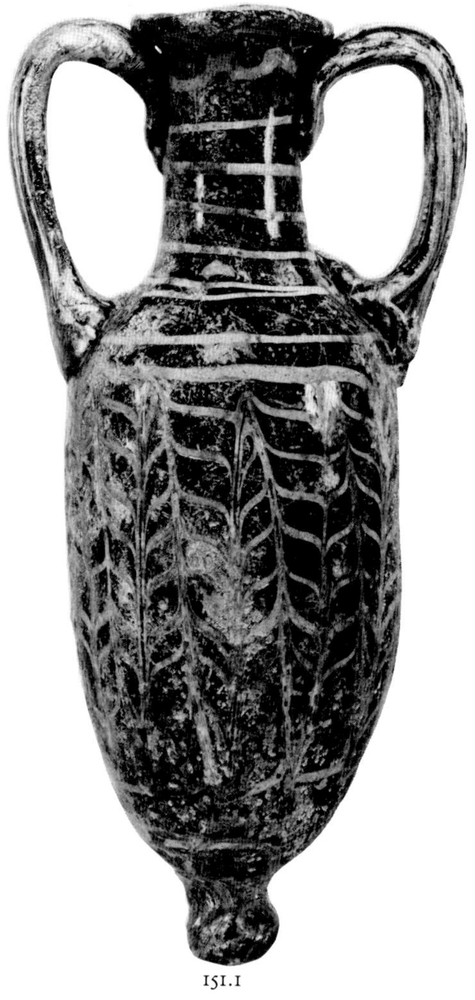

151.1

handles and end knobs, and the short neck, curving handles, quasi-cylindrical body, and large end knob.[4] In later Hellenistic examples the handles become more vertical, the body ovoid, the end knobs elongated, and the handles and end knobs are made almost exclusively of colorless glass.[5] Examples most similar to the Walters vase have been found on Cyprus and the Syrian coast, where they were probably made to hold the famous perfumes of Syria, comprising rose oil, unguent of lilies, and oil of the saffron blossom.[6]

1. D. Barag, *Catalogue of Western Asiatic Glass in the British Museum* (London, 1985), I, 31.
2. D. Harden, "Core-formed Glasses of the Alexandrians," *Alessandria,* 400–404.
3. D. Harden, *Catalogue of Greek and Roman Glass in the British Museum* (London, 1981), I, 128.
4. Ibid., 129; 131, no. 352; 132, no. 353.
5. Ibid., 129.
6. Ibid., 129.

Cast Glass Bust of Sarapis
Second century

47.106. Blue glass. Purchased in 1925. Ht, 7.9 cm; W, 4.3 cm; Th, 4.1 cm. Hole beneath for attachment; neck and chest on right side of hole broken away. Edge of modios and tip of nose broken away; abraded across forehead and front of hair; pitted over surface.

Head and bust of facing male has a short beard arranged loosely in coils; his mustache has drooping tips. Wavy hair falls beneath his ears and is surmounted by a tainia and a modios bearing in relief a frieze of wheat sheaves. The beginning of an undergarment is visible, and his mantle lies over his left shoulder.

Exhibitions and Catalogues: *Pagan and Christian Egypt,* Brooklyn Museum (Brooklyn, January 23–March 9, 1941), no. 109.

Publications: D. K. Hill, ''Material on the Cult of Sarapis,'' *Hesperia* 15 (1946) 65–66, fig. 5; L. Castiglione, ''La statue de culte hellénistique du Sarapieion d'Alexandrie,'' *Bulletin du musée hongrois des beaux-arts* 12 (1958) 26, no. 12, fig. 16; G. J. F. Kater-Sibbes, *Preliminary Catalogue of Sarapis Monuments,* Études préliminaires aux religions orientales dans l'empire romain 36 (Leiden, 1973), 201, no. 1072.

The god Sarapis represented an assimilation of Osiris and the bull god Apis. While he may have originated in the Pharaonic period, the deity did not enjoy widespread popularity before the Hellenistic age when, in partnership with Isis, his cult spread widely over the Mediterranean. Clement of Alexandria relates two traditions concerning the origin of the god's principal statue, both that it was brought from Sinope under Ptolemy II (308–246), and that an image was created in Egypt by an artist named Bryaxis, working at about the same time.[1] This latter statue, Clement tells us, was molded from a pulverized mixture of many substances, including metal and stones, and, was stained a dark blue, or kuanos. The blue color of the Walters bust echoes this latter tradition, but the link may only be coincidental, because Roman portrait busts in blue glass are also known.[2] The Walters head is unusually close to those works believed to be the most faithful reflections of the god's statue. The beard falls in two large coiled locks on the chin, the end of the mantle is brought over the left shoulder, and, in its undamaged state, individual locks of hair

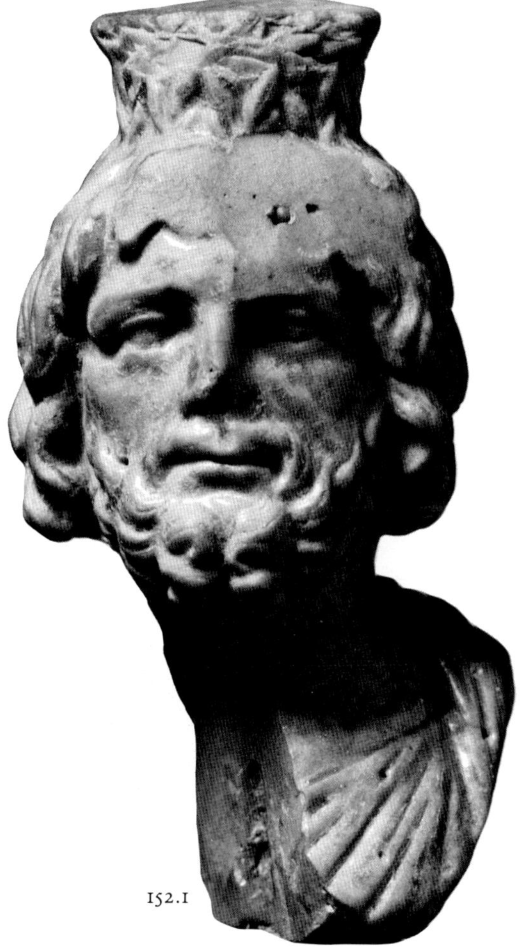

152.1

fell forward over the brow.[3] This degree of accuracy, as well as the quality of workmanship, suggest a date for the Walters bust not long after the prototype was completed. The piece thus appears to be a rare example of Ptolemaic cast glass, and possibly a more expensive version of replicas in faience, which the bust recalls in fabric and color. Noteworthy is the unmodeled blocklike area on the back, a traditional feature in Egyptian sculpture where it is the conventional location for inscriptions.

1. See Pollitt 279; Clement of Alexandria, *Protrepticus,* IV. 43P.
2. Compare two busts of Augustus. See D. Harden, ed., *Glass of the Caesars* (Milan, 1987), 21–22.
3. For the tradition of the Sarapis statue, see E. Reeder Williams, ''A Bronze Bust of Serapis at the Johns Hopkins University,'' *BABesch* 52–53 (1977–78) 201–207.

Accession Number	Catalogue Number	Accession Number	Catalogue Number	Accession Number	Catalogue Number
22.226	30	48.278	80	54.1160	47
22.407	29	48.285	77	54.1169	48
23.6	28	48.288	86	54.1170	46
23.7	39	48.289	82	54.1624	70
23.21	40	48.290	83	54.2016	73
23.22	6	48.294	84	54.2365	68
23.25	7	48.295	94	54.2372	58
23.26	2	48.296	81	54.2380	53
23.40	38	48.297	75	57.375	131
23.69	27	48.298	76	57.376	131
23.81	31	48.302	11	57.385	133
23.83	35	48.303	78	57.386	132
23.84	24	48.304	79	57.581	122
23.86	33	48.309	104	57.582	122
23.87	36	48.315	103	57.598	129
23.88	34	48.364	107	57.610	121
23.90	25	48.366	108	57.611	121
23.98	19	48.368	105	57.909	42
23.99	32	48.370	106	57.910	43
23.100	22	48.421	109	57.911	67
23.137	15	48.491	102	57.1021	137
23.140	16	48.1714	90	57.1022	142
23.141	18	48.1748	101	57.1027	134
23.155	17	48.1916	100	57.1490	126
23.173	26	48.1934	91	57.1496	118
23.174	5	48.1946	92	57.1498	119
23.177	1	48.2022	10	57.1499	119
23.185	4	48.2525	87	57.1524	130
23.217	20	48.2527	89	57.1540	128
23.220	3	48.2528	88	57.1541	127
23.222	14	48.2538	12	57.1671	120
23.229	21	54.598	50	57.1672	120
23.230	23	54.699	74	57.1698	136
23.239	13	54.702	57	57.1699	135
23.241	37	54.710	69	57.1730	124
42.103	143	54.741	65	57.1731	124
42.110	144	54.742	64	57.1732	123
42.190	139	54.743	45	57.1733	117
42.856	138	54.744	54	57.1843	41
42.934	145	54.948	71	57.2021	116
42.1319	141	54.954	72	57.2022	116
42.1339	140	54.1001	52	57.2073	125
47.87	151	54.1005	44	59.526	146
47.106	152	54.1006	66	59.527	147
48.73	8	54.1045	61	59.530	148
48.84	9	54.1046	62	59.531	150
48.86	95	54.1050	63	59.723	149
48.117	96	54.1053	56	71.18	112
48.128	97	54.1067	60	71.493	110
48.129	99	54.1075	49	71.557	115
48.130	98	54.1076	51	71.608	113
48.272	93	54.1103	59	71.609	114
48.277	85	54.1107	55	71.616	111